NEW YORK UNIVERSITY SERIES IN SELECTED ECONOMIC WRITINGS

BOOKS IN THE SERIES

Selected Economic Writings of William J. Baumol
Edited by Elizabeth E. Bailey

•

Selected Economic Writings of Fritz Machlup
Edited by George Bitros

•

Selected Economic Writings of Oskar Morgenstern
Edited by Andrew Schotter

•

Selected Economic Writings of Abba P. Lerner
Edited by David C. Colander

•

Selected Economic Writings of W. Arthur Lewis
Edited by Mark Gersovitz

•

Selected Economic Writings of Abba P. Lerner

Edited by
David C. Colander

Associate Professor
of Economics
University of Miami

New York • New York University Press • 1983

Library of Congress Cataloging in Publication Data

Lerner, Abba Ptachya, 1903–1982
Selected economic writings of Abba P. Lerner.

(New York University series in selected economic writings)
Bibliography: p.
Includes index.
1. Economics—Addresses, essays, lectures.
I. Colander, David C. II. Title. III. Series.
HB171.L629 1983 330.1 82-18835
ISBN 0-8147-1385-8

Manufactured in the United States of America

PREFACE

As is usual, an editor is indebted to a great many people and I am no exception. Colin Jones and Despina Papazoglou of New York University Press saw the project through to its completion. Without them, there would be no book. Daliah Lerner put up with Abba and me as we went through the selections and made our assumption—that any real world needs would somehow be met—come true. Without her help, encouragement and support, there would be no us. William Baumol, Irv Sobel, Charles Rockwood and Leonid Hurwicz, all gave suggestions and encouragement.

The acknowledgements page (p. vi) lists the journals and publishers who gave permission but it does not recount the many individuals who actually did the bureaucratic paper-pushing: the secretaries, administrative assistants and editors who make up the publishing profession. I thank them all, as I do my secretary, Debbie Rogers, who organized the permission gathering process and Julia Durney who helped with editing and indexing.

But most of all I want to thank Abba for writing the articles and for being everything that is embodied in his name. I am proud to consider myself a Lernerian economist.

Acknowledgments

Grateful acknowledgment is made to the following for permission to use essays which appeared in their publications:

The American Economic Review
The American Scholar
Atlantic Economic Journal
Ballinger Publishing Company
Bulletin of the Atomic Scientists (published by the Educational Foundation for Nuclear Science)
The Canadian Journal of Economics and Political Science
Challenge (published by M. E. Sharpe)
Eastern Economic Journal
The Economic Journal (published by Cambridge University Press)
Economica
International Cultural Foundation Press
International Labour Review (published by the International Labour Office)
Journal of Economic Literature
The Journal of Political Economy (published by the University of Chicago Press)
Martinus Nijhoff (distributed in the U.S.A. by Kluver Boston, Inc.)
McGraw-Hill Book Company, Inc.
Michigan State University Press
National Association of Secondary School Principals
National Council for the Social Studies
National Education Association
The Review of Economic Studies
The Review of Economics and Statistics (published by the North-Holland Publishing Company)
Social Research
Times Books, a division of Quadrangle/The New York Times Book Co., Inc.
The University Review (predecessor of *New Letters* magazine)
Western Economic Journal (predecessor of *Economic Inquiry*)
Yivo Bleter (published by the YIVO Institute for Jewish Research)

FOREWORD

To explain the particular animus of Abba Petachya Lerner on grounds that contribute to an understanding of his writings we have to understand not only his "bent of mind" but also the background circumstances which shaped his basic concerns and preconceptions.

By the time Lerner entered the London School of Economics after a decade's "career" as a capmaker, Hebrew school teacher, Rabbinical student, and small businessman, he brought from the predominately Jewish section of the London East End a unique amalgam of interests, and linguistic competence, combined with the ability to draw those very subtle distinctions which are the hallmark of rabbinical training.

The forces which led Lerner to study economics stemmed from his desire to determine his own position which initially led him to focus upon an intellectually amorphous body of writers representing the various Socialist contenders including Stalinists, Trotskyites, Social Democrats, Labor Zionists and Syndicalists. Initially he was greatly influenced by Maurice Dobb, whose works seemingly lent academic credence and respectability to Marxism. That same restless curiosity led him to the works of Thorstein Veblen, whose ideas seemed more relevant to the class oriented British society of the late 1920s than those of Alfred Marshall whom Abba had also read.

The prevailing economic and social conditions, which along with anti-semitism, profoundly affected and disturbed Lerner, also contributed to his desire to find solutions to what he then regarded as capitalist associated problems of exploitation, income inequality, poverty and unemployment. These problems which he linked to "welfare" influenced his desire to master economics in order to see whether the corpus of economic theory was compatible with democratic socialism.

From the inception of his studies at LSE Lerner monopolized the school's major prizes and fellowships beginning with the first year essay prize and culminating in the prestigious Leon Post Graduate Fellowship for 1934–1935. The latter fellowships were not simply the result of brilliance as a student: they were also based upon at least eight major articles in such journals as *Economics, Review of Economic Studies,* and the *Economic Journal*. These very early articles which emphasize diagrammatic representation show great technical and expository ability and evidence an already high degree of sophistication in the innovative application of economic concepts to theoretical issues.

An earlier hitherto unpublished article written during Lerner's third "undergraduate" year at LSE, reveals this great combination of expository lucidity combined with penetrating analysis. What this recently discovered work, published herein under the title of "Paleo-Austrian Theory," demonstrates, is his early ability through imaginative three dimensional analysis, to generalize and extend the particularized Hayekian version of the average period of production upon which it is based. Had the article been published then it would have removed the Hayekian formulation from subsequent criticism by Frank Knight and the subsequent reformulation by Sir John Hicks. This article shows that Abba even as a "sophomore" student was able to reconcile neo-classical economics, to which on logical grounds he was being increasingly drawn, with his socialist convictions.

Had anyone attempted to predict the close intellectual and personal relationship between Lionel Robbins and Lerner that prediction would have been labeled "ridiculous." Nevertheless, Robbins, a tall, aristocratic looking, Oxford educated member of the establishment and acknowledged conservative, who already was an established name in the profession, and the slight, Jewish, self-educated socialist found far more in common than the political and social class differences which seemingly divided them. What they shared was intellectual drive, the gift for logical analysis, and highly innovative "bents" of mind.

Two articles published in 1934, "The Concept of Monopoly and the Measurement of Monopoly Power" and "Economic Theory and Socialist Economy," show a transition from the sophisticated graphical—but still graduate school and "talmudic" oriented—representation of theoretical concepts to more substantive issues. In the "Monopoly" article Abba focuses upon the welfare implications of monopoly and finds the existing, primarily Marshallian oriented, concepts either deficient or inadequately specified for measuring welfare losses attributed to "monopoly." The almost simultaneous Robinson and Chamberlinian developments, whose essentials Lerner incorporated into his final draft, somewhat reduced the impact of this work, but no one reading it in the context of his time would deny that the work made an original, albeit lesser noticed contribution towards a key element in what Shackle was to later call the "Age of High Theory." The statement in that article, "In applying the particular mechanisms to the whole economy we get the appropriate reductio ad absurdum" indicates Lerner's growing awareness of the limitation of partial equilibrium concepts and presages his subsequent receptivity to an aggregative approach.

In the "Socialist Economy" article and in his related rejoinder to Maurice Dobb, Lerner reconciles his growing acceptance of the tenets of neo-classical theory with his socialism, thereby adding to a debate beginning in the late 19th century when such neo-classical notables as Von Wieser and Barone, had argued that marginal valuation based upon individual preferences would easily become the rule in a socialist society. Meanwhile Abba had been exposed to the work of Ludwig Von Mises, Friedrick von Hayek and Lionel Robbins who argued against Socialism on grounds that Socialist managers could not take into account individual preferences and could not even begin to make the complex marginal calculations necessary to even approach the Walrasian equilibrium conditions.

In his articles on socialist economics Abba argues against this view and demonstrates that the tenets of competitive theory are as applicable to a democratically organized socialist society as a capitalist one. He states "consumer preference maximization is completely within the spirit of socialism." After arguing that a pricing system based on marginal yields is needed for a modern economy to function efficiently he contends that their possible relevance under socialism is even greater than under capitalism since a socialist state is more likely to ascertain and act upon the true marginal social yields and costs. In doing so he corrects some problems in Oscar Lange's formulation, pointing out that the social dividend should be distributed with no connection to the wage in order for it not to interfere with the optimal distribution of resources.

The direction and nature of Lerner's career interests changed profoundly when he received the Leon Post-Graduate Study for 1934–1935 which financed his study at Cambridge. That fellowship put him in close contact with J. M. Keynes in that critical period in which the *General Theory* was being written and simultaneously discussed in graduate seminars. Abba soon found himself convinced by Keynes' arguments that welfare losses due to unemployment were far greater than those emanating from allocative inefficiency. His continuing preoccupation with unemployment increasingly led him to conclude that Keynes' analysis provided a practical basis for solution of the most crucial problem confronting Western society. Thus, in 1936 he wrote his first work to receive world wide attention, "Mr. Keynes' General Theory." In this article "approved by Keynes," which was labeled by the ILO editors as a clarified or simplified popularization for sophisticated but non-theoretically oriented policy makers, he not only distilled the essence of Keynes' work but also made original substantive contributions to it.

Abba was among the first to recognize that Keynes' analysis was based upon the practical unattainability of the underlying assumptions of the neo-classical full employment equilibrium model, and thus on that basis labeled, as he still does today, the Keynesian scheme as a "policy" rather than a "theoretical" revolution. Nevertheless, he predicted that the "General Theory" would lead to a massive change in economic thinking especially among "practical men dealing with economic problems because Keynes has shown that what the ordinary man felt in his bones can be justified by keen analysis."

Abba's move to the United States in 1937 only served to accelerate his already impressive rate of publication. By 1944 when *The Economics of Control* appeared, he had already published over 30 articles in major U.S. journals, a substantial proportion of which were devoted to interpreting, clarifying and correcting Keynes. His most noteworthy articles written during this period were "The Economic Steering Wheel," "Functional Finance and the Federal Debt," and "Some Swedish Stepping Stones" which anticipated the Post-Keynesian developments at least two decades later.

To many, including myself, Abba's masterpiece is *The Economics of Control,* some of whose chapters are cited herein. This work integrated Lerner's views on democratic socialism, consumer sovereignty, income distribution and macro-economics and explained how each was merely an example of a deviation between marginal social costs and benefits. This work respecified the notion of a welfare optimum from one solely based upon productive (or allocative) efficiency to one in which distributive efficiency is accorded equal importance.

The optimum marginal welfare conditions now labeled as Lange-Lerner had previously been stated by others but Lerner's particular specification and synthesis with the functional finance mechanism of control was a novel one. These specified micro-economic optimal conditions were amplified through Lerner's delineation of functional finance control techniques, e.g., taxation and subsidization, by means of which a government could optimize welfare by facilitating a close approximation of the equation of marginal social costs and benefits (even in the case of market imperfections).

In this work Lerner's support of socialism is modified. He unequivocally states, "The fundamental aim of socialism is not the abolition of private property but the extension of democracy. Where competitive enterprise works best in the social interest it should apply."

In "The Economics of Control" Lerner was well aware that what he termed the basic distributive theorem of utilitarian marginalism, "namely, income equality," applies only to a given social income and could involve an irreconcilable conflict with maximization of social income. The latter depends upon human effort which can be affected adversely by failure to receive income payments deemed consonant with the maximum expenditure of effort. Although Lerner had put that patently "uncomfortable" matter aside, his awareness of the unsatisfactory state of his defense of income equality later brought him back to the issue, and his 1978 article "Utilitarian Marginalism" (Nozick-Rawls), showed that the resolution of this issue was a major career concern. His attempt to reconcile these apparently dichotomous aspects of welfare, and salvage substantial income equality through delineation of "necessary and unnecessary" payments is ingenious, to say the least. Whether that solution is practical or politically feasible—a recurring question in all of Lerner's major reform proposals—is another issue.

One possible explanation for the failure of *The Economics of Control* to achieve more widespread recognition as a modern classic is that many who were willing to accept its micro-economic implications not only identified the work with Lerner's early socialism but also were sufficiently disturbed by its apparently radical ideas of functional finance and income equality, to be unable to treat the work on its merits. At the same time many of those who would have been receptive on ideological grounds to Abba's overall solutions felt betrayed because of his apparent renunciation of socialism.

The Keynesian and Post-Keynesian Lerner: Inflation and Stagflation

According to John Von Neuman all theories have their origins, and possible demises, in empirics, and the unexpectedly rapid inflation of the immediate post-war era provided such an empirical test for the Keynesian formulation. Thus, from 1945 onward, concern with the rising price level and its relationship to the "completeness" of the Keynesian schema is accorded primary emphasis in Lerner's writings. His thinking has been manifested in four distinct phases, each one of which represents an increasingly sophisticated formulation of original ideas.

The first phase which perhaps is best represented by the two articles selected, "Money as a Creature of the State" and "The Inflationary Process," emphasizes the incompatibility of free collective bargaining with full employment and stable prices; the second phase is characterized by his distinction between high and low full employment; the third by sellers inflation; and the fourth might be summarized as the expectational inflation phase.

The first phase reflecting Lerner's reaction to trade union demands for large wage increases in 1945–46, which were rationalized through "vulgarized" Keynesian purchasing power arguments was that higher wages could only trigger an increase in the price level. His growing belief that the twin goals of functional finance, namely, full employment and stable prices, were proving incompatible with free collective bargaining, led him to conclude in his 1947 "Money" article that the only way the State could maintain the value of its money would be through an incomes policy, which would link wage increases to increased productivity.

In his "Inflationary Process" article Lerner emphasizes the point he has consistently made throughout his career, namely, that any incomes policy either must replicate market differentials or fail. In the same work he delineated his perception of the tradeoff between unemployment and inflation. A one percent reduction in employment sacrifices

2–3 percent of real national product; a one percent increase in inflation would result in only a $^{1}/_{16}$ percent real reduction.

Lerner's evolving position is evidenced in his *The Economics of Employment*. The high and low full employment concept, only one of the original features of this work, represented a further progression of his conception of Keynesian economics.

One can see in this distinction between high and low full employment an anticipation of both the essence of stagflation and of the Phillips curve approximately a decade before either of these concepts became common currency among economists. He had incidentally anticipated stagflation even earlier when he stated in late 1947 "Nevertheless, the worker's bargaining power may still be too great for price stability even when economic activity is below the optimum level."

The majority of both Lerner's intellectual supporters and foes alike regard this distinction between high and low full employment as a "cop out", which reflected his unwillingness at that time to face up to the basic flaw in the Keynesian analysis. In his 1966 Ely Lecture titled "Employment Theory and Employment Policy," he acknowledged that by stating that as a consequence of having "brainwashed himself" he was unable to grasp that what seemingly constituted a verbal paradox was in reality a theoretical one. In his inimitable style as a phrasemaker he put the matter thusly, "In my first encounter with the indecent entrance of the inflation diagram on the stage before his cue was called, i.e. before full employment was reached, some remnant of this brainwashing made me give the full employment (albeit low full employment) to the point where the dragon first appeared . . . to legitimize the dragon's premature entrance."

Lerner's reluctance to accept the logical implications of his "premature" recognition of the essence of the Phillips curve is evident in other remarks in the same article. Although not questioning the curves' empirical foundation he nevertheless stated, "We cannot do business with the dragon (through some deflationary fiscal-monetary mix) by feeding him a certain number of jobs . . . . and, between the political and morally impermissible catastrophic depression that crushes Sellers Inflation and the excess demand of Buyers Inflation the effects on prices and inflation are questionable."

The 1957–59 period, characterized by recession and a rising price level, provided the backdrop for Lerner's (and Sidney Weintraub's) Sellers Inflation phase, the conceptualization of which clearly delineated the beginning of the Post-Keynesian era. In a series of articles, typified by "Sellers Inflation and Inflationary Depression," he not only contrasted Buyers Inflation (Inflation I) with Sellers Inflation (Inflation II), the latter resulting from combined claims of sellers in excess of 100 percent of the produce, but he also expressed his fears regarding an economy trapped permanently between high and low full employment in a situation of "administered recession" compounded by an "administered inflation."

Abba's 1972 book *Flation* introduces his fourth phase expectational inflation or Inflation III, which results from "defensive behavior," that is, the attempt to raise wages and prices to defend relative real incomes in anticipation of expected generalized price increases.

A major formulation of Lerner's position regarding Keynesian economics is embodied in a provocative 1977 article in *Social Research* in which he demonstrates his mastery of succinct summation. He defines the Keynesian phases as follows: "*Pre-Keynes:* With a stable money supply prosperity and price stability require only that wages (prices) behave themselves, i.e., adjust to the money supply. *Keynes:* With steady wages (prices) prosperity requires only that the money supply behave itself and adjust to the wage and price level. *Post-Keynes:* Both money supply and wages must behave themselves. For prosperity money supply must adjust to wages (prices). For price stability the average wage can rise only with an increase in productivity.''

These and other articles in the late 1970s such as ''Keynesianism, Alive If Not So Well at Forty'' reflect Lerner's continuing desire to correct certain misconceptions about Keynesian analysis, as well as to ''defend'' the temporal relevance of both the Keynesian and Post-Keynesian formulations.

Notwithstanding these shifts in terminology and emphasis during his more than three Post-War decades of writing on employment and inflation Abba has consistently maintained that full employment should not be jeopardized by deflationary policies directed indiscriminately against all forms of inflation; that such policies directed against cost-administered inflation are destined to fail, that departures of any consequence from full employment would be far more harmful to national economic welfare than inflation, and that an incomes policy such as his proposed Market Anti-Inflation Plan, which, like his 1948 plan would replicate market generated wage and policy differentials, is the only viable way to maintain full employment without inflation.

This emphasis in the Post-War era upon Lerner's macro-economic writings should not obscure the fact that in many of those aspects of micro-economic theory, methodology, ideology, and the political process which characterized his pre-World War II efforts he still maintained, what to others less gifted than he would have constituted, an impressive rate of publication.

In all of his varied works over a career spanning six decades Abba Lerner has consistently manifested his eternal optimism, that the full force of his considerable mental and intellectual powers can be employed to generate new ideas which will improve the human condition, and that through rational intellectual discourse he can persuade us to adopt them.

Irvin Sobel
Professor of Economics and Philosophy
Florida State University

CONTENTS

PART ONE
MICROECONOMICS

A. Partial Equilibrium

[1]

The Diagrammatical Representation of Elasticity of Demand

By A. P. LERNER
(*London School of Economics*)

THE very neat and simple diagrammatical representation of Elasticity of Demand that Marshall gives in connection with the ordinary demand curve, where quantities are measured along the X axis and prices along the Y axis, tends to make people use that form of diagram when some other form would be more helpful for the problem in hand. It therefore seems worth while to show that the elasticity of demand can be shown as simply and as neatly on any other form of demand curve.

Marshall's formula is $\frac{PT}{Pt}$ in Fig. 1.[1] This ratio is seen more easily in $\frac{OA}{At}$ which can be measured on the scale provided for measuring the ordinates. This immediately suggests how we can measure the elasticity of demand in connection with the marginal receipts curve. R the marginal receipts curve corresponding to the demand curve D in Fig. 1 will cut PB at Q so that $PQ = At$. This is because the marginal receipts are equal to the price of the added unit minus the loss due to the fall in price on all the units sold. Measuring p, price, on the vertical axis and q, quantity along the horizontal axis, the loss due to the fall in price is seen to be equal to the rate of fall of price per unit multiplied by the number of units affected. This is $-\frac{dp}{dq}q$ or geometrically $\frac{At}{AP}AP$, which equal At. Since $PQ = At$ and $OA = BP$, e, the elasticity of demand, can be expressed by $\frac{PT}{Pt}$ or $\frac{OA}{At}$ or $\frac{BP}{PQ}$. The last expression can be expressed verbally by saying that the elasticity of demand is equal to the price divided by the difference between the price and the marginal receipts. This way of putting it may help us to discover business men's estimates of the elasticity of demand for their products and appears to offer possibilities of a measure of the degree of monopoly power of a firm, but that is by the way. It will be noticed that the expression agrees with the well-known property of the marginal receipts curve of lying above the horizontal axis where e is greater than unity, of lying on the axis where e is equal to unity and of lying below the axis where e is less than unity.

The property of e being equal to $\frac{p}{p-r}$ where p equals price and r equals marginal receipts enables us to show e on the aggregate demand

[1] *Principles*, p. 839.

39

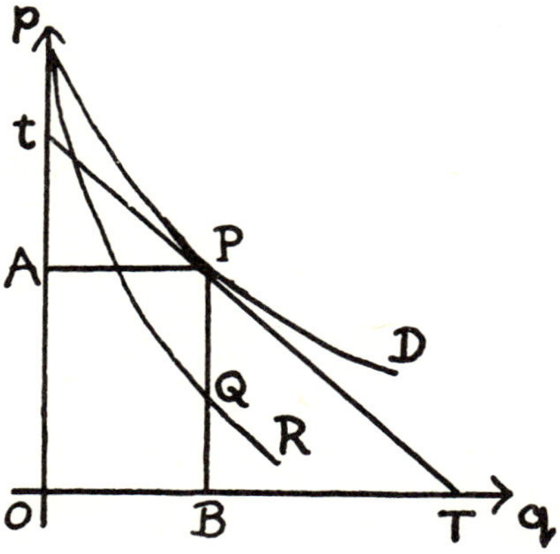

FIGURE 1

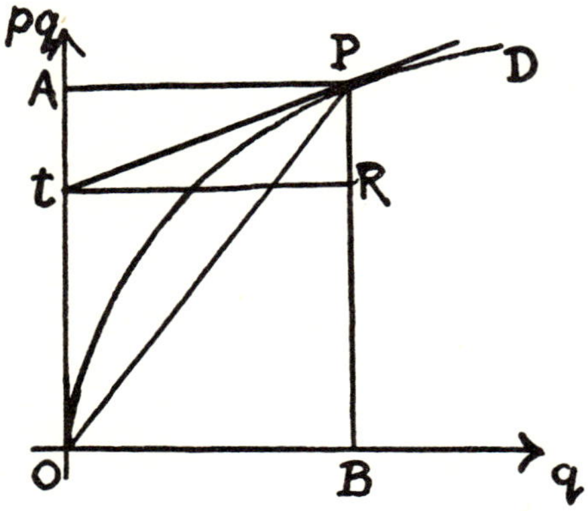

FIGURE 2

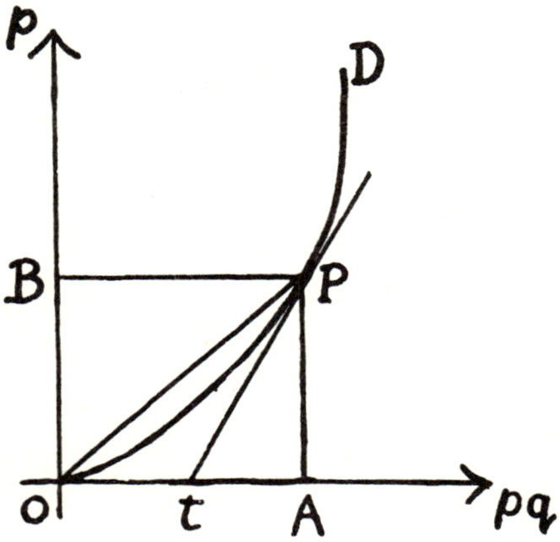

FIGURE 3

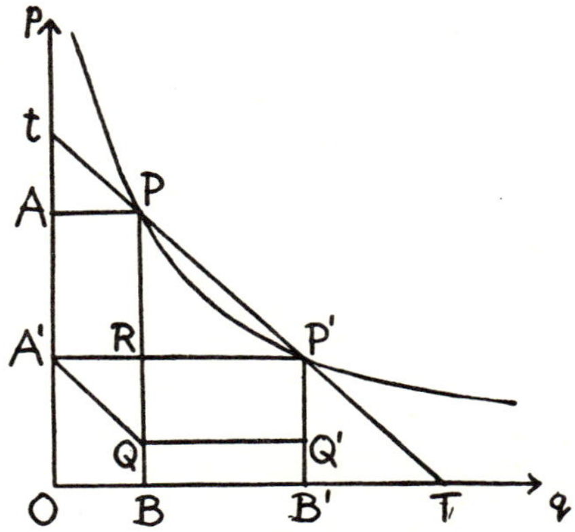

FIGURE 4

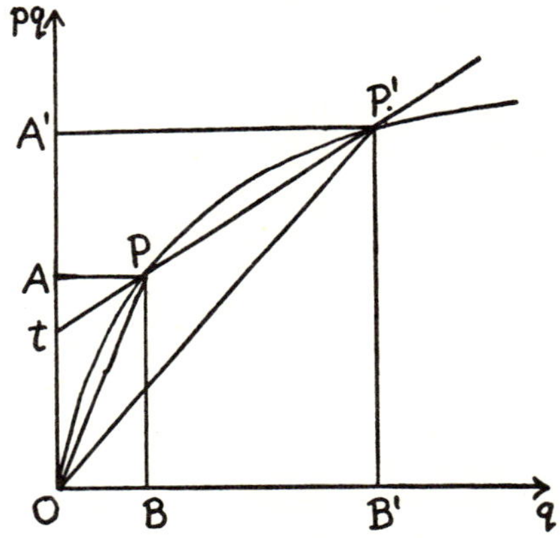

FIGURE 5

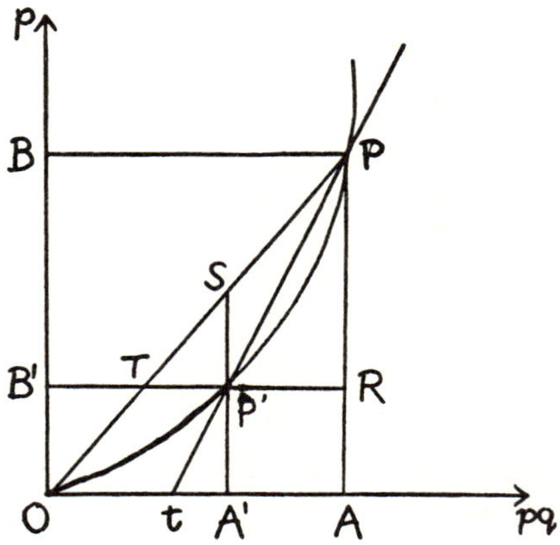

FIGURE 6

curve (fig. 2) where the horizontal axis measures q and the vertical axis measures pq (outlay or price times quantity). Price is represented by $\frac{PB}{OB}$ and marginal receipts by the tangent $\frac{PR}{tR}$ which equals $\frac{At}{OB}$ so that e is equal to

$$\frac{\frac{PB}{OB}}{\frac{PB}{OB}-\frac{At}{OB}}=\frac{PB}{PB-At}=\frac{OA}{Ot}$$

The concept of "arc elasticity" introduced by Dr. Dalton,[2] can also be represented diagrammatically in the various forms of demand curves. It is, however, necessary first to clear up some difficulties which have arisen around the concept of "arc elasticity."

Dr. Dalton's modification of Marshall's diagram is seen in Fig. 4, where the tangent of Fig. 1, which represented an infinitesimal change in price at P, is replaced by a chord which represents a finite fall of price from BP to B′P′ or a rise of price from B′P′ to BP. Dr. Dalton measures the arc elasticity in the first case (taking the higher end of the arc as base) as $\frac{PT}{Pt}$ and in the second case (taking the lower end of the arc as base) as $\frac{P'T}{P't}$.

This ambiguity is noted by Dr. Dalton, who declares that the difference between the two elasticities will not generally be large, and is seized upon by critics who show that it can be very large and who imply that this makes the whole concept of arc elasticity practically useless,[3] particularly as the arc elasticity will also vary with the size of the arc.[4] The objections seem most conclusive when we note with Dr. Dalton that "For a constant outlay curve, the point elasticity of demand is always equal to one, but the arc elasticity is never equal to one. The arc elasticity of such a curve is always greater than one for a fall in price and an increase of demand and always less than one for a rise in price and a decrease of demand." It is, of course, only a matter of terminology, but if constant outlay is to be separated from unit elasticity it would seem best to call the measure something other than "elasticity."

But all these objections can be avoided by a simple correction to Dr. Dalton's formula. The elasticity of demand for the arc PP′ is quite unambiguously $\frac{P'T}{Pt}$ whether one is considering a rise in price or a fall, and there is no bother about choosing a base. If $P'T=Pt$, $e=1$, the proportional change in price is equal to the proportional change in demand and the outlay is unchanged. For then $tP'=tT-P't=tT-tP=PT$, and,

[2] *The Inequality of Incomes*, pp. 192 ff.
[3] Schultz, *Statistical Laws of Demand and Supply*, pp. 8-14.
[4] Marschak, *Elastizität der Nachfrage*, p. 7 n.

by similar triangles, tA′P′ = PBT and tAP = P′B′T, so that rectangle OP = tOT − PBT − tAP = tOT − P′B′T − tA′P′ = rectangle OP′.

Similarly it can be shown that if P′T > Pt the fall in price will be accompanied by a more than proportionate increase in the amount bought so that outlay increases, and vice versa.

Diagrammatically, the ambiguity in Dr. Dalton's formula is due to the attempt to give the arc elasticity without specifying the relevant arc (i.e. both end points). Each of Dr. Dalton's alternative formulations involved the knowledge of the slope of the chord and the position of *only one end point* and may be described as an attempt to give the *arc* elasticity of a *point*. It is not surprising that an undefined arc has an indefinite elasticity. What is surprising is in the first place that the chord, which corresponds to any finite movement along a demand curve, and for which the tangent is only the representative in the limiting case of an infinitesimal movement, should have been forgotten in going back from the limit to the real case and supplanted by one or the other of its extremities, and in the second place that critics should have condemned the whole concept on account of this slip.

Arithmetically, the slip amounts to an attempt to measure elasticities in relationships between *percentage* changes in price and demand instead of in *proportional* changes, and, of course, the same proportional change (say 3 : 4) is expressed differently in percentage terms according as to whether it is an increase (when it appears as 33 per cent.) or a decrease (when it is 25 per cent.). Since the changes of price and quantity are always in opposite directions, a different ratio between the changes will appear according as to which is measured as an increase and which as a decrease. That is, according as to whether we are considering a rise or a fall in price.

The formula here suggested avoids this ambiguity by measuring all changes in the same way—as increases. The proportional change in price, expressed as an increase, is $\frac{AA'}{OA'}$ or $\frac{PP'}{TP'}$ and the proportional change in quantity expressed as an increase is $\frac{BB'}{OB}$ or $\frac{PP'}{tP}$. The latter divided by the former is the elasticity of demand and this gives us $\frac{P'T}{Pt}$. It would, of course, be just as correct to measure all changes as percentage decreases so that we would get as our measure of elasticity $\frac{PT}{P't}$, but the first seems simpler.

Mathematically there seems to be some æsthetic objection to the use of arc elasticity, but on this I do not feel competent to give an opinion.

It might appear that the ambiguity in Dr. Dalton's formula has not really been avoided, for the alternative formula $\frac{PT}{P't}$ will not give the same numerical result as the formula suggested here in the first place, $\frac{P'T}{Pt}$, except when elasticity is unity. It will give a smaller figure for elasticities greater than unity and a larger figure for elasticities less than unity. Which figure, if either, is the " true " elasticity?

The answer is that there is no " true " arc elasticity and that either formula gives a satisfactory index of what is wanted, namely, the degree to which a given fall of price calls forth an increase in the quantity bought. One is no truer compared with the other than a centigrade temperature is truer as compared with the corresponding fahrenheit temperature. It is only a matter of choosing a scale. The scale depends upon what is to be meant when it is said that one proportional change is twice (or any other integral or fractional number of times) as great as another proportional change. Is the proportional change which is twice as great as 3 : 4 (which is the same as 4 : 3), 3 : 5 or 2 : 4 or $2\frac{1}{2} : 4\frac{1}{2}$ or what?

The most logical way seems to be to say that a proportional change A shall be considered twice as great as another proportional change B if, as an operation[5] it gives the same result as when B as an operation is applied twice in succession[6] and in the same direction. This would make the proportional change which is twice as great as 3 : 4 equal to $3:4 \times 3:4$ or $3^2 : 4^2$ or 9 : 16 or $3 : 5\frac{1}{3}$. More generally, the proportional change which is n times as great as a : b is $a^n : b^n$.

This is pointed out by Schultz[7] who seems, however, to consider that this is the only " right " way. It is obviously not suitable for simple diagrammatical treatment, but this does not matter, for other scales are just as satisfactory. In the formula suggested $\left(\frac{P'T}{Pt}\right)$ where all changes are considered as percentage (or fractional) additions, the common-sense view is taken that by twice the increase from 3 to 4 is meant the increase from 3 to 5. More generally, the proportional change that is n times as great as the proportional change $a : a + \Delta a$ is $a : a + n\Delta a$. Every point on this scale will correspond to one and only one definite point on the more " logical " scale, and it can therefore be used just as satisfactorily. In Fig. 4, if the proportional change in demand is n times as great as the proportional change in price then $\frac{BB'}{OB} = n\left(\frac{AA'}{OA'}\right)$

$$\frac{PP'}{Pt} = n\left(\frac{PP'}{P'T}\right)$$

$$\text{and } \frac{P'T}{Pt} = n$$

and is a simple, adequate and unambiguous measure of the elasticity of demand of an arc of a demand curve.

We can now turn to the diagrammatical representation of arc elasticity on the different kind of demand curves. Corresponding to the formula $\frac{OA}{At}$

[5] A. N. Whitehead, *An Introduction to Mathematics*, pp. 79 ff.

[6] " The sum of two operations is the single operation which has the same effect as the two operations applied successively." *Ibid*, p. 80.

[7] *Loc. cit.*

of Fig. 1 we have $\frac{OA'}{At}$ in Fig. 4, which is obtained directly by projecting the primary formula on to the Y axis.

Corresponding to the second formula for Fig. 1, $\frac{PB}{PQ}$, we have $\frac{P'B'}{P'Q'}$ of Fig. 4 where Q is obtained by drawing A′Q parallel to PP′ meeting PB in Q and drawing QQ′ parallel to the X axis to meet P′B′ in Q′. The rectangle QP′ will then be equal in area to the rectangle A′P so that the area of the rectangle BQ′ will measure the excess of the rectangle OP′ over the rectangle OP, that is the increase in outlay following the fall in price and the attendant increase of demand, and B′Q′ will measure the increase in receipts per unit of increased output or the rate of marginal receipts for the range indicated by the arc. The elasticity is equal to price divided by the excess of price over marginal receipts $\frac{P'B'}{P'Q'}$ and this agrees with the other formula, since P′B′=OA′ and P′Q′=RQ=At (for triangle RQA′=triangle AtP).

Corresponding to Fig. 2 we have Fig. 5[8] where, applying the principle of price divided by the excess of price over marginal receipts, we get

$$\frac{\frac{P'B'}{OB'}}{\frac{P'B'}{OB'}-\frac{A't}{OB'}}=\frac{OA'}{Ot}$$

as the arc elasticity corresponding to the point elasticity $\frac{OA}{Ot}$ in Fig. 2. In Figs. 3 and 6[8] we have the other kind of integral curve where the ordinate measures p and the abscissa measures pq. In Fig. 6 the quantity bought at the higher price is $\frac{OA}{AP}$ (outlay divided by price) or $\frac{OA'}{A'S}$ where S is the point where the perpendicular through P′ meets OP. The quantity bought at the lower price is $\frac{OA'}{A'P'}$. The proportional change in quantity is therefore $\frac{P'S}{A'P'}$ while the proportional change in price is $\frac{BB'}{OB'}$. e therefore $=\frac{\frac{P'S}{A'P'}}{\frac{BB'}{OB'}}=\frac{P'S}{BB'}=$ $\frac{P'S}{RP}=\frac{TP'}{TR}=\frac{Ot}{OA}$. The same formula $\frac{Ot}{OA}$, will give the elasticity of demand for Fig. 3 which represents the limiting case where P and P′ coincide.

[8] In all figs. P′ corresponds to a lower price than P.

[2]

The Concept of Monopoly and the Measurement of Monopoly Power[1]

I

MONOPOLY, says the dictionary, is the exclusive right of a person, corporation or state to sell a particular commodity. Economic science, investigating the economic aspects of this legal right, found that they all resolved themselves into the implications of the power of the monopolist—as distinguished from a seller in a competitive market—arbitrarily to decide the price of the commodity, leaving it to the buyers to decide how much they will buy at that price, or, alternatively, to decide the quantity he will sell, by so fixing the price as to induce buyers to purchase just this quantity. Technically this is expressed by saying that the monopolist is confronted with a falling demand curve for his product or that the elasticity of demand for his product is less than infinity, while the seller in a purely[2] competitive market has a horizontal demand curve or the elasticity of demand for his product is equal to infinity.

The monopolist is normally assumed to tend to fix the price at the level at which he makes the greatest profit or " monopoly revenue." This monopoly revenue constitutes a levy upon the consumers that the monopolist is able to appropriate for himself purely in virtue of his restrictive powers *qua* monopolist, and it is the consumers' objection to paying this levy that lies at the base of popular feeling against the monopolist.

In addition to this it is claimed that monopoly is harmful in a more objective sense. A levy which involves a mere transference from buyer to monopolist cannot be said to be harmful from a social point of view unless it can be shown that the monopolist is less deserving of the levy than the people who have to pay it; either because he is in general a less deserving kind of person, or because the transference will increase the evils of inequality of incomes. But the levy is not a mere transference. The method of raising it, namely, by increasing the price of the monopolised commodity, causes buyers to divert their expenditure to other, less satisfactory, purchases. This constitutes a loss to the consumer which is not balanced by any gain reaped by the monopolist, so that there is a net social loss.

The nature of the loss here loosely expressed seems to have defied attempts at more exact exposition, the difficulties encountered on these attempts having

[1] The great advances made in the subject of this article since the major part of it was written—particularly in the work of Mr. Chamberlin and Mrs. Robinson—have rendered many parts of it out of date. In preparing it for publication, while cutting out some of these parts, I have been so much under the influence of this recent work that I cannot say how much of what is here published is really my own.—A. P. LERNER.

[2] " Pure " competition is different from " perfect " competition. The former implies perfection of competition only in respect of the complete absence of monopoly and abstracts from other aspects of perfection in competition. This useful distinction is suggested by Chamberlin. See his *Theory of Monopolistic Competition*, p. 6.

even induced some to declare that this commonsense view of a social loss is an illusion, while more careful sceptics prefer to say that nothing " scientific " can be said about it. The account given above clearly will not do as a general and accurate description of the nature of the social loss. Where a consumer spends as much as before on the monopolised commodity when the price is raised, he cannot be said to divert expenditure to other and less satisfactory channels, and where he spends more[1] upon the commodity than at the lower competitive price it might even be argued that there is a net social gain in so far as the consumer is induced to spend more on the commodity which is more urgently needed and less on other commodities! There seems little to choose between this argument and the counter-argument, that as long as the elasticity is greater than zero some consumer (or unit of consumption) is induced to change the direction of his expenditure so that he suffers the uncompensated inconvenience which constitutes the net social loss. Does this mean that if a man's demand is completely inelastic (so that the increased price brings no diminution in the amount of the monopolised commodity consumed and the whole of the levy is sacrificed ultimately in the form of other commodities) the expenditure of the income, as diminished by the amount of the levy, is not interfered with by the existence of the monopoly ?—i.e. that if he had paid the levy in cash and prices were not affected he would have reduced his consumption of other commodities in the same way ? Or is it more reasonable to suppose that a rise in a particular price will always tend to diminish purchases of the dearer commodity, where a cash levy (prices remaining unchanged) would diminish all expenditures in the same proportion so that if the same amount of the monopolised commodity is bought at the higher price, a cash diminution in income of the size of the levy would

[1] Where as much or more is spent on a commodity when the price is raised the elasticity of demand is equal to or less than unity. This may appear incompatible with the condition of monopolistic equilibrium that elasticity of demand shall be greater than unity (as long as marginal cost is positive). There is, however, no incompatibility, for the two elasticities of demand are different things. The elasticity that has to be greater than unity for monopolistic equilibrium is the elasticity at the *point* on the demand curve corresponding to the position of monopolistic equilibrium. The elasticity that is equal to or less than unity when the amount spent on the commodity remains unchanged or increases as the price is raised, is the elasticity over the *arc* of the demand curve from the point of competitive equilibrium to the point of monopolistic equilibrium. The arc elasticity in this sense will normally be less than the point elasticity, as will appear from the diagram. If tT is the demand curve (here drawn a straight line), P' the point of competitive equilibrium, and P the point of monopolistic equilibrium, then the *point* elasticity at the monopoly equilibrium will be $\frac{PT}{Pt}$ while the *arc* elasticity will be $\frac{P'T}{Pt}$, which is smaller. The arc elasticity must be smaller unless the demand curve is so concave (upwards) that it shows a constant or increasing point elasticity as price is lowered. The point elasticity at the competitive position will, of course, be $\frac{P'T}{P't}$. For the explanation of this definition of " arc elasticity," see my note on " The Diagrammatical Representation of Elasticity of Demand," in No. I of the REVIEW.

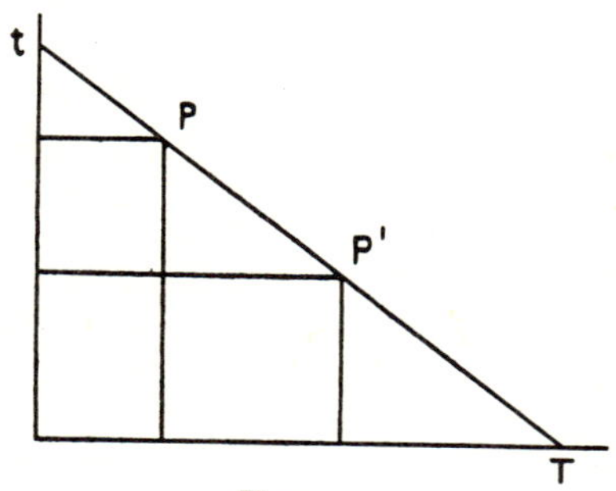

FIGURE I

have *increased* the demand for that commodity? The problems do not seem to be amenable to treatment on these lines.[1]

The commonsense attitude is, however, not easily balked. Another attempt was made to deal with the problem by Marshall, by means of the apparatus of consumers' surplus. If it is assumed that the marginal utility of money is unchanged, or that the change is so small that it may legitimately be neglected, it can be shown that the money value of the consumers' surplus lost is greater than the monopoly revenue gained, so that we have a theoretical measure of the net social loss due to the monopoly. There are, of course, many important weaknesses in this treatment, and some ways of applying it are completely wrong. The marginal utility of money can be considered unchanged only if we are considering a small change in the price of only one commodity. This makes it impossible to add the consumers' surplus obtained by an individual from different goods. Quite wrong is any attempt to speak of the consumers' surplus of a community and to derive it from the communal demand curve. And there are other traps to be avoided in this connection which are quite well known. But the exclusive preoccupation of teachers of economics with putting their pupils on their guard against these insufficiencies and dangers has tended to make them deny the problem with which the concept of consumers' surplus was intended to deal—the net social loss and its nature. It is not intended here to deny or even to belittle the dangers and confusions attendant on the use of the concept of consumers' surplus, but it does seem that some light can be thrown on the problem by its use.

From the consumers' surplus approach there has emerged a clarification of the rent element in monopoly revenue. It is only in the case of constant or decreasing average cost that the amount of monopoly revenue is necessarily less than the loss of consumers' surplus. The monopoly revenue will be greater if the average cost curve rises steeply enough. This gave the impression that the monopolistic restriction brought about a net social gain so that the competitive output was too great and it would be beneficial to tax industries which were "subject to diminishing returns." In correcting this view it was shown that against the monopoly revenue was to be reckoned not only the loss of consumers' surplus, but also the reduction in rents as compared with those receivable under competition. If the reductions of rent is not allowed for, the diminution of costs of the marginal units, as output is restricted, is attributed to all the *infra*-marginal costs where there has been no reduction in social costs, but only a transference of income from the receivers of rent. In the accompanying Fig. 2 AR is the average revenue or demand curve (which, to avoid the quarrels over consumers' surplus, we can consider as the sum of a number of identical demand curves of similar individuals), MR is the marginal revenue curve, AC is average costs, and MC is marginal costs. P' will be the competitive point where output is OM' and price is $M'P'$, and P, which is perpendicularly above

[1] In the last few months Dr. J. R. Hicks and Mr. R. G. D. Allen have been making investigations on these lines and have demonstrated by means of the indifference curve apparatus that, with continuous indifference curves, an absolutely inelastic demand curve must be accompanied by a negatively sloping expenditure curve. This means that a change in income (prices remain unchanged) would bring about a change *in inverse direction* of the amount of the commodity bought. They have not been interested, however, in the problems dealt with in this article.

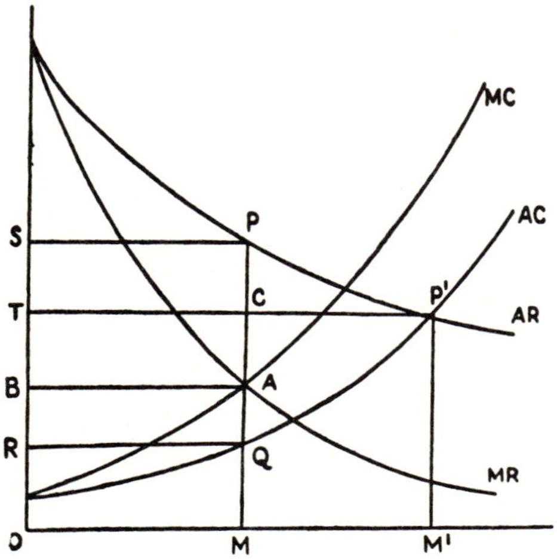

FIGURE 2

A, where *MR* and *MC* cut, will be the monopoly point where output is *OM* and price is *MP*. Consumers' surplus lost is equal to *SPP'T*, while monopoly revenue is *SPQR*, which may be greater. But against this must be reckoned the loss in rents, *RQP'T*, so that there is a net social loss of *PQP'*.

One is tempted to divide the monopoly revenue *SPQR* into two parts, *SPCT* and *RQCT*, and to say that the former is the monopoly revenue extracted from consumers while the latter is the monopoly revenue extracted from receivers of rent or producers' surplus. It is exactly parallel to the extraction of monopoly revenue from the receivers of consumers' surplus, but is obtained in virtue of the monopolist being confronted with a rising supply curve instead of with a falling demand curve. It is a gain obtained by a " single " buyer instead of a gain obtained by a " single " seller. The appropriate parallel name for it would be *Monopsony Revenue*.[1] This dichotomy of the monopoly revenue is based on a comparison of the monopoly position with the competitive position.[2] *PC* is the rise in price and *QC* is the fall in average cost, so that these quantities multiplied by the monopolistic output give the monopoly revenue and the monopsony revenue respectively.

It will, however, not do to compare the monopoly position with the competitive position for the purpose of making the dichotomy, for by this procedure it is made to depend upon the shape of the curves for outputs between the monopolistic output *OM* and the competitive output *OM'*, which may be a long way from it. It does not seem reasonable that the degree of monopsony or monopoly at output *OM* should be dependent upon what happens to demand or cost curves in the vicinity of output *OM'*. And apart from this the taking of the competitive output and price as a base from which everything is to be measured leads to more concrete inconsistencies. Thus we may attempt to find the amount of monopoly revenue, (in the more exact sense, that is, not including monopsony revenue) by considering what it would be if the average cost were constant at the competitive level so that there was no monopsony. *AC* and *MC* would then coincide with *TP'*, and the monopoly

[1] Joan Robinson, in *The Economics of Imperfect Competition*, introduces the word Monopsony, but does not speak of Monopsony Revenue.

[2] By monopoly position is meant a position in which the demand curve does not appear horizontal to all the firms in the industry. The simplest case of this is when there is only one firm which coincides with the whole industry, and that is what is shown in Fig. 2 at the monopoly position *P*. Monopoly is essentially a property of *firms* and by a monopolistic industry is meant nothing more than an industry in which *firms* have downward sloping demand curves. And, of course, only a firm is interested in maximising monopoly revenue. If the demand curve for the whole industry is horizontal, the industry is in a competitive condition, but that is only because in this case every firm in the industry must also have a horizontal demand curve—even if there is only one firm.

revenue would not be *SPCT* but some other larger amount, for the output could not be *OM* but some other amount. If we reverse this process, assuming that the demand curve and the *MR* curve are horizontal, we again find that the monopsony revenue is not *RQCT* but some other larger amount, and the output is not *OM* but, again, some other amount.[1]

The direct comparison of monopolistic with competitive equilibrium further assumes that cost conditions are the same and that demand conditions are the same. Neither of these is likely, and the combination of both is much less likely.

A more reasonable procedure for the allocation of the gains as between monopoly and monopsony revenue is to take as a basis not the price which would obtain if there were neither monopoly nor monopsony, but instead of that the actual conditions of the monopoly-monopsony equilibrium. With the given demand curve pure[2] monopoly output could only be *OM* if the horizontal *AC* curve were coincident with *AB*, in which case the monopoly revenue would be equal to *SPAB*. With the given *AC* curve the pure monopsony output could only be *OM* if the horizontal demand curve is coincident with *AB*, in which case the monopsony revenue would be equal to *RQAB*, and *RQAB* and *SPAB* do add up to the monopoly-monopsony revenue *SPQR*.

From this it appears that the monopoly revenue per unit of output, *AP*, is the excess of price over marginal cost, so that the mark of the absence of monopoly is the equality of price or *average* receipts to *marginal* cost, and the mark of the absence of monopsony is the equality of *average* cost to *marginal* receipts.[3]

The test more usually accepted is the equality of average costs to price or average receipts. It is this equation which is regularly given as the definition of

[1] In Fig. 2, where both *AR* and *AC* are concave upwards, the output under monopoly without monopsony would be less than *OM*, and the output under monopsony without monopoly would be greater than *OM*. The outputs are given by the abscissae of the points where *TP'* is cut by *MR* and *MC* respectively. If *AR* and *AC* are convex, the outputs would move in the opposite direction. If they are straight lines, or if the convexity of one is just offset by the concavity of the other, the output will be the same as when the monopoly and monopsony are found in combination. If the elimination of monopsony changes the output in one direction, the elimination of monopoly would change output in the other direction, and *vice versa*.

[2] By *pure monopoly* is meant a case where one is confronted with a falling demand curve for the commodity one sells, but with a horizontal supply curve for the factors one has to buy for the production of the commodity; so that one sells as a monopolist but buys in a perfect market. Similarly, *pure monopsony* stands for perfect competition in the market where one sells, but monopsony in the market where one buys—being confronted with a horizontal demand curve but a rising supply curve. *Pure monopoly* is monopoly free from all elements of monopsony. *Pure monopsony* is monopsony free from all elements of monopoly. *Pure competition* stands for freedom from all elements of both monopoly and monopsony. The *purity* of monopoly or of monopsony has nothing to do with the *degree* of monopoly or monopsony.

[3] *Marginal* cost and *marginal* receipts are, of course, always equal to each other in any equilibrium, whether monopolistic or monopsonistic, or both or neither. It is, therefore, possible to express the same relationships in terms of the equality of price or average receipts to marginal receipts and the equality of average costs to marginal costs. But this procedure rules out conditions of disequilibrium together with monopoly or monopsony, so that to affirm this would be merely to say in other words that the demand or supply curve is horizontal, so that by definition there is no monopoly or monopsony. The relationships given in the text are not the merely mathematical relationships between an average and its corresponding marginal curve, but between real conditions of costs on the one hand and of receipts on the other. It will be seen below that these relationships will not always coincide with the tautologous alternatives suggested in this footnote.

" competitive " position,[1] and a suggestion like the one here given is likely to meet with a lecture on the impropriety of comparing averages with marginal values. It would seem, however, that the orthodox point of view is not only based upon too great a readiness to consider perfect competition as the ideal type of economic phenomena towards which all things tend, but are deterred more or less only by " frictions " (for in perfect competition all these equations become identical), but is in some measure induced by the habit of using straight lines in diagrams dealing with monopoly, and thus missing the problem. For in this case, AB of Fig. 2 would coincide with $P'T$, and the two dichotomies of the monopoly-cum-monopsony revenue are identical.

The point at issue is not merely a verbal one of definition—a quibble as to what it is better to call the " competitive " position. The importance of the competitive position lies in its implications of being a position which in some way or another is better than other positions. It is the position in which the " Invisible Hand " has exerted its beneficial influences to the utmost. It has become the symbol for the social optimum. Its importance for us here is in giving us a basis against which we can compare the effect of monopoly in order to see the social loss, if any, that the existence of a monopoly brings about. Is the social optimum that position at which prices are equal to average cost, or that at which price equals marginal cost and average cost equals marginal revenue ?

The social optimum relative to any distribution of resources (or income) between different individuals (and we cannot here go into the problems connected with optimum distribution) will be reached only if the resources which are to be devoted to satisfying the wants of each individual are so allocated between the different things he wants, that his total satisfaction would not be increased by any transference of resources from the provision of any one of the things he gets to any other thing he wants. This would show itself in the impossibility of any individual being put in a preferred position without putting another individual in a worse position. We may adopt this as our criterion or test of the achievement of the relative optimum. If in any set of circumstances it is possible to move one individual into a preferred position without moving another individual into a worse position (i.e. such that the original position is preferred to it by the individual affected), we may say that the relative optimum is not reached ; but if such a movement is impossible, we may say that the relative optimum has been attained. The conditions which must be satisfied if the optimum is attained can be formulated quite simply.

Any change in the position of any individual means a change in the quantity of goods (and services) he consumes. For any such a change to take place it is necessary that there shall be either (*a*) a *similar* change in the total quantity of goods produced or (*b*) an *opposite* change in the total quantity of goods consumed by others, or (*c*) some combination of (*a*) and (*b*). In the case of (*a*), consumption by other people need not be interfered with by the change,

[1] Even Mrs. Robinson defines " competitive output " and " competitive price " as that output or price at which $AC = AR$ or price (*op. cit.*, p. 160), although she demonstrates most clearly in other parts of the book how this condition ($AC = AR$) is also reached in monopolistic or imperfectly competitive equilibrium.

the whole change in the consumption by one individual being covered by changes in production. In the case of (*b*), there need be no change in production, any increase in the consumption of particular goods by one individual be provided by decreases in their consumption by others, and any decreases in the consumption of other goods by one individual being covered by increases in their consumption by others. In case (*c*) both kinds of compensating movements take place, but these can be separated and dealt with as cases of (*a*) and (*b*) so that no special treatment is necessary.

If a change in the consumption of various goods by one individual which improves his position is compensated solely by a movement of type (*a*), consumption by all other individuals need not be affected. This means that the effect of the movement from the previous position was to make one individual better off without making any other individual worse off. The previous position could not, therefore, have been an optimum position. One condition, then, of the optimum position is that any change in the quantity of goods consumed by any individual which improves his position cannot be compensated by a movement of type (*a*).

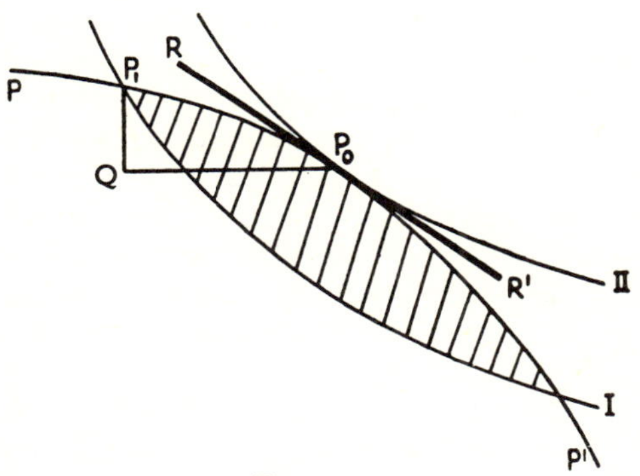

FIGURE 3

This is illustrated in Fig. 3,[1] PP' is a section of the displacement cost curve (or production indifference curve) of the whole community. I and II are consumption indifference curves of one individual. The indifference curves are superimposed upon the displacement cost curve, so that the point on the indifference map which represents the quantities of the commodities X (measured horizontally) and Y (measured vertically), consumed by the individual in the initial position, coincides with the point on the communal displacement cost curve which represents the total amount of the commodities (X and Y) produced in the whole community in the initial position. If P_1 is this position, a movement from P_1 to any point above I represents a movement favourable to one individual. Compensating movements of type (*a*) from P_1 are, however, limited to points below PP'. The shaded area in the diagram represents positions to which movements from P_1 are favourable to one individual and can be compensated by movements of type (*a*). Thus a movement from P_1 to P_0 represents a diminution in the production of Y by an amount P_1Q and an increase in the production of X by an amount QP_0;[2] accompanied by a similar change in one individual's con-

[1] I am indebted to Mr. V. Edelberg for the suggestion of the application of the indifference curve apparatus to the problem in this manner.

[2] It is not necessary that all or any of the identical units of factors set free from the production of Y should be used in the production of X. They, or a part of them, may go to the production of a third commodity Z, as substitutes for other factors which are released to produce the additional X; and there may be any number of such steps. This, of course, does not mean that every commodity is a *direct* displacement cost for every other commodity at the margin (in the

sumption which moves him on to the higher indifference curve *II*; while the quantities of goods remaining to be consumed by other people are unaffected.

It is, of course, not necessary that any improvement should go up to the highest possible point—here P_0. A movement from P_1 to any other point in the shaded area indicates an improvement, but leaves room for still further improvement.

Such a movement is possible as long as the indifference curve cuts the displacement cost curve, giving an overlapping (shaded) area. Our first condition for the optimum position can be expressed by saying that these curves must not cut.

If the curves are smooth this will mean that they are tangential as at P_0, but our condition is satisfied without the tangency of the curves, if either (or both) of the curves changes directions suddenly at the point where the curves meet or that it forms an angle. What is necessary is merely that the curves shall meet at P_0 without cutting. This condition must be fulfilled for every individual in the community.

The movement of one individual to a preferred position, may, however, be covered by opposite changes in the consumption of others. This, too, can be examined in the same diagram. Let *I* and *II* represent the same indifference curves as before, but let *PP'* represent now not the displacement cost curve, but the indifference curve of any other individual, turned through 180° around the common point which shows the combinations of goods consumed by the individuals. If the indifference curves cut, as they do in our diagram if P_1 is the common point, there is an overlapping area, shaded in the diagram, showing the possibility of improving the position of one without worsening the position of the other. A movement from P_1 to P_0 improves the position of *one* individual and leaves the other at another point on the same indifference curve *PP'*, and, therefore, not worse off. Movements from P_1 to any intermediate point in the shaded area would make both individuals better off. In order to satisfy the condition of the optimum it is therefore again necessary that there should be no gap between the curves, i.e. that they should not cut. If they are smooth, it means that they are tangential, and that the slopes of the indifference curves of both individuals were parallel in the initial position, since the turning of a curve through 180° does not change any slopes.

The diagrammatical treatment restricts one to the consideration of only two commodities. This does not matter for the present purpose, since the relationships described have to obtain for every pair of all the commodities in the economy. This is because the failure of the conditions to be satisfied for *any* pair of commodities shows a possibility for improvement which is incompatible with an optimum position.

If both of these conditions are satisfied, as between each individual's indifference curves and the communal displacement costs curve on the one

sense that factors can move directly from one to the other without economic loss), as would be the case if each factor had the same marginal productivity in all uses—universal substitutability of factors at the margin. It only means that there is some path, however indirect, whereby a diminution in the production of one commodity permits an increase in the production of any other commodity, leaving the quantity of the rest of the commodities unaffected. That is what is meant by drawing a displacement cost curve for any two commodities.

hand, and as between each individual's indifference curves and every other individual's (inverted) indifference curves, on the other hand, it is impossible to improve the position of any individual without worsening the position of some other individual. The optimum position, relative to the distribution of income between individuals, is attained.

Can we make any use of such a complicated set of conditions? If it were necessary to investigate separately the slopes of the indifference curves of all individuals for all pairs of commodities in order to discover whether the conditions are satisfied, it would be most profitable to discontinue this analysis at once. But there is no need for all this. We need merely assume that some of the indifference curves are smooth at the positions representing the amounts consumed by the individuals, and that each individual, in buying goods for his own consumption, considers the price as given. Under these conditions the relative prices of each pair of goods in the market will accurately reflect the slopes of the indifference curves where these are smooth; and for those cases, where an indifference curve forms an angle, the ratio between the prices will give a line (RR' in Fig. 3) of such slope that the indifference curve will lie wholly *above* it, meeting it but not cutting it if it is superimposed on the consumption point P_0. The mere existence of a free market in consumption goods thus satisfies the second of our two conditions.

The first condition is satisfied if the price ratio on the market, represented by the slope of the line RR', is such that the displacement curve lies wholly *below* it, meeting it at the production-consumption point P_0, but not cutting it. If the displacement cost curve is smooth and, therefore, tangential to RR', this will mean that the price ratio is proportional to the marginal displacement costs, which condition is satisfied if *price is equal to marginal cost.*

From this analysis we see that the optimum is reached when the price reflects the alternatives given up at the margin, whether this alternative is considered in physical terms of some other commodity or whether we go direct to the satisfactions that the physical alternatives represent. The loss involved in monopoly can be seen in the divergence between price and this marginal cost. The loss involved in monopsony is of exactly the same nature, and a parallel analysis is rendered unnecessary if we translate the rising supply curve that is seen by the monopsonist into a falling demand curve by considering the purchase of A for B as the sale of B for A. This loss is avoided only if price to the consumer (AR) is equal to marginal cost (MC), and if the wages of labour (AC) are equal to its marginal product ($=MR$). If we prefer we may put the latter statement in the form of demand. The price of leisure demanded by labourers (AR) (which is his wage) must be equal to the marginal cost of his leisure (MC) (which is equal to the marginal product of the labour withdrawn).

II

In considering the degree of monopoly in a particular field one's first inclination seems to be to hark back to the etymological meaning of the word and to see how close the situation is to the conditions which accompany a "single seller." On this line one would say that there is complete monopoly if there is actually only one seller, and that the monopoly element diminishes as the number of sellers increases. One could construct some kind of index of the degree of monopoly, such as the inverse of the number of sellers, which would give values ranging from unity in the case of this kind of " complete " monopoly to zero in the case of an infinite number of sellers.

The most obvious of the many reasons why this will not do is that there may be a very high degree of monopoly (in any sense other than that of the formula for such an index), even where there are many sellers, if one or two sellers control a sufficiently large proportion of the total supply. For this reason one turns instead to discover how great a proportion of the total supply is controlled by one or a few individuals or organisations. The same information may also be sought more indirectly by inquiries into the size of firms.

This procedure, however, is still quite inappropriate for measuring the degree of monopoly if we are interested in its economic and social implications of control over price and social loss as discussed in the first part of this paper. This is seen most clearly when we observe that control by a single firm of 100 per cent. of the supply of a commodity for which the demand is infinitely elastic (which will always be the case if there is some equally satisfactory substitute available at a constant price) is absolutely unimportant and has no economic significance, while a " partial " monopoly of a commodity for which the demand is inelastic may be able to raise price by reducing output and is clearly a much more effective case of monopoly.

The statistical method of measuring monopoly, besides missing the main issue in this way, encounters enormous practical difficulties in which investigators can hardly hope to avoid getting entangled. The problems of allowing for changes in taste and technique, in transport and in business organisation, of dealing with firms making many products and of discovering the degree to which different firms compete with one another or mitigate the competition by Gentlemen's Agreements, trade conventions, business alliances, and so on, are just a few worth mentioning, but there is one that interests us particularly here, and that is the relatively simple one of defining the commodity.

A man may have a considerable degree of monopolistic power although he is in control of only a very small part of the supply of a commodity if he is afforded some protection from the competition of the rest of the supply by the cost of transporting other supplies to his market. Under these conditions the price of the commodity will be different in different places. The best way of dealing with this is to declare that objects having the same physical characteristics are not the same goods if they are at different places. Location is an essential and distinguishing characteristic of economic goods, and the only relationship between the prices of similar goods in different places is that which results from the possibilities of transforming the one good into the other by transporting it from the one place to the other.

And location is not the only variant of this kind, but rather the simplest species of a large genus, and is useful for a simplified exposition of the problems involved. Every specialised gradation of every particular quality of every " commodity " may be treated as " distance," and the cost of changing the quality to a particular grade as the cost of " transport." Some of these problems are dealt with by Hotelling in his article, " Stability in Competition," *Economic Journal*, 1929, p. 41, where he gives examples ranging from the sweetness of cider to the service of churches.

To these variants must be added also all fictitious variations, such as are successfully imposed upon the minds of buyers by skilful advertising, as well as the tendencies of customers to buy from one seller rather than from another by sheer force of habit. Here the " distance " is the fictitious difference in quality or the goodwill of the customer, while the " transport costs " are the costs involved in overcoming the " goodwill " whether by reducing price or by counter-advertisement.

This splitting up of the conception of a commodity of course multiplies the number of commodities indefinitely, and seems to create monopolies in the most unexpected places. Carried to its logical extreme, every firm now becomes a monopoly, since it is impossible for more than one unit of product to be in the same place. But even without going to such extremes it becomes impossible to apply the simple measures of monopoly that we are criticising. Further difficulties are yet to arise.

While the idea of considering the same things at different places as different goods seems to have spread considerably, the full revolutionary implications of this step forward in the picturing of the equilibrial forces do not seem to have been quite realised.

In calling the same thing at different places different commodities, we have rejected the criterion of physical similarity as a basis for the recognition or classification of commodities and have put in its place the principle of substitutability at the margin.

If the same thing at a different place is not the same commodity it is only because the difference in its location prevents it from being substituted for, or used in the same way as, the same thing here. But this principle can be applied in the converse form too. With substitutability as the principle it is no longer necessary for different units of the same commodity to have the same physical characteristics as long as they are substitutable at the margin for the purpose that the buyer wants them. This means that if one pound of coal gives me the same heating power as four pounds of wood, that both of these items cost the same on the market, and I am indifferent as to which I have, then one pound of coal and four pounds of wood represent the same number of units of the same commodity. It means, further, that if I am indifferent as to whether I have one hundredweight of coal every week during the winter, or an overcoat to keep me warm, then a winter's coal and an overcoat are equal quantities of the same commodity. Further still, if I am indifferent as to whether I have a wireless set for £10 or whether I have the satisfaction of saving ten Chinese children from starvation, the wireless set in London is the same quantity of the same commodity as £10 worth of rice in China ; while if I get the same satisfaction from a £100 motor-car here and now as I could from a Mediterranean cruise next year, which costs £100 plus the accumulated interest on the money, then the motor-car here and now and the Mediterranean cruise next year are equal quantities of the same commodity. Physical qualities, spacial and temporal position are irrelevant now that we have the ultimate criterion of substitutability at the margin. If any quantity or complex of goods and services can be substituted at the margin for any other quantity of goods and services (and therefore have the same market value), then they are both equal quantities of the same commodity. It would perhaps be best to give terminological recognition to such a break with traditional usage by speaking of " units of accommodation " instead of units of commodities.

If this way of looking at things seems paradoxical, it is only because we have not yet completely freed ourselves from the crudely materialistic conception of goods with which the Physiocrats and Adam Smith were the first to wrestle. The inadequacy of a purely physical criterion of commodities is obvious when we consider the enormous physical difference which we neglect if they do not affect the qualities in which we are interested (that is which affect our satisfactions), of which we are often completely unconscious, but which are of so much importance to Mr. Sherlock Holmes. Physically there are no two similar articles even apart from location. If two objects are considered to be items of the same good, it is only because they are " good for " the same purpose—always, ultimately, the satisfaction of a want. It is futile to say that the motor-car and the Mediterranean cruise satisfy different wants until we are able to define " similar " wants otherwise than as wants that are satisfied by physically similar objects. There is no *qualitative* criterion of wants. Wants can only be considered as similar when the person who feels them displays equal concern for their satisfaction and thus shows them to be equal in *quantity*. To follow any other course is to sacrifice the logic of the science to the irrelevant convenience of the shopkeeper.

It may be objected that this concept of commodity is so abstract and elusive as to be unusable. That is perfectly correct. But therein lies a great part of its advantages. It cannot be used like the more material conception to drown the theory in irrelevant statistics. It puts an end to attempts, here, to find a measure of monopoly in terms of the proportion of the supply of a commodity under single control and clears the way to a better understanding.

Another line of approach that suggests itself is to compare the amount of monopoly revenue with the total receipts, and to take this ratio as a measure of the degree of monopoly power. Allowance is thus made for the size of the industry or the firm. We will obtain values ranging from 0 in the case of perfect competition to 1 where the whole of receipts is monopoly revenue, and at first glance all seems well.

This procedure will, however, not do, for what we want in the measure of monopoly is not the amount of tribute individuals can obtain for themselves from the rest of the community, by being in an advantageous monopolistic position, but the divergence of the system from the social optimum that is reached in perfect competition. From this point of view the monopolist gains are not to be distinguished from rents of scarce property that he owns, or any other source of individual income. The independence of the monopolist gain from the social loss can perhaps most clearly be brought out by a consideration of how far they can vary independently. The limiting case is seen where the demand curve for the product of a monopolist coincides over considerable range with his average cost curve. Here the monopoly revenue is zero wherever the monopolist produces within this range, yet he has control over price, and the social loss will be different according to what output the monopolist decides to produce. It clearly will not do to say that the degree of monopoly power in such a case is zero.

If the average cost curve is horizontal such a divergence cannot occur. The firm can only change output while keeping monopoly revenue zero if the demand curve is also horizontal, and that means perfect competition in either case and no social loss. But in such a case we are comparing not merely monopoly revenue with total receipts, which is the same as the ratio between average receipts minus costs and average receipts (and which is also seen in the ratio between average costs and average receipts), but also *marginal costs* with *average receipts*, and it is in divergence between these, as we have seen above, that the essence of monopoly is to be found.

In such cases (where the cost curve is horizontal) the ratio of monopoly revenue to total receipts coincides exactly with the ratio of the divergence of price from marginal cost to price, and it is this latter formula that I wish to put forward as the measure of monopoly power. If P = price and C = marginal cost, then the index of the degree of monopoly power is $\frac{P-C}{P}$.

It will be observed that this formula looks like the inverse of the formula for the elasticity of demand. It differs from it only in that the item marginal cost replaces the item marginal receipts. In equilibrium as normally conceived marginal costs coincide with marginal receipts so that our formula becomes identical with the inverse of the elasticity of demand. It will be best to consider this as a special case.

In this special case we can find the degree of monopoly power via the elasticity of demand. The determination of this elasticity of demand is not to be confused with that of Pigou and Schultz in finding the elasticity of demand (as part of the demand function) for a materially (physically) defined commodity on a market. What we want here is the elasticity of demand for the product of a particular firm. This is much easier to obtain, for it is only when he knows the shape of the demand curve for his product that any entrepreneur can obtain his maximum profit; and he is, therefore, always applying himself energetically to obtaining as accurate an estimate as possible of this elasticity. This does not mean that the entrepreneur will be able to fill in the elasticity of demand on a questionnaire form. He will rarely know what the term means. But his unfamiliarity with the technical jargon of economists must not be held to show an ignorance of so primary a principle for intelligent business management as the urgency of knowing the effect of price changes on sales. His behaviour in running the business for maximum profit will enable any student to deduce the (estimated) elasticity of demand from the firm's cost curve and the selling price. From the average cost curve the marginal cost curve can be derived. The marginal cost is equal to the marginal receipt, output being adjusted so as to make them equal if profit is maximised. The elasticity of demand is equal to the price divided by the difference between price and marginal cost—it is the inverse of our formula for the measurement of the degree of monopoly power.

In finding the degree of monopoly in this special case " via the elasticity of demand " we found that the easiest way of finding the elasticity of demand was via the degree of monopoly. We may, therefore, leave out the elasticity of demand altogether and just keep to our formula all the time. In the special case both come to the same thing, but we must use the new formula and not the inverse of the elasticity of demand whenever we consider cases where the maximum monopoly revenue is not obtained in practice.

This may be accidental, as when the monopolist does not know the shape of his demand curve and his estimate of the elasticity of demand at the actual output is erroneous ; or it may be intentional. The price and output may intentionally be fixed in a manner which does not give the maximum monopoly revenue :

(*a*) When the monopolist is not working on purely business principles, but for social, philanthropic or conventional reasons sells *below* this price commodities which it is considered socially desirable to cheapen—as when a public authority supplies cheap transport facilities—or sells *above* this price commodities which are considered socially harmful—as may be done by a State liquor monopoly.

(*b*) When the monopolist is working on purely business principles, but keeps the price and his profits lower than they might be so as to avoid political opposition or the entry of new competitors. The second could, perhaps, better be considered as a case where the demand is more elastic in the long period, taking into account the contingent competition, than in the short period, and where the monopolist takes a long period view.

In all such cases our formula is not equal to the inverse of the elasticity of demand ; but wherever there appears a divergence between the two it is our formula and not the inverse of the elasticity of demand which gives the measure of what we want. In the first case—where the monopolist's estimate of the elasticity of demand is erroneous—the consumers will in every way be in exactly the same position as if the elasticity were what the monopolist thinks it is. If he over-estimates the elasticity of demand he will sell a larger amount at a lower price. If he thinks the elasticity is infinite—i.e. that if he produced less he would not be able to get a better price—he will make price equal to marginal cost, and the effect on consumers will be the same as if there were perfect competition.[1] The unused monopoly power will be there, but being unknown and unused it is, economically, as if it were not there. For practical purposes we must read monopoly power not as *potential* monopoly, but as monopoly *in force*.

If the monopolist underestimates the elasticity of demand he will sell a

[1] Mrs. Robinson has pointed out to me that the delusion that elasticity is infinite would persist only if *MC* happened to equal price already. This is the easiest case for the correction of a mistaken estimate in the process of adjustment to it. The same possibility exists with any estimated elasticity of demand as long as the marginal cost and the estimated marginal receipts do not coincide and so preclude any adjustments.

smaller quantity and at a higher price than at the point of maximum monopoly revenue. The only difference between this and the previous case is that the monopolist's error brings a loss to consumers instead of a gain. The monopolist himself, of course, loses by the error in either case. The consumer here has to pay a higher price or else do without. It is again just as if the elasticity of demand were what the monopolist thinks it is. This may sound as if the monopoly *in force* is here greater than the *potential* monopoly power, but the inverse of the elasticity of demand at the maximum revenue point does not really give the potential monopoly power. It gives just that degree of monopoly power which it is necessary to put into force in order to obtain the maximum revenue and which is in force where the maximum revenue is being obtained. The monopolist always has powei in excess of this ; but as the employment of it can only bring him a loss, he normally does not use it intentionally. If he chooses to use it he can, of course, for the exercise of this power consists of diminishing the amount he produces. Potential monopoly power is only used to its maximum when the monopolist stops all production. What our formula gives is the degree of monopoly power in force.

The same arguments apply to cases where the maximum monopoly revenue is not obtained for social, philanthropic or conventional reasons or for the purpose of avoiding political opposition or contingent competition. In the last case, our procedure saves us all further investigation into the complications involved in considering the length of the period upon which the demand curve is based. The appropriate costs to be reckoned are those of the present, or rather of the immediate future, so as to enable us to measure temporary monopolies. The degree of monopoly over a long period is perhaps best expressed in an average of the short-period monopolies over the period.

The primary unit to which our measure of monopoly applies is the firm in the very shortest period. In order to get a measure of monopoly over a period we had to take an average of such coefficients of monopoly. In order to get a measure of monopoly over an industry we have to follow the same procedure and find an average of monopoly of the separate firms included in the industry. The " industry " is to be considered as a group of firms, chosen for the purpose of the special investigation. It is quite unnecessary, for this purpose, to say anything at all about the " commodity " which the " industry " produces, nor is there any need to be able to draw demand or supply curves for the industry. All the difficulties of definition of " commodity " or " industry " are completely avoided.

More strictly a simple average of the degrees of monopoly in firms may be used to indicate the degree of monopoly in an industry only in the very limited sense of the degree of monopoly *at that stage*. It is not a measure of the degree to which the application of the resources of the community to the production of the products of the " industry " diverges from the social optimum. That depends upon two other sets of conditions in addition to this *local* element of monopoly.

The first of these is the degree of monopoly in the firms (or " industries ") producing the raw materials for all the previous stages in the production of the products. The restriction of productions in any stage has its effects in all the succeeding stages. The final degree of reduction of product will depend upon the degree of monopoly in all the preceding stages. These have to be aggregated so as to give the tendency to divergence from the social optimum in the whole series of the production stages of the product ; this phenomenon may be called the transitiveness of monopoly.

Theoretically, this can be done quite simply. What we want is the divergence between the price of the product and its marginal *social* cost. If in all the previous stages price is equal to marginal cost, the marginal cost to the firm is also the marginal social cost. If in any stage there is a divergence, price being above marginal cost, that divergence is a gap in the social cost. The social cost can then be calculated by multiplying the price by a factor for each stage in production, each factor being the ratio of the marginal cost to the price in the corresponding stage. Thus, if there are five stages and in each stage the degree of monopoly is $\frac{1}{5}$, marginal cost over price in each stage is $\frac{4}{5}$, the social cost is $(\frac{4}{5})^5$ of the price of the final product, and by our formula the " social " degree of monopoly is $1-(\frac{4}{5})^5$.

Practical difficulties that arise in attempts to measure the " social " degree of monopoly, or different products may be attacked by any of the tricks of the trade of mathematical statistics. It may be necessary to assume average degrees of monopoly in separate stages and to calculate " social " degree of monopoly by the number of stages, and so on ; but it is not intended here to discuss anything but the simplest theoretical implications.

The second set of complicating considerations arise when we ask the even more ambitious question : What is the (social) degree of monopoly in the society as a whole ? From this general point of view the conditions for that optimum distribution of resources between different commodities that we designate the absence of monopoly are satisfied if prices are all *proportional* to social marginal cost. If the " social " degree of monopoly is the same for *all* final products (including leisure) there is no monopolistic alteration from the optimum at all. The absolute height of " social " degrees of monopoly becomes completely unimportant.

This is because if the "social " degree of monopoly is the same for all products it *must* be equal to zero in real terms. For from the social point of view, the marginal cost of any product is always some other product. If the " social " degree of monopoly for product A is positive, this means that the price of A is greater than the price of some other product B which is the alternative foregone. The price of B cannot then be greater than the price of A. If both degrees of monopoly are equal they must both be zero.

What is important is the deviations between the degrees of monopoly ; and it is this which must be measured in order to answer our question. A suitable measure for this is the standard deviation of the " social " degrees of monopoly of all final products in the society.

Another complication arises in the growingly important cases where it is found to be profitable to extend or maintain the amount sold, not by reducing price but by expenditure on advertising, salesmanship, gifts, coupons and beautiful wrappings—all of which can be subsumed under the heading of " marketing costs." In such cases what becomes of the elasticity of demand ?

In the recent cost controversy, "marketing costs" were eagerly seized upon in attempts at a conciliation between decreasing costs and competitive equilibrium.[1] Such arguments may be described with some justification as contriving to exhibit decreasing costs at peace with competitive equilibrium by the device of leaving out of account the marketing element in the costs which is increasing so rapidly that *total costs* are not decreasing at all; the contradiction being hidden by a separation of "productive" from "marketing" costs.

This solution of the problem cannot, however, be dismissed as mere word-jugglery. It does show the actual working of the forces involved, and it is only the terminology that is unfortunate. What we have here is not perfect competition but *monopolistic* or *imperfect* competition. Chamberlain and Robinson have developed a more satisfactory line of attack on these problems, but how are we to find the falling demand curve which will entitle us to put these cases into this category and enable us to deal with them in the same way?

In order to obtain this it is essential to separate productive from marketing costs. The marketing costs involved in selling a given quantity of product must be subtracted from the gross receipts, just as if they were all direct or indirect reductions in price, leaving a definite total and average net receipts. For each quantity produced different prices may be charged and different marketing costs incurred. For each output some combination of prices charged and marketing costs incurred will leave a maximum average (and total) residue after subtracting the average (or total) marketing costs, and this maximum is the relevant Average Net Receipts for that output. The locus of such points will be the Average Net Receipts curve for the firm, and this is the "demand curve" which we need. This average net receipts curve and the corresponding marginal net receipts curve have to be used in conjunction with the "productive" cost curves which we may call "net" cost curves.

If the average net receipts curve is negatively inclined, one proceeds just as in the simple analysis of imperfect competition where there are no selling costs. The firm equates its marginal net cost to its marginal net receipts, and the degree of monopoly is equal to average net receipts over average net receipts minus marginal net costs, and the divergence of the position from the social optimum is illustrated by the fact that production is not carried on at the minimum average cost, but the firm produces less than this optimum output, stopping at a point where the average net cost curve is tangential to the average net receipts curve. The social loss, if any, due to the expenditure of resources on advertising is *not* taken into account in the measurement of monopoly. The measure will be the same whether the marketing costs are large or small, and whether they are given to the consumer in forms corresponding to cash, or whether they have important influences on his tastes for good or for bad. The social effects of different kinds of advertising constitute a quite separate problem.

If the average net receipts curve is horizontal where the marginal net costs curve cuts it, there is no monopoly. The existence of marketing costs is quite another matter.

[1] As by R. Harrod in his article on "The Law of Decreasing Costs," *Economic Journal*, Dec. 1931.

B

But there is no reason why the average net receipts curve should not slope upwards! It may well be that a larger quantity can be sold at a higher price at the same or a smaller *average* cost of marketing, and there is no ground for considering such a combination of circumstances as in any way exceptional. We must apply the same analysis here and not be deterred if the results at first appear a little strange.

If the firm with a rising average net revenue curve has a constant cost curve, or can acquire more of the product from other firms without affecting its marketing possibilities, we have another form of the paradox of the incompatibility of equilibrium with a horizontal demand curve and a falling average cost curve below it. The marginal revenue and the marginal cost curves cannot meet until the conditions are changed. Either the receipts curves must begin to fall or the cost curves must rise.

The interesting case—the one which can remain in equilibrium in these conditions—is the case where the average costs of the firm rise after a time as output increases, and where it cannot obtain more from other firms at the same price, either because the other firms' costs rise or because to do this would interfere with the reputation of the firm and upset its marketing possibilities.

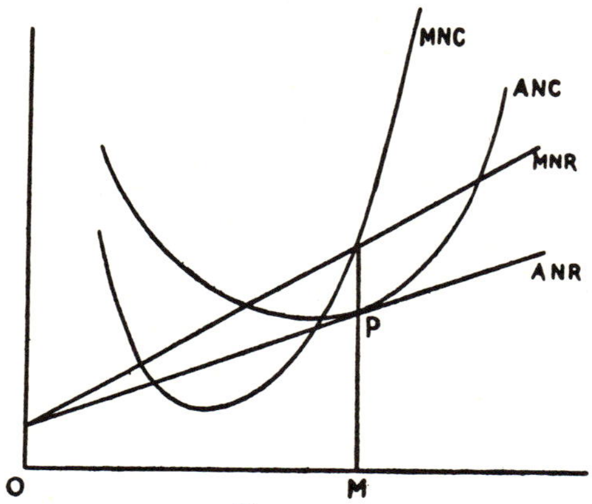

FIGURE 4

This is shown in Fig. 4, where the firm is in equilibrium producing an output OM.

Average net receipts (ANR) are equal to average net costs (ANC), and marginal net receipts (MNR) are equal to marginal net costs (MNC). The degree of monopoly is here *negative* since marginal cost is greater than average receipts. This may appear surprising, but it merely means that the divergence from the social optimum is in the direction opposite to that usually brought about by monopolies. Instead of the firm producing *less* than it should, it is producing *more*; the same kind of social harm is done, and it is reflected in the same way by the excess of the average cost over the minimum.

In finding an average degree of monopoly in an " industry," positive and negative monopolies may cancel out in whole or in part. Does this harm our apparatus?

I do not think it does this at all. It rather brings out the true nature of our measure as an index of *divergence* from an optimum. In any group of firms taken together to make an " industry," divergences may, and should, be expected to some extent to cancel out. For we are now considering the application of resources to this " industry " as against the rest of the economy. If of two firms within the " industry," one is producing too much and the other too little from the point of view of the economy as a whole; the industry may not be producing either too much or too little. The maladjustment becomes a local affair which we must neglect in this larger consideration.

When our " industry " becomes the whole society, there cannot be too much or too little resources used, and as we have seen above, all the individual positive and negative monopolies must cancel out. This does not mean that society as a whole must always be in an optimum position, nor does it take any meaning away from the concept. It only means that the larger the fraction of the whole society one wishes to examine, the less legitimate is it to use particular analysis. In applying the particular mechanism to the whole economy we get the appropriate *reductio ad absurdum*. What is relevant for general analysis is not the *sum* of individual degrees of monopoly but their *deviations*. The standard deviations as suggested above may perhaps be used one day to give an estimate of the divergence of society from the social optimum of production relative to a given distribution of income.

A. P. LERNER.

London.

[3]

II.—THE DIAGRAMMATICAL REPRESENTATION

By A. P. LERNER
(*London School of Economics*)

THE interesting concept of elasticity of substitution developed by Dr. J. R. Hicks in his *Theory of Wages* might be more easily handled by some people if it could be expressed in diagrammatical form, so that the elasticity of substitution could be read off in the same way that the elasticity of demand is read off a demand curve. It will be attempted in this note to show how such a curve could be produced.

Consider the curve II′, neglecting the rest of the diagram. Measuring two factors of production X and Y along the axes, the curve II′ represents quantities of the two factors which can be used to produce the same amount of product, so that any point P on the curve means that the given quantity of product can be produced by means of OM of X and MP of Y; OM being equal to the abscissa of P and MP its ordinate. The slope of the curve at any point represents the ratio at which one factor can be substituted for the other without changing the amount of product, so that at P, X and Y are substitutable for each other in the ratio of ML of X to MP of Y (PL being tangential to II′ at P). This ratio is the inverse of the ratio between the marginal productivities of the factors. The elasticity of substitution, it will be remembered, measures the degree to which the substitutability of one factor for another varies as the proportion between the factors varies. In figure 1, the substitutability of the factors for each other is measured by the tangent or slope of the curve at any point. At P it is equal to $\frac{MP}{ML}$ or the quantity of Y that a unit of X can replace if we are considering the substitutability of X for Y, or $\frac{ML}{MP}$ in terms of the substitutability of Y for X. This is obvious from the symmetry of the diagram, and in the rest of the note we shall speak only of the substitutability of X for Y.

The ratio between the factors at the point P is $\frac{OM}{PM}$. If we can now construct a curve which measures along the X axis the ratio between the factors, and along the Y axis the substitutability of X for Y, the elasticity of such a curve will give us the elasticity of substitution, or the proportional change in substitutability as a function of the proportional change in ratio, in the same way as the elasticity of a demand curve gives us the proportional change in price as a function of the proportional change in quantity.

Such a curve can be constructed geometrically from the II′ curve. Choose a unit of Y and a unit of X arbitrarily. Measure off the unit of Y along the Y axis equal to OA. From A draw a line AA′ parallel to the X axis. Join OP, and let OP or OP produced cut the line AA′ at Q.

In Figure 2, mark off ON along the X axis equal to AQ, and draw a perpendicular to the X axis NS. Now mark off NR along the X axis equal to the chosen unit of X, and from R draw a line parallel to PL in Figure 1. This line will cut NS at a point we will call P′. In the same way a series of points like P′ can be drawn in Figure 2, each corresponding to a point like P on the II′ curve in Figure 1. The locus of such points will be a descending curve if the II′ curve is convex to the origin. The curve in Figure 2 will be our substitution curve, the elasticity of which will measure the elasticity of substitution. The abscissæ will measure the proportion of X to Y; thus since OA = 1, $ON = AQ = \frac{AQ}{OA} = \frac{OM}{MP}$. The ordinate of Figure 2 will measure the substitutability at the corresponding point; thus, since NR = 1, $NP' = \frac{NP'}{NR} = \frac{MP}{ML}$. This treatment, of course, can be applied to any two factors which we have here referred to generally as X and Y.

If II′ is a straight line the tangent to the II′ curve is constant and so NP′ is constant. This gives us a horizontal substitutability curve signifying infinite elasticity of substitution. This is because a straight II′ curve shows the absence of any resistance to the continued substitution of one factor for another at a constant rate.

If II′ is a rectangular hyperbola or curve with elasticity unity, the elasticity of substitution will also be unity. This is because the slope of a rectangular hyperbola at any point is always equal and opposite to the slope of the line joining that point to the origin. Since the first is $\frac{MP}{ML}$ the ordinate of the substitutability curve and the second is $\frac{MP}{OM}$ the inverse of the abscissa, the ordinate and the abscissa will vary inversely giving a constant product and a rectangular hyperbola with elasticity unity.

The greater the convexity of II′ towards the origin the less will be the elasticity of substitution, the limiting case being reached when there is a finite change of slope of the II′ curve at a point—the curve is broken into two parts which make an angle at the point of $<180^{\circ}$ above the point so that the angle points downwards. The sudden change of slope is reflected in the substitutability curve by a sudden vertical fall so that at that point the elasticity of substitution is zero.

If II′ is concave towards the origin instead of convex, the substitutability curve will slope upwards. This can be described as showing an elasticity of substitution " greater than infinity " or as a negative substitutability. In this case there is no question of absence of resistance to continual substitution, but rather of encouragement to continual substitution. It is a case of increasing returns to changes in ratio and is incompatible with competitive conditions for, at a given ratio between the prices of the factors, costs can be reduced or output increased by substituting either factor for the other.

In another note in this journal Mr. P. M. Sweezy arrives independently at a similar curve obtained by a different process for the special case when the factors are labour and " time." Mr. Sweezy, instead of using the II′ curve, considers the variations in the amount of product from a given quantity of labour as the time of production is varied. The increase of one factor while the other is constant has results which are identical with the substitution of one factor for another only if the production function is homogeneous, i.e. if there are no economies or diseconomies of scale. If that assumption is made, Mr. Sweezy's argument amounts to the same as mine; but it is, of course, only applicable (as Mr. Sweezy shows) for the special case where one of the factors is " time." It must also be noted that one cannot identify " time " with the factor " capital," for although both must increase together, capital, in most senses of the word, will increase in a greater ratio than " time." My own formulation seems to have the advantages (*a*) of being applicable to any factors whatsoever; (*b*) of not assuming homogeneity in the production function or the absence of any economies or diseconomies of scale; and (*c*) of involving no mathematics.

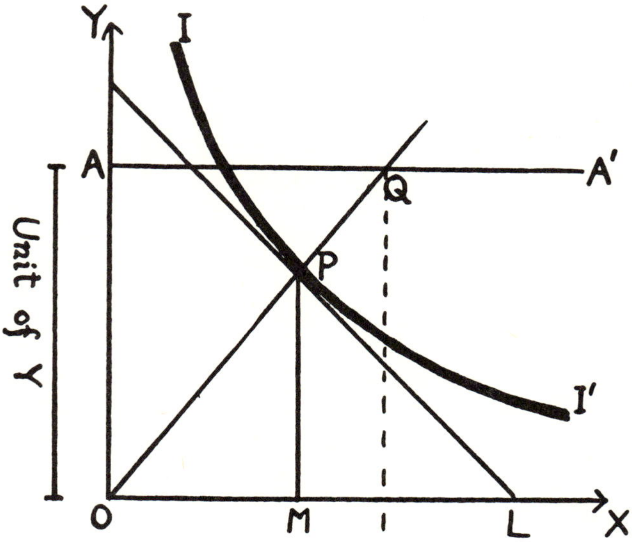

Fig I

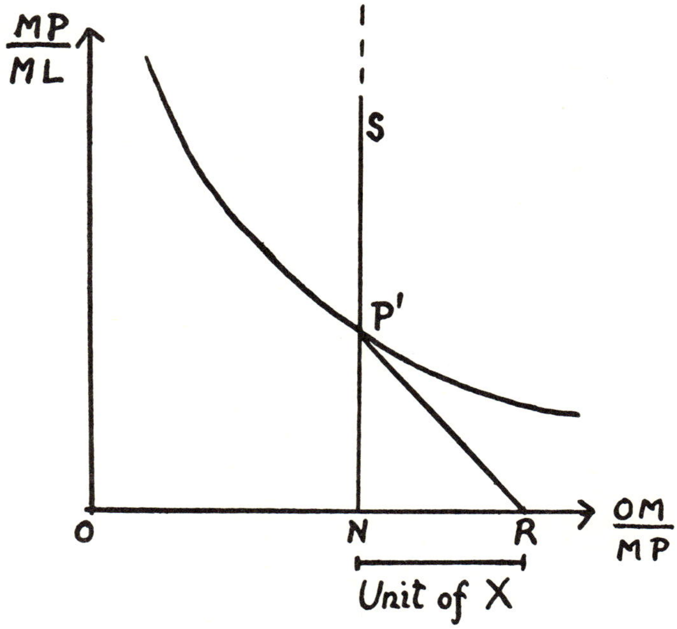

Fig II

[4]

The Analysis of Demand

The first part of this paper attempts to construct a more complete, more systematic and more symmetrical formulation of the Hicksian analysis of demand. The second part endeavors to integrate substitution effects. income effects and complementarities in a more general alternative approach to the analysis of demand.

I. *A Suggested Reformulation*

John R. Hicks' valuable separation of demand into income effects and substitution effects [2, Ch. 2] and his analysis of the substitution effect into complementarity and substitution [2, Ch. 3] are difficult for students to handle, partly because of a certain unnecessary asymmetry and partly because of the use of the word "substitution" for two different purposes.

The asymmetry occurs in the dichotomy of goods into the rather special class of "inferior goods." of which one buys less when real income is increased (relative prices remaining the same), and the much more general class of all other goods. A symmetrical dichotomy might be to divide goods into those which increase less than in proportion to the increase in income and those which increase more than in proportion. Hicks' segregation of inferior goods is more useful than this symmetrical dichotomy, but the benefits of segregating inferior goods could be retained in a more complete and yet symmetrical analysis that marked off a "normal" area from "inferior goods" at one extreme and "superior goods" at the other extreme. A parallel asymmetry appears in Hicks' dichotomy of the substitution effect into complementary goods and all other goods which he calls substitute goods. Here, too, a trichotomy could separate out an opposite extreme, symmetrical with complementarity, leaving a middle range between the two extremes.

The other difficulty that sometimes confuses students is Hicks' use of the same root both in the term "substitution effect" to refer to the change in the amount of a good bought in response to a change in its relative price (as contrasted with the "income effect" or the response to a change in real income) and in the term "substitute good" to refer to a particular kind of substitution effect; namely, the effect of a reduction in the amount of one good bought when more of another good is bought (as contrasted with a "complementary good" where there is an increase instead).

To avoid these difficulties I suggest the following set of nine definitions:

1. *Income effect:* The change in the quantity of good[1] bought as a result of change in real income, relative prices remaining the same.

[1] Throughout this article, "good" stands also for any *group* of goods whose relative prices are unchanged.

2. *Inferior good:* A good of which less is bought (and therefore has less income spent on it) when income increases. (Income elasticity of demand is negative.)

3. *Superior good:* A good of which so much more is bought when income increases that more than the whole increase in income is absorbed (and less is therefore left available to be spent on everything else). (Income elasticity of demand is greater than the ratio of total income to the amount spent on the item.)

If any good is inferior, then the remaining good (or all the remaining goods taken together) must be superior because more than the whole increase in income is left to spend on it; and conversely, if any good is superior, the remaining good (or all the remaining goods taken together) must be inferior because there is less income left for it (or them).

4. *Normal good:* A good of which more is bought when income increases, but not so much more as to leave less income for everything else. (Income elasticity of demand is positive, but less than the ratio of total income to the amount spent on the item.)

It is possible for all goods to be normal, but they cannot all be inferior and they cannot all be superior. These relationships are illustrated in Figure 1 where the arrows represent possible directions of movement in the quantities of X and Y bought as income is increased from the initial point P.

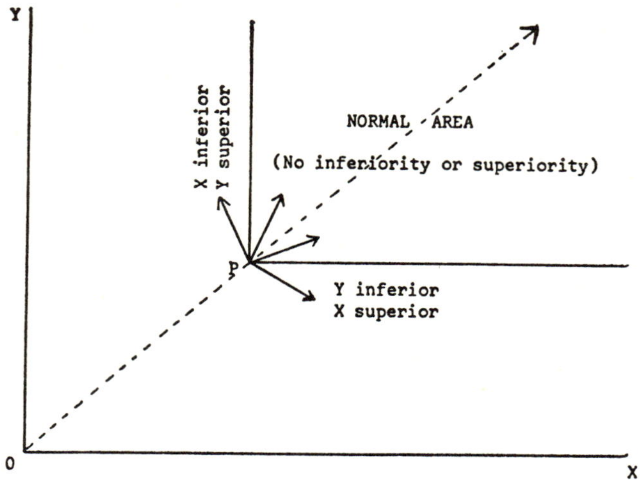

FIGURE 1

The NE quadrant (with respect to P) shows the case when X and Y are both normal so that more of both is bought when income increases. The NW quadrant shows X inferior and Y superior. The SE quadrant shows Y inferior and X superior. The dotted arrow passing through P from the origin is the symmetrical dichotomy suggested above, but rejected in favor of the trichotomy into inferior, normal and superior. In terms of the dichotomy, an arrow through

P steeper than OP would show Y superior and X inferior and a flatter arrow would show X superior and Y inferior, leaving no area at all for "normality."

Hicks' formulation distinguishes only between the NW quadrant where X is inferior and all the other possible directions for the arrows where X is not inferior. It can also be applied in reverse to distinguish only between the SE quadrant where Y is inferior and all the other possible directions of the arrows where Y is not inferior.[2]

If a group of goods taken together is inferior (i.e., less is spent on them when income is increased), not all of the goods in the group have to be inferior individually. Some of the individual goods and some subgroups may increase in quantity (and therefore have more spent on them) when income increases —i.e., they may be normal or even superior. But at least one of them must be inferior. If less is spent on all of them together, but more than before is spent on some of them, it must be even more true of the remaining ones that less than before is spent on them.

If a group of goods is superior, it is similarly true that not all of them have to be superior individually. But in this case it is possible that no member of the group and no subgroup will be superior. All the members of a superior group and all the subgroups may be "normal" in that although more of each is bought (and more spent on it than before) no single one has more than the whole increase in income directed to the increased expenditure on itself, and some may even be inferior.

To avoid one of the uses of the word "substitution" while refining the analysis of Hicks' "substitution effect," we shall speak instead of direct and indirect price effects.

5. *Direct price effect:* The effect of a change in the price of a commodity on the quantity of that commodity bought (the real income level being kept constant by an adjustment of money income).

The direct price effect is always negative, i.e., the quantity change (if any) is in the opposite direction to the price change. The cheapening of a commodity can never by itself result in less of it being bought.[3]

6. *Indirect price effect:* The effect of a change in the price of a commodity

[2] Students (and teachers) are frequently tempted to say "superior" for noninferior and to suppose that in this they are following Hicks. Hicks does speak of "the inferior good and the superior substitute which replaces it" [1, p. 66], but only to refer to a particular substitute, and does not call "noninferior" goods in general "superior goods."

[3] Prestige goods are only apparent exceptions. If the only thing that is reduced is the price that actually has to be paid, more, never less, will be bought. A change in the price that other people *think* you pay can work the other way, but that is not a genuine price effect.

Similarly with the case of expectations. If price reductions establish an expectation of further reductions, purchases may drop, but it is not the reduction or what one actually has to pay that is responsible for this. It is the *expectation* of future price reduction that is responsible Such an expectation would be only *more* restrictive if it were not for the reduction in what actually has to be paid. In the case of an inferior good, too, the reduction in what has to be paid for additional units can only be responsible for *increasing* the amount bought even if the income effect (of the money saved by the price reduction) should more than offset this in a "Giffen" case.

on the quantity bought of *another* commodity (the real income level being kept constant by an adjustment of money income).

In the case of two commodities only, the indirect price effect can only be positive, i.e., the quantity of the other commodity must move in the same direction as the price of the first commodity. If X becomes relatively cheaper and more of X is bought, this must be accompanied by a decrease in the amount of Y if the real level of income is not to go up; and conversely, a rise in the relative price of X which reduces the amount of X bought must be accompanied by an increase in the quantity of Y.

In the case of more than two commodities, three cases are possible: complementarity, its opposite, and competitiveness.

7. *Complementarity:* If more of Y is bought when more of X is bought (because X has become cheaper), then Y is complementary with X.

If Y is complementary with X, X must also be complementary with Y. More of Y is bought only if the increase in X makes Y more effective. This means that the effectiveness of X and Y together is greater than the sum of the effectiveness of each of them separately, and that means that an increase in Y makes X more effective and X is complementary with Y.

For example, suppose that initially X and Y each cost $1 a unit and are used in such quantities that their marginal worth is just equal to their price. The price of X is then reduced to 90 cents per unit and the quantity of X is expanded until an additional unit is worth no more than 90 cents while the quantity of Y is held constant. If Y is complementary with X (so that there would be tendency for more of Y to be bought), this means that an additional unit of Y has become worth more than its price. Let us say it has become worth $1.05. A unit of X and a unit of Y *together* are then worth at least $1.95. (They would be worth more than this to the extent that adding another unit of X would increase the worth of Y still more.) This means that the use of an additional unit of Y (which costs $1) raises the marginal worth of X from 90 cents to at least 95 cents and that means that X is complementary with Y.

Whenever Y is complementary with X, Z must be related to X in an opposite manner. If increase in X (due to a reduction in the price of X) is accompanied by an increase in Y, there will have to be a reduction in Z sufficiently great to keep the individual on the same level of real income even though both X and Y have increased. It may seem that the natural name for this relationship would be *substitution,* which suggests a natural counterpart to complementarity. This, however, will not do for two reasons:

(a) The counterpart to complementarity, like complementarity itself, is applicable only to the case where there are three or more variables. Yet, it is almost impossible to avoid using the word substitution when referring to the replacement of one input by another or of one output for another in response to a price change where these are the only two variables and complementarity and its counterpart cannot arise.

(b) The term substitution suggests that what is involved in the counterpart to complementarity is a very high degree of substitutability—i.e., that if Y is complementary with X, this is because so much of Z is displaced by the relatively cheapened substitute X that more of Y has to be brought in to maintain the level of real income. But the phenomenon we are concerned with cannot be explained by a high substitutability of X for Z. Even if we take the very highest conceivable degree of substitutability, namely the case where X and Z are completely identical items and therefore absolutely perfect substitutes, a cheapening of X results in Z being completely displaced by X. There would then be more of X than there previously was of X and Z together, because some additional X would displace some of Y (some X will be substituted for some Y). There would therefore have to be *less* Y than before so that Y could not be complementary with X. The relation between Z and X that is a reflection of complementarity between Y and X is not substitutability, but something basically different.

We must therefore avoid the word "substitution" and instead speak of "anticomplementarity."

8. *Anticomplementarity:* If, when X is cheapened and more of it is bought so much less of Y is brought that there is more money left for Z (even though less money than before must be available for Y and Z together) then Y is anticomplementary with X.

There must be less money left for Y and Z together because if this were not so when we have more X, the real income level would be greater, and we are still assuming that money income is being adjusted so as to maintain the same level of real income.

If Y is anticomplementary with X, Z must be complementary with X since more of Z is bought when more of X is bought. (There is more money left to buy Z at an unchanged price.) The converse is also true. If Y is complementary with X, Z must be anticomplementary with X—i.e., so much less of Z is bought that more money is left for Y (otherwise more of Y could not be bought and Y could not be complementary with X).

9. *Competitiveness:* If less of Y is bought when more of cheapened X is bought, but not so much less as to leave more money for Z, then Y is neither complementary nor anticomplementary with X, but a competing good.

It is possible for all goods (other than X) to be competing with X, but it is not possible for all to be complementary with X or for all to be anticomplementary with X because, as we have seen, if Y belongs to either of these last two categories, Z must belong to the other, and vice versa.

A group of goods that is complementary with X may contain goods and subgroups of goods that are not individually complementary, but competing or even anticomplementary with X. In that case, the remaining goods as a subgroup must be even more complementary with X. Since more than before is spent on the complementary group as a whole and less than before is spent on the competing and anticomplementary goods within the group, there must be a still greater increase in the amount spent on the remaining members of the group. At least one of its members must therefore be individually complementary with X.

A group of goods that is anticomplementary with X may similarly contain members of a subgroup of members that are not anticomplementary, but

There is no difficulty in making this comparison because if X and Z are perfect substitutes, an appropriately chosen unit of X is exactly equivalent to a unit of Z.

competing or even complementary with X. But, in this case, it is possible for *none* of its members or subgroups to be anticomplementary with X individually. If some are complementary (so that more is spent on them than before), the remaining members, as a group, will be even more anticomplementary with X. But all the members of any anticomplementary group may be competitive, in that although less is spent on each member than before, no single member or subgroup (which we may call Y') has so much less spent on it that more money is left for Z' (the group of all goods other than X and Y'), and some may even be complementary.

Hicks' "income effect," "inferior good," and "complementarity" have the same meanings as here. Hicks' "normal good" may be either a superior good or a normal good, his "substitution effect" may be either a direct price effect or an indirect price effect, and his "substitute good" may be either an anticomplementary good or a competing good.

II. *Substitution Effect: An Alternative Approach*

The following device is an attempt at an alternative approach to Hicks' "substitution effect." It tries to combine the symmetrical dichotomy mentioned in the beginning of Section I with the trichotomies developed thereafter and it grows directly out of Hicks' extension of the analysis of consumption to the analysis of production. It yields a more general formulation that assimilates income effects to the price effects.

Definition 1—An *element* is an input or an output, outputs counting as positive elements and inputs as negative elements.

Definition 2—A *variable* element is an element that varies in quantity in response to price changes.

> *Theorem 1*—In any economic situation, the changes in the variable elements in response to a change in the relative price of a variable element will never all be in the same direction. If one element increases, at least one other element will decrease, and vice versa.

This is because in any economic situation an increase in an output must be accompanied either by a decrease in some other output or by an increase in some input (which is a decrease in an element, inputs being counted negative). Similarly, a decrease in an input (which is an increase in an element) must be accompanied either by an increase in some other input or by a decrease in some output. If this is not so, the original situation must have been an uneconomic one in which it was possible to get something for nothing. Conversely, a decrease in all the elements that varied would indicate a deliberately wasteful decrease in output or increase in input, implying a departure from an economic situation if such a situation existed in the first place. This theorem seems to correspond to the elimination of income effects by fixing the "nonvariable" elements that constitute the framework within which we are working, leaving room only for relative price effects on the variable elements. (We shall see below that this is not quite so.)

Definition 3—The *direct price effect* is the effect of a change in the relative price of an element on the ratio between the quantity of that element and the quantity of all the other variable elements taken together. (This corresponds to definition 5 of Section I.)

Theorem 2—If the prices of the variable elements all change in the same proportion, so that there is no *relative* change in their prices, there will be no effect on the quantities of any of them.

Since there is no change in the relative price of any pair of variable elements, there is no reason for substituting one for another or for changing the rate of transformation of one into another. A proportional change in the prices of all the variable elements does mean a proportional change in the opposite direction of the relative prices of all the fixed elements relative to the prices of the variable elements, but the quantities of the fixed elements, by definition, cannot be changed.

Theorem 3—Any direct price effect is always positive. The quantity of the element changes in the same direction as the relative price absolutely, as well as in relation to the other variable elements.

This means that a cheapening of an input relatively to the prices of the other elements, if it has any effect at all, will always result in an increase in that input (which is a decrease in the element), and that an increase in the price of an output if it has any effect at all will result in an increase in its output. (The changes might be very small or, in the limiting case zero, but never in the opposite direction.)

Theorem 4—Any response to a change in the price of one variable element in the quantity of the other variable element (or in the quantity of all the other variable elements taken together if there is more than one) is always negative; the quantity—absolutely as well as relatively to the first variable element—changes in the direction opposite to the change in the relative price of the first variable element.

This is because the change in the relative price of the first variable element constitutes an opposite change in the relative price of the second variable element (or the group of all the other variable elements) and the positive direct price effect of the latter constitutes a negative response to the first price change.

Where there are only two variable elements, these relationships can be expressed as follows:

(a) Where both of the variable elements are inputs, e.g., factors of production, one will be substituted for another if its relative price falls. Our device here merely changes the sign—the increase in the relatively cheapened factor is a decrease in one element, and the decrease in the other factor is an increase in the other element.

(b) Where both of the variable elements are outputs, and the price of one output rises relatively to the price of the other, the first will be substituted in production for the second.

(c) Where one of the two variable elements is an input and the other is an output, we find ourselves dealing not with substitution, but with increases or decreases in *production* (the transformation of one element into another). An increase in the price of the product (or output) relatively to the price of the factor (or input) will result in an increase in the output of the product (an increase in one element) accompanied by an increase in the input of the factor (a decrease in the other element); and conversely for an increase in the relative price of the factor.

Where there are more than two variable elements, we may treat the situation in the same way by considering all the other variable elements (other, that is, than the first, whose relative price has changed) as a single second variable element.

This gives no trouble where all the other variable elements are outputs (which have the same sign as elements) or where all the other variable elements are inputs (which have the opposite sign). The matter is a little more troublesome where some of them are outputs and some are inputs. In that case, an increase in the quantity of the "second element" will consist of the increase in the value of the outputs minus the increase in the value of the inputs (or plus the decrease in the value of the inputs), all of course weighted by their unchanged prices.

If the change in the quantity of the first element is accompanied by opposite changes of exactly the same proportion for every one of the other elements, so that the ratio between these is unaffected, it is obvious that they can be treated as a single item and that is the end of the story. Only the direct price effect is operative. But a change in the price of one element, and the consequent change in the ratio of this element to the others taken together, may have an *indirect* effect on the proportions between the other elements. Thus, if the variable elements are all inputs, a decrease in the price of input A, while bringing about the substitution of A for other inputs, may also result in a second input B being substituted for the remaining inputs (which we may now consider together as a third input C). The same indirect effects are of course also possible if the elements are outputs or if some are inputs and some are outputs.

Definition 4—The *indirect price effect* is the effect of a change in the relative price of one variable element on the proportion between a second variable element and the remaining variable element of elements. (This corresponds to but is different from definition 6 of Section 1.)

The direct price effect can be measured by the (direct) elasticity of substitution (or by the elasticity of transformation) which is the proportional change in relative price divided into the proportional change in the relative quantities of the two elements, or groups of elements) involved.

The indirect price effect can be measured by the *cross*-(or indirect) elasticity of substitution (or transformation) which is the proportional change in the relative price of the first element divided into the proportional change in the ratio between the second and third elements.

If A, B, and C are the variable elements, the direct elasticity of substitution or transformation (the measure of the direct price effect of a reduction in the relative price of A) is equal to the proportional change in the relative price of A (relatively, that is, to the prices of B and C) divided into the proportional change in $A/(B + C)$, when $(B + C)$ is the value of the combination of B and C measured at their old prices. The cross-elasticity of substitution or transformation (the measure of the indirect price effect) is equal to the proportional change in the relative price of A divided, not into the proportional change in $A/(B + C)$, but into the proportional change in B/C. If this measure is positive for B, it is negative for C and vice versa, with a dividing line where both are zero and there is no indirect price effect.

The indirect price effect becomes particularly interesting when it is so great that it is able to reverse the direct price effect on the quantity of one of the "other" elements (i.e., other than the one whose relative price has changed). This will be the case only if the increase in, say, B on account of the indirect price effect (i.e., its being substituted for C) is greater than the decrease in B on account of the direct price effect (i.e., greater than the decrease in B that would have taken place if there had been no indirect price effect and the decrease in $(B + C)$ had consisted of exactly proportional reductions in B and in C).

Definition 5—Two elements are *complementary* with each other if a change in one (resulting from a change in its relative price) is accompanied by a change in the other in the same direction. (This corresponds to definition 7 of Section I.)

As we have seen, this could happen only if the indirect price effect exceeds the direct price effect.

Definition 6—Whenever two elements are complementary with each other, the third variable element (or all the others taken together, if there are more than one) is *anticomplementary* with them. (The cross-elasticity is just as great for the third element as for the second, only in the other direction.)[5] (This corresponds to definition 8 of Section I.)

Definition 7—Elements that are neither complementary nor anticomplementary with each other are *competitive* with each other. (This corresponds to definition 9 of Section I.)

Competitive elements may show positive or negative indirect price effects, but these are not strong enough in the positive direction to result in complementarity or strong enough in the negative direction to result in anticomplementarity.

We may now rewrite Theorem 1 more concisely as:

Theorem 1′—The elements in an economic situation cannot all be complementary with each other.

We can also see now that this is only a special case of a still more general theorem:

Theorem 1″—The indirect price effects (or the cross-elasticities of substitution or transformation) cannot be all positive or all negative.

This is because every indirect price effect that is positive for B, because it increases the ratio B/C, must be negative for C because it *ipso facto* reduces the ratio C/B.

All these relationships are most easily seen where the variable elements A, B, and C are all inputs. A fall in the relative price of A will result in more of A being used as it is substituted for the other variable inputs. There may be a

[5] Note that although "indirect price effect" is different in Section II, "complementarity" and "anticomplementarity" have the same meaning as in Section I.

reduction in both B and C, in which case A is competitive with both of these. But it is also possible for one of them, say B, to be complementary with A. Although its price has not fallen, more of B is used because more of A is used. C will then have to decrease all the more, not only because A has been substituted for $(B + C)$ (in the direct price effect), but also to offset the still greater increase in B at the expense of C (in the indirect effect). This reflects C's being anticomplementary with A. Since A must be complementary with B if B is complementary with A, C must be anticomplementary with B as well as with A.

The only remaining possibility is for A to be complementary with C and therefore anticomplementary with B, when B will have to be anticomplementary with C too. This is completely symmetrical with the case just considered and exhausts all the possibilities where the three variable elements are all inputs. In any triad, either all pairs are competitive or one pair is complementary and the other two pairs are anticomplementary.

The analysis is identical for the case where the variable elements are the outputs X, Y, Z, except that, unlike the inputs, these all have the same sign as elements. (We will now use the letters A, B, C, etc., only for inputs and the letters X, Y, Z, etc., only for outputs.) An increase in the price of an output X will result in more of it being produced. This may be accompanied by a decrease in all the other outputs Y and Z, in which case there is no complementarity or anticomplementarity in production. All the elements are competitive. On the other hand, one of the other outputs, say Y, may increase. In that case, we say that Y is complementary with X and we also have to say that Z is anticomplementary with X and that Z is anticomplementary with Y (since X is complementary with Y); and conversely, when Z is complementary with X, Y must be anticomplementary with X and with Z. As in the previous case, complementarity arises only if the cross-elasticity of substitution is sufficiently greater than the direct elasticity of substitution.

But this still does not exhaust all the cases covered by Theorem 1. What if one of the variable elements is an output and the other are inputs, output X and inputs A and B being the variable elements?

A decrease in the price of A will result in an increase in the input of A (a decrease in this element). This may result in the other elements all increasing. More of the cheapened input A (less of element A) works with less of input B (more of element B) producing more of output X (more of element X). There is no complementarity and no anticomplementarity, and all the elements are competitive with each other.

But it is also possible for one of the other elements to be complementary with A and to decrease when element A decreases. Suppose element B is complementary with A. Element B then decreases (input B increases). Element X will then have to be anticomplementary and increases all the more. We may then say, if we wish, that input B being complementary with input A, more of B has to be used together with the increased A, with a correspondingly large increase in output X. Here complementarity looks perfectly normal.

More interesting is the case where the element that is complementary with input A, is an output so that when input A increases (element A decreases), output X (and element X) decreases. Here we have the case of regression [2, p. 93] where the cheapening of a factor of production and an increase in its use leads to a decrease in output! Regression is nothing but complementarity between an output and an input, but it does not look so normal.

We can handle this better by looking at a reduction in the output of X as the feeding of the lost output back into the process, treating it like an input and giving this imaginary input the name D ($\equiv -X$). Similarly we may treat a saving in the input of factor B as an increase in the output of the economized input item, giving this imaginary output the name W ($\equiv -B$). We now have complementarity of D with A. More of input D is used together with more of input A (both of these elements decreasing) in order to produce a large increase in W which is anticomplementary with A. Formally, this is just like the case above where there was also a large increase in output (there of X, here of W) even though this called for using more of another factor (there B, here D) and we have more of both factors producing more of the product. Retranslating this into our original letters, we can say that the complementarity of X with A means that a cheapening of A makes it worthwhile to forego some output of X in order to save on the input of B, since the release of large quantities of B reduces the output of X by very little (because B is anticomplementary with A and with X).

Still more interesting is the case (with the same variable elements A, B, and X) in which there is an increase in the relative price of X. The direct price effect is an increase in element X (and output X). If there is no complementarity, the other elements both diminish. This means that the inputs of A and B both increase and we have the familiar normal increase in production in response to an increase in the price of the product, by increasing all the factors of production.

But suppose element A is complementary with element X. Then the increase in X is accompanied by a movement of element A in the same direction. But an increase in element A is a decrease in input A! This is the other side of regression. This may be dealt with analogously. Treat the saving of a unit of factor A as the production of a unit of an imaginary product called V ($\equiv -A$). Then complementarity of V with X means that as more of X is produced, it is worth devoting more of factor B to the production of V—i.e., to the economizing of A. But there is another and a more attractive way of dealing with this case: A is nothing but an inferior good in the production of X and B is therefore a superior good.

There remains only the case where there is one input and two outputs. But since we can freely translate outputs into inputs and vice versa, this is symmetrical if not identical with the case we have already considered.

What may seem surprising is how the concept of inferior goods crept into our discussion. Inferior and superior goods belong to the income effect which seems to have been left behind when we assumed the "other elements" fixed, concentrating on the direct and indirect price effects that comprise what Hicks called the substitution effect.

The answer seems to be that it depends on what are the other elements fixed. As long as all the outputs or products are fixed, we may say that real income is fixed and we have only price effects and no income effects. Only inputs or factors of production are variable and we can speak only of complementary, competing, and anticomplementary inputs—the substance of Hicks' substitution effect. Similarly, if all the inputs or factors are fixed and only outputs or products are variable, we can speak only of complementarity, competition, and anticomplementarity in production.

But as soon as we permit some of the variable elements to be inputs and others to be outputs, the line between income effects and price effects becomes impossible to apply because holding the other elements constant no longer means the same as holding the level of real income constant. A rise in an output price relatively to an input price (which is the same as a fall in an input price relatively to an output price) induces an increase in input and in output and this is an increase in income; and conversely, a fall in output price relatively to input price induces a decrease in income.

Worse still, even in the case where the variable elements are all inputs or are all outputs, the line disappears as soon as we recognize that economizing a factor is equivalent to increasing a product, and increasing a product without decreasing any other product is clearly congruent with an income effect. Complementarity between an input and an output means that when the output is increased, the input is diminished, so that the input is inferior. When inputs in general are increased so as to produce more of the output, less is used of the inferior input. Complementarity between an input and an output also means that when the input is increased, the output is diminished so that the output is a regressive good. Just as complementarity turns out to include inferiority and regression, so anticomplementarity turns out to include superiority and progression (antiregression). We get inferiority or superiority if the output price changes relatively to the other prices, and regression or progression if it is the input price that changes relatively to the other prices. The inferiority, normality, and superiority of inputs and the regressivity, normality, and progressivity of outputs turn out to be only other sets of names for the three basic relationships between elements: complementarity, competitiveness, and anticomplementarity. Hicks' income effect turns out to be a special case of the indirect price effect, which in turn is a part of Hicks' substitution effect.

All these relationships are illustrated in Figure 2 where *A*, *B*, and *C* stand for inputs and *X*, *Y*, and *Z* stand for outputs. In the trios of capital letters forming the headings of the various columns, a line (marked *c*) connecting two letters, indicates that the two elements represented by the letters are complementary; and a small *a* between two letters indicates that the two elements are anticomplementary. The absence of such a line or letter indicates the absence of complementarity and of anticomplementarity so that the elements are competitive. The plus and minus signs represent increases or decreases in outputs or inputs resulting from the changes indicated at the left of the row, and for every plus there must be a corresponding minus. The signs would have to be reversed for inputs if we were to keep to the language of elements and that would make it easier to check on the symmetry and on the equality of plus and minus signs, but it seems to be easier to follow the meanings if we keep to the

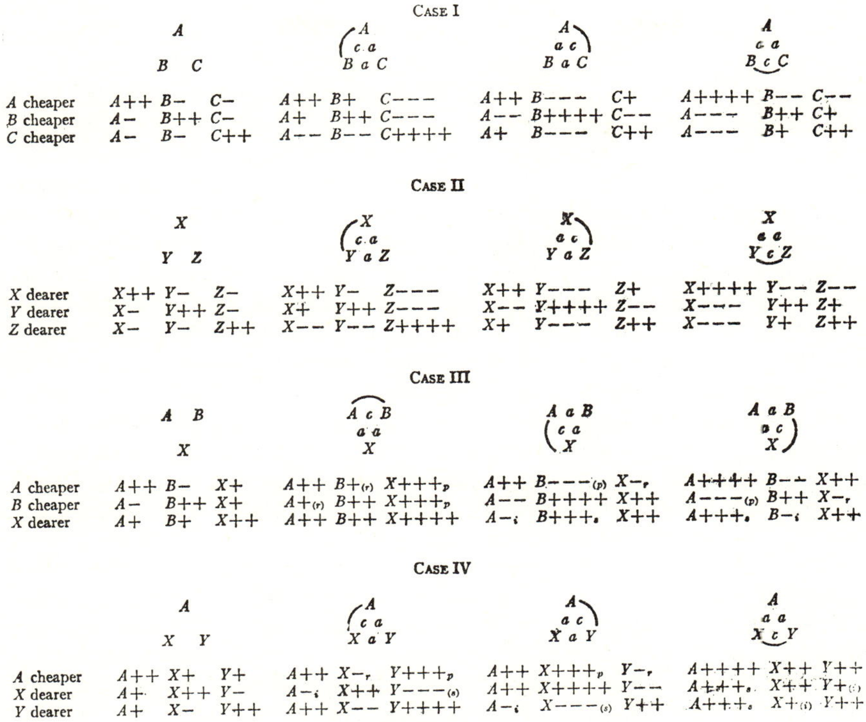

Figure 2

English usage. The number of plus or minus signs indicate the number of influences that would cause the element to vary in the direction indicated. They must not be understood to indicate the *size* of a change because a single influence in one instance might be quantitatively greater than as many as four influences in another instance. It must also be remembered that the anticomplementarity the third element with the two complementary elements refers only to all the other elements (other, that is, than the complementary pair) *taken as a whole* if there are more than one of them. Any proper subset of these may be competitive or even complementary with the complementary pair.

In Case I of Figure 2, the three variable elements are all inputs. (If there are more than three, all those left after two have been considered may be treated as the third element.) The first column shows three competitive inputs. There are two plus signs attached to the *A* in the first row of the first column to indicate that *A* is substituted for *B* as well as for *C*. The minus signs attached to the *B* and the *C* show the other side of the same substitution. The number of plus signs in each case must therefore be equal to the number of minus signs. The same relationship is seen in the next two rows in this column.

The second column in Case I shows *A* and *B* complementary so that *A* and

C are anticomplementary as also are B and C. The first row here differs from the first row in the first column because the complementarity between A and B means that there is an indirect price effect causing B to be substituted for C to such a degree that the $B-$ is turned into a $B+$. This is balanced by the two additional minus signs attached to the C, one to balance the removal of the original minus attached to the B and another to balance the plus put in its place. As before, the total number of plus signs is equal to the total number of minus signs. The second row shows the same thing for a cheapening of B instead of a cheapening of A. The third row is different because it is now not one of the complementary inputs that is cheapened, but the one that is anticomplementary with the other two. The cheapening of C causes C to be substituted for both A and B. But the complementarity causes A to be reduced further because there is less of its complement B, and it causes B to be reduced further because there is less of its complement A. A and B therefore given an additional minus each and two more plus signs are added to C as more of it has to be added to compensate for both of these further contractions if output (and any other elements) are to be held constant. The next two columns of Case I follow exactly the same principles.

Case II shows the completely symmetrical relationships for three variable outputs X, Y, and Z, Case III shows two variable inputs A and B, and one variable output X, and Case IV shows one variable input A and two variable outputs X and Y. An inferior input is indicated by i, a superior input by s, a regressive output by r, a progressive output by p. (These subscripts are put in parentheses where inputs are treated as outputs or outputs as inputs.)

The blurring of the line between income effects and price effects is a result of an ambiguity of the word "income" that is inevitable as soon as it is applied to more than one homogeneous item. In the analysis of income, this is avoided by treating the utility produced by the consumption goods (plus or including saving), or the level of income, as such a single homogeneous item. In the analysis of production on the same line as consumption, it seems natural to consider the restriction imposed by a constancy of the "other elements," when some are varied in response to changes in relative price, as corresponding to the restriction imposed by a constancy of the level of income. This is most natural when the "other elements" which are kept constant consist of all the outputs or products. The analogy still seems to make some kind of sense, as indicating a given level, where the constant "other elements" consists of all the inputs. The analogy is clearly invalid where the varied elements include an input and an output because that permits production and consumption to increase or decrease, but it is only the *visibility* of the invalidity that is affected. The same trouble exists even when the variable elements are all inputs or all outputs. The increase in one output at the expense of a decrease in another output is no different from an increase in an output at the expense of an increase in an input; and a decrease in one input at the cost of increasing another input is no different from a decrease in an input at the cost of decreasing an output. They are just like an increase or a decrease in production.

One is tempted to avoid these embarrassments by simply defining an increase in an output as an increase in output-income, and an increase in an input as an increase in input-income. It is in relation to increases in output-income that an input may be inferior or superior, and it is in relation to an increase in input-income that an output may be regressive or progressive.

Our framework, however, still prevents a "Giffen case" from appearing. A "Giffen case" means an increase in an output when its price falls (or an increase in an input when its price rises); i.e., an element moving in the opposite direction to the change in its price.This can occur only if something other than the change in relative prices permits an increase in the element which more than offsets the direct price effect which, according to Theorem 3, is always positive, i.e., in the same direction as the price change. That something must mean not merely an increase in output-income or in input-income but an increase in income in the general and original sense of an increase in all the elements or an increase in some elements without any elements decreasing, and that is ruled out by Theorem I. Since an input is a negative element, income, or the sum of *all* the elements, consists of output-income minus input-income. Our elimination of income changes in this general sense does not prevent the emergence of inferiority, superiority, progression and regression as aspects of complementarity and anticomplementarity, but it does prevent the emergence of a Giffen effect.

A. P. LERNER*

REFERENCES

1. J. R. HICKS, *A Revision of Demand Theory.* Oxford 1956.
2. ———, *Value and Capital.* Oxford 1939.

* The author is professor of economics at Michigan State University, East Lansing, Michigan. He is indebted for a number of clarifications and corrections to discussion with students and colleagues and especially to Boris Pesek.

[5]

CONSUMER'S SURPLUS AND MICRO-MACRO

ABBA P. LERNER
Michigan State University

THE recent proliferation of suggestions for different measures of consumer's surplus seems to be a symptom of the eagerness of many economists to discredit the concept, to nullify Hicks' rehabilitation of it, and to disassociate themselves from it. The first part of this article attempts to simplify the issue by weeding out some of the plethora of different measurements that are the fruit of an excessive product differentiation in definitions of consumer's surplus. The second part consists of some speculations as to whether some of the unease behind the ingenuity in product differentiation does not arise from the concept's failing to lend itself to the current Procrustean fashion of forcing all economic analyses into one or the other of two boxes labeled "macro" and "micro."

I

By the consumer's surplus gained or lost by a change in price, I mean the money value of the benefit that the consumer gets from a price reduction in a free market or of the damage that he suffers from a price increase. This, it seems to me, is what Marshall had in mind when he spoke of consumer's surplus. The concept is examined carefully by Hicks,[1] who suggests that it can be measured by what he calls the "equivalent variation" (E), the *money subsidy* a consumer would have to get, in lieu of a price reduction, to benefit him as much as the price reduction would have done, or by the *money tax*, in lieu of a price increase, that would hurt him just as much as the price increase would have done.

One of the things that have made many economists uneasy about the concept of consumer's surplus is that it generally has a different measure according to the direction in which it is measured. The subsidy that is equivalent to a price reduction from $5 to $4 will normally be greater than the tax that is equivalent to the price increase from $4 to $5. This, however, is only the natural result of the *income effect*—the change in the demand for the commodity due to the change in real income (or utility level).

If there were no income effect—that is, if the good were just on the borderline dividing inferior goods from non-inferior goods, the income elasticity of demand being exactly zero—the subsidy E would be exactly equal to the tax E. There would be only the *substitution effect* or *direct price effect*. The reduction of the price of a commodity from $5 to $4 would result in an increase in the amount of it bought as it is substituted for other items that have not become cheaper, and an increase in its price from $4 to $5 would result in an exactly equal decrease in the amount bought as the other items are substituted for it in exactly the same degree. There would be complete symmetry between the increase and the decrease in price, and the subsidy equivalent to the price reduction would be exactly equal to the tax equivalent to the price increase.

But if the cheapened commodity is not an inferior good (so that an increase in real income *increases* the demand for it), then the increase in real income due to the price reduction will result in a *secondary increase* in the amount bought (the income effect) over and above the substitution or direct price effect. The secondary increase in the amount bought *increases* the benefit yielded by the price reduction, so that the equivalent subsidy E has to be greater than in the absence of any income effect. Similarly, a price increase, by reducing the real income, brings about a secondary *reduction* in purchases, and this diminishes the damage from the price increase, so that the equivalent tax E is smaller than it would be in the absence of any income effect. The subsidy E will there-

[1] J. R. Hicks, *Value and Capital* (Oxford, 1939), pp. 38–41; and his *A Revision of Demand Theory* (Oxford, 1956).

76

fore be greater than the tax *E* on both counts.

In the case of an inferior good, it is the other way around. A price reduction is not so beneficial, and a price increase is more damaging, so that the subsidy *E* is smaller and the tax *E* is greater.

Hicks also develops the concept of *compensating variation* (*C*). This is the tax or subsidy which must *accompany* a change in price so as exactly to offset or compensate for the benefit or the damage. But this measure is already given by *E*. As Hicks shows in *A Revision of Demand Theory*, *C* for any price change is equal to *E* for the reverse price change. This is because the same income effect is involved in each case. When a price is reduced from $5 to $4, thus raising the level of real income, the compensating variation *C* is the tax that reduces the real income to the original lower level from which it was raised by the price reduction. When a price is *not raised* from $4 to $5, and real income is not lowered, the equivalent variation *E* is the tax that would lower real income from the same higher level to the same lower level as the price increase from $4 to $5 would have lowered real income if it had taken place. It is therefore identical with the compensating variation *C* for the reverse price change.

The difference between the *E* and the *C* for any price change (which is the same as the difference between an *E* for any price change and the *E* for the reverse price change or the difference between the *C*'s for the same pair of opposite price changes) could not arise for Marshall because he was neglecting the income effect. (This is the significance of Marshall's assumption of "constant marginal utility of money.")

Hicks describes two more "consumer's surpluses,"[2] which he calls the *equivalent surplus* (*e*) and the *compensating surplus* (*c*). The equivalent surplus *e* is the same as *E*, except for the stipulation that the consumer must not change the amount he buys (at the unchanged price) even though he might want to do so because of the tax or subsidy.[3] To compensate the consumer for this stipulation, *e* must be a greater subsidy, or a smaller tax, than *E*.

The compensating surplus *c* is the same as *C* except for the same stipulation, namely, that the consumer must not change the amount he buys (at the new price) even though he might want to do so because of the tax or subsidy that compensates for the price change. To compensate the consumer for this stipulation, *c* must similarly be a greater subsidy or a smaller tax than *C*.

Figure 1 shows the case of a non-inferior good. *O* is the initial income measured along the *Y* axis, and *A* is the chosen point showing how much of *X* the individual buys at the price indicated by the slope of *OA*. When the price is lowered to that shown by the slope of *OB*, the individual moves to *B* instead. An increase of income from *O* to *S* is equivalent to the price reduction, because with no change in prices it would permit the individual to move to *C*, which is as good as *B* (on the same indifference curve). *OS* is therefore the subsidy *E* that measures the consumer's surplus gained by the price reduction.

If we started with the price *OB* (so that the individual chose point *B*) and then raised the price from *OB* to *OA*, the individual would go to *A* instead. A decrease in income from *O* to *T* (without any price increase) would harm him just as much as the price increase since it would make him move to *D*, instead of to *B*, and *D* is just as good (or as bad) as *A*. *OT* is therefore the tax *E* that measures the consumer's surplus lost by the price increase. *OS*, the subsidy, is greater than *OT*, the tax, because the triangle *OQS* is greater than the similar triangle *TRO*, because *Q* is to the right of *R*.[4]

[2] Taken from A. M. Henderson, "Consumer's Surplus and the Compensating Variations in Income," *Review of Economic Studies*, 1940–41, pp. 117–21.

[3] "We consider his position before he makes any further adjustment in consumption as a result of the change in his income." (*A Revision of Demand Theory*, p. 100.)

[4] This is because *C* and *B* must be to the right of *A* and *D*, respectively (to show that at higher incomes more is bought of non-inferior goods), and

If the stipulation is made that the tax or subsidy must not change the amount bought, the individual is prevented from moving to the preferred point *C* or *D*, but may only move directly north or directly south from *A* or from *B*. The subsidy *e* must therefore be *Os*, which is greater than *OS*, to enable him to reach *c*, the first point due north from *A*, which is as good as *B* (or *C*). Similarly, the tax *e* will be *Ot*, which is less than *OT*, and yet suffices to move him due south from *B* to *d*, which is as bad as *A* (or *D*).

The case of an inferior good is shown in Figure 2, where *OS* is less than *OT* because *Q* is now to the left of *R*.[5] If the stipulation is made that the tax or subsidy must not change the amount bought, the constraint now works in the opposite direction, but it is still onerous and so the subsidy must still be greater and the tax smaller. *Os* would therefore be greater than *OS* and *Ot* smaller

Q must lie between *C* and *B*, while *R* must lie between *A* and *D*. If *C* should lie to the left of *D* (which it happens to do in Fig. 1, but this need not be so) it is possible to distort the curves so as to make *Q* lie to the *left* of *R*. To do this one would have to make the indifference curves very convex in the vicinity of *C* and *D* and very straight over the rest of the range between *C* and *B* and between *D* and *A*. This would make the straight part of the upper curve very close to the price line *OB* and flatter than the straight part of the lower curve which would be very close to the steeper price line *OA*, indicating that over this range *X* is an *inferior* good—an increase in income would result in a *decrease* in the amount of it bought. A similar distortion is possible in the case of the inferior good of Fig. 2, where the distortion would make the good non-inferior over a part of the range. No such peculiar cases can arise, however, if *C* is to the right of *D* in Fig. 1 or if *A* is to the right of *B* in Fig. 2 and there is no horizontal overlap between *CB* and *AD*.

[5] Just as *C* is to the left of *A*, and *B* is to the left of *D*, to show that when income increases, less is bought of the inferior good (see n. 4).

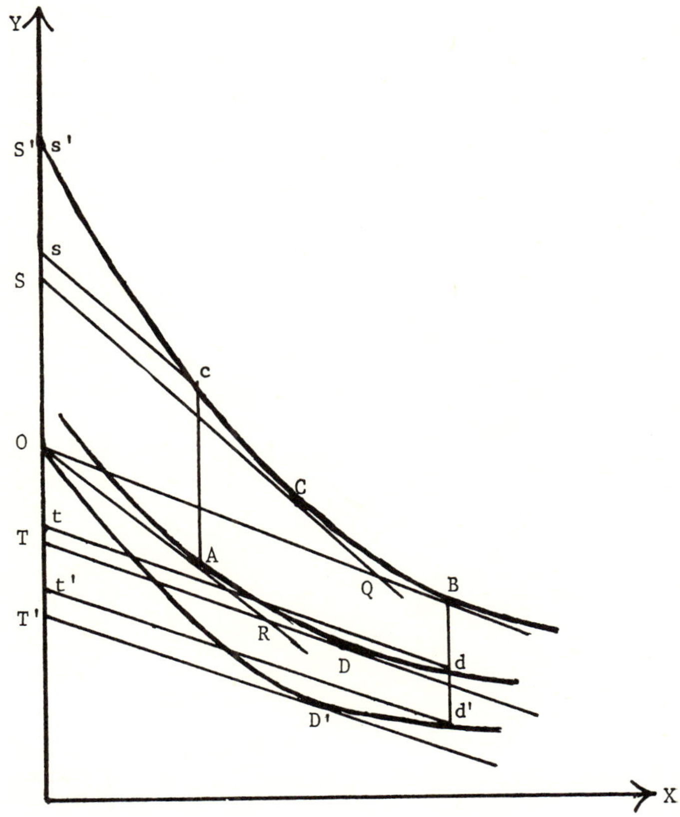

Fig. 1

than OT, just as in the case of a non-inferior good. But Os would still be less than Ot (although these will differ by less than do OS and OT) if X is consistently inferior over the range between A and B. This is because Os is equal to Ac, the vertical distance between the indifference curves at A, and Ot is equal at Bd, the vertical difference between the same indifference curves at B, and for an inferior good the vertical distance between indifference curves diminishes as one moves to the left.[6]

These stipulations make c and e rather queer concepts. They arise from reading Marshall too literally. Marshall did speak of consumer's surplus as the difference between the price paid for each unit and the price the consumer would be just willing to pay for it, but he was certainly not considering the application of this formula to situations in which the consumer could not freely buy just as much as he wanted to. Here, as in other cases pointed out by Hicks, a problem arises only because Marshall used language that becomes inadequate when the income effect is not neglected.

Hicks seems to feel this and to defend the concepts e and c on the ground that they are useful in considering the introduction of a new commodity or the elimination of an old one. He argues that in such a case E is arbitrary since the (imaginary) price of a non-available commodity is indefinite, while e is not arbitrary as long as there is some

[6] The slope of the indifference curve at B is equal to the slope at D and therefore less (flatter) than at d. The slope at c is less than at C and therefore less than at A (where it is the same as at C). If this relationship holds throughout the range, the line cB must be flatter than the line Ad so that Ac $(=Os)$ must be less than Bd $(=Ot)$. (This refers to Fig. 2; the opposite is true, of course, in Fig. 1 where cB must be steeper than Ad.)

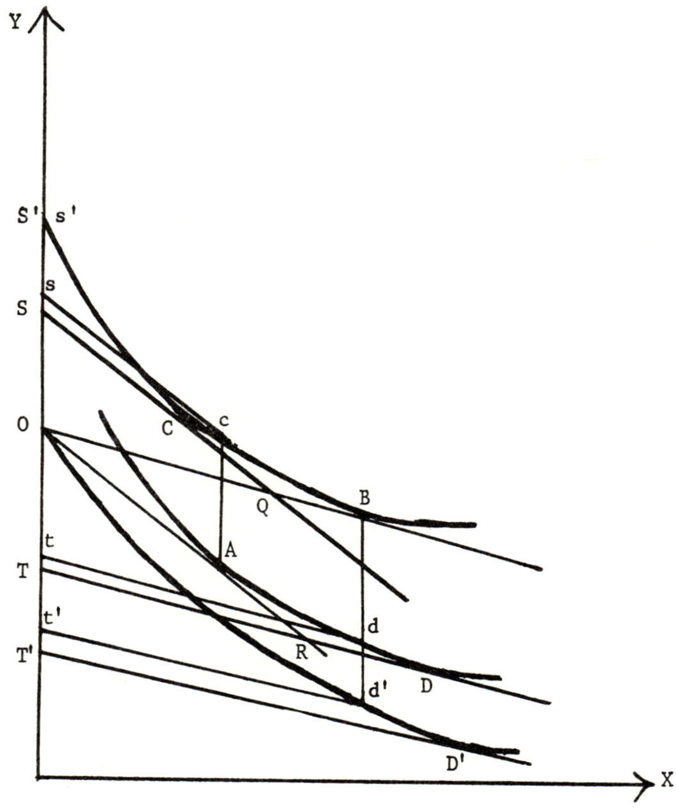

FIG. 2

subsidy which would be equivalent to making the commodity available and some tax which would be equivalent to eliminating it from the market. But in that case, the subsidy E is indistinguishable from the subsidy e, because the stipulation that distinguishes e from E becomes meaningless. The quantity consumed of the non-available good is zero in any case. The subsidy E cannot change the amount consumed any more than the subsidy e.

There is, in any case, no need to consider any imaginary price of a non-available good. In the case of the introduction of a new good, there is no higher price. There is instead a zero consumption of the non-available good. O then takes the place of A (the lower indifference curve passes through O), and S' (the point where the higher indifference curve, which passes through B, touches the Y axis) takes the place of both C and c. The consumer's surplus gained from the introduction of the good is OS'—the subsidy E that is sufficient to raise the consumer from O to the same income level (the same indifference curve) to which he would move (at B) if the good had become available at the price indicated by the slope of OB.

On the other hand, in the case of the elimination of an old commodity, the tax E raises no problems that are avoided by using the tax e instead. The tax (E or e) that is equivalent to the elimination of a commodity is that which moves the individual down to a point (D' or d') on the indifference curve that passes through O. The consumer's surplus that would be lost by the elimination of the commodity can still be measured by E or OT', and there is no reason for the stipulation that would make it e or Ot'. (One could instead say that A would coincide with O, and C would coincide with S', as they would for prices equal to or greater than indicated by the slope of the tangents to the indifference curves at O and S', respectively, at which prices none of the good would be bought—just as if it were not available at any price.)

There is therefore no need for the queer "consumer's surpluses" e and c. We can take into account the income effect that Marshall neglected and still manage comfortably with *only one* consumer's surplus, namely E, the tax of the subsidy that would have the same effect on real income if it took the place of the price change considered.[7]

II

I find it difficult to avoid the impression that the proliferation of measures of consumer's surplus is a result as much as it is a cause of the unease engendered in many economists by the concept. It is a kind of demonstration of non-involvement in a somewhat disreputable business. Consumer's surplus nevertheless seems to me to be of very great use not only as a heuristic device for showing students of economics the benefits from an increase in the freedom of trade, but also for indicating where one should look for indications and estimates of the social benefits or damages from many an important governmental or other policy decision.

It may be that the prejudice against the concept is due to its not fitting into the now well-established dichotomy of economics into microeconomics and macroeconomics. In each of these fields it is easy to provide entertaining arguments that seem to show either that consumer's surplus is unnecessary or that it is wrong. In the microeconomic field it is possible to show that the optimum position (which maximizes consumer's surplus) can be described more simply without using the concept. In the macroeconomic field it can be shown that there is no possible measure for the *total* of consumer's surplus of an individual or the total

[7] Fritz Machlup makes an analysis similar to the above in his review of *A Revision of Demand Theory* (*American Economic Review*, March, 1957, pp. 119–35) and esp. in the diagram on p. 123, which considers several additional proposed measures of "Hypothetical Income Variations." However, Machlup does not indicate the common-sense reasons here suggested why the subsidy E (or C) differs from the tax E(or C); neither does he attempt to consider whether any of the suggested measures of consumer's surplus by different hypothetical income variations makes more sense than the others.

benefit that he enjoys from being able to buy at the current market prices everything that he does buy.

This is seen more clearly if we put the question in a slightly different way. We may ask how much money a consumer would pay for the right to continue to buy at the current price something that he is now buying. If we are fascinated by the infinitesimal calculus and ask this question for the strictly microeconomic marginal unit of a commodity, the answer is *zero*. The consumer is not willing to pay anything, because that is the essential nature of the marginal unit. If he were getting any net benefit from buying it instead of spending the money on something else, he would buy more of the item in the first place and the unit in question would no longer be marginal.

If we are hypnotized by the macroeconomic revolution in economic thought and ask the same question for the totality of *everything* to which the consumer applies his money (including his saving) the answer is again *zero*. He is not able to pay anything for the privilege of continuing to buy what he is now buying at the same prices as before, because he has no money whatsoever left over for this purpose. He is already applying all his money to the previous purposes. In the strictly microeconomic case he is *unwilling* to pay anything that could be the measure of consumer's surplus. In the strictly macroeconomic case he is *unable* to.

If we do not insist that the consumer continue to buy everything that he buys when he is free to buy as much as he wants to at the current prices, he could be made to give up as much of his income as would reduce him to the same degree of misery as would be achieved by cutting him off from the market entirely. The measure we get boils down in almost all circumstances to hardly more than an approximation to his total money income; it is not a useful measure of his benefit from being a member of the economy.

The true moral of the story is not, however, that we should dispense with the notion of a money measure of consumer's surplus and with attempts ever to estimate it. The true moral is that consumer's surplus does not belong either to strict miocreconomics or to strict macroeconomics but is somewhere in between. We can get meaningful answers to our questions only if we ask how much a consumer would pay for the right to continue to buy, or to avoid being prevented from buying, at the current price, some significant but not very large part of what he is buying. It must be significant, so as to include infra-marginal units, since it is only for the sake of these, where there is some consumer's surplus, that he would be willing to pay any ransom. It must not be a large part of what he buys because he will then not be able to pay the ransom and still have the money to exercise very much of the ransomed right.

If we keep to what we may call "*macro-marginal*" problems, when we have neither infinitestimal nor all-embracing but merely *significant* purchases to examine for consumer's surplus, we can avoid the paradoxes. The notion of consumer's surplus can help us to consider and compare the social costs and the social benefits of changes in taxes, trade restrictions, or degrees of monopoly, of social services, indivisible investments, and policies and plans of many kinds. We must (on occasion) leave the splendid heights of mathematical microeconomics or the soul-satisfying sweep of all inclusive closed macroeconomic models if we are to deal with many of the practical problems of economic policy whose habitat is in the less romantic macromarginal middle ground.

[6]

A NOTE ON THE DIMINISHING MARGINAL UTILITY OF INCOME

Abba P. Lerner
Queens College and The Graduate CUNY Center,
and Florida State University, Tallahassee

Ever since Sir John Hicks' rehabilitation [1,2] of Marshall's "Consumer's Surplus," innumerable books and articles (including some of my own) have followed Hicks in measuring consumer surplus not by Marshall's area under the demand curve and above the price, but by variations in income *equivalent* to, or *compensating* for, a change in the price of a commodity.

In the familiar Figure 1, lowering the price of X from that shown by the budget line D (X *D*earer) to that shown by budget line C (X *C*heaper) increases utility by as much as it would be increased by an increase in income of A (measured in terms of Y). Raising the price of X back to the previous level (going back to budget line D from budget line C) lowers utility by as much as it would be lowered by reducing income by B. But B is smaller than A! Thus there seem to be two *different* changes in income (measured in terms of Y), both of which are equivalent to *the same* difference in utility. (The changes in income can as well be measured in terms of X. Those are shown as A′ and B′.)

This paradox has been explained as reflecting the diminishing marginal utility of income. At a higher income it takes a larger quantity of income, with its smaller marginal utility, to bridge the same utility gap.[1]

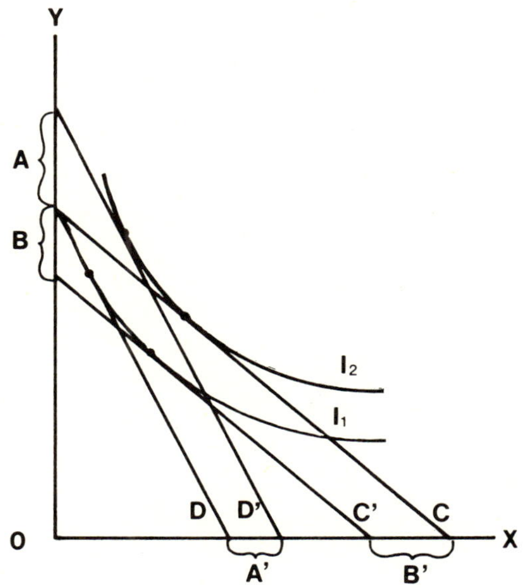

Figure 1, X Normal

That something is wrong with this becomes obvious when we consider what happens if X is an inferior good, when an increase in income, as from D to D′, causes *less* of X to be consumed. B is then greater than A, as is shown in Figure 2. On the same logic this would have to be explained as reflecting *increasing* marginal utility of income.[2]

This paradox, like all paradoxes, is dispelled by clarification. Here the clarification comes from realizing that diminishing (or increasing or constant) marginal utility of income has nothing to do with the case.

A, the increase in income (in terms of Y) that is equivalent in utility gain to the reduction of the price of X, is figured at the *higher* price of X shown by D or D′. It is the vertical distance between D and D′ *in either direction,* and so it is also the *decrease* in income that corresponds, at the higher price of X, to the same utility loss.

B, the *reduction* in income equivalent to the price increase, is figured at the lower price. It is the vertical distance between C and C′ and so it is also the equivalent *increase* in income at the lower price of X. A can thus be compared with B more easily by considering them *both* as the different changes in income, for the different prices of X, that would produce the same difference in utility level.

If X is a normal good, some part of any increase in income is spent on X. If X is dearer, more money is required for the same increase in utility. If X is an inferior good (Figure 2), *less* of X is bought when income is increased, so that money is *saved* on X, rather than more *spent.* If X is dearer, more money is saved, so that it takes a smaller gift to achieve the same increase in utility. Diminishing marginal utility of income does not come into the picture.

The borderline between X normal and X inferior, when there is no income effect, would be represented by "vertically parallel" indifference curves (i.e., a constant vertical distance between the two indifference curves), when A and B would be equal. This condition has been called "constant marginal utility of money" or "constant marginal utility of income." This too is unwarranted and has no more to do with the case than increasing or diminishing marginal utility of income.

Another way of demonstrating the irrelevance of diminishing marginal utility of income is to point out that *only one difference* in utility levels is considered—that between

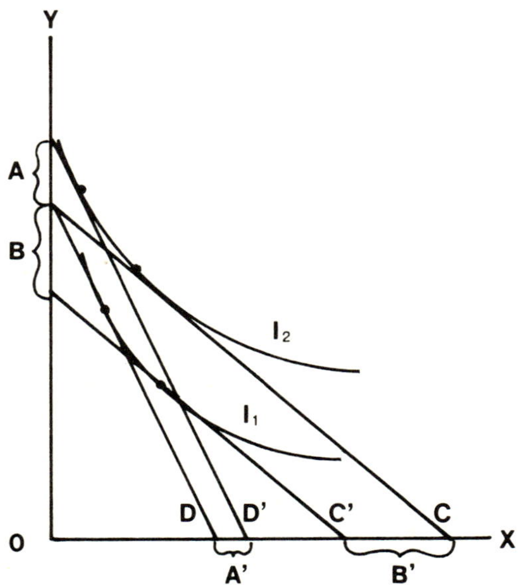

Figure 2, X Inferior

the two utility levels represented by the two indifference curves I_1 and I_2. There are no successive changes in income which would have to be compared to tell whether the marginal utility is diminishing or not.

The source of our paradox is a confusion between the marginal utility of income (the difference between different levels of utility pertaining to *different* indifference curves) and the marginal substitutability of Y for X (indicated by the slope of an indifference curve at a point on it). A is greater than B if there is diminishing marginal substitutability of Y for X as Y is increased, X being held constant. This is the case if X is a normal good. An increase in income (as from D to D′ or from C′ to C) will then be shared between buying more of X and buying more of Y. If an additional quantity of Y is given as a present to such a consumer, he will exchange some of the Y for some additional quantity of X so as to restore the marginal substitutability of Y for X to equality with the unchanged ratio between their prices. The dearer is X, the less he benefits from any given gift of Y, and the larger will be the gift required to bring him up to the same level of utility. A is greater than B.

If X is an inferior good, Y is a *superior* good.[3] Y's marginal substitutability for X *increases* as Y is increased, X being held constant. An increase in income, prices being held constant, will cause him to buy *less* of X. This means that he will spend on additional Y the whole increase in income *plus what he saves in buying less of X*. If an additional quantity of Y is given to such a consumer, he will reduce his purchases of X, using the savings to buy still more of Y. The dearer is X the more he can save in this way and the smaller is the gift of Y required to bring him to the higher utility level. A is now less than B.

What this means is that A and B are not really changes in income! Changes in income are represented by movements of the whole budget line D or C. A and B are the different changes in Y that are equivalent to the different changes in income that yield that same change in utility at the different prices of X. It is *normality*—i.e., the diminishing marginal substitutability of Y for X (X constant) and the diminishing marginal substitutability of X for Y (Y is constant) that makes the equivalent variation in income greater for higher prices of X; and it is *inferiority of X* (implying the superiority of Y)—i.e., *increasing* marginal substitutability of Y for X (X constant), which makes the equivalent variation smaller for higher prices of X.

In this clarification geometry and English seem to be better tools than mathematics. Arithmetic would seem to be better still. The money gift (or find) which is as good as the price reduction from, say, $5 to $4, would normally be spent, in part, on X at $5. The money tax (or loss) which is as bad as the price increase from $4 to $5 takes away money some of which would have bought some X at $4. The gift (A) must therefore be greater than the tax (B). But if X is an inferior good, on which money is *saved* rather than more spent when income is increased, then it is the other way round.

APPENDIX

The primary source of the confusion between marginal utility of income and marginal substitutability of Y for X seems to be Alfred Marshall's apology in his statement that ". . . in the discussion of consumer's surplus, we assume that the marginal utility of money to the individual purchaser is the same throughout. Strictly speaking we ought to take account of the fact that if he spent less on tea, the marginal utility of money to him would be less that it is . . . But these changes of consumer's rent (being of the second order of smallness) may be neglected on the assumption, which underlies our whole reasoning, that his expenditures on any one thing, as, for instance, tea, is only a small part of his whole expenditure.'' [4] p. 842.

But what Marshall is neglecting is not the diminishing marginal utility of money or even the marginal utility of income. It is the *income effect* on the quantity of X bought. Hicks showed that the neglected income effect is positive for non-inferior goods and negative for inferior goods, and that it vanishes at the borderline between them, which he called ''constant marginal utility of income'' when there is nothing for Marshall to neglect. But this borderline case also has nothing to do with constancy or otherwise of the marginal utility of income. It the case of constancy of the marginal substitutability of Y for X, X being held constant.

One is tempted to declare Marshall innocent of the confusion on the ground that by his ''marginal utility of money'' he did not mean marginal utility of income at all but only the income effect on the amount bought. This is supported by his describing the Giffen case as an exception. Inferiority was thus considered doubly negligible—as negligible even in relation to the negligible normal income effect. The Giffen case *is* an exception, and even an especially extreme exception—*to normality of the income effect*. It is no exception to the diminishing marginal utility of income. But all this does nothing to diminish the effectiveness of Marshall's apology for neglecting ''the diminishing marginal utility of money'' in propagating the confusion.

NOTES

1. E. J. Mishan, for example, writes ''The two different measures arise simply from the fact of the diminishing marginal utility of money . . . the sum of money required to express this difference is larger for an addition to an individual's money income than for a subtraction from it.'' ([4] pp. 100–101).
2. Mishan, after demonstrating that *A* is greater than *B* for normal goods, suggests that ''there should be no trouble in tracing out the same or symmetrical conclusions for 'inferior' goods,'' ([4] p. 101). It is not clear whether Mishan recognized that ''symmetrical'' here means ''opposite.''
3. In much of the literature any non-inferior good is called ''superior.'' It would seem more normal to call such goods ''normal goods,'' leaving the term ''superior goods'' for the case when the income effect is just as extreme as in the case of inferior goods, but in the opposite direction. Thus I define ''*Superior good:* A good of which so much more is bought when income increases that more than the whole increase in income is absorbed (and less is therefore left available to be spent on everything else). (Income elasticity of demand is greater than the ratio of total income to the amount spent on the item.)'' [3] p. 784. On this definition if, and only if, any good (or combination of goods) is inferior, the other good (or all the other goods taken together) is superior; and *vice versa*.

REFERENCES

1. R. G. D. Allen and J. R. Hicks, ''A Reconsideration of the Theory of Value,'' *Economica*, 1934.
2. J. R. Hicks, *Value and Capital*, Oxford, 1939, pp. 38–41, and *A Revision of the Theory of Demand*, Oxford, 1956.
3. Abba P. Lerner, ''The Analysis of Demand,'' *The American Economic Review*, September 1962, pp. 783–797, with Mathematical Appendix by Hirofumi Uzawa, pp. 797–801.
4. E. J. Mishan, ''Realism and Relevance in Consumer's Surplus (reprinted from *Review of Economic Studies*, 1948) in *Welfare Economics*, New York, 1969.
5. Alfred Marshall, *Principles of Economics*, 8th Edition, Macmillan, London, 1920.

B. General Equilibrium: International Trade

[1]

The Diagrammatical Representation of Cost Conditions in International Trade

By A. LERNER

IN the *Weltwirtschaftliches Archiv* for July 1930 Dr. Haberler suggests that Barone's figures for the treatment of International Trade need not be restricted to conditions of constant costs, as Barone's rectilinear figures might seem to imply, but can be supplanted by production indifference curves. In this connection the following constructions suggest themselves.

(1) In fig. 1 ab and a'b' are production indifference curves of two countries in the same two commodities, say wheat measured along the horizontal axis and cloth measured along the vertical axis (so that any point p on the curve represents the possibility of the country producing np wheat + mp cloth). The negative slope of the curves represents the necessity of producing less of one commodity in order to produce more of the other, and the convexity (upwards) of the curves, or increasing negativeness of the slope from a to b represents the condition of

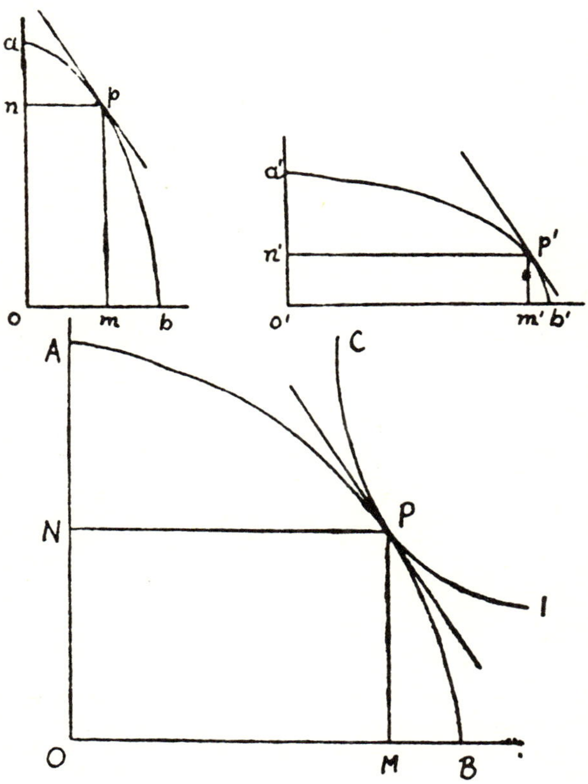

Fig. 1.

346

increasing marginal cost of the production of one commodity in terms of sacrifice of the other.

To obtain a composite production indifference curve for the two countries taken together: Along the Y axis mark the point A so that OA = oa + o'a'. From A draw that part of the curve ab or a'b', starting from a or a', whose slope is the least negative. Continue this slope to the point where it becomes parallel to (or just as negatively inclined as) the beginning of the other curve. Continue to add increments taken from these curves *in order of least negative slope* until the curves are exhausted. When this occurs the curve AB will have been formed so that B will be on the X axis and OB equal to ob + o'b', since the sum of the downward movements of the increments of which AB is made up = the sum of the downward movements of the curves ab and a'b' = oa + o'a' = OA, while the sum of the horizontal movements similarly = ob + o'b'.

The curve AB will be the compound production indifference curve of both countries taken together. OA will represent the amount of cloth the countries can make if they concentrate all the resources on cloth-making. The least negative parts of ab or a'b' represent those transferences of resources from cloth-making to wheat-growing which give the greatest amount of wheat per unit of cloth sacrificed. As the process continues and we transfer more and more resources from cloth to wheat, less profitable transferences have to be made—more and more negatively inclined increments of curve are added until at OB all the resources are applied to wheat and the output is equal to the sum of the amounts of wheat that each could produce separately, ob + o'b'. The gains from international trade cannot take place when both countries are producing only one and the same commodity. These gains, when they are possible, are shown in the middle region of the curve AB which here gives greater values of x and y than the separate curves.

(2) To show the conditions of international trade, let a consumption indifference curve[1] CI touch AB in P. At P draw

[1] The consumption indifference curves in this paper are curves which show by their slope at any point the rate at which the commodities will exchange against one another when the quantities produced are those indicated by the co-ordinates of that point. It may be objected that they are not pure "indifference" curves as their shape would depend on the distribution of resources and would be affected by what is actually produced. This, however, does not matter, for although one cannot say that the community is "indifferent," in terms of absolute satisfaction, to the different points on an indifference curve, yet the *behaviour* of the community with respect to these curves is exactly comparable to that of an individual with respect to his true indifference curves. This, I think, could be demonstrated, but

the tangent to the two curves. Draw tangents to ab and to a′b′ parallel to this tangent, and from the points of contact P, p, and p′ draw perpendiculars PM, PN, pm, pn, p′m′, and p′n′ to the axes. Then, in equilibrium, the total production of wheat will be OM of which om is produced in the first country and o′m′ in the second country, while the total production of cloth will be ON, with *on* produced in the first country and o′n′ in the second.

The production in the two countries indicated by the diagram is a possible condition of equilibrium because:

(*a*) on + o′n′ = ON while om + o′m′ = OM. AN is equal to the total downward movement of the curve AP, but this curve is less negatively inclined throughout than the tangent at P and must therefore be made up of those parts of ab and a′b′ which are less negatively inclined than the tangent, i.e. it is made up of ap and a′p′, so that its total downward movement (AN) is equal to the downward movements of its two components an and a′n′.

$$\begin{aligned} AN &= an + a'n'. \\ OA &= oa + o'a' \\ OA - AN &= oa - an + o'a' - a'n' \\ ON &= on + o'n' \end{aligned}$$

Similarly OM = NP = the sum of the horizontal movements of AP and therefore of ap + a′p′ = np + n′p′ = om + o′m′.

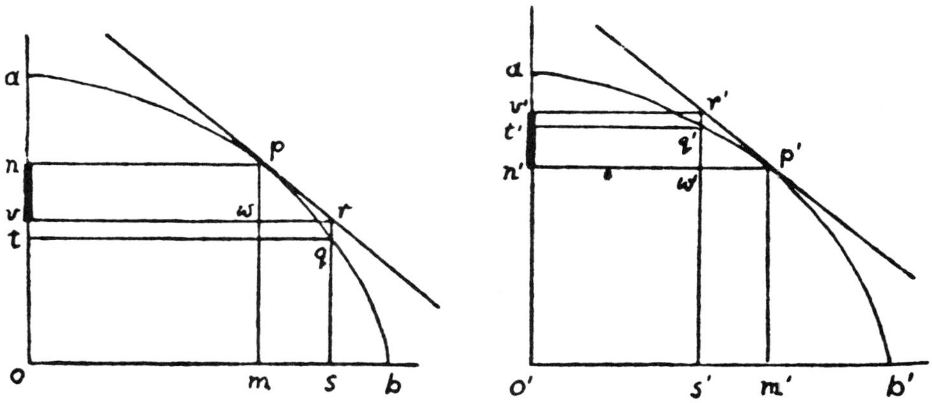

Fig. 2.

(*b*) The tangents are parallel at p and p′, signifying that agreement between relative marginal costs, and therefore of relative prices, which is necessary for international trade equilibrium.

it is not necessary here, where all that is done, after all, is to describe equilibrium conditions.

The position indicated in the diagram is the only one which satisfies the conditions of equilibrium because :

(*a*) No other position can give as large a product. If we start from a position like the one indicated, we can only get another position producing the same amount of one of the commodities by increasing the production in one of the countries and decreasing it in the other by an equal amount. If we do this we will always find the amount of the other commodity has diminished. In fig. 2, starting from a position of equilibrium as shown in fig. 1, an attempt is made to find another position of equilibrium producing the same amount of wheat by shifting from om and o′m′ to os and o′s′ so that ms = m′s′. Since the tangents at p and p′ are parallel and wr = ms = s′m′ = w′p′, the triangle pwr = the triangle r′w′p′, so that pw = r′w′ and nv = v′n′. But since the curves are convex, nt, the diminution in cloth-production in the first country, is greater than nv, while n′t′, the increase in cloth-production in the second country, is less than v′n′ and so less than nv. That is to say the amount of cloth produced is less than in the position from which we

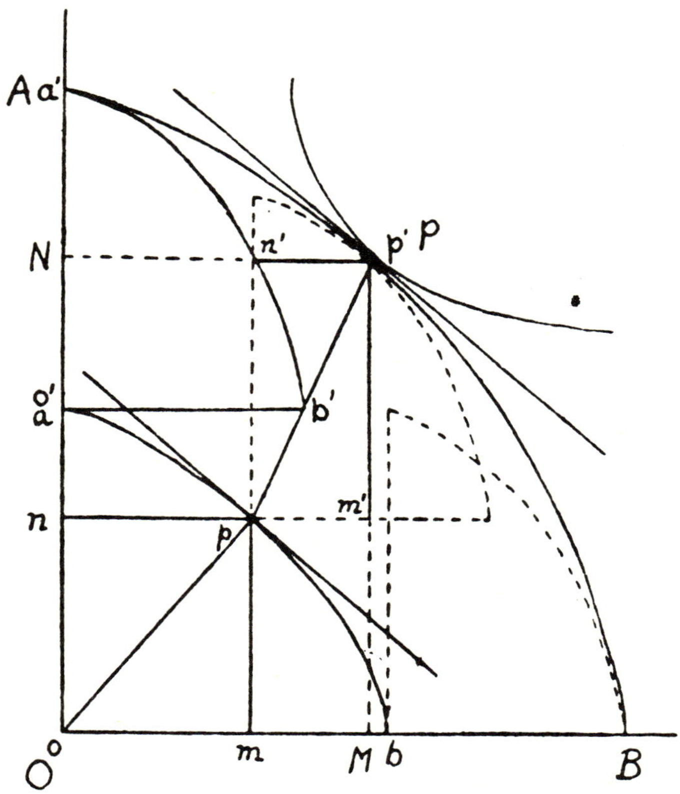

Fig. 3.

started and so cannot be a position of equilibrium. This is more easily seen from the fact that

(*b*) at q and q′, the points on the curves representing the production in the new position, the tangents will not be parallel, since the tangent at q will be more negatively inclined than that at p or p′, while the tangent at q′ will be less negatively inclined. This means that the relative prices of the commodities will be different in the two countries—a condition clearly incompatible with equilibrium.

(3) All diagrams of this kind can be obtained by the alternative method of imagining one of the curves being moved round the other curve so that its axes remain parallel to the axes of the other while its origin is kept on the other curve, then the curve marked out by the parts of the moving curve furthest from the origin of the stationary curve will be the compound indifference curve, the outer curve representing the optimum combinations of the production of both countries. This is illustrated in fig. 3, and is applicable to all shapes of curves, nor does it matter which curve is kept stationary and which is moved round. Although this way is more vivid it has the disadvantage of not showing so clearly, at first sight, what shape the compound curve will have.

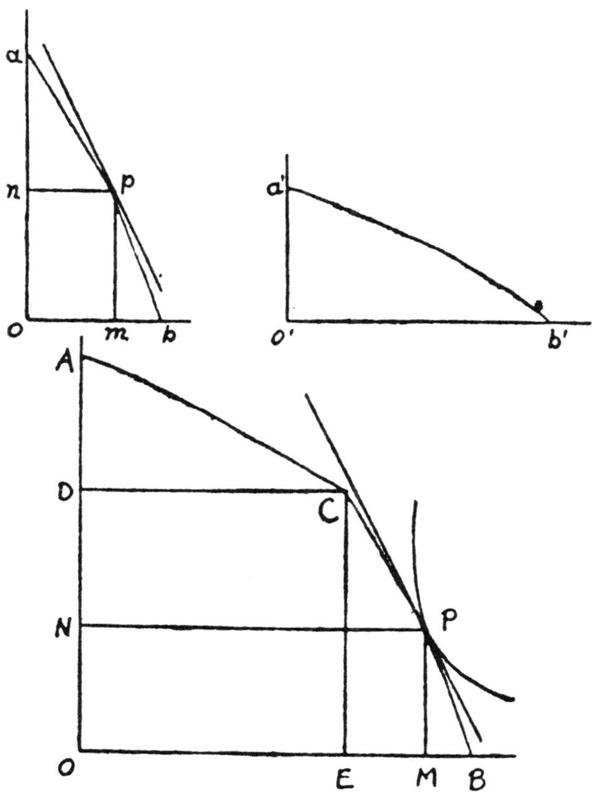

Fig. 4.

(4) The rules given in section (1) for the construction of the compound production indifference curve can be directly applied to a number of cases simpler than the one there given. Where every part of one of the curves is less negatively inclined than any part of the other curve, the whole of one curve will be incorporated in the composite curve before the next is started.

This will be the case whether the conditions are those of increasing cost, as represented by convex curves, constant cost, as represented by straight lines, or decreasing cost, as represented by concave curves, or whether one country has increasing and one decreasing cost. The compound indifference production curve AB, will in each of these cases be made up of two parts, AC, which is simply a′b′ transported, and CB, which is ab transported, so that ADC = a′o′b′ and CEB = aob.

Under these conditions it can be shown that at least one of the countries must completely specialise, producing only one commodity, and this is brought out in the diagrams by the impossibility of drawing parallel tangents to the two curves.

The possible gain from international trade is indicated in these cases by the outward slope of the curve from A and B towards C and the projection of C at the point of most effective international specialisation, when each country is producing only the commodity for which it is better fitted. This projection is seen to be weakened by increasing costs and is sharply emphasised by decreasing costs.

Since C is a projecting point it may lie on a consumption indifference curve at a point where the tangent to it will not be parallel to any possible tangents to either ab or a′b′. This means that the conditions of production represented by the point C (complete specialisation by both countries) does not uniquely determine the relative prices of the two commodities but leaves them only limited by the shapes of the constituent curves between the relative prices indicated by the tangents to ab at a and to a′b′ at b′.

This freedom is least with increasing costs, is greater with constant costs and is greatest with decreasing costs. Within these limits the relative prices are determined entirely by the consumption indifference curves. This is important in so far as C is a projecting part and therefore very likely to lie on a maximum consumption indifference curve. It becomes more important with constant than with increasing costs and still more important with decreasing costs for the double reason that in this order

(*a*) the point C projects more, and

(*b*) the field for unhampered decision of relative price by demand alone becomes wider.

The same argument will apply to projecting points arising below, and it must be borne in mind that this kind of discontinuity can also arise in the curves for one country.

(5) By an argument similar to that of fig. 2 it can easily be proved that with two concave curves (that is with decreasing costs), one country at least must specialise. Just as the argument of fig. 2 will apply not only to

(*a*) two convex curves, but also to
(*b*) one convex curve and one straight line, and
(*c*) one convex and one concave curve *where the convexity is greater than the concavity,*

so the argument here will apply not only to

(*d*) two concave curves, but also to
(*e*) one concave curve and one straight line, and
(*f*) one concave and one convex curve *where the concavity is greater than the convexity.*

There remain two intermediate cases :

(*g*) two straight lines (which must be parallel if they are to be considered as capable of having parallel tangents), and
(*h*) one concave and one convex curve *where the concavity is just equal to the convexity.*

In these two cases production is indeterminate, the same product, within certain limits, being obtained whether there is specialisation or not.

(6) The compound production indifference curve formed from two concave curves, will be of the form shown in fig. 5

AEC = DHB = aob, AFD = CGB = a′o′b′.

ACB and ADB must be considered as alternative curves each made up of aob and a′o′b′ in succession, but the two compound curves having them in different order, and the " effective " production indifference curve AKCLDRB must be considered as made up of sections taken from these alternative curves.

To find the distribution of production in the two countries, mark the point P where the highest consumption indifference curve touches AKCLDRB and draw the perpendiculars PM and PN to the axes. P will be on either ACB or ADB. Of these two consider only the curve on which P lies. This curve is made up of ab and a′b′ and P will be on the section corresponding to one of these. Mark a point p or p′ on the original curve at the corresponding spot (by " parallel tangents " or by measurement from A, B, C or one of the axes) and draw perpendiculars to the axes pm and pn or p′m′ and p′n′. The

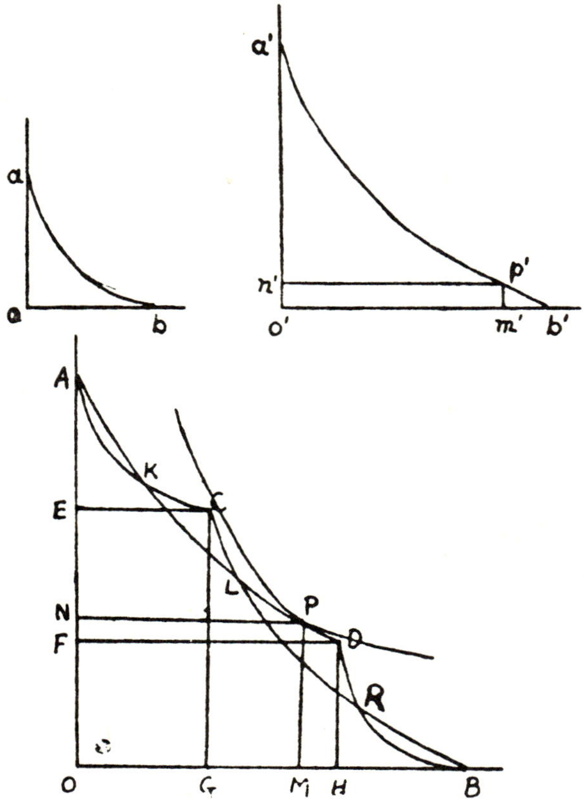

Fig. 5.

point p or p′ will mark the production in this country. The other country will specialise entirely in the commodity of which this country is not producing the amount indicated by P.

C and D are protruding points of specialisation where the economies of decreasing cost are best realised and seem very likely to lie on maximum consumption indifference curves. K, L and R are points which allow of two alternative arrangements of production as they are upon both the ACB and upon the ADB curves, it seems, however, very unlikely that any of these should lie on a maximum consumption indifference curve. The relative prices of the commodities are indeterminate at these points between the limits indicated by the two tangents that can be drawn to the two curves at each of the points and would be decided by conditions of demand.

This procedure will also be applicable where there is one concave curve and one straight line and where there is one concave and one convex curve *if the concavity is greater than the convexity,* these being the group a, b and c of section 5. In these two latter cases, however, the curves cannot cut more than once and in any of the cases they may not cut at all.

(7) A consideration of how curves of the same shape are compounded leads us to the conclusions that

(*a*) where the curves are parallel straight lines representing relative costs constant and the same in both countries, we have a position the converse of that at the point C in section 4. Prices are fixed by supply conditions independently of demand, while the distribution of production is a matter of complete indifference.

(*b*) With similar convex curves, the compound curve will differ from the constituent curves in nothing but scale. The industries will be in the same relation to each other in both countries.

(*c*) With similar concave curves, the relative size of the two countries becomes relevant. Where one country is larger than the other we will get fig. 5. As the disparity increases C and D move away from each other, and conversely. When the countries are of the same size C and D coincide as also do the alternative curves ACB and ADB. This means that the size of the country is important where there are decreasing costs since these, being profitable, will be carried to the limit, i.e. one country must always specialise as shown in section 4. The duality of the curve means that it does not matter which country will specialise.

(8) With one concave and one convex curve, if one is more inclined throughout than the other, we get the simple case of addition dealt with in section 4. Where the curves contain points of similar slope, we must consider whether the concavity is greater than the convexity or vice versa.

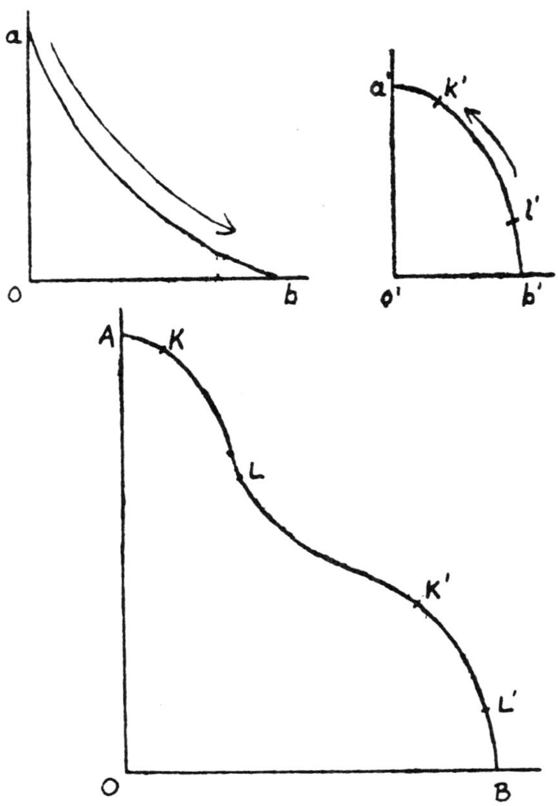

Fig. 6.

If the concavity is greater, we can proceed exactly as in the case of two concave curves (section 7). When the convexity is greater we must follow the principles of section (1) where there were two convex curves. There is, however, the complication that in order to keep on points of parallel tangency we have to go *up* one curve while we go *down* the other, so that in drawing the compound curve we must *subtract* bits corresponding to bits of one curve while we *add* bits of the other. This is shown in fig. 6. The slope at k′=that at b and the slope at l′=that at a. AKL is the same shape as a′k′l′ and K′L′B the same as k′l′b′. LK′ is equal in length to ab−k′l′ and is obtained by adding bits of ab while subtracting bits of k′l′ of the same change of slope. No part of ab is incorporated in AB until we come to L because although the slope at K is the same as the slope at b, the part of ab in the vicinity of b is not approachable until the distance along the curve from a has been traversed and we cannot incorporate any of the curve in the vicinity of a until at L we have a slope the same as that at a. In applying the consumption indifference curve to this figure it must be remembered that between A and L as also between K′ and B the first country is completely specialising and only between L and K′ can we apply " parallel tangents."

The two humps of this diagram mean that in these ranges of supply advantage can be taken of the decreasing costs in the first country through its specialisation, while the hollowness of LK′ represents the loss of these economies when specialisation has to be given up.

As ab becomes more concave, it goes through the same change of slope in a shorter length of line, and so LK′ which=ab−k′l′ becomes smaller and L and K′ approach one another. When the concavity is just equal to the convexity L and K′ coincide and the compound curve is made up entirely of sections of a′b′. In this case the first country must always specialise unless, as is almost inconceivable, the protected point L (=K′) lies on a maximum consumption indifference curve. If ab becomes still more concave, concavity becomes greater than convexity, a case already dealt with.

If ab becomes less concave, it gets through less change of slope and k′ and l′ tend to approach. LK′ will become less concave too and longer. In the limit, when ab becomes a straight line, k′ and l′ coincide, as also do K and L as well as K′ and L′, while LK′ becomes a tangent joining the two humps, is equal in length and slope to ab, and will join two sections of AB which if put together will make a curve like a′b′.

In this way can be illustrated the conditions, say, under which each country will produce some of each commodity. These are :

1. Points of parallel tangency.
2. At least one curve must be convex.
3. If the other is concave the convexity must be greater than the concavity.
4. The indifference consumption curve must touch the compound curve at a point of parallel tangency.

Which means:

1. There must be possible some arrangements of production for which relative (marginal) costs will be equal in the two countries.
2. At least one country must be producing under conditions of increasing costs.
3. These increasing costs must be increasing more rapidly than decreasing costs, if any, are decreasing in the other country.
4. The demand must be such as to bring production to a point of equal relative (marginal) costs in the two countries.

(8) It is perhaps hardly necessary to point out that these curves do *not* tell how much is gained by international trade. That must depend, in part, upon the shape of the consumption indifference curves and upon how the demand they represent is distributed between the two different countries. If the consumption indifference curves of the separate countries when applied to the separate home country production indifference curves give the same production as is indicated by the application of the joint consumption indifference curve to the compound production indifference curve, then no gain is possible from international trade (nor is any international trade possible) even in the most favourable-looking cases of decreasing cost and relative advantages throughout. On the other hand, in such an unlikely looking case as the two similarly shaped convex curves, where there are no decreasing costs to be exploited or comparative advantages to be obtained, there can still be great gains from international trade if one country wants much cloth and the other wants much wheat; for in these conditions international trade will avoid the increasing costs that specialisation would entail.

[2]

1934]

The Diagrammatical Representation of Demand Conditions in International Trade

By A. P. Lerner

In a previous article,[1] concentrating on cost conditions, I avoided the complications on the side of demand, representing these by what I loosely called " consumption indifference curves." I made it clear in a footnote[2] that these, being applied to " countries " and not to individuals, are not the ordinary curves which show combinations of commodities to which an individual is indifferent; but the legitimacy of the procedure still remains to be vindicated.

I

1. The objection is that one cannot say that a community is definitely better or worse off in one of two positions if some of the individuals in the community are better off and others are worse off, so that one cannot draw indifference curves for a community. The same objection might be raised in the case of an individual. If a man has more food but less fuel, how are we to balance the quite different feelings of satiation and cold that he experiences and say which is the greater ? The answer is a behaviourist instruction to observe the results of the action which takes place when the various forces have worked themselves out and the individual makes a decision. The same procedure might be adopted in the case of the community. It, too, can just as tautologically be said to prefer that which is acquired by the community to that which might have been acquired in its stead. It is true that the decisions of the community depend upon the distribution of property among the individuals of the community and on their consequent differential pull, but it is no less true that the decision of the individual depends upon the relative pull of his different

[1] " The Diagrammatical Representation of Cost Conditions in International Trade," Economica, August 1932. [2] *Ibid.*, p. 347.

appetites. In both cases these pulls have to be taken as given, and the greater readiness to accept them in the latter case seems to be nothing more than individualist prejudice.

2. Of greater validity is the objection that the distribution between individuals in a community itself depends upon what is being produced, so that the production and consumption indifference curves cannot be drawn separately and then applied to each other. This independence is not assured in the case of the individual either, for it is quite likely that the kind of work done influences the individual's tastes. But these objections are covered by a more serious one which applies to individual indifference curves as well as to " collective indifference curves " (or curves which show by their slope at any point the relative prices of the commodities or the rate at which they are exchanged when available in the quantities indicated by the co-ordinates of the point). These curves cannot be considered as known over the whole surface or even over any considerable area, but only at or near the point where the individual or community happens to be. In the case of the individual it is because it is only in this vicinity that he has learnt by experience the effects of small changes, and also because changes in what he produces may affect his tastes. In the case of the community it is because the price ratio will depend not only on the quantities of the commodities available, but also on what the people are engaged in producing as well as on the relative wealth of the individuals in the community.

3. The result is that both for the individual and for the community we must use not continuous indifference curves, but only the knowledge of marginal rates of substitution or relative prices (represented by slopes which may be considered as tangents to consumption indifference curves) at points on the production indifference curve or the line of exchange which can actually be reached.[1] The individual or community will then move along these paths until a point is reached where the slope is tangential to the path and equilibrium is attained. Multiple equilibrium is of course possible in both cases.

This type of reasoning can be substituted wherever in my previous article I have applied " collective indifference curves " to countries or combinations of countries, without affecting the arguments there put forward.

[1] These slopes need not, of course, be considered as part of one system of consumption indifference curves as the system may be considered as changing in shape as one moves along the path.

II

4. The construction given above seems the simplest for dealing with the problem raised by the troublesome "consumption indifference curve" of my previous article, but another approach to the problem has led to what appear to me to be much more interesting constructions.

Consider an individual's indifference curves. Following the usual assumptions of diminishing utility we find his consumption indifference curve sloping down from left to right and convex to the origin. If we follow up this curve towards the right we see it getting flatter and flatter until a point is reached where it is horizontal. At this point the marginal utility of commodity X has fallen to zero since a small increase in the quantity of X without any change in the quantity of Y leaves us on the same curve. If it reaches the X axis and disappears before becoming horizontal we have to take a higher curve, and we will finally get one which becomes horizontal (unless the desire for the commodity is insatiable). It may continue horizontal for some time and will do so as long as additional quantities of X are indifferent to the individual, but after a time additional X becomes obnoxious and our individual will only be indifferent to an addition of the discommodity X if it is made up for by an *addition* of some of commodity Y. The curve will turn upwards. With the increasing degree of discommodity of X and diminishing utility of Y, he will require larger and larger quantities of Y to make up for each additional unit of X that he has to suffer. The curve will become steeper in its upward turn until it becomes vertical. This happens when the marginal utility of Y has fallen to zero, and our individual cannot be compensated for additional quantities of X by any additions of Y. The curve continues upwards vertically as long as additional quantities of Y are indifferent, but when Y too becomes obnoxious and a discommodity, our individual has to be compensated in some way if an addition of some of the discommodity Y is to leave him in an indifferent position. Giving him more X will not compensate him, for X is here also a discommodity, but he can be compensated for suffering more Y *by being made to suffer less* X. This means that the curve will turn back, going upwards to the left. The increasing disutilities of the discommodities will make the curve turn more and more to the left, making it concave downwards.

The same, of course, holds if we follow up the consumption

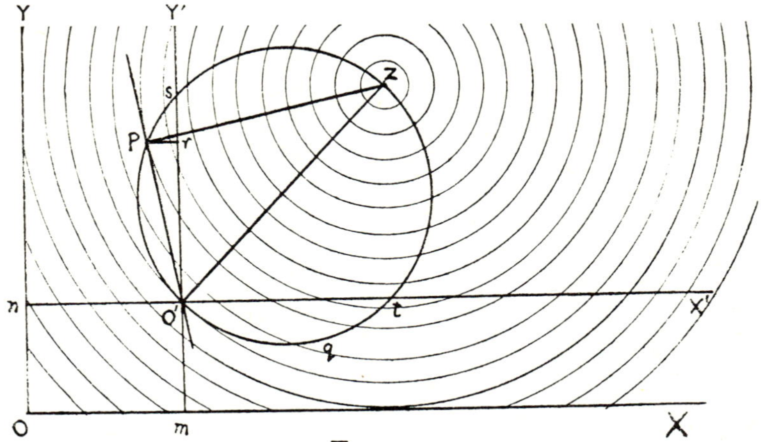

FIG. 1

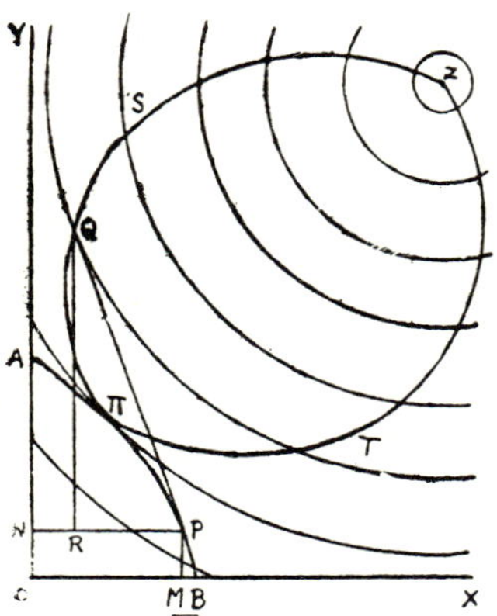

FIG. 2

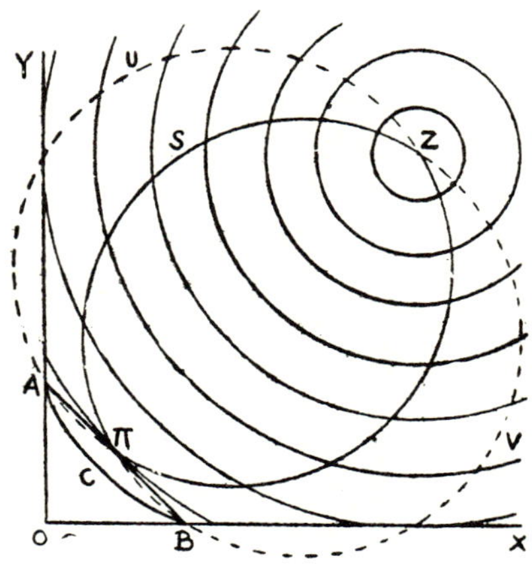

FIG. 3

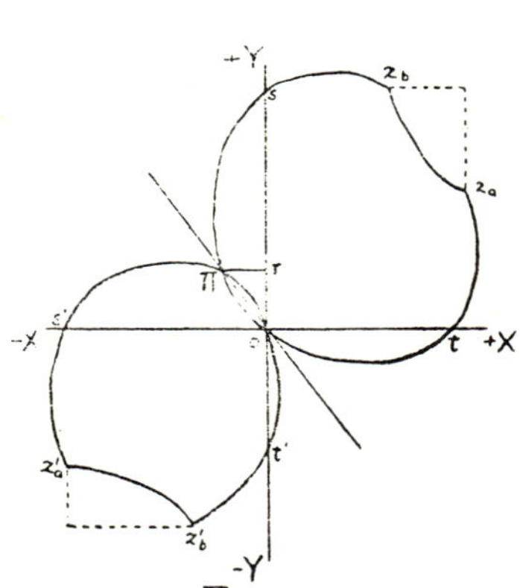

FIG. 4

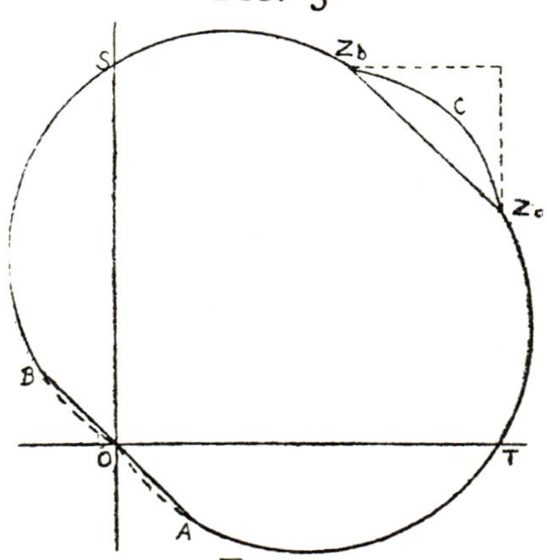

FIG. 5

indifference curve in the other direction. As we follow it from the initial position to the left it becomes steeper and steeper until it is vertical. It then turns round to the right, becomes concave downwards, becomes horizontal, and then turns down to the right, still concave downwards, where it meets the other end of the curve where we left it at the end of the last paragraph. The curve is thus shown to form a circuit which in our diagram we can draw as a circle. A higher one will form a circle contained within this circle showing the consumption or possession of larger quantities of X and Y in the regions where they are scarce commodities, and smaller quantities in the regions where they are superabundant nuisances. A lower one will form a larger enveloping circle showing smaller quantities of commodities and larger quantities of nuisances. We thus get a series of concentric circles covering the whole of the area between the axes. The higher curves are smaller circles within circles. The highest converges to a point which shows that combination of X and Y where they are neither commodities nor discommodities, but both have a marginal utility of zero. They are neither scarce nor superabundant. There is just the right quantity, and any addition to or subtraction from that quantity of either would diminish our individual's well-being. Such a series of concentric consumption indifference curves are shown in Fig. 1 with Z the point of "Bliss" marking the centre of the system.

5. From any point O′ which marks the quantities of the commodities (Om of X, On of Y) that an individual possesses, we can draw a curve which will show us how much trade the individual will do at any market price and in what direction he will trade, i.e. whether he will trade X for Y or Y for X. This curve is the locus of all points from which tangents to the consumption indifference curves pass through O′. With circular indifference curves with centre Z this will give us the circle having the diameter O′Z, since at any point P on the willingness-to-trade or demand curve the tangent PO′ is at right angles to the radius ZP and the locus of the apexes of right-angled triangles on the same hypotenuse is a circle. If the line of exchange is represented by the slope of O′P the individual will move along it to P where the slope of the indifference curve or his subjective scale of preference is identical with the market rate of exchange or the objective scale of preference, giving up Pr of X for O′r of Y (Pr perpendicular to O′Y′). Remembering that circles are here used as ideal types

for any kind of circuit, we may say that all demand curves are circular.

6. It should be observed that the sections of the demand curve O′Ps and O′qt are the familiar Marshallian willingness-to-trade curves.[1] If we take O′ as our origin and O′X′ and O′Y′ as our axes, there will then be measured not the quantities of X and Y consumed or possessed by the individual, but only quantities that he gives and receives in exchange. If the rate of exchange is that indicated by the tangent to the demand curve at O′ (which is also the tangent to the indifference curve at O′) there will be no trade. Any other line of exchange through O′ cuts the demand curve at some other point which marks the quantity of trade done, the commodity acquired being measured positively and the commodity given up being measured negatively. Thus with the line of exchange O′P there is acquired the amount of Y measured positively along O′r and there is given up the amount of X measured negatively along rP giving the total movement O′P. A normal price line will be negatively inclined as normally some of one commodity has to be given up to get some of the other. A vertical line of exchange would mean that Y can be obtained without changing the holding of X, i.e. it is a free good. Y would then be acquired until the point s is reached where its marginal utility is zero. A horizontal line of exchange would similarly lead to a free acquisition of O′t of X. A positively inclined line of exchange would mean that every acquisition of a quantity of one commodity has to be accompanied by a certain proportionate *increase* of the holding of the other good—a negative price. The most advantageous line of exchange would be O′Z which would allow of movement to the point of " Bliss " and is as good as having both goods acquirable and disposable without cost.[2]

7. A similar demand curve can be constructed for an

[1] *Pure Theory of International Trade*, L.S.E. Reprints, and *Money Credit and Commerce*, Appendix J.

[2] All this probably looks like the remotest possible kind of pure abstraction, but this completion of an old line of thought has already proved of service in several real problems. It shows how Marshall's " normal case " of international trade supply-and-demand curve is merely the elastic part of the demand curve ; that if Marshall had followed up his curves he would have found that every " normal " curve became " abnormal," and that every " abnormal " curve begins by being " normal." It shows further that every demand curve starts off with an elasticity of infinity which ultimately falls, as price falls, to a zero elasticity. It demonstrates more clearly than any other treatment the fact that what a person or country will trade, what are export goods and what are import goods, depends upon these relative prices.

individual who instead of a stock of commodities as in Fig. 1 has the possibilities of production of a P.I.C.[1] as in Fig. 2. Here the demand curve is the locus of all points on the C.I.C.s from which points tangents to the C.I.C. are also tangential to the P.I.C. (or meet the P.I.C. at either of its extremities), and the C.I.C. and the P.I.C. are on opposite sides of the tangent. The tangency of the line of exchange to the P.I.C. represents the necessity of goods alternatively producible at the margin having the same value—otherwise there is a possibility for gain by transferring production from the one with the lesser value to the one with the greater value. Where the line of exchange touches an extremity of the P.I.C., the individual is specialising completely in one commodity, and there is no possibility of producing more of it by any sacrifice in the production of the other. If the rate of exchange is that indicated by the slope of PQ the individual will produce at P, i.e. OM of X and ON of Y, and will exchange PR of X for RQ of Y moving from P to Q, PQ being tangential to AB at P and to a C.I.C. at Q. It is necessary for the C.I.C. and the P.I.C. to be on opposite sides of the line of exchange, for if both are on the same side it will be possible to reach a higher C.I.C. by moving on a parallel line of exchange from an adjacent point on the P.I.C.

8. To get this demand curve it is not necessary to assume, as is assumed in Fig. 2, that costs are increasing. Fig. 3 shows the demand curve with constant or decreasing costs. Keeping in mind our assumption of a given market rate of exchange between the commodities, it is clear that with decreasing cost the individual will always specialise in either X or Y, since at any rate of exchange he can thus get more than if he produced some of each. Thus if ACB in Fig. 4 is his P.I.C. a straight line at any slope whatever from either A or B can bring him to a position at least as high as Π on his system of C.I.C.s If costs are constant the P.I.C. is the straight line AΠB. At the rate of exchange indicated by the slope of this line, Π will be the point of consumption, but production is indifferent anywhere along AΠB since Π can be reached by exchange from any point along the line. At any price other than this a position preferred to Π can be reached by specialising and producing at A or at B, and the demand curve is the locus of points on the C.I.C.s from which tangents can be drawn to A or B, keeping the P.I.C. and the C.I.C. on opposite sides of the tangent. The demand

[1] P.I.C. stands for Production Indifference Curve and C.I.C. stands for Consumption Indifference Curve.

curve will be composed of sections of circles like the demand circle of Fig. 1 having AZ or BZ as diameter. These circles are ΠTZUA and ΠBVZS, and the demand curve is made up of the sections ΠTZ of the one and ΠSZ of the other, as only these sections have the C.I.C. and the P.I.C. on opposite sides of the tangent. In the case of constant costs we have to take into account the possibility of producing at other points on the P.I.C. and reaching Π by exchange, so that at the price indicated by the slope of AΠB there can be exchange up to BΠ of X for Y and up to AΠ of Y for X. This is not so for the case of decreasing costs. We can therefore say that for constant costs the demand curve is AΠTZSΠB, while for decreasing costs it is limited to the circuit ΠTZS.

9. This demand curve gives us the alternative and more interesting way of finding the equilibrium of trade between two " countries." The point where the demand curve touches the P.I.C. is the same point at which a C.I.C. touches it—Π in Figs. 2 and 3. So that instead of saying that an isolated individual with increasing or constant costs will produce at the point on his P.I.C. where a C.I.C. is tangential to it, we may say that he will produce at the point where it is touched or cut by the demand curve. The case of decreasing costs raises a special difficulty that will be dealt with below. The advantage of thus substituting the demand curve for the C.I.C. lies in the fact that while the C.I.C.s of two individuals cannot be added in any way, the demand curve *can* be added and applied to the compound P.I.C. thus giving us the production of the two individuals when they trade with one another. If we consider the P.I.C. AB in Fig. 2 to be the compound P.I.C. of two individuals obtained as described in my previous article, the compound curve ΠTZQ can be obtained as described below. We need three diagrams, one for each individual separately and one for the combination of the two. Since all these diagrams will look alike we can take Fig. 2 to stand for all of them, making clear to which we are referring in the text by following the notation of my last article and using lower-case letters for the first individual, lower-case letters dashed for the second individual, and capital letters for the compound case.

Having got the compound P.I.C. AB from ab and a′b′ take points p, p′, and P where parallel lines are tangential to the curves or touch their extremities, and draw these parallel lines. Mark off q and q′ where these lines cut or touch the demand curves πszt and π's′z′t′ respectively. On the tangent at P parallel to pq and p′q′, mark off Q so that PQ=pq+p′q′ in length and direction, so that where pq is drawn in the sense or direction opposite to p′q′, PQ will be equal in length to the difference between these two lines and will be in the sense of the longer line. Where pq is equal in length and opposite in sense to p′q′, PQ will be equal to zero, P and Q will coincide, and we will have the point where the compound demand curve touches the compound P.I.C.—that is *Π* in Fig. 2. The compound demand curve will be the locus of all points Q obtained in this manner from parallel lines of all possible slopes.[1]

At any price represented by the slope of the parallel lines pq, p′q′, and PQ, pq represents the amount and direction of trade the first individual is willing to do, and p′q′ the amount and direction of trade the second individual is willing to do. Unless pq and p′q′ are opposite in sense, unless, that is, one wishes to trade some X for some Y while the other wishes to trade Y for X there can be no trade between them. And unless pq is equal to p′q′ in length, the supply will not be equal to the demand and there will ensue a change in price. Trading equilibrium can therefore only be reached when pq is equal and opposite to p′q′ and that as we have seen is where PQ is equal to zero. The price in equilibrium will be that represented by the tangent to the compound P.I.C. where it is touched by the compound demand curve, i.e. by the tangent to AB at *Π*. At that price production must be as indicated by the ordinates of *Π*.

10. The relation of these individual demand curves to international trade becomes clear when it is observed that the compound demand curve can again be added in the same way to any other such demand curve whether primary or compound. The compound demand curve in conjunction with the compound P.I.C. shows in PQ the amount and direction of trade

[1] In the compound case of Fig. 2 there will therefore be no C.I.C.s, but only price-slopes on the P.I.C. AB, and on the demand curve *Π*SZT. At *Π* the price-slope would be the same as the slope of the P.I.C. and that of the demand curve. On all other points of the demand curve the price-slopes would be such that if continued they would form the lines of exchange tangential to the P.I.C. or touching its extremities. As one moved along the demand curve from *Π* to Z by either route, the price-slope, identical with the slope of the demand curve at *Π*, would cut it at a greater and greater angle (just as in moving from *Π* to A or B) until at Z it becomes perpendicular to the demand curve and disappears. A price-slope at any point on the P.I.C. would represent the knowledge of the price that would obtain for that combination of production if there is no trade with outsiders, i.e. outside the individuals included in this compound case. A price-slope at any point on the demand curve would show the price that would obtain if the point were reached by producing where the ratio of alternative marginal products is equal or nearest to the price and trading with outsiders.

that the individuals taken together are willing to do at each price. Where both are willing to trade in the same direction, PQ is the simple arithmetical sum of pq and p′q′; but where one wishes to do some trade with the other individual the amount of trade that the two individuals taken together are willing to do with outsiders is less than the amount of trade that one of the individuals would be willing to do by himself, the limiting case being that just described when the two individuals just satisfy and compensate each other's willingness to trade, and the combination, at the price shown by the tangent at Π will do no trade. The one individual will trade pq and the other p′q′, but these being equal and opposite pq+p′q′= PQ=zero.

The addition of demand curves can thus be continued without limit, and so one can conceive of demand curves for " countries " being built up without any comparison or addition of different individuals' utilities, and the distribution of production between " countries " is determined.[1]

11. This presentation has further the advantage over the treatment in the first part of this article that it shows the amount of trade carried on between the two " countries " in pq, which is, of course, equal to p′q′ for the equilibrium position

[1] The P.I.C.s of " countries " are of course not obtained by merely adding up the productive possibility of all the separate individuals in a country, but to a much greater extent by the combination of individuals into firms which enables them to take advantage of specialisation. It is difficult to bring this into consideration when using the highly abstract simplification of having two commodities only, but the difficulty might be overcome by regarding the *entrepreneur* as well as the owners of employed factors as having such employment as a possibility of production—a point on their P.I.C.s—which gives them the quantities of the commodities that they get in this way as the return from that possibility. There arise further difficulties from the interdependence of such productive possibilities, but these do not seem insuperable either. The purely technical possibilities must be taken by the economist as given, and can be expressed by a P.I.C. for the " country." For increasing and constant costs the only possible price relationship of the products is given for any productive distribution or point on the curve by the alternatives producible at the margin. This, in conjunction with the technical conditions, gives the rewards of every factor, which with the individual C.I.C.s gives the individual demand curves which can be added and applied to the technically given curve of productive possibilities. The equilibrium position will be that at which the collective demand curve touches the P.I.C. at the point from which the calculation started. That is, at that production where the market exchange relationship is equal to the ratio at which the goods are alternatively producible at the margin. Where there is not this coincidence there arises a tendency to produce more of the commodity which has the relatively higher price, and this movement by increasing the relative cost and/or diminishing the market exchange ratio of the commodity whose production is increased tends to bring about the coincidence and persists until the coincidence is brought about. The case of decreasing costs raises special difficulties which will be dealt with below.

when PQ=O. We can extract these quantities of " willingness to trade " and consider them separately.

In Fig. 4 we will measure positively quantities of X and Y that the first country will acquire at different exchange ratios, and we will measure negatively quantities that it will give up at these exchange ratios. As we wish to relate the willingness-to-trade of the first country to the willingness-to-trade of the second country we must measure negatively the quantity that the second country acquires, since these are the goods that the first country gives up ; and we must measure positively the goods that the second country gives up, for these are the goods that the first country acquires.

The "pq"s and the "p′q′"s of Fig. 2 are the willingnesses-to-trade of the first and second country, and we have only to transfer these lengths in their appropriate directions to Fig. 4 measuring them all from the origin of the system of co-ordinates. The " pq "s will be transferred directly as measured, and will give us the willingness-to-trade or demand curve $otz_az_bs\Pi o$ while the " p′q′ "s have to be transposed in sense before they are transferred so that we get $ot'z'_bz'_as'\Pi o$. Only at the price ratio represented by the slope of the line $o\Pi$ does supply equal demand. That is therefore the equilibrium rate of exchange between the first and second country, the first country giving up Πr of X for *or* of Y, the second, of course, doing the reverse. Thus p′q′ which was equal and opposite to pq, having been reversed, now coincides with it in $o\Pi$. It can be seen that the section of the diagram near the origin in the top left-hand quarter is the familiar Marshallian construction. If the two " circles " are tangential at the origin there will be no trade between the countries. If conditions of production as well as tastes are identical in the two countries, the two demand curves will be similar in shape and symmetrical about the origin and will therefore be tangential at the origin, thus signifying the absence of trade. If the circles cut in the lower right-hand corner, trade will be in the reverse direction, that is, the first country will give up Y for X instead of X for Y.

12. The break in the demand curve z_az_b (and in the same way $z'_az'_b$) represents the quite negligible possibility of the point of " Bliss " in Fig. 2, being approachable by a line of exchange from the P.I.C. Lines of exchange which make this possible must be positively inclined, showing a negative price of each commodity in terms of the other, so that in order to acquire any quantity of one, instead of *giving up for it* a quantity

of the other it is necessary to *accept with it* a quantity of the other commodity. There will be no point on the P.I.C. having such a positive slope, so that the line of exchange will have to connect z with one of the extremities. Since at z the C.I.C. contracts to a point, it cannot be said to lie on one side or the other of the line of exchange so that we cannot follow the rule of connecting it with that extremity which would leave the P.I.C. on the opposite side. We must therefore consider it as capable of being reached from either extremity. It is reached from a when the line of exchange is az, being the extreme end of that part (tz) of the demand curve which is reached by a line of exchange from a and which is part of the " circle " having the diameter az. It is reached from b when the line of exchange is bz, being the extreme end of that part (sz) of the demand curve which is part of the " circle " having the diameter bz. All the " pq "s or quantities and directions of exchange that correspond to the section of the demand curve πqsz (Fig. 2) are shown in Fig. 4 in the section of the willingness-to-trade curve oΠsz_b, oz_b being the limiting line of exchange bz. Similarly the other half of the demand curve πtz of Fig. 2 is shown in otz_a of Fig. 4, oz_a being the counterpart of az. This leaves $z_a z_b$ unaccounted for. This is the part of the willingness-to-trade curve which corresponds to the rates of exchange between oz_a and oz_b. In Fig. 2 these prices are the lines of exchange between az and bz. In this range of prices, the optimum production for the individual would be that from which he could reach z by exchange. It is no longer necessary for the line of exchange to be tangential to the P.I.C. or to be limited to its extremities, for these conditions only apply to cases where shifting the line of exchange in one direction or the other (without turning it) could bring the individual on to a higher C.I.C. This cannot apply here, for there is no higher point than z. For all rates of exchange, then, between az and bz production will be at the point where ab is cut by the line of exchange drawn from z. This gives us $z_a z_b$ of Fig. 4 which is identical in shape with ab but reversed. The corresponding break $z'_a z'_b$ in the other willingness-to-trade curve will be identical in shape with a′b′, but not reversed, since the inversion of every p′q′ will have cancelled this inversion.

All this is seen more clearly when we consider the constant and increasing costs of Fig. 3 and the extraction of the willingness-to-trade curve in Fig. 5. Whereas in Fig. 2 only part of the demand curve consists of sections of the circles whose diameters are the lines joining z to the extremities of the P.I.C., in the case of the constant and increasing cost curves of Fig. 3 the demand curve is formed entirely from sections of such circles except for the straight line sections *Π*A and *Π*B in the case of constant costs as shown in section (8) above.

The demand curve for constant costs A*Π*TZS*Π*B is shown in the willingness-to-trade curve in two sections. A*Π*TZ is seen in OATZ$_a$ and ZS*Π*B in Z$_b$SBO, while Z$_a$ is joined to Z$_b$ by a straight line, since the inversion of the straight P.I.C. does not affect its shape. This gives us the willingness-to-trade curve OATZ$_a$Z$_b$SBO.

In the case of decreasing costs the demand curve *Π*TZS of Fig. 3 is shown again in two sections: *Π*TZ by ATZ$_a$ and ZS*Π* by Z$_b$SB. Z$_a$ is joined to Z$_b$ by a line inverse in shape to the P.I.C., and therefore concave to the origin, shown by Z$_a$CZ$_b$. Between A and B the willingness-to-trade curve has a gap. This gap is the most important part of the diagram, for it indicates the special difficulties arising in the case of decreasing costs. How trade, if any, will take place if the other country's willingness-to-trade curve as a result of this gap misses the willingness-to-trade curve ATZ$_a$CZ$_b$SB cannot be established without a further elucidation of the fundamental assumptions.[1]

III

13. The difficulties that arise in connection with decreasing costs are due to the fact that any individual or " country " with a decreasing costs P.I.C. will always specialise, producing only X or only Y if there is any exchange ratio which can be taken by the individual or " country " as given. At any exchange ratio production will be at an extremity of the P.I.C.

This will not matter at all if the trade is done between this country and a country with increasing costs at an exchange ratio at which the two countries' " willingness-to-trade " are equal and opposite, and at which the other country will not be specialising—i.e. it will not be producing at an extremity of its P.I.C. but at some intermediate position on it. In this case everything is determinate. The exchange ratio is equal to the ratio between the quantities of goods alternatively produced at the margin in the increasing costs country; and at that exchange ratio supply will be equal to demand. This will be

[1] I am indebted to Mr. A. Emanuel for bringing to my notice this indeterminacy in the case of decreasing costs.

shown in the willingness-to-trade curve of the increasing costs country missing the gap in the willingness-to-trade curve of the decreasing costs country, and cutting this curve at a point which shows the trade done and the exchange ratio.

There is no serious difficulty even if both countries have decreasing costs, if when both are specialising, each in a different commodity, there is some exchange ratio at which their "willingnesses-to-trades" are equal and opposite. This would be shown in their willingness-to-trade curves cutting, both gaps being avoided. In this case there will be no indication of the exchange ratio from the production side in the form of the ratio between alternatively producible quantities of the different goods at the margin, but the exchange ratio is sufficiently determined by the condition of making supply= demand, and that is given by the intersection of the willingness-to-trade curves. This kind of one-sided determination is not peculiar to decreasing costs, but arises whenever both countries specialise and is mentioned in my previous article (p. 351).

14. The real difficulties arise when we have a country with decreasing costs which does not specialise. In my previous article (p. 352) I indicated that with two countries both having decreasing costs, one at least must specialise; this suggests the possibility that the other might not, and indeed in Figs. 5 and 6 of that article I describe conditions where one country with decreasing costs does not specialise. This seems to contradict the proposition put forward in this article that a country with decreasing costs *must* specialise if there is any market rate of exchange. The apparent contradiction is due to a difference of basic assumptions. If conditions of perfect competition are assumed, as they have been so far in this article, with everybody confronted with an *exchange ratio* which he takes as given rather than with a demand curve, then a decreasing costs country must specialise. But if the decreasing costs in a country are considered to have had their natural effect of leading to monopoly, then the monopolistic country is no longer faced with an exchange ratio but with a demand curve, and may find it advisable to restrict production of the commodity in which it would otherwise have specialised, and apply the resources set free in this way to produce some of the other commodity. The tendency to monopoly will show itself in the impossibility of obtaining an equilibrium position as long as competitive conditions prevail, for on account of the gaps in the willingness-to-trade curves, there may be no prices at which the supply is

equal to the demand. In these cases we must apply the principles of Monopoly Theory.

If this impasse is reached in the case where one country has increasing costs and one country has decreasing costs, we may consider the decreasing costs country as the monopolist. The monopolist can be considered as having, on the one hand, a set of real C.I.C.s, and on the other hand his P.I.C. as well as the *possibility of exchanging different quantities at different prices* with the other country. We have to add to his *production possibilities* his *exchanging possibilities* to get his total *possibilities of acquisition*. This can be represented by the curve obtained by moving the other country's willingness-to-trade curve (the lower " circuit " of Fig. 4) round his P.I.C., keeping the origin on the P.I.C. and the axes parallel and marking out the parts of the moving curve farthest from the origin in the way described in my previous article on p. 250, section (3). The equilibrium point will be where the resulting Acquisition Indifference Curve reaches a highest C.I.C. The distribution between production and exchange is determined exactly, as is the distribution between production in the two countries in the completely analogous additions of the P.I.C.s of two countries in my previous article.

The same procedure may be followed in the case of two countries both having decreasing costs. If one of them acts as a monopolist and the other accepts his price, we get a determinate equilibrium in exactly the same way. A completely different equilibrium will be reached if the countries reverse their roles, and the second country acts as the monopolist while the first accepts the prices. If both countries try to act the monopolist, and neither adjusts himself to the price proposed by the other, there develops a problem of tacit or open bargaining with a wide range of possible bargains and no determinate exchange equilibrium. The problem resolves itself into a simple case of bilateral monopoly.

15. Monopoly may of course also arise in the case of increasing costs, and in this case, too, the same reasoning holds good. As compared with the position reached under perfect competition the " terms of trade " will be turned in favour of the monopolist and against the competitive country, and the monopolistic country may be said to have gained by this change. This corresponds to Edgeworth's argument for small import or export tax.[1]

[1] *Papers*, vol. ii, p. 39.

16. Finally it should be noted that the constructions both of this and of my previous article apply to any kind of trade, between individuals, towns, regions, countries, and continents as well as between social classes or between people at different points of time; and that it is only an historical accident of the development of Economic Theory that all these problems are called " International Trade."

[3]

The Symmetry Between Import and Export Taxes

By A. P. Lerner

This note does not arrive at any conclusions not previously obtained by Bastable, Marshall and Pigou, but it shows the nature of the slip which led Edgeworth to conclusions contrary to theirs, and demonstrates the applicability of Marshall's "offer curve" apparatus to the elucidation of this problem.[1]

If there are two countries, *e* (England) and *g* (Germany), and two goods E and G which are produced by them respectively under conditions of perfect competition and in the absence of transport costs, tariffs or capital movements between the countries, the equilibrium of international trade is depicted by fig. 1. Along the axes are measured

[1] Edgeworth, in an article on "The Pure Theory of International Trade" (*Economic Journal*, 1894, p. 435), writes: "The want of symmetry between the effects of restriction, and in particular taxes, on exports and imports, is perhaps the conclusion which can be most peculiarly and exclusively attributed to the mathematical method. The truth does not seem to have been attained by the ordinary methods." The peculiar result is not due to the use of mathematical methods but to an error in their use committed by Edgeworth. He attributes to the manner in which a tax is collected effects which are really due to the form in which it is spent. This results from the ambiguity, in discussing barter conditions, of the phrase "a tax on exports". On page 624 of the same number of the *Economic Journal*, in a further article of the same series, Edgeworth points out that Bastable in his "International Trade" disagrees with this conclusion, but he fails to meet the point.

In the *Economic Journal*, 1897, p. 397, in a review of the second edition of Bastable's "International Trade", Edgeworth recants his general proposition about the asymmetry of import and export taxes, but maintains that it is still true in the case of taxes imposed *in kind*. He seems here to be aware that it is not really the form of imposition of the tax that matters but its expenditure by the government, for he is careful in his second line of defence to say "Let a tax be imposed . . . and *consumed by the Government*, *or at any rate not sold* . . ." (my italics). He refers also to some very obscure footnotes in his series of articles on "The Pure Theory of Taxation" in the *Economic Journal* of 1897, which he alleges to contain recantations of his error. Yet in the collected papers (Vol. II, p. 39), published in 1925, the sentence quoted at the head of this note is repeated without significant alteration, although a good deal of the argument which appeared originally to justify it is left out. The omission is pointed out in a footnote which declares the missing argument "to be true only of some import taxes *in kind*" (Edgeworth's italics).

The essence of the true theory is to be found in Marshall's *Money Credit and Commerce*, pp. 181–182, and an admirable summary of the discussion is available in Pigou's *Public Finance*, pp. 198–200. One purpose of this note is to exonerate the "mathematical method" from Edgeworth's error—a task in which I am emboldened by my experience in having repeated this error in a Seminar at the London School of Economics.

quantities of the goods E and G. Any radiant from the origin (like OR) indicates a rate at which E can be exchanged for G (e.g. ON of E for NS of G). The curves e and g are the offer curves of the countries. They indicate the amount of trade the inhabitants of the country are willing to do with the other country at each rate of exchange or price. (E.g. at the price indicated by the radiant R, Germany wants to move from O to S, giving up NS of G for ON of E, while England wants to go as far as T, giving up OL of E for LT of G.) The supply of E for G is greater than the demand and the rate of exchange becomes less favourable for England ; the radiant moves to the right to signify that a larger amount of E must be exchanged for each unit of G. The equilibrium position is reached when the radiant passes through the point where the offer curves cut. S coincides with T at P where OM of E is exchanged for MP of G, since both countries are willing to do just the same amount of trade. Supply is equal to demand.

The imposition of a tax, whether on imports or on exports, has the effect of making the price for traders in England different from that for traders in Germany, since some of the goods are intercepted at the customs house and appropriated by the tax collector. If the tax is on G and German traders give OD of G for DC of E (fig. 2), English traders receive only AB of G in exchange for the OA of E that they give up, BC being taken by the tax collector. The price to German traders is shown by the radiant Rg, while that to English traders is shown by Re.

These radiants form a *pencil*, the amplitude of which is a measure of the size of the tax, irrespective of whether E or G is the subject of the tax. The amplitude of the pencil must be measured not by the angle between the radiants but by drawing a perpendicular from any point on one of the radiants to the axis lying beyond the other radiant, and measuring the proportion of this perpendicular that lies within the pencil. The measure of the pencil is therefore $\frac{CB}{CA}$ or $\frac{BF}{BH}$ which are equal to each other—signifying the irrelevance for the measure whether E or G is taxed —since $\frac{CB}{CA} = \frac{CF}{CO} = \frac{BF}{BH} \left(= \frac{KC}{KD}\right)$. A pencil of the amplitude shown in figure 2 indicates a 40 per cent. tax if imposed entirely on imports (G) or entirely on exports (E), or both an import and an export tax of such size that the sum of their effects is equal to a 40 per cent. tax.[1]

Thus in place of the single price-radiant which was swung round to make supply equal to demand we have a pencil which must similarly be swung round to the equilibrium position, its amplitude being determined by the size of the tax or taxes and independent of whether they are imposed on imports or exports.

The point (U in fig. 2) where Re cuts the e curve shows the supply of E and the demand for G by English traders. The point (C) where Rg cuts the g curve shows the supply of G and the demand for E by German traders. It is at once clear that the supplies and demands thus given will never equal each other however much we swing the pencil round in either direction, since these points, lying on different radiants, can never coincide. If we draw a right-angle (CTU) parallel to and in the same sense as the axes, so that its upper extremity (C) lies at the point where the g curve is cut by Rg and its right hand extremity (U) lies at the point where the e curve is cut by Re, its vertical arm (CT) will measure the excess in the supply of G over its demand, while its horizontal arm (TU) will measure the excess of the supply of E over its demand.[2] But our right-angle, measured in this way, is nothing but the *absolute* measure of the amount of the taxes. Obviously our inability to find the equilibrium position where supply equals demand was due to our leaving out of account the demand by the government out of the proceeds of the tax.

We can now go ahead. Given the amplitude of the tax and the proportion in which the government (which here includes any beneficiaries from the taxation) consumes

[1] E.g. two taxes of 20 per cent. and 25 per cent. have a joint effect of 40 per cent. since if these percentages are subtracted consecutively from any item there will remain 60 per cent, of the original amount whatever the order in which this is done. In Fig. 2 if T bisects CB. CT represents a 20 per cent. tax on G and TU a 25 per cent. tax on E. $\left(\frac{KC}{KD}=\frac{40}{100}, \frac{CT}{CB}=\frac{KU}{KB}=\frac{KS}{KC}=\frac{20}{40}.\ \frac{SC}{SD}\right.$ = the rate of tax on E $= \frac{KC-KS}{KD-KS}=\frac{20}{80}=$ 25 per cent.). Alternatively the pencil may be considered as the sum of the two adjacent pencils which would be traversed by CT and TU respectively, remembering that in adding the measure of the pencils, they must be summed as consecutive percentage subtractions, so that 20 per cent. + 25 per cent. = 40 per cent.

[2] Some readers may find it more satisfactory to imagine C and U to be connected by a *rectangle*, with sides parallel to the axes (CTUS in fig. 2) of which the left side and the base constitute our rightangle. The excess of the supply of G over its demand is then measured by the *height* of the rectangle, while the excess of the supply of E over its demand is measured by the *width* of the rectangle. Similarly we may call CT the *height* of our rightangle and TU its *width*.

E and G, we can find the equilibrium position by swinging the pencil round until the ratio between the length of the arms of the rightangle $\left(\frac{CT}{TU}\right)$ corresponds to the ratio in which the government consumes G and E. Thus in fig. 2, the government demand for CT of G and TU of E meets the excess of supply by the traders, supply is equal to demand and we have the equilibrium. If the pencil were swung slightly towards the right, the rightangle would become flatter and wider, so that with the same government demand there would be an excess of the supply of E over the demand and an excess of the demand for G over its supply. This would make E cheaper relatively to G so that the pencil would swing back again towards the left to the equilibrium position.

In the limiting case where the government consumes only E, the rightangle reduces to a horizontal line which traverses the pencil and meets the offer curves. Where only G is consumed by the government it becomes a vertical line.

From this examination it becomes clear that whether the tax is collected in G or in E makes no difference since this plays no part in the determination of the equilibrium position. We can draw another rightangle which shows the tax in the form in which it is collected. This taxation rightangle, like the government consumption rightangle, must fit into the pencil, since the pencil measures the amplitude of the tax, but, unlike the consumption rightangle, it need not meet the offer curves in its extremities. That was necessary for the consumption rightangle only because the government expenditure had to raise the traders' demands to their supplies.

The taxation rightangle is transformed into a consumption rightangle by a movement of one of its arms along one of the radiants until it reaches the offer curve. Thus in fig. 2, if the tax had been raised entirely in G, the taxation rightangle would have had the limiting shape of the vertical line CB. The government would then exchange G for E with English traders, moving the right extremity of the rightangle along Re from B to U and the corner of the rightangle from B to T, the rightangle acquiring the shape CTU and becoming a consumption rightangle. If the tax had been collected entirely in E, the initial taxation rightangle would have been a horizontal line traversing the pencil and passing through U and T. The excess of E over UT would then be exchanged by the government for TC of G. Edgeworth's error may be considered as the failure to distinguish between these two rightangles.

One extremity of the taxation rightangle may be expected to touch an offer curve, otherwise it can be transformed into a consumption rightangle only by moving the arms along *both* radiants. This would mean that the government exchanges G for E as well as E for G—which is not impossible, since the prices at which it can do this are divergent so that a profit emerges, but such an excursion of the government into active participation in foreign trade is unnecessary, for these profits are just what would flow to it from the taxation on the trade when done by the traders.

The apparatus we have been developing enables us to see the final equilibrium position resulting from the imposition of a tax of given size, given the ratio of its consumption between E and G, without drawing any of the magnifications, projections or other distortions of the offer curves that Edgeworth found necessary and which led to his slip. All we need do is to fit a government consumption rightangle of the appropriate dimensions into the offer curves. Figures 3, 4 and 5 all show the two limiting cases of government consumption being restricted to E (C_1U_1) or to G (C_2U_2) and one intermediate case with some of both E and G being consumed (CTU). In fig. 3 both offer curves are elastic. In fig. 4 both are inelastic. In fig. 5 e is elastic while g is inelastic. This figure can be turned round to show the reverse case.

From a cursory study of these figures it appears that in all cases (*a*) English traders are better off (U_1 is further along e so that more G is bought and on better terms) while German traders are worse off the greater the ratio of government consumption of E ; (*b*) English traders will be better off than in the absence of the tax (apart from any benefit they may derive from the government consumption) if the proportion of the tax (measured in G) that is spent on E is greater than the elasticity of the g curve over the relevant range;[1] and conversely that German traders will be better off than in the absence of the tax if the proportion of the tax (measured in E) that is spent on G is greater than the elasticity of the e curve. (*c*) In this latter case, the English nation, including those who enjoy the government expenditure, will be worse off than if there had been no tax, in the sense that the new position, including the government consumption, is one which is on a lower indifference curve as indicated by the offer curve. This raises many difficulties, but there is an unambiguous loss if at the same time the g curve is inelastic, for this gives a position (C_2 in fig. 4) where England gives up more E and receives less G than in the absence of the tax.

So far we have spoken in barter terms, but to suppose that the tax is raised in money and the money then spent on the commodities hardly affects even the form of the argument. There is the same divergence between the prices to the traders in the different countries, the same gap between the radiants of the pencil, and it is filled in the same way by the government demand. It enables us to consider the possibility of the government taxing imports or exports but not spending the money at all. In this case one must consider the rentier beneficiaries from the ensuing deflation as being the recipients of the taxation proceeds, and it is the form taken by their additional purchases that determines the effect of the tax.

In inserting a rightangle to represent the government demand, we have been assuming the proportions between government consumption of E and G as given. It is obvious that this is not fixed but will depend upon the relative prices of E and G. Closely bound up with this is the implicit assumption that the shapes of the traders'

[1] This can be demonstrated with the help of fig. 2. Suppose the g curve to turn down (since it must be inelastic, otherwise it is impossible for the proportion of the tax spent on E (which < 1) to be equal to the elasticity) and to pass through C and U. Draw a straight line through C and U, meeting the G axis in M and the E axis in N, and continue UT to meet OG in L. (This construction is not shown in the figure.) Then the elasticity of the offer curve (*cf.* Lerner, "Elasticity of Demand," *Review of Economic Studies*, Oct., 1933, p. 44, and p. 40, fig. 5) is $\frac{LO}{MO} = \frac{TB}{CB}$ which is the proportion of the tax, measured in G which is spent on E. In this case U, the English traders' equilibrium, will be at the point of intersection of the offer curves so that they do just the same trade as in the absence of the tax—the whole of the tax burden falls on the foreigner. If, however, the proportion of the tax spent on E were greater than this, the price of E would rise relatively to that of G, the pencil would swing round to the left, and U would move to a point on e further from the origin, indicating that the English traders buy more G and on better terms. The foreigner pays more than the whole of the tax.

offer curves (which include the demand for imports) are independent of the taxation and the expenditure by the government. Both of these complications can be dealt with at the same time. The e curve can be stabilised by segregating all the influences which might be considered to affect it and incorporating them in the *government demand curve.* This is in accordance with our procedure of including all demand by beneficiaries from government expenditure in the government demand.

The government demand curve is the curve SC in fig. 6, which is a kind of small replica of the e curve, something like the embryo orange that one finds in a Jaffa. US is the size of the tax measured in E. At the price Rg—which is the price at which the government can convert E into G —it moves the top end of the rightangle from S to C. Instead of inserting a rightangle we have to insert the wedge CSU, moving U down the e curve, SU meanwhile contracting so as to measure the same size of pencil, until the radiant (from the origin) passing through S meets the government demand curve just at the point where it cuts the g curve.

This is not quite satisfactory in so far as it implies that the shape of SC is independent of the size of the tax collected. An improvement on this is to consider there to be a series of SC curves, more or less parallel to each other and starting from different points on US and US continued. Each of these curves shows the government demand curve corresponding to the size of the tax, measured in E, as indicated by the distance of the bottom of the curve from U along US. This series of curves is then moved down in the same way until the curve which begins at the point along US corresponding to the size of the tax is in a line with the origin and with the point where it cuts the g curve. The line through these points is Rg and this gives the equilibrium position as shown in fig. 6, the government consuming CT of G and TU of E.

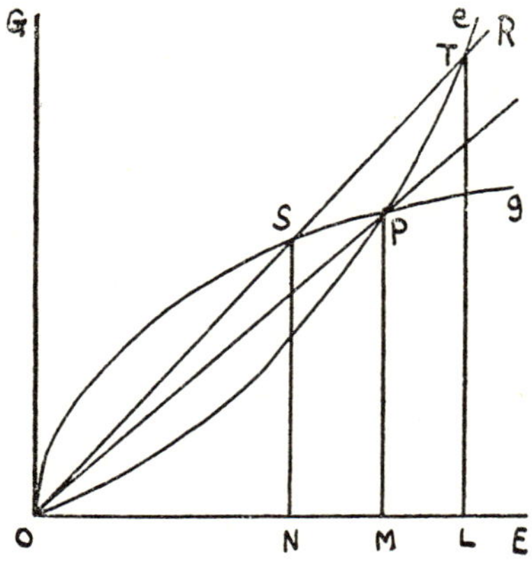

Fig. 1.

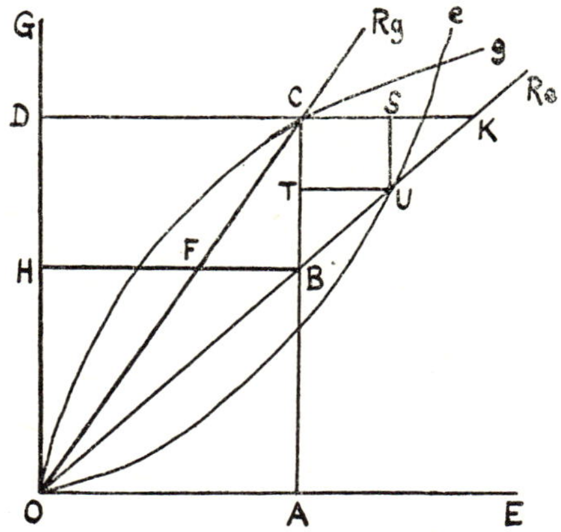

Fig. 2.

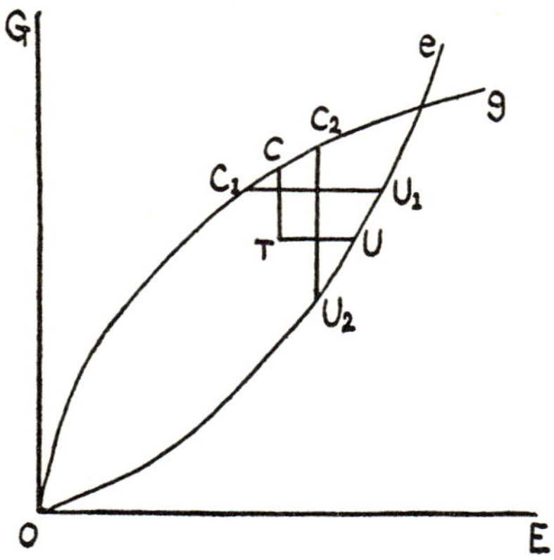

Fig. 3.

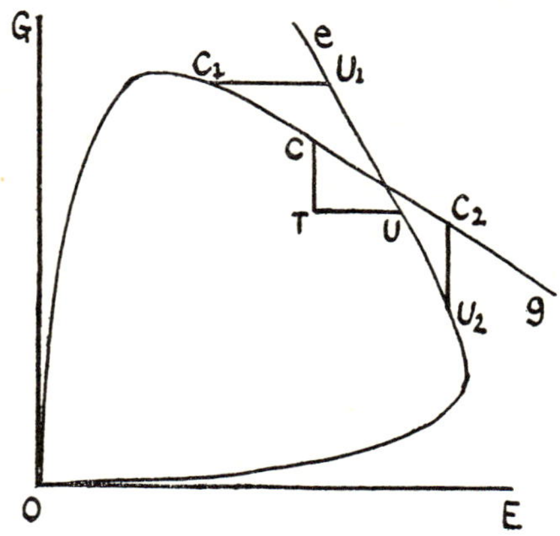

Fig. 4.

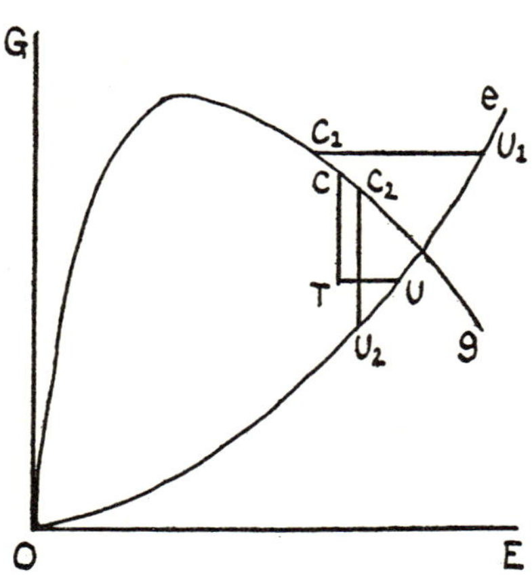

Fig. 5.

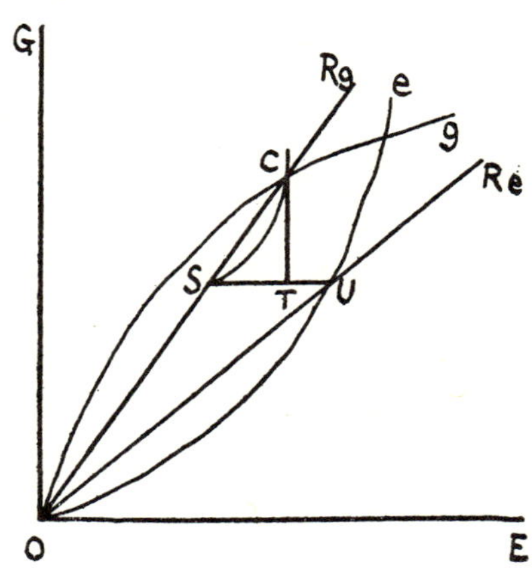

Fig. 6.

[4]

1952]

Factor Prices and International Trade

By Abba P. Lerner

(The following article was prepared by Professor Lerner for a seminar at the London School of Economics in December 1933. It is the paper referred to by Professor Samuelson in his article, "International Factor-Price Equalisation Once Again", Economic Journal, *June 1949, p. 181. It is reproduced here as it was originally written; and it will be of value to students both for its place in the history of ideas and also for the geometric technique employed to demonstrate conditions for the equalisation of factor prices.)*

1. Following the accepted tradition of International Trade Theory, let us make the following usual assumptions:

(1) Factors are not allowed to move between countries.

(2) Finished commodities can move between countries without cost.

(3) Perfect competition.

(4) There are only two countries, two commodities and two factors.

To which we add

(5) The same technical knowledge is available in both countries.

From (2) and (3) it follows that the same commodities must have the same price in both countries (all prices being converted on to a common basis at the current rate of exchange) and also the same cost of production wherever they are produced.

A first glance at these considerations would seem to suggest that there must be complete specialisation in at least one of the commodities unless factor prices are the same in both countries. For if in equilibrium one factor is cheaper in one country than in the other, the other factor must be dearer or else the first country would export both commodities and import neither. From this it would follow that the commodity which used a larger proportion of the cheaper factor would have a lower cost in this country than in the other so that the conditions of equilibrium would be upset by any difference of factor prices as between the two countries.

2. This seems to fit in with the general view that divergent scarcities of factor are the moving forces behind international trade. In lieu of the export of *factors* which are unable to move, there are exported commodities which contain the services of cheaper factors in a greater proportion than the commodities which are imported. This movement extends until either (*a*) complete specialisation has already been reached, i.e. there is no commodity being produced abroad which contains a greater proportion of this cheaper factor than any commodity produced at home, or (*b*) the price of the cheaper factor has risen to equality with its price abroad. *Therefore, if both commodities are produced in both countries, the equilibrium must be of the second type, i.e. factor prices must be the same in both countries.*

3. Against this it is often objected that it is impossible for factor prices to be the same if the ratio between total quantities of the factors is different in the two countries. For if factor prices are the same, the proportion in which factors are combined in the production of commodities must be the same, so that some of the factors would remain unemployed and so change the price.

This argument is based upon a confusion between two ratios: the ratio between the factors in the production of a particular commodity, and the ratio between the quantities of factors in a country. There is no need whatever for these to be the same. The larger proportion of a factor in one country can be taken up in the production of the commodity which uses a larger proportion of this factor, if this commodity is produced in a greater proportion to the other commodities in this country than in the other country. Thus if in countries 1 and 2, commodities A and B are made from factors X and Y, if the factor prices are the same in both countries, the factors will be combined in the same proportion in both countries for the production of each commodity. Suppose one unit of X and one unit of Y combine to make a unit of A, and one unit of X and 5 units of Y combine to make a unit of B. Then the proportions between the factors in each country can be anything between 1 : 1 and 1 · 5. If in country 1 there are 100 X and 200 Y and in country 2 there are 100 X and 400 Y, all this means is that the proportion of B to A manufactured will be greater in country 2 than in country 1. There will be made altogether 100 units of A and 100 units of B. Country 1 producing 75 A and 25 B and country 2 producing 25 A and 75 B, all the factors being used. For every combination of factors and set of coefficients, there will be a distribution of production between the countries which will just use up all the factors.

Nor is it necessary to assume fixed coefficients of production as the above arithmetical example might seem to imply. Fig. 1 shows how the factors of a country are distributed between the production of two commodities for all proportions between the quantities of the commodities.

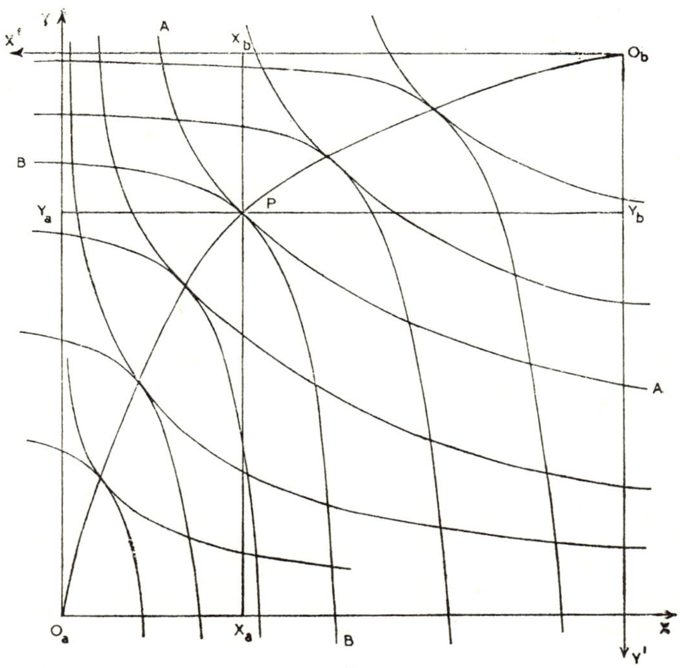

Fig. 1

Along O_aX and O_aY are measured quantities of the factors X and Y used in the production of commodity A. The curve A and all the other similarly shaped curves which are convex to the origin O_a are isoquants of the commodity A—each curve showing different combinations of X and Y which together produce the same quantity of commodity A. The point P on the curve A indicates that O_aX_a of X and O_aY_a of Y can produce the quantity of A to which that particular curve A corresponds. There are an infinite number of such curves filling the space between the axes. All the isoquants are assumed to be similar in shape (for the same commodity), differing only in scale.[1]

The axes O_bX^1 and O_bY^1 and the curves like B which are convex to the origin O_b represent exactly the same thing for commodity B instead of A. The point P on the curve B indicates that O_bX_b of X and O_bY_b of Y can produce that quantity of B to which that particular curve B corresponds.

The origin O_b (and the whole system of axes and curves connected with it) is so placed that the co-ordinates of O_b with respect to the origin O_a (or the co-ordinates of O_a with respect to the origin O_b—which amounts to exactly the same) measure the total available factors of production X and Y in the country. Any point within the rectangle formed by the two pairs of axes will give two pairs of co-ordinates, one for each system. The first pair will represent quantities of factors used in the production of commodity A and the second pair will represent quantities used in the production of B. The sum of these will be equal to the total supply of the factors.

Not all points in this rectangle represent economic distributions. These are limited to the curve O_aPO_b which is the locus of points where A isoquants and B isoquants touch each other. From any other point it is possible, by moving towards this curve, to increase the output of one or both of the commodities. This curve shows all the possible distributions of the factors between the commodities as conditioned by the technical knowledge represented by the isoquants, the quantities of the factors, represented by the relative positions of the two systems, and the economic consideration of producing as much as possible with given resources, represented by the choice of points where isoquants are tangential. Where, on this curve, production will take place will depend upon conditions of demand in this country

[1] This means that the production function is homogeneous and there are no economies of scale. This is assumed throughout this article, for, if there are economies of scale, there must arise complete specialisation in at least one of the commodities (i.e, one of the commodities, at least, will be produced in only one country) so that the problem with which we wish to deal cannot arise.

and upon the desire to trade by the other country (which depends upon both the technical conditions in the other country and upon conditions of demand there). This curve shows what possible ratios of factors in the production of any commodity are compatible with the existing ratio of factors in the country.

4. The argument given in sections (1) and (2) is not sufficiently rigid and certain limitations have to be imposed upon the propositions enumerated. It will, however, be found to provide a substantially reliable rough expression of the correct theory.

If A and B are the *prices* of the commodities, X and Y the *prices* of the factors, K and L the respective quantities of X and Y used in the production of a unit of A, M and N the quantities used in the production of a unit of B and the subscripts 1 and 2 indicate to which country the prices or quantities refer, we can express the conditions of equilibrium in the equations :

$$\left.\begin{aligned} A_1 = K_1 X_1 + L_1 Y_1 = K_2 X_2 + L_2 Y_2 = A_2 \\ B_1 = M_1 X_1 + N_1 Y_1 = M_2 X_2 + N_2 Y_2 = B_2 \end{aligned}\right\} \quad .. (1)$$

These equations are satisfied if factor prices are the same in both countries, for in that case the proportion of the factors used in each commodity must be the same in both countries, all the subscripts disappear and the equations become identities.

5. Contrary, however, to what seems to be implied in the simple reasoning of section (1) this is not the only solution. There are possible two other types of solution, but these depend upon such unlikely conditions that they may fairly be said to be of theoretical rather than practical interest even when comparing them with the abstract theoretical problem which we have so far discussed.

The first of these two "theoretical" solutions[1] refers to the case where the ratios of the factors are the same in each country for *both* commodities. It is then possible for factor prices to be different in the two countries, one factor cheaper in one country and the other factor cheaper in the other country, while the argument of section (1) could not be applied as there is no commodity "which uses a larger proportion" of any factor. Against the objection that in

[1] Suggested to me by Mrs. J. Robinson of Cambridge.

this case the two commodities are economically " one commodity " the view was held that this identity of factor proportions need not be true for all price relationships, but only for those reached in the equilibrium position.

It can be shown that these conditions are not sufficient to assure equilibrium. If $\frac{K_1}{L_1}=\frac{M_1}{N_1}$ and $\frac{K_2}{L_2}=\frac{M_2}{N_2}$ it is still possible to have the case indicated by the equations

$$\left.\begin{array}{l} A_1 = 2X_1 + 3Y_1 = 5X_2 + 2Y_2 = A_2 \\ B_1 = 4X_1 + 6Y_1 = 15X_2 + 6Y_2 = B_2 \end{array}\right\} \quad .. \quad (2)$$

where the coefficients of production, K, L, M and N of equations (1) are replaced by figures which satisfy the conditions of equal ratios of factors for both commodities in each country as well as the general condition of a positive and finite elasticity of substitution. It is obvious that both of these equations cannot be true whatever the prices of the factors. Unless factor prices are the same in both countries (in which case K, L, M and N would have to be the same too) it is necessary that $\frac{K_1}{M_1}=\frac{K_2}{M_2}$ and also, which would follow, that $\frac{L_1}{N_1}=\frac{L_2}{N_2}$. This is only likely to be the case if the technical conditions of production of the two commodities are identical over a considerable range, so that, economically, they are *one commodity*.

6. The second " theoretical solution " is indicated by the following values of the terms in equations (1).

X_1	Y_1	K_1	L_1	M_1	N_1	X_2	Y_2	K_2	L_2	M_2	N_2
10	3	3	16	2	20	7	5	4	10	5	9

Substituting these in the equations we get :

$$\left.\begin{array}{l} A_1 = (3 \times 10) + (16 \times 3) = (4 \times 7) + (10 \times 5) = A_2 = 78 \\ B_1 = (2 \times 10) + (20 \times 3) = (5 \times 7) + (9 \times 5) = B_2 = 80 \end{array}\right\} \quad .. (3)$$

Here neither factor prices nor proportions of factors are the same, yet the equations are satisfied. This case definitely shows the simple argument of section 1 to be erroneous. The special condition under which such solution may be possible will be best shown by a diagrammatical treatment of the problem.

7. Fig. 2 shows two isoquants, A and B, for unit quantities of the two commodities. By our assumption of equal technical knowledge they are applicable to both countries.

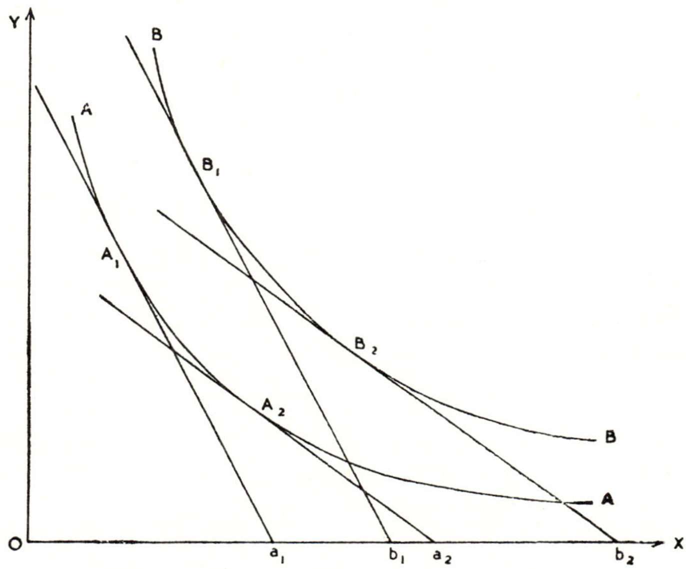

Fig. 2

Let a pair of parallel tangents be drawn to the two isoquants at A_1 and B_1 to cut the X axis in a_1 and b_1 and another pair of parallel tangents at A_2 and B_2 to cut the X axis in a_2 and b_2. The slope of the first pair of parallel tangents represents the price ratio of the factors in country 1, and the slope of the second pair of tangents represents the price ratio of the factors in country 2. All combinations of factors indicated by the co-ordinates of points on a tangent will have the same total value at the price ratio indicated by the slope of the tangent. Factors will be used in the proportions indicated by the co-ordinates of the point where these tangents touch the isoquants, for these are the points where, at the given factor-price ratio, any expenditure on factors gives a maximum output of the commodity. In country 1 the quantities of factors per unit of commodity will be measured by the co-ordinates of A_1 and B_1 and in country 2 they will be measured by the co-ordinates of A_2 and B_2.

Since the value of a unit of a commodity is equal to the value of the factors it incorporates, and since all points on a tangent represent the same value, the value in country 1 of a unit quantity of A will be equal to the value of a_1 of factor X, and a unit of B will be equal in value to b_1 of factor X. In country 2 commodities A and B will be worth a_2 and b_2 respectively in terms of factor X. The conditions of equilibrium, that relative commodity prices are the same in both countries, can then be represented by the formula

$$\frac{a_1}{b_1} = \frac{a_2}{b_2}$$

8. If factor prices are the same in both countries, this condition is satisfied for curves of any shape and for all factor-price relationships, for the two pairs of parallel lines coincide and become one pair of parallel lines, $a_1 = a_2$ and $b_1 = b_2$.

9. Equilibrium may be reached with factor prices different in the two countries if the proportions in which the factors are used are the same for both commodities in each country but not the same in both countries. This is Mrs. Robinson's case and is shown in Fig. 3. It can also be easily seen that

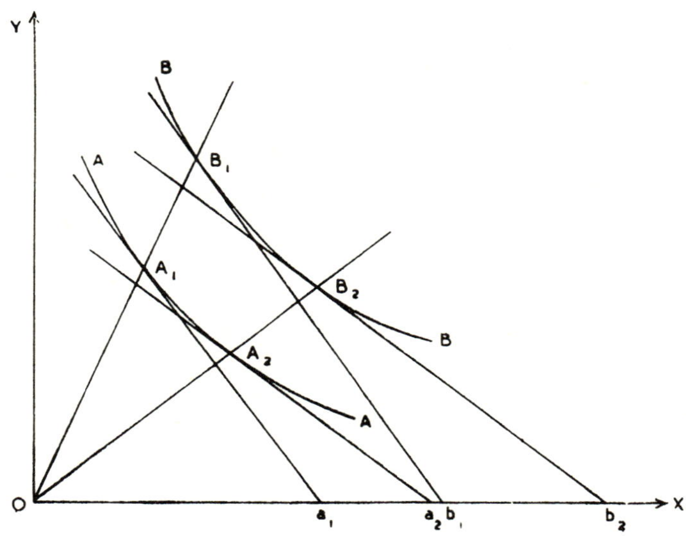

Fig. 3

these conditions are not sufficient for the equilibrium to be reached, for, by similar triangles, $\frac{a_1}{b_1} = \frac{a_2}{b_2}$ only if $\frac{OA_1}{OB_1} = \frac{OA_2}{OB_2}$. The meaning of this and the likelihood of its happening will be investigated below when we come to analyse possible relationships between the isoquants of the different commodities.

10. Of all possible relationships between the shapes of the isoquants for the two commodities, the most likely case seems to be that in which one commodity will use a relatively larger proportion of one of the factors, whatever the relative prices of the factors in the country. If B is the commodity which at all factor-price ratios uses a relatively larger proportion of X, this will be shown by the two different isoquants being so shaped that if two parallel tangents are drawn to them at A_1 and B_1 in Fig. 4, OA_1 will be steeper

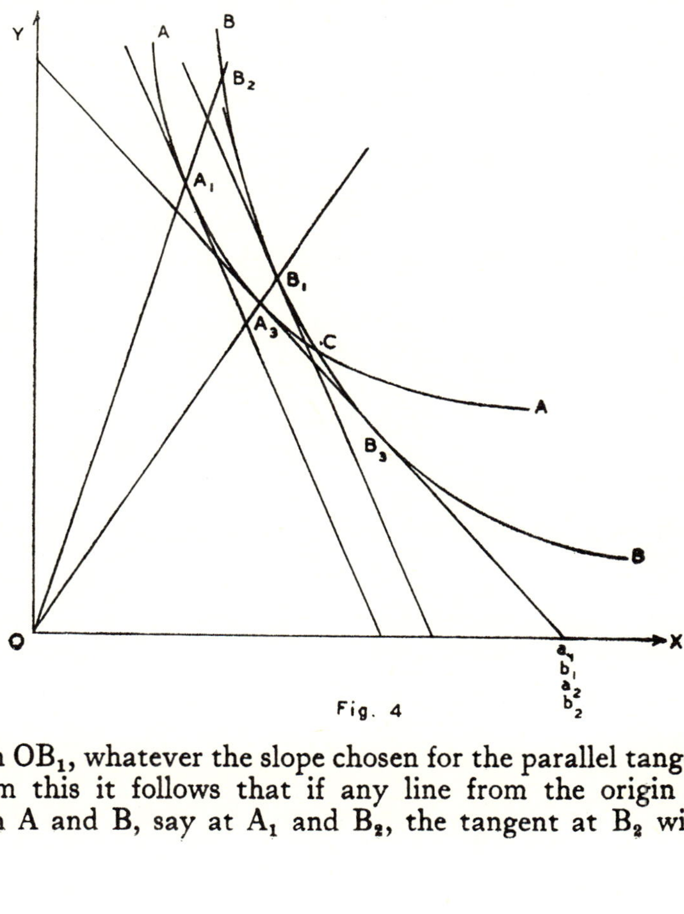

Fig. 4

than OB_1, whatever the slope chosen for the parallel tangents. From this it follows that if any line from the origin cuts both A and B, say at A_1 and B_2, the tangent at B_2 will be steeper than the tangent at A_1 because the tangent at B_2, which is to the left of B_1 will be steeper than the tangent at B_1 which is parallel to the tangent at A_1.

This means that if for each factor-price ratio the corresponding quantity ratio of X to Y is greater for B than for A, then it will also be true that for every quantity ratio of X to Y the corresponding price of X (relatively to that of Y) will be greater for B than for A. B will only give up using a greater proportion of X if X is dearer for it than for A.

Remembering that there are an infinite number of both kinds of curves—all of the same shape but differing in scale (the homogeneous production function) we may further say that no A curve can be cut more than once by the same B curve and vice versa. We can see the reason for this if we imagine OB_2 swinging round from the Y axis towards the X axis. The steeper slope at B_2 than at A_1 means that as long as B is above A the curves are convergent until they cut at C, and then they diverge all the time so that they cannot come together to cut again.

For curves of this nature the only solution is that of equal factor prices in both countries unless there is complete specialisation in at least one commodity in the sense that not more than one of the commodities is produced in *both* countries. The second solution (Mrs. Robinson's) is not possible because at no price relationship will the proportion of the factors be the same for both commodities. The third solution suggested in section (6) above cannot apply for it shows B using a smaller proportion of X (relative to Y) than A at the factor-price ratio of country 1 but using a greater proportion at the factor-price ratio of country 2.

The impossibility of any solution other than the first can be demonstrated diagrammatically. Suppose the Fig. 2 to represent equilibrium conditions so that $\frac{a_1}{b_1} = \frac{a_2}{b_2}$. Since the production functions are homogeneous we can obtain a curve of a different size but of the same shape by changing the size of our unit quantity. Consider a B curve smaller than that drawn in Fig. 2 in the proportion $\frac{a_1}{b_1}$. The tangent to this curve for country 1 will coincide with the tangent A_1a_1. Since $\frac{a_1}{b_1} = \frac{a_2}{b_2}$ the tangent B_2b_2 will coincide with

A_2a_2. We shall then have two lines each touching the two same isoquants and this is necessary for equilibrium.

But in Fig. 4 it is impossible to draw two lines each of which touches both A and B. Only one line can do this—the one touching them at A_3 and B_3. Full equilibrium with curves of this form can therefore only take place if the prices of the factors are the same in both countries.

11. If a pair of curves A and B cut in two places (C and D in Fig. 5), one curve must be more convex than the other.

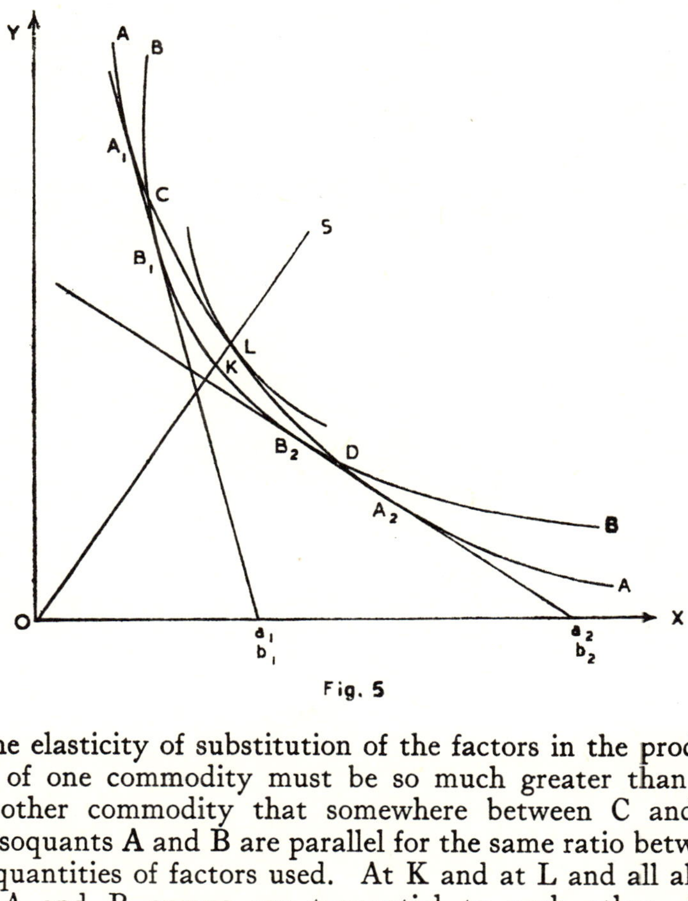

Fig. 5

The elasticity of substitution of the factors in the production of one commodity must be so much greater than for the other commodity that somewhere between C and D the isoquants A and B are parallel for the same ratio between the quantities of factors used. At K and at L and all along OS, A and B curves are tangential to each other. The relative quantity of X for any factor-price ratio is greater for B than for A above OS and smaller below OS. Every tangent to both an A and a B curve must touch both either *on the same side of* OS or *on* OS.

In the former case one other tangent can touch the same two isoquants *on the other side of* OS. The factor-quantity ratios as between the two commodities will be reversed in the two countries. The same commodity (A) will be able on account of its greater elasticity of substitution to use relatively more in each country of that factor which is cheaper in that country, and thus maintain the same price relationship to the other commodity. This is the state of the arithmetical solution in section (6). It will be possible, however, at *only one* factor-price relationship in each country for any factor-price relationship in the other country. This will be at the point where the change in the proportion of the factors used *just balances* the differences in factor prices as between the two countries. This solution is clearly possible only as an unlikely coincidence.

12. The case where two curves A and B cut each other in three places is shown in Fig. 6 where they cut at C, D and E.

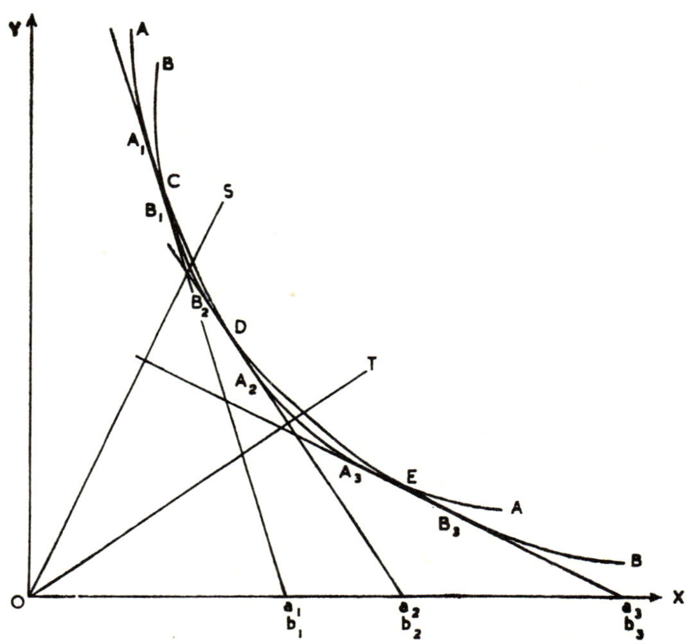

Fig. 6

It will here be possible to draw three different lines each of which touches both A and B, each line representing a different possible factor-price ratio in a different country, all three countries being in international trade equilibrium. There will also now be two lines radiating from the origin, OS and OT, along which A and B curves touch each other. The points of tangency of any line with the curves A and B will be either *both* above OS, in which case B_1 will be *below* A_1, or *both* between OS and OT, when B_2 will be *above* A_2, or else *both* below OT, when B_3 will be again below A_3.

In comparing country 1 with country 2 and in comparing country 2 with country 3 in Fig. 6, we have exactly the same case as that described in the section (11). But in comparing country 1 with country 3 we have a new phenomenon. In country 1 factor X is dear and in country 3 X is cheap. In both countries commodity B uses relatively more of X as compared with commodity A. Yet prices of both commodities are equally affected by the change in the price of the factors.

This is because the gain of the commodity (B) which uses a larger proportion of the cheapened factor (X) in virtue of the saving in the cost of the quantity initially used is offset by the loss due to its not being able to increase its proportion of the cheapened factor in as great a ratio as the other commodity (A) which uses a smaller proportion of this factor.

This solution, too, can be seen to be a very unlikely case as again for any factor-price ratio in country 1 there is only one corresponding factor-price ratio in country 3 where the counterposed forces are just equal and an equilibrium is attained. There appears to be no mechanism whereby such a position would be approached so that it must be considered as an unlikely accidental solution that would be immediately upset by any change in data if indeed it ever happened to be hit upon.

13. A tangent to both curves at the same point, which would have to be on a line of the type of OS or OT, would show a special kind of equilibrium, having some of the qualities of all the different types considered, and therefore also partaking of the attribute of stability. It would show not only the same factor prices in both countries, which is a sufficient condition for stable equilibrium, but also the ratio of factors the same for both commodities, not only in each country but, which would follow from this and from the equality of factor prices, in both countries.

14. It is not necessary to go on to consider curves which cut more than three times. It can be seen that curves which

cut n times have n possible common tangents and n-1 " radiants of tangency " as OS and OT may be called. The more often curves cut, the more alike they must be in shape, and we may say that the more often they cut, the closer they approach identity of shape. Curves may be expected to be identical rather than cut many times.

The likelihood of a solution of the type illustrated in Fig. 3 can be indicated by considerations of this kind. We have seen above (section (10)) that in any equilibrium in which factor prices are different in the two countries, two common tangents can be drawn to the two curves. This means that, in Fig. 3, another B curve, say B^1, touches both A_1a_1 and A_2a_2. Since all our curves represent homogeneous functions, and A and B have parallel tangents (= equal slope) at A_2 and at B_2, A and B curves must touch each other along OB_2. Similarly, they must touch each other along OA_2. B^1 will therefore touch A_1a_1 and A_2a_2 at the same points where these are touched by A, namely at A_1 and A_2.

This is shown in Fig. 7. OS and OU are " radiants of tangency ", and there must be another " radiant of

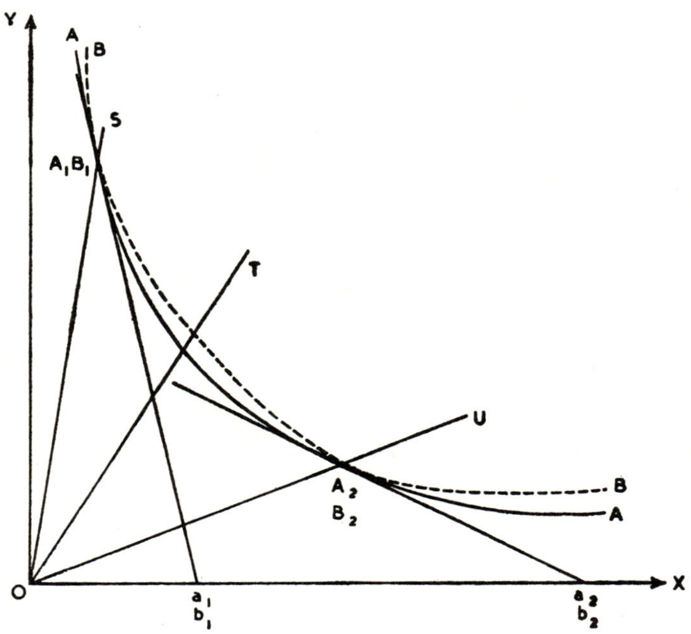

Fig. 7

tangency " between these (unless the curves are identical throughout in which case these cover the whole surface) and it is here shown in OT. Three " radiants of tangency " must mean curves cutting four times. This is seen to be the case, for the B curve immediately below B^1 must cut A in four places, once on each side of A_1 and A_2.

We see then that the equilibrium of Fig. 3 demands isoquants which cut four times without becoming identical. But this is not all. If we consider the B curve immediately above the one drawn we shall see that it does not cut A at all. This means that not only must there be B curves which cut A on A curve four times, but that any B curve which does not cut A four times *must not cut it at all.* Either four or none. Only if this is the case will any B curve *touch* an A curve twice.

Further, coincidence is necessary for this equilibrium even if we are given isoquants of this form. There are only two factor-price ratios in any country which make this equilibrium possible and if one of these is reached the equilibrium is not possible unless the factor-price ratio in the other country is the other of this pair of factor-price ratios which are shown in the two tangents in Fig. 7.

From all this we may conclude that if two (or more) commodities are produced in each of two (or more) countries, between which commodities can move and in which the same technical knowledge is available, then in any stable or reasonably likely equilibrium physically similar factors, even though they may not move between the countries, will have the same price in each country.

Roosevelt College,
Chicago, 5.

[5]

CHAPTER 28. FOREIGN TRADE III (*IN A CAPITALIST ECONOMY*)

In a capitalist economy there are many more reasons for expecting deviations from the optimum situation which would result from free trade (and which would be identical with that achieved by a universal adherence to the Rule). quite apart from the more general deviations that result from the absence of perfect competition throughout the economy.

Particular interests are able to harm the economy as a whole by insistence on protective devices in lieu of harmless but unpopular compensation.

First, there are a series of interferences with free trade because of sectional interests which stand to gain by the tariffs and quotas and other impediments to free trade and which consequently are deaf to the irrelevant argument that the economy as a whole must lose by the restrictions. To the same category belongs the resistance of organized labor to the immigration of cheap labor or the importation of the products of cheap labor. Such immigrant labor, getting only its marginal product, can only enrich the community as a whole, but labor in direct competition with it may lose. It is true that society could afford to compensate all who suffer from such competition from foreign dumping or cheap labor, but society shows no signs of doing this and so the sectional interests go ahead and usually succeed in getting some protection. Each protection is a burden on all the other parts of the economy, so that the net result is likely to be that *everybody* is worse off than if nobody were protected, but even if they were all aware of this each interest would want the other protections to be removed before its own was touched, and so we have the kind of impasse that is seen most dramatically in disarmament conferences.

Among the arguments used as weapons by the various interests seeking protection and endeavoring to persuade everybody that the protective measure is not only their just due but really good for everybody else, there are innumerable sophisms that economists have industriously, and in general fruitlessly, exposed for generations. However, a few of the arguments are sound.

Even "taxing the foreigner" is not carried out scientifically.

One of the sound arguments is that it is possible to tax the foreigner by a tariff that would reduce the price the foreigner received for his product and so the price to the domestic buyer would rise by less than the amount of the tax—the rest of the tax is paid by the foreigner. This will be recognized as indicating an elasticity of supply of the imported good that is less than infinite so that the price falls if less is bought. This situation permitted the collectivist economy to increase its income by restricting purchases. It is, however, unlikely, even in this case, that the tariff urged at the instigation of a sectional interest will be the one which would maximize the benefit to the country from the restriction of imports. In the capitalist society, moreover, there is seldom any call for the corresponding restrictions on exports, which could benefit the country in the same way at the expense of the foreigner, because there is usually no sectional interest that would gain by this restriction. How the optimum restriction of imports and exports could be attained in a controlled economy with free enterprise, if the gain from exploiting the foreigner should be considered worth striving for, will be examined in the next chapter.

The most serious foreign trade problems of the capitalist economy are connected with employment. We have examined the process by which full employment may be reached in a capitalist economy that is complete in itself—that is, with no foreign trade—if the amount of money is given and the rate of interest is permitted to adjust itself to it, equalizing the demand for money to hold with the amount of money available to be held. In examining this process we noted a number of points at which it is likely to be stalled. When we bring in the complications of foreign trade we find there are still other difficulties in the way of the automatic movement to and maintenance of full employment in an uncontrolled capitalist economy.

The typical capitalistic monetary system is the gold standard. Instead of a fixed amount of money, which we assumed in Chapter 22, there is a fixed gold value of the monetary unit. This is maintained by the government either by actually issuing gold coins of a fixed weight or by buying and selling gold for the currency at a fixed price. The machinery for this is fundamentally the same as that we have described for counterspeculation. The government, by offering to buy or sell unlimited quantities of any good, can keep its price constant. Such buying and selling is the only effective way of pegging a price. The passage of a law that declares any other price illegal would merely be evaded by subterfuges of unending ingenuity. A country on the gold standard, by offering to buy or sell unlimited amounts of gold at a given price, pegs the price of gold in terms of the currency and therefore also the value of the currency in terms of gold.

The conveniences of the gold standard are insufficient to make up for the hindrances it imposes on a policy for full employment.

Once the gold standard is established, there are considerable conveniences in keeping it unchanged at the same price of gold as long as the other countries do so too. This results in a practically constant price of foreign exchange which is very useful to importers and exporters, and by providing a simple rule for the management of the currency it serves as a check on the hasty impetuousness that many people believe (contrary to all experience) to be the natural characteristic of governmental action. These conveniences tend to be exaggerated until the maintenance of the price of gold is identified with the notion of upholding the national honor and even in some mystical way with national solvency.

Fear of losing gold is met least objectionably by raising interest rates.

The danger of a country's being forced off the gold standard arises from the possibility that the demand for gold (which the government guarantees to buy and sell in unlimited quantities at a fixed price) will exhaust the government's stocks and the government will no longer be able to sell gold at the guaranteed price. The price of gold will then rise in terms of the currency, so that the value of the currency falls in terms of gold, and the national honor is besmirched. Monetary policy is therefore primarily directed toward preventing such a situation. This is done by raising the rate of interest, through a restriction of the supply of money and of credit, whenever there are any signs of the possibility of a net outflow of gold from the coffers of the monetary authority. This would happen whenever the amount of gold *demanded* from the government monetary authority in exchange for money was greater than the amount of gold being *offered* to the government in exchange for money. Gold withdrawn from the reserves of the monetary authority is for the most part sent abroad to purchase foreign money from the governments of other countries on the gold standard to pay for a balance of imports whose value exceeds the value of the exports (the rest of the foreign money being obtained from the foreign purchasers of the exports). The import balance (the excess of the value of imports over the value of the exports), which is usually called an unfavorable balance of trade, is the cause of the outflow of gold. Because the supply of foreign currency available from the proceeds of the exports is not sufficient to satisfy the demand for foreign currency to pay for the imports, the price of foreign currency, which is demanded by the importers who have to get the foreign currency to pay their foreign suppliers, rises on the foreign exchange market. This goes on until it is cheaper, instead of buying foreign exchange on the market, to obtain it by the indirect method of buying gold from the government (at the guaranteed rate), exporting it, and purchasing the foreign currency from the foreign government with this gold at the fixed rate established by the foreign country's gold standard.

The restriction of credit and the resulting high rate of interest tend to correct the outward flow of gold in three ways which we shall consider in the order of the speediness of their action. First, the high rate of interest makes it profitable for idle funds to be kept in this country rather than in the other countries where the interest they earn is lower. Foreigners and citizens who had foreign money loaned out at interest abroad call in these loans, exchange the currency for the currency of this country, and lend it out here at the higher rate of interest. This increases the supply of foreign currency offered for our own currency on the foreign exchange market, so that the need for foreign exchange by the importers can be satisfied, the price of the foreign currency falls back to normal, and there is no need for gold to be exported.

This is only a temporary alleviation, for there is a limit to the amount of idle money that can be moved freely from one country to another in this way. When it has all moved where the rate of interest is higher, the gold movement will be resumed if there is still an excess of imports over exports.

It should be noted that this will work only if there is complete confidence in the continued maintenance of the gold standard. If the rise in the rate of interest is interpreted by the capitalists who own the idle funds as an attempt to keep on the gold standard that might fail in its purpose, they will move their capital *out* of the country rather than into it. They will endeavor not to have their wealth in terms of our currency, which is in danger of depreciation in terms of the other currencies if we are eventually forced off the gold standard at the old gold parity, but to have their wealth in terms of other currencies, or in terms of gold, which would then appreciate in terms of our currency. The high interest that may be earned in the meantime will be relatively insignificant.

This may lead to severe unemployment, which gives rise to pressure for import duties.

The second way in which the high rate of interest checks the flow of gold out of the country is by its effect on the level of economic activity in the country. The high rate of interest reduces investment. This cuts down income and so consumption and income fall in accordance with the propensity to consume until the lower level is reached where the gap between income and equilibrium consumption is equal to the lower level of investment. With this lower level of income, consumption of all kinds is reduced, including the consumption of imported goods. This tends to correct the import balance and to check the outflow of gold. If this should not be sufficient, and gold continues to flow outward, the monetary authorities will restrict the supply of loans still further until enough unemployment has been created to reduce imports to the level necessary to check the outward flow of gold. Clearly this is not a desirable solution.

The third way in which the high rate of interest checks the gold flow works *through* the second. The lower level of activity and the unemployment tend to lower the prices of factors of production and the cost of products of all kinds, including the cost of exports. This causes exports to increase, together with the level of economic activity in general including imports, until full employment is reached again. There will be a lower level of prices in this new position which induces foreigners to buy more of our exports, and so there is enough supply of foreign currency to permit even that quantity of imports to be bought and paid for which accompanies a fully employed economy, and there is no tendency for gold to flow out any more.

The difficulties in the way of this third and final solution are the same as those we have already noted in Chapter 22, so that the second phase, with considerable unemployment, is likely to hold the stage for a considerable and even indefinite period.

This strange situation in which the maintenance of full employment is sacrificed to the relatively insignificant consideration of stabilizing the value of gold or of foreign currencies (which is classically portrayed in the economic history of England from 1925 to 1931) gives rise to a powerful argument for a general tariff. This would discourage imports and eliminate the import balance. The danger to the gold standard would be removed without plunging the economy into a depression.

Export subsidies violate the spirit of the gold standard.

The only real objection to a general tariff for this purpose is that the depression is only temporary (it is hoped) while the tariff is likely to become a permanent barrier to trade that would have to be raised again the next time there was an import balance. This objection can be met by adding a subsidy to exports at the same rate as, and to be paid out of, the tax on imports. The subsidy would encourage international trade just as much as the tariff would discourage it. By this means the gold flow can be stopped without harming international trade and so the gold standard can be maintained without sacrificing either employment or the benefits from the international specialization of production that international trade makes possible.

But this is only a pretended maintenance of the gold standard. The tax on imports and the subsidy to exports come to the same thing as a tax on the purchase of foreign currency (to pay for the imports) and a subsidy on the sale of foreign currency (obtained from the sale of the exports), and everything is just as if foreign currency had been permitted to appreciate in terms of the domestic currency (or the domestic currency permitted to depreciate in terms of the foreign currency and in terms of gold) by the amount of the tax or the subsidy. It would be better and far simpler to have an open depreciation of the currency rather than this disguised form of it which more than anything else would appear to foreigners as unfair competition that calls for retaliation.

Capital movements can cause the same difficulties.

The same problem arises if *mei* and the rate of interest should happen to rise abroad or fall at home. We have seen that this would result in a flow of lending abroad, which would make for an excess demand for foreign currency and an outward flow of gold. In the equilibrium situation this would be offset by an excess outward flow of export goods, on balance, which, by itself, would have led to an inflow of gold. Unfortunately this equilibrium does not come about any more automatically than the maintenance of full employment. Under the gold standard, the export balance would come about only after the outward flow of gold had called forth a restriction of credit and a rise in the rate of interest which had discouraged domestic investment and economic activity in general (in addition to temporarily checking the amount of foreign lending), and the depression had sufficiently reduced wages and cost and prices to make exports cheap enough to induce foreigners to buy enough more of them to balance the effects of the foreign lending. (In this they would be helped by the decrease in imports because domestic goods would now be relatively cheaper to buy compared with imported goods.) As before, there is a considerable likelihood of stalling in the second phase with the equilibrium in the exchange market brought about by the decrease in imports that results from the poverty of the depression artificially induced by the raised rate of interest.

The same difficulties may arise *within* a country. One region may find a decrease in the demand for its product from the other regions, or *mei* may be higher in other regions. This leads to an import balance of goods or an export balance of lending, or both, and money is drained out of this region just as it would be drained out of one gold standard country to another under like circumstances. The high rate of interest discourages investment, so economic activity declines and there is unemployment until wages and costs have been sufficiently reduced to restore the demand by the other regions for the products of this region. Any depreciation of the local currency which would avoid the necessity for unemployment and local cost reduction is, of course, impossible. If this works out satisfactorily within a country, the gold standard advocate can argue, why can it not operate internationally? Does not our argument for flexible exchanges also logically commit us to a demand for currency autonomy for every region, district, and village?

The prerequisite for a single currency (or gold standard) area is effective freedom of movement of goods, people, and capital.

The answer is that the region within the country differs from an independent country in the important respect that it enjoys the free movement of goods, of people, and of investment into the other regions of the same country. An import balance that causes money to flow out of one region means an export balance in another region where money is flowing in, and economic activity is at an unusually high level. The inhabitants of the first region can move without restriction into the prosperous region. This does not mean that there cannot be depressed areas within a country, but it does mean that these are not likely to be very serious if it is easy to get a job by moving into the other area, and in any case the depressed area will be recognized as a responsibility of the country as a whole. This is not true for separate countries. Tariffs and quotas interfere with trade, and the movement of people from country to country is seriously limited. It is only because of these restrictions that a rigid enforcement of fixed exchange rates between the values of the currencies of different countries can be so very harmful. If there were complete freedom of movement of goods, investment, and people, an international currency system would be as sound as a single monetary system for a country within which the three freedoms of movement are realities, and a properly managed gold standard system might be one way of arranging this.

Stable exchanges are a result of this—a symptom that cannot safely be established by decree.

The conveniences of having a single monetary system might then be sufficient to make it worth while to undertake the trouble of having to make minor adjustments in the levels of local wages and costs instead of merely adjusting the value of the local unit of money. But the *first* step in bringing about this desirable state of affairs is to remove the hindrances to movement. As a result of this freedom of movement of products, investment, and people, the prices of the factors and the *mei* are made equal in the different countries, prosperity is more equally enjoyed by all countries, and there will be less need for variations in the relative values of the different currencies to maintain full employment. When these changes are sufficiently small, even though the exchanges are free to move up or down, *then* will be the time to consider the conveniences and inconveniences of fixing a single monetary system for the whole world. It will not be a very important matter, for substantial stability of the exchanges will have been reached before the issue arises. But to try to establish it before the underlying conditions of stability (that is, the freedoms of movement) have been established is certainly to attempt to establish world unity by decreeing one of its symptoms—like attempting to establish good health by commanding everybody to display a glowing complexion.

Where demands are inelastic the automatic mechanism works the wrong way.

There are other circumstances that render the automatic maintenance of full employment still more precarious. If unemployment succeeds in reducing wages, costs and prices, the economy passes from the second to the third phase. Exports are increased because they are cheaper and imports are cut down because with the lower incomes not so many of them can be afforded and cheaper domestic goods are substituted for them. But this does not necessarily mean a correction or even an improvement in the import balance, for that is concerned not with the amounts of physical goods but only with their *values*. At the lower price of exports foreigners will buy more of them, but unless the quantity of exports increases in a *greater proportion* than their prices fall, that is, unless the foreign elasticity of demand is greater than unity, the *value* of the exports will not increase. If the elasticity of demand is less than unity, the value of exports will *decrease* and that would make the import balance greater than ever. The situation might still be saved by the decrease in imports, which *must* involve a decrease in the value of imports. But if the demand for imports is very inelastic the decrease may not be sufficient to make up for the decrease in the value of the exports. If the elasticity of demand for imports is greater than zero by the degree to which the elasticity of demand for exports is below unity, the two influences will just offset each other and the fall in domestic prices will have no effect at all on the import balance; and if the elasticity of demand for imports is less than this the import balance will actually *increase* as a result of the fall in price so that gold will flow out even faster than before and the crisis will get worse and worse. It should be noted that at the critical point; where the elasticity of demand for imports is just as much above zero as the elasticity of demand for exports is below unity, the sum of two elasticities is unity. If this sum is greater than unity, a fall in the price level tends to correct the import balance and to check the gold flow; if it is just equal to unity, the fall in prices has no effect on the import balance; and if it is less than unity, the fall in prices *increases* the import balance and renders the situation even more critical.

The critical point is where the *sum* of the elasticity of demand for imports *plus* the elasticity of demand for exports is equal to unity.

For example, if the elasticity of demand for exports is unity, the quantity of exports increases in the same proportion as the price falls (together with the domestic price level) so that the value of the exports will remain the same. If the elasticity of demand for exports is less than unity, say one third, the quantity bought will increase only one third as much as the price falls and then the total value of the exports will fall. Suppose the price of exports falls 3 per cent. This will result in an increase in exports of 1 per cent so that total value of exports will fall about 2 per cent. Now suppose the elasticity of demand for imports to be two thirds (so that the sum of the two elasticities is equal to one). Then the decrease in income and in domestic prices of 3 per cent is equivalent to a 3 per cent increase in the price of imports (for that is their *relative* increase) and will lead to a decrease in the amount bought, and in their value, of 2 per cent (two thirds of the change in their relative prices because the elasticity of demand for imports is two thirds). The values of imports and exports move together and the import balance is unchanged. If the sum of the two elasticities is less than unity, there will be a "perverse" movement of the import balance.[1]

[1] To complete this argument it must be added that, as prices fall in this country, there is a parallel tendency for increased activity and rising prices abroad where there is an export balance and an inflow of gold. This would mean that the 2 per cent decrease in the value of the imports and exports would not be absolute, but only relative to the new prices and incomes abroad, but they would still equal each other, and so

This state of affairs could not be set right by reducing the value of the currency. That would avoid all the harmful effects of the preliminary phase with a depression at work to reduce the prices, but if the sum of the elasticities is less than unity it would not correct the first situation any more than the fall in prices does. The import balance would increase in the same way and bring with it a further depreciation in the value of the domestic currency which would only make matters still worse.

To correct such a situation it is necessary to *raise* the value of the currency instead of lowering it. The automatic adjustment by lowering prices is not only unnecessarily painful, but works in the wrong direction. It is not only nasty, but it is no medicine, for it only aggravates the disease.

The tendency to assume that elasticities are high shows undue optimism.

These possibilities are usually ignored or else pointed out as queer but practically unimportant cases. This is due in part to the tendency in economic writings to assume elasticities to be high because that would fit in better with the ideas of perfect competition on which, until recently, economic analysis was based, and partly to the related habit of assuming a world with many small countries, none of them large enough to influence prices appreciably. If this were true, such low elasticities as those here discussed, where the sum of two of them is less than unity, could be relegated to the realm of *curiosa*. But there are now large economic empires with tremendous control over the price at which they will buy, especially in the short period; and more important still is the proliferation of tariffs and quotas and exchange clearing schemes that are used as "defenses" against a country which reduces its costs or the value of its currency, or which tries to reduce its import balance by subsidizing exports. These have the effect of reducing the elasticity of demand for its export. Indeed where the exports are fixed by quotas the demand is exactly zero. When such

there would still be no change in the import balance. It is likely that import and export prices would not move as much as domestic prices because they are influenced more by conditions abroad, but this consideration affects both imports and exports symmetrically and does not affect the essence of the argument.

a country has cut its imports to the very minimum in its efforts to correct its balance of payments, the demand for the remaining imports will be very inelastic too. We then have the phenomenon just analyzed, which is not at all uncommon in times of international depression. One country after another is forced off the gold standard, finds its currency depreciating without this affording much relief, and is able to find a stable position only after a long fall in the value of its currency and the introduction of special restrictions on trade have so altered the situation that the elasticities are no longer so low.

[6]

OPEC—A Plan—If You Can't Beat Them, Join Them

ABBA P. LERNER*

The Problem

The "New Economic World Order" plan to transfer some wealth from rich countries to poor countries has been almost completely eclipsed by OPEC's much more successful plan to transfer wealth from oil-importing countries—not to poor countries but to Oil Producing and Exporting Countries—OPEC.

As the development of alternative sources of energy encounters unexpectedly severe problems in pollution, in increasing costs and in a public outcry against nuclear energy, OPEC is discovering that there is no apparent limit to its power of extortion. As long as its victims compete against each other for oil, instead of combining against the extortion, OPEC can turn the rich countries into poor countries. But what could the oil importing countries do if they did combine? The use of force is too costly and too dangerous—and could be counterproductive.

The Solution

If we can't beat them we can join them! In charging $26 per barrel of oil instead of a "fair price" of, say, $6 (the pre-OPEC $3 price adjusted for the decline in the purchasing power of the dollar), OPEC is in effect collecting a "sales tax" of $20. Other producers of oil (and of oil substitutes) have, in effect, already "joined" OPEC by imposing the same "sales tax" on the energy *they* supply.

They are indeed *compelled* by the market to charge the OPEC price. But the "sales tax" nature of their price increase (as "free riders" on the OPEC wagon) is recognized in the U.S. Government's attempt, via the "windfall profits tax," to have the IRS appropriate the domestic producers' revenues from this "sales tax" (minus a "handling charge" of some 80 percent).

Unfortunately, there is no way to get back any of the "sales tax" imposed by OPEC and other foreign suppliers of oil and oil-substitutes, but *the U.S., and other oil importing countries, can also "join" OPEC by imposing a countervailing purchase tax on energy equal, on each purchase, to the excess of the actual price over the "fair price."* The purchase tax should also be imposed on purchases from the domestic and other non-OPEC producers of oil and oil-substitutes (who have "joined" OPEC).

The Benefits

1) The excess of the consumers' price over the "fair price" would be shared equally between the suppliers and (the governments of) the importing countries. (If we had acted right at the beginning of OPEC, we could have been sharing this excess equally with OPEC all the time, but it's no use crying over the spilt billions). Half of the excess price (the purchase tax revenue) would be available to compensate those for whom the price increase is too great a burden. The recipients of the compensation should of course have to pay the same high price for oil and oil-substitutes as anybody else if they are not to be tempted to use them wastefully. Since only the poor would be compensated for the price increase, a great part of the revenue from the purchase tax would be available for reduction of income taxes or for other purposes.

2) The price of energy to consumers would

*Florida State University. Presidential address of the Ninth International Atlantic Economic Conference, Freeport, Bahamas, February 10-15, 1980.

have to cover both the "sales tax" and the purchase tax–in our example $46 ($6 + $20 + $20). This would reduce the demand. A resulting oil glut could then kill the cartel bringing an end to both the "sales tax" and the purchase tax.

3) If the import price nevertheless stays at $26, and the price to the consumer is raised to $46 by the oil purchase tax, each barrel of reduction in consumption would reduce the oil producers' "sales tax" revenues by $20.

4) The purchase tax would prevent domestic production of energy at costs between $26 and $46 per oil barrel equivalent. As long as we can get oil from OPEC at $26, incurring costs greater than $26 is a waste of resources, impoverishing the nation even more than it is being impoverished by having to pay $26 for imported oil instead of the "fair price." The purchase tax prevents this waste of resources by reducing the after-tax price obtained by domestic producers to $26. This renders unprofitable any production that costs the country *more* than the imports but leaves profitable the production of oil and oil-substitutes that cost the country *less* than the imports.

By far the most important result would be:

5) The purchase tax would discourage further increases in price (i.e. in "sales tax") and even induce reductions, because

a) If a supplier increases his "sales tax" by one dollar the increase in the consumer's price will be two dollars, because of the parallel increase in the purchase tax, so that the reduction in sales would be twice as great. Even if the consumers should still pay out more money (for less energy) the supplier would get only half of any such increase in payments. The other half would go to the parallel increase in the purchase tax. This would greatly reduce the profit from an increase in "sales tax."

b) Conversely, if a supplier lowers his "sales tax" by one dollar the reduction in the consumer's price will be two dollars, because of the parallel decrease in the purchase tax, so that the resulting increase in sales will be twice as great. This would greatly reduce the loss from the reduction in the "sales tax."

c) The doubled reduction in sales from an increase in the supplier's "sales tax" could even turn the profit into a loss; and the doubled increase in sales from a "sales tax" reduction could even turn the loss into a profit. In this latter case, the purchase tax would make it worthwhile for OPEC to reduce their "sales tax." The parallel reduction in the purchase tax would then double the price reduction to consumers.

d) A reduction in output by OPEC (or any) producer would raise the price to the consumers. But half the increase goes to the purchase tax, so that only the remaining half of the increase would go to increase the "sales tax" per unit. This may be insufficient to offset the reduction in the "sales tax" revenue from the reduced sales, and so could make the reduction in output unprofitable.

e) Any individual supplier always faces a greater proportional response of sales to a change in his "sales tax" than is faced by the OPEC combine. A reduction in *his* "sales tax" increases *his* sales in a greater proportion. The doubling of his already greater increase in sales from a change in his "sales tax" would therefore be even more likely to make the profit from a reduction in his "sales tax" (and a defection from OPEC) a temptation he could not resist.

The Theory

Economists call these doubled changes in sales from a given change in price, a doubling of the "elasticity of demand." The elasticity of demand is a measure of the degree of competition faced by a seller, and its inverse, the smallness of the elasticity of demand, is a measure of the monopoly power exercised by a seller. Doubling the elasticity of demand means reducing the monopoly power by half, thereby making the market twice as competitive.

The Conclusion

Unfortunately, serious discussion of the oil purchase tax Plan is certain to be distracted by debates on the reality of the global oil shortage. The global oil shortage may be an unscientific fiction. If so we will forever keep on finding oil more rapidly than we use it, and perhaps also soon enjoy unlimited cheap energy from radiation-free nuclear fusion. On the other hand, the OPEC price may in fact be no greater than the proper economic price if we must take into account an urgent need to conserve oil for coming painful years of greater and greater scarcity, to say nothing of the desirability of discouraging the use of oil on account of pollution effects.

Which of these views (or what intermediate position) is correct does not matter for the Plan. In either case the excess of the current price over the pre-OPEC price is not necessary to make the current production profitable. The domestic oil producing industry was not considered an unprofitable one even before it joined OPEC, and it would now, even after paying the oil purchase tax, still be getting the OPEC price.

An excess of a price over and above what is needed to induce the production of any commodity is what economists call "surplus" or "rent." Others call it "gravy." The excess of the price of oil (and its substitutes) to the consumer over the "fair price" is just such "gravy." Who gets the gravy, while of overwhelming interest to actual and potential recipients, has very little to do with making the supply of oil available.

This note can only give a general idea of the Plan. Many variations are possible. The purchase tax could be, say, *twice* the excess of the oil import price over the "fair price." Two-thirds instead of half of the "gravy" would then go to the governments of the importing countries for alleviating the suffering (and for other purposes), and there would be a much stronger discouragement of price increases and encouragement of price reductions by the oil suppliers. The elasticity of demand would then be multiplied by three. The market would become *three times* as competitive and the degree of monopoly power would be reduced by two-thirds.

The "fair price" could also be figured in different ways. Theoretically the compensation should be based on a more sophisticated measure of the OPEC-caused increase in the cost of basic needs. There are undoubtedly many more ways in which the plan can be modified and probably improved.

The oil purchase tax Plan is basically a plan by which the U.S., and other oil importing countries, could weaken, and perhaps ultimately destroy, OPEC's powers of extortion, meanwhile taking a share of the "gravy," and using this to compensate low income citizens who are badly hurt by the price increases.

The automatic objection to this plan is that it would raise the price above the already horribly high level. But it must be recognized that if we do nothing OPEC will get more and more used to expanding their extortion while we get more and more used to submitting to it. When the "sales tax" was raised from $18 to $20, and a larger increase had been expected, this was greeted as "good news." As I write these lines the "sales tax" is $20. By the time you read this it will undoubtedly be much higher.

We must be willing to accept the price increase from the oil purchase tax (and its accompanying compensation to the more grievous sufferers) as an escape from still greater future OPEC price increases (without the compensations).

C. General Equilibrium: Welfare Economics

[1]

Economic Theory and Socialist Economy

ECONOMIC discussions of socialist problems fit peculiarly well into the dialectical system of theses, antitheses and syntheses. Not to go back any further than is necessary for the understanding of the present state of this argument we can take as our primary thesis that view which is most closely connected with, and can be represented by, the name of Mises.[1]

According to this view, the economy of a socialist society is bound to be shattered upon the rock of *Wirtschaftsrechnung*. In the absence of the unhampered markets of a competitive capitalist economy, there can be no possibility of maintaining that rational economic calculus which is essential to the efficient organisation of production. Universal chaos and destitution will be the only outcome of following the mirage of a socialist commonwealth.

The antithesis to this view was that of the socialists, and particularly of those who were engaged in the building up of a socialist society. They simply denied both the relevance and validity of the " Mises " arguments, and considered them as baseless and calumnious inventions for turning the mind of the multitude away from the socialist path. The arguments were denounced as meaningless anti-socialist propaganda, produced by reactionary professors sacrificing their interest in scientific truth at the altar of class interest. They might be the victims of a class ideology which made it impossible for them to envisage a society in which their class had lost its place or they might be mercenarily selling their theories to the Capitalist for cash. In either case their arguments were just part of the spate of anti-socialist " bogey stories " that might have to be met by anti-capitalist propaganda but did not deserve serious discussion. The department to deal with " Mises " was not the " Gosplan " but the OGPU.

Of the attempts which have been made to bring about a synthesis between the economists' and the socialists' points of view, that outlined by Mr. H. D. Dickinson[2] may be taken as representative. The demands for *Wirtschafts-rechnung*, prices and markets are no longer considered as anti-socialist tricks or even as bourgeois illusions. But it is maintained that a socialist economy can supply these at least as efficiently as a Capitalist or private exchange economy and probably much more efficiently ; and a rough sketch is made of the way in which a socialist society would be able to do this.

[1] In this article I have used the names of Mises, Dickinson, and Dobb as standing for certain well-defined typical attitudes to the problem rather than as standing for the individuals to whom they belong, and in particular two articles recently written by Mr. Dickinson and Mr. Dobb as representative of the kind of expression that these attitudes tend to find. As this may occasionally make my argument against particular attitudes look like personal attacks, I would like to make it clear in advance that that is far from my intention, and to take this opportunity of expressing my indebtedness to the writings of Professor Mises in my economic education, and to Mr. Dobb for having largely inspired my decision to take up economics as well as for my interest in the subject of this article.

[2] *Economic Journal*, June, 1933.

In the first attempts at the application to a socialist society of economic principles developed in the study of capitalist society, it is inevitable that many slips will be made in the difficult task of separating the elements which are common to both societies from those which belong only to one. Differences have to detected which were not seen previously because for the previous purposes they were irrelevant. The result of this kind of difficulty is that where the concepts have not been sufficiently refined, where a complex thing appears simple, there will be transferred from the capitalist to the socialist society institutions and organisations which find themselves in conflict with their environment. This kind of error is seen in Mr. Dickinson's use of statistically determined demand curves. In the capitalist society it is perhaps possible to get some estimate of a demand curve upon the assumption, among many others, that all other prices are constant. Mr. Dickinson transfers curves drawn up in this way to the socialist economy where in his scheme they have to be added together, thus contradicting the assumption in each case that other prices are constant. In addition to errors of this kind there are a number of other weaknesses, mostly related to those made famous by Cassel such as the assumption that price is a function of only one variable (after paying lip-service to Walras), the crude form of the purchasing power parity theory, and a misunderstanding of the relation between long and short term interest rates, as well as a number of smaller slips in connection with Infant Industries and comparative costs, state power over exchange rates, and the treatment of composite demand.

These errors—if indeed I am found to be right in suggesting that they are errors—do not seriously detract from the merit of Mr. Dickinson's work. They rather emphasise the extreme difficulties of investigation in a vast unexplored region, and are so much to be expected in such pioneer efforts that their absence should arouse the utmost suspicion. I mention them here, not in order to discuss them in detail—I hope to make that attempt elsewhere—but because they are typical of all those efforts at synthesis of which I take Mr. Dickinson's essay as representative, and because of the reactions they bring about in the socialist camp.

Socialists are suspicious in the extreme of such new-found allies coming from the " idealogical " centre of the enemy's camp. The attempt to base the socialist economy on a rationally worked-out system of prices and markets may be a subtle scheme of sabotage for building the socialist society on rotten foundations. In any case, such a foundation is by its nature not impervious to reasoned criticism. The cautious guardians of socialism are for retaining the superior strategic fastnesses of simple faith. The heresy must be eradicated. Against the " Dickinson " thesis is raised the antithetic slogan: " The categories of capitalist economy are inapplicable to the socialist society," and in the resulting attack on the thesis the exigencies of war demand the complete disregard of those idealistic rules of peace-time discussion: the canons of logical consistency. Of this antithesis Mr. Dobb's article[1] is an excellent example and will serve as a distinguished representative of its type.

[1] *Economic Journal*, December, 1933.

ECONOMIC THEORY AND SOCIALIST ECONOMY

Preliminary to the main statement of the case there is launched a general attack upon the " alleged " neutrality of economic science. Thus Mr. Dobb quotes Professor Robbins' statements : (*a*) " Economics is unconcerned with norms and ends " and (*b*) " the corollaries of economic theory do not depend upon facts of experience of history, but are implicit in our definition of the subject-matter of economic science as a whole," and uses the questionable methodology of (*b*) to discredit (*a*), neglecting the possibility that (*a*) may be right while (*b*) is wrong, even though both propositions are put forward by the same man in the same book.

The equilibrium theorist, complains Mr. Dobb, while pretending to a scientific aloofness from any norms, is often led to describe certain positions as " maxima " and when he does that he, " of course, tacitly appeals to a norm." But is not Mr. Dobb here fathering his own personal ends on to the " equilibrium " economist ? A maximum of the kind the " equilibrium " economist talks about is reached if the marginal productivity of all factors bear to each other the same proportions in all industries. This is a maximum only in the sense that when such a position is reached it is no longer possible to increase the output of one industry without diminishing the output in other industries. But where is the illegitimate " norm " in declaring these to be the conditions of such a maximum ?

What happens is that Mr. Dobb believes such a maximisation to be a good thing, but when he makes that personal judgment he imagines himself to be reading the thoughts of the " equilibrium " economist. In the same sort of way we might say that when an engineer is engaged on plans for maximising the energy output of an engine for a given amount of fuel, he is, " of course, tacitly appealing to a norm." It is, however, not his own norm but somebody else's ends for which he is catering, and the one who is paid this compliment should give thanks rather than scold.

If on the other hand the maximum is one which Mr. Dobb is not inclined to consider as an optimum, as may be the case with the maximisation of a monopoly revenue, all that he need do is to refrain from calling it an optimum. And if the monopolist does consider it an optimum, one cannot put the blame on the economist.

The central point of Mr. Dobb's attack is directed against what he calls " the economists' assumption of the ' sacredness ' of consumers' preferences." If we allow for Mr. Dobb's skilful exploitation of the discrediting word " sacredness " we find that all that this amounts to is that some economists in searching for " maxima " which might be useful have considered that a principle likely to be accepted by socialists might be that of giving people what they want where there is no good reason for a contrary policy. Mr. Dobb appears to argue that a free pricing system is necessary in order to give people what they want, but to deny the advisability of so doing. It is only by disputing this end that Mr. Dobb rejects the means.

As an economist I cannot, of course, "adjudicate" the correctness or legitimacy or " goodness " of such an end. As a human being and a sympathiser with socialist ends, it seems to me that a maximisation on such lines is completely in the spirit of all socialist ideals and particularly sympathetic to the slogan of " scientific socialism "—" . . . to each according to his needs." A superior contempt for the tastes and judgment of the " masses," and a paternal solicitude in choosing for the people what is good for them, does not seem to me to be the avoidance of an unscientific major premise about " sacredness." It consists rather in supplanting the democratic assumption that—in the absence of vitiating factors—people try to get what they like, by the much more suspect proposition that somebody else (the Government, Mr. Dobb ?) knows better than the people themselves what is really good for them.

When Mr. Dobb wrote his *Russian Economic Development* (published in 1928) he was on the " Dickinson " side. The change in his attitude on this matter of who chooses is, of course, a case of the development of personal taste, and *de gustibus non disputandum.* But although it is not possible to argue about the rightness or wrongness of the attitude, a possible sociological explanation is of the greatest interest.

In the course of the years that have elapsed since Mr. Dobb wrote the Excursus to his *Russian Economic Development*, the Government of the Workers' Republic has shown itself to be more and more the expression of a bureaucratic class and less and less the Dictatorship of the Proletariat. The universal tendency of a governing class to identify the community with itself so that it sees its own interests as the socially desirable, and its own attitude as the general will—not exorcised by the sign of the Hammer and Sickle or adequately countered by the vaccine of official Marxist Philosophy—obtains in Russia as elsewhere. The governing class in Russia tends more and more to see the problems of the country and of the Revolution through the spectacles of the bureaucrat. And nothing is more characteristic of that outlook than a contempt for the masses, and an impulse to run their lives for them much more efficiently than the common herd could themselves. The people become more and more a somewhat recalcitrant material for the weaving of social patterns pleasing to bureaucratic aesthetics ; and the usurpation of the individual's freedom to choose his own way of life is justified by minor variants of the ancient plea of apologetic tyrants : " It's for their own good ! "

This attitude of the governing class, however, is not restricted to the participants of privilege. Apart even from sycophantic aspirants for favours from the privileged, it is possible and even common for the attitude to spread to men who do not stand to profit personally by upholding such a regime. Particularly so is this the case with the governmental attitude of the U.S.S.R. Sympathisers with the aims of the Proletarian Revolution have concentrated all their hopes on the Soviet Union and have identified the Government of Russia with their hopes for the salvation of humanity. Under such circumstances it is inevitable that they should be affected by the mental climate that surrounds that Government. This is what appears to have happened to Mr. Dobb.

Of course, not all communists are affected in this way—indeed, one may say that this is a fundamental deviation from the communism of Marx and Lenin—but liberal-minded critics of Communism are also prone to take the behaviour of the Russian government class as representative of Communists in general and to declare " scratch a would-be planner and you usually find a would-be dictator ! "[1]

But if it is impossible to argue about attitudes, it is still possible to show that even if Mr. Dobb's attitude is accepted his conclusion does not follow. Whether it is the consumer himself or whether it is somebody else who decides what is good for him, the same problem remains. All that happens is that the place of the consumer is taken by the other person or body who does the choosing for him. In the formal analysis this person or body now *is* the consumer. Without the pricing system that Mr. Dickinson, and once Mr. Dobb, were seeking to develop it is impossible for an economic system of any complexity to function with any reasonable degree of efficiency. All Mr. Dobb's arguments and illustrations to the contrary are erroneous or irrelevant. While starting out with the argument that pricing is not necessary, Mr. Dobb soon finds himself in the company of " Mises " in dogmatic assertions of its impossibility. Like Mises, he assumes the pricing system transferred *unaltered* from a perfectly competitive economy and then wishes to surprise us by showing that it does not fit a socialist society. Either there are unequal incomes and therefore " plural voting " in the money demand for consumers' goods or else different scarcities of different kinds of labour find no expression in costs of production. " Mr. Dickinson cannot have it both ways " (p. 592).

Mr. Dickinson, however, does not try to have it both ways. His adaptation of the pricing mechanism may be faulty or clumsy, but Mr. Dobb does not attempt to improve upon it or even to point out where it is wrong. He just ignores it in true Mises style as a sacrilegious attempt to improve on a "perfect " price mechanism. Especially curious is the first horn of the bogus dilemma. The urgency for exact equality of voting goes ill with the bureaucratic contempt for the intelligence of the voter. But this, again, is nothing but the exigency of war. In the name of the OGPU one may attack " Dickinson " with the sword of Mises in the left hand and the club of Hitler in the right.

Thus from the fact that the advertiser and the press magnate " both damage the sacredness of the popular verdict pretty ruthlessly ; in both spheres it would seem that bad money drives out good " (p. 591), the moral is drawn—not that harmful advertisement and press magnates should be abolished in a socialist state, but that the popular verdict is to be ignored. In Mr. Dobb's metaphor it will be not that bad money should be suppressed, but that we must go back to barter. Against this bass of the complete authoritarian, there resounds the tenor of the 100 per cent. Mises : " For this fundamental relation between the production of immediately consumable goods and the production of capital goods [the automatic index of a free market in consumption goods] can afford no criterion " (p. 592) ; but it is unfortunately drowned by the bass : " In judgments of the future the ' natural ' individual is notoriously unreliable " (p. 593). Both voices may here be correct, but all this thunder merely means again that the competitive price system has to be *adapted* to a socialist society. If it is applied *in toto* we have not a socialist but a competitive society. Authoritarianism objects to any pricing.

[1] Professor L. C. Robbins' *The Scope and Significance of Economic Science*, p. 113n.

Intransigent Liberalism objects to any amendments to the Liberal machine. But why need we take any notice of either ?

In pointing out that in a socialist society there is no excuse for the illusion that there is a " natural " rate of interest by which the socialist community must be ruled, Mr. Dobb is quite right. But neither is there any excuse for this illusion in any other kind of society. In any society the rate of interest must reflect the marginal productivity of waiting, but what that will be depends upon the amount of saving and investment. The illusion to which reference is made appears to be an identification of the money rate of interest which correctly reflects real marginal productivity of capital and that real rate of interest that would accompany some optimal rate of saving. But in claiming to overthrow the illusion Mr. Dobb seems to be going too far. He wishes to reject the constituents of the confusion. The optimum-rate-of-saving element may be questioned, but consideration of the actual productivity of waiting is fundamental.

Mr. Dobb goes on to show how one can get a satisfactory approximation to the " relative maximum " reached by application of the principle of least cost without the use of any pricing mechanism. He here gratuitously assumes that all economic losses due to a distribution of resources other than that which would be indicated by the pricing mechanism would only be temporary ; he seems to consider that such losses could only occur in connection with the application of free capital as between industries ; and he assumes that the most important and most difficult of such disequilibria are those which " offend against what we may call the *technical* rigidities of the economic system ; as, for instance, if the requisite ratio between coal-cutters and coal-trucks is not observed " (p. 595).

In suggesting that offences against technical rigidities are likely to be adjusted without the intervention of any principles about marginal yield, Mr. Dobb seems to imagine that the problem is practically solved. But it is precisely where there are *technical* rigidities that maladjustments are " visible to the naked eye," and here, in the most favourable case for direct adjustment, the experience of Russia has been most disappointing. The enthusiastic newspaper campaigns for such things as the provision of spare parts in accordance with the number of tractors may be beautiful examples of the splendid spirit of self-criticism, but the recurring cycles of the same criticisms say little for the effectiveness of this method of remedying such situations. And it is easy to see why. In a complicated economy there are always large numbers of such adjustments necessary. They cannot all be the subject of newspaper campaigns, and in the absence of price indications their relative seriousness is not easy to determine. Which are dealt with and which neglected will depend upon the local channels of influence and wire-pulling capabilities.

Nor are Mr. Dobb's examples of disequilibrium without technical rigidities of the type which is most important, yet most difficult if not impossible to detect " by the naked eye." He supposes that planning authorities " finance technical advance in certain directions more liberally than in others ; that they put lifts in some office buildings and not in others ; that they install a

ECONOMIC THEORY AND SOCIALIST ECONOMY

conveyor system in the boot manufacture of one locality, but not in neighbouring woollen cloth factories " (p. 595). The implication is that you ought to have the lift and conveyors in both, and that the disequilibrium will shortly be remedied. It is, however, not at all obvious that *all* office buildings should have lifts even if some should, nor does the installation of conveyors in a boot factory imply the appropriateness of conveyors in a woollen factory. It is necessary to know the productivity of the conveyor in the two cases. It may well be that with the given available capital the conveyor should have been established in the woollen factory, but is " uneconomical " in the boot factory.

But even if we assume the office buildings so similar, and the productivity of the conveyors so obviously equal that it is clear that either both or neither should have them, the main problem remains. Are we to have lifts or conveyors ? Without a pricing system the economy reverts to Blind Man's Buff.

In endeavouring to minimise the importance of this equalisation of marginal yield, Mr. Dobb calls it a " relative maximum " (p. 594) and casts doubts upon its objectivity. He is " tempted to the suspicion that to strive after such a maximum is very like looking in a dark room for a black hat that may be entirely subjective, after all " (p. 594).

The maximum is relative in the sense that the application of resources will be different if consumers' tastes are different (whether these are the actual consumers or the authoritarians who choose for them) and if the State decision as to the amount to be saved and invested is different. But given these, there can be no doubt about the objective nature of the maximum. If the marginal productivity of different factors do not bear to each other the same ratio in the production of different commodities, it will be possible, by re-shuffling the factors to produce *more* of some or all of the commodities produced, without producing less of anything or applying more resources or energy to production. The loss involved in not having such an adjustment of factors will be seen in the difference in the concrete commodities produced.[1] Any reference to the utility differences are irrelevant and only illegitimate attempts to belittle the importance of pricing. A further attempt " to define such loss as ' loss of utilities ' through time which would need some objective standard of time-preference " (p. 595) is based upon a confusion between the loss from violating the principle of equal marginal yield with a loss resulting from a deviation from some implied optimum rate of saving and investment. The former has nothing to do with the latter which Mr. Dobb introduces here, presumably because its objectivity is in doubt, and tries to father on to Mr. Dickinson.

Mr. Dobb tries further to safeguard himself by claiming that " What is lost by failing to attain this maximum may well be of a lower order than the

[1] The loss described above is, of course, quite apart from the loss arising because the commodities produced are not those that the consumer would prefer, but this loss is not capable of such objective demonstration, and if one chooses to say that the decisions of authorities are to be preferred, there is no room for argument. A pricing system strives to eliminate both kinds of loss. I am inclined to consider the loss due to the replacement of the actual consumer by the bureaucrat as considerably the more important of the two, but more stress is laid on the former in this article because even the avowed bureaucrat has to recognise departures from the objective maximum.

probable error in any scale of economic priorities established by a free market or in any other way " (p. 594).

This implies (*a*) some transcendental optimum other than that shown " by a free market or in any other way " ; (*b*) that error from such transcendental optimum is of equal importance to the loss from the chaotic state of industry in the absence of economic adjustment ; and (*c*) that the two kinds of loss are alternative instead of additive. It seems fairly clear that (*b*) and (*c*) fall both on their own account and on account of their dependence upon the impermissible major premise (*a*).

In the face of all these difficulties, which are quite distinct from the question of freedom of consumers' preference for all the society, it may appear strange that the governing class, even if completely bureaucratic, does not use the pricing instrument for its own ends. The reason for this can also be seen in the character of bureaucracy.

To some extent, of course, it is due to a lack of understanding of the possibilities of pricing for the socialist economy, but that should not prevent pricing systems from being studied with a view to such possibilities instead of their being denounced as " bourgeois." The main explanation must be sought in the bureaucrat's jealousy for his own power.

Just as the bureaucracy tries to free itself from the direct democratic control of the masses whom it comes to despise, so it is anxious to be above and beyond the external control of a still more democratic pricing machine to which it would in certain respects be subservient. It tends to solve all problems by precedent or by handing them on to higher and still higher officials. It believes that to the question, " How is this economic problem decided ? " the statement, " It is decided by Gosplan " is an answer. The process is described by Trotsky in connection with inflation : " The bureaucracy has rid itself not only of political control on the part of the masses, but also of the automatic control on the part of the chervonitz."[1]

The bureaucratic outlook in which all the economic difficulties of planning are dissolved in the rosy reflection of omnipresent and omnipotent red tape is seen in Mr. Dobb's recipe : " In a socialist society the rate of interest, the level of wages, and the distribution of resources between constructional and finishing trades are all elements in a single decision taken by the State as to the distribution of resources between present and future." Prices, markets, or other means of reducing the innumerable kinds of resources and products to some common measure do not seem to be necessary. Compare with this the estimate of a great revolutionary leader who has had practical experience of the problems :

> " If there existed the universal mind, that projected itself into the scientific fancy of Laplace ; a mind that would register simultaneously all the processes of nature and of society, that could measure the dynamics of their motion, that could forecast the results of their inter-reactions, such a mind, of course, could *a priori* draw up a faultless and an exhaustive economic plan, beginning with the number of hectares of wheat and

[1] L. D. Trotsky, " Soviet Russia in Danger," in *The Communist*, June, 1933.

down to the last button for a vest. In truth, the bureaucracy often conceives that just such a mind is at its disposal; that is why it so easily frees itself from the control of the market and of Soviet democracy."[1]

"The innumerable living participants of economy, State as well as private, collective as well as individual, must give notice of their needs and of their relative strength not only through the statistical determinations of plan commissions but by the direct pressure of supply and demand. The plan is checked and, to a considerable measure, realized through the market. The regulation of the market itself must depend upon the tendencies that are brought out through its medium. The blueprints produced by the offices must demonstrate their economic expediency through commercial calculation."[2]

"Economic accounting is unthinkable without market relations."[3]

It would appear that Mr. Dobb, afraid of appearing to share "the professional pride of economists" (p. 594), has left it to the revolutionary to state the economic problem.

So far I have been dealing with those arguments which, while professing to guard socialism from "counter-revolutionary elements and "Bourgeois Economics," really plead for the safeguarding of bureaucratic irresponsibility. There is another element in Mr. Dobb's article[4] with which I would like to deal and which is more specific to it. This consists of a number of points which are not in harmony with the main contentions, and which are due to the fact that Mr. Dobb is too good an economist to be a perfect bureaucrat.

Mr. Dobb does not really despise consumers' preferences so much or he would not suggest that the State should take steps to influence tastes (p. 592). Nor is he really against the application of the established economic categories to a socialist state. This is seen when he comes to a positive problem in which he wishes to illustrate the difference between the two kinds of economy. Mr. Dobb considers that when periods of capital accumulation coincide with periods of great technical progress, business men tend to underestimate the future fall in the rate of interest. From this he deduces that instead of the principle of equality of marginal yield the socialist society should have some other principle, peculiar to itself, for the regulation of its investments: ". . . it would be economical to invest in the new technical processes in

[1] L. D. Trotsky, *Soviet Economy in Danger*, pp. 29-30, Pioneer Publishers, New York. This pamphlet also gives a very clear, honest, and informed account of the kind of disproportionality that has arisen in Russia precisely because of the substitution of bureaucracy for *economic* mechanism.

[2] Op. cit., p. 30.

[3] Op. cit., p. 33.

[4] Apart from a number of points to which I can attach no clear meaning, and whose obscurity, I suspect, springs from a common source. Thus there seems to be an objection to applying the same pricing principles to both Capital and Labour "since the two categories of cost are incurred by dissimilar agencies (or persons)" (p. 593). To this statement is appended a note saying that "In the manner in which equilibrium theory is usually stated there is assumed to be a complete formal parallelism between demand and supply. But this formal treatment neglects this very significant difference of fact." The proposition is put forward that "the pricing of property depends upon the level of wages (i.e., the supply of price of labour) relative to productivity, modified by the rate of saving" (p. 593). The suggestion is thrown out that the assignation of costs to resources just because they are scarce, such as land, is somehow a mere "convention" (p. 596). But Mr. Dobb could perhaps explain these puzzles had he more space.

advance of that fall of the interest rate which would later render them profitable: in other words to violate the principle of equimarginal returns and apply a *different* time-discount to different sections of an industry and of the economic system, investing part of the available capital resources in ways which yield, not the normal interest-rate of to-day, but what will be the normal rate, say, ten or twenty years from now. The advantage would consist in the lower obsolescence and the longer term of usefulness of the plant. To take a fanciful example: if one did not realise that in five years' time one would be rich enough to build a palace, one might built oneself a house destined later to become redundant. But if one had been able to forecast the windfall of five years hence, it would have paid to forego the house and live in a bungalow in the interim, and with the difference commence to lay the foundations of the palace" (pp. 596-597).

But there is here no new principle whatsoever. If the bungalow is less comfortable than the house there is here a different amount of saving. If the bungalow is just as comfortable as the house, the difference is merely a question of the degree of foresight. To say that there will be more foresight in a socialist economy does not mean that the economic principles are different. With the same degree of foresight a competitive economy would also build a bungalow and a palace, for the anticipated fall in the rate of interest would have its effect on long-term borrowings at present. If the rate of interest is five per cent. for the next five years and three per cent. thereafter, it will be possible to borrow for ten years at about four per cent. Under such conditions an investment for different periods would have a *different* time discount in a competitive society. What has happened is that the economist in Mr. Dobb has seized hold of an inadequate formulation in Mr. Dickinson's scheme, and wishes to cry out "Bad Economics," but the bureaucratic censor mistranslates it "Bourgeois Economics."

* * *

To summarise. The presumption is that since scarcity is common to both kinds of society, there may be applied to the socialist society much that has been learnt by the study of the implications of scarcity in a capitalist society. If the criterion of what people would like to have is to play any part in deciding what things shall be provided for them, there is necessary a market on which the consumer can express his choice and on which the prices reflect the alternative-product costs of the various commodities at the margin. If the consumers (in the ordinary sense) are not to be trusted to choose for themselves, the same pricing mechanism is necessary as a guide to the aristocracy which chooses for them (and which formally constitutes the consuming body). But even if all decisions about what people should consume are made by a single dictator or by a very small oligarchy which can reach all decisions by agreement in the council chamber, an elaborate pricing mechanism will still be necessary to make possible the comparison of the marginal productivities of all original means of production and intermediate products in all stages of the manufacture of all commodities in order to achieve the purely technical maximisation of the output of commodities in the proportions decided upon.

ECONOMIC THEORY AND SOCIALIST ECONOMY

In declaring that " Planned economy will have its laws, as has *laissez faire* economy ; it will have its economic accounting and its calculation," Mr. Dobb warns us against false analogies, and rejects all attempts at the adaptation of price mechanisms from capitalistic to socialistic society. Analogies may, of course, mislead, but just as analogies cannot prove anything, neither can they disprove any contention in whose service they are used. Great care must be exercised in examining such contentions, and one must be prepared to reject any and every one of them if sufficient reason is given. But the reason must be specific to the particular point. To bring against the thesis that an analogy can be applied the antithesis that it is in some way a " false " analogy is as futile as it is easy. Every analogy is false somewhere or it would be not an analogy but an identity. What is wanted is not an antithesis, but an analysis to show exactly what elements have to be discarded and a synthesis in which the tested fruits of the analogy are scientifically established. So far no case has been made out against the application of the general principles, and of bogey cries of " Bourgeois " and "Analogies " no notice can be taken. In detailed criticisms of this work Mr. Dobb's services would be of great value, but if he lends himself to the general condemnations of all attempts, discouraging investigators and discrediting their efforts, he will be hindering the development of socialist economy by a particularly vicious form of economic sabotage.

London. A. P. LERNER.

[2]

THE REVIEW OF ECONOMIC STUDIES

A Rejoinder

It is clear from Mr. Dobb's reply that my article on Economic Theory and Socialist Economy can easily be misunderstood.

There are two distinct issues on which I differ from Mr. Dobb, and it is perhaps because he insists on mixing them up that he sometimes feels his arguments to be a little beside the point and complains of an invisible opponent. The first issue is purely one of values. I think it desirable that individuals should have the maximum of freedom in the conduct of their lives, and believe that this implies that any individual should be allowed to have what he prefers whenever it makes no difference to what other individuals can have. I further consider that such a state of affairs can only be approached if there exists a free market in consumption goods. I do not believe that any State is likely to exist where the members of the government do not believe themselves better judges than the consumer as to what is best for him in at least some branches of consumption. If I had the power I would want to interfere with people's consumption myself, but I still believe that well-meaning regulation of other people's lives does more harm than good. I am perfectly aware, as Mr. Dobb concedes on p. 148 but immediately forgets, that a free market in consumption goods is not enough, so that I cannot understand the plebiscite analogy unless Mr. Dobb wishes to suggest either that I say that a free market does guarantee the fulfilment of consumers' choice—which I do not say—or that because it is insufficient it is unnecessary—which does not follow. I have little faith in the efficacy of questionnaires, etc., as mechanisms for deciding what to *give* people (although they can have enormous importance in suggesting what to *offer* them on the market). For even if it were possible to get a minutely accurate idea of what the average man wants, the average man may nevertheless not exist. The bed of Procrustes would not be much more comfortable even if made with scrupulous accuracy to fit the length of the average man.

In my article I do not concentrate on this issue, because being a value judgment it does not lend itself to useful discussion. If Mr. Dobb does not consider the fulfilment of individuals' choice as important, we can do more than register a difference in our outlook. I concentrate instead on the second issue which does not rest on value judgments, but should be capable of proof or disproof. The proposition that I wish to establish is that when the State has decided what it is going to do as to the fulfilment or non-fulfilment of individuals' choice, setting up its own system of priorities, it will not be able to achieve its ends with any reasonable degree of efficiency without the use of a price system. And by a price system I do mean a price system. Not a mere *a posteriori* juggling with figures by auditors, but prices which will have to be taken into consideration by managers of factories in organising production.

Of course, this is intended for a society of some complexity. If the State decrees that everyone shall spin his own loincloth, tend his own goat, and spend the rest of the time in contemplation of the dialectic, it will probably manage without a price system. How much more so in a world where there are only two (homogeneous) products and only two (homogeneous) factors of production. It will be quite easy, if each producer is also completely familiar with the production function of the other product, and is kept informed at all times of all variations in demand, and in the supply of factors and in changes in technical knowledge, for the technical expert to work out whether it is possible to increase the output of both products by a re-shuffling of factors. This will be the case whenever the ratio between the marginal productivities of the factors is not the same in both industries, and if the State tells the technical expert in what proportion it would like the increase to be divided between the two industries, the technician will be able to arrange it for them. Where there are thousands of products and thousands of factors, being combined in thousands of different ways in millions of different productive units, and where a re-shuffling of factors may have to be of a most complicated kind, it seems to me that it would not be so easy to find the technical expert who knows all that is going on everywhere. Yet it is possible to enlist each producers' separate knowledge of the ratio between the marginal productivities of factors in his own workshop, and to integrate this knowledge in the service of society by the use of the price mechanism. If every producer so regulates his production as to make the marginal productivities of factors proportional to their prices on a market, and if the prices are moved so as to equate the producers' demands to the supply, the problem can be solved without waiting for the super-technician.[1] Curiously enough, people who are concerned for the solution of this problem should such a universal mind, which can consider and decide everything at once, not happen to be available, are called Utopian by those who think the matter will look after itself.

The parable of the mountains rests upon the confusion of the two issues. What I am saying is that whatever mountain is chosen (and I have my own preference—which is the first issue) the technique of climbing will still be of use. Only the price-mechanism is more than a technique of climbing—it is a means of discovering which way leads up and which way down the mountain.

The transcendental maximum which Mr. Dobb introduces is the position that is reached only if people get what they want when they choose " correctly " (i.e., if there is no " error " in the " scale of economic priorities established by a free market or in any other way " (see *Economic Journal*, December, 1933, p. 594). I do not know what is meant by " correctly " unless it means " as I would choose for them ".) The maximum that I refer to is obtained when people get what they want to the extent that the State wishes them to get what they want, and the State gets what it wants (for its citizens) as far as objective conditions (resources and technical knowledge) permit.

[1] I do not follow Mr. Dobb's footnote (1), p. 146. I believe that the condition of diminishing returns, though necessary for competitive equilibrium, is not sufficient to determine uniquely any " most productive combination ". It is possible to increase both products whenever the ratio between the *actual* marginal productivities are different in the two industries. Whether these productivities are increasing or decreasing at equal or at different rates, or whether one is increasing and the other decreasing, are considerations whose relevance escapes me. The ratio between the marginal productivities is, of course, a technical fact (though it depends upon the outputs of the industries, and is independent of the market valuations of the products only if the outputs are independent of market valuations), so that my disagreement with Mr. Dobb here belongs to the second issue and concerns the likelihood of such technical improprieties being avoided without their being brought to the notice of the man on the spot in the form of a divergence between the ratio between the technical productivities of factors and the ratio between their prices.

Mr. Dobb the economist emerges again for a moment when he says incidentally that commodities using more capital should be priced higher than commodities using less (footnote (1), p. 151) a maxim derived from Bourgeois economics which could be of great value for the present Soviet Economy, but he disappears again before noticing that the introduction of H.P. is merely an improvement in the capital market for consumers (footnote (1), p.148).

I confess that my use of the terminology of dialectics was facetious. Apart from its occasional convenience as a pigeon-holing device and as a vehicle for methodological platitudes, I can see no use in it except for the wrapping up of questionable arguments in a confusion that protects them from criticism ; as was done, for instance—talking of plebiscites—when the Comintern persuaded communists in the Saar and elsewhere, for several months, that they should support the return to Germany. I do in my article concentrate on similarities between a socialist and a capitalist economy, because my aim is to utilise existing knowledge. All science consists in such a movement from the known to the unknown. If it is the duty of the dialectician to concentrate on differences and to condemn attempts at finding similarity among difference (there is all the world of difference between this and the pointing out of errors in particular arguments), his function to me is indistinguishable from that of those bishops and physicist-philosophers who do not rejoice in the progress of science but rather gloat in the contemplation of some manifestations of ignorance, in a worship of the Mysterious, the Indeterminate, the Unknown, the Different.

London. A. P. LERNER.

[3]

CHAPTER 6. SIMPLE PRODUCTION II (*UNDER PERFECT COMPETITION*) THE WELFARE EQUATIONS

Under certain conditions free enterprise leads to the optimum use of resources without any Rule expressly designed to bring it about.

Under certain circumstances it is possible for the optimum division of a factor between its different products to be reached in a capitalist economy with production carried on by business firms that are not subjected to any rule expressly devised to bring about this result. The owner (or manager) of each firm seeks to maximize his profit and this leads him to expand production whenever the extra cost involved is less than the extra revenue that results from having a larger output to sell. In the same way it would lead him to contract production if the saving from using a unit less of the (scarce) factor is greater than the loss from having a smaller amount of product to sell.

If there is *perfect competition in buying* the price of the factor is equal to the marginal cost to the buyer.

When the extra cost is equal to the extra revenue there is no profit in either expanding or contracting production.

The extra cost to the firm of employing another unit of a factor is equal to the price of the additional unit of the factor *plus* the increase in pay which the firm is forced to grant, as a result of its increased demand for the factor, to the other units of the factor in its employ. Thus if the manager of the firm is employing 100 units of a factor at $1 each, paying out $100, and the employment of one more unit would raise the price of all units to $1.01, the extra cost of employing another unit would be greater than the price. It would exceed the price ($1.01) by the 100 extra pennies that each of the other 100 units would be able to get because of his increased demand—a total of $2.01. This can be calculated another way. The manager believes that if he were to employ another unit he would have to pay for all the 101 units at $1.01 each, a total of $102.01, which is $2.01 more than when he employs 100 units. The extra cost of employing another unit is $2.01 while its price is $1.01.

If the manager does not believe that employing another unit of the factor will increase the price (usually because he is only one of many employers of the same factor), the second item disappears in the calculation of the extra cost of employing another unit. The 101 units simply cost $101 instead of $100 for 100 units, and the extra cost of employing another unit, $1, is equal to the price of the factor.

Such an absence of any influence over price is called *perfect competition in buying*.

If there is *perfect competition in selling* the price received for the product is equal to the marginal revenue.

The extra revenue that the firm obtains from employing another unit of a factor is equal to the value of the extra or marginal product *minus* the loss in revenue that the manager believes will come from the reduction in price because of the increased supply. Thus, suppose a firm was producing and selling 200 units of product at 50 cents each, so that the total revenue was $100, and that employing another unit of factor would increase output from 200 to 202 units and this would lower the price to 49½ cents. The extra revenue would be equal to the value of the extra 2 units (99 cents) *minus* 200 times ½ cents (or $1). In this case the extra revenue is actually negative, *minus* 1 cent. This too can be calculated the other way. If 202 units were produced and sold at 49½ cents each, the total revenue would be $99.99—1 cent less than what is obtained from the sale of 200 units at 50 cents each. If the price fell only to 49¾ cents, the extra revenue would be 49½ cents. This figure is obtained by subtracting 200 times ¼ cent (or 50 cents) from 99½ cents (twice 49¾). Revenue is $100.49½ instead of $100. As long as there is some fall in price the extra or marginal revenue is less than the value of the marginal product.

If the manager of the firm does not believe that the increase in his output will have any effect on the price, then again the second (and negative) item disappears in the calculation of the extra revenue. The 202 units will net $101 instead of $100 for 200 units. The extra revenue of $1 equals the value of the marginal product. Such an absence of influence on the price of the product is called *perfect competition in selling.*

If there is perfect competition throughout the economy individual enterprisers seeking to maximize their profits behave just as if they were following the Rule.

We have seen (p. 72) that the principle followed by the firm seeking to maximize its profit is as follows: "If the extra revenue from employing another unit of any factor is greater than the increase in cost, increase output (for that will increase the profit). If the fall in revenue from employing a unit less of a factor is less than the fall in cost from so doing, decrease output (for that will increase the profit). If the rise or fall in revenue from changing the quantity of a factor used is equal to the rise or fall in cost, continue producing at the same rate (since the change would not increase the profit)." We have just seen that if there is perfect competition in buying the change in cost from using one unit more or one unit less of the factor is exactly equal to the price of the factor, so that we may say "the price of the factor" instead of "the rise or fall in cost." We have also seen that if there is perfect competition in selling the change in revenue from varying output by employing a unit more or a unit less of the factor will change the revenues by exactly the value of the marginal product, so that we may say "the value of the marginal product" instead of "the rise or fall in revenue." If we substitute these phrases into the principles for maximizing profit it reads as follows:

"If the value of the marginal product of any factor is greater than the price of the factor, increase output. If the value of the marginal product is less than the price of the factor, decrease output. If the value of the marginal product is equal to the price of the factor, continue producing at the same rate." This is identical with the Rule given the manager of production in the controlled economy (see p. 64) and would lead in exactly the same way to the optimum allocation of the factors among the various products.

This is illustrated by the welfare equations which must be satisfied if the optimum is to be reached.

The discussion as developed so far may be expressed by the following chain of five equations between six items, which describe the situation in each productive unit when the optimum division of each factor among its different products has been accomplished by private profit-seeking firms when perfect competition in buying and in selling exists in every productive unit throughout the whole of an uncontrolled economy. These may be called *the welfare equations*. The six items are:

1. *The Marginal Social Benefit* (*msb*). This is the benefit to society (*i. e.* the net benefit to all the members of society affected) from the particular increment of output of product considered.
2. *The Value of the Marginal Product* (*vmp*). This is the physical increment of output of product being considered, multiplied by the price paid for it by the consumer. If the increment is exactly one unit of product, the value of the marginal product will equal the price of the product (*p*).
3. *The Marginal Private Revenue* (*mpr*). This is the increase in revenue (positive or negative) received by the producer as a result of producing and selling the increment in output.
4. *The Marginal Private Cost* (*mpc*). This is the increase in cost incurred by the producer as a result of increasing the quantity of factor he purchases in order to be able to produce the increment of output.
5. *The Value of the Marginal Factor* (*vmf*). This is the physical increment of the factor of production (that is needed to make the increment of product) multiplied by the price per unit paid for it and received by the owner of the factor. If the increment is exactly one unit of factor, the value of the marginal factor will be equal to the price of the factor (*pf*).
6. *The Marginal Social Cost* (*msc*). This is the sacrifice to society from having the marginal factor used up here so that it is not available for use elsewhere. It is the "social marginal opportunity cost" referred to on p. 66. It is the alternative marginal social benefit that the marginal factor could have produced if it had been used elsewhere.

The five equations are:

(1) Marginal Social Benefit = Value of Marginal Product

This equation is satisfied if there is an optimum allocation of consumption goods and if the purchaser of the good is the only individual in society who is affected by the purchaser's use of the product. In that case the amount of money paid for it measures the usefulness of the product to the purchaser and so to the society of which he is the only individual affected.

(2) Value of Marginal Product = Marginal Private Revenue

This equation is satisfied if there is perfect competition in selling the product. The producer is then not able to influence the price of the product by varying the output, so the extra revenue he gets from an increment in output is simply the physical increment in output multiplied by its price.

(3) Marginal Private Revenue = Marginal Private Cost

This equation is satisfied if the producer maximizes his profit. This involves expanding output as long as the marginal private revenue is greater than the marginal private cost and contracting output as long as it is less; the equilibrium position where profits are maximized thus being reached only when these two values are equated.

(4) Marginal Private Cost = Value of Marginal Factor

This equation is satisfied if there is perfect competition in buying factors of production. The producer is then not able to influence the price of the factor by varying the quantity of it that he buys, so the extra cost of buying the increment of factor is simply the physical quantity of the factor multiplied by its price.

(5) Value of Marginal Factor = Marginal Social Cost

This equation is satisfied if the first four equations hold for all the other production units in the economy using the factor so that the value of the marginal factor equals the alternative marginal social benefit from using the factor in these other uses.

These five equations may conveniently be written out in abbreviated form thus:

$$msb = vmp = mpr = mpc = vmf = msc$$

The optimum allocation of factors between different uses is attained if the first of the six items is equated to the last and $msb = msc$ with only one equation instead of five. This would represent the task that confronts a Ministry of Economic Planning which tries to utilize the factors of production in the best possible manner by shifting resources directly from points where they are less useful to others where they are more useful until they are equally useful in all uses.

The method of the collectivist economy described in Chapter 4 can be represented by these three equations:

$$msb = vmp = vmf = msc$$

The first of these, $msb = vmp$ (equation 1, p. 76), is satisfied if there is an optimum allocation of consumption goods such as can be brought about by a free market as described in Chapter 1. The second, $vmp = vmf$, is given by the Rule that the managers of all production units must obey. The third equation, $vmf = msc$ (equation 5), is satisfied if all the other managers of production (who have to pay the same price for the factor) make this price equal to the value of alternative marginal product, since *msc* is nothing but the alternative *msb*.

The Welfare Equations

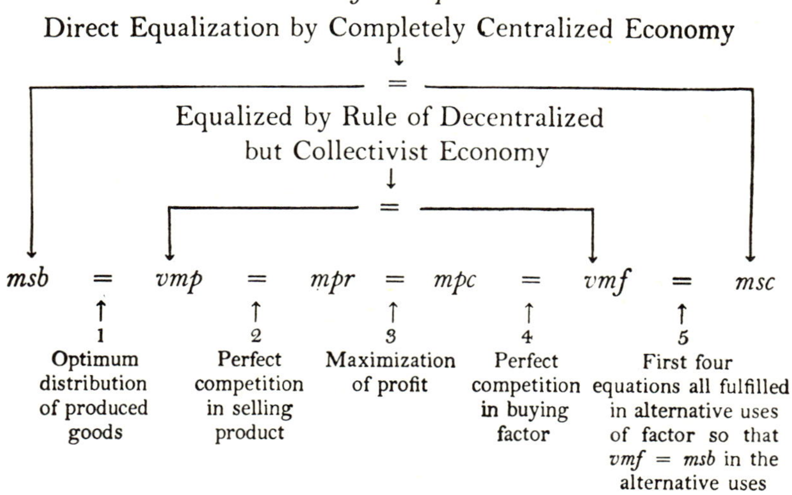

If these five conditions are satisfied, an optimum allocation of factors among the different products is reached in a capitalist economy.

[4]

CHAPTER 9. AN ALTERNATIVE FORMULATION OF THE WELFARE EQUATIONS. EQUALITY AND PROPORTIONALITY

There is an alternative formulation of the principles we have so far examined. To give it here will serve three purposes. It will make the principles stand out more clearly by showing them from a slightly different angle; it will provide an alternative terminology that is more natural and more convenient for some of our problems; and it will connect the present formulation more closely with previous writings in the field.

Adjustment of production so as to reach the optimum may be considered in terms of the factor or in terms of the product, and there are two corresponding formulations of the Rule and of the welfare equations.

If we consider every adjustment in shifting resources from one use to another as the shifting of *one unit of factor* at a time, the marginal quantity of factor is always one unit and the value of the marginal factor is the same thing as the price of the factor. We can then substitute *pf* (the price of the factor) in place of *vmf* in the series of equations that must be satisfied if the optimum use of resources is to be achieved in a free enterprise economy. The series of equations will then appear in the form

$$msb = vmp = mpr = mpc = pf = msc$$

where *msb* and *msc* stand for the marginal social benefit and the marginal social cost where one unit of *factor* is shifted from one use to another.

It is just as legitimate to start instead with *a unit of product* and consider the effects on the economy of producing a unit more or a

96

unit less of the product. The series of equations will then take the form

$$msb = p = mpr = mpc = vmf = msc$$

Where p is the price of the product (per unit) and *msb* and *msc* stand for the marginal social benefit and the marginal social cost involved in producing an additional unit of product instead of leaving the resources needed for this to produce something else.

The analysis of the conditions under which these equations are satisfied follows the previous analysis very closely. The centralized bureaucratic state would try to make $msb = msc$ in both senses, for if it is carried out in one sense it is also carried out in the other. The difference is merely one of the unit in which the adjustment is expressed. If a unit of factor could at the margin be used to produce either 2 baskets of fruit or 4 pounds of meat, the price of a basket of fruit would have to be twice the price of 1 pound of meat, say 60 cents for a basket of fruit and 30 cents for a pound of meat. The *msb* of a unit of factor applied to the production of fruit would be measured by the value of 2 baskets of fruit or $1.20. The *msc* is measured by the value of the 4 pounds of meat that have to be sacrificed because the unit of factor is producing fruit instead of meat. These 4 pounds at 30 cents a pound are worth $1.20, so $msb = msc$.

Exactly the same situation is described in our second formulation. The *msb* of a unit of fruit (a basketful) is measured by its price at 60 cents. Its *msc* is measured by the value of the meat that is sacrificed because the production of this basket of fruit used up some quantity of factor that might have produced meat. The quantity of factor is half a unit. Half a unit of factor could have produced 2 pounds of meat. Meat is 30 cents a pound, so 2 pounds are worth 60 cents. This is the *msc* of a basket of fruit, and *msb* still equals *msc*.

The same thing may be done the other way around starting with 1 pound of meat as the unit. Its price is 30 cents, and this measures its *msb*. One pound of meat at the margin uses up $\frac{1}{4}$ unit of factor which could have produced $\frac{1}{2}$ basket of fruit. The *msc* of 1 pound of meat is measured by the value of this $\frac{1}{2}$ basket of fruit which is sacrificed (to permit the 1 pound of meat to be produced), and $\frac{1}{2}$ a basket of fruit is worth 30 cents. Again *msb* = *msc*.

(Of course we have had to use prices to indicate *msb* and *msc*. The centralized bureaucratic state that tries to equalize them without using the price mechanism would be giving itself an unnecessarily difficult if not impossible task.)

So it does not matter which way we define *msb* and *msc*. Their equalization means the same thing on either definition. It is only necessary not to mix the two up and go from one of the meanings to the other in the middle of the analysis because that would render the argument quite invalid. However, this should not be difficult to avoid since it is always necessary to mention the item whose *msb* and *msc* is being considered.

The Rule may be expressed in terms of the marginal cost instead of the marginal quantity of factor.

A similar translation of the Rule as given to the managers of the collectivist economy is possible. The managers could be instructed to adjust their output to make *p* = *vmf*, which comes to the same thing as making *vmp* = *pf*. In either case, *vmp* is equated to *vmf*. Consider the grower of fruit who adjusts his output so that *vmp* is equal to *pf*. The price of (a unit of) the factor is $1.20. Its marginal product (*mp*) is 2 baskets of fruit, *vmp* is $1.20 (2 baskets at 60 cents each), and *vmp* = *pf*. Applying our second formulation to the same situation, we find that *p* (the price of the product) is 60 cents. The marginal factor (the quantity of factor needed to produce the unit of product at the margin) is half a unit of factor, and *vmf*, its value at $1.20 a unit, is 60 cents. If *vmp* = *pf*, *p* = *vmf*.

In the same way it can be shown in terms of the new formulation how perfect competition in buying and selling brings about the optimum division of each factor between its different products. In the capitalist economy *msb* = *p* if there is a free market in the goods purchased and an optimum allocation of goods, *p* = *mpr* if there is perfect competition in selling products; *mpr* = *mpc* if the firms maximize their profits; *mpc* = *vmf* if there is perfect competition in buying factors, and *vmf* = *msc* if the first four equations are fulfilled for all the other firms so that *vmf* = the alternative *msb* which is the same thing as the *msc*.

The second formulation is more natural in some ways, and parts of it are more frequently used by economists. That is why it is sufficient to say *p* for price instead of *pp* for price of the product. Similarly *mr* for marginal revenue and *mc* for marginal cost are frequently used in the sense in which we have used *mpr* and *mpc*. The *p* for private is usually omitted because most economists are most of the time engaged only in considering private interests that may lead to equilibrium prices and outputs so that they do not find it necessary to make explicit mention of the private nature of the marginal revenue and the marginal cost they are concerned with. On the other hand, *vmf* (the value of the marginal quantity of factor) and *mf* (the marginal quantity of factor) are not commonly used terms though *vmp* and *mp* (the marginal product), its exact opposite, are very common. Yet these are perfectly symmetrical; *mp* is the quantity of product that results from applying one more unit of the factor; *mf* is the quantity of factor that must be added to produce one more unit of product.

This is misleading until it is pointed out that marginal cost really stands for the value of the marginal quantity of factor.

The neglect of *mf* in the literature has led to a slightly misleading formulation of the Rule for production in the collectivist economy. The Rule is usually given in terms of equating *p* not to *vmf* but to *mc*. Strictly speaking, this is wrong, for we have seen that it is only if output is adjusted so as to make *p* = *vmf* that the optimum allocation of factors is achieved. The error is, however, usually corrected by pointing out the implied assumption that there is perfect competition in buying factors (so that *mc* = *vmf*) or that the manager in calculating *mc* disregards any influence he may have in affecting the price of the factor. This amounts to changing the meaning of *mc* to make it mean the same as *vmf*. Consequently the formulation of the Rule in terms of equating *p* to *mc* is not actually wrong but only misleading.

Of the two formulations of the Rule to be followed for the optimum division of a factor among its different products we shall more frequently use the first. That is, we shall prefer to use the formulation in terms of *the unit of factor* that is added or subtracted from a particular use or shifted from one use to another, rather than the formulation in terms of the unit of product and the effect of producing a unit more or a unit less of product. This is the form in which the Rule was originally given on p. 64. If for some special purpose it seems desirable to take a unit of the product as the starting point, the Rule would instruct the manager of production to increase or decrease his output of the product until its price (*p*) is equal to the value of the marginal quantity of factor (*vmf*). The original formulation is to be preferred in general because it shows up more clearly the fundamental nature of the problem as one of choosing between alternative uses of a scarce factor of production.

Making the price *proportional* instead of equal to marginal cost was believed to be enough,

From the table on p. 89 and the accompanying analysis it would appear that for optimum division of a factor among its different products it is not really necessary that there be perfect competition throughout but only that there be the same degree of imperfection of competition in the alternative use of the factor. If the meat producers also combine to form an organization, they might make their *msb* twice their *pf*, and then there would be an optimum allocation of factors between fruit and meat. The table of p. 89 would now look like this:

	msb	*vmp*	*mpr*	*mpc*	*pf*	*msc*
Fruit	$2.00	$2.00	$1.50	$1.50	$1.00	$2.00
Meat	$2.00	$2.00	$1.50	$1.50	$1.00	$2.00

with *msb* = *msc* for both fruit and meat.

If this were correct the Rule for the controlled economy would have to be changed accordingly. Instead of instructing managers to adjust production until *vmp* is *equal* to *pf*, it would be sufficient to order them to make *vmp proportional* to *pf*; the ratio to be given to all producers by the Ministry of Economic Planning. Only if this ratio happened to be unity would the Rule appear in the form we have given it. On our second formulation the Rule would be to adjust production until *p* was in some given ratio to *vmf*, the ratio again to be the same for all producers and dictated by the Ministry of Economic Planning. Whatever the ratio determined by the Ministry of Economic Planning, the different *vmp's* and *pf*'s (or *p*'s and *vmf's*) would be *proportional* and *msb* would be equal to *msc*.

However, this is not quite correct although it was held to be so until very recently.

It is not possible for all the industries which use a factor to do what one of them alone could do. The fruit growers can double the price of fruit by restricting output and shifting the displaced factor to the production of meat. The meat growers can double the price of meat by restricting output and shifting the displaced factor to the production of fruit. But it is not possible for both of these things to be done at the same time. If both industries attempt it, the displaced factor of production will not be absorbed but will remain unused. (Of course, there are other industries besides meat and fruit in which the factor might be absorbed, but we are using these two to represent all the different industries for which the factor of production might be used.) If the factor stays unused we shall certainly not have an optimum division of the factor among its different uses. Its *msb* will fall to zero and certainly below *msc* which is measured by the value of the meat or fruit that a unit of it could produce.

It may be possible for the price of the factor to fall until it is all employed even though in both fruit and meat *vmp* is twice *pf* (and $p = 2\ vmf$). The factor will then be ideally divided between producing fruit and producing meat. The income of the owners of the factor will be less and the income of the managers of production will be greater. If the monopoly is owned by the owners of the factor in proportion to their ownership of the factor, there will be no real difference, for each owner will get just as much more as a shareholder in the monopoly as he gets less as an owner of the factor. If the distribution of monopoly profit is determined in any other way, some will be richer and some will be poorer, but this will be purely a matter of the division of income among different individuals and will not directly affect the division of the factor between the two uses. (It may do so indirectly if the division of income results in a change in the relative demand for meat and fruit, but this would not prevent an *optimum* division of the factor between fruit and meat for the new demand conditions.)

but proportionality cannot be universal unless it is really equality.

If the *proportionality* instead of equality between the price of each factor and the value of its marginal product were established in *all* uses, this would not distort the optimum division of the factor among its products but would only change the division of income If *vmp* were everywhere greater than *pf* in the same proportion, less income would go to the owners of the factor and more would go to the monopolists in charge of production. These would in effect be collecting tribute from the owners of the factor. But there would still be an optimum division of the factor of production among the different products in accordance with the demand for products corresponding to the new distribution of incomes. In every firm *msb* would be equal to *msc* in the manner illustrated by the table on p. 100.

However, this is not significant because *it is not possible for the ratio* between *vmp* and *pf* (or between *p* and *vmf* or between *vmp* and *vmf*) *to be the same in all uses* of all factors unless this proportion is *unity*. In other words, they cannot *all* be proportional unless they are *equal*.

This is illustrated in the allocation of labor power between labor and leisure,

The most important of all factors is without any doubt *labor*, and labor always has the alternative of not working but providing leisure for the individual who is the owner of his own labor. For the optimum allocation of labor as between work and leisure it is necessary that the *vmp* of a little more labor should be *equal* to *pf*, the price of the factor labor or the wage payment for the extra amount of labor. If the worker is free to work the extra hour or not, he will work up to the point where the disutility of another hour's work (which is the same thing as his valuation of another hour's leisure) is measured by the payment for the extra hour's work. He will therefore equate the *msb* of leisure to the pay he gets for his work. But this *msb* is the alternative *msb* to his working, and therefore the *msc* of employing him in industry. If then his *msb* in industry is not *equal* to his wage, *msb* will not be equal to *msc* and we will not have the optimum division of the factor labor between production and leisure.

If the *vmp* of an extra hour's labor is not equal to *pf* (the price or wage of labor), the worker will work either too much or too little. It is wasteful for him to sacrifice an hour of leisure which is worth, say, $1 to him if the net result of his work is that the product is increased by only 50 cents' worth of goods. This is wasteful because the worker is willing to give up more than 50 cents' worth of goods to take the place of what he would add to the total product and he would still be better off by not working while nobody else need be any worse off. If his *vmp* is greater than his *pf* or wage he will not work as much as is desirable. If his *vmp* is $2 and his wage is $1 an hour he will refuse to work beyond the point where his valuation of an hour's leisure rises above $1. The worker refuses to work another hour because, while the wage is $1, he values the hour at, say, $1.25. He would be glad to work another hour for $1.50, and it would be socially desirable for him to do so, for even if he were paid $1.50 for the additional hour there would still be a net benefit of 50 cents for the rest of society out of his marginal product which is worth $2. That is why it is necessary that *vmp* be not merely *proportional* but *equal* to *pf*, for labor.

and in other decisions not subject to the Rule.

The same reasoning would apply to any other factor of production which can be freely directed to producing something without needing the consent of a manager who is subject to the Rule. All cases of competitive speculation would come under this category. Any hoarding of goods from one period to another or any kind of production that might be carried on by small producers on a purely competitive basis would satisfy these conditions unless the activity was subjected to the Rule. This would be unnecessarily cumbersome; would deprive the economy of the advantages of a freely competitive sector where the optimum use of resources was brought about automatically without the supervision and administrative problems necessary elsewhere. Moreover, it would be very difficult to prevent speculators from carrying on their beneficial trading activities secretly and illegally in a way that could not be prevented without a costly system of police supervision and espionage that would be of great danger to democracy. For all these reasons it is necessary to keep to the first formulation of our Rule which instructs managers to adjust production so as to make $vmp = pf$. If vmp must equal pf in these special cases (which are very important ones), it must also be made equal in all other cases if it is to be *proportional* in general.

There are two points to be added to this digression. First, the idea of a worker varying his hours to adjust his marginal valuation of leisure to his wage may seem fanciful when workers are only too glad to get any job and will work whatever hours the employer asks in order to keep their jobs. Even so, workers have many indirect ways of adjusting their hours of work or their output both individually and collectively. In an economy where full use is made of resources, either because it is a controlled economy or because full use comes about by accident in an uncontrolled economy, more satisfactory provision can be devised to give this very important freedom of choice. Technical conditions of production may dictate certain limitations in any individual factory, but it is possible, if industry should be organized with the welfare of the workers as clearly in mind as the whims of the customers, for a worker to be able to choose between different factories with different hours of work, different holiday arrangements, and so on. The choice of how much to work is important in free economies now and can be given much greater scope in a controlled economy which considers this as important for a worker as it is for a woman to be able to choose between 200,000 different kinds of silk hose.

The other point is to guard against a misunderstanding. It might seem to be implied that if the wage is raised a worker will always work more hours and vice versa. This does not necessarily occur. If the wage is raised, the incentive for working another hour is raised by that much. But by the same act the income of the worker is raised, and that may raise even more the amount of money he is willing to sacrifice for another hour of leisure. Under these circumstances, raising his wage will not make him work harder but on the contrary may result in his working fewer hours.

This, however, does not upset our argument. Making the wage equal to the value of the worker's marginal product still improves on the division of the factor among its alternative products not only by adjusting the value of the marginal product but by varying the value of the alternative product, leisure. It is only a bad habit we all have of forgetting that leisure is just as important as any other product of labor. Perhaps we tend to lose sight of it because it is not to be seen on the transmission belt in the factory.

[5]

Chapter Nine

Principles of Efficient Economic Policy

Economic policy has five main channels of action: (1) action *on behalf* of the market, directed at creating the basic conditions for the proper working of the price mechanism; (2) action *on* the market, directed at improving its functioning; (3) action *through* the market, directed at dealing with external effects and with social priorities by means of adjustments in the price structure; (4) action *within* the market, directed at achieving particular objectives as one of the participants in the market; and (5) action *outside* the market, directed at setting up centralized, administrative, economic mechanisms where these are more efficient than the decentralized market mechanisms.

Action on Behalf of the Market

Only the government can create the conditions for the proper functioning of the market. For this it must provide effective legislation on which commercial transactions can be based, providing security of property rights and reducing uncertainty in business operations. The government must regulate the activities of organizations and institutions, private or public, which are powerful enough to be able to abuse the market and impair its proper functioning. The government must devise and improve laws in many varied fields directed at perfecting, stabilizing and simplifying the operation of the market mechanism and increasing its reliability.

The government must also support the distribution of truthful information on the possibilities of production and consumption and the quality of products and of their components while preventing false and misleading publicity.

Action on the Market

As we have seen, there are a number of phenomena that are liable to disturb the proper functioning of the price mechanism. Price rigidity prevents the consumer from obtaining all he wants to buy at the given prices, and prevents the producer from selling all the output it is worth his while to produce. Monopoly and monopsony, price discrimination, administrative restrictions on the volume of trade, are all similarly harmful. The harm common to all these is that they prevent the market from establishing the socially desirable equality between the marginal rates of substitution in consumption (for consumers) and the marginal rate of transformation in production (for producers).

It is the government's responsibility to remove or neutralize forces that would distort the "correct" price structure required for economic efficiency. The government can eliminate monopolies, monopsonies, and cartels, both of buyers and of sellers, by prohibiting the setting of maximum or minimum prices and by outlawing price discrimination. The government can also ensure correct prices by operating directly on the market, buying and selling any quantities supplied or demanded at appropriate, marginal, social-cost prices. These would have to be provisional prices, adjusted from time to time to changes in cost and demand conditions.

There are those who believe that in order to ensure economic efficiency the government must intervene and fix both the quantities and the prices. For this they propose the setting up of teams of economists who will compute exact costs of production and prescribe both the outputs and the prices.[a] This is no way to achieve economic efficiency. No matter how exact the computations by the teams, it is quite impossible for them to take into account the continual changes in the conditions of production, to consider technological changes and determine their rate of adoption, or to anticipate the changes in demand.

"Fixed prices" and "correct prices" are mutually contradictory terms. Obtaining correct prices is possible only if the prices are not fixed but flexible. Fixing prices and outputs conflicts with the principle of prices changing in accordance with movements in cost and demand as these adjust to each other. Even if we could arrange for current computations to keep up with all changes in adjusting prices and outputs, the best they could do would be to achieve what is reached anyway by the price mechanism.

Action through the Market: Taxes and Subsidies

The government acts through the market mechanism by applying taxes and subsidies, changing the prices so as to alter the behavior of producers and consumers. One must distinguish here between two cases: the case where the government wants to change the production and consumption of a *specific* product, and the case where the government wants to change the level of consumption *in general.*

[a] In Israel, a system similar to this operates in agriculture. Teams within the Ministry of Agriculture compute the costs of production, fix producers' prices, determine the areas to be cultivated and allocate the areas among the producers. Marketing councils operating under the authority of the Ministry of Agriculture regulate the flow of products going to the market (see Chapter 22).

Changing Specific Consumption. The government will want to change the output and consumption of a specific product if the product involves external benefits or costs, or because of a social preference. In these cases, a gap must be created between the price to the producer and the price to the consumer. If the quantity of output and consumption is to be increased, the price paid by the consumer must be reduced below the price received by the producer, and the government must provide a subsidy which will cover the difference between the two prices. For products having external benefits, the subsidy per unit of product should be equal to the marginal external benefits. Consumption will then be increased until there is equality between the marginal cost of production and the marginal *social* utility (the purchaser's marginal utility, plus the external marginal utility). On the other hand, when the purpose is to reduce output and consumption because of external costs, the same principle requires the price to the consumer to be higher than the marginal cost of production by the amount of the marginal external cost or disbenefit. The price will then be raised to equality with the marginal *social* cost.

Changing Consumption in General. Taxes and subsidies can be directed toward achieving general objectives not especially related to any specific product. In an inflation caused by excess demand, an increase in taxes can help to reduce the excess demand. In depression, subsidies can reduce unemployment. Such taxes and subsidies contribute to economic stability and thereby increase economic efficiency. They can also aid in achieving social objectives. For example, progressive taxation and subsidies to those with low incomes reduce the inequality of income.

Taxes and subsidies can thus help to achieve general or social objectives; however, as they are levied on incomes and on specific goods and services, they damage economic efficiency. This damage stems from the gap created between the price to the producer and the price to the consumer, which upsets the equality between the marginal substitutibility and the marginal transformability. To achieve the objectives of taxes and subsidies while minimizing the damage to economic efficiency, taxes and subsidies that have the least possible effect on the behavior of producers and consumers should be chosen. A tax that does not influence consumers' and producers' behavior is called a *neutral* tax.

A lump-sum tax is an outstanding example of a neutral tax. This is a tax levied on an individual at a fixed amount (not necessarily the same for everybody) without considering his income, his expenditures or his market behavior. Accordingly, such a tax will not affect the equality of the marginal rates of substitution to the marginal rates of transformation. A *per capita* tax (the same for everyone) increases the inequality of income, while a universal *per capita* subsidy reduces the inequality of income, again without diverting the economy from economic efficiency.

Taxes and subsidies levied against some goods and services but not against all are not neutral; they result in changes in price which cause consumers to shift from the taxed to the untaxed or more lightly taxed items. These are presumably less needed (and therefore not previously chosen) so that there is a decrease in economic efficiency. However, if the price change does not greatly influence the amount demanded or supplied, the departure from efficiency will be small.

A tax of this type, whose influence is small, is that on the rent of all land. Landowners cannot raise their rents because that would remove part of their land from being used at all. Accordingly, landowners will be forced to absorb the whole burden of the tax. The rent will remain at the original level, the use of the land will not change, and economic efficiency will remain undamaged. Increasing or decreasing taxes of this type alters the division of incomes and can contribute to the stabilization of the economy without touching economic efficiency. Taxes levied on goods consumed by rich people hurt efficiency very little, where the demand for these products does not depend much on the price. A tax of this type, since it falls on those with high incomes, is similar to a progressive income tax.

The greater the number of goods and services taxed, the less will be the consumer's opportunity of substituting untaxed goods for the taxed ones. There will be a smaller shift to inferior, untaxed substitutes, and a smaller loss of efficiency. The substitutes must be inferior or they would have been chosen even without the tax. If the tax is levied at an equal rate on all products, as well as on leisure, efficiency will not be affected at all, because consumers cannot avoid the tax by shifting from taxed products to any substitute. A general tax is thus a neutral tax. Income tax is a relatively efficient tax since it is equivalent to a tax on all the goods and services purchased out of the taxed income.

Income tax is not quite a general tax because it is not levied on the leisure of the worker. Leisure is thus made relatively cheaper. An income tax induces the worker to increase his leisure time, that is to say, to work less than is appropriate for economic efficiency.[b] Furthermore, the income tax is not levied on goods and services which the individual produces for himself. This too harms economic efficiency. The income tax also harms efficiency because it discriminates against saving, since the tax is usually levied not only on the income that is saved but also on its fruits—the future interest income.

A tax aimed at changing the consumption of a particular product may simultaneously serve to bring about a desired general change in overall con-

[b]This inclination to work less may be offset, or even more than offset, by an opposing tendency: with a reduction in after-tax income, people are inclined to work harder to make up for the loss. But even then less work is done than economic efficiency would call for, taking into account the lower net income. The marginal utility of leisure is less than the marginal utility of the alternative marginal product from working, though *both* marginal utilities may be higher for the worker who, because of the income tax, enjoys less goods as well as less leisure.

sumption. If the government is interested in raising the level of education and is also interested in increasing the income level of the poor—and the majority of people with low education levels are in low-income brackets—then educational subsidies granted to the children of the poor will serve both objectives together. This is a case where the subsidy serves two objectives at the same time—one specific (education), and the second general (division of income).

It is nevertheless necessary to distinguish between these two purposes or we can easily find ourselves with an inefficient tax. Assume, for example, that to increase the income of the poor, they are supplied with clothing at especially low prices. If for some reason we are particularly interested in increasing the consumption of clothing by the poor, then the policy achieves two purposes at the same time. But if there is no such special interest in clothing consumption, the measure is inefficient. The poor will no doubt benefit by getting more clothes, but the consumption of clothing will rise above the efficiency level. Their marginal substitutability of clothing for other goods and services will be reduced below that for other consumers, and below the marginal transformability of clothing into other goods and services. The greater the subsidy to clothing, the greater the harm to economic efficiency. It would be more efficient to give the same subsidy in the form of cash. They would then not be tempted to buy more clothing in order to get more subsidy, but would divide the money subsidy among different goods and services in the way they consider best. They would be better off, the gain coming entirely out of the greater efficiency of the economy.

The same logic applies to a bread subsidy given to bakers. The price of bread being the same for all consumers, they all have the same marginal substitutability of bread for all other products. But because the price of bread is below the producers' marginal costs, the marginal transformability of bread into other products is lower than the marginal substitutability, and economic efficiency suffers. The poor do spend a high proportion of their income on bread, and the bread subsidy improves their situation in relation to the more well-to-do. But if they got the same subsidy in cash, they would spend it in a manner that would benefit them more. This is the meaning of damage to economic efficiency.

Action within the Market

In the case of natural monopolies there are two ways for the government to ensure economic efficiency. One way is to regulate the monopolies; the other way is for the government itself to run the monopoly. Education is another example. It could be entrusted to private institutions with government subsidies, because of the resulting external benefits, but the government could also set up a network of schools by itself.

In addition to public services, such as telephone, electricity, water and gas, and in addition to services yielding external benefits such as health and education, the government can operate in any field whatsoever if it believes that this would increase economic efficiency. In every such instance the objective is not maximum profit but only greater economic efficiency. A government company can enter a monopolized industry in order to make it competitive. But if the government company reaches an agreement with the monopolistic firm so as to increase the profits of both firms, the government company will have failed to achieve the purpose for which it was established.

If a natural monopoly is more efficient when run as a government operation than as a private firm under governmental regulation, the government should run it. But if the private firm is more efficient, and the cost of government regulation is less than the difference in efficiency, then private operation is to be preferred.

The government operates within the market also for its own purposes The government is a huge organization employing many workers and buying and selling different goods and services. As such, it participates in the market just like any other consumer or producer, but on a tremendously large scale. Here too the government should apply the principles of economic efficiency. It should buy and sell in the market at competitive prices and not exploit its monopolistic and monopsonistic powers. Moreover, it must buy in the cheapest market and itself produce the services it needs if that reduces its costs. Thus, the government must behave like any private firm, choosing the cheapest of the many options, producing the item itself, buying it, accepting the lowest tender for the same quality, subcontracting, and so forth.

But when the government buys goods or services in an imperfect market, it should use the method that maximizes the efficiency of the *economy* even if this does not minimize the cost to the government *company*. It must not exploit its monopolistic and monopsonistic powers to increase its profits, but operate within the framework of the price structure—the given set of prices—meticulously maintaining the equality of the value of marginal product to the value of the marginal factors (which would be the marginal cost if the government enterprise had no monopsony power). Thus the government can play its part, as a consumer and as a producer, to increase economic efficiency by its appropriate participation in the market.

Action outside the Market

Action outside the market pays no attention to market prices. It is appropriate for public goods and for the large centralized firms, which have already been discussed. In these areas the centralized method is superior to decentralization.

Here the government is confronted with two problems: first, how large the output should be; second, who should be the producer. Since market prices cannot reliably provide a basis for determining size of output, another system of evaluation is required. For example, in order to determine the size of the defense services, research must be conducted into the external benefits from this service and all the alternative outputs that must be given up in order to achieve this output. In order to determine the size and location of an industrial center, research must be conducted into all the effects of these decisions throughout the society.

These problems can be tackled by methods of research and analysis that have been developed in economics, sociology, mathematics and related fields. Complete solutions to such problems cannot be guaranteed, but these research techniques can certainly assist us in approximating overall economic efficiency.

Although decisions of this nature are inescapable responsibilities of government, it is not essential for the government to be the organization that carries them out. Consider, for example, the construction of a dam for flood prevention. The decision is the government's, but construction does not have to be done by a government office. In every situation the task should be assigned to the organization most efficient in the particular task—public or private, centralized or decentralized. In achieving this, the market mechanism can be of help, for example by means of competitive tenders, and by private and public companies on an equal footing.

[6]

The American Way of Business

PART ONE: ANALYSIS

By Oscar Lange and Abba P. Lerner

I. Strengthening the Economic Foundations of Democracy

When contrasted with private enterprise, collectivism stands for public enterprise. This contrast is not to be confused with collectivism *versus* individualism as alternative philosophies of social organization. The issue between individualism and collectivism is whether the ultimate purpose of society is the well-being of the individual and his development for the greatest enjoyment of the good life, all the organizations of society being justified only by their usefulness for the individual, or whether the individual must be sacrificed for some greater collective good such as the power or grandeur or glory of the nation, the state, or the race.

Reasonable discussion about purposes is impossible unless they can be viewed as themselves alternative means to some agreed upon more remote objective. The conflict between the individualist and the collectivist philosophies of social organization does not seem to be reconcilable in this way. The present war in its most meaningful aspect is just such a conflict. In the Nazi and Fascist concept the individual is only a cog in a machine, only an instrument to be sacrificed without question for the greater glory of the State, the race, or the emperor. To the freedom loving nations the race is a disappearing survival of earlier tribal thinking (or rather feeling) and the State and the emperor are instruments to be used only as long as they remain effective means for improving the life of the individual. This is nowhere expressed more clearly than in the preamble to the Declaration of Independence.

Whether individualism or collectivism is accepted as the goal or end of human co-operation there remains the question whether the *means* to be utilized in achieving this aim is to be public enterprise or private enterprise. It would seem more natural for collectivist societies to be biased in favor of public enterprise and for individualist societies to be biased in favor of private enterprise. But that this is not a necessary relationship is to be seen in the considerable use of private enterprise in Germany, Italy, and Japan even though their social philosophy is clearly and explicitly collectivist, while in Soviet Russia private enterprise has been almost completely exterminated and public enterprise erected in its place even though the avowed purpose of the Soviet Union is to serve better the development of its individual members. Indeed, the idea of abolishing private enterprise came from socialist thinkers who believed that this change would actually further the development and freedom of the individual.

II. Private Enterprise

In the United States today most people take it for granted that the natural form of economic activity is private enterprise. Most people make their living by working for employers who are in business not primarily to serve consumers, but for profit. No doubt the initiators and managers of these private enterprises like to feel that they are useful to society and even believe most of the advertisements which tell the public how useful they are. But they would not be in business if it did not promise to be profitable. To the charge that some of the activities are not really in the social interest, they plead that if they themselves did not carry on these business enterprises somebody else would. Indeed this plea is usually true and they do not deserve special blame. A man who sees a chance of making a fortune by persuading people to buy a useless or even moderately harmful patent medicine cannot really be blamed for going into such a business if he knows that any self-sacrifice in refusing to provide such a product will mean only that somebody else will do it instead and might sell the public something even more harmful.

But if the initiators and managers of private enterprises can escape the blame when their products are harmful to society they cannot at the same time claim credit for producing the things that are beneficial to society. It must be recognized that their aim, when they go into business, is to make money and the good or the harm done to society is a secondary matter even though there may be a temptation to claim credit when it does good and to evade responsibility when it does harm.

Of course private enterprise is not permitted to engage in every activity that it finds profitable. Society has found it necessary to circumscribe the field within which private enterprise is permitted to operate. Slavery, for example, or the manufacture and distribution of the more noxious drugs and poisons are prohibited. Nor is private enterprise permitted to run its business without considerable and growing regulations in the interest of society. There are restrictions and penalties on the importation of certain goods (although these restrictions are usually imposed only for the benefit of special interests that are able, by disguising themselves as social interests, to get special consideration of their profits or job opportunities). Furthermore, there are restrictions on conditions of work in the interest of safety and sanitation, and provisions for compensation for injuries to employees in the course of their work. There are regulations about hours of work, minimum wages, and the age of employees. There are regulations with respect to the organization of workers in trade unions and employers must observe "fair labor practices." There are social security taxes on workers and employers and a large number of other regulations by Federal, state, and local governments that circumscribe the freedom of private enterprise in all sorts of ways.

In a special category are those private enterprises which are called *public utilities* where, in addition to the foregoing general regulations, there is a special regulation of the prices they may charge for their service and the conditions under which they must provide the service to the public. These public utilities are industries which the courts have ruled to be "informed with a public interest" in the sense that the consumer is not in a position to bargain with the producer by threatening to get the service from a competitor. Such a threat is clearly of no significance to the providers of electric current, gas, water, many forms of transportation, or telephone service. It has therefore been felt that the consumer needs special protection and so there has grown up a system of public-utility regulation which prevents the making of exorbitant profits by the suppliers of such services and ensures the provision and maintenance of the services. In these fields there is still private enterprise in the main, but the provision of the services is so hedged by restrictions of various kinds that it becomes difficult to say whether the final result is not closer to public enterprise than to private enterprise in that more of the important decisions of what should be provided and how it should be provided are made by public officials regulating the enterprise than by the private owners of the enterprise.

III. Public Enterprise

There is also in every country a section of the economy that is frankly undertaken by public enterprise. The postal service, the Armed Forces, the police, the law courts, elementary and secondary education, fire protection, and sanitation are provided by organs of society consciously organized to provide these social services to meet recognized social needs. We too easily take the public provision of these services for granted, not realizing that they were developed only in the face of determined and sincere opposition by men who believed that the provision of such services was outside the province of government and constituted a threat to the liberty of the subject. Indeed it must be confessed that the "collectivization" of education, of the Armed Forces, and of the police certainly looks more like a threat to personal liberty than the present proposals for general and adequate social security which are also being opposed by some as deadly dangers to the freedom of the individual.

IV. Private Property and Public Policy

The public regulation of private enterprise and the islands of public enterprise in the economies with which we are familiar are, however, not the most significant delimitations of private enterprise. There are others more fundamental and more likely to be overlooked. These are the legal and social framework within which private enterprise operates..

The concept of private property itself is not a natural one with which we are born, although it appears almost as such to us who grow up with it all around us. In many civilizations it does not exist at all and the members of such civilizations find it incomprehensible when they first come across it (or rather when it first comes across them—backed with sufficient military force to make them respect it even if they do not understand it). What things are subject to private property and what things are not is a matter of extremely complicated law. In general it may be said that the decisions as to what things shall be subject to the rules of private property and recognized by the courts have on the whole been decided in the light of whether it would serve society better for the particular kind of property right to be recognized. *Our system of private property, when considered as a whole, is itself an elaborate piece of public enterprise, designed in the general social interest.*

The underlying idea of the mechanism is to establish a way of life in which individuals, when they try to benefit themselves, will be benefiting society as a whole whether that is their intention or not.

This is illustrated in the simplest kind of property—the right of the individual in the product of his own hands. It is in the social interest that the soil should be cultivated so that the crops will be available for society to consume. If the cultivator of the soil had no greater claim than anyone else to the crops that he brought forth with the sweat of his brow, he would have no incentive to work hard to produce them. He would find it more pleasant to go fishing and then collect whatever somebody else had cultivated. The land would thus not be very efficiently and industriously cultivated except by men filled with a strong desire to do things for their neighbors, and there are not enough of such men to keep any society going. But if the cultivator of the soil is given a right over his crop and is protected in his enjoyment of the crop, he will work hard to produce it, and when he has produced it he will sell it and there will be plenty on the market for others to buy. Private property will have harnessed the self-interest of the farmer in the service of society as a whole. This harnessing of private interest for the general good is the essence of all social organization.

A particularly vivid example of the social usefulness of private enterprise was provided by the New Economic Policy, adopted in Russia by the Communists in 1921, which permitted a limited amount of private enterprise in trading and in production. This led to a rapid increase in output and improvement in distribution that saved the country from complete ruin after the calamities of the war, the revolution, and the civil war, simply by making it profitable to producers and traders to produce what the country was starving for and carry it to where it was needed by people who by producing something themselves (or in some other way) could get the wherewithal to pay for it.

Yet private property, while it has by and large tended to perform this vital service, was never carefully and consciously planned from the beginning for this purpose and it certainly was not adjusted to fit in with changing technical conditions of production. Rather, it grew, in a sense naturally, slowly through the ages. It was amended as pressures for its amendment became very strong, frequently only after violent conflict as when the laws of property over human beings were changed by the American Civil War or when the laws of property in land were changed in the old world only after many agrarian uprisings. The result is that the potential social advantages of property laws are realized only imperfectly. To some it seems as if the conditions of production have changed so fundamentally that the laws of private property have now completely outlived their usefulness and are only a drag on the further development of society. This is indeed the Marxian thesis, which goes to an extreme in maintaining that there no longer is any useful part to be played in the future of our society by the private ownership of the instruments of production. As we shall see below there is no need to make any such unverifiable prophecies as to the course of the future development of the techniques of production and the influence of these on the social organization that would harness them best in the social interest.

What we can say is that since the development followed a kind of unconscious evolution it naturally tended to lag behind the ever increasing rate of change in technique. Without going to the extreme of declaring that private enterprise has lost *all* its usefulness we may be entitled to examine the actual state of affairs to see how adequately it serves our purposes at the present time and whether our existing mixture of private and public enterprise is the best that we could now devise. Perhaps we should have more private enterprise and less public enterprise in our mixture or perhaps it should be the other way. We may even be able to discover some general principles which would permit us to make the best use of both the public-enterprise instrument and the private-enterprise instrument, both of them directed to increasing the efficiency of our society and both subservient to the individualist philosophy of giving the individual ever greater freedom to develop his personality and to enjoy the good life.

For this we must examine the actual machinery more closely, for only in this way can one hope to find an answer to the question of private enterprise *versus* public enterprise. One must be prepared for such an inquiry not to give all the marks to one of the contestants. It may not even tell one which scores more points than the other. But it may perform the much more useful purpose of indicating what each instrument is best suited for and to show how to make them work together for the general social good of society.

V. Rules for Public Enterprise

One may begin with the public-enterprise mechanism and examine the obvious claim that it must work in the social interest because it is specially intended for that purpose and is not distracted by any considerations of private profit. This claim takes too much for granted since it is inevitable that any public enterprise will be run by the same kind of people who operate the economy at present. These men rarely have either the noble character or the power to act purely in the interests of the social welfare, and even if they had both there is the question whether they would know what it is they should do in the social interest. Nearly all of them must work for superiors whom they will try to please, whether to keep their jobs or get promotions or because they are interested in the efficiency of the organization and believe that this is forwarded by their obeying orders. In fact, the man who works in a public enterprise has to follow certain rules which in most cases are of the same kind as those he has to follow in a private enterprise. What we have to consider then is what are the *rules* that should govern the behavior of those who run enterprise if the result is to be the best service of the needs of the members of society.

It is true that in many fields of public enterprise the rules followed are nothing but copies from the field of private enterprise taken over just because the managers of the public enterprise had no principles of their own and frequently thought the rules developed by private enterprise had universal validity—never going behind them to see how they were related to the social interest or whether they were related at all. In many cases, they followed the principles of private enterprise out of mere force of habit or because they believed the adoption of other rules would constitute unfair competition with private enterprise. But we must, without prejudice, ask ourselves what rules should be prescribed for the operators of public enterprise to make them serve society best, and compare the results with the achievements of private enterprise in a variety of situations.

In the first place, the products of public enterprise should be sold on a free market with the same price for the same good for everybody.[1] Each consumer will then tend to adjust his expendi-

[1] The same good at different places or at different times may be considered different goods so that there can be differences of price to correspond to the difficulty of changing the time or place of the service, but at the same time and place the price should be the same for all.

ture between the different products so that he could not further improve his condition by buying a dollar's worth less of the one to set free a dollar with which to buy more of the other good. This means that an additional dollar's worth of any good that he could buy is no more useful to him than the dollar's worth of the other good that he would have to give up in order to be able to buy it; and this is true for all the individuals who have to pay the same prices for all the goods that they buy. The result is that no individual's valuation of something that somebody else has is any higher, *relatively* to his valuation of what he has himself than the corresponding relative valuation by the individual who possesses it.

AN IDEAL DISTRIBUTION

Everyone is at least as satisfied with what he has as he would be with anything that anybody else would be willing to give him in exchange for it. In other words the different goods are distributed between the different consumers in the *ideal proportions* so as to satisfy any differences in tastes or in the kinds of things that the different individuals need. Any other distribution of the different goods among the different individuals would not satisfy this condition and hence would not be ideal. Under any other than this ideal condition, it would still be possible to improve on the situation by reshuffling goods between different individuals, giving each consumer more of what he values relatively more highly and transferring from him to others what others value relatively more highly. This would benefit both by permitting them to have things that they preferred. But such a reshuffling would merely be an imperfect move toward the ideal distribution that is achieved in the first place by merely charging everybody the same price and permitting all consumers to buy freely the amounts that they would like to buy.

It is true that some individuals might be getting more than is desirable of *all* goods, so that their *absolute* valuation of goods in general might be considered too low. The remedy for this is to give them less *money* to spend (or take some of their money away by taxes), so that they buy less of goods in general, thus leaving more for other people. But their *relative* valuation of what they have would still be the same as anybody else's so it would not be possible in this case to improve the situation all around, making *everybody* better off, by simply reshuffling the different goods.

EXAMPLES FOUND IN RATIONING

This issue is especially relevant at the present time because our current rationing schemes are devices for distributing goods otherwise than by a free market with the same price for all. It therefore has the defects we have just indicated. I have more sugar coupons than I really need and should like to have more meat coupons. My neighbor would like to exchange some of his meat coupons for some of my sugar coupons. Both of us would be happier for the exchange and nobody would be any worse off, yet the exchange is illegal, and even if I evade the law by inviting him to cake in exchange for his inviting me for a steak, this is a clumsy and inefficient way of improving the distribution of goods between consumers.

The reason for rationing is that the distribution of money income is so uneven that, when some things such as meat or gasoline become more than usually scarce, a free market would enable the rich to bid the price up so high that the rest would not be able to get any of the scarce goods at all. The remedy would be not necessarily to ration at all but to restrict the expenditure of the rich by taxation while leaving them free to distribute their restricted demand as they wish between the different scarce goods. This would prevent the rich from getting all the scarce goods away from the poor while at the same time permitting those who had a greater need for one of the scarce goods to get more of it at the sacrifice of other scarce goods. Nobody would have a right to grumble if one man bought more sugar than another by cutting down on his meat, since everybody who wished could do the same.

Such schemes of dealing with serious scarcities by limiting or otherwise seriously restricting the expenditure by the rich on scarce goods rather than by rationing the individual scarce goods have not generally been accepted. There is nevertheless a tendency for such a situation to be approximated as a result of gradual improvement in the methods of rationing even though the initiators of the improvements are not in the least aware that they are moving in this direction.

This can be seen as the ration coupons take on more and more of the qualities of money. First they are specific for a certain quantity of a single product. Then it is found convenient to combine the rationing of several goods under one rationing plan as in the case of meat and butter in the United States or in the case of many different kinds of clothing which come under a single system of point rationing as in England and Germany. Then it is found advisable to change the point values of the different items included in the point-rationing system in accordance with changes in their demand or supply. Retailers are given the right to change the point value when they find that their stocks, of meat for example, are in danger of deterioration, but in order to prevent this from being abused, it has been ruled that it be permitted only when the money price is reduced at the same time as the price in points, so that there is a bargain price in the one form of money (ration points) only when there is a bargain price in the other form of money (currency). Now plastic coins are used in lieu of the points. These are used again and again just like ordinary money. Every new improvement makes the point system more like the conventional money system with the crucial difference that the distribution of points is on an equalitarian basis which does not permit some to "hog" the scarce goods.

At the same time as the physical machinery of the point-rationing system is made to work more and more like the normal money mechanism, the area to which the point rationing applies shows signs of being extended to cover more different items for the sake of permitting the individual to choose between them. This is not so clear from the purely American experience where the point-rationing method was applied from the beginning to quite large groups of goods, but point rationing was a late development in the other countries which suffered from acute scarcities earlier than we did and in disregard or ignorance of the principles here developed started out with individual rationing of each different item. Here we are benefiting from the experience of the English and the Germans in avoiding the greater inconvenience of having a large number of different ration cards, each for a different rationed article. The completion of this consolidation and simplification of rationing procedures would mean only one system of ration points, and when these points come to be used exactly like the other ordinary kind of money we have in fact reached the system of limiting the spending power of the rich over goods that have become scarce.

Probably the real reason for not adopting this more satisfactory system right from the beginning, instead of by a complicated and uncomfortable improvement and consolidation of particular rationing, is that the direct method is immediately recognized as a tremendous equalization of real purchasing power, a demoting of ordinary money from many of its most important functions and a depreciation in its real value. This sounds too revolutionary and perhaps even communistic to be applied openly, but, since the objectives are necessary for the effective prosecution of the war effort, the same things are permitted and even welcomed when the rôle of money is degraded indirectly and less conspicuously by the development of rationing. It is only reasonable to expect that when a thing is done, so to speak, clandestinely and in large measure unconsciously, it will not be done as efficiently as if it were done openly and with a clear recognition of the issues. At any rate the natural history of rationing illustrates most emphatically the usefulness of the price mechanism as an instrument for bringing about the most satisfactory distribution of a given supply of goods among a population.

A public enterprise economy would bring about the ideal distribution of the available goods by permitting consumers to buy the goods they prefer at the stores, charging everybody the same price for the same good at the same time and place. Some enthusiasts for public enterprise, who call themselves socialists or even collectivists, tend to reject the use of the price mechanism for this purpose. This seems to be due to the association of the use of money with the evils of the system of society that they wish to supersede and is in the same category of foolish sentimentality as the desire to do without machinery or without police or without clothes or other irrational associations of all the evils of society with a single instrument or aspect of it. This is attributable to insufficient understanding of the nature of the instrument and how it could be used for purposes held precious by the critic.

EQUATE FACTOR PRICE TO VALUE OF MARGINAL PRODUCT

Next comes the question of how public enterprise would go about producing most efficiently the goods that are needed in the desired proportion. One of the desirable conditions to bring about this end is to have the productive activity of society decentralized. This is to permit all the detailed decisions to be made on the spot by men who know what they are doing rather than to leave to the central planning board the impossible task of deciding everything. The managers in charge of particular production units can, to a great extent, choose between the use of different materials and different methods of production. For wise decisions of this nature it is essential to know the relative importance of the different productive resources for the rest of the economy. This knowledge would enable the manager to choose those resources which involve a smaller sacrifice in their withdrawal from alternative uses. It is impossible for the manager of every factory to know what each productive factor would be used for if he did not use it—or even whether it would be used at all rather than left unemployed. What he needs is some simple indication of the usefulness for alternative production of each of the goods that he might use. Such an indication of the alternative productivity of each factor is provided in its *price.* For this we must have *markets* for the factors in which the price equates the supply to the demand, with appropriate rules governing the demand for the factors of production by the various managers in charge of the public enterprises.

The proper rule is that each manager should *increase* the quantity of any factor (or any combination of factors) that he uses if the price of the factor is *less* than the value of the additional output that the additional quantity of the factor makes possible, and should *decrease* the quantity of any factor if its price is *greater* than the value of the decrease in output resulting from the decrease in the factor. In general the application of the rule will mean that the price of each factor will be neither greater nor less but *equal* to the value of the difference in output that a variation in the factor brings about.

If the manager follows this rule, the price paid for each factor will be equal to the value of the additional product that a unit of the factor could add to the product in any alternative use. If the price of the factor is greater than the value of the additional product that an additional unit would add to any manager's output, the rule enjoins him from using another unit of the factor and this is good because if he did he would bring about a loss of output elsewhere that is valued more highly than the increase in his own product. An additional dollar's worth of what he is producing would entail the loss of more than a dollar's worth of some alternative product and that would be socially wasteful.

On the other hand, if the price of the factor is less than the value of what it adds to the manager's output, the rule says he should use more of the factor (and produce more of the product) until this situation has been changed. In this case a dollar's worth of the factor, the use of which involves a decrease in alternative uses of a dollar's worth of some alternative product, is able to add *more* than a dollar's worth of product for the manager under discussion so that there is a net social benefit in taking some of the factor from the alternative use and using more of it here.

An understanding of the nature and working of our rule for governing the amount of any factor to be used by each manager of production is essential for the clarification of the issue between private and public enterprise.

If the criterion by which we judge collectivist and private enterprise is solely the efficiency in the use of society's resources in satisfying the needs of the individual members of society, the crucial test must be the degree to which either method approximates the ideal just described. If the value of the marginal product[2] of any one factor is the same in every use, either because the *rule* we have promulgated is accurately adhered to by all the managers in a public-enterprise economy or as a result of some other method (and we shall see that there are other ways in which it can be brought about), then social production is as efficient as it is possible to make it with available resources and managerial knowledge and skills. It is then impossible to increase the product by shifting resources between different uses or by changes in the technique or organization of production.

It should be noted that this involves a procedure which looks very improper to anyone who automatically transfers to the management of public enterprise the concepts of accounting and sound business that are proper for private enterprise but they have no necessary relevance for public enterprise. The application of the rule for extending the use of every factor of production up to the point where the value of the marginal product is no greater than the price of the factor can have the result of extending the output of a unit of production not only beyond the point of maximum profit, but also beyond the point where total costs are just covered by total revenue.

[2] The marginal product of a factor is defined as the amount by which the output is increased or decreased by adding or subtracting a unit of the factor.

PRICE EQUALS AVERAGE COST

The point of maximum profit is easily abandoned as not necessarily in the *social* interest, but the rule's complete disregard of whether there are any profits or even losses goes much more against the grain. Many socialists have indeed been so much influenced by the principles of making ends meet, or of not operating at a loss, that they have proposed, instead of the rule which we have seen to be essential for efficiency, a rule for extending production to the point where price is equal to *average* cost. This would eliminate both profits and losses, and if generally applied might be an improvement insofar as it meant that monopolistic restrictions on production, where they had been successful in bringing about profits to the monopolist, would be prevented. But this would merely be an accidental and only partial correction of a socially uneconomic use of resources that our rule eliminates completely.

The alternative rule of making the *average* cost equal to the price of product will not correct monopolistic restriction of output below the socially desirable if it is applied to profits that arise for reasons other than monopoly. For example, if the coal industry is nationalized (any compensation for the owners of the mines being taken out of the general funds of society) and the mines are then operated up to the level of output at which the price of coal is equal to the average cost in the industry as a whole including the low-cost and high-cost mines, then the marginal cost[3] of producing coal will be greater than the price. In other words, the marginal product of labor and other resources applied to coal production will be less than the price of these factors. This is wasteful because it means that a dollar's worth of these resources (which are worth a dollar because they could produce a dollar's worth of some product other than coal) adds less than a dollar's worth of coal. It would be better if such resources were used to produce the other products instead. The consuming public would be better served. It is only if the value of the marginal product of each factor is the same in every use to which it is put that the most effective use is made of the resources of society.

These examples may have given the impression that following the rule increases the efficiency of the economy only by causing

[3] Marginal cost is defined as the extra cost of producing an additional unit of a product.

shifts between different products—there being always less of one product for the sake of producing more of another product, the latter being considered preferable because the consumers offer to pay a higher price for it. If this were all, it might be possible for one who did not care for the judgment of consumers as to what they prefer to pooh-pooh the rule as an attempt to maximize something that is only subjective and largely the product of taste-creating advertisements. But the usefulness of the rule is by no means limited to this improvement of the nature of output as judged by the consumers, by giving them more of something they value higher instead of something they value less highly. Only about a tenth or fifteenth of the total output of industry is of this nature. The great majority of products are sold to producers and in this case the gain from following the rule will mean that the manufacturer will be able to get something for which he is willing to pay more instead of something for which he is only willing to pay a smaller amount. He is willing to pay more for one product rather than another only because he is able to add more to his own output with it than with the alternative. This means that there is a net increase in output from the proper use of the rule. The gain is *objective* in the sense that it does not depend on our acceptance of the choice of the consumer but can be directly measured in a greater output of the same product. A large part of the greater efficiency of capitalist production as contrasted with the modes of production of pre-capitalist times is due to such consideration of the *prices* of factors by manufacturers in deciding whether to use one factor rather than another or in deciding whether to use a method which uses one set of factors instead of a method which uses another set of factors.

WAGE EQUALS VALUE OF MARGINAL PRODUCT

Another implication of the rule is that the factors of production are paid the value of their marginal product. This is important in determining the ideal intensity and the length of labor insofar as the laborer is able to choose how much he shall work. His wage being equal to the value of his marginal product (which is what he contributes to society by working the additional hour) he will work the additional hour if the contribution to society is valued more highly than his leisure and he will not work the additional hour if the leisure is valued more highly than the product.

A payment for labor that is not equal to the value of the laborer's marginal product will result in either more work or less work than is socially most desirable. If the wage is less than the value of the marginal product, the worker will be induced to work less than is socially desirable. He will refuse to work an additional hour for a dollar as soon as he reaches the point where an hour's leisure is worth more than a dollar to him. This is wasteful if the value of the marginal product is more than a dollar—say two dollars. If he had been paid something between a dollar and two dollars, he would have worked and both he and the consumer who is willing to pay two dollars for the product would have been better off. There is a corresponding social loss if the relationship is the other way. A wage greater than the value of the marginal product will have the effect of inducing the worker to work an additional hour even though he would, for the sake of the leisure, have been willing to forego more money than is sufficient to compensate the consumer for the product that would not then be produced.

Paying for work at a rate equal to the value of the marginal product is the ideal *intensity* of reward. It makes the private benefit from an additional unit of work exactly equal to the social benefit yielded by the product of the work, so that the individual, although he is concerned only with maximizing his own welfare, is under these conditions induced to work just as much as is in the general social interest. This again satisfies the most fundamental principle of successful social organization—to make everybody, while acting in his own interest, do just that which is in the social interest and to do neither too much nor too little of it.

[7]

Marginal Cost Pricing in the 1930's

By ABBA P. LERNER*

I have to treat this assignment as a chapter for my autobiography, since I cannot separate it from the beginning of my interest in economics.

My first contact with economics was the introductory lecture of a course in economics in evening classes offered by the London County Council in the East End of London in 1919. The lecturer was a young man from Cambridge who spent the whole hour telling us how wonderful was a certain Professor Alfred Marshall. I did not believe anyone could be as wonderful as all that and I did not continue with the course or have any further contact with economics until I went to the London School of Economics exactly ten years later.

I came to the London School of Economics *(LSE)* as a socialist, with Marxist inclinations and with some rather grandiose notions of turning bourgeois economics to socialist use. I could not yet have been cured of my first vision of the Russian Revolution as the emancipation of man from subservience to money, the root of all evil, since I remember being utterly confused when Professor Postan showed me a letter from a Russian professor who had been sent to Siberia for bourgeoise deviations in his writings in ichthyology. I could not believe that Postan was lying, or that he had been deceived. On the other hand I was not ready to believe that Russia had become such an insane tyranny, so that for quite a while this remained an "unsolved puzzle."

I fell in with a group of revolutionary socialists at the school, finding great enlightenment in the idea of The Class Struggle, until I decided that although explaining the world in terms of two classes was an improvement on supposing perfect harmony and community of interests, a closer approximation to the real world was obtainable by considering more than two interest groups. In this escape from the Marxian duality I was helped by observing in a fellow Marxist, a convert from some Christian fundamentalism, a horror at something I had said which he saw as an incredibly heretical departure from "belief in" the class struggle. But my full emancipation may have come much later. Indeed I remember meeting Max Radin in Berkeley in 1938 when he teased me on having flirted with the Fourth International instead of sticking with the democratic Second International, and I provided him with a surprisingly durable source of amusement by telling him that it was because I had learned to count beyond two.

My own shift of interest from the Third to the Fourth International, from Communism to Trotzkyism, occurred in 1931. (I say shift of interest rather than conversion, because, although there was a period in which the class struggle seemed to me a useful abstraction, I was never able to accept either the labor theory of value or dialectical materialism.) In 1931, a communist fellow student, who was proficient in Russian, had come back from a tour of the Ukraine as a translator and reported the impending mass starvation imposed on the peasants by the forced grain collections. For this he was denounced as a Trotzkyist and he then indeed became one, and I became a Trotzkyist "fellow traveller."

Before I began my studies at *LSE,* a friend who had been there for a year or two, got me to read a couple of books to prepare for *LSE.* I remember being quite impressed with the idea of consumer's surplus, and that he tried, unsuccessfully, to persuade me that it was not a good idea at all. It was apparently looked down upon at *LSE.* I had also read Henry George, and found him quite impressive, both on free trade and on "the single tax" on land values, and had been completely taken in by Veblen as the only man who dared bring scientific method to social

*Queens College, City University of New York.

problems. I was thus greatly puzzled by the amusement displayed by John R. Hicks, who was my tutor in the first year, when I told him what I had read in economics.

At the end of my first year I sat down to consider what I had learned during the year. While my wife was complaining that all she ever heard when I was talking with my friends was "equilibrium," it seemed to me that the only thing I had learned was the idea of "marginal." I was quite depressed. It seemed to me that I should have learned that in a few hours at the most. But since then I have come to wish that more of my students would be able to master the concept of "marginal" properly by the time they sat for their bachelor's degree.

This brings me to the topic of my paper. I became a rabid marginalist, fanatically enthusiastic about the principle that economic efficiency, which is, of course, socially desirable, required every product price to be equal to the marginal cost (more strictly to the value of the additional factors required to produce an additional unit of the product where this is equal to the value of the alternative products sacrificed).

I remember reaching the conclusion that retail stores should charge the marginal cost of making each sale, and since it took the salesman no more time to sell a larger quantity than a smaller quantity, the addition to the cost of the material should be the same, so that the total price would be less per unit the greater the amount bought. I toyed with the idea of approximating this by having the shops sell everything at cost, and charge the customer a fee for entering the shop, which would pay for the provision of the retailing services, and with similar extensions of the marginal cost pricing principle. My fellow socialists were outraged at such devices, which would penalize the poor, and I was forced prematurely to the conviction that what was wrong with the poor was not the prices they have to pay but that they had too little money—that the solution of poverty lay not with the manipulation of prices but with the distribution of money income.

My enthusiasm for marginalism did not at first have any special connection with socialism or with socialist pricing. It first was directed to the social inefficiency of monopoly in raising price above marginal cost and thus interfering with my newly discovered Invisible Hand and its promise of economic efficiency. I had many arguments with those who, in objecting to the monopolist charging more than the *average* cost, seemed to me to be carried away by anger at (or perhaps jealousy of) the profits enjoyed by rich monopolists, or by deep concern at the exploitation of the poor customers who had to pay his exorbitant prices. To me these seemed irrelevant and sentimental interferences with the economist's job of avoiding the waste, the misallocation of resources, from prices above or below the marginal cost. Anger or jealousy about the receiver of the "monopoly profits" and concern about the exploitation of customers who had to pay the monopoly prices, obscured the economics. They distracted attention from efficient versus inefficient use of resources, to the quite different problem of some people being richer and some poorer than one would like them to be. Here too I felt that the issue was one of the distribution, or perhaps the redistribution, of *money,* and furthermore, it was not really the redistribution between monopolistic sellers and the "exploited" buyers of such goods, but between rich and poor. It was perfectly possible for "exploiting" monopolists to be poorer than "exploited" customers. Once more I was led to the conclusion that excessive wealth and excessive poverty were matters concerning not the prices of commodities but the distribution of income and wealth.

It seems obvious that socialist societies must be just as concerned with economic efficiency as capitalist societies, or at least that economists, concerned with efficiency, must see that efficiency is a matter of importance for both forms of social organization. But I do not think I thought of marginal cost pricing as particularly relevant to socialism until I found myself in debate with socialists who objected to the view that socialist societies should make use of this principle.

I had an exchange of articles with Maurice Dobb who seemed to believe, at the time, that pricing of any kind was inconsistent with the rational planning of the economy in physical terms which would be possible when capitalism had been replaced by socialism, so that neither marginal cost nor average cost had any place in socialism.

Durbin and Dickinson and a number of others argued in favor of socialist societies charging the average cost. I remember especially having long discussions on this with Dickinson at a meeting of English economists in Oxford. It seemed to me (naturally) that all the logic was on my side, and that only irrelevant arguments were put forward against marginal cost pricing in a socialist society. These stressed such issues as the difficulty of figuring the marginal cost, while the average cost could easily be reached (after the event). One only had to divide what had turned out to be the total cost by the number of units sold. Sometimes they dwelt on the difficulties of distinguishing between long-run and short-run marginal cost.

I cannot here go into the details of these objections to marginal cost pricing and their refutation. I came away from these discussions with the feeling that the widespread popularity of average cost pricing had two different causes. One was a failure to distinguish between the concept of perfect competition, a *means* for achieving economic efficiency that is possible under some circumstances, and economic efficiency itself as the *end* which perfect competition could serve. Price equal to average cost, one of the results of perfect competition, was mistakenly assumed to be the condition necessary for economic efficiency. The other and more important cause of addiction to average cost pricing was a happy point of coincidence of certain elements in the basic prejudices of sentimental socialists and sentimental capitalists. The socialists felt that profit was immoral and even wicked, so that they could not accept any policy that permitted price to be above average cost and thus gave rise to the objectionable phenomenon of profits. The capitalists felt that losing money must mean that something is basically wrong, since the natural purpose of economic activity is to *make* money. Furthermore they objected strongly to the subsidies that would have to be provided where marginal cost pricing would make the price less than the average cost, and to the taxes that would be necessary to pay for the subsidies. Average cost pricing thus formed a happy meeting ground in which the capitalist and the socialist sentimental prejudices could coexist with the minimum of friction.

It was at this stage that Oscar Lange came to London and wrote an article on market socialism for the *Review of Economic Studies,* of which I was the managing editor. He laid down the same principle of charging the marginal cost for everything, and I was of course delighted to have this article in the *Review,* as were all the other editors. But Lange got caught in the puzzle of what to do if the sum of the marginal costs did not add up to the total cost, which would be bound to happen unless the marginal costs, on the average, happened to be just equal to the average cost.

Lange's solution was to make a compensating adjustment to the wage, multiplying the price paid for labor by a bonus proportional to the wage, which made the pay greater than the marginal cost by just enough to absorb the surplus.

My contribution was to point out that this would be a departure from the efficiency principle. The surplus could be distributed in any way whatsoever that seemed good to the authorities, provided it was *not* related to the wage. Relating it positively to the wage would not only discriminate in favor of those who already had a higher wage, aggravating the inequality of income regrettably required for economic efficiency, but would also cause a departure from the efficient use of resources. Lange quickly saw my point and accepted the correction.

Strangely enough, on rereading my article, I find it repeating the very error in Lange's article which I was correcting. I speak of the principle of having prices of products *proportional* to marginal cost as a sufficient condition for efficiency in the allocation of resources between the production of different products. If the price of a product is, say, twice the marginal cost, all is still well if the price of the product is also twice the marginal cost in all the alternative uses of the factors. If $2 is the price of a product whose marginal cost is $1, the resources set free by producing one unit less of this product could be used to produce two dollars worth of other products (with a marginal cost of $1). One could say that the *social* marginal cost is really $2, the value of the alternative product or products that had to be sacrificed to make possible the production of two dollars worth of *this* product. The $1 is the *private* and not the *social* cost. Distributing the surplus *in proportion* to the wage, as initially proposed by Lange would still leave price *proportional* to marginal *private* cost and equal to marginal *social* cost. I was thus doing exactly what I was criticizing Lange for doing, even while successfully persuading him that he was wrong!

The trouble with Lange's original rule, as well as with the formulation in my "correction" of his rule, was that the rule cannot be applied universally in all the other uses of the factors. The use of labor time for leisure, for "do it yourself" or for private exchange of services with a friend or neighbor made the private marginal cost *equal* to the price or value of the product, so that universal *proportionality* of marginal cost to price could be attained only by the special proportionality of *equality* of price and marginal cost.

This more satisfactory formulation was not developed until later. (It is in my *Economics of Control,* published in 1944, twelve years after I had started working on it.) Nevertheless, the agreement between Lange and myself on the necessity of having the wage *equal* to and not merely *proportional* to the marginal product, shows that although my formulation was faulty our understanding of the issues was correct.

It somehow seemed natural, both to Lange and to myself, in those days, to suppose that the revenues from the sale of all products at marginal cost would exceed the total cost, i.e., that in general the marginal cost would be above the average cost. There would then be a surplus available which I later (in my *Economics of Control*) called a "social dividend" to be distributed equally among the whole population as the simplest and most efficient way of alleviating poverty or increasing equality. We did not anticipate the growth that has taken place in government spending on armaments and on much more complicated and much less efficient ways of helping the poor and various other groups disguised as deserving poor. (I have never been able to understand the scorn poured by Marxists on Bernard Shaw's insistence of equality as the essence of the socialist ideal.) More recently it has received much publicity as Milton Friedman's "negative income tax."

In my gropings toward the maximum social benefits to be derived from marginalism I had originally given practically no attention to administrative problems, and had almost automatically pictured socialist society as some sort of universal government enterprise which would instruct all the managers, who would be government employees, to follow the marginal cost pricing principle. I remember being surprised by Lange's acceptance of naturally small private enterprises, "farmers and barbers," as perfectly compatible with socialism. I had never thought of this but found it immediately acceptable. In general it seems to me that no disagreement between Lange and myself on economic theory ever survived an hour's discussion, although I understand that many economists have written on differences between our approaches of which I am quite unaware.

Perhaps marginalism has continued to be my hangup, but I still feel that this principle is not fully exploited by many modern economists. The egalitarianism behind the suggested equal division of Lange's excess of average price over average marginal wage cost, my "social dividend" or Friedman's negative income tax, I see *economically* justified as a more efficient way of using income to provide satisfaction to individuals. It is based on my assumption that other people, like myself, have their well-being increased by having more income, and that, like myself, they experience diminishing marginal utility of income as a result of some element of rationality in their use of their income. They quite often choose to spend their money on what they find *more* rather than *less* satisfying, so that an additional dollar means less to a man when he is richer if he can spend it only on the less satisfying goods he avoids buying when he is poorer. In the absence of knowledge of the *absolute level* of the satisfaction of others, the best way of distributing the surplus (over what is necessary to induce the production of the income) is to divide it equally. This is how my learning some economics at *LSE* gave a rational meaning to my egalitarian impulses.

The empathy that makes me attribute utility, rationality and diminishing marginal utility, to individuals other than myself does not extend to society. I do not attribute to society either a level of utility or a diminsihing marginal utility of income. While an individual's preferences can indeed be considered as an *ordering* of social states, I see no reason for assuming that social decisions involve a social ordering. This assumption seems to me very much like the assumption that statisticians used to make that index numbers ought to behave just like natural numbers and conform to the reversal test, so that Paasche and Laspeyres would have to be identical.

Thus when Kenneth Arrow says that "the outcome of a social choice procedure (whatever you call it) is an ordering," I get lost. I would think that the outcome of a social choice procedure would be not an ordering but a *choice*—a choice of a social policy. This choice will, of course, result in social states which some individuals will look forward to with hope, and some with dread.

What I find much more important than the, to me idle, talk of social orderings is that the restriction of *individual* preferences to *orderings* constitutes a flight from marginalism. The various invariances of individual orderings with respect to monotonic transformations, only serve to banish the assumption that others, like myself, have diminishing marginal utility of income, and destroys the rational basis for egalitarianism as efficiency.

But egalitarian impulses will out. Other rationalizations are sought, and this has led to a plethora of other, or apparently other, reasons for advocating the egalitarian distribution of surplus. Rawls finds it in fairness and/or justice. His "original state" allegory is certainly a most dramatic way of saying "let us not be biased," but in his "maximin" principle I see no basis (in spite of his denials) other than the assumption of diminishing marginal utility of income or an infinite risk aversion, or perhaps both.

Arrow and Amartya Sen find it in *"equity."* I have just had some intensive discussion on this subject with Sen. He rejects the utilitarianism on which I base my case for the equal distribution of surplus. Instead he turns to equity (or, more modestly, to his "weak equity principle") aimed not at maximizing utility but at *equalizing* it. He would always, therefore, advocate the transfer of "some" income from happier to less happy individuals, irrespective of their income. The "some," I think, betrays Sen's discomfort at having to take income from a happy poor person and give it to a miserable rich person, even if the loss to the former is greater than the gain to the latter. (You would presumably know if this was the case if you knew which was the happier and which the more miserable.) I see neither the possibility nor any desirability in equalizing the utility levels of different individuals, nor indeed of any or "some" movements in that direction.

Arrow's equity principle seem to come to the same thing as Sen's. I see in both a retreat from marginalism, reminiscent of the addiction of pre-Lange-Lerner socialist egalitarians to the principle of having price equated to average cost, but, of course, on a much more sophisticated level. They are forced by their abhorrence of the subjective basis for assuming individual diminishing marginal utility of income, *without comparing them,* to rest their egalitarianism on the much less defensible *comparison* of the actual levels of individual total utility.

[8]

On Optimal Taxes With an Untaxable Sector

By ABBA P. LERNER*

In the absence of externalities the optimal allocation of resources between different uses is reached by setting the prices of products at marginal (opportunity) cost—the price of the alternative product—so that the consumers' demand will cause that alternative to be produced which they prefer to consume.

I

If for any reason more money must be collected from the public, the optimal allocation of resources will be preserved if the money is raised by "ideal" taxes, namely taxes which do not entail social damage by inducing resources to be shifted to less urgently desired purposes for the sake of avoiding the taxes. Such ideal and "unavoidable" taxes are (1) a "lump sum" tax and (2) a uniform tax on all uses of resources. A lump sum tax makes shifting irrelevant, and a uniform and universal tax cannot be avoided by shifting since the same tax is waiting wherever the resources are shifted. Lump sum taxes being impractical or perhaps impossible, this gives us *the first rule* of ideal taxation: Maintain the *proportionality* of price to marginal cost by having a uniform *tax rate* on all uses of resources by means of an ad valorem tax on *all* final output. *Equalize* T/MC, the ratio of the *tax* to the *marginal cost*. This would *eliminate* or prevent any social damage and the outcome would be Pareto optimal.

But it is no more possible to tax *all* final outputs than to have lump sum taxes. Some uses of resources, like leisure, do it yourself, or undeclared mutual services, are *untaxable*, and it will not do to tax only *some* of the outputs proportionately. We are therefore left with the question: How should *taxable* uses be taxed?[1]

The first category to be chosen for taxation consists of items with completely inelastic demand or completely inelastic supply. This works like a lump sum tax since there is no elasticity of output with respect to the tax and no shifting at all.

If enough money cannot be raised in this way (because as tax rates are increased, output must be affected—i.e., some "tax elasticity of output" emerges), taxes will have to be imposed where there is some tax

* University of California, Berkeley. This paper was inspired by the article by Professors William J. Baumol and David F. Bradford in this issue, and gained very much from correspondence with them. It also benefited from discussion with my colleagues George Akerlof and Avinash Dixit, and would have benefited still more if I had listened to them more carefully.

[1] The treatment of this question constituted a significant part of my contribution to the "Lange-Lerner" socialist economics. It took the form of rejecting a proportional *negative* tax (social dividend). "Dr. Lange declares that the social dividend must be distributed as a percentage on the wage rate if it is not to interfere with the ideal distribution of labour between different occupations (p. 21). This seems to me to be an error . . . If the social dividend is made proportional to the wage, there will be an undue attraction of workers to the occupation with the greater wage on account of the greater social dividend obtainable there in addition to the greater wage" (Lerner, 1936 p. 73). The issue is also dealt with in *The Economics of Control*, ch. 9 "Equality and Proportionality" pp. 96–105, where the headlines read: "Making price *proportional* instead of equal to marginal cost was believed to be enough . . . but proportionality cannot be universal unless it is really equality. . . . This is illustrated in the allocation of labor power between labor and leisure."

elasticity, and therefore some shifting of resources and some social loss. The taxation should then be concentrated where the tax elasticity is least since that is where the shifting is least.

T, the *tax* per unit, will be equal to $P-MC$, the excess of P, the *price* of the product, over MC, its *marginal cost*. But if P measures the marginal utility of the product to the consumer and MC measures the marginal disutility of producing it (basically the marginal utility of the alternative product foregone), then $P-MC$, or T, will also be the measure of MSD, the *marginal social damage* per unit reduction of this output and the consequent shifting of resources to the alternative use. If the total social loss (from a given amount of tax revenue to be collected) is to be minimized, the ratio between the extra damage due to, and the extra revenue collected by, a marginal tax increase must be the same everywhere. Otherwise a shift of taxation could increase tax revenue even while reducing the social damage. This gives us a *second rule* of ideal taxation: Adjust the tax rates on the different items so as to *equalize* T/MTR (where MTR is the *marginal tax revenue* from that tax increase which reduces output by one unit). This would not eliminate, or prevent, social damage but would *minimize* it and the outcome would be a "quasi-optimal" second-best solution of the problem.

The equalization of T/MTR implies the equalization of $T/(T-MTR)$. Since T, the tax per unit, is also ATR, the *average tax revenue*, this also implies the equalization of $ATR/(ATR-MTR)$. But average tax revenue over average *minus* marginal tax revenue is nothing but the elasticity of output with respect to the tax or the *tax elasticity*. The second rule may, therefore, also be expressed as: *Equalize the tax elasticities*. This form of the second rule may be seen as the result of concentrating the taxation where the tax elasticity is least, since any inequality of tax elasticity would be removed by shifting taxation from where the elasticity is greater to where it is less.

II

It must be recognized, however, that only if the shifting of resources is from the taxed sector to an untaxed sector of the economy does MC measure the usefulness of the alternative product, and only in that case is T or $(P-MC)$ equal to MSD. Equalizing tax elasticities (in equalizing T/MTR) thus minimizes only that part of the social damage which is due to the shifting of resources from the taxed sector to the untaxed sector. But equalizing the tax elasticities for different items with different demand elasticities and different supply elasticities involves *different tax rates*. These different tax rates will bring about a faulty allocation of resources between the different activities *within* the taxed sector. The loss from *this* misallocation of resources would be not merely minimized but *eliminated* by following not the second rule but the first rule, i.e., by equalizing not T/MTR but T/MC.

Thus we see that the second rule is appropriate where the shifting is only from a taxed to an untaxed sector, while the first rule is appropriate where the shifting is only to another part of the taxed sector (as would be the case if all uses of resources could be, and were, taxed).

What we need is a rule that is applicable whether the resources shifted by a tax remain in a taxed sector or go to the untaxed sector or are divided between the two sectors. For this we can use a more general rule that encompasses both the first rule and the second rule: *Let the tax on each use of resources be equal to the tax on the alternative use*. There will then be no incentive to shift any resources to another (and inferior) use so as to avoid the tax. This would not merely minimize any social damage from the taxation, it would *eliminate* it and the outcome would be Pareto optimal.

III

To be able to apply this more general rule, we would have to know in each case what the alternative use is and what taxes would fall on this alternative use. If the alternative use is entirely in the untaxable sector of the economy, the item in question should not be taxed either. It must be assimilated to the untaxable sector in a larger *untaxed* sector, reducing the taxable sector to a smaller *taxed* sector. On the other hand, if the alternative use is entirely in the taxed sector, the tax must be the same as in the alternative use. The two uses should be assimilated and considered as a single industry for our present purpose.

If there are only these two possibilities, then the required tax revenue should be raised by a uniform ad valorem tax on all sales in the taxed sector. Indeed, in such a case, a whole of the taxed sector can be considered as a single assimilated industry with absolutely inelastic demand or absolutely inelastic supply. No resources can be shifted out of it, and the tax is "unavoidable" and ideal, just like a lump sum tax.

But these two are not the only possibilities. There will be items from which only a *fraction* of the resources shifted will go to other parts of the taxed sector, the rest going to the untaxed sector. On such an item, if it were the only one of its kind, the ideal tax is this fraction of the otherwise *uniform* tax just mentioned, since that would be the amount of the tax on the alternative use of the resources. But the existence of such items means that there must exist sectors with various *lower* tax rates. The ideal tax for each good would, therefore, have to be adjusted further to allow for the different fractions of the shifted resources which would go to various sectors subject to different tax rates.[2,3]

IV

It would not seem possible to work out all these complications. They could be avoided if we could consider only the damage due to the shifting of resources from the taxed sector to the untaxed sector of the economy, neglecting the damage caused by the shifting of resources between the different parts of the taxed sector taxed at different rates. In that case we could simply apply *the second rule:* Equalize T/MTR. But the second rule is appropriate only if there is no substitutability, either in consumption or in production, between the different taxed items taxed at different rates, or if only a small sector of the economy is to be taxed (possibly because only a small sector is technically taxable) so that the shifting of resources among the different parts of the taxed sector can be considered small enough to be neglected, the bulk of the shifting being from the taxed to the untaxed sector of the economy.

The complications could also be avoided if we could do the opposite and consider only the social damage due to the shifting of resources between the different parts of the taxed sector, neglecting the social damage caused by the shifting of resources from the taxed to the untaxed sector. In that case we could simply apply *the first rule:* Equalize T/MC. But the first rule is appropriate only if there is no substitutability, either in consumption or in produc-

[2] My colleague Avinash Dixit has developed a mathematical formula which seems to correspond to such an application of the more general rule!

[3] It should be noted that one of the results of this would be that the tax rate would be lower the greater the degree to which it would cause resources to be shifted from the taxed to the untaxed sector, both directly and indirectly (i.e. via being shifted to other parts of the taxed sector which are being taxed at a lower rate because more of *their* resources are shiftable, directly or indirectly, to the untaxed sector, etc.).

tion, between the taxed and the untaxed sectors, or if the untaxed sector is very small so that the shifting of resources from the taxed to the untaxed sector can be considered small enough to be neglected. Where there is significant substitution both between the two sectors as well as between the different parts of the taxed sector, neither rule can be ignored and we cannot bypass the complications. A simplifying compromise must then be sought between the two conflicting rules.

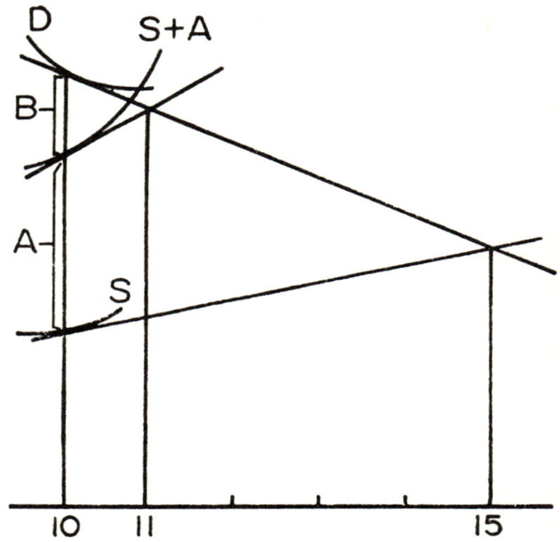

FIGURE 1

V

Such a compromise could be based on the simplifying assumption that all resources shifted by a tax would be divided between the taxed and the untaxed sectors in proportion to their size; i.e., if the taxed sector is twice as big as the untaxed sector, twice as much of any shifted resources would go to other parts of the taxed sector as would go to the untaxed sector.

On this assumption the proportions of the revenue raised in accordance with the two different rules should be in proportion to the relative size of the taxed and the untaxed sectors of the economy. Thus if the taxed sector is twice as great as the untaxed sector, two-thirds of the required revenue should be raised by tax *A*, a uniform proportional tax on marginal cost, and one-third of it by a non-uniform tax *B*, concentrated where the tax *B* elasticities are least so as to equalize these for the different taxed items. (The imposition of each tax would of course reduce the revenue from the other tax, and if this had not been taken into account the tax rate would have to be recalculated.)

The combination of the two taxes, since it leaves the *B* tax elasticities equalized, looks something like the abandonment of our first rule in favor of the second. But this is not so. It is only the *B tax elasticities* that are equalized, not the overall tax elasticities. Only in the limiting case where *all* shifted resources go to the untaxed sector does tax *A* disappear. The formula then degenerates into the second rule. In the converse limiting case, where none of the shifted resources would go to the un-

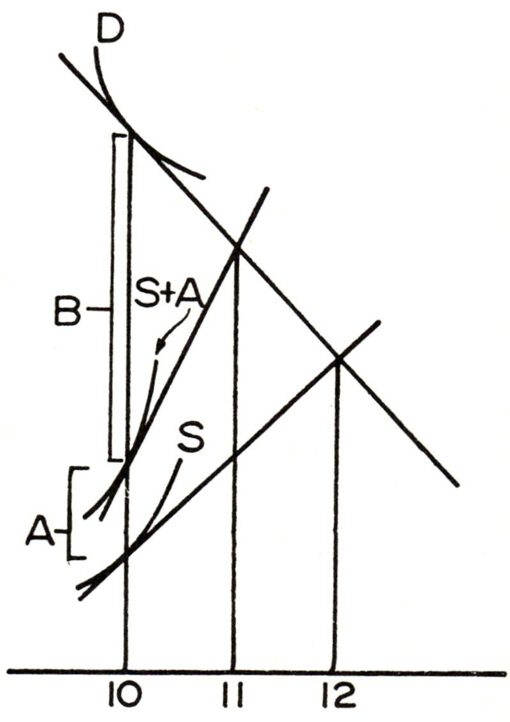

FIGURE 2

taxed sector, tax *B* disappears and the formula degenerates into the first rule.

Figures 1 and 2 show the tangents to the demand curves (*D*), to the supply curves (*S*) and to the supply-plus-tax-*A* curves ($S+A$), at the equilibrium output of 10 units. In both figures tax *A* is 100 percent on marginal cost (supply) and the *B* tax elasticities are 1/10 in each case. The overall tax elasticities, however, which would have been equalized by the application of the second rule, are 5/10 and 2/10, or $\frac{1}{2}$ and $\frac{1}{5}$, respectively.

Appendix

1. "*The Mislaid Maxim*"

In their article, "Optimal Departures from Marginal Cost Pricing," Baumol and Bradford (hereafter referred to as BB) survey the literature on the subject and rediscover in it a "mislaid maxim" which seems to me to overemphasize somewhat the departures from the principle of marginal cost pricing, as in their conclusion that "Generally prices which deviate in a systematic manner from marginal cost pricing will be required for an optimal allocation of resources." The mislaid maxim consists of a "basic theorem" which "has been stated in a number of different ways . . ." and which BB summarize in four different variants.

1) If prices are quasi-optimal the ratio between the marginal profit yields of unit changes in the *prices* of any two goods will be equal to the ratio between their output levels.

2) For each product, the deviation of the quasi-optimal price from marginal cost must be proportionate to the difference between the product's marginal cost and marginal revenue (i.e., its marginal social welfare cost must be proportionate to its marginal contribution to the profit requirement). This result holds only in the case where cross-elasticities are all zero.

3) For each product, the percentage deviation of quasi-optimal price from marginal cost must be inversely proportionate to its price elasticity of demand. This result also holds only where cross-elasticities of demand are zero.

4) Quasi-optimal prices must yield outputs that deviate by (approximately) the same proportion from those which would result from pricing at the marginal costs corresponding to the quasi-optimal output levels.

Of the four variants of the "mislaid maxim" the first, which requires "that the ratio between the marginal profit yields of unit changes in the prices of any two goods be equal to the ratio between their output levels," is derived by BB from a concern not with the *social damage* but with the *consumer's loss* from having to pay a higher price (which loss, for a unit increase in price, is identical with the output level). This loss, it should be noted, is still there even if the demand is absolutely inelastic, though the tax is then "unavoidable," equivalent to a lump sum tax, and causes no shifting of resources and *no social damage* at all.

Nevertheless, with the assumption of a constant *MC* or supply curve (which would be the case if we let the prices of all inputs supplied in the economy be fixed, and let competition eliminate economies and diseconomies of scale), it can easily be shown to follow from our second rule. If we so choose the (arbitrary) size of the units in which the output is measured as to make the tax rate per unit the same for both goods, equal *absolute* increases in *P*, will constitute equal *proportional* changes in *T*. With the tax elasticities the same (our second rule), *equal absolute* increases in *P* (since they constitute *equiproportional* increases in *T*) will be accompanied by *equiproportional* decreases in output. If the output of one of the goods was three times as great as that of the other before the increase in *P*, it will still be three times as great after the increase in *P*, and the yield in profit (or tax revenue) from a unit increase in price (or tax) would also be three times as great, thus satisfying the required proportionality between marginal yield and level of output.

This is shown in Figure 3 where *OR* measures the normalized *T*. The increase in revenue from the increase in price per unit is shown in the horizontal rectangle RD, the loss in revenue from the reduction of output is shown by the vertical rectangle CD and the marginal profit yield from the price increase by the difference $RD-CD$. If the output of the other good, with the demand curve P^*, is three times as great, the corresponding rectangles will also be three times as great. RD^* has the same thickness as RD but is three times as long, and C^*D^* has the same height as CD but is three times as wide since the demand curve P^* is three times as flat. The marginal profit yield, $RD^*-C^*D^*$, will therefore also be three times as large and proportional to the three times larger output level.

The equalization of the ratio between the marginal tax yield and the output level seems to have no economic meaning. It is therefore somewhat strange that the formula should give the right answer. The explanation of the paradox is that an economically meaningful relationship is hidden within it.

The proportionality between output level (x) and marginal yield (y) derives from the proportionality between the areas of the rectangles RD and RD^*, which measure the consumers' loss (l) and the rectangles CD and C^*D^*, which measure the social damage (d). We thus have proportionality in *four* items, x, y, l, and d. The meaningful relationship, hidden behind the proportionality of x and y, is the proportionality of y and d. The equalization of the ratio between marginal yield and output level turns out to be an obscure way of expressing the equalization of marginal tax yield and marginal social damage—an equalization that minimizes the total social damage for a given total tax yield.

However, BB's first variant will be right only where there are constant costs and where all the shifting is into the untaxed sector of the economy. It can be generalized to cover increasing (or decreasing) marginal costs by substituting "taxes on" for "prices of," making it read: "that the ratio between the marginal profit yields of changes in the *taxes on* any two goods be equal to the ratio between their output levels." It then becomes equivalent to our second rule. But to deal with shifting within the taxed sector we have to turn to our first rule.

The second variant, which "calls for the deviation of [ ] price from marginal cost for each product to be proportionate to the difference between its marginal cost and its marginal revenue" is identical with the first form of our second rule (equalize T/MTR) where $T=(P-MC)$ and $MTR=(MR-MC)$ (MR [*marginal revenue*] including the marginal tax and MC excluding it).

The third variant requires that "for each product the percentage deviation of [ ] price from marginal cost must be inversely proportional to its price elasticity of demand." Like the first, it can be derived from our second rule in combination with the assumption of constant marginal cost. If the marginal cost is constant, our second rule (Equalize the tax elasticities) is equivalent to making the tax rate inversely proportional to the elasticity of demand. This is shown in Figure 3. Taking the horizontal MC curve beginning at 0 as the base, the height of the P (or demand) curve above the MC (or supply) curve measures T (the tax per unit). At point D this will be equal to CD. The tangent of the demand curve at D (AB'') shows us that

$$e_T \text{ (the tax elasticity)} = BD/DA$$

If the base line from which P (the price, including the tax) is measured is OB' or $O''B''$, for two different goods, then

$$e_D \text{ (the elasticity of demand)} = B'D/DA \quad \text{or} \quad B''D/DA$$

$$T/P \text{ (the \textit{tax rate})} = \frac{CD}{C'D} \quad \text{or} \quad \frac{CD}{C''D} = \frac{BD}{B'D} \quad \text{or} \quad \frac{BD}{B''D} = \frac{BD/DA}{B'D/DA} \quad \text{or} \quad \frac{BD/DA}{B''D/DA} = \frac{e_T}{e_D}$$

Since e_T is a constant, the same for all the taxed industries, T/P, the tax rate, is inversely proportional to the elasticity of demand for the different products. (This, BB's third variant, must however be measured as a percentage of the *price* and not of the *marginal cost*—it is T/P not $T/MC[=T/(P-T)]$ that must be proportional to the elasticity of demand.) Here they pay their respects to marginal costs being "not generally constant" and point out that Ramsay, Pigou and Boiteux did take *elasticity of supply* into account.

The arguments supporting the second and third variants make use of the "simplifying assumption" that the cross-elasticities are all equal to zero. If this is taken strictly, it means that there is no shifting at all of resources to alternative (and less preferred) untaxed or more lightly taxed products. The resources set free are just those required to satisfy the requirements of the government (or there may be no resources set free at all if the purpose of the taxation was only to prevent overall excess demand inflation). It also means that the demand elasticities will all be *equal* (at unity, since if there is no change in expenditure on any other item, there cannot, with the same total income, be any change in the expenditure on "this" item). All the variants of the second rule which say the tax must be proportional to the elasticity of demand then become indistinguishable from our first rule which says that the tax must be *proportional.* Period. (The elasticity of supply has been eliminated from the picture by the assumption of constant costs.) But the situation is stranger still. *Any* tax system whatsoever is now optimal since there can in any case be no shifting and no social damage from the switching to less preferred goods for the sake of avoiding taxation.

If the assumption of zero cross-elasticities is taken to refer only to the taxed items, then any shifting of resources *within* the taxed sector is assumed away and there remains only the possibility of the shifting of resources from the taxed to the untaxed sectors of the economy. The second rule, and any variant of the maxim which implies it, then minimizes the damage from this shifting, and is quasi-optimal.

The fourth variant ". . . [ ] prices must yield outputs that deviate by (approximately) the same proportion from those which would result from pricing at the marginal costs . . . ," is more general than the first and third, as is claimed by BB, in that it does not depend on constant costs. Like the other three variants it fails to deal with the social damage from tax-induced shifting of resources within the taxed sector. It is *less* general than the other variants in that it will be true only if the supply and demand curves are straight lines (or are of exactly offsetting opposite convexities) so that the tax revenue curves (T' in Figure 3) obtained by subtracting the supply curves (vertically) from the demand curves (which would show the output corresponding to each level of tax per unit of output) are straight lines. However, if these curves are approximately straight, the result will be approximated.

2. *Constant Costs*

The assumption of constant cost, by making the elasticity of supply infinite, is responsible, in the first and third variants and in much of the literature, for an undue concentration on the elasticity of demand and for obscuring the completely symmetrical relevance of the elasticity of supply, or of the MC.[4] Thus, if the supply (or MC) curve is less than infinitely elastic (represented in Figure 3 by MC') and the demand curve is infinitely elastic (represented by the horizontal line OC^*), the tax (EC) that equalizes the tax elasticity constitutes a *tax rate* (here represented as T/MC and seen as EC/EC' or EC/EC'') inversely proportional to the elasticity of *supply* instead of to the elasticity of demand. If neither the supply curve nor the demand curve is infinitely elastic (and they are represented by P and MC' respectively) the tax (ED or SR) that equalizes the tax elasticities constitutes a *tax rate* proportional to a *combination* of the elasticity of supply and the elasticity of demand. It is equivalent to a tax rate on the buyer of $CD/C'D$ or $CD/C''D$, i.e., proportional to the inverse of the elasticity of demand, *plus* a tax rate on the seller of $EC/$

[4] This is what enables BB to be satisfied with the four variants of the second rule.

$C'E$ or $EC/C''E$, i.e., proportional to the inverse of the elasticity of supply.[5]

The assumption of constant costs is not merely a slip or a simplification. It is the result of a widespread confusion of (a) the distinction between *demand* and *supply* with (b) the distinction between *preferences* (among outputs or inputs) and the *technically given production possibilities*. The *sound* consideration that social damage from tax-avoiding shifting of resources can consist only in faulty allocation in relation to *preferences* (if only final products are taxed) is thus translated into the *unsound* conclusion that only the elasticity of *demand* is relevant.[6] This can be seen in the figure used by BB in their article where the possibility of any producers' surplus is eliminated by the assumption of constant cost. The rectangles (CK and CE_b) between the horizontal marginal cost curve CC' and the demand curve D_b represent the transfer of income from the consumer to the monopolist as monopoly revenue (or to the government as taxes) at prices P_0 and P_1. The increase in this transfer from an increase in P (or T), namely CE_b *minus* CK or P_0E_b minus R_bK, is the increase in net (monopoly or tax) revenue. Subtracting from this the part (P_0E_b) which consists of the higher price paid by the consumer on the reduced output

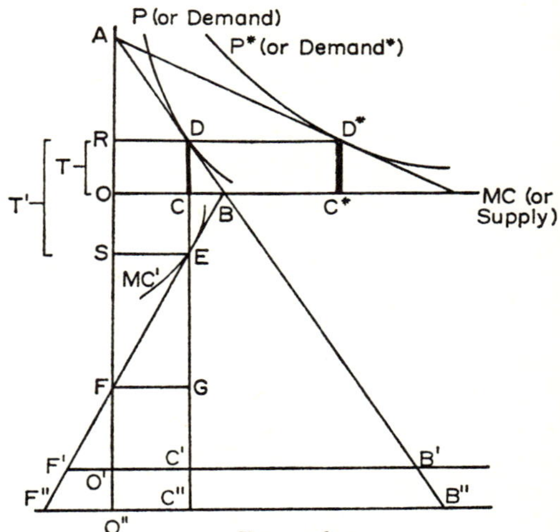

FIGURE 3

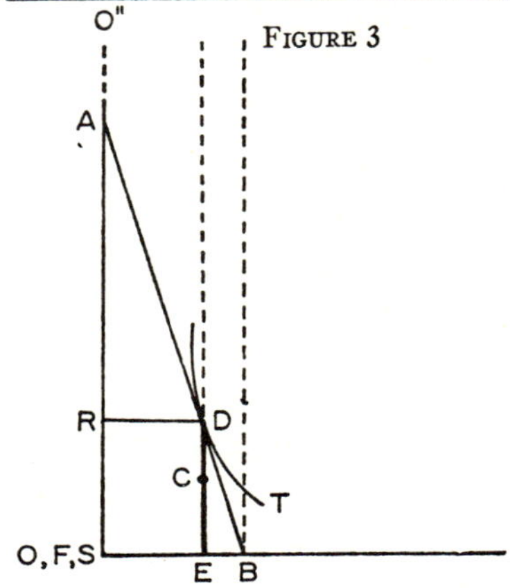

FIGURE 4

—approximately his loss of consumers' surplus—we are left with the *minus* item (R_bK) and the conclusion that "the rise in price will have caused a net reduction in net revenue *plus* consumer's surplus that is measured by the shaded area R_bRKE_b."

This conclusion is not incorrect, but it throws a very dim light on the subject. The shaded area R_bRKE_b does measure the degree to which the loss of consumer's surplus is greater than the gain in revenue, but it is not instantaneously clear that this difference is the measure of the social loss. That it is indeed the measure of the social loss can be seen directly, without reference to the loss of consumer's surplus, to the gain in (monopoly or tax) revenue, or to the difference between these, by simply noting that

[5] I am indebted to my colleague Avinash Dixit for discussions that lead to the clarification of this relationship. I am also indebted to Vladimir Simonek of the Prague School of Economics for reminding me that the neglect of the elasticity of supply would be even more troublesome in socialist societies where there is a very strong tendency to neglect the demand side rather than the supply side. Their readers would be disturbed by a diagram like Figure 3 where, at least initially, the falling demand curves are much more prominent than the rising supply curve. It might be useful, therefore, to show the tax revenue curve separately from the demand curve and more clearly as one that depends on *both* the supply and demand curves. This is done in Figure 4 where T, the tax revenue curve, is made up of the vertical distances, taken from Figure 3, between the rising marginal cost or supply curve MC' that passes through E and the falling demand curve P that passes through D. The tax per unit is ED or SR and the tax elasticity is seen directly as BD/DA.

[6] As is claimed, e.g. by Diamond and Mirrlees, p. 14, in terms of an alleged basic asymmetry between demand and supply.

the shaded area represents the social damage from the shift of resources from "here," where the value of their marginal product is between OP_0 and OP_1, to "there" where their marginal product is equal to the (constant) marginal cost OC.

3. *Inputs as Negative Outputs*

The mathematically elegant device of treating inputs as negative outputs obscures the damage caused by the shifting of resources when the tax discourages the producer rather than the consumer. The mathematician may retort that his algebra has included all these effects in his "negative outputs," but rising supply curves are not made flat by calling inputs negative outputs. That eliminates only such increasing MC as is due to diminishing utility of negative inputs (e.g. of "not working"), but it leaves such increasing MC as is due to diminishing transformability of one output into another on account of heterogeneity of productive resources.[7] The treatment of inputs as negative outputs can easily mislead one into taking the asymmetry between subjective preferences and objective production possibilities as an asymmetry between demand and supply, and thereby seduce even economists who are not allergic to consumer's surplus into disregarding such social damage as consists not of the reduction of (consumer-producer's) surplus from negative outputs but of the reduction of *rents* on intra-marginal *nonhuman* productive resources.

The lumping together of *rents* with producer's surplus from *human* inputs, and then transposing both together into consumer's surplus from negative outputs, does indeed translate all possible social damage into the destruction of consumer's surplus. But such a procedure obscures rather than brings out the asymmetry between demand and supply that is fundamentally the difference between subjective (human) preferences (between different outputs or inputs) and objective production feasibilities.

Nevertheless, a careful use of the device of treating inputs as negative outputs can serve to clarify a distinction that is perhaps more fundamental than that between consumer's surplus and producer's surplus. This is the distinction between (a) the social damage from taxation in inducing *subjectively inferior consumption* (including the provision of such inputs, treated as negative outputs, as are regarded as inferior to, i.e. more objectionable than, alternative inputs) and (b) the social damage from taxation in inducing *objectively inferior production* (the use of inputs, between which there are no human preferences, to produce a less valuable output).

The first kind of social damage includes both consumer's surplus and producer's surplus. It consists of that part of the social damage which is caused by the taxation inducing a movement against *human* resistance of consumer-producer's diminishing marginal *subjective* substitutability, which is represented by the convexity (downward) of indifference curves or surfaces, and which may be called *subjective social damage.* The second kind of social damage consists of the social damage which is caused by the taxation inducing a movement against *technical* resistance, diminishing marginal *objective* substitutability, which is represented by the convexity (upward) of the opportunity curves or surfaces, and which may be called *objective social damage.*

In Figure 5 the imposition of a tax on X (but not on Y) causes the equilibrium to move along the production opportunity curve AB (which shows what combinations of X and Y are available for consumers after any using up of resources by the government) from P on indifference curve I to Q on the lower indifference curve I_t. The difference between the slopes of the two

[7] It eliminates them from the MC curve, but they are only translated (in "space" as well as in language) into negative slope in the demand curves for the negative output. The negative outputs would have to be retranslated into positive inputs and the tax on them, based on the inverse of their elasticity of demand retranslated into a tax on the input based on the inverse of their elasticity of supply (unless the Internal Revenue could be educated into imposing the appropriate taxation on the negative outputs in accord with their elasticity of demand). But that would still not cover that part of the increasing MC which is due to technical diminishing transformability of one output into another.

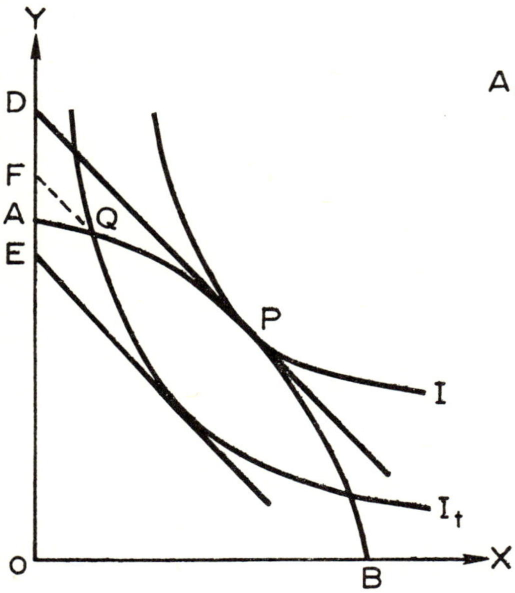

FIGURE 5

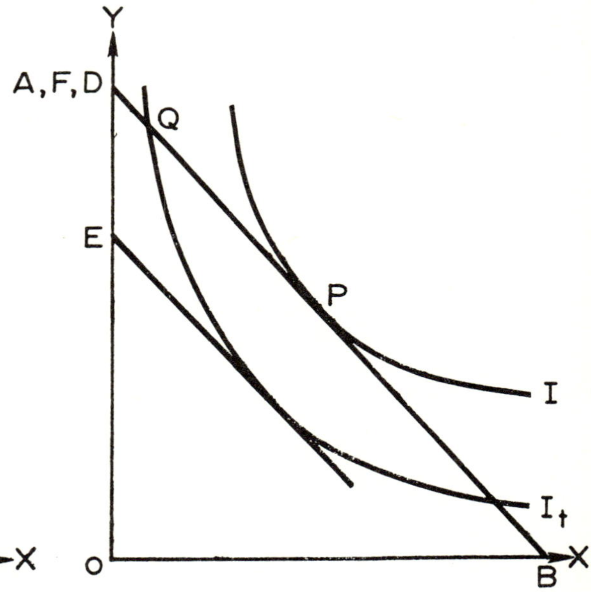

FIGURE 6

curves at Q is equal to the tax rate on X. The social damage is equivalent to an income reduction DE, but the value of the output, which is the income of the owners of the factors of production, will have fallen only by DF (both being measured in terms of Y at the no-tax relative prices).

The amount of social damage is determined in part by the convexity of the indifference curve (or rather the degree to which the slope of successive indifference curves is greater as one moves up the opportunity curve from P to Q) and in part to the convexity of the opportunity curve itself as one moves up it, since both of these affect the position of Q and the level of I_t. The convexity of the opportunity curve is responsible for the reduction DF in income to the owners of the factors of production. This is the *objective* part of the social damage. The convexity of the indifference curves (or the degree to which their slope becomes steeper as one moves up along BA) is responsible for the rest, the *subjective* part of the social damage, FE.

The point may be highlighted by considering the extreme cases. If there are no objective resistances to switching between the production of X and the production of Y, so that the opportunity curve is a straight line, we see in Figure 6 that there is no objective social damage. DF disappears. In this case, if we call inputs involving human preferences negative outputs, we are justi-

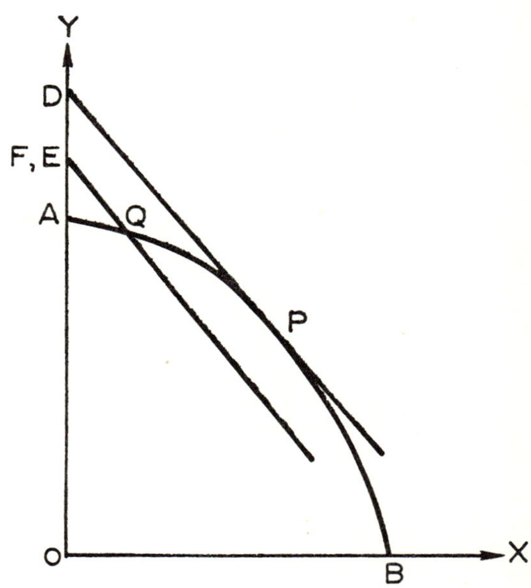

FIGURE 7

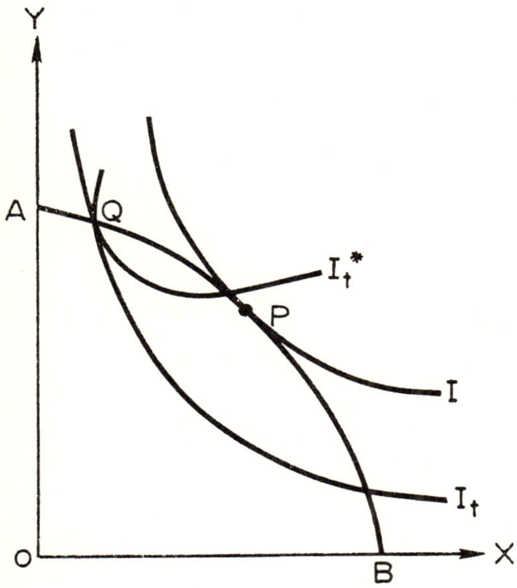

FIGURE 8

fied in assuming constant costs and in either calling all the social damage a loss of consumer's surplus or in saying that the producer's surplus is taken care of together with the consumer surplus.

If there are no subjective resistances to switching between the consumption of X and Y, so that the indifference curves are straight lines, we see in Figure 7 that there is no subjective social damage. FE disappears. The social damage (DE) consists entirely of the decrease (DF) in the income of the owners of the factors of production. The consumers (including the consumers of negative output) are faced by no price changes. They had no consumer's surplus in the first place and have lost none. It is only as owners of the factors of production that they have lost income as the tax induced them to shift against *objective* resistance and their *rents* have diminished by the total amount of the social damage. In both of these extreme cases there is no change in relative prices and thus no "index number" ambiguity about the amount of social damage.

If there are neither subjective nor objective resistances, both the opportunity curve and the indifference curve are straight lines. There is then no social damage at all. If the indifference curves have the same slope as the opportunity curve, a tax on X reduces its output to zero and no tax can be collected. Consumers are not forced onto a lower indifference curve and the owners of factors of production have no reduction in income. If the indifference curves do not have the same slope as the opportunity curve, only one of the two goods is produced, a tax on it can be considered either as a "lump sum" tax or as a "universal" proportional tax and again there is no social damage.[8]

REFERENCES

W. J. Baumol and D. F. Bradford, "Optimal Departures from Marginal Cost Pricing," *Amer. Econ. Rev.*, June 1970, *60*, 265-83.

P. A. Diamond and J. A. Mirrlee, "Optimal Taxation and Public Production," mimeo. working paper 22, M.I.T., 1968.

A. P. Lerner, "A Note on Socialist Economics," *Rev. Econ. Stud.*, Oct. 1936, *4*, 72-76.

———, *The Economics of Control*. New York 1944.

[8] The transfer of income from the owners of relatively cheapened productive resources to the owners of those which have gone up in price, and from the consumers of goods that have become more expensive to the consumers of goods that have become cheaper, may so change "collective preferences" as to make P inferior to Q. But this could happen only if the transfer of income brought about a strong shift in preference for Q as compared with P such as would be indicated by the new in difference curve I_t^* in Figure 8 instead of I_t. Since this possibility is no more likely than the opposite, which would *increase* the inferiority of Q to P, it may be disregarded until some positive evidence for it should appear.

D. Distribution Theory

[1]

CHAPTER 3. THE OPTIMUM DIVISION OF INCOME

In Chapter 1 we separated the problem of the division of income among the individual consumers of a society from the problem of the allocation of existing goods of all kinds to make up each consumer's portion. We studied the latter problem, concentrating on the nature of an optimum allocation of goods, and concluded that it could most satisfactorily be brought about by giving sums of money to the different consumers in accordance with whatever principles of the division of income were adopted in our controlled economy and then permitting consumers to buy the goods they prefer in the stores at prices which are adjusted to make the demand for each good equal to its supply. We must now consider the problem of the division of income, remembering that this issue is involved in every decision or action that would make one consumer better off at the expense of another.

Money income can be used to represent real income even if prices change.

The device of paying out sums of money to the consumers and letting them bid for the various goods available goes a long way toward providing us with a mechanism for dealing with the problem of the division of income, but it is not quite self-evident that the problem of how much of goods in general shall go to any consumer is completely identical with how much *money* (money income) shall be given to him.

One consumer may be made better off at the expense of another, without any change in their money incomes, by an alteration in the prices at which they can buy goods. If the price of meat rises while the price of fruit falls, the vegetarian is made better off and the meat eater is made worse off even though their money incomes are unchanged.

However, if there is some other independent principle that determines the prices of all the goods available, we can take the money income as a measure of the real income in actual goods and services consumed. We have such an independent principle in the principle of maintaining an optimum allocation of goods. Whatever the principle of division of income adopted, the prices of the various goods are determined at the level which makes the demand for each good equal to the supply, and so we can take the money incomes as a measure of the real incomes.

This does not mean that the prices will not change and that such changes will not make some people better off and others worse off even though their money incomes remain the same. It does mean, however, that we must disregard such changes when they are a result of changes in demand for the various goods or changes in the supply while the optimum allocation of goods is maintained. If we could say that in the old situation the actual relative well-being of the consumers was just what we wanted it to be, then, when prices changed, we would want to make some adjustment in the money incomes to offset the change in prices and leave the consumers in the same relative position as before. But we have no way of directly comparing the well-being of different consumers. Our only objective general indication is their money income, and this has not changed. We may have good reason for believing that one consumer is better off than he was before and that another is not as well off as he was before, but we have no more reason for supposing that the old situation is better than the new one (that is, is more like the situation we wish to bring about) than from supposing that the new one is better than the old one.

To obtain a criterion for the optimum division of money income we must assume that different people enjoy similar satisfactions.

This somewhat unsatisfactory state of affairs is an unavoidable result of the impossibility of measuring the satisfactions of different consumers on the same scale. We avoided this difficulty in Chapter 2 by having recourse to *relative* valuations or marginal substitutabilities, which are ratios between objective goods like meat and fruit. How can we overcome this obstacle in our study of the distribution of income and in our search for an optimum division of income?

We can solve this problem if we add two more assumptions to those we made in Chapter 2. We assumed there that the consumers in the economy were capable of feeling satisfaction and that whenever they could choose among two or more alternatives they chose the one that yielded the greatest satisfaction.

The first of the additional assumptions is that the satisfactions experienced by different people are *similar* in the sense that they are the same kind of thing. In other words, that it is not meaningless to say that a satisfaction one individual gets is greater or less than a satisfaction enjoyed by somebody else. When a man says, "Thy need is greater than mine," he may be right or wrong, but even if it is not possible to discover whether he is right there is no need to insist that he is delirious. That the satisfactions experienced by different people are the same kind of thing is incapable of proof. The only justification for making this assumption is that, while there are a few philosophers who argue that we cannot know this, there are no men whose behavior does not suggest the acceptance of the assumption. To reject it would in fact deny meaning even to the assertion that anyone other than myself is capable of feeling *any* kind of pain or pleasure.

This assumption gives meaning to the concept of maximizing the total of the satisfactions experienced by all the individuals in a society. The condition that has to be satisfied if this object is to be attained is that no part of the consumption goods or the income of the society shall go to any individual but the one who can obtain the greatest satisfaction from its consumption. If the income is divided among the individuals enjoying it in such a manner that this criterion is satisfied, then any change in the division would involve the substitution of a smaller (or at best an equal) satisfaction for each one that is lost, so that nothing could be gained by any change.

We must also assume that the principle of *diminishing marginal utility of income* holds generally.

Although there is now a clear enough concept of the achievement of our goal, there does yet not appear to be any conceivable way of doing anything toward bringing it about. It would seem to be necessary to discover how much satisfaction every individual would obtain from every unit of income before the appropriate distribution of income could be attained. The practical possibility of an attempt to reach the goal is brought a little nearer when we make use of the second additional assumption—*the principle of diminishing marginal utility of income.*

This principle asserts that the amount of satisfaction that every individual obtains from his income depends upon the size of his income in such a manner that he always gets more satisfaction from a larger income, *and that the extra satisfaction he gets from a given increase in his income* (the marginal utility of income) *is less if his original income is greater.* Thus an increase of income from $2000 to $2100 would increase his satisfaction by less than when his income is raised by a similar amount from, say, $1000 to $1100. The greater a man's income, the less significant to him is a given absolute rise in income. The principle is called one of diminishing utility because if we considered a man's income to be increased by consecutive equal increments, say, from $1000 to $1100, $1200, $1300 . . . etc., then the extra satisfaction attained by each *raise* (the *marginal* utility of income) would *diminish* from raise to raise because each time he would be receiving the same increase but starting from a higher initial level.

The principle of diminishing marginal utility of income can be derived from the assumption that consumers spend their income in the way that maximizes the satisfaction they can derive from the goods obtained. With a given income, all the things bought give a greater satisfaction for the money spent on them than any of the other things that could have been bought in their place but were not bought for this very reason. From this it follows that if income were greater the additional things that would be bought with the increment of income would be things that are rejected when income is smaller because they give less satisfaction; and if income were greater still, even less satisfactory things would be bought. The greater the income the less satisfactory are the additional things that can be bought with equal increases in income. That is all that is meant by the principle of diminishing marginal utility of income.[1]

If we now consider the shifting of a small amount of income from one individual to another, we know that the loss to the one and the gain to the other would be equal to the marginal utilities to the individuals of their respective incomes. If the marginal utilities were unequal, there would always be a gain—total satisfaction would be increased—by taking a small amount of income from the individual with the lower and giving it to the individual with the higher marginal utility of income. Such a redivision of income would be in accordance with the idea of giving to him who had the greater need.

The shifting of income from an individual with a smaller to one with a greater marginal utility of income need not stop after one unit of income had been shifted. The inequality between the marginal utilities would probably not have disappeared, so the operation would be repeated and for the very same reason. The principle of diminishing marginal utility of income indicates, however, that sooner or later the procedure will come to a stop. For as the income of the receiving individual increases the marginal utility of his income diminishes in accordance with this principle. At the same time the marginal utility of the shrinking income of the other individual will increase. As this goes on, the difference becomes less and less until ultimately the marginal utilities of the incomes of the two individuals become exactly equal to each other. When such a division of income has been reached, nothing more

[1] This argument assumes that the different satisfactions obtained from the consumption of different goods are independent of the size of the income and therefore of the other goods consumed. The effects of taking into consideration these *complementarities* are considered below. The principle of diminishing marginal utility of income is not to be confused with the principle of diminishing substitutability (*M*) of one good for another. The former is derived from introspection and the assumption of rationality of choice. The latter rests on the firmer base of the observed phenomenon that individuals do not spend all their income on one single good. The former refers to the effects of *additions* to income, the latter to the effects of the *substitution* of one good for another.

can be done to make the total of the satisfactions of the two individuals any greater. Total satisfaction is maximized by that division of income which equalizes the marginal utilities of the incomes of all the individuals in the society. Individuals with greater capacities for satisfaction than other individuals will be given incomes sufficiently larger to bring them to the point where the diminishing marginal utility of income has made their *marginal* utility just equal to that of the individuals with smaller capacities for satisfaction (or desires or needs) and smaller incomes. Everybody's marginal capacity for enjoying income will be equalized and we will have achieved a fulfillment of the principle: To each according to his needs.

The maximization of total satisfaction by equalizing the marginal utility of income is impossible,

Here we come up against a serious difficulty. Our assumptions that individuals are capable of feeling satisfactions and that their satisfactions are the same kind of thing have given meaning to the concept of maximizing total satisfaction, while the principle of diminishing marginal utility of income has simplified the task to one of equalizing the marginal utilities of income to all the individuals in the society. But we have no means of doing this. There is no way of discovering with certainty whether any individual's marginal utility of income is greater than, equal to, or less than that of any other individual.

If any two individuals were known to have exactly the same capacity of distilling satisfaction out of income, it would also be known that an unequal division of income between them would make the marginal utility of the larger income less than the marginal utility of the smaller income and that an equalization of income would equalize their marginal utilities and maximize the total utility enjoyed by both together. If it were known that one had a greater capacity for satisfaction (at all income levels), it would also be known that an equal division of income would result in a greater marginal utility of income for the one with the greater capacity for satisfaction, so that it would require an unequal division of income, more going to the one with a greater capacity for satisfaction and less going to the one with a smaller capacity for satisfaction, to equalize the marginal utilities of income and maximize the total satisfaction. But these things are not capable of being discovered. Every individual could declare that he has exceptionally high capacities for satisfaction and so should be given more income than anybody else if total satisfaction is to be maximized; and there is no way of testing the validity of such a claim.

but the maximization of *probable* total satisfaction is attained by an equal division of income.

In the absence of the possibility of discovering, and hence of equalizing, the marginal utilities of income to different individuals it is not possible to maximize the total of satisfactions. It is, however, still possible so to divide income as to maximize the *probable* total satisfaction, making this greater than the *probable* total satisfaction that would result from any other distribution of income. If it is impossible, on any division of income, to discover which of any two individuals has a higher marginal utility of income, the probable value of total satisfactions is maximized by dividing income *evenly*.

That this is so is seen from the consideration that a transfer of income from a richer to a poorer individual would increase total satisfaction if both individuals had the same capacities for satisfaction, for in that case the shift of income would be a movement toward the equal distribution which would make their marginal utilities equal. Such an equality of capacities for satisfaction cannot, however, be assumed to be the case. The richer individual may have either a greater or a smaller capacity than the poorer. If the poorer man has a greater capacity, the gain is increased on that account. If the richer man has the greater capacity, the gain is diminished on that account (and may even be converted into a loss). The possibility of an increase in gain offsets the possibility of the diminution of gain since they are equally likely to occur in any particular case. There remains the net gain that is seen by itself in the case of equal capacities but which becomes only a *probable* gain on account of the possible increase or diminution of the gain which arises with unequal capacities.

This argument is illustrated by Figure 1. Curves AA' and BB' show the marginal utilities (measured vertically) of different amounts of income (measured horizontally from either end) enjoyed by two different individuals *A* and *B*. The curves are drawn sloping downward away from the vertical axes so as to conform to the principle of diminishing marginal utility. If an income of $200 per month is divided equally between *A* and *B*,

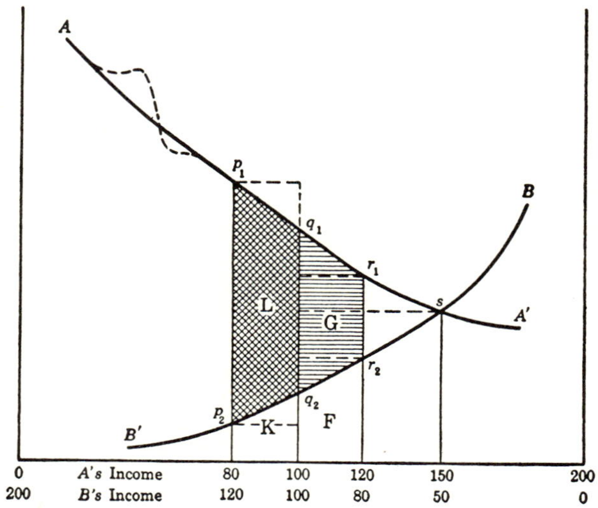

Figure 1

the marginal utilities of income to them will be represented by the height of q_1 and q_2 respectively.

A is represented as having a greater capacity for satisfaction, so his curve is drawn higher up. With the same income as *B*, the marginal utility of his income is greater than *B*'s, q_1 is greater than q_2. From this it follows that a small diversion of income from *B* to *A* would increase the total of satisfactions. This is illustrated in the figure by supposing *A*'s income to be increased by $20 while *B*'s income is reduced by the same amount, the total income of the two being kept constant, $80 + $120 = $200. The area F + G represents the increase in *A*'s satisfaction, while the area

F shows the decrease in *B*'s satisfaction. The net *gain* is shown by the shaded area G and is positive as long as *A*'s marginal utility is greater than *B*'s. Total satisfaction would be increased by departing further and further from the initial equalitarian distribution, shifting income from *B* to *A* until the marginal utilities are equalized at *s*, *A* having $150 and *B* having only $50. The total gain would be measured by the area q_1sq_2.

This cannot be done because we have no way of discovering how high the marginal utility curves are or even which of the two curves is higher. Let us again suppose ourselves to start with an equal division of income between two individuals, and consider what we *can* know about the effects on total satisfaction of a departure from the equalitarian distribution. We are now unable to use the curves in the figure and have to make guesses about them. All that we know is that they slope downward away from the vertical axes because of the principle of diminishing marginal utility of income and that one of the curves may be higher than the other.

If now a small shift is made from one individual to another, it may be a shift of the nature of the one considered above, as from *B* to *A*, that is, from an individual with a smaller marginal utility of income to one with a greater marginal utility. In that case there is a net increase in total satisfaction like that indicated by the shaded area G. But it is just as possible that the shift of income will have been from an individual with a greater to one with a smaller marginal utility of income. In that case the change would be of the nature of a shift from *A* to *B*. *B*'s gain would be indicated by the area K and *A*'s loss would be shown by area K + L, so that total satisfaction would have been *diminished* by a net *loss* indicated by the double-hatched area L.

Such a blind shift from an equal division of income is just as likely, then, to increase as to diminish total satisfaction, and if there were a very large number of cases, it might be expected that about half of the shifts would increase total satisfaction and the other half would diminish it. This would leave us indifferent as to the distribution of income in our desire to maximize total satisfaction but for one other thing that tips the scale. Although the probability of a loss is equal to the probability of a gain, every time a movement is made away from an equalitarian division the probable *size* of the loss is greater than the probable size of the gain. This is shown in the figure where, because of the slopes of the curves, given by the principle of diminishing utility of income, the double-hatched area L (which represents the *loss*) is greater than the shaded area G (which represents the *gain*). Out of 100 million shifts away from an equalitarian distribution of income in a large population, it could be expected that about 50 million would increase total satisfaction and about 50 million would diminish it. In about 50 million cases the shift would be beneficial (from *B* to *A*), and in the other 50 million cases it would be harmful (from *A* to *B*). The total increase in satisfaction received in the beneficial shifts would come to about 50 million times the shaded area G in the figure, while the total loss of satisfaction suffered in the harmful shifts would amount to about 50 million times the double-hatched area L. There would be an almost certain social loss. From this we obtain our conclusion that *if it is desired to maximize the total satisfaction in a society, the rational procedure is to divide income on an equalitarian basis.*

Complications arising from complementarity and irrationality do not affect the general conclusion.

We can now consider a complication we have so far ignored. The argument on which we based the principle of diminishing marginal utility of income is strictly valid only on the assumption that the utilities or satisfactions that an individual derives from the consumption of different goods are independent of each other. If these utilities have complementary relationships, it is possible for the marginal utility of income to increase instead of diminishing with increased income. Items that are rejected and not bought when income is low may nevertheless have a higher utility when a higher income enables them to be bought because the fact that other things are being consumed by the individual increases the utility of these items. Thus it may be that at a low level of income an individual who would have to choose between fine clothes and an automobile might choose the clothes rather than the automobile, not because the clothes gave a very great amount of utility but because without the fine clothes she would not dare to show herself in the automobile so that the latter by itself would be almost worthless. An increase in her income which enables her to buy the automobile as well as the clothes would then be much more significant than the increase which permits only the clothes to be bought because it enables both clothes and automobile to be fully displayed and enjoyed. The marginal utility of the clothes in the absence of an automobile might be represented by 5 units. The marginal utility of an automobile in the absence of the fine clothes would then be, say, 2. But the utility of the combination of fine clothes *and* the automobile might be 20. The utility of the first increment of income would then be 5 and the utility of the second increment of income would be 15. This would be an example of increasing marginal utility of income.

Complementarities can be positive, as in the example here given, where the possession or consumption of one good enhances the satisfaction yielded by another, or negative, when the possession or consumption of one good is a substitute for another good and diminishes the additional satisfaction that it can provide. In the one case it tends to mitigate and may occasionally even more than compensate for the principle of diminishing marginal utility of income and give rise over some range to increasing marginal utility of income. It does this by creating a kind of discontinuity (making the satisfaction obtainable from clothes plus automobile one indivisible item) which shows itself in a "bump" on the marginal utility curve, possibly even making a part of the curve slope upward with increasing income. In the other case—when it is negative—the complementarity reinforces the principle of diminishing marginal utility of income.

These two tendencies may be expected to have about equal value in the absence of more particular information, so that we would have the marginal utility of income diminishing with the same average intensity as in the absence of any complementarities but subject to irregularities which may sometimes be intense enough to make the marginal utility of income increase for some income ranges. The principle of diminishing marginal utility therefore reduces to a probability in any particular case, but this is all that is needed as a guide to the selection of that division of income which maximizes the *probable* total of satisfactions in the society.

Second, it is not necessary for our purpose to suppose that the expenditure of income is *always* conducted in a perfectly rational manner. As long as some considerable proportion of expenditure is governed by a rational choice of items that yield a greater rather than a smaller satisfaction, the marginal utility of income will *in general* decline. There will again be irregularities, caused by irrationality in expenditure, that may either increase or decrease the rate of decline, and now and then a particularly serious irregularity may actually bring about an *increase* in the marginal utility of income over a range. This, too, does not affect the *probability* of a generally declining marginal utility of income, which is all that we need for our argument.

The acquisition through experience of capacity to enjoy income may be an argument for equalizing income gradually rather than suddenly.

Third, it might be argued, with some plausibility, that the experience of having a larger income develops a man's tastes and capacities for enjoyment, so that the marginal utility curves of rich men should be considered to be higher than those of poor men. From this it would follow that an ideal distribution of income would give more to people who have been richer. The converse of this, too, may be argued with about the same plausibility, on the ground that a man with a high income gets used to the luxuries that he can afford so that he consumes them almost automatically, hardly noticing that he does so and so getting practically no enjoyment out of what would give a great thrill to the poor man unused to these expenditures. This would offset the first argument and strengthen the case for maximizing aggregate satisfaction by equalizing incomes. However, even if the first consideration were known to outweigh the second, and even if of the two arguments *only* the first were found to have validity, it would still be true that probable aggregate satisfaction is maximized by an equalitarian division of income. But this would now only be true in the long run. In the long run—in the absence of any knowledge of or belief in racial superiorities—different individuals' capacities for *acquiring* the power of enjoying income can be put in place of the *actual* capacity for satisfaction that we have considered above, and the same results will follow. In the long run probable aggregate satisfaction is maximized by an equalitarian distribution of income. In the short run, however, there is a difference. It would be best, if experience of higher income had the effect of *raising* the curve of marginal utility of income, temporarily to leave more than the average of income with those whose income has been higher. This consideration is of importance together with many other considerations in the *dynamic* problem which we are not here discussing, of how rapid should the *transition* from a previous unequal to an ideal equalitarian distribution of income. It cannot affect our conclusion that if it is desired to maximize satisfaction the ideal to be aimed at is an equality of income.

If acquisitiveness indicated greater capacity to enjoy income, an unequal division would be the optimum,

A qualification might appear to be necessary for differences in income due to greater effort. When an individual works longer hours or applies himself more assiduously to his work there is a presumption that he has a greater use or need for the extra income he gets from the extra effort and should get a larger income.[1] This does not follow. A man works harder only when the wage plus the attractiveness of the work itself (or minus the irksomeness of the work) in relation to his enjoyment of the alternatives of leisure or taking his work easy, his *M* of pay-plus-work for leisure, is greater than for others who prefer not to make the extra effort. There is no more reason for believing that he works harder because an additional dollar is worth more to him (in which case he should get a larger income) than that he works harder because the marginal disutility of work or the marginal utility of leisure

[1] I am indebted for this observation to Dr. Carl T. Devine, now of Johns' Hopkins.

is less for him (in which case he should get a smaller income). But even if this qualification should be justified it does not seriously affect our conclusions.

but concessions that have to be made for other reasons would meet this point too.

As we shall see, the principle of equalizing income does not preclude permitting those who so wish to sacrifice some of their leisure for extra income. This opportunity is especially valuable for those who value money income more and tends to correct this deviation from the pure theorem here enunciated by permitting these individuals to get a higher income by working harder. It should be remembered moreover that it is only where greater effort and not chance or inheritance causes inequality that this consideration is relevant, and in these cases it will be necessary to permit some inequality for the quite different reason that the principle of equality would have to compromise with the principle of providing such incentives as would increase the total of income available to be divided.

Our argument also assumes that satisfaction is derived only from one's own income,

Implicit in our argument for the equalitarian division of income are several other assumptions of a more negative character which amount to little more than the assumption that there is no special reason for preferring an unequal division. One of these is the assumption that each individual's satisfaction is derived only from his own income and not from the income of others. If the poor derive more satisfaction from seeing the splendors of the very rich than from an alleviation of their own poverty the argument might be upset (though even so they would be free to contribute to a Society for the Provision of Spectacular Expenditures and get the spectacles more economically). On the other hand, the pain that even those who are not poor get from the existence of poverty and the envy that the poor feel for the rich would tend to strengthen our argument for equality. Sometimes the spectacular expenditure of the rich is identified with cultural values. This is an extremely precarious thesis and rather less plausible than its converse that spectacular expenditure by the rich tends to destroy cultural values and distort rather than develop true artistic appreciation. But in any event these considerations merely stress the "probability" nature of our conclusion. If we knew the effect in every particular case it is virtually certain that an *unequal* division of income would be the best possible, and the consideration raised in this paragraph would have to be taken into account, as well as the marginal utility curves, but in the absence of this unattainable knowledge our conclusion in terms of probabilities still holds.

and that individuals are equally sensitive to increases as to decreases in income.

Another implication of our argument for equality of income is that the marginal utility of income is the same, for any individual with a given income, whether we consider his income to be increased or decreased. But it is possible that a man feels an increase in income from $2000 to $2100 less keenly than he would feel a decrease in income from $2100 to $2000. Or he might feel the latter more keenly than he feels the former. If a diminution in income is felt more keenly than an increase, any redivision of income (which must involve a diminution as well as an increase) is harmful just because it is a change. This is clearly seen if we consider a redivision that neither increases nor decreases the inequality of the division of income. If income is shifted between two individuals in such a way that their relative position is exactly reversed, there is no difference in the degree of inequality, yet there is a net loss because the gain is felt less keenly than the loss. Even if the inequality is reduced by the shift the harm from the act of redivision may be greater than the benefit due to the superiority of the new division over the old division. This consideration might appear to upset our conclusion in favor of redivision of income from the existing unequal division to an equalitarian division. However, this is not really so.

But even if these assumptions are not warranted the general conclusions still hold.

This comes to the same as the problem already considered of the rich who were supposed to have acquired a greater sensitivity to income. Greater sensitivity to diminutions of income than to increases in income would merely lead to the conclusion that redivision would be slow. If the sensitiveness to diminutions of income is so much greater than the sensitiveness to corresponding increases of income that the benefit from an increase in income is quite negligible in comparison with the pain of the decrease in income, nobody's income should be reduced, but it would still follow from our analysis that no income above the average should be increased and that no member of the new generation should be given an income above the average, for in the determination of new incomes to new members of the population the problems from acclimatization to high income need not be allowed to arise in the first place. In less extreme cases there should be some redivision of income from rich to poor but at a slow rate, the rate of redivision being that at which the harm done by the change itself is just great enough, at the margin, to offset the gain from the improvement in the division of income. A more rapid rate of redivision would do more harm than good (at the margin) while a less rapid rate of redivision would mean the abandonment of some benefit from improved division which is greater than the harm done by the additional change that this would entail.

If consumers were more sensitive to increases in income than to decreases, the queer conclusion would follow that *any* change would be good unless it made the new division more unequal than the old; and even in that case there would remain a net gain if the change were followed by a change back to the previous division. The final division of income would be the same as in the beginning, but of the intervening increases that were followed by decreases and decreases followed by increases there would remain a net gain from the greater sensitiveness to the increases. This is indeed the exact opposite, as might be expected, of the situation where decreases were felt more keenly than increases. There the change had to be checked and minimized even if the final results of the change were good. Here change is good in itself quite apart from the benefits from an improvement in the division of income. On this hypothesis the best thing is to have all income fluctuating as widely and as rapidly as possible though it would still be desirable for the fluctuation to be around an equalitarian base if the greatest satisfaction is to be obtained from a given total income with a given degree of change. This conclusion should be sufficiently strange to permit us to rest content, until such time as we get some knowledge on the subject, with the implication that consumers are equally sensitive to increases and decreases in income. This we can do with a clear conscience since our conclusions are not being put forward as a proposal for the immediate redivision of income on a perfectly equalitarian basis, but merely as a solution of the theoretical question of what would be the division to be aimed at if a *given* total income were to be divided in the most effective manner for the maximization of total satisfaction.

There are other arguments that are frequently adduced to support the policy of equality of income. It may be argued that an equalitarian division of income is more "fair" than any other or that it is favorable to the development of a feeling of comradeship and friendliness. It may be hailed as a corollary of the notion of the Brotherhood of Man, or it may simply be proposed as an end in itself with a direct aesthetic appeal unmarred by any rationalization or logic chopping. For most people who sympathize with the conclusions of this chapter these other more direct and more easily understood arguments usually have a greater appeal. The argument here developed is, however, not supererogatory. Its purpose is to bring to light the implications hidden in *obiter dicta* that propositions about the division of income belong to the realm of value judgments and that arguments based on the concept of maximizing total utility have no meaning, so that the economist, as such, can say nothing about an equalitarian division of income, while as a member of society all that he can say is that he likes it or dislikes it.

To reject the conclusion that the optimum division of income is an equal one is not more impartial or scientific than to accept the assumptions on which it is based.

What our analysis brings out is that the maintenance of a dignified and "scientific" impartiality on this proposition contains just as much of value judgment as the conclusion that an equalitarian division maximizes the probable total of satisfactions enjoyed by the individuals in the society. For, unless we have made a mistake in our argument, the refusal to accept the conclusion can rest only on the refusal to accept one or both of our two primary assumptions—that is, a refusal to suppose that other people have any capacity for feeling satisfactions and/or a refusal to suppose that all people enjoy satisfactions of a similar or comparable character. We may dismiss the former as so arrogant as to render it too unlikely that any sane person would really hold it (though a solipsistic philosopher might make some such statement during office hours), and the latter because it makes a distinction between individuals that could be defended only by the exponents of Nazi biology.

It is important to note that the argument given above in favor of an absolutely equalitarian division of income is not directly applicable to practical policy. It is the solution to the problem of maximizing the probable total of satisfactions that can be attained by the member of society from a *given* income. As soon as other objectives are introduced which come into conflict with this one a compromise has to be made. It will probably also be desired to produce as great an income as possible for division among the members of society, and if a greater total income would be produced if the division of income were less equalitarian, a compromise cannot be avoided.

The general argument does not rule out particular cases where some reason may be given for particularly high or particularly low needs, for instance, of invalids on the one hand or ascetics on the other. But wherever there is no good specific reason for inequality the general principle holds that if we would maximize satisfaction from a given total social income the rational procedure is to equalize individual incomes.

[2]

Distributional Equality and Aggregate Utility: Reply

By A. P. LERNER*

The formulation of the argument for distributional equality by William Breit and William Culbertson is an improvement on that of *The Economics of Control* and is much more effective in class. Their generalization of the proposition to the case of increasing marginal utility (of income) offset by a greater degree of diminishing marginal utility elsewhere, is also an improvement. Their point that Paul Samuelson did not escape the "equal ignorance" assumption is well taken.

Ambiguity, being a case of lack of clarity is a charge that can never successfully be refuted. However, I would like to deny a switching of conclusions. Perhaps the ambiguity would have been avoided if I had added the following words in Roman type to the italicized sentence quoted: "*. . . if it is desired to maximize the total satisfaction in a society, the rational procedure*, in the absence of the knowledge that would enable us to equalize the marginal utilities, *is* to maximize the probable total satisfaction—i.e., *to divide income on an equlitarian basis*." The theorem on page 32 is not "bolder" than the "meek and mild" one of page 29. It is the same proposition.

The ingenous device of the 100 million coconut islands in one way does more than is claimed for it and in another way, does less. If it were possible to divide the total population into pairs which had the same utility functions, the equalization of income within each pair would *never* involve a "wrong" movement to be offset by a "right" one. That is why there is certainty of improvement from equalization on every island. Furthermore, there would be an absolute maximization, with certainty, of the total satisfaction of the pair on each island from their joint income.

On the other hand, the parable assumes that the combined incomes of the pairs have somehow already been equalized; that for every individual in the half of the total population with incomes less than the mean, his "partner" in the other half of the population (with an identical utility function) has an income greater than the mean by the exact amount that his is *less* than the mean. (This implies incidentally that no individual has an income as much as twice the mean unless his "partner" has a zero income.)

If this is not the case, some islands will be richer than others. We will then have to equalize the incomes of the islands before we could conduct Breit and Culbertson's experiment. The parable, therefore, while not necessary for the "meek" proposition that income equalization maximizes the *probable* total satisfaction, is not sufficient for the "bold "proposition (to which I have never subscribed) that income equalization increases total satisfaction with *absolute* certainty.

Breit and Culbertson's development of their parable reflects the same discomfort they have seen in others. The pair on the island are not satisfied with the proof that the equalization of the incomes has *maximized their probable* satisfaction. Sharing a widespread human craving for certainty, they want to be *quite sure* that they have at least *increased their actual* total satisfactions. This assurance is unfortunately not available as long as the utility functions are unknown.

Breit and Culbertson also are seeking for a certainty of gain in a "much bolder and more interesting proposition regarding realized satisfactions" instead of the maximization of a mere probability, and are accurately represented by the island pair they have invented. They have imagined a certainty of gain only by imagining the discovery of identical-utility twins. But the whole point of the

* University of California, Berkeley.

argument is that in the absence of knowledge of the utility functions (so that we cannot equalize the marginal utilities—with different incomes for individuals with different utility functions and equal incomes for those, like the island pairs, with identical utility functions) we nevertheless still have the probability proposition.

There can be no absolute certainty of gain from any redistribution between individuals of whose utility functions we are ignorant. Nevertheless, if I were offered 11 cents for every "head" in return for 10 cents for every "tail" on 100 million tosses of an unbiased coin, I would consider the probability of gain certain enough.

[3]

Utilitarian Marginalism (Nozick, Rawls, Justice, and Welfare)

Abba P. Lerner*

One purpose of this article is to show the relationship of Robert Nozick's "Entitlement" and John Rawls' "Justice" to the utilitarian marginalism that derives from the classical economic approach to the distribution of income.[1] Nozick and Rawls claim to derive guides for income distribution from general principles of justice. But general rules for the distribution of income cannot be derived from abstract principles of justice because "justice" has no objective meaning. For any individual, justice is what he considers fitting, or *just fitting* the situation. It has been used to defend the traditional, like slavery; the inevitable or natural, like death and genetic differences; the expected, like hanging for stealing a sheep; the unexpected, like catastrophes called "acts of God"; and the satisfaction of revenge, sometimes called just punishment or punishment to fit the crime. It is hard to think of any inhumanity–one is tempted to say injustice–that has not at some time been defended as Demanded by Justice. I shall try to show that Nozick's and Rawls' suggestions for the desirable distribution of income are in fact based fundamentally, if not correctly, on nothing but (utilitarian) claims that they would yield higher levels of satisfaction.

A second purpose of this article is to examine the interdependence between two aspects of social efficiency–*distributive efficiency* in the division, or sharing, of the social income among the different members of society, and *productive efficiency* in the allocation of the different productive resources among their different uses and of the different consumer goods among the different consumers of the incomes so divided, and their relation to the capitalistic and socialistic principles of economic organization.

More logical terms would be "division" of the social income and "allocation" of the different goods and services, but the traditional separation of economics into "production" and "distribution" is far too well established. We shall occasionally, however, find it convenient to speak of "allocative" efficiency to refer both to the different factors of production and the different consumption goods and services.

I. "Entitlement"

Nozick claims that his theory of "Entitlement" is rooted in "the laws of nature." In his "state of nature" individuals have perfect freedom to order their actions and dispose of their possessions as they think fit within the bounds of the laws of nature. This freedom requires the state to be minimal, its function limited to the provision of a justice system for the enforcement of contracts and the protection of its citizens against violence, theft, and fraud.

The entitlement theory states that a person is justly entitled to any holdings bestowed on him by nature or justly acquired by inheritance, or by free exchange for justly acquired holdings, i.e., when their acquisition has not violated any

*Queens College, CUNY and FSU.

[1]The references are to Robert Nozick, *Anarchy, State and Utopia* (New York: Basic Books, 1974) and John Rawls, *A Theory of Justice* (Cambridge, Mass.: Harvard, 1971).

individual's natural rights. If any natural rights have been violated in the acquisition or the transfer of holdings, such injustice should be rectified. Thus, whether a distribution is just depends on how it came about.

Nozick advances the usual economic arguments about the advantages of the division of labor, specialization, comparative advantage, and free exchange. Cooperation comes about through contract and exchange among individuals. Since the resulting distribution of income and wealth depends on the exchange ratios or prices at which the exchanges are made, justice depends on the prices being "fair." The prices in free exchange are judged as "fair" because people freely choose to make exchanges, and to transfer entitlements, with no restrictions on the freedom to trade with any other party on mutually acceptable terms.

There can be no serious objection to Nozick calling free exchange, and its effects, "just." Nobody is harmed by a free exchange and so there is at least nothing "unjust" about it. On the other hand, redistribution of income or wealth by the government (in taxing some to provide income or services to others) is declared by Nozick to be coercive and therefore "unjust." Nozick's "justice" therefore requires that redistributive actions by the government be limited to what cannot be avoided in financing the justice system.

But although the word "justice" is not very meaningful to me (and I remember that for a large part, perhaps a majority, of the world's population free exchange is criminal rather than just) I am in agreement with the substance of Nozick's argument. The situation *after* a free exchange is preferable (on utilitarian grounds) to the situation *before* the exchange. There is a net gain. Some have benefited from the exchange and none have been harmed. Nozick, however, draws a quite different conclusion. His conclusion is that the set of holdings after the exchange is a just one. In his enthusiasm for the net gains from exchanges freely undertaken, in that it can only benefit the parties to it so that the changes brought about may be called just, he goes on to attribute this virtue of the *change* to *the total situation* after the change—to the new distribution of income and wealth—and declares that too to be just.

This assumes that the distribution was a just distribution before the exchange, and therefore could not be improved upon (made more just?) but only worsened by any redistribution. The application of this argument must ultimately credit "nature" with providing the *initial* inheritances in some just manner. But we have no reason to presume that "nature" somehow knows what it is doing and therefore distributes initial endowments of property and of abilities according to some concept of justice. Professor Israel M. Kirzner (in his article in this volume "Entrepreneurship, Entitlement, and Economic Justice") is more consistent than Nozick in attributing the virtues of an *act* of free exchange to the distribution of income and wealth in a *regime* of free exchange. He seems to defend the distribution "brought about" by free exchange (i.e., in existence after some free exchange) as just, and therefore not to be disturbed by any redistribution, even if the previous distribution is known to have been unjust.

Nozick's attribution of justice to the distribution existing in a free exchange economy seems to be based on a misunderstanding of the significance of "marginal product" for economics. There were one or two economists who claimed that paying a factor its (his?) marginal product is "just" because that is "what he (it?) produces." But almost all economists reject this argument. Accepting it would indeed made them the "apologists for capitalism" that Marxists accuse them of being. In this context paying "what he produces" means paying a *person* the value of the marginal product, either of his own personal activity or of the land or capital goods which he happens to own. There is certainly not much to the argument that a person *deserves* (is "entitled" to) what is the result of his good fortune in inheriting these either legally or genetically. The proposition is an empty one from which no moral conclusion can be drawn. Nozick's attempts to bolster the proposition by reference to natural law do not make it any less vacuous.

There is, indeed, a powerful social reason why the price paid for the use of a factor should be equal to the value of its marginal product. But it is based not on justice, and not even on any concern at all as to who is going to receive that payment, as we shall see below. Its purpose is to serve the productive (allocative) efficiency of the economy by getting the factor to go to that use where the value of the marginal product is greatest, and not to a less important use where the value of its marginal product is less.

The distribution of income and wealth is, of course, affected by the degree of freedom of exchange, but it also depends on the distribution *before* the exchange; and that is the result of history. History is also a part of nature. And history is full of much that can certainly not be called just. To take seriously Nozick's final principle that rectification is called for where some injustice has been perpetrated, we must look into all the bloodshed, the invasions, the massacres, the oppressions, the enslavements throughout the history and prehistory of mankind. We would find very little justice left in the distribution to be protected by the minimalist state. Nozick's recommended "rectification" would call for just that kind of governmental intervention and redistribution that he rejects as "coercion."

We could claim that free exchange will yield a just distribution only by following Kirzner in completely disregarding both history and nature and "let the dead past bury its dead." This would require us to believe that all the inequalities of inheritance of property as well as of human capacities would have been rendered insignificant by the current benefits from a regime of free exchange and free enterprise for a generation or two.

II. Maximin

Rawls comes very much closer to an economist's treatment of the subject. In his "difference principle" he implicitly recognizes the emptiness of "justice" and, by the device of redefinition, replaces it by "fairness." His basic principle is "Justice as Fairness." Fairness is the attribute of judgments made with no special preference for benefits to the judge himself. It is the absence of bias. Rawls dramatizes this most strikingly by his use of the concept of the "original position." In the imagined "original position" one is asked to choose between possible worlds into which to be born without knowing one's status, wealth, abilities, preferences, or luck. There is no possibility of distinguishing between oneself and others, and consequently one can only choose in a completely impartial way. Other writers in this field have defined the word "moral" in the same way that Rawls defines "just," namely, as unbiased or impartial. A "moral preference" is thus a preference for what is good for people in general with no special consideration for what is good for oneself or one's friends.[2]

I find myself in complete sympathy with Rawls' "moral" or "fair" approach to the problem of the distribution of income, but in applying it he makes the opposite error from that of Nozick. Whereas Nozick claims *too much* for the benefits from the equalization of relative marginal utilities by free exchange, extending these virtues to whatever distribution happens to exist (giving the credit to "nature"),

[2]Adam Smith defined moral rules of behavior as what would be recommended by an "impartially sympathetic observer." Professor John C. Harsanyi argues that "a value judgment would show the required impersonality if the person who made the judgement had to choose . . . in complete ignorance of what his own position (and the position of those near to his heart) would be within the system." (*Journal of Political Economy*, October, 1953: pgs. 434–435.)

Rawls pays *too little* attention to the possibilities of marginal adjustments.

One of the functions of economists, and indeed one of their persistent burdens, is to keep on reminding people that there are *degrees* of almost everything. Thus, most recently, public interest in the environment has raised a cry for the *abolition* of various kinds of pollution, and economists have had to try to teach that there is an optimum *degree* of almost every kind of pollution. And for such improved adjustments we need the discrimination of marginal analysis.

Rawls distinguishes only between the "worst off" group in society and everybody else, giving no indication of the probabilities of being in one or another group, or of the level of income of the rest of the population and its distribution among them. He naturally comes to the conclusion that anybody who is deciding into which kind of world he would rather be born would protect himself by choosing that kind of world in which its worst off are not so badly off. It would, of course, be more desirable to be born into a world where one had a better chance of being better off, or of being much better off rather than not so much better off. But this marginal analysis is played down by Rawls, and in its absence any rational person, if he is forced to be "moral" or "just" (in the sense of "unbiased") by being put in the "original position," would indeed follow Rawls' "maximin" principle. He would maximize the minimum income by choosing to be born into that kind of world in which the worst off group is better off than the worst off group in any other of the possible worlds.

Rawls views the initial or "natural" distribution of material assets, as well as of natural abilities, as "morally arbitrary," so that no person has a moral claim to any particular product share. Those who would be better off (if paid the value of the marginal product of their work and of the material factors they owned) should make transfers to the worse off. This is only just (i.e., fair) because it brings the distribution closer to what would be chosen if there were no bias, namely, what would be chosen in the "original position."

Rawls also says that the better off in society make transfers to the worse off in order to gain and maintain their cooperation. This argument can be turned around. One can just as logically argue that the worse off give rewards to the better off to induce them to cooperate and make the worse off not as badly off as they otherwise might be. But this argument is not really basic to Rawls' model of the impartiality or morality of the choice in the "original position." It is, of course, a fact that there are transfers from the rich to the poor in the actual world, but that is not because of a widespread acceptance of Rawls' maximin principle. It is more due to the partial but very general acceptance of the utilitarian arguments with the marginal analysis which Rawls plays down.

It would seem that Rawls avoids marginal analysis because of an over-reaction to the Nozick type of error—his misuse of marginalism to defend the final distribution of income in a competitive free exchange economy as morally justified—and he throws out the baby with the bathwater. But by combining marginal analysis and utilitarian theory with the principle of "fairness" (with or without the dramatic device of the "original state") we can improve on Rawls' analysis even though in some cases we get the same conclusions.

III. Distributional and Productive Efficiency

In Bentham's utilitarianism, the general satisfaction of the community is measured by the sum total of the individual satisfactions or utilities. It is democratic and egalitarian, each individual's satisfactions receiving equal weight. Because of some philosophical difficulties in the meaning of *total* utility, some economists have instead spoken of maximizing *average* utility. But this too involves adding the total utilities of individuals, and philosophical difficulties remain. It is possible to avoid all these difficulties by speaking instead of *marginal* utility to individuals from the consumption of goods and services. To compare the marginal utilities of individuals we do not have to go into the much more troublesome issue of measuring, or even estimating, any individual's *total* utility.[3]

If a gain in utility by an individual to whom a dollar of income is transferred is greater than the loss of utility by the individual from whom the dollar is taken (i.e., the marginal utility of income is greater to the first individual than to the second), then the shift of the dollar is an improvement because the gain is greater than the loss. If it is considered desirable to distribute a given total income most efficiently—to provide a larger rather than a smaller marginal utility wherever possible—this objective is achieved only by a distribution of income which makes all the marginal utilities of income equal. (It has to be a *given* total income so that the amount of income taken from one is equal to the amount given to the other.) This is the condition for the efficient distribution of income.

Distributional efficiency, the principle governing the efficient division of income among the different individuals, is exactly parallel to productive efficiency, the principle governing the efficient allocation of resources among their different possible uses. That is obtained by shifting every resource from any point where the value of its marginal product is less to where it is greater. Only when these are equalized everywhere, and such further shifts are therefore no longer possible, is the efficient allocation of resources achieved. The same is true of the allocation of a consumer's income among the different consumption goods available to him. Its efficient allocation requires the equalization of the marginal utilities (which are the marginal products) of his different expenditures on the different consumption goods. This is included in our "productive efficiency."

---

[3]Having discovered that *ordinal* welfare functions are sufficient for microeconomic welfare theory in explaining market behavior in terms of observed acts of choice that reveal individual preferences, economists have rejected *cardinalism*, which had been used to explain market behavior in terms of unobservable individual utilities (although it can also be used exactly like ordinal utility).

Comparing the marginal utilities of income of an individual at different income levels (in discussing diminishing marginal utility of income), does not mean resorting to cardinality. Cardinality does imply the possibility of such comparisons, but the converse is not true. It is true that if we could compare the marginal utilities throughout the whole possible range of income, we would be able to reconstruct the whole cardinal utility function and to measure the *total utility*. But the comparison of total utilities does indeed suffer from the meaninglessness that has improperly been attributed to *all* utility comparisons. The comparison of *marginal* utilities is *not* meaningless.

The measurement of temperature has often been suggested as an analogy to the measurement of utility. But I have never been accused of meaninglessness when I said that I feel more keenly the difference between 60° and 65° in the swimming pool than that between 65° and 70°. However, it does not make any sense to ask how keenly I feel the *total* temperature of the water—whether my zero is Celsius' or Fahrenheit's or Kelvin's.

The resistance to the comparison of marginal utilities is very strong, and it seems to rest on the feeling that it is our duty to choose between ordinality and cardinality, and while ordinality does not permit such comparisons, the more permissive cardinality is itself outlawed. But for the comparison of marginal utilities, we do not have to assume *full* cardinality. What we need is a less forbidding name for that *part* of cardinality which is assumed in the comparison of *marginal* utilities. I find "marginalism" to be an adequate name, but that may be only because I was never properly trained in symbolic logic so that I am not tempted to call this cardinality. That may also be why the argument as put forward by me in 1934 was very slow of acceptance—even frowned upon as an unfortunate flaw in my *Economics of Control*—while Harsanyi's use of it in 1953 and 1957 was hailed by Paul Samuelson as a "rehabilitation of cardinal utility" which constituted "a rare quantum-jump breakthrough in welfare economics." But it is not really a rehabilitation of cardinal utility (even though Harsanyi himself says he might as well call it that). It is a smaller jump, and as such, even more to be admired as an important breakthrough.

Allocative efficiency is reached automatically in a free competitive market. If any factor of production has marginal products of different value in different uses, it would pay somebody to shift some of the factor from where the value of the marginal product is less to where it is greater. The difference would be a net gain or profit. But the market does not in the same way way equalize the marginal utility of income. In a free competitive market it is the *owner* of every factor who is paid the value of the factor's marginal product. Each individual's income is equal to the marginal product of each factor multiplied by the number of units of that factor that he owns. His income is represented by the area of the rectangle (OE) in the diagram. The height of the rectangle (SE) shows the price or pay per unit of the factor, while its length (OS) shows the quantity he owns. There is no reason for assuming that the distribution of ownership, and consequently of income, would be such, and that the capacity of individuals to enjoy income would be such, as to make the marginal utility of income to all the different individuals anything like equal. Equalization of the marginal utilities can therefore be achieved only by transferences of income from those with smaller marginal utilities of income to those with greater marginal utilities until the marginal utilities had all become equal.

Some of such transferences are voluntary gifts (charity) to those whose needs seem greater (i.e., who seem to have a greater marginal utility of income). These gifts diminish the inequality but clearly they do not eliminate it. Further equalization of the marginal utility of income can therefore come about only by government redistribution of income–denounced by Nozick (and Kirzner) as coercion and contrary to "justice" since it interferes with the complete liberty of the state of nature.

We have considered these objections to attempts to combine distributive with allocative

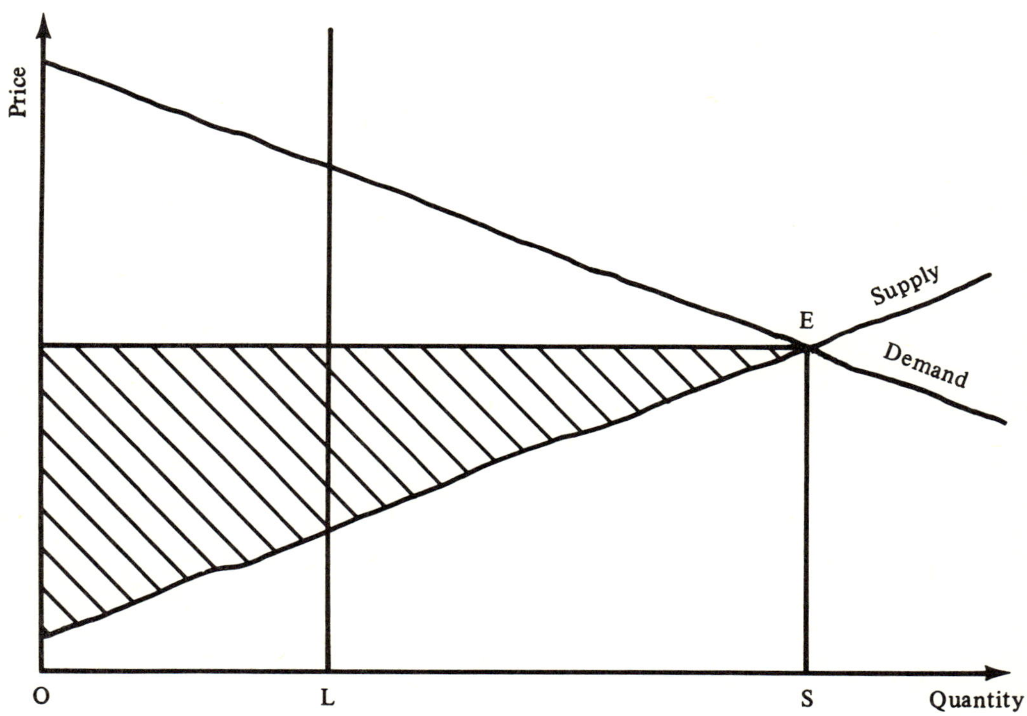

efficiency, and there are some more hurdles, but I shall try to show that these can all be overcome.

We have seen that distributive efficiency–the optimal division of income–is obtained only if the marginal utility of income is equal for all individuals. In trying to achieve this by re-distribution of income we immediately come up against a serious difficulty. There is no way of discovering whether any individual's marginal utility of income is greater than, equal to, or less than, that of any other individual! Every individual could declare that he has an exceptionally high capacity for satisfaction and so the marginal utilities of income could be equalized only by giving him more income than anybody else; and there is no way of testing the validity of such claims.

IV. Income Equalization–Maximizing Probable Gain

Nevertheless it is possible to redistribute income so as to maximize the *probable gain*. The probable gain from any redistribution is maximized by dividing the income *equally*. This proposition rests on the following assumptions: (1) other consumers besides me are capable of feeling satisfactions; (2) every individual gets more satisfaction from a larger income than from a smaller income; (3) whenever a consumer can choose among two or more alternatives he chooses the one that yields the greatest satisfaction; (4) the satisfactions experienced by different people are *similar*, so that it is not meaningless to say that the satisfaction which one individual derives from an additional unit of income is greater, or that it is less than, the satisfaction that would be derived from it by another individual.

From these assumptions (essentially, that others have feelings, and some rationality, like me) it follows that the marginal utility of income is diminishing. The *extra satisfaction the individual gets from a given increase in his income* (the marginal utility of income) *is less if his original income is greater.*[4] (This can be represented by a downward sloping curve of the marginal utility of income.)

The establishment of the principle of diminishing marginal utility of income is of crucial importance. If indeed consumers spend their income in a way that maximizes their satisfaction, the things bought give a greater satisfaction than the other things that could have been bought instead with the same income, but were not bought for this very reason. It therefore follows that if income were greater, the additional things that would be bought would be "next best"–the things that are rejected when incomes are smaller because they give less satisfaction. And if income were greater still, even less satisfactory things would be bought. The greater the income, the less satisfactory are the additional things that remain to be bought with the additional increase in income. That is all that is meant by the principle of diminishing marginal utility of income.

I further invoke three more assumptions which somewhat complicate the issue and might seem to cast some doubt on the principle of diminishing marginal utility of income. I will show that even if these three additional assumptions are not warranted, the general conclusion still holds. Initially I assume further (5) that the different satisfactions

[4] My initial statement on the principle of the diminishing marginal utility of income appears in Abba P. Lerner, *The Economics of Control* (New York: The Macmillan Company, 1944, Chapter 3). In that work I discuss both distributive efficiency and productive efficiency but I do not adequately integrate them, leaving the implication that a compromise between two contradictory principles is required i.e., that *both* principles have to be compromised. In the present article I argue that this is not the case. It is possible for only *distributive* efficiency to have to give way, while productive efficiency is untouched; the limitation to the full achievement of distributive efficiency is due not to the necessity of satisfying the basic condition for productive efficiency, but to quite different forces.

obtained by a person from the consumption of different goods are independent of the size of his income and therefore of the other goods consumed. Initially I assume (6) that the experience of having a larger or smaller income does not develop or dull a person's tastes or capacities for enjoying income. Initially I assume (7) that an individual derives more satisfaction from an extra $1.00 of income for himself than from an extra $1.00 of income for anyone else.

Consider a transfer of income from a richer to a poorer individual. If both individuals have *the same* overall capacity for deriving satisfaction from income (which would be represented by *identical* downward sloping curves of the marginal utility of income) such a transfer would yield a net gain. For in that case the poorer individual has a higher *marginal* utility of income. (The identical marginal utility of income curve is *higher* at the point corresponding to the smaller income.)

Such overall equality of capacities for satisfaction cannot, however, be assumed to be necessarily the case. The richer individual may have either a greater or a smaller capacity than the poorer one (a higher or a lower marginal utility curve). If the poorer person has the greater capacity, the gain is increased on that account. If the richer person has the greater capacity, the gain is diminished on that account. It may even be converted into a loss. The possibility of an increase in gain offsets the possibility of a diminution of gain since these are equally likely to occur in any particular case. The net gain (which is a certainty in the case of equal capacity) then becomes only a *probable* gain on account of the possible increase or diminution of the gain which arises with unequal capacities. *Every transfer of income from a richer to a poorer individual therefore shows a probable gain.* From this it follows that the rational procedure is to keep shifting from richer to poorer until the income differences have disappeared, i.e., to divide a given total income *equally*.

I shall now consider the complications mentioned above. The argument for diminishing marginal utility of income holds strictly throughout every individual's whole income range only on the assumption (assumption 5) that the satisfactions than an individual derives from the consumption of different goods are independent of each other. If these utilities have complementary relationships it is possible for the marginal utility of income to increase with increased income instead of diminishing. Items that are rejected and not bought at one income level may nevertheless be bought at a greater income not just because they are "next best" although less satisfying than what is bought at a lower income, but because other things are now being consumed by the individual and these increase the utility of the new items.

Complementarities can, however, be either positive or negative, and negative complementarity *reinforces* the principle of diminishing marginal utility of income. Only positive complementarity tends to mitigate, and may occasionally even reverse, the diminishing marginal utility of income. It does this by creating a kind of discontinuity which, if it is powerful enough, can raise a "bump" on the marginal utility curve, possibly making a portion of the curve slope upward with increasing income.

But the "bump" always has a second side which, when the complementarity effect has been exhausted, must make the curve fall *more* than it rose (if it actually did rise). The marginal utility of income will still be diminishing with the same *average* intensity but will be subject to irregularities. The principle of diminishing marginal utility therefore reduces to a probability. But this is all that we needed anyway.

A similar answer can be given to the objection that many decisions are foolish or hasty or based on insufficient or faulty information, so that they do not result in that expenditure being chosen which yields the greatest satisfaction. The results of such decisions are a matter of luck or chance. But as long as a significant part of the decisions are based on deliberate judgement and reliable information, our conclusion still holds. These decisions will lead to desired results more often than the opposite, and their results in any particular case will *probably* be preferable to the results of the deliberately rejected choices, so that the results of every actual choice will still *probably* be preferred to the results of the rejected choices; and that again is all that we need.

Another problem arises if we relax assumption (6). The experience of having a larger income may develop a person's tastes and capacities for enjoying income so that the marginal utility curves of rich people would be higher than those of poor people. An ideal distribution of income would then give more to people who have been richer. The converse of this too may be argued with about the same plausibility. A person with high income gets used to luxuries so that he hardly notices items that would give a great thrill to a poor man unused to them. This would reverse the first argument and *strengthen* the case for equalizing incomes. However even if the first consideration were known to outweigh the second, and even if of the two arguments only the first were found to have validity, there would still be a *probable* gain from an egalitarian division of income. But this would now be true only in a longer run. If experience of higher income really had the effect of *raising* the curve of marginal utility of income, it would be best *temporarily* to leave more than the average of income with those whose levels of income has been higher. This still does not alter our conclusion. It only addresses itself to how rapid should be the *transition* from a previous unequal to an ideal egalitarian distribution of income, and to the importance of avoiding the establishment of inequalities of income in the first place.

Some might argue that a person feels a greater increase in satisfaction from a given income *increment* than he would feel from the same-sized income *decrement*. But this comes down to the same problem already considered—that of the rich who are supposed to have acquired a greater sensitivity to income. Greater sensitivity to diminutions of income would merely lead to the conclusion that redistribution should be gradual. It would still follow from our analysis that no income above the average should be increased and that no member of the new generation should be given an income above the average, so that the acclimatization to high income should not arise in the first place. But where it has arisen, the *speed* of redistribution of income from rich to poor must be limited to the rate of redistribution at which the harm by the change itself is just great enough, at the margin, to offset the gain from the improvement in the distribution of income. A more rapid rate of redistribution would do more harm than good at the margin, while a less rapid rate of redistribution would mean the abandonment of some benefit from improved distribution that is greater than the harm that would be done by the greater rate of change.

A qualification might appear to be necessary for differences in income due to greater effort. When an individual applies himself more assiduously to his work this might be held to indicate that he has greater use or need for the extra income derived from the extra effort. Some might contend that such an individual should receive a larger income. This does not follow. A person works hard only when the wage plus the attractiveness of the work itself (or minus the irksomeness of the work), in relation to the opportunity cost of the alternative leisure forgone, is greater than for others. But there is no more reason for believing that a person works harder because an additional dollar is worth more to him than that he works harder because the marginal disutility of work or the marginal utility of leisure is less for him. We know only that these are less in relation to the marginal utility of consumption goods. But it is all of these marginal utilities *combined* that constitute the marginal utility of income and there is no reason here for believing that that is higher or lower than for others.

Assumption (7) is that each individual derives more satisfaction from an increment to his own income than from the same increment to the income of others. If the poor derive more satisfaction from seeing the splendors of the rich increase by $1.00 than from the alleviation of their own poverty by $1.00, our argument might be upset, but then they could, and would, donate some of their income to the rich until this were no longer the case. Conversely, the pain that even those who are not poor get from the existence of poverty, and the envy that the poor feel for the rich, would tend to strengthen the argument for equality.

Sometimes the spectacular expenditure of the rich is identified with cultural values. Because cultural values are relative within a society this appears an extremely precarious thesis. In any event, our primary theorem remains intact. The rule for the most efficient distribution of any given income is to distribute it equally.

V. Material Incentives

It might seem that this conclusion, no matter how inescapable it is to all but those who have the arrogance to deny our basic assumptions that others, besides them, have feelings and some rationality, is rendered practically worthless by its complete dependence on the assumption of a *given* income, i.e., that the amount of income to be distributed is independent of how it is distributed. But there would certainly be less income produced if there were no material incentives for work and for efficiency. Payment for work equal to its marginal productivity is also a very important part of the general rule for productive efficiency–that the price paid for every factor of production should be equal to its marginal product. Thus, there appears to be a fundamental conflict between distributive and productive efficiency that would be absent only in extreme situations where the value of the marginal product of all kinds of human effort has fallen to zero.

Examples of this could be a condition of *absolute plenty* (sometimes called "full communism") where productivity (capitalist or socialist) has outstripped the desire for goods and services (perhaps as a result of a philosophy of simpler living) or a condition of *absolute shortage* of land, tools and materials to work with–as in a besieged fortress (or in other cases of catastrophic overpopulation). We have never experienced absolute plenty, when there would be no distributive problem anyway, and in cases of extreme shortages, when total income is more or less given, income inequality has usually been diminished, in real terms, by egalitarian rationing. This indicates a general recognition of the distributive efficiency of egalitarianism and its dominance where productive efficiency becomes unimportant.

(It is of interest to note that on the assumption of a given total income to be shared, the maximin principle also yields the same result as the utilitarian marginal analysis. This is because the average income is then also the maximin income.)

But we live in a world where productive efficiency is of the utmost importance. For the richest countries it can be argued that greater productivity alone would merely raise "keeping up with the Joneses" to a higher intensity while speeding up the depletion of the planet's natural resources, and that only an increase in distributive efficiency could improve the condition of man. But for most of the world even the complete equalization of income would merely spread the misery from the vast majority to all. Only an increase in output (per capita, of course) could bring significant relief.

Since material incentives are necessary to induce productive efficiency to increase the output–the income available to be distributed–the rule for the efficient distribution of a *given* income seems supremely irrelevant.

These issues present no problem for Nozick. His assumption of the justice of the distribution of holdings in a regime of free exchange removes any concern for efficiency of distribuion, while his implied assumption that "nature" continually updates the laws that define property rights so as to eliminate all externalities, thus maintaining productive efficiency through the automatic competitive equalization of the prices of all factors to the changing value of their marginal social products.

Rawls, however, recognizing that changes in property rights and other social arrangements affect both the size and the distribution of the social income, is constrained by his maximin principle to approve of changes which increase output only if they improve the condition of the "worst off" group (or in case of a tie, of the next-worst-off group). Utilitarian marginalism also recognizes that differences in property rights and other social arrangements affect the size and distributions of the social income, but it leads to Rawls' maximin conclusion only on the assumption of a universal absolute and overriding risk aversion. Absolute risk aversion would still lead a perfectly unbiased person to declare that he would have chosen the maximin world to be born in. But it would not make it moral for him to choose that for others unless he could assume that every one else suffers from the same absolute risk aversion. Furthermore, it raises the doubly difficult philosophical question whether the unborn judge in the "original position" should be supposed to know what his risk aversion or risk preference is (or would be?).

Rawls claims, however, that he does not base his maximin principle on marginal analysis and absolute risk aversion but on everybody, including those in the "worst off" group, having some "common property rights" in whatever can be produced in society, and so also in any increases on output. But this, if I understand it correctly, is a complete departure from his basic idea of Justice as Fairness, as guaranteed by the "original position," and is close to some Nozick-like notion of "entitlement."

Since the equal income theorem applies only to the distribution of a *given* total income, anything which *increases* somebody's income without reducing anyone else's income must be accepted as a pure gain. Utilitarian marginalism here leads to the rule that the price paid for anybody's extra (marginal) effort should be equal to the extra (marginal) product, bringing us back to the principle of allocative efficiency—the efficient allocation of time between work and leisure. The marginal effort will then be undertaken by everybody as long as this is beneficial to him, while there is just as much product left for everybody else. There is a net gain. Some are better off and none are worse off, even if none of those in the worse off group are among the beneficiaries.

If, as seems very likely, an increase in total income and wealth eases transfers from rich to poor and there is an increase in such transfers, we have an improvement in both productive and distributive efficiency. But is it possible to work more systematically toward achieving both types of efficiency?

VI. Unnecessary Payments

This appears to involve a fundamental conflict of mutually inconsistent principles. The rule called for by the principle of distributive efficiency stands squarely on a *given* or fixed income to be distributed. The rule called for by the principle of productive efficiency rests roundly on an *augmentable* income, maximised by paying the worker the value of his marginal product. How can this circle be squared?

The circle *can* be squared to the degree that *some* of the marginal product need not be paid. That part can then be treated as belonging to a *given* "surplus" which can be subjected to the distributive efficiency rule of equal distribution.

(This use of the surplus, though *possible*, is of course not *necessary*. Surplus has been appropriated throughout the ages for all sorts of other purposes.)

Until recently, it was not uncommon for economists to argue that income taxes and inheritance taxes could improve distribution without interfering with production. As long as the marginal tax is less than 100%, it was argued, the point of maximum profit is not moved, and production is not affected. This has now gone out of fashion. Income is not pure profit and income taxes reduce the incentive to earn income. Only lump-sum taxes are seen as neutral, and they are not practical and are considered a theoretical curiosum. Also half forgotten is an older unpractical theoretical museum piece—the "faculty tax"—for eliminating income inequalities from work (inherited income having perhaps already been dealt with by progressive taxation of inheritances). The "faculty tax" is a lump sum tax equal to a person's ability to earn income (his "earning faculty") *minus* the average income. (If one's "earning faculty" is less than the average income, his tax becomes a *negative tax*—a subsidy.)

The impracticability of the "faculty tax," like the popular demand for abolishing pollution or Rawls' exclusive concentration on the "worst-off" group, can be alleviated by bringing in the economist's all-purpose solvent—their gradualness, continuity, or marginalism. What cannot be done in one fell swoop can be done by degrees; and in fact it is being done by degrees all over the place by lump sum taxes in various guises—or is it disguises?

The telephone user pays a lump sum tax (in this case a negative one—a subsidy) in the form of getting a certain number of calls free. As long as he uses more than this number of calls, what he is charged per call by the telephone system could be the marginal cost, which is the proper degree of discouragement. The "small business" may get some loans at specially low rates of interest, but if it still has to borrow some more money at the current rate, this does not cause it to use any of the capital inefficiently. Here again is a hidden lump sum subsidy. When a fixed amount of gas is sold by the producers to the distributors at less than the market price, the difference in money received is exactly equivalent to a lump sum tax paid by the former to the latter. But as long as this does not apply to marginal production, the effect is again purely distributional. It has no effect on productive efficiency. Farmers in Israel (and elsewhere) are given a certain amount of water at much below cost. But as long as this supply is not enough fully to satisfy the demand, and they buy additional water (at a price that covers the marginal cost) up to the point where the price is equal to its marginal product, and if the farmers would be operating in any case, there is again a pure lump sum subsidy—a transfer of income that does not interfere with productive efficiency—that may be a contribution to distributive efficiency.

The general principle underlying the possibility of increasing distributional efficiency without diminishing productive efficiency is illustrated in our accompanying diagram, which shows the number of hours worked (OS) and the wage rate (SE), E being the equilibrium point at which supply is equal to demand. The rectangle (OE) represents, in its area, the price (SE) times the quantity (OS), the total amount paid.[5]

In this figure the supply curve shows that smaller amounts would be supplied at lower prices. The shaded area within the rectangle (lying above the supply curve) thus represents payments over and above what is necessary to make the supply available. Only the unshaded part of the rectangle, (that part of it which lies below the supply curve) represents the "necessary" payment that the suppliers have to get to be willing to make the supply available. The rest is "surplus" or "unnecessary payment." The full-price (SE) is what has to be paid for the marginal unit, but all the other units could be obtained for less. This is shown by the supply curve being lower to the left of E.

Paying for *all* the units at the same marginal rate, may seem natural or even necessary, but this is only because it is our habit to start count-

[5]The development of this diagram appears in Abba P. Lerner, "The Economics and Politics of Consumer Sovereignty," *Proceedings of the American Economic Association*, (May 1972): 261.

ing from zero. But this procedure is arbitrary. The count could begin at any other point—at, say, half the standard number of hours. If the standard number of hours of work in a particular industry is 6 hours, then counting the hours for the purpose of computing the pay would begin only after 3 hours of work.

VII. Degrees of Socialism

The later this count begins, i.e., the greater the number of "unpaid" hours, the more of the product would be left as a part of the "given" social product available for "free income" to be distributed in accordance with distributive efficiency, and the greater will then be the degree to which the society could be said to be socialistic.

This looks rather like a trade-off between allocative and distributive efficiency, but that is not the case. As long as the *marginal units* of factor services are paid their marginal product any increase in "unpaid" hours, and the consequent decrease in "paid" hours, is not at the expense of productive efficiency.

Coming back to our diagram, consider the possible vertical lines, like that at L, which could be drawn parallel to the ordinate as points from which we begin to count the "paid" hours. If we start at 0 on the extreme left, paying all the units at the marginal rate, we have the pure free exchange system with the allocation favored by Nozick and honored by him as "natural." Moving the vertical line all the way to the right up to the point of intersection E, would mean having no "paid" hours at all with the whole of the output available for distribution in accordance with allocative efficiency. This is the other limiting case of pure socialism via the lump sum "faculty tax" and the equal distribution of income.

VIII. Resistances

A close approximation to such complete equalization of income is unpractical, but not because it would interfere with productive efficiency. It is unpractical only because the population is not prepared to accept such extreme equality of income. The supplier will not be willing to supply his services unless the pay he gets for his "paid" hours covers the "necessary payment for all the hours he works." The "lump sum" tax that takes the form of the "unpaid" hours must not be too great.

If L in our diagram represents the point at which we start the pay, the total pay will be shown by the area of the smaller rectangle LE. If the area LE is less than the unshaded part of the larger rectangle OE, he will not willingly supply the "free" hours of work for the sake of the earnings of the "paid" hours that follow.

If L is the point at which these two areas (LE and the unshaded area of the larger rectangle OE) are just equal, then starting the pay at any point between O and L would provide varying degrees of distributional efficiency but would retain complete allocative efficiency throughout. Starting the pay later, between L and S, would not work. It would be "too socialistic."

The objective of trying to achieve as much distributive efficiency as possible without sacrificing any allocative efficiency can thus be expressed as trying to move L, the point from which the pay begins, as far to the right toward S as possible. But the area LE cannot be reduced below the "necessary payment." What determines the necessary payment?

The payment that is necessary to obtain the use of a factor for a particular purpose is what the factor could get in the best paid alternative use. In a society organized with the social purpose of maximizing both kinds of efficiency, the alternative marginal rate of pay is technically determined by the value of the alternative marginal product. But the L point in the alternative occupation, the point at which the pay begins, is under the central government's control. The total alternative earnings, and thus the necessary payment, can thus be made very low indeed. The L point can be shifted quite far toward S. This is limited only by the remaining options that cannot be government controlled. These are the myriad devices that can be invented by workers who do not feel that they are being treated fairly or justly and which will ultimately force the authorities to grant conditions that eliminate such resentment.

High among these resistances to "too much socialism" are the established traditions of *inequalities* of pay for different occupations. It is these feelings of the *propriety* of certain income differences that constitute the resistance to the "socialistic" distributional efficiency, and it is these that have to be weakened if greater distributive efficiency is to be attained while protecting maximum productive efficiency.

Another possible approach would be to set the L point at the same number of "unpaid" hours for everybody, with all workers free to work more hours and be paid the value of the marginal product for the additional hours, or to work fewer hours and be docked the value of the marginal product of the reduced hours from their "free income." This would induce the high marginal product workers to increase their efforts and their hours of work, and their already high total pay, until the increased marginal disutility of work rose to equality with the marginal utility to the worker of the high marginal pay; and conversely it would induce the low marginal product workers to cut down their efforts and their hours of work, and their already low total pay, until the marginal disutility of the work is reduced to equality with the marginal utility of the low marginal pay. Work with high value of marginal product would then become doubly attractive and conversely work with very low value of marginal product would become doubly unattractive.

Workers would then be induced to move from work with low marginal product to work with high marginal product. Both of these responses would tend to equalize the marginal product as well as the marginal pay, the distribution of marginal effort and the number of hours worked, and thus also the individual incomes. It would improve both allocative and productive efficiency, while at the same time acclimatizing the public to more egalitarian and more socialistic distribution.

As this develops, the L point can be moved further to the right, and the "unpaid" hours and the "free income" increased. But all the time the increase in distributional efficiency does nothing to diminish productive efficiency. What limits the degree of distributional efficiency and the speed with which additions to it are achieved is not the protection of productive efficiency, but the traditions of legitimate inequalities, the political power of pressure groups, the threats of strikes, and, most of all, the inefficiencies from apathy in work which often cannot be distinguished from the conscious or unconscious sabotage of productive efficiency that grows out of feelings of resentment at whatever is deemed "unjust."

Such a development of increased distributional efficiency can properly be said to make society more socialistic. But whether it makes it less capitalistic is not so clear. It has to be so if capitalism stands for income inequality or distributional inefficiency—as it certainly has come to mean for many people. But if capitalism stands for making use of free exchange and competition in markets for the purpose of maximizing productive efficiency, then there is nothing anticapitalist in the socialism of greater distributional efficiency through "unpaid" inframarginal hours of work (and other productive factors) and "free income."

While such redistributions are usually given names with socialist connotations there are equally appropriate capitalistic words. Instead of being called "social grants" or "welfare payments" or even the hybrid "negative income tax," one could declare every citizen to have become a capitalist—to have inherited shares in "The Grand National Corporation," or even in specific local or multinational corporations, and the "free income" to be nothing but the dividends he is entitled to because they are earned by the shares he owns.

IX. Summary

I have presented three recipes for desirable income distributions, each claiming to yield higher levels of human satisfaction. But only my argument about the tandem nature of allocative and distributional efficiency and the diminishing marginal utility of income is based clearly on an analysis of the expected effects on human satisfactions.

Nozick's theory of *entitlement* justifies the distribution reached in a free exchange economy, presuming that all factors are "naturally" paid the value of their marginal product, and that such payments are "just." Rawls' *Maximin* principle can be derived on utilitarian principles, from an imagined choice in "the original position" only on the assumption of an overriding absolute risk aversion. It can also be reached from a concern limited to the welfare of the "worst off" or by jettisoning Rawls' Justice as Fairness (together with his "original position") and subscribing to a belief in some Nozickian "entitlement" of the "worst off" to a share in any *increase* in total social income.

The basic distributive theorem of utilitarian marginalism—that distributive efficiency calls for income equality—is strictly applicable only for a *given* total social income. Since the total social income is not given but depends on human effort, a compromise has to be made. The equality theorem must be adjusted to induce individuals to cooperate in exercising their full capacities. But it is argued that within a wide range the equalizing redistribution of income can take place without reducing total output. This is shown in an analysis of "necessary" and "unnecessary" payments which is illustrated in our diagram.

Utilitarian marginalism points the way to a combination of the maximization of productive efficiency, given the degree of perfection and competitiveness of the market, with a simultaneous maximization of distributional efficiency, constrained only by social, conventional and political resistances to extremes of egalitarianism. My colleague at Florida State University, Professor E. Raymond Canterbery has suggested that this policy be called the pursuit of the *Maximax*.

[4]

WELFARE ECONOMICS AND THE SCITOVSKY PARADOX

Abba P. Lerner
QUEENS COLLEGE of The City University of New York

If a change from situation A to situation B makes some people better off and none worse off, B is better than A. If the change makes some better off and some worse off, but those who gain compensate those who lose and still have some gain left over, B is again better than A. After the compensation some are better off and none are worse off.

If the change benefits some and hurts others, and the gains are great enough to enable the gainers to compensate the losers, but (for whatever reason) the gainers do not compensate the losers—it was argued (originally by Kaldor) that there is, in some sense, an "increase in output." The increase in output is not merely physical, which might mean more of things that people do not want. The new output is capable of making everybody better off. But it is accompanied by a shift in distribution so that some people find themselves worse off while others gain more than the whole increase in output. Unless the shift in distribution is a bad one, and so bad that it more than offsets the benefit from the "increase in output," B should still be considered better than A.

Scitovsky then showed that it is possible on this criterion to have B better than A *and* A better than B! Those who gained by the change from A to B would gain more than enough to compensate completely all who lost by the change. But if this change took place, without the compensation, a switch back from B to A would also enable the beneficiaries to compensate the losers and still have some gains left. This is the paradox; and it has scared away from welfare economics altogether many economists who had been rather leery of welfare economics to begin with.

The paradox is illustrated in Figure 1. PP is a production possibility curve showing what combinations of X and of Y can be produced. There are two communal indifference curves, one corresponds to the production of the quantities of X and Y as shown by position A and it passes through point A in the diagram. It shows the combinations of X and Y which could leave each individual as well off as at A. Each point on the indifference curve measures the sums of the quantities of X and Y consumed by each individual at the welfare level of A at the different relative prices indicated by the slope of the communal indifference curve at that point. The other communal indifference curve passes through B and shows the corresponding combinations of X and Y, which, in the same way, could leave each individual as well off as at B.

Figure 1 shows B above the A indifference curve and A above the B indifference curve. This must be so if B is to seem better than A from position A while A seems better than B from position B, as is required by the Scitovsky paradox. The figure shows us that the paradox can occur only if the B indifference curve is tilted to the left (counterclockwise) in relation to the A indifference curve, as shown by the arrows in the diagram.

Something similar to the Scitovsky paradox appears even in cases where there is no tilting of indifference curves. In Figure 2 we have only one set of indifference curves and it is independent of what is being produced. It may represent a single individual or a society in which all individuals have identical tastes. Here the movement from A to B, which means producing more X (and less Y) is an improvement. B is better than A. From position B a movement to C in the opposite direction, producing less X (and more Y), is now an improvement. From C a movement to D, producing more X (and less Y), is an improvement and so on. We have alternating movements in opposite directions like those of Figure 1.

All of these alternating movements in opposite directions can be seen as aimed at the optimal position Z (where an indifference curve is tangential to PP) but overshooting the mark, first in one direction and then in the other. In Figure 1, however, unlike Figure 2, the reverse movement from B could lead *all the way back* to the original position A. This is possible because the shift from A to B tilts the indifference curve to the left and it gets tilted back again, to the right, by the shift back from B to A. In spite of this difference what we have here is again a case of going too far in the right direction and having to backtrack each time the goal is over-reached.

This becomes clearer if we assume *continuity* in the tilting of the communal indifference curve in response to movement along PP. This assumption of continuity would seem no less justifiable than the assumptions of continuity that enable us to draw continuous indifference curves, individual or communal, or a continuous PP curve. As production moves down PP from A in the direction of B, the indifference curve is continuously and gradually tilted to the left. At A the indifference curve is steeper than PP, at B it is flatter than PP. Somewhere between A and B the indifference curve must pass from being steeper than PP to being flatter than PP, and at that point, it must have the same slope as PP. This is where the indifference curve is tangential to PP and is shown at Z in Figure 1. Z is the optimal point which would be overshot each time in alternating movements between A and B.

It might even be that at A, B looks like the optimal point Z, i.e., the point where PP would just be touched by a higher indifference curve if we could draw one corresponding to production at A; and that similarly, A might look like "Z" from position B. But there is no way of drawing such higher communal indifference curves, since they are not anchored on the specific income distributions and on the other influences that depend on where production happens to be. This objection does not apply to communal indifference curves A, B and Z, since each of these refers only to the distribution of income (and other influences) as determined by production at A, B or Z respectively.

Movement along PP could also tilt the communal indifference curve in the opposite direction, i.e., to the right (clockwise). This is shown in Figure 3 for a shift down PP. The tilt would be to the left for a shift *up* PP. At A, A* might seem to be the optimum. But a movement from A to A* would tilt the communal indifference curve to the right and A* would be found not to be a "Z." In this case, instead of the target being overshot, the aim falls short and further movement *in the same direction* is called for instead of a reverse movement. Similarly, at B, B* might seem to be the point to be reached, but the movement of production from B to B* (*up* PP) would tilt the communal indifference curve to the left and the "Z" would have moved further away from B. In this case the optimal point Z is further from A and from B than it seems. The optimum (which is also the equilibrium point) is in this case made harder to reach by the tilt. In the Scitovsky paradox case, it is made easier to reach. The Scitovsky type of tilt has an effect similar to making the indifference curves set (if we had an indifference curve set) more convex so that the equilibrium is more stable. The forces moving the economy to equilibrium are stronger. Tilting in the opposite direction has the opposite effect and is similar to making the indifference curves less convex so that the equilibrium is less "tight."

Figure 4 illustrates a more extreme form of the counter-Scitovsky tilt. At A, B looks like the optimal point, but when B is reached the optimal point seems to have moved down to C. At C, it seems to have moved further down to D and so on. Where the steepening of the communal indifference curve resulting from its being tilted to the right by the movement down PP is sufficient to prevent it from being surpassed by the increasing steepness of the PP curve as one moves down it, equilibrium would not be reached until we got to the corner at Z where there is complete specialization on X with no Y produced at all. All this could just as well go in the opposite direction with complete specialization in Y. An even more special case would be where the indifference curve is tangential to PP to begin with and tilts to the right in just the degree to which the PP curve gets steeper as one moves down it. It would then remain tangential to PP as production moved along PP in either direction and we would have indeterminacy or neutral equilibrium.

But why should the communal indifference curve tilt in either direction? There seem to be three possible explanations. A Scitovsky type tilt would mean that as relatively more of a product is produced the relative desire for it is diminished. Consumers become less fond of it, or become more fond of the other product of which less is being produced. This is over and above the diminishing *marginal* substitutability on account of there being more of this product available and less of the other. This direction of tilting thus *strengthens* the forces leading to an equilibrium. The three possible reasons for such tilting are: 1. there is an illusion that increases the desirability of what we do not have and which disappears or is reversed when we get it. "The grass is always greener in the other field." 2. Producing less Y and more X increases the income of those who are relatively more fond of Y. These are now rich enough to be able to compensate those who would lose by the return to A. 3. Production of less Y and more X affects the tastes of the producers. They become less fond of X or more eager for Y.

The opposite tilting would, of course, be caused by the opposite causes. Instead of envy for what we have not, there would be an exaggerated appreciation of what we have. Instead of increased relative income for those who prefer the disappearing product, we would have the enrichment of those who are more fond of what is becoming more plentifully available. Instead of producers disliking what they make they are enthusiastic about their own products. Unfortunately these apparently more socially attractive responses would *diminish* the effectiveness of the market mechanism while the responses underlying the Scitovsky paradox strengthen it.

The Scitovsky paradox is sometimes expressed somewhat differently. It is said that while the would-be gainers from a movement (from A to B) are able to more than compensate the losers from the movement, the losers are able to more than compensate the would-be gainers in bribes to have them refrain from the movement. I do not see how this is possible. If the potential gain to the gainers is greater than the potential loss to the losers it cannot at the same time be true that the potential loss to the losers is greater than the potential gain to the gainers. It is the increased wealth in situation B of those who prefer situation A (or the increase in the degree of preferences for A) that makes it possible for them to compensate those who prefer situation B. These changes in wealth or in tastes is not taken into account in the construction of the communal indifference curves out of the individual indifference curves. This construction is based on the initial distribution of wealth and on the initial sets of individual preferences. If all these things could be taken into account, neither the Scitovsky paradox nor the other kinds of tilting of the communal indifference curve would arise.

The reader may have noticed a certain lack of patience on my part for communal or social indifference curves. My impatience is due in part to my remembering a device I used many years ago which enables me to deal with problems of the kind discussed here without making use of such communal or social indifference curves. All that is needed is a *slope of relative prices* for each point on PP. These relative prices (P_x/P_y, the price of X in terms of Y) will be the resultant of the different incomes of the members of society that derive from the demand for the factors of production owned by them. Their incomes provide the weight given to their different tastes for the different products. In the absence of any tilting one would expect that the relative price of X in terms of Y would fall as one moved down PP producing more X and less Y. At the same time, as more of X and less of Y is produced, more and more resources which are relatively less efficient in the production of X have to be taken away from the production of Y. Only those relatively more efficient in the production of Y remain there. More and more resources which are relatively less efficient in the production of X have to be mobilized to increase its production. The marginal cost of producing X in terms of the alternative Y (C_x/C_y) will be increasing. This is shown in the increasing steepness in the PP curve itself as one moves down it. At A, the slope of relative prices is greater than the slope of PP. The price of X in relation to the price of Y is greater than the marginal cost of X in relation to the marginal cost of Y. This indicates that more X and less Y should be produced. At B, the slope of relative prices is flatter than PP. The relative marginal cost of X is greater than the relative price of X, indicating that less X and more Y should be produced. Somewhere between A and B the slopes must become equal. This is where we have the equilibrium and the optimum at Z, where the relative marginal costs are just equal to relative prices and no shift in production is called for.

For those who find it difficult (or somehow insufficiently rigorous) to consider such movements of relative slopes as one moves along PP, the argument can be spelled out in further detail. In Figure 5, the slopes are translated into vertical heights. At A, P_x/P_y is greater than C_x/C_y. At B, it is the other way around. Somewhere in between the two curves have to cross. Their heights, and the relative prices and relative marginal costs they represent, are equal at Z.

The assumption of continuity shows that the conditions that lead to the Scitovsky paradox strengthen the forces that lead to the optima of welfare economics and should rally economists to welfare economics rather than encourage the tendency of some economists to keep away from it and to disparage it. The Scitovsky analysis, however, regains all its strength if we consider the possibility that there is no continuity—that only position A and B are available and nothing in between. It is then no use showing that a better position Z would exist, of which the Scitovsky paradox helps us to become aware, if there were continuity. It shows us that free enterprise may succeed in maximizing regret. Whichever of the alternatives is chosen, the current relative prices will make the foregone alternative seem to have been a lost better opportunity. If we have a sufficiently long period, or sufficient flexibility in the shifting of resources from the one to the other alternative, we could find ourselves wasting our substance in continually scrapping and rebuilding our plants instead of using them to produce outputs for consumption. In the more extreme case of complete flexibility we could be turned into a communal Buridan's ass frozen into an inability to choose between the alternatives.

But all such difficulties are no particular criticism of welfare economics. They show the inapplicability of microeconomics for macro decisions. These are inevitably political decisions where the invisible hand, which operates ultimately on each economic unit being able to neglect its impact on the totality, must give way to the visible hand of an administrator who has to try to act "dialectically," i.e., taking everything into account. Not least among the instruments that could guide him would be macro-marginal welfare economics which deals with decisions in case of indivisibilities—as in Chapter 16 of my *The Economics of Control*.

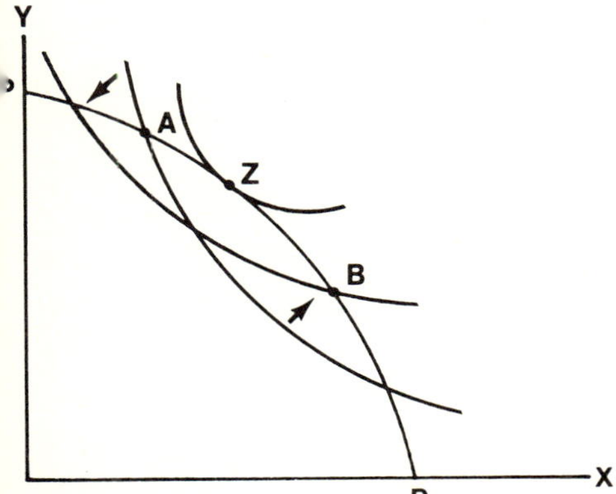

Figure 1

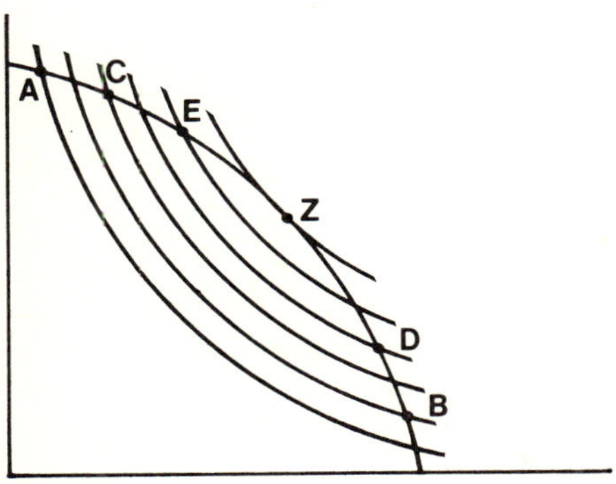

Figure 2

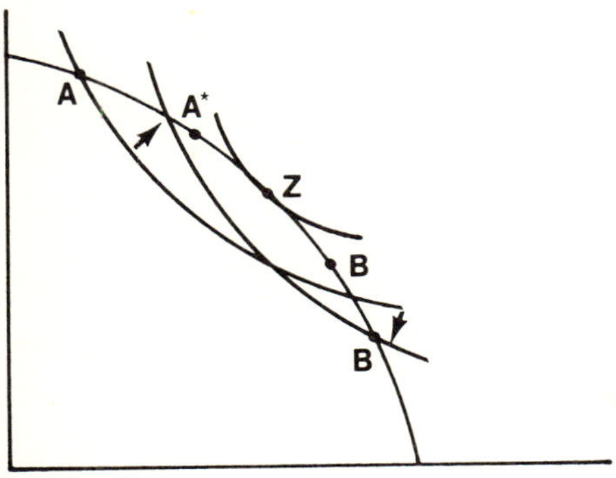

Figure 3

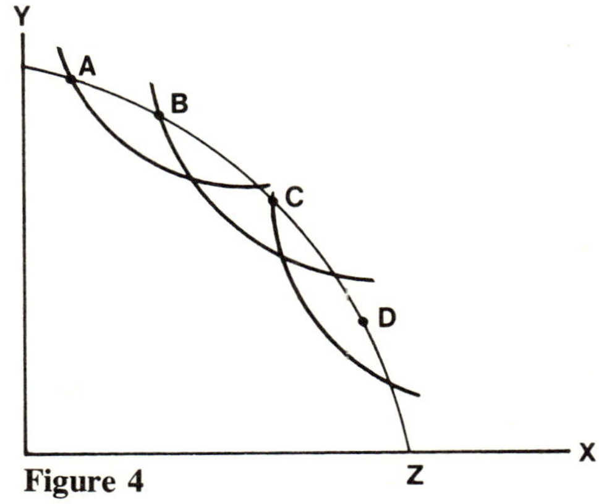

Figure 4

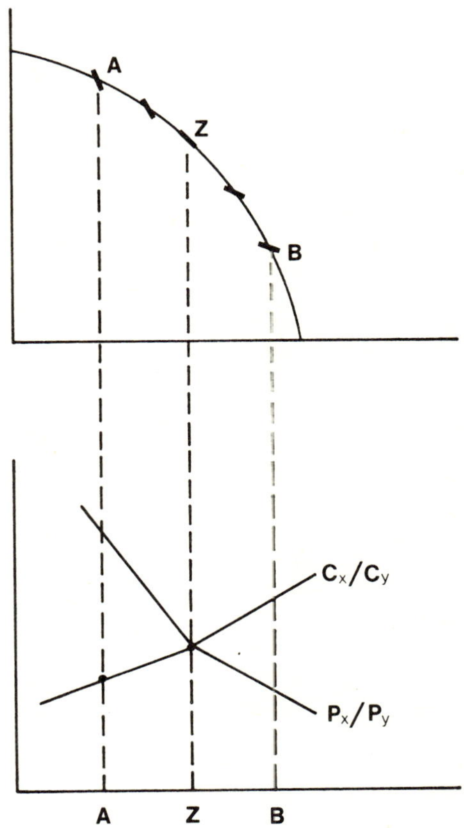

Figure 5

PART TWO
MACROECONOMICS
A. Functional Finance

[1]

Mr. Keynes' "General Theory of Employment, Interest and Money"

by

A. P. LERNER
London School of Economics

In an important book recently published[1] *Mr. Keynes has attempted to solve the general problem of variations in the volume of output and employment. As the book is largely an attack on the adequacy of the existing orthodox economic theory as a means for handling the problems of fluctuations in employment, trade cycles, and the like, it is clear that it has an important bearing on many of the questions which are at present in the forefront of the interests of the International Labour Organisation. The argument, however, which deals primarily with questions of theory and only in the second place with the application of this theory to practice, is by no means easy to follow, partly from the intrinsic nature of the subject, partly from the highly specialised terminology employed. The Office has therefore thought that many readers of the* Review *would welcome an account in simpler terms of the main argument of the book. This is the purpose of the following article, whose author is thoroughly familiar with Mr. Keynes' writings. It should be added that the article has been read in manuscript by Mr. Keynes himself, who has expressed his approval of it.*

THE object of this article is to provide as simple as possible an account of the most important line of argument that runs through Mr. J. M. Keynes' book *The General Theory of Employment, Interest and Money*, so that, except perhaps in some details of presentation, it contains nothing original. I have endeavoured, where possible, to follow the traditional

[1] John Maynard KEYNES: *The General Theory of Employment, Interest and Money*. London, Macmillan, 1936. XII + 403 pp. 5s.

— 2 —

use of language more closely than Keynes does, as I have found that this renders the argument both more intelligible and more acceptable to those who are not familiar with the oral tradition of Cambridge. While necessarily simplifying the argument considerably in order to be able to encompass it in an article of appropriate length, I do not think I have left out anything fundamental. In discovering what are the points in the argument or its presentation at which students are liable to jib, I have learnt much from innumerable discussions with economists and students in London, Cambridge and Geneva, and of these certainly the most helpful was Dr. Gottfried Haberler, who has been working towards similar results along a quite different route. I must add that I would certainly not have been able to attempt this task were it not for the time I spent in Cambridge in 1934-35 while Leon Fellow of the University of London.

* * *

Keynes wishes sharply to distinguish his own system from what he calls the " classical " economics. By that he means the orthodox body of doctrine, first conceived in fairly complete outline by Ricardo, and developed by almost all economists of repute from that time on, both in England and elsewhere, which finds its present culmination in the works of Pigou. Keynes is so keen on making clear the difference between the classical and his own scheme that he perhaps over-emphasises it, willingly taking this risk in order to be certain of avoiding the other error, which he considers more dangerous, of permitting a reader to overlook the revolutionary nature of the change. He has no patience whatever for the interpreter who would try to read Keynes' views into the classical writers. This is not at all—as is frequently suggested—because that would diminish his claims to originality (in fact I believe he is over-generous in his estimate of how near the Mercantilists and the Monetary Cranks were to his thesis) but because he is convinced that such identification is made plausible only by obscurity. Keynes therefore complains that " Those who are sufficiently steeped in the old point of view simply cannot believe that I am asking them to step into a new pair of trousers, and will insist on regarding it as nothing but an embroidered version of the old pair that they have been wearing for years. " [1]

[1] *Economica*, Nov. 1931, p. 390.

— 3 —

I have insisted at some length on this because it helps to explain the extraordinary psychological resistance to Keynes' new argument that is always displayed by classical economists. (I shall use this word throughout in Keynes' sense.)

It is this psychological resistance that so frequently leads people to reject a proposition of Keynes' as a paradox and then to turn uneasily and, almost in the same breath, to scorn it as a platitude. " It's absolutely wrong "—"we all knew that before!"

The last sentence in Keynes' preface reads : " The difficulty lies, not in the new ideas, but in escaping from the old ones, which ramify, for those brought up as most of us have been, into every corner of our minds." I would like to underline that sentence.

* * *

Keynes is concerned with the problem of unemployment. The classical view is that in the absence of State interference or other rigidities, the existence of any unemployment will have the effect of lowering wages.

This follows immediately from the definition of unemployment, for any man who is not in employment but who does not try to get work at a lower wage is no more considered to be unemployed than the man who refuses to work overtime or on Sundays. At the current wage he prefers leisure to employment. He may be idle but he is not unemployed—at any rate he is not involuntarily unemployed. If he really wanted to work, if he were really unemployed, he would offer himself at a lower wage and this would reduce the level of wages. Unemployment is incompatible with equilibrium.

The reduction of wages, the argument goes on, will make industrial activity more profitable so that business men will employ more people. As long as there is any unemployment wages will fall, and as long as wages fall profits rise, and as profits rise employment increases until all the unemployed are absorbed in industry and we have equilibrium and no more unemployment.

Unemployment can therefore persist only if the State, or the Trade Unions, or some other institution prevents the unemployed from offering their services at lower wages and so from setting in motion the automatic mechanism which leads to equilibrium and full employment. What is necessary, therefore, is simply to remove the rigidity and allow the unemployment to liquidate itself by reducing wages.

Keynes accepts neither the definition nor the argument. Like the classical economists he is concerned only with *involuntary* unemployment, but he defines as *involuntarily* unemployed a man who would be willing to work at a lower *real* wage than the current real wage, whether or not he is willing to accept a lower *money* wage. If a man is not willing to accept a lower *real* wage, then he is *voluntarily* unemployed, and Keynes does not worry about him at all. But there are millions of people who on Keynes' definition are unemployed but who fall outside of the classical definition of unemployed, and these provide one of the most pressing of modern social problems. These are willing to work for less than the current real wage—they would be willing to work for the current money wage even if the cost of living were to go up a little—yet they cannot find jobs. What determines the number of people in a society who find themselves in this position ? Or to put the question the other way round, what determines the number of people who do find employment ? The object of Mr. Keynes' book is to indicate the road leading to the answer to this question.

The classical refusal to consider these men as really involuntarily unemployed resolves itself into a recipe for finding them employment. They have only to agree to accept lower wages and they will find work. Keynes objects to this procedure of economists on two separate grounds. His first objection is on the practical ground of the uselessness of tendering advice that one knows will not be accepted, even if it is sound advice. It is time for economists who wish to give statesmen practical advice to realise that money wages are sticky—that workers will, in fact, refuse to reduce money wages.

But Keynes' main objection consists of a denial of the theory which is put forward as an excuse for the treatment. If money wages are reduced it does not follow that there will be any increase in employment. A general reduction of wages will reduce marginal costs, and competition between producers will reduce prices of products. Equilibrium will be reached only when prices have fallen as much as wages, and it will not pay to employ more men than in the beginning. The workers, who are able to make agreements with their employers about their *money* wage, cannot adjust their *real* wage. If they could reduce their real wage more would be employed, but they can only attemp to reduce their real wage by reducing their money wage at the existing price level. This, however, only brings about a proportionate fall in prices so that they are in fact not able to vary their *real* wage. That is why their unemployment is *involuntary* even if they refuse to accept a lower money wage. For that would not have the desired effect of reducing the real wage and increasing employment—it would merely remove a certain stability of prices.

It has hardly been disputed that a cut in money wages, by reducing costs, will have some tendency to reduce prices, but it remains to be shown why prices should fall *proportionately* to the reduction in money wages so that there is *no* fall in the real wage and so *no* increase in employment in the manufacture of consumption goods. (Employment in investment industry depends on other factors considered below. For the time being this is taken as given.)

Whether this will be the case or not cannot be decided at all by looking merely at the effect of the wage cut upon *costs*. It is necessary also to consider the effect of the wage cut upon *demand*; whether directly or whether indirectly through the change in employment that might be initiated by the first impact of the wage cut. Until we bring this into the picture we have not sufficient data to be able to decide what the result must be.

This has made it possible for one eminent economist to argue that a cut in money wages will increase employment, and for another eminent economist to argue that a cut in money wages will not increase employment. The first is able to show that his thesis is consistent with the cost conditions; for with a larger volume of employment—with more labour applied to the given productive equipment of society—the marginal productivity of labour is less, marginal costs are higher relatively to wages; prices (which, with the same degree of imperfection of competition, must in equilibrium bear the same ratio to marginal costs) are also higher relatively to wages, so that the workers by cutting their money wages have been successful in reducing their *real* wages. The second is also able to show that his conclusions are consistent with the cost conditions; for if there is no increase in employment, marginal costs will fall as much as wages, and prices have to fall in the same proportion as costs, so that there is no change in real wages. Further, each economist is able to accuse the other of assuming his conclusions, and then each can complain of the pot calling the kettle black. So that we have an infinite regress but no answer to our question.

The necessity of bringing in the demand side is seen even more clearly if we suppose for a moment that wages are the only item that enters into marginal costs and that marginal costs are constant. In this case there is no inverse relation between employment and real wages. If wages are cut, marginal costs fall in the same proportion as wages whether there is an increase in employment or not. There will be no fall in real wages, but that tells us nothing about the volume of employment. To get the answer to our question we have to consider the effects of the wage cut on demand, direct as well as indirect.

The essence of the analysis whereby Keynes obtains the result that there will be no change in employment comes from a consideration of demand conditions. If there is initially an increase in employment—and, since employers very often think that a wage cut is a good thing, this impact effect is very likely—the demand conditions will be such as to bring about losses which tend to induce the entrepreneurs to curtail employment until the previous equilibrium level of employment is restored. Similarly, if the impact effect is to reduce employment, this will bring about profits which induce entrepreneurs to raise employment to the previous level.

The losses that accompany an increase in employment in the manufacture of consumption goods are due to the tendency of people, whose income is increased, to increase their expenditure by *less* than the increase in their incomes. This means that the increase in revenue from the sale of the larger output of consumption goods is less than the increase in the outlay on their production so that there emerges a net loss. This loss may be mitigated, but not entirely escaped, by the withholding of stocks with the intention of selling them at a more propitious moment, but this procedure, while diminishing losses, has the effect of building up superfluous stocks. The losses and the accumulation of stocks both tend to reduce employment, and these forces must persist and accumulate as long as employment remains above the equilibrium level. The whole of this phenomenon is reserved for the case where the initial effect of the wage cut is to diminish employment.

We must now consider how all this works if items other than wages enter into marginal costs. Where this is the case these

— 7 —

other items are payments for the use of productive resources which, in the short period, are fixed in supply. This is because they accept whatever they can get, their reward falling relatively to wages until all those that are of any use whatever are employed.

If, then, wages are reduced, the attempt to substitute labour for these other productive resources will increase employment and may reduce the earnings of these resources. As long as these earnings have not fallen in the same proportion as wages, costs and prices will not have fallen as much as wages but will have fallen more than the rewards of the other productive resources. Real wages will be lower while the real reward to the other productive factors will be greater. More men will be employed, and the total real income will be greater ; since with more men employed on the given resources a greater real product is forthcoming. The aggregate real income of the other productive resources is increased, since the quantity employed is unchanged and the real rate of reward is increased. The aggregate real income of labour may be greater or less than in the beginning, according as the increase in employment is greater or less than the reduction in the real wage.

As long as this situation remains, prices have not fallen as much as wages have been reduced ; and the workers have been able to reduce their real wages by reducing their money wages and thus to increase employment. Such a position cannot be expected to persist, but contains within itself forces which will still further reduce the rewards of the factors other than labour until costs and prices have fallen proportionately to wages, and real wages and employment are back again at the original level.

In the situation we have just described total real income is greater than in the initial position, because more men applied to the same equipment produce more goods. There is an increase in the total real costs of the consumption entrepreneurs exactly equal to this increase in real income (since the incomes of the factors of production are the costs of the entrepreneurs). Out of this extra income some will be saved, so that the total receipts of consumption entrepreneurs increase (in real terms) less than their outgoings. Entrepreneurs make losses which cause them to restrict their (output and) demand for productive resources. This goes on as long as more men are employed than in the initial equilibrium and as long as the real

— 8 —

reward of the productive resources other than labour is greater than in the initial position. These two phenomena disappear at the same time, since the tendency to substitute labour for other productive resources, which led to the increase in employment in the first place, disappears just at the point where the real reward to the other productive factors has fallen in the same proportion as prices and wages. A new equilibrium is reached only when employment has gone back to its original level and the reward of the other resources has fallen to their old *real* level. This will only be when their prices have fallen in the same proportion as wages. As long as these have fallen only in a smaller proportion than wages, prices will be higher than before relatively to wages and lower than before relatively to the reward of the other productive resources, and the disequilibrium described will continue.

In a longer period it will be possible to increase or decrease the supply of productive resources other than labour by varying the application of current factors of production to their manufacture, so that the above argument, which rests on the fixity of supply of productive resources other than labour, would not apply. But there will be no inducement to vary their supply since their price, determined in the longer period by their cost of production, will have varied in just the same proportion as wages. There is therefore no point in departing—except as a temporary mistake—from the initial level of employment.

This does not mean that a reduction of money wages may not have all sorts of indirect influences which ultimately react on the level of employment. There will be effects on the demand for money, on the rate of interest, on entrepreneurs' expectations of future prices or rather of the relation of these future prices to present costs, on the distribution of wealth and spending—all these and other influences will have an effect on the number of people that entrepreneurs consider it profitable to employ—but these work in divergent directions and some of them only after a considerable interval, so that nothing can be said as to the effect of the sum of these influences on employment as a result of a reduction in wages until a complete set of assumptions have been provided as to the form and strength of these influences. Before we have all this information we must either assume them to cancel out and say that there is no effect on employment, or else, if we wish to be more realistic, we must say that what happens to employment if money wages are reduced will depend upon other conditions, so that employment might go either up or down. Anything might happen. There is no simple rule such as the classical economists envisage relating the level of employment to the money wage.

If the level of employment is not affected in any simple way by the money wage, what is it that does determine the amount of employment ? Before answering this question it is useful to contemplate some very simple equations.

The income of the whole society is earned by the members of the society in producing either consumption goods or other kinds of goods. We call these other goods investment goods. This gives us our first equation. The total income of society (Y) is made up of the income earned in making consumption goods (C) and the income earned in making investment goods (I). $Y = C + I$.

Now C, which stands for income earned in making consumption goods, must also stand for the amount spent on buying consumption goods, since these two are in fact the same thing. (Similarly I stands also for the amount of money spent on investment goods). The aggregate amount of saving in any period (S) is defined as the excess of aggregate income in the period over the expenditure on consumption goods. This, the almost universal definition of Saving, gives us our second equation $S = Y - C$ (Definition).

From these two equations it follows that saving must always be equal to investment. $S = I$.

This appears rather peculiar to many people when they first meet it, since there is obviously no mechanism whereby any individual's decision to save causes somebody to invest an exactly equal amount. Mr. Keynes has ineradicably impressed that upon the mind of everyone who has read his *Treatise on Money*. And of course Keynes was right in this. Yet there is no paradox.

It is perfectly possible for any individual to save more without investing more himself. The proposition applies only to *aggregate* saving and investment. Neither is it necessary that aggregate investment should increase whenever any individual decides to increase the amount that he saves. This would be so if an increase in an individual's saving left unchanged the amount saved by all other individuals together, so that it always meant an increase in aggregate saving. But we cannot assume that, because the individual must decrease his expenditure on consumption goods to the extent that he increases his saving. This diminution in C (if others have not changed their expenditure on consumption goods) diminishes Y (by diminishing the income of those who sell consumption goods) and therefore leaves (Y — C), which by definition is S, the same as before. Others have saved as much less as he has saved more, so that aggregate saving is unchanged and equal to the unchanged I. If there is no change in I there can be no change in S.

Individuals deciding how much to spend out of their incomes seem to be able to decide how much to save, and if we consider one individual in a large society, this has sense, because the effect on his own income of an individual's expenditure on consumption goods can be neglected. But if we take society altogether and neglect the effect of changes in expenditure on total incomes, we naturally get into trouble, for we are then making the contradictory assumptions (*a*) that when people save more they spend less on consumption goods and (*b*) that the people who sell consumption goods do not receive any less. And nobody expects to get sensible results by deduction from contradictory assumptions, not even those who are most scornful of the canons of " bourgeois " logic.

The classical view that an individual, in deciding to save more, increases the aggregate amount of saving (S), can be supported by another argument which does not, at first sight, appear to be quite as illogical as that just given. We must leave this however until we have examined the classical theory of the determination of saving and investment and the rate of interest.

A more common-sense objection to the proposition that saving and investment must always and inevitably be equal to each other is to be found in the query whether the identity of these two cannot be upset by *hoarding*. In the case of any individual it is clear that there is no need for his saving to be equal to his investment. When an individual saves more than he invests he is said to *hoard* the difference. Why cannot society do the same ? And if society hoards (or dishoards) will that not make saving greater (or less) then investment ?

We must note more carefully what is meant by " hoarding ". Our individual who invested only a part of his saving was left with the difference in cash. His store of money has increased and it is in fact this increase in his store of money that *is* his hoarding. Any individual who saves more than he invests in any period increases his holding of money by the difference. Any individual who increases his store of money in any period must have saved more than he invested in the period by jus that amount.

The question " Can the society hoard ? " means, then, nothing else than " Can the society increase its store of money ? " This will depend upon whether the monetary authority has increased the amount of money in the society during the period we have been considering, or whether it has not.

If the monetary authority does not increase the amount of money it is impossible for the society to hoard. If any individual hoards other individuals have to dishoard to the same extent, for it is impossible for anybody to increase his store of money without somebody else diminishing *his* store of money as long as the total store is unchanged. There cannot therefore be any *net* hoarding (or dishoarding) by all the members of the society taken together, so that there cannot for the society be any excess of saving over investment (or of investment over saving). S = I.

If the monetary authority does increase the amount of money, then there not merely *can* be net hoarding by the whole society, but there *must* be net hoarding exactly equal to the increase in the society's holdings of money. This does not mean that there is any divergence between saving and investment. There is indeed an excess of saving over investment by the individuals who are left with the extra money that has been put into the society and which must be in somebody's hands. But this is exactly balanced by the expenditure of money by those individuals who borrowed the extra money from the monetary authority (the banks). These borrowers were enabled by the banks to consume or to invest out of borrowed money that was not part of their income. In so far as they spent the money on consumption this constituted negative saving which has to be subtracted from the excess saving by the hoarders. The rest of the borrowed money is invested and provides the investment that balances the excess saving and shows again the inevitable equality of saving to investment. We always get back to this really very obvious if not very informative bit of arithmetic. It only appears strange or suspicious because of the habit of looking at the saving from the point of view of the individual who has got his income and is wondering whether to save it or not. He is naturally unable to see the whole social process. Our suspicions should vanish when we realise that all that the proposition says is that the excess of total income over income earned in making consumption goods is equal to the income earned in other ways.

What we have done now is to replace the suspect proposition that S = I by the even more suspect proposition that it is impossible for a society to hoard if the banks do not increase the amount of money. Does this imply that everything that has been said in economic discussions about the effects of hoarding is sheer nonsense ?

This is of course not the case. The trouble arises from a confusion of two meanings of " hoarding ". When people consider, say, the deflationary effects of hoarding they are talking sound and important sense. But if they are to use the word " hoarding " in the sense we have used it so that it indicates an excess of saving over investment, they should speak of the deflationary effects of " attempts to hoard ". These effects are of the utmost importance. They involve a reduction of prices, of profits, of employment, of incomes, of prosperity generally and of many concomitants of these. But they do not involve an increase in hoarding—in our exact sense of increasing the money held—unless the amount of money is increased. It is only saying the same thing in other words to show that an attempt by people to save more than they invest will diminish consumption and incomes and employment, etc., but will never succeed in making saving greater than investment.

We see then that decisions of income receivers as between spending and saving do not affect the aggregate volume of saving but do determine the size of both income and consumption. The difference between them, which is the amount actually saved, is determined by those who decide the size of I (which is equal to the excess of income over consumption because it is that part of income which is not earned in making consumption goods).

If we have given the size of I, we can say that Y is determined by the propensity to save. If we suppose that the amount people save depends only on the size of their income, and that it increases with the size of income, we can see that income must be at that level where the amount people wish to save is equal to I.

As long as income is below this level people will wish to save less than is being invested, i.e. they will want to spend on consumption goods more than is being earned in making consumption goods, and since these two are identical this means that they will *wish* to spend on consumption goods more than they *are* spending on consumption goods. This will lead to increased demand and profits in the manufacture of consumption goods which will lead to an expansion of employment and income until this level is reached. People then wish to save just as much as is being invested, i.e. they spend on consumption goods an amount that is less than their income by exactly the expenditure on (= the earnings in the manufacture of) investment goods, i.e. they spend on consumption goods just as much as is earned in making consumption goods, i.e. just as much as the cost incurred in making consumption goods. There is neither profit nor loss but equilibrium. If employment and income had risen above the level where people wish to save just as much as is being invested, losses would have emerged to bring incomes and employment down again to the equilibrium level where people wish to save just as much as is being invested. S = I. Although there is no mechanism whereby decisions about saving bring about an equal value of investment, which is what makes the equation suspicious, because of the long-standing habit of expecting the influences to work *from* saving *to* investment, *there is* a mechanism whereby decisions to invest bring about an equal amount of saving, which is what makes the equation true. I = S."

From the expenditure on consumption at this level of income we can derive the number of men employed in making consumption goods—for there is a functional relation between this number of men and expenditure on their product. Similarly, from the expenditure on investment goods we can derive the number of people at work in making the investment goods. This gives us the total number of men employed. This number is determined by the amount of investment and the propensity to save (or its complement : the propensity to consume, which is the relationship between income and consumption). The propensity to consume may also depend upon other things, such as the rate of interest. These can be brought in and they fit quite well into the theory, but it is a reasonable simplification to assume that small changes in the rate of interest will affect different people in opposite directions ; and the net effect may here be neglected.

There remains to be considered what determines the rate of investment. It is in the analysis of this that some of the more subtle and more valuable innovations in the theory are made by Keynes. Investment consists in the application of productive resources to the manufacture of capital goods. Capital goods are goods which are valuable on account of services they are expected to yield in the future. The efficiency of a capital good, or the rate of return over cost, as Irving Fisher calls this, is the rate of yield of the capital good, i.e. it is that rate of discounting the expected future yields of the capital good which makes the sum of the discounted yields equal to the cost of making it. For example, if it costs £300 to make a machine which gives off two services, one in one year's time which is then worth £220 and one in two years' time which is then worth £121, the efficiency of this machine is 10 per cent., because if the values of the services are discounted at the rate of 10 per cent. down to the present, the sum of their values is £300. ($£220 \times \frac{100}{110} = £200$, $£121 \times \left(\frac{100}{110}\right)^2 = £100$, and $£200 + £100 = £300$.) The *marginal* efficiency of any particular type of capital good is the efficiency of the marginal item of that type of capital good, in the use where its installation would show the greatest possible efficiency. The marginal efficiency of capital in general is the highest of the marginal efficiencies of all capital goods that still remain to be made.

It should be noted that the marginal efficiency of any capital good is described in the same way (has the same dimensions) as the rate of interest, so that it can be measured against it. It is a percentage of so much per annum. But it must on no account be confused with the rate of interest. The rate of interest is the rate at which money has to be paid for the privilege of borrowing money; or, from the point of view of the lender, it is the rate at which one is remunerated in money for the service of lending money.

There is, however, a certain relationship between the rate of interest and the marginal efficiency of capital. For it will pay entrepreneurs to borrow money in order to increase the rate of construction of capital goods—which is the rate of investment—as long as the rate of interest is less than the marginal efficiency of capital. As the rate of investment increases the best opportunities for investment are used up, and the marginal efficiency of capital diminishes. This happens in two ways. As the amount of capital increases, the expected values of the services of new capital goods fall as these have to compete with a larger supply of existing capital goods. This will be a very slow process since the rate at which capital is increased—the output in a short period—is small relatively to the existing stock of capital goods. But the other way in which the marginal efficiency falls is operative in the short period. As the rate of investment increases, the marginal cost of making capital goods increases, and this immediately tends to reduce the marginal efficiency of capital to the rate of interest. For each rate of interest there is a corresponding rate of investment. This relationship is the schedule of the marginal efficiency of capital.

The schedule of the marginal efficiency of capital is sometimes called the demand curve for savings because the entrepreneurs, who undertake the investment and have to obtain the funds to finance it, are conceived to obtain them from the savings of individuals which when summed constitute the "supply" of savings. This is important in so far as it is brought in to explain the amount of investment that takes place, and upon the amount of investment depends—as we have seen—the amount of employment which is the *quaesitum* of the whole book.

It is clear that the amount of investment undertaken by entrepreneurs in any given position, given the marginal efficiency schedule of capital, will be determined by the rate of interest. The crux of the matter lies then in the theory of the determination of the rate of interest.

According to the classical theory, the rate of interest is given by the supply and demand schedules for savings. The rate of interest is the price of savings and that amount of saving and investment comes about that is indicated by the intersection of these demand and supply schedules. If the supply of savings is greater than the rate of investment the rate of interest will fall so as to bring them into equilibrium and *vice versa*. Savings and investment are brought into equality with each other in an equilibrium by the movement of the rate of interest.

This line of reasoning is not merely wrong—it is meaningless. The equations on page 9 show that savings can never be different from investment whatever the rate of interest, so that it is nonsense to say that the rate of interest brings them to equality with each other. This can be shown in another way. The supply schedule of savings in this scheme is supposed to be independent of the demand curve for saving (which is the marginal efficiency schedule of capital). This means that, given the rate of interest, the amount of saving is independent of the amount of investment and also of the size of people's incomes. In fact of course it is ridiculous to assume that this is so, for what happens is that if there is an increase in investment, incomes increase immediately so that saving is increased by exactly the amount that investment is increased. The supply curve does not keep still. Whatever the point one takes on the demand curve the supply curve moves to the right or to the left so that it intersects the demand curve at the point taken.

We can now consider the alternative argument, referred to above, which is sometimes put forward in defence of the proposition that any individual, in deciding to save more, thereby increases S, the aggregate amount of saving of the whole society. Instead of assuming that when an individual saves more and spends less on consumption goods the seller of consumption goods continues to receive the same amount as before, so that Y, the aggregate income of society, is unaffected, it is assumed that whenever an individual decides to increase his saving by a certain amount, either he or somebody else always increases investment by the same amount. This increases the incomes of those engaged in the production of investment goods by as much as the income of the producers of consumption goods diminishes, so that Y, the aggregate income, remains the same. C, the expenditure on consumption goods, has diminished, and (Y — C) or S has increased as much as the first individual increases his own saving.

There are two difficulties about this argument. The first is that there is no satisfactory indication of any mechanism in a monetary economy whereby the decision to save necessarily carries with it an instantaneous and equal decision to invest. The second difficulty is that if there were some mechanism which did make somebody decide to invest exactly as much as anybody saved, the classical explanation of the determination of saving and investment would be upset in a manner similar to the one we have indicated. For this would mean that the investment curve—which constitutes the demand curve for the supply of savings—coincided throughout with the supply curve of savings. At each rate of interest people decide to save a certain amount (supposing for the moment that the supply curve of saving is not shifted about by changes in income due to changes in investment)—and if there is some mechanism whereby an individual's decision to save calls into being an equal amount of investment, then saving again equals investment throughout (though not for the reasons given above).

— 17 —

There is only one curve, which is both the supply curve and the demand curve for savings, so that the rate of interest remains unexplained.

This argument sometimes takes the form of assuming MV (the amount of money multiplied by its velocity of circulation) as unchanging. This means that the total amount spent altogether both on consumption and on investment is unchanged, so that if £1 less is spent on consumption £1 more must be spent on investment. This assumption is frequently very tacit, and when made explicit it appears in extremely innocent-looking forms like assuming " other things remaining the same " or considering what happens " in the absence of hoarding ". This really means that unless something special from outside—" hoarding "—intervenes, we may expect MV to remain constant and that any decision to save will somehow result in somebody investing an equal amount. This criticism of the illegitimate and sometimes unconscious assumption of a constant MV is not Keynes' way of dealing with the argument. He usually refuses to have anything to do with such simple " quantity equations ". Dr. Haberler, however, concentrates on this line of attack, which is only a more orthodox (and more complicated) route that leads to the same conclusions as are obtained by Keynes.

There remains unexplained what it is that determines the rate of interest. The explanation of this is given by Keynes, who derives it from the inadequate theories of the Mercantilists by an easy development of a line of thought that had been shut out of economic theory for over a century. This line of thought has only recently been coming back into respectable economics under very heavy disguise in the writings associated with such esoteric concepts as the " natural rate of interest " and " neutral money ".

The rate of interest is what people pay for borrowing money. It is what people who have money—cash—obtain for lending it to other people instead of holding it themselves. It is not payment for saving, for one can save without lending the money saved ; and in that case one does not get any interest payments. On the other hand one can lend money out of what one previously held ; and in that case one gets interest payments without saving. The relevant demand is then the demand to *hold* money. The supply is simply the total amount of money that there exists. This demand schedule Keynes called *Liquidity Preference*, and it is the intersection between the liquidity preference schedule and the supply of money (which is a perpendicular line if the amount of money is fixed) that gives the rate of interest upon which the whole thing depends. The higher the rate of interest the greater the cost—in terms of interest forgone—of holding money and the smaller the amount of money people will want to hold. Conversely, if there is an increase in the amount of money the rate of interest will fall until people want to hold the larger amount of money. They are induced to want to hold more money by the fall in the rate of interest, for then, to some people, the convenience and feeling of security of holding cash can be satisfied to a greater extent because the cost is less.

Our conclusion is that the amount of employment can be governed by policy directed towards affecting the amount of investment. This may be done either by lowering the rate of interest or by direct investment by the authorities. There may be difficulties for institutional or psychological reasons in reducing the rate of interest to sufficiently low a level to bring about that rate of investment which, with the existing propensity to consume, is necessary in order to bring about full employment. It is because of such difficulties that Keynes thinks that public works are necessary, and may become more and more necessary as the wealth and capital equipment of the community increase. For this means that on the one hand people wish to save more out of the larger income corresponding to full employment while on the other hand the accumulation of capital lowers the marginal efficiency schedule of capital. Equilibrium with full employment is then possible only at lower interest rates than are practicable unless either (*a*) investment is increased by State production of capital goods whose efficiency is less than the rate of interest or which for any other reason would not be manufactured by private entrepreneurs, of (*b*) the propensity to save is diminished—consumption increased—by State expenditure on social services or by redistribution of income from the rich to the poor, or by any other means.

The reader may have noticed a considerable similarity between this last argument and the classical argument that was so vehemently attacked on pp. 15 and 16. Here in fact an equilibrium is indicated by the intersection of demand and supply curves for savings. What the argument amounts to is that if for institutional reasons the rate of interest cannot be brought down to the level which equates the supply and demand, the demand curve must be moved to the right or the supply curve moved to the left until they meet at a level of the rate of interest that *is* practicable. But what was impossible in the classical explanation of the rate of interest is permissible here because for this argument we were assuming full employment in order to be able to consider what are the necessary conditions for that to exist. There is then a given income so that there is a given supply schedule of savings. The criticism of the classical explanation of the determination of the rate of interest is that its argument—in assuming a given supply curve of savings—is implicitly assuming a given degree of employment, namely, full employment. And it is not useful to consider what determines the amount of employment on the assumption that there is full employment—or even to discuss the determination of the rate of interest under those conditions without considering whether in fact there is any force which will bring about full employment.

Keynes' conclusion that the amount of employment has to be governed by operating on the amount of consumption and investment, *via* the rate of interest or otherwise, may seem at first sight to be a very small mouse to emerge from the labour of mountains. Everybody has known that cheaper money is good for business, and so is any increase in net investment or expenditure. But except for occasional lapses from scientific purity to momentary commonsense, the pundits of economic science have been declaring that people should practice more thrift. There has been a weakening of this attitude recently—I am not clear to what extent this is due to the cyclical fluctuation in the attitude of economists and how much to the influence of Keynes' ideas and some parallel development by J. R. Hicks and the Swedish writers. But we must not forget that it is not so very long ago that we had Professor Robbins and Mr. Keynes on the wireless respectively advising the world to save more and to spend more. And there is still in Milan a World Institute for the Encouragement of Thrift. It will be a long time before the view that thrift " since it enriches the individual can hardly fail to benefit the community " is seen to be an important example of the common logical error of composition. What Keynes has done is to show that what the ordinary man has often felt in his bones can be justified by a keener analysis than has so far been applied to the problem. He has shown further that it is *only* by working indirectly on these same determinants that any other remedies can ever work. Thus, even in the case when a reduction of money wages increases employment it does so only in so far as it indirectly reduces the rate of interest. The direct effect is merely to reduce both prices and money incomes, leaving the *real* situation as before. At the lower price level people find that they need less money to carry on their business, so that if there is no change in the amount of money its supply is greater than the demand to hold it, and the attempt of money holders to lend the spare money to others, or to buy other assets for money, raises the value of the other assets and reduces the rate of interest. The reduction of the rate of interest does the trick by making a larger rate of investment profitable. Incomes then increase, in accordance with the propensity to consume, until a level of income and employment is reached which induces people to save at a rate equal to the greater rate of investment. From this it follows that any objections that may be raised against the dangers inherent in lowering the rate of interest in an attempt to increase employment apply just as much or as little to the policy of increasing employment by lowering wages, since that works only *via* lowering the interest rate. It is not denied that there are any dangers, but such as they are, they are inherent in *any* successful attempt to increase employment. To run away from these is to refuse to be cured because that will make it possible to become sick again.

To seek the alleviation of depression by reducing money wages, rather than by directly reducing the rate of interest or otherwise encouraging investment or consumption, is to abandon the high road for a devious, dark, difficult and unreliable path, for no better reason than that the dangers that await one at the common destination are more clearly seen when it is approached by the broad highway.

[2]

THE ECONOMIC STEERING WHEEL

The Story of the People's New Clothes

A. P. LERNER

Our economic system has frequently been put to shame by displaying it before an imaginary visitor from a strange planet. It is time to reverse the procedure. Imagine yourself instead in a Buck Rogers interplanetary adventure, looking at a highway in a City of Tomorrow. The highway is wide and straight and its edges are turned up so that it is almost impossible for a car to run off the road. What appears to be a runaway car is speeding along the road and veering off to one side. As it approaches the rising edge of the highway its front wheels are turned so that it gets back onto the road and goes off at an angle making for the other side where the wheels are turned again. This happens many times, the car zig-zagging but keeping on the highway until it is out of sight. You are wondering how long it will take for it to crash, when another car appears which behaves in the same fashion. When it comes near you it stops with a jerk. A door is opened and an occupant asks if you would like a lift. You look into the car and before you can control yourself you cry out, "Why!. There's no steering wheel!"

"Of course, we have no steering wheel!" says the occupant rather crossly. "Just think how it would cramp the front seat. It is worse than an old fashioned gear-shift lever and it is dangerous. Suppose we had a steering wheel and somebody held on to it when we reached a curb! He would prevent the automatic turning of the wheel and the car would surely be overturned!. And besides we believe in Democracy and cannot give any one the extreme authority of life and death over all the occupants of the car. That would be Dictatorship."

"Down with Dictatorship," chorus the other occupants of the car."

"If you are worried about the way the car goes from side to side," continued the first speaker, "forget it! We have wonderful brakes so that collisions are prevented nine times out of ten. On our better roads the curb is so effective that one can travel hundreds of miles without going off the road once. We have a very efficient system of carrying survivors of wrecks to nearby hospitals and for rapidly sweeping the remnants from the road to deposit them on nearby fields as a reminder to man of the inevitability of death."

You look around to see the piles of wrecks and burned out automobiles when the man in the car continues. "Impressive isn't it? But things are going to improve. Do you see those men marking and photographing the tracks of the car that preceded us? They are going to take those pictures into their laboratories, and pictures of our own tracks too, to analyze the cyclical characteristics of the curves, their degree of regularity, the average distance from turn to turn, the amplitude of the swings and so on. When they have come to an agreement on their true nature we may know if something can be done about it. At present they are disputing whether this cyclical movement is due to the type of road surface or to its shape or whether it is due to the length of the car or the kind of rubber in the tires, or the weather. Some of them think that it will be impossible to avoid the cycles unless we go back to the horse and buggy, but we can't do that because we believe in Progress. Well, want a ride?"

The dilemma between saving your skin and humoring the lunatics is resolved by your awakening from the nightmare, and you feel glad that the inhabitants of your own planet are a little more reasonable. But are they as reasonable about other things as they are about the desirability of steering their automobiles? Do they not behave exactly like the men in the nightmare when it comes to operating their economic system? Do they not allow their **economic** automobile to bounce from the curb of depression to the curb of inflation in wide and uncontrolled arcs? Through their failure to steer away from unemployment and idle factories are they not just as guilty of public injury and insecurity as the mad automobilists of Mars?

Page Two

The outstanding problem of modern society is just this. All the other really important problems such as wars and fascism are either caused or aggravated by the failure to solve this one. What is needed more than anything else is a mechanism which would enable us to regulate our economy so as to maintain a reasonable degree of economic activity: on the one hand to prevent any considerable unemployment of resources and on the other hand to prevent the stresses of the over-employment of resources and the disorganization that we know as inflation. We need a regulator of employment—a mechanism for the maintenance of prosperity.

The instrument that can do this is as readily available as the steering wheel for automobiles, yet it is not installed and operated. Instead, all our universities are engaged in studying and adding to the enormous literature about the path travelled by the economy when no steering wheel is used—the study of the business cycle.

Effects of Uncontrolled Spending

In our present fairly competitive economy based on fairly free enterprise the level of economic activity is determined by how much money is being spent on the goods and services that can be produced. The immediate effect of a decrease in spending is either the accumulation of unsold goods or a decrease in prices. These effects are soon followed by a reduction in orders to manufacturers and a decrease in employment and output until any prices that may have fallen will be restored to their normal relationship to cost. Conversely the immediate effect of an increase in spending is to deplete stocks or raise prices and this will soon be followed by an increase of orders to manufacturers. The increased orders to manufacturers will increase employment and output until the normal relationship between prices and cost has been restored. The greater spending of money is met (after a period of adjustment) by a larger supply of goods to be purchased, and prices and cost are not permanently affected in any great measure. But if there are no unemployed resources available it is impossible for employment or output to increase, so that prices do not fall back again to normal but stay higher. If the increased spending is not absorbed by an increase in the supply of goods it must show itself in higher prices for the same supply of goods.

Nor is this the end of the story. The manufacturer cannot increase output where there are no unemployed resources available. But the increased orders at higher prices induce manufacturers to **try** to increase their output to take advantage of the unusually high profits. In so doing they try to get men and materials away from each other by offering higher wages and prices (or merely agreeing to their demands for higher wages and prices). This raises the money incomes of labor and of the owners of other instruments of production and results in a further increase in spending. Increased spending increases incomes, and increased incomes increase spending and so the process becomes cumulative with prices rising (and the value of money falling). If this process is permitted to continue by a monetary authority which provides the increasing amount of money that is needed as prices rise, we are in the midst of an inflation. Such an inflation disorganizes the economy and works great hardship on those with fixed or only slowly adjustable money incomes, and ruins those with savings cautiously tied to the depreciating money.

The aim of any reasonable regulation of the level of economic activity in society (which we may call "employment" for short) must be to arrange that the rate of spending be neither too small, which would cause unemployment, nor too great, which would cause inflation. A satisfactory level (or range) of employment must be chosen, and the total rate of spending must be raised when employment is too low, and curtailed when employment rises too near the full employment mark where inflation would set in.

If the rate of spending happens to satisfy this criterion, employment is adequate and there is no need for any special measures. If there is not sufficient spending so that employment is too low, then the difference can be made up by the government. The government can spend money **directly** on public works or **indirectly** by paying out more to people who would be only too glad to spend it, such as pensioners or people on relief or taxpayers whose taxes are reduced. If there is too much spending so that there are signs of the beginnings of inflation, the government can correct this either by decreasing some of its own spending, direct or indirect, or by collecting more in taxes and thus leaving less in the hand of the taxpayers for them to spend. This gives us the first rule for the regulation of employment:

1. The government shall maintain a reasonable level of demand at all times. If there is not enough spending so that there is excessive unemployment, the government shall reduce taxes or increase its own spending. If there is too much spending the government shall prevent inflation by reducing its own expenditures or by increasing taxes.

Most of the time our present economy seems to suffer from too little rather than from too much spending, so that to correct this disposition it would be necessary for the government on the whole to spend more or to decrease its tax revenues, or both. Where is the money to come from?

The simplest answer is "from the printing press". After giving this answer it is usually necessary to wait for the listener's eyebrows to fall back a little and to help this movement by pointing out four things: (a) This is not identical with inflation. (b) An increase in the amount of money in existence is of no importance for the economy unless it leads to an increase in **spending** by somebody. (c) An increase in spending is just what is needed to bring about an increase in employment, and (d) As long as it is possible for the supply of goods to increase along with the increase in spending, there would be no (permanent) increase in prices.

This does not mean that the government would have to keep on printing more new money forever week by week and year by year to maintain prosperity. As the stock of money increased it would in various ways lead to an increase in spending by private individuals and corporations who wished to diminish their holdings of large quantities of profitless cash, and this would make it necessary for less spending to be undertaken by the government. When there is so much money in existence that the rate of private spending is enough to provide a satisfactory level of employment, the government will not have to spend any more than it raises in taxes, and the printing presses can be stopped.

Money and Investment

The stock of money, through its influence on the rate of spending, can thus be the equilibrating factor which keeps employment at a reasonable level. Nevertheless, it might not be considered desirable to reach this particular equilibrium. One of the many reasons for this is that such a policy might be considered to entail over-investment in the sense that too large a portion of the resources of society is devoted to investment for the future, and too little is left for current consumption.

If the stock of money increases and the members of society find themselves holding larger and larger amounts of fruitless money (since the money that is in existence or "in circulation" is always held by somebody), they will attempt to make some profit by lending it out to borrowers or by exchanging it for interest-yielding forms of wealth. This will raise the price of securities and lower the rate of interest. At the lower rate of interest it becomes worthwhile to borrow money to undertake investments which do not yield very much. If the government prefers to feed the present generation better, say by continuing with children's allowances (and does not want to increase taxes because that would also bear heavily on current consumption), it will not like to see the reduction in the rate of interest because that would call forth spending on these not very useful investments, and this increase in spending would make it necessary for the children's allowances to be stopped (or for taxes to be increased) if there is not now to be too much spending. Too much spending, it will be remembered, causes inflation.

The government can continue its spending on children's allowances and yet prevent the rate of interest from falling if it prevents the amount of money from increasing. It can do this by **borrowing back** the money that it spends.

On the other hand the government might in different circumstances wish to en-

Page Four

courage private investment, and in that case it could do the opposite. It could for there can be no other explanation of the idea that it is unfair for the govern-**lend** rather than borrow money on the capital market (or repay some of the national debt in cash, which comes to the same thing) and in this way increase the amount of money, lower the rate of interest, and increase investment. This brings us to the second rule, which is not as fundamental as the first but helps to complete the sketch of the economic mechanism:

2. By borrowing money when it wishes to raise the rate of interest and by lending money or repaying debt when it wishes to lower the rate of interest, the government shall maintain that rate of interest which induces the optimum amount of investment.

These two rules provide the mechanism for guiding the modern economy— the missing steering wheel. The principles are not really very difficult.[1] Why have they not been applied long before now?

Breaking with Tradition

First there is the breach with tradition. The approach is unorthodox. Spending by the government must be regarded not as something to be done when it can be "afforded" or when it is essential to prevent starvation, but as a regular and painless way of maintaining prosperity, to be undertaken when the society is poor on account of unemployment rather than when it is prosperous and appears to be able to afford luxuries. Taxes must be regarded not as a means to which the government has to resort in order to get money in the same way as an individual has to work to earn his living, but as merely a device for reducing the income and therefore also the expenditure of members of society. The quantity of money must be regarded not as something to be regulated strictly according to the sacred rules of some gold standard with which the government has no right to interfere, but as something that is of no account in itself and should be completely subservient to the rules for maintaining the right amount of spending and investment. An increase in government debt must be regarded not as a measure of last resort to be undertaken only in extreme emergency and in limited degree, but as a matter of very little consequence, the national debt and the rate at which it is being increased or repaid being completely subjected to the rules for maintaining prosperity and preventing inflation. It is only to stress this breach with tradition that the third "rule" is provided:

3. If either of the first two rules conflict with the principles of "sound finance" or of balancing the budget or of limiting the national debt, so much the worse for these principles. The government press shall print any money that may be needed in carrying out these rules.

Yet the conflict with tradition does not seem by itself a sufficient explanation of the failure of modern society to regulate the level of economic activity. The fundamental logic of the new position is quite easily demonstrable. It is almost self evident that while the individual can be sent to prison for manufacturing money, the government need not fear the FBI, so that it must be governed by different principles in this respect than is the individual. A firmly established modern state is perfectly well able to borrow money or print money if it is in need of money, so that it is foolish for it to behave like a bankrupt monarch whose credit is so low that he can hardly borrow, who has little or no power over the scarce metal that is used for money within his realm and who must perforce limit his private spending to the taxes that his parliament or his rudimentary fiscal machinery permits him

[1] Non-economists who wish to read a little more about the scheme will find useful an article by the present author entitled "Total Democracy and Full Employment" in **Social Change** for May, 1941, (published by New America at 3929 Ellis Avenue, Chicago, 35c). A more complete outline of the theory can be found in another article by the present author entitled "Mr. Keynes' General Theory of Employment," in the **International Labor Office Review,** October, 1936, in **An Introduction to the Theory of Employment** by Joan Robinson, Macmillan, 1938. **An Introduction to Economic Analysis and Policy** (part I) by J. E. Meade and C. J. Hitch, Oxford Univ. Press, 1938, also relates this to the other main economic problems. **The General Theory of Employment Interest and Money** by J. M. Keynes is the source of all the other recent writings on the subject, but not easy to read. **An Economic Program for American Democracy** by Seven Harvard Economists, Vanguard Press, 1938, is a very clear little book that points the moral of the theory. Very recently J. P. Wernette of the Harvard School of Business Administration has written an excellent book that goes to the roots of the matter and yet is readable for non-economists. It is called **The Control of Business Cycles,** Farrar and Rinehart, 1941.

to collect. The existence now of other ways of obtaining the money needed for state purposes permits the modern state to tax or not to tax according to which policy has the better effect on the body politic. Policy can be directed in accordance with the **effects** of taxing, which are undoubtedly to decrease the money in the hands of the taxpayer and to permit him to spend less. The advisability of taxation depends only upon whether this reduction in income or wealth and the consequent reduction in spending is socially desirable.

Similarly with the national debt. In spite of newspaper editorials it is being recognized more and more generally that a nation does not get poorer any more than it gets richer when the internally owned national debt increases. All that happens is that the citizens as members of the state owe more to themselves (i. e. to each other) as holders of government stock. While a debt by one nation to other nations or the citizens of other nations is a burden comparable to the debt of a man to other men, the debt of a nation to its own citizens is not comparable in this way and is not a "burden" on the nation.

These arguments are simple to pose and difficult to argue against. They easily convince the unsophisticated and are accepted after a struggle by almost all economists who have not grown too old to change their habits of thought. Something more than tradition, therefore, must be sought as an explanation of their general failure to be applied to practical government.

In the second place one must consider to what extent the management of employment is held up by resistance from vested interests. These too would not seem to be strong enough to overcome the pressure of all who would gain from the maintenance of prosperity. Workers would be secure in their jobs and in the knowledge that other jobs are not difficult to get. Capitalists would be making profits on a scale that in the past has only been experienced in short periods of boom. Nor need this gain involve any man's loss, for it can all come out of the avoidance of waste from underemployment—waste that for the United States during the single decade 1930-1939 is estimated at much more than two hundred billion dollars worth of real goods and services that might have been produced—an amount more than four times as great as that represented by the highly publicized imaginary burden of our record national debt.

Who Would Be Hurt

Apart from such specialists as bankruptcy lawyers the only people who **might** lose by the maintenance of prosperity would be the insurance companies, the banks and the endowed institutions who live on the pure interest from safe investments. These would find their incomes cut if the maintaining of prosperity necessitated a reduction in the rate of interest. The insurance companies and banks, insofar as they do not make it up in the greater volume of business that goes with prosperity, would have to find other ways of making ends meet such as investing in industry or charging higher premiums and service charges, but they are in a position to look after themselves. The endowed institutions, universities, research foundations, hospitals and the like might encouner difficulties, if private gifts are not sufficiently increased as a result of general prosperity, but even a most generous compensation would be a negligible cost compared with the benefits of prosperity. There should be no strong resistance here.

Then there are the ideological resistances which are to some extent bound up with the deadweight of tradition, but less susceptible to change through enlightenment because they are based on dogma rather than on mere inertia. There is a dogma of the right and a dogma of the left.

The dogma of the right says that it is improper for the government to go into business or to interfere with business. It is all but blind to the concept of business activity as a way in which the needs of society come to be provided, and looks upon a business simply as a privately owned source of income—a "racket" to which the business man is entitled by virtue of discovery or conquest. Usually this is covered up by some rationalization, for there can be no other explanation of the idea that it is unfair for the government to compete with business even in cases where it is shown that the consumer would benefit. The consumer is not the person considered when it is the question of somebody muscling in on one's racket.

Now it is possible for the government to regulate prosperity without competing with anybody besides the banks, and it is even possible to compensate the banks for any loss without making any appreciable inroads into the benefits of prosperity. But the principle of the government having to regulate the level of business activity is bad for the morale of the captains of industry who could no longer be regarded by themselves or by others as the source of all blessings of our age of progress. Furthermore, any interference by the government is a dangerous precedent. It will lead to other actions being demanded of it in the general interest, which definitely would conflict with the private interests of monopolists and others. This seems to be the reason why the ideological champions of the extreme right have denounced as bolshevism the first hesitating (not to say wobbly) steps of the New Deal in the direction of maintaining prosperity by governmental regulation of total spending.

The dogma of the left says that it is improper for private business to compete with the government. It is based upon a belief that only 100 per cent collectivism can solve the problems of society and that private enterprise for the sake of profit is not only unjust and exploitative, but must inevitably bring with it the wastes, the disorganization and the unemployment that has been associated with capitalism in the past. This seems to be the reason why the New Deal was in the beginning so foolishly labeled "fascistic" by many communists and socialists. Again there would seem to be little force behind either of these ideological oppositions insofar as business men prefer profits to principles, workers prefer employment to empty theories, and neither group is easily swayed by the professional interests of the organizers of communist parties or of associations of manufacturers.

Timidity of Proponents

All of these resistances would be of little avail, were it not for weakness in the other camp, the proponents of organized prosperity. A kind of timidity makes them shrink from saying anything that might shock the respectable upholders of traditional doctrine and tempts them to disguise the new doctrine so that it might be easily mistaken for the old. This does not help much, for they are soon found out, and it hinders them because in endeavoring to make the new doctrine look harmless in the eyes of the upholders of tradition they often damage their case. Thus instead of saying that the size of the national debt is of no great concern, it has been argued that the increase in the national income will permit the interest on the national debt to be raised without increasing taxes.[2] Instead of saying that the budget may have to be unbalanced, and that this is insignificant compared with the attainment of prosperity, it is proposed to disguise this fact by having an elaborate system of annual, cyclical capital and special budgets as in Sweden.[3]

But infinitely more depressing than these particular timidities, which weaken the forces working for the organization of prosperity, is a more general capitulation before the prejudices of the public. A great majority of the people to whom the theory of controls is explained will say, "I can see that you are right but most people will not be able to see it, so that there is no chance of anything being done." The number of people who take this attitude is most alarming. This is the attitude of the more intellectual persons. Equally discouraging is the attitude of less intellectual (or rather less self-confident) members of the public who will say, "It seems all right to me, but I am not an expert and I suppose there is something wrong that I can't see." And in this way policy is stalled. The intellectuals are afraid to push the proposal because of unjustified contempt for the public (or perhaps because of subjective

[2] **An Economic Program for American Democracy**, p. 72. On the whole this book is not very guilty of the timidity about which I am complaining. Some other examples are mentioned in my references to Mr. Hitchcock in my note on "Peace and Finance" in the March, 1941, issue of the **University Review**, p. 196.

[3] E. Lindahl, **Studies in the Theory of Money and Capital**, London, Allen and Unwin, 1939, Appendix on "The Problem of Balancing the Budget," and see A. P. Lerner, "Some Swedish Stepping Stones in Economic Theory," **Canadian Journal of Economics and Political Science**, November, 1940, pp. 580, 590 and passim, for a fuller criticism of this particular timidity.

doubts as to their own superiority), and the public is afraid to accept arguments that they understand perfectly well because the "intellectuals" (for whom they have an unjustified reverence) have not come out for them.

With one important difference the situation is like that of the famous emperor in the story who was persuaded to parade before his people in his underwear by the charlatans who claimed that the imaginary new clothes they had made for him were so fine that no one could feel them, and so beautiful that no one who was foolish or dishonest or unfit for his office could see them. And so neither the emperor nor any of his courtiers or his people would admit that they saw no clothes until they were betrayed by an unintimidated child. So it is with the problem of organizing prosperity. The scholars who understand it hesitate to speak out boldly for fear that the people will not understand. The people, who understand it quite easily, also fear to speak out while they wait for the scholars to speak out first. The difference between our present situation and that of the story is that it is not the emperor but the people who needlessly go naked and hungry and insecure and discontented—a ready prey to less timid organizers of discontent for the destruction of civilization.

At the present time the National Defense Program promises to provide a temporary sufficiency of spending without any conscious organization of prosperity. This gives us a breathing space in which the principles of organized prosperity can be spread until they are so widely understood that they can be applied within the framework of our democratic society even while the democracy in it is widened and deepened. If this challenge is not met, it will not be possible for democracy to stand. It is therefore incumbent upon all who care for a free society to investigate and propagate the democratic organization of prosperity.[1]

[1] There are many ways of doing this and many organizations which can help. The organization which seems to me to view the matter most intelligently and to tie it up most consistently with the other major problems of society is the group calling itself New America and producing the excellent quarterly journal **Social Change,** at 3929 Ellis Avenue, Chicago, Illinois.

[3]

CHAPTER 13

High Full Employment and Low Full Employment

FUNCTIONAL FINANCE is directed not only at preventing depression but also at preventing inflation. It aims to keep total spending from going too high just as much as it aims at preventing total spending from going too low. But more attention is usually paid to the prevention of depression and unemployment because this is probably a more important problem than the prevention of inflation. This concentration has led many people to suppose that Functional Finance is directed entirely or almost entirely toward depression, and they have, in fact, called it "depression economics," meaning perhaps thereby to imply that as soon as there is no longer a depression Functional Finance becomes inapplicable and we have to go back again to "sound finance."

Functional Finance is not the same as "depression economics."

Now it is true that when the upside-down economy of depression no longer exists, we have something like the world of classical economics, in which there is always full employment. But this is only a superficial similarity. The recognition of the current existence of full employment, whether the full employment is accidental or the result of policy, is not the same thing as the classical assumption that we always and naturally have full employment so that we do not have to worry about the possibility of too little spending or of too much spending. Even if there is full employment we still have to think about the danger of spending becoming too small or becoming too great. The principles of Functional Finance are just as applicable and just as necessary in preventing spending from being too great as in preventing spending from being too small. Functional Finance may be more important for the prevention of depression because the prevention of depression is more important than the prevention of inflation, but it is not merely depression economics.

The distinction between deflationary and functional unemployment is inadequate.

Avoiding both inflation and depression means achieving full employment. But we have already seen that full employment is not as clear a concept as might be wished. A preliminary attempt was made near the beginning of this book (in Chapter 2) to diminish the ambiguity or elusiveness of the concept of full employment. There we made the distinction between deflationary unemployment and frictional unemployment and said that Functional Finance could be directed only at removing deflationary unemployment. In other words, deflationary unemployment is that unemployment which can be cured by simply increasing total money demand for goods and services. Frictional unemployment is the unemployment which remains and which cannot be removed by merely increasing total money spending still more. It can be reduced only by the removal of the particular frictions which prevent unemployed men and unfilled vacancies from getting together. When all the remaining unemployment is frictional unemployment we have "full employment."

But when we look at this more closely we find that there is no such simple line between frictional unemployment and deflationary unemployment. There is a large volume of unemployment which we cannot dismiss from consideration by merely saying that it is frictional and can be cured only by the removal of particular frictions.

One way in which this problem is often expressed—usually by critics of Functional Finance—is to say that there is a region (between depression and inflation) where we have *both* depression and inflation. If in a condition of depression the rate of money spending is increased, a point is reached at which further increases in money spending would not bring about any permanent increase in employment but would only cause inflation. Yet at this point the number of unemployed will be much greater than that made necessary by the real technical frictions.

In the United States of America it is technically possible for the number of unemployed to be reduced below 2 million. This is proved by the fact that in 1946 and 1947 the number of unemployed *was* less than 2 million while the economy was working very satisfactorily. The number of *frictionally* unemployed in the strict technical sense must have been less than 2 million. Yet if the number of unemployed is reduced below 6 million or thereabouts, wages and prices begin to rise and we have some inflation. This is what is meant by saying that there is a range—namely, between 6 million unemployed and 2 million unemployed—when we have both depression and inflation. The lower extreme of this range, at which there are 6 million unemployed but at which wages and prices begin to rise, we shall call "low full employment." The upper extreme of the range, where all the unemployment is truly frictional in the technical sense, we shall call "high full employment." [1]

The disturbing influence is the bargaining power of labor.

The special influence that causes wages and prices to rise even though the number of unemployed is much greater than what is

[1] These two numbers, 2 million and 6 million, are merely guesses. It may be that more accurate numbers would be 1½ million and 4½ million. Considerable investigation would be necessary to get more reliable estimates, and the numbers themselves may change with changing conditions. But there are two such numbers that correspond to high full employment and to low full employment, and the two numbers will be used throughout this book as shorthand expressions for whatever the true numbers might be of those that would be unemployed in the conditions of high full employment and low full employment.

made necessary by real frictions is the excessive bargaining power of the workers. If there are less than about 6 million unemployed in the United States of America, the bargaining power of the workers is excessive. The pressure for higher wages by workers is greater than the resistance to wage increases by employers, and wage rates tend to rise more rapidly than the over-all increase in labor productivity. Employers are unwilling to suffer interruptions in production because business is pretty good. Other workers are not easy to find. Employers may even bid up wages in attempts to expand rapidly to take advantage of relatively good business. And so wages rise.

As wages rise, costs rise and the prices of the products rise. The possibility of raising the prices of the products is a most important consideration in persuading employers to pay the higher wages. The increase in prices destroys the expected benefit for the workers from the increase in wages. They can buy no more goods now with their higher money wages than they were able to buy before with their lower money wages. This leads to a demand for another wage increase to give the workers the expected increase in their real wage, of which they consider themselves to have been cheated by the price rise, and the next round of wage increases leads to another price increase, another disappointment, and another demand for wage increases; in this way we get the spiral of inflation.

It is not impossible for a wage increase to start off a depression rather than an inflation. This could happen if the wage increase took place at a time when conditions of demand, or perhaps some sort of price control, prevented the increase in cost from being passed on in higher prices. But these are rather special cases. In the former case the impossibility of passing on the increased wages in higher prices would indicate that we were on the verge of falling below even the low full employment into a condition of depression. The increase in wages would not bring about the depression; the depression was about to descend on the economy anyway. The wage increase would rather have the opposite effect of preventing the fall in prices and the expectations of further falls in prices which would have aggravated the depression. In the second case the stabilization of the price level by price control changes the whole picture and makes it necessary for the wage level to adjust itself to the price level. As we shall see below, this would interfere with the possibility of achieving high full employment.

If we are to keep to the formulation of Chapter 2, according to which all unemployment that cannot be cured by more spending is called "frictional unemployment" and is compatible with full employment, we shall have to say that we have full employment even when there are 6 million unemployed in the United States. Any increase in spending has the effect not of increasing the level of employment but merely of raising wages and prices. The 6 million would therefore have to be classified as frictionally unemployed. But only 2 million of the 6 million are unemployed for reasons that are really frictions in the normal sense of the word. It is the bargaining power of workers that causes wages to rise as soon as the number of unemployed is reduced below 6 million. Excessive bargaining power can therefore be considered a kind of friction. It is not a technical friction. We may call it an economic friction. If something could be done to remove this economic friction we would be able to reach the much higher level of employment with only 2 million unemployed. But as long as the economic friction remains and the reduction of unemployment below 6 million causes inflation, we have to say that full employment means having 6 million people unemployed. This is the low level of full employment. The elimination of the economic friction would permit us to reach the high level of full employment with only 2 million unemployed.

Overfull employment can only be temporary.

It is of course possible for money demand to raise employment above the low level of full employment so that there are less than

6 million unemployed. The output of goods and services would be increased too. But such "overfull" employment cannot be maintained. Wages and prices will rise. They may at first rise quite moderately, but that is only because workers are being deceived and are not realizing that their higher money wages are being eaten up by higher prices. With, say, 3 million unemployed the bargaining power of workers is able to raise wages by, perhaps, 15 per cent per annum. But this is true only as long as workers are assuming that prices are going to stay constant (or, what is more likely, they have not thought about changing prices at all). The increase in money wages is taken to be an increase in what they can buy with their wages. It will not take the workers long to discover that prices are in fact rising so that a much greater increase in money wages is needed to provide the expected increase in real wages that they have bargained for. But they can never catch up with the rising prices. They are like the proverbial donkey carrying the proverbial carrot in front of his nose. The more rapidly wages are increased the more rapidly prices will increase. In short the rise in prices and wages becomes cumulative and self-accelerating.

It is possible for the inflation to continue for a while, but as it accelerates in the way described, greater and greater increases in money spending are needed to maintain the same level of employment. If the inflation is maintained for some time at an ever-increasing rate, we get the disruptions of the economy that come from the establishment of expectations of the inflation continuing further still and at still faster rates. The rate of spending increases even faster than at the rate needed for maintaining the same level of employment, and we get a still higher level of employment and of course a still greater bargaining power of workers and still greater pressures for higher wages and still more rapidly rising prices. But instead of this leading to more production and higher levels of living, the opposite happens. It is found to be more profitable to buy things quickly, before their prices rise, than to produce things. Production therefore falls. All the normal criteria for distinguishing relatively more useful from relatively less useful activities break down. Many necessities run short because the factors of production have been shifted to the production of much less useful things or to the characteristic activity of the inflation—running to buy something before someone else gets there or before the price is raised.

This process must come to an end before very long. It may be stopped soon by a shortage of money. But even if the monetary authorities cooperate in keeping the inflation going by creating all the money needed as prices keep on increasing, even to astronomical figures, as in the European hyperinflations after both world wars, the inflation comes to an end when the inflation is no longer endurable, and some new kind of money is adopted to take the place of the old money, which becomes completely worthless.

It is not possible to maintain a level of employment which is so high that it makes the bargaining power of labor great enough to make wages rise more rapidly than the productivity of labor. Such a high level of employment is self-destructive because it brings about and then depends on the maintenance not merely of rising prices but of prices that are rising at an ever-increasing speed. This cannot be maintained and so it is impossible to reduce the level of unemployment permanently below the 6 million level as long as such a low level of unemployment has the effect of giving excessive bargaining power to labor.

Greater bargaining power does not help labor as a whole.

In the last few paragraphs there has been much emphasis on the evils of excessive bargaining power of labor. This emphasis is easily denounced as showing an antilabor attitude. But such a denunciation would be based on an assumption that an increase in labor's bargaining power is good for labor, enabling labor to make a better bargain in real terms and to get a larger share in the national income. This assumption, plausible and even "self-evident" as it appears to many, is completely unfounded.

During the inflation that is brought about by an excessive rise in money wages (*i.e.,* the excess of the rise over the increase in the productivity of labor) it is difficult to say what may happen. In the confusion some workers may find that for a time their wages rise more than the prices of the goods they buy. Most workers will find the opposite to be the case. And when the inflation becomes severe enough to disrupt the economy, almost everyone will be worse off. But when the inflation is stopped or if the inflation is prevented from developing cumulatively, the great bargaining power of labor will be found not to have done labor as a whole any good at all.

This is because an over-all change in wages in general without any change in the relation of particular money wage rates to each other has no necessary effect on the real wage rates or on the real situation in the economy as a whole. A general rise in money wage rates (relative to productivity) results in a proportional general rise in prices and in money incomes, so that in real terms everything is just as it was before.

Representatives of workers are prone to believe that a general increase in money wage rates would increase the real wages of workers at the expense of the owners of other factors of production (whom for our present purposes we may call their employers). Representatives of workers therefore tend to favor increases in money wage rates. Representatives of employers are prone to think the same, and for this reason they in turn tend to frown on general increases in wage rates. But in both cases the tendency to believe that to raise money wages will benefit workers and harm employers is the result of thinking of the effects of money wage increases only in a single trade or only in a single firm and then assuming, quite falsely, that the general effect of a general increase in money wages is the same as the local effect of a local increase in money wage rates.

When it is remembered that a *general* increase in wage rates raises the costs of all competitors and increases the incomes of the workers it becomes evident that prices will not stay the same but will rise. And furthermore it can be shown that the rise will be in the same proportion as the general increase in wages, so that the workers are not able to buy any more with their higher money wages and the employers will be able to obtain just as much real profit as before. The workers do not gain from the general increase in money wage rates and the employers do not lose anything from it until there is the inflationary disorganization of production.

Labor's share is determined by more basic social institutions.

Unless there is a fundamental change in the general institutions of society, in the degree of monopoly or the degree of competition, there will remain the same degree of markup between costs and prices—the same range of profits in the different occupations resulting from the existing degree of competition or monopoly. For this reason prices will rise in the same proportion as costs. The difference between costs and prices, or in other words the profits, will also increase in the same proportion as wages and prices, but the higher money profits will not mean higher real profits any more than the higher money wages mean higher real wages.

It might be argued, and it too frequently is argued, that not all costs are wages, so that costs will rise less than wages and therefore prices will rise less than wages. But this objection seems plausible only as long as we forget what these other costs are. The cost of raw materials and other nonwage costs of any firm are nothing but the prices of the products of other firms and consist of the costs plus profit markup in these other firms. If the other firms' costs consisted entirely of wages, their prices, which are the nonwage costs of our first firms, would rise in the same proportion as wages. All costs, including "nonwage costs," would therefore rise in the same proportion as wages, and prices would rise in the same proportion too. To the extent that the other firms also have nonwage costs we have to bring in still other firms whose products constitute *their* nonwage costs. The analysis can be complicated in this way indefinitely, but the result is always the same. When all the effects are taken into account the conclusion is always that prices will rise in the same proportion as money wage rates if there is a general increase in money wage rates in the economy as a whole.

Another way of showing that this is what must occur is to consider the effects on the economy if costs and prices in general did not rise in the same proportion as wages. It would then be profitable for all producers to try, wherever possible, to replace labor by machinery or land or other factors of production whose costs have risen less. This would constitute an increase in demand for all these other factors which would keep on forcing their prices up. Only when their prices had risen as much as money wages in general would this pressure cease and the previous equilibrium relationship between all prices including wages be restored.

The proposition that raising money wages leaves unchanged the real wage and the fraction of the national income going to labor is equally true for all levels of employment. It is just as true for a condition of depression as for a condition of full employment and for exactly the same reasons. It is true that the level of economic activity itself can and does have important effects in determining what share of the national income goes to labor. If there is an increase in the level of economic activity, with no change in the fundamental economic and social institutions that determine the way the national income is shared between labor and the rest of the economy, there will be a smaller *proportion* (but a larger absolute amount) going to labor and a larger proportion going to others. But if the level of economic activity remains constant, an increase in money wages in general results in a corresponding increase in prices which leaves real wages just where they would have been in the absence of the general increase in money wages and prices.

To point out this truth is not the same thing as refusing to be interested in increasing the share of the national income that goes to labor. It is only to point out that raising the general level of wages is not a way of achieving the object. Extremely impatient people, however, are prone to get angry with a signpost, however accurate it may be, that tells them that the way they want to go is not going to lead to the place they want to get to. This chapter is not concerned with policies that really would increase labor's share. It is concerned with pointing out that a general increase in money wages must not be assumed to be the same thing as or even to lead to an increase in real wages.

Bargaining power is *effective only for* relative *wage rates.*

An increase in the money wages of a *section* of the economy is different. Even though the products made by the workers whose wages are raised may themselves rise, there will be no such rise in the prices of the goods made by the other workers whose wages are left behind. The prices of their products will also stay behind. The worker with the *relatively* higher wages will enjoy an increase in his real wage. He will be able to buy more goods and services with his wages (that is, if he remains in employment—which is much less certain now that his product is dearer relatively to the product of the workers whose wages have not been raised). That is why he wants to raise his money wages whenever he can.

But we have seen that if *all* sections get their wage rates increased they find that the prices of what they buy rises in the same proportion as their wages so that their expected gains turn out to be empty. Their disappointment only causes them to ask for another and bigger money wage increase. They will of course be disappointed again and as many times as they try this trick.

In time they may learn that they cannot win at this game, but unfortunately this discovery does not stop the inflationary process.

Understanding is not enough to prevent inflationary pressures.

It does not help very much for the workers or their representatives to understand that the increases in money wages must turn out to be merely nominal—that price increases will inevitably take away all that seems to be gained by the money wage increases. Such understanding by workers and their leaders cannot by itself stop the process of rising wages and prices and inflation because no group of workers will want to be left behind in the race. Even though this is a race in which however fast you run you stay where you are, it is also a race in which if you do not run as fast as the rest you will be moving backward—you will find that the prices of what you buy rise faster than your wages—and your real income actually falls. And if you should run faster than the others your income will in fact be greater because your wages will have risen faster than the prices of the things you buy that are made by other workers whose wages have not risen as much as yours. In this way the fruitless race to inflation and disaster can go on and on, faster and faster, and cannot be stopped by merely making the runners aware of the general futility of the race. Each dares not stop as long as the others are running, and so the race goes on.

A reserve army of unemployed seems to be necessary for stability.

It is of course possible to put an end to this inflationary race by the simple application of Functional Finance. A restrictive fiscal and monetary policy can reduce effective demand to the level at which the inflationary spiral is stopped by the unwillingness of employers to grant wage increases and by the reduction of the workers' pressure for them. But this way of preventing inflation would mean giving up the benefits of a high level of employment and introducing a reserve army of some 6 million unemployed men in order to reduce the excessive bargaining power of the workers. This sounds very much like the Marxian doctrine that a reserve army is necessary for the maintenance of capitalist society. Keeping 6 million unemployed instead of the 2 million made necessary by real technical frictions means a cut in the national income of some 15 billion dollars per annum. Clearly it would be most desirable to have a more economical and a socially less objectionable way of preventing inflation.

Low full-employment equilibrium depends on wage rigidities which we cannot hope to remove.

In the next chapter we shall consider a plan for eliminating this reserve army of unemployed, but before we go on to that we must consider an apparent theoretical difficulty. How can we have two full-employment equilibria, a low level of full employment with 6 million unemployed which seems to be stable but undesirable, and a high level of full employment with 2 million unemployed? [2]

If we had the perfect flexibility of wages that is sometimes assumed in economic theory, Functional Finance would indeed tend to move the economy to the high level of full employment. As long as there were more than 2 million unemployed there would be a tendency for wages and prices to fall and it would clearly be appropriate for the total level of spending to be increased. In this way the high level of full employment would be reached and maintained.

The wage rigidity that prevents wages and prices from falling and high full employment from being reached by the simple application of Functional Finance does not depend upon the great strength that collective bargaining and trade unions have reached at the present time. Even weak trade unions can cause a great deal of trouble to an employer who attempts to cut wages, and

[2] I am indebted in the following section to discussions with Professor Armen A. Alchian of the University of California at Los Angeles.

this will make him hesitate to do so. Even if there were no trade unions at all, the mere idea that a certain wage rate is reasonable or right or proper or fair—that it is antisocial to reduce wages—is sufficient to establish that degree of wage rigidity downward which can make a low level of full employment a stable position. Employers themselves feel that it is not nice to reduce wages or that they will not be well looked upon if they do. If no wages can fall, wages will rise in those areas where there is a *relative* scarcity of labor. If there are more than 6 million unemployed there is plenty of labor in almost every labor market. But if there are less than 6 million unemployed there will be scarcities of labor in some parts of the economy. Wages will rise in these parts but will not fall elsewhere. There is therefore an increase in the general level of wages and, if the increase is greater than the over-all increase in productivity, an increase in prices, and this starts the inflationary spiral.

The automatic achievement of high full employment through Functional Finance therefore depends on an absence of any conception of fair wages, on an immediate readiness of employers to reduce money wages as soon as there is the slightest excess of supply of labor over the demand in any labor market, and on an immediate readiness of the workers to accept such money wage reductions. The kind of flexibility of wages that is necessary to give a single high full-employment equilibrium is therefore not likely ever to exist and is of no practical significance. We cannot expect Functional Finance alone to give us high full employment.

Without Functional Finance even perfect wage flexibility would not give automatic high full employment.

It is even more difficult to imagine high full employment being reached automatically *without* the application of Functional Finance, no matter what extremes of flexibility of wages are assumed. But it is useful to look into this because there are some neoclassical economists who seem to like to argue that all our employment problems are due to wage and price rigidities. If there were perfect flexibility of wages and prices, anything less than high full employment would result in falling wages and prices. This could lead to the expectation of further declines in wages and prices and to a *reduction* in employment or an accelerated aggravation of the unemployment because an expected further fall in prices makes investment and economic activity in general look much less profitable. There would be an increase in the desire to hold cash (which would be continuously appreciating in purchasing power as prices fell), and this would feed the depression still further. We could in short have a *hyperdeflation* that could be economically much more devastating than any hyperinflation—economic activity could be reduced to near zero, and it is most likely that some violent political upheaval would put an end to the process if it were permitted to continue by a government faithful to the end to the tenets of classical economic theory.

There is a limit to hyperdeflations in that there is a certain amount of money in the economy which does not disappear in the course of the hyperdeflation and which becomes more and more valuable as prices fall. A great deal of money does disappear; much credit money, whether issued by banks or by others, may be destroyed, and therefore you could get wages and prices continuing to fall along with the terrible disruption of the economy. But there is a core of money which does not disappear—gold and the hard money provided by government. As the hyperdeflation proceeds, the value of the stock of money becomes so great and the people who own this money are so rich that this will overcome their tendency to hoard the increasingly valuable money. They will increase their demand for goods and services and this will put an end to the hyperdeflation and to the depression.

It is doubtful whether anybody ever seriously suggested this as a practical way of governing our economy. The large volume of money which we need for the smooth working of a modern economy is already so great in relation to the national income that wages and prices could fall for a long time before the end of this road was reached. We must recognize, however, that the increase in the value of the stock of money when prices fall is a significant item, and it is probably true that modern Keynesian economists and protagonists of Functional Finance have paid insufficient attention to this element.

A less fantastic proposal of anti-Functional Financiers is that the volume of money income should be stabilized by monetary authorities.[3] This would then give the high level of full employment if you could remove all the frictions and rigidities we have spoken about. This is true. The only objection is that there is no feasible way of removing the rigidities. It would not be sufficient to weaken the most powerful trade unions or even to destroy them. It would not be sufficient to destroy all trade unions. Social security would have to be abolished. Workers' savings and credits would have to be taken away. There would have to be removed from the minds of both workers and employers the idea of a fair or decent wage rate. There is no practical possibility of removing the ideas of fairness of wages and of the defenses that workers have against wage reductions and there is very doubtful desirability in doing so. If the rigidities are not removed, stabilizing money income would prevent hyperdeflations, but it would be compatible with quite severe depressions and much more than 6 million unemployed.

Our problem is then: How can we get from low full employment, with 6 million unemployed, to high full employment, with not more than 2 million unemployed? How can we abolish the reserve army of unemployed without falling into inflation and destroying the stability of our economy?

[3] Presumably by the monetary and fiscal instruments of Functional Finance but with the aim of stabilizing the volume of money income instead of with the direct aim of full employment.

Summary.

The more frequent consideration of depression than of inflation in connection with Functional Finance has led to its being called "depression economics." But this is incorrect; Functional Finance is just as applicable to the prevention of inflation as to the prevention of depression. Achieving full employment means avoiding both depression and inflation, but there are serious ambiguities in the concept of full employment. These are insufficiently removed by the distinction between deflationary unemployment and frictional unemployment. There is a range between depression and inflation where wages and prices are rising even though there are more unemployed than can be blamed on frictions in the normal sense. In this range one can see indication both of depression and of inflation.

The influence that causes wages and prices to rise even when there are large numbers of unemployed is the excessive bargaining power of labor. The bargaining power of labor is excessive whenever it causes wages to rise more rapidly than over-all productivity. This causes prices to rise *pari passu* with wage increases so that there is no real wage increase but only inflation. Excessive bargaining power by workers may be called an "economic friction" to distinguish it from real or technical frictions that form a more "genuine" limitation to the attainable level of employment and output. The elimination of economic friction would permit the high level of full employment to be reached.

Even without the elimination of economic friction increased total spending can raise employment above the low full-employment level (*i.e.,* unemployment can be reduced below the 6 million level) but this can only be temporary. This is because "over-full" employment causes inflation, and inflation cannot be continued indefinitely.

To call labor's bargaining power excessive is not to be against the interests of labor. Excessive bargaining power of labor does not increase the real wage or the share of the national income going to labor. An over-all change in the level of wages causes a proportional change in the level of prices. Labor men tend to favor and employers tend to frown on general wage increases because they assume, quite falsely, that a general wage change has the same effect as a local wage change. But the real wage is determined by more basic social institutions, such as the degree of monopoly, which are unaffected by the level of money wages. This is true for all levels of economic activity. To point this out may be disappointing to labor if it removes an illusion.

A *section* of the economy *can* increase its real wage by raising its money wage relatively to the rest of the economy, but if all sections try this we have inflation. The inflation cannot be prevented by mere enlightenment as to the effects of wage increases because nobody can afford to keep out of the inflationary race. And stopping the inflation by Functional Finance means establishing low full employment and maintaining a reserve army of 4 million unnecessarily unemployed people.

The stability of the low level of full employment depends on downward wage rigidities. It is impractical to propose their abolition because that would involve not merely destruction of trade unions but impoverishment of all workers, abolition of social security, and removal of the general feeling, shared by both workers and employers, that there is a "fair wage" which it is undesirable to lower. Furthermore such a complete removal of wage and price rigidities would subject the economy to the danger of hyperdeflations that would be more devastating than hyperinflations. Together with Functional Finance the abolition of all wage and price rigidities would result in high full employment. Together with a policy of stabilizing the level of money income hyperdeflations would be prevented, but there could still be very serious depression. But since the abolition of all wage and price rigidities does not seem feasible, we are left with our problem of how to get high full employment without inflation.

[4]

FUNCTIONAL FINANCE AND THE FEDERAL DEBT

BY ABBA P. LERNER

APART from the necessity of winning the war, there is no task facing society today so important as the elimination of economic insecurity. If we fail in this after the war the present threat to democratic civilization will arise again. It is therefore essential that we grapple with this problem even if it involves a little careful thinking and even if the thought proves somewhat contrary to our preconceptions.

In recent years the principles by which appropriate government action can maintain prosperity have been adequately developed, but the proponents of the new principles have either not seen their full logical implications or shown an over-solicitousness which caused them to try to save the public from the necessary mental exercise. This has worked like a boomerang. Many of our publicly minded men who have come to see that deficit spending actually works still oppose the permanent maintenance of prosperity because in their failure to see *how* it all works they are easily frightened by fairy tales of terrible consequences.

I

As formulated by Alvin Hansen and others who have developed and popularized it, the new fiscal theory (which was first put forward in substantially complete form by J. M. Keynes in England) sounds a little less novel and absurd to our preconditioned ears than it does when presented in its simplest and most logical form, with all the unorthodox implications expressly formulated. In some cases the less shocking formulation may be intentional, as a tactical device to gain serious attention. In other cases it is due not to a desire to sugar the pill but to the fact that the writers themselves have not seen all the unorthodox implications—perhaps subconsciously compromising with their own orthodox education. But now it is these compromises that are under fire. Now more than ever it is necessary to pose the theorems in the purest form. Only thus will it be possible to clear the air of objections which really are concerned with awkwardnesses that appear only when the new theory is forced into the old theoretical framework.

Fundamentally the new theory, like almost every important discovery, is extremely simple. Indeed it is this simplicity which makes the public suspect it as too slick. Even learned professors who find it hard to abandon ingrained habits of thought have complained that it is "merely logical" when they could find no flaw in it. What progress the theory has made so far has been achieved not by simplifying it but by dressing it up to make it more complicated and accompanying the presentation with impressive but irrelevant statistics.

The central idea is that government fiscal policy, its spending and taxing, its borrowing and repayment of loans, its issue of new money and its withdrawal of money, shall all be undertaken with an eye only to the *results* of these actions on the economy and not to any established traditional doctrine about what is sound or unsound. This principle of judging only by *effects* has been applied in many other fields of human activity, where it is known as the method of science as opposed to scholasticism. The principle of judging fiscal measures by the way they work or function in the economy we may call *Functional Finance.*

The first financial responsibility of the government (since nobody else can undertake that responsibility) is to keep the total rate of spending in the country on goods and services neither greater nor less than that rate which at the current prices would buy all the goods that it is possible to produce. If total spending is allowed to go above this there will be inflation, and if it is allowed to go below this there will be unemployment. The government can increase total spending by spending more itself or by reducing taxes so that the taxpayers have more money left to spend. It can reduce total spending by spending less itself or by raising taxes so that taxpayers have less money left to spend. By these means total spending can be kept at the required level, where it will be enough to buy the goods that can be produced by all who want to work, and yet not enough to bring inflation by demanding (at current prices) *more* than can be produced.

In applying this first law of Functional Finance, the government may find itself collecting more in taxes than it is spending, or spending more than it collects in taxes. In the former case it can keep the difference in its coffers or use it to repay some of the national debt, and in the latter case it would have to provide the difference by borrowing or printing money. In neither case should the government feel that there is anything especially good or bad about this result; it should merely concentrate on keeping the total rate of spending neither too small nor too great, in this way preventing both unemployment and inflation.

An interesting, and to many a shocking, corollary is that taxing is *never* to be undertaken merely because the government needs to make money payments. According to the principles of Functional Finance, taxation must be judged only by its effects. Its main effects are two: the taxpayer has less money left to spend and the government has more money. The second effect can be brought about so much more easily by printing the money that only the first effect is significant. Taxation should therefore be imposed only when it is desirable that the taxpayers shall have less money to spend, for example, when they would otherwise spend enough to bring about inflation.

The second law of Functional Finance is that the government should borrow money only if it is desirable that the public should have less money and more government bonds, for these are the *effects* of government borrowing. This might be desirable if otherwise the rate of interest would be reduced too low (by attempts on the part of the holders of the cash to lend it out) and induce too much investment, thus bringing about inflation. Conversely, the government should lend money (or repay some of its debt) only if it is desirable to increase the money or to reduce the quantity of government bonds in the hands of the public. When taxing, spending, borrowing and lending (or repaying loans) are governed by the principles of Functional Finance, any excess of money outlays over money revenues, if it cannot be met out of money hoards, must be met by printing new money, and any excess of revenues over outlays can be destroyed or used to replenish hoards.

The almost instinctive revulsion that we have to the idea of printing money, and the tendency to identify it with inflation, can be overcome if we calm ourselves and take note that this printing does not affect the amount of money *spent*. That is regulated by the first law of Functional Finance, which refers especially to inflation and unemployment. The printing of money takes place only when it is needed to implement Functional Finance in spending or lending (or repayment of government debt).[1]

In brief, Functional Finance rejects completely the traditional doctrines of "sound finance" and the principle of trying to balance the budget over a solar year or any other arbitrary period. In their place it prescribes: first, the adjustment of total spending (by everybody in the economy, including the government) in order to eliminate both unemployment and inflation, using government spending when total spending is too low and taxation when total spending is too high; second, the adjustment of public holdings of money and of government bonds, by government borrowing or debt repayment, in order to achieve the rate of interest which results in the most desirable level of investment; and, third, the printing, hoarding or destruction of money as needed for carrying out the first two parts of the program.

II

In judging the formulations of economists on this subject it is difficult to distinguish between tact in smoothing over the more stag-

[1]Borrowing money from the banks, on conditions which permit the banks to issue new credit money based on their additional holdings of government securities, must be considered for our purpose as printing money. In effect the banks are acting as agents for the government in issuing credit or bank money.

gering statements of Functional Finance and insufficient clarity on the part of those who do not fully realize the extremes that are implied in their relatively orthodox formulations. First there were the pump-primers, whose argument was that the government merely had to get things going and then the economy could go on by itself. There are very few pump-primers left now. A formula similar in some ways to pump-priming was developed by Scandinavian economists in terms of a series of cyclical, capital and other special budgets which had to be balanced not annually but over longer periods. Like the pump-priming formula it fails because there is no reason for supposing that the spending and taxation policy which maintains full employment and prevents inflation must necessarily balance the budget over a decade any more than during a year or at the end of each fortnight.

As soon as this was seen—the lack of any guarantee that the maintenance of prosperity would permit the budget to be balanced even over longer periods—it had to be recognized that the result might be a continually increasing national debt (if the additional spending were provided by the government's borrowing of the money and not by printing the excess of its spending over its tax revenues). At this point two things should have been made clear: first, that this possibility presented no danger to society, no matter what unimagined heights the national debt might reach, so long as Functional Finance maintained the proper level of total demand for current output; and second (though this is much less important), that there is an automatic tendency for the budget to be balanced in the long run as a *result* of the application of Functional Finance, even if there is no place for the *principle* of balancing the budget. No matter how much interest has to be paid on the debt, taxation must not be applied unless it is necessary to keep spending down to prevent inflation. The interest can be paid by borrowing still more.

As long as the public is willing to keep on lending to the government there is no difficulty, no matter how many zeros are added to the national debt. If the public becomes reluctant to keep on lending, it must either hoard the money or spend it. If the public hoards, the government can print the money to meet its interest and other obligations, and the only effect is that the public holds government currency instead of government bonds and the government is saved the trouble of making interest payments. If the public spends, this will increase the rate of total spending so that it will not be necessary for the government to borrow for this purpose; and if the rate of spending becomes too great, *then* is the time to tax to prevent inflation. The proceeds can then be used to pay interest and repay government debt. In every case Functional Finance provides a simple, quasi-automatic response.

But either this was not seen clearly or it was considered too shocking or too logical to be told to the public. Instead it was argued, for example by Alvin Hansen, that as long as there is a reasonable ratio between national income and debt, the interest payment on the national debt can easily come from taxes paid out of the increased national income created by the deficit financing.

This unnecessary "appeasement" opened the way to an extremely effective opposition to Functional Finance. Even men who have a clear understanding of the mechanism whereby government spending in times of depression can increase the national income by several times the amount laid out by the government, and who understand perfectly well that the national debt, when it is not owed to other nations, is not a burden on the nation in the same way as an individual's debt to other individuals is a burden on the individual, have come out strongly against "deficit spending."[2] It has been argued that "it would be impossible to devise a program better adapted to the systematic undermining of the private-enterprise system and the hastening of the final catastrophe than 'deficit spending.' "[3]

These objections are based on the recognition that although every dollar spent by the government may create several dollars of

[2]An excellent example of this is the persuasive article by John T. Flynn in *Harper's Magazine* for July 1942.

[3]Flynn, *ibid.*

income in the course of the next year or two, the effects then disappear. From this it follows that if the national income is to be maintained at a high level the government has to keep up its contribution to spending for as long as private spending is insufficient by itself to provide full employment. This might mean an indefinite continuation of government support to spending (though not necessarily at an increasing rate); and if, as the "appeasement" formulation suggests, all this spending comes out of borrowing, the debt will keep on growing until it is no longer in a "reasonable" ratio to income.

This leads to the crux of the argument. If the interest on the debt must be raised out of taxes (again an assumption that is unchallenged by the "appeasement" formulation) it will in time constitute an important fraction of the national income. The very high income tax necessary to collect this amount of money and pay it to the holders of government bonds will discourage risky private investment, by so reducing the net return on it that the investor is not compensated for the risk of losing his capital. This will make it necessary for the government to undertake still more deficit financing to keep up the level of income and employment. Still heavier taxation will then be necessary to pay the interest on the growing debt—until the burden of taxation is so crushing that private investment becomes unprofitable, and the private enterprise economy collapses. Private firms and corporations will all be bankrupted by the taxes, and the government will have to take over all industry.

This argument is not new. The identical calamities, although they are now receiving much more attention than usual, were promised when the first income tax law of one penny in the pound was proposed. All this only makes it more important to evaluate the significance of the argument.

III

There are four major errors in the argument against deficit spending, four reasons why its apparent conclusiveness is only illusory.

In the first place, the same high income tax that reduces the return on the investment is deductible for the loss that is incurred if the investment turns out a failure. As a result of this the *net* return on the risk of loss is unaffected by the income tax rate, no matter how high that may be. Consider an investor in the $50,000-a-year income class who has accumulated $10,000 to invest. At 6 percent this would yield $600, but after paying income tax on this addition to his income at 60 cents in the dollar he would have only $240 left. It is argued, therefore, that he would not invest because this is insufficient compensation for the risk of losing $10,000. This argument forgets that if the $10,000 is all lost, the net loss to the investor, after he has deducted his income tax allowance, will be only $4,000, and the rate of return on the amount he actually risks is still exactly 6 percent; $240 is 6 percent of $4,000. The effect of the income tax is to make the rich man act as a kind of agent working for society on commission. He receives only a part of the return on the investment, but he loses only a part of the money that is invested. Any investment that was worth undertaking in the absence of the income tax is still worth undertaking.

Of course, this correction of the argument is strictly true only where 100 percent of the loss is deductible from taxable income, where relief from taxation occurs at the same rate as the tax on returns. There is a good case against certain limitations on permissible deduction from the income tax base for losses incurred, but that is another story. Something of the argument remains, too, if the loss would put the taxpayer into a lower income tax bracket, where the rebate (and the tax) is at a lower rate. There would then be some reduction in the net return as compared with the potential net loss. But this would apply only to such investments as are large enough to threaten to impoverish the investor if they fail. It was for the express purpose of dealing with this problem that the corporation was devised, making it possible for many individuals to combine and undertake risky enterprises without any one person having to risk all his fortune on one venture. But quite apart from corporate investment, this problem would be met almost entirely if the maximum rate of income tax were reached at a relatively low level, say at $25,000 a year (low, that is, from the point of view of the rich men who are the supposed source of risk capital). Even if all income in excess of $25,000 were taxed at 90 percent there would be no discouragement in the investment of any part of income over this level. True, the net return, after payment of tax, would be only one-tenth of the nominal interest payments, but the amount risked by the investors would also be only ten percent of the actual capital invested, and therefore the net return on the capital actually risked by the investor would be unaffected.

In the second place, this argument against deficit spending in time of depression would be indefensible even if the harm done by debt were as great as has been suggested. It must be remembered that spending by the government increases the *real* national income of goods and services by several times the amount spent by the government, and that the burden is measured not by the amount of the interest payments but only by the inconveniences involved in the process of transferring the money from the taxpayers to the bondholders. Therefore objecting to deficit spending is like arguing that if you are offered a job when out of work on the condition that you promise to pay your wife interest on a part of the money earned (or that your wife pay it to you) it would be wiser to continue to be unemployed, because in time you will be owing your wife a great deal of money (or she will be owing it to you), and this might cause matrimonial difficulties in the future. Even if the interest payments were really lost to society, instead of being merely transferred within the society, they would come to much less than the loss through permitting unemployment to continue. That loss would be several times as great as the *capital* on which these interest payments have to be made.

In the third place, there is no good reason for supposing that the government would have to raise all the interest on the national debt by current taxes. We have seen that Functional Finance permits taxation only when the *direct* effect of the tax is in the social interest, as when it prevents excessive spending or excessive investment which would bring about inflation. If taxes imposed to prevent inflation do not result in sufficient proceeds, the interest on the debt can be met by borrowing or printing the money. There is no risk of inflation from this, because if there were such a risk a greater amount would have to be collected in taxes.

This means that the absolute size of the national debt does not matter at all, and that however large the interest payments that have to be made, these do not constitute any burden upon society as a whole. A completely fantastic exaggeration may illustrate the point. Suppose the national debt reaches the stupendous total of ten thousand billion dollars (that is, ten trillion, $10,000,000,-000,000), so that the interest on it is 300 billion a year. Suppose the real national income of goods and services which can be produced by the economy when fully employed is 150 billion. The interest alone, therefore, comes to twice the real national income. There is no doubt that a debt of this size would be called "unreasonable." But even in this fantastic case the payment of the interest constitutes no burden on society. Although the real income is only 150 billion dollars the money income is 450 billion—150 billion in income from the production of goods and services and 300 billion in income from ownership of the government bonds which constitute the national debt. Of this money income of 450 billion, 300 billion has to be collected in taxes by the government for interest payments (if 10 trillion is the legal debt limit), but after payment of these taxes there remains 150 billion dollars in the hands of the taxpayers, and this is enough to pay for all the goods and services that the economy can produce. Indeed it would do the public no good to have any more money left after tax payments, because if it spent more than 150 billion dollars it would merely be raising the prices of the goods bought. It would not be able to obtain more goods to consume than the country is able to produce.

Of course this illustration must not be taken to imply that a debt of this size is at all likely to come about as a result of the application of Functional Finance. As will be shown below, there is a natural tendency for the national debt to stop growing long before it comes anywhere near the astronomical figures that we have been playing with.

The unfounded assumption that current interest on the debt must be collected in taxes springs from the idea that the debt must be kept in a "reasonable" or "manageable" ratio to income (whatever that may be). If this restriction is accepted, *borrowing* to pay the interest is eliminated as soon as the limit of "reasonableness" is reached, and if we further rule out, as an indecent thought, the possibility of *printing* the money, there remains only the possibility of raising the interest payments by taxes. Fortunately there is no need to assume these limitations so long as Functional Finance is on guard against inflation, for it is the fear of inflation which is the only rational basis for suspicion of the printing of money.

Finally, there is no reason for assuming that, as a result of the continued application of Functional Finance to maintain full employment, the government must always be borrowing more money and increasing the national debt. There are a number of reasons for this.

First, full employment *can* be maintained by printing the money needed for it, and this does not increase the debt at all. It is probably advisable, however, to allow debt and money to increase together in a certain balance, as long as one or the other has to increase.

Second, since one of the greatest deterrents to private investment is the fear that the depression will come before the investment has paid for itself, the guarantee of permanent full employment will make private investment much more attractive, once investors have got over their suspicions of the new procedure. The greater private investment will diminish the need for deficit spending.

Third, as the national debt increases, and with it the sum of private wealth, there will be an increasingly yield from taxes on higher incomes and inheritances, even if the tax rates are unchanged. These higher tax payments do not represent reductions of spending by the taxpayers. Therefore the government does not have to use these proceeds to maintain the requisite rate of spending, and it can devote them to paying the interest on the national debt.

Fourth, as the national debt increases it acts as a self-equilibrating force, gradually diminishing the further need for its growth and finally reaching an equilibrium level where its tendency to grow comes completely to an end. The greater the national debt the greater is the quantity of private wealth. The reason for this is simply that for every dollar of debt owed by the government there is a private creditor who owns the government obligations (possibly through a corporation in which he has shares), and who regards these obligations as part of his private fortune. The greater the private fortunes the less is the incentive to add to them by saving out of current income. As current saving is thus discouraged by the great accumulation of past savings, spending out of current income increases (since spending is the only alternative to saving income). This increase in private spending makes it less necessary for the government to undertake deficit financing to keep total spending at the level which provides full employment. When the government debt has become so great that private spending is enough to provide the total spending needed for full employment, there is no need for any deficit financing by the government, the budget is balanced and the national debt automatically stops growing. The size of this equilibrium level of debt depends on many things. It can only be guessed at, and in the very roughest manner. My guess is that it is between 100 and 300 billion dollars. Since the level is a result and not a principle of Functional Finance the latitude of such a guess does not matter; it is not needed for the application of the laws of Functional Finance.

Fifth, if for any reason the government does not wish to see private property grow too much (whether in the form of government bonds or otherwise) it can check this by taxing the rich instead of borrowing from them, in its program of financing government spending to maintain full employment. The rich will not reduce their spending significantly, and thus the effects on the economy, apart from the smaller debt, will be the same as if the money had been borrowed from them. By this means the debt can be reduced to any desired level and kept there.

The answers to the argument against deficit spending may thus be summarized as follows:

The national debt does not have to keep on increasing;

Even if the national debt does grow, the interest on it does not have to be raised out of current taxes;

Even if the interest on the debt is raised out of current taxes, these taxes constitute only the interest on only a fraction of the benefit enjoyed from the government spending, and are not lost to the nation but are merely transferred from taxpayers to bondholders;

High income taxes need not discourage investment, because appropriate deductions for losses can diminish the capital actually risked by the investor in the same proportion as his net income from the investment is reduced.

IV

If the propositions of Functional Finance were put forward without fear of appearing too logical, criticisms like those discussed above would not be as popular as they now are, and it would not be necessary to defend Functional Finance from its friends. An especially embarrassing task arises from the claim that Functional Finance (or deficit financing, as it is frequently but unsatisfactorily called) is primarily a defense of private enterprise. In the attempt to gain popularity for Functional Finance, it has been given other names and declared to be essentially directed toward saving private enterprise. I myself have sinned similarly in previous writings in identifying it with democracy,[4] thus joining the army of salesmen who wrap up their wares in the flag and tie anything they have to sell to victory or morale.

Functional Finance is not especially related to democracy or to private enterprise. It is applicable to a communist society just as well as to a fascist society or a democratic society. It is applicable to any society in which money is used as an important element in the economic mechanism. It consists of the simple principle of

[4] In "Total Democracy and Full Employment," *Social Change* (May 1941).

giving up our preconceptions of what is proper or sound or traditional, of what "is done," and instead considering the *functions* performed in the economy by government taxing and spending and borrowing and lending. It means using these instruments simply as instruments, and not as magic charms that will cause mysterious hurt if they are manipulated by the wrong people or without due reverence for tradition. Like any other mechanism, Functional Finance will work no matter who pulls the levers. Its relationship to democracy and free enterprise consists simply in the fact that if the people who believe in these things will not use Functional Finance, they will stand no chance in the long run against others who will.

[5]

THE BURDEN OF DEBT

Abba P. Lerner

"But look," the Rabbi's wife remonstrated, "when one party to the dispute presented their case to you you said 'you are quite right' and then when the other party presented their case you again said 'you are quite right,' surely they cannot both be right?" To which the Rabbi answered, "My dear, you are quite right!"

MESSRS. Bowen, Davis, and Kopf have shown [1] that the real burden of a project using up resources in the present can be shifted to future generations by internal borrowing, providing one defines "generation" in a particular way. It is just as easy to prove that all politicians are economists or that all economists are dunces, provided one defines "economist" in a particular way. But even if I call the tail of a sheep a leg that will not turn sheep into quintapeds. The issue is of course terminological rather than substantive. It is nevertheless one of the utmost importance because the conclusion reached by Bowen *et al.*, although not incorrect on their own definitions, is bound to be misinterpreted as meaning what it seems to be saying in English and as indeed implying that most politicians understand economics better than the economists — most, if not all, of whom are dunces.

Bowen, Davis, and Kopf are absolutely right when they agree that there is "absolutely nothing" wrong with the standard argument of modern economists that the real burden of a debt can ***not*** be shifted to future generations if it is defined as "the total amount of private consumption goods given up by the community *at the moment of time the borrowed funds are spent.*" But President Eisenhower "appears convinced that the costs of debt-financed public projects can be passed on to future generations." Like the Rabbi in the story, Bowen *et al.* want to say that he too is right, but in their enthusiasm they even say that the purpose of their note "is to suggest that in this instance it is the President who is — in at least one highly important sense — right," [2] thus clearly implying that the economists are wrong.

To make the President appear right, Bowen *et al.* redefine "present generation" to mean the people who lend the money to finance the project, and they redefine "future generation" to mean the people who pay the taxes that are used to repay the principal and the interest on the loans. The perversity of the redefinitions is obscured by supposing that the lenders ("this generation"), are all 21 years old at the time of the execution of the project when they lend the money and by supposing that they are repaid 44 years later, on their 65th birthday, with funds obtained at that time from 21-year-old taxpayers ("the next generation"). The burden is thereby shifted from "this generation" to "the next generation."

What has been proved, if we obstinately insist in expressing the conclusion in English, is that it is possible to shift the burden from the Lenders to the Taxpayers or, we might say, from the Lowells to the Thomases. The Lowells are better off and the Thomases are worse off than if the Lowells had been taxed to raise the money for the project in the first place.

The "red herring" nature of having the Lowells lend the money now (so that we can call them the present generation) and having the Thomases pay the taxes in the future (so that they can be called the future generation) jumps to the eye if we note that the shifting of the real burden of the project from the Lowells to the Thomases (or indeed of any other burden) could take place just as well at the time of the project (or at any other time) by simply taxing the Thomases instead of the Lowells.

No economist, so far as I am aware, has ever denied the possibility of borrowing or of lending or of taxing some people instead of others, or of any combinations of such oper-

[1] W. G. Bowen, R. G. Davis, and D. H. Kopf, "The Public Debt: A Burden on Future Generations?" *American Economic Review*, L (September 1960), 701–706.

[2] *Ibid.*, 701, where President Eisenhower is quoted as saying, "Personally, I do not feel that any amount can be properly called a surplus as long as the nation is in debt. I prefer to think of such an item as a reduction on our children's inherited mortgage," in his *State of the Union Message*, January 7, 1960.

ations. And if we redefine Mr. Eisenhower's words so that they mean only that such operations are possible, then indeed the words used by the President constitute a true statement. But there is no reason for supposing that the President was trying to use any language other than English, and what the President said is simply wrong (in English), unless indeed all the economists (including Bowen *et al.*, as well as J. M. Buchanan, who plays similar linguistic tricks [3]) are absolutely wrong.

The real issue, and it is an important one, between the economists and Mr. Eisenhower is not whether it is possible to shift a burden (either in the present or in the future) from some people to other people, but whether it is possible *by internal borrowing* to shift a real burden from the present generation, in the sense of the present economy as a whole, onto a future generation, in the sense of the future economy as a whole. What is important for economists is to teach the President that the latter is impossible because a project that uses up resources needs the resources *at the time that it uses them up*, and not before or after.

This basic proposition is true of all projects that use up resources. The question is traditionally posed in terms of the burden of a *public* project financed by *privately* held internal debt; but the proposition is quite independent of whether the project is public or private as well as of whether the debt is private or public. The proposition holds as long as the project is financed *internally*, so that there are no outsiders to take over the current burden by providing the resources and to hand back the burden in the future by asking for the return of the resources.

It is necessary for economists to keep repeating this basic proposition because one of their main duties is to keep warning people against the fallacy of composition. To anyone who sees only a part of the economy it does seem possible to borrow from the future because he tends to assume that what is true of the part is true of the whole. It *is* possible for the Lowells to borrow from the Thomases, and what this borrowing does is to shift a burden from the Lowells to the Thomases in the present, and then to shift an equal burden from the Thomases to the Lowells in the future when the loan is repaid. To the Lowells (and to anyone else who sees only the Lowells) the combination of these two shifts looks like the shifting of a burden from the present into the future or the shifting of resources from the future into the present. To the Thomases, of course, the transactions will look like the opposite, namely, the shifting of a burden from the future into the present or the shifting of resources from the present into the future. But the borrowing and the repayment do not make a Time Machine. There is no shift of resources or of burdens between different points in time. It is possible for a *part* of the economy (the Lowells) to shift *its* burden into the future only as long as *another part* of the present economy (the Thomases) is ready to take it over for the intervening period. It is not possible for *the whole* of the present generation to shift a burden into the future because there are no Thomases left to play the magician's assistant in the illusion.

This is not to say that there is no way at all in which the present generation can shift a burden onto future generations. Our proposition is only that this is not done by internal borrowing. We can impoverish the future by cutting down on our investment in capital resources (or by using up or destroying natural resources) that would have enabled future generations to produce and enjoy higher standards of living. There is even a possible connection between internal debt financing and this way of really impoverishing future generations. If full employment (or some other level of employment) is somehow being maintained, and if the conditions of the borrowing and the kinds of people from whom the borrowing is done are such that they reduce consumption by less than consumption would have been reduced if the money had been raised instead by taxes, then there will be more consumption and there will therefore have to be less investment. The borrowing will then have reduced the real resources inherited by future generations.

But there is no *necessary* connection. It would almost certainly not work this way in the conditions of 1960. Whether the borrow-

[3] In his *Public Principles of Public Debt* (Homewood, Illinois, 1958).

ing increases or decreases consumption depends on the nature and on the conditions of the borrowing on the one hand and of the alternative — the taxation — on the other hand. Furthermore, at the present time, when we have considerable unemployment and unused capacity, an increase in consumption is more likely to lead to *more* investment (out of unutilized resources) and therefore to an *increase* in the productive resources inherited by future generations. And it is quite certainly not these complicated considerations that are responsible for the President's belief that internal borrowing increases and repayment reduces "our children's inherited mortgage." In any case even the *possibility* of a genuine impoverishment of future generations by an induced reduction in investment is *explicitly* ruled out by Bowen *et al.* when they say that the resources consumed by the project "*must* entail a contemporaneous reduction in private consumption." [4]

Any genuine impoverishment of future generations must be the result of *not* reducing private consumption by the full amount of the resources used up in the project so that some of these resources must come out of alternative investment (if we rule out the use of unemployed resources). It is only the curtailed alternative investment outside of the project that can tend to impoverish future generations (although this might be more than made up for them by the benefits that these same future generations will derive from the project in question).

We can also impoverish the future by using up in the production of armaments too much of the resources that would have gone into investment; and we can equally impoverish the future by an over-economy in armaments, or by skimping in our contribution to the building of a healthy world, so that we invite aggression or foster resentments and revolutions. But both of these possibilities are completely independent of whether we borrow or tax.

[4] *Ibid.*, 703, my italics.

Semantic playfulness like that of Bowen *et al.* seriously sabotages economists in their important task in educating the public to the appreciation of an important truth. By their ingenious redefinition of "generations" they have made it more difficult to point out just where the fallacy of composition is perpetrated. It is perpetrated when a part of the economy (as in their definition of this or that generation) is taken for the whole (as in the usual meaning of a generation as *all* the people living at a certain date); and this is exactly what Bowen *et al.* do when they say that President Eisenhower (speaking English) is right.

They have taken a true proposition — i.e., that some people can shift a burden into the future by borrowing from other people — and rewritten it in such a manner that almost everyone will read in it the false proposition that the nation as a whole can filch resources from the future by internal borrowing (public or private), thereby impoverishing future generations. It is unfortunately the false proposition that is implied in the statement by the President, and believed by many people in positions to make vital decisions. The false belief may well contribute to a failure of the free nations to take the steps necessary to maintain and extend freedom in the world. There is even a clear and present danger that because of a baseless fear of impoverishing future generations by leaving them with a larger internal debt (which they will owe to themselves), we may fail to protect them from nuclear war and/or totalitarian domination; the confusion sown by Bowen *et al.* tends to increase that danger. It is to be hoped that these authors will tell the President that they were using a special language of their own and didn't mean what they seemed to be saying when they seemed to be denying a proposition with which, as they themselves declare, there is "absolutely nothing" wrong.

[6]

CHAPTER 23

Economics, Politics, and Administration

WE HAVE now concluded our treatment of the *economics* of employment, but a word or two must be added on the *politics* and the *administration* of employment policies in general and of Functional Finance in particular. This is especially necessary because of the frequency with which opponents of measures like Functional Finance move from economics to these other fields. They very often agree, after protracted argument, that "the economics is perfectly correct." But since "a man convinced against his will retains the same opinion still" this agreement does not prevent them from continuing their opposition. They then try to justify the continued opposition on different grounds. No longer able to charge economic illiteracy, they take refuge in charges of political impossibility or administrative unfeasibility.

The central purpose of the book is to help remove the confusions and misunderstandings that are in the way of a wholehearted utilization in our society of the economic steering wheel referred to in Chapter 1. The rest of the book is an amplification of Chapter 1, developing explicitly the income analysis on which it is based, considering some of the objections and difficulties in the way of its full application, and considering some closely related issues like the national debt, the international aspects of employment policies, and the problems that would arise *out of* the achievement of full employment. All through the book it has been necessary here and there to touch on political and administrative aspects of employment policies. In this chapter we shall try to pull some of these elements together.

371

The political philosophy of Democratic Functionalism shows that there is no conflict between freedom and order.

The social and political philosophy of Functional Finance is that of Democratic Functionalism, of which Functional Finance is a part. Democratic Functionalism calls for the application of the humanistic principles of classic liberalism to modern problems and to modern techniques of dealing with them. It consists of the *functional* principle that all social institutions—ancient or modern, actual or potential—should be judged only by their effectiveness in carrying out their functions in the social interest and the *democratic* principle that in estimating the social interest, there should be no discrimination between different men or groups of men, for that would be undemocratic, but that all men should be considered equally worthy.

One corollary of Democratic Functionalism is that the much spoken of conflict between freedom and order in society is a delusion and a snare. It is *never* necessary to choose between freedom and order. It is not even necessary to look for a *compromise* in which some of each is sacrificed for some of the other. Order is nothing but an instrument for maximizing the total freedom in society by lessening the freedom of some people to do what they want to do when that limitation increases by *more* the freedom (which includes the ability) of others to do what *they* want to do. It follows that the maximum or order is identical with the maximum of freedom. A sacrifice of freedom for the sake of order is as senseless as any sacrifice of an end for the sake of the means for its own achievement.

The acceptance of a rule can turn political into economic problems and make them solvable.

There is, of course, often a conflict between the interests of different people or of different groups of people. In such conflicts it is inevitable that some interests, some freedoms should be sacrificed for the sake of others. Unless there is some accepted principle or rule that determines the nature of the settlement, the conflict of interest gives us a *political* problem. This means that the settlement is nothing but a resultant of the forces that the interested parties can bring to bear on the issue. The settlement is then truly a *compromise,* with complete disregard of the interest of one or other of the parties as a limit of the range of possible compromises.

Where there is a generally accepted principle or rule for determining the nature of the settlement, a genuine solution is possible which is not a mere compromise or resultant of immediate forces. If the rule is one which limits freedom only where the limitation is necessary for the sake of greater freedom, then both freedom and order are maximized. The limitation of the smaller freedoms constitutes the order necessary for the enjoyment of greater freedoms.

The principle or rule necessary for providing a genuine solution must be directed at the *content* of the settlement and not merely at the *manner* in which the settlement is reached. The institution of democratic procedures for resolving differences by majority vote does not change the basically political nature of conflicts or the compromise nature of their settlement. The substitution of ballots for bullets diminishes the amount of naked violence but does not constitute a principle or rule to take the place of the pressure of the conflicting forces in determining the content of the settlement of the issues voted on.

The principle of freedom is such a rule.

An important step toward the replacement of arbitrary compromise by a rule is to be found in the principle of freedom. This is the principle that anyone may do whatever he prefers to do as long as this does not affect the ability of other people to do what *they* want to do. This principle enables purely economic problems to be separated out from the complex of social relations, and to the purely economic problems we can apply relatively simple procedures of getting optimum solutions in terms of maximization of the benefit to those who are affected.

The principle of freedom is seen most clearly in the imaginary case of the distributist society in which individuals can produce the things they want by themselves in their own houses or gardens. In the absence of interdependence in production there is no political problem involved. Nobody else is affected by anyone's industry or laziness. We get the optimum solution by permitting each individual to maximize his satisfaction by working just as hard and as long as seems best to himself.

In a modern economy where industry must be highly integrated if it is to be productive enough to keep us all alive, let alone maintain our high standards of living, the principle of freedom still permits us to extract purely economic problems and to solve them by a maximizing process just as in the imaginary distributist society. This trick is done by establishing markets and prices and paying for effort at a money rate equal to the value of the marginal product of the worker. Paying anyone the value of his marginal product means that whether he works more or works less exactly the same is left over for the rest of society to enjoy. The social benefit is maximized by permitting each worker to work just as hard and as long as he finds it best to do in his own interest. Society is not interested in applying any pressure on him to work more or to work less, and he is not able to apply any pressure on society by threats of working more or of working less. Freedom is maximized.

What all this means is that we can convert a political problem into an economic problem by applying to it some generally accepted rule that makes the solution determinate rather than arbitrary. We can then solve the problem by a process of maximization. Economists can show determinate solutions not because they are smarter than political scientists but because the economic problems are just those problems for which a generally accepted principle has become applicable so as to make its solution determinate.

The principle of democracy is another.

The opportunities for solving political problems by turning them into economic problems are, however, severely limited by the condition that nobody may be harmed by the solution that maximizes the benefit to those affected. This is still true even after making full use of the principle of compensating (out of the benefits yielded by the maximizing procedures) those who would otherwise be harmed. (Whether such compensation is considered as an extension of the principle of private property or as replacement of private property by other institutions may seem important to those who like to think of themselves as devotees of capitalism or of socialism but is not of interest to Democratic Functionalism.) In all cases where some may be benefited (*i.e.,* have their freedom increased) only by methods which would hurt others (*i.e.,* diminish *their* freedom to do what they want) the problem is still political and can be settled only on the arbitrary basis of a resultant of the forces brought to bear by the interested parties.

This remaining jungle can be reduced to order by the general acceptance of an additional principle or rule. This is the principle of democracy. The general acceptance of the principle that all men are to be considered equally worthy would permit the benefits and the damages to be put in a single scale. A determinate solution emerges if we let the greater outweigh the lesser.

The combination of the principle of freedom with the principle of democracy tells us, for example, how the total income of society should be divided among the population. Effort should be paid for at a rate equal to the value of the marginal product, and the rest of the national income should be divided equally among all the population (except for clear cases of special need such as blind persons or those requiring special medical attention).

Any other income, unless it is indirectly necessary in applying the principles of freedom and of democracy, can be justified only on the basis of other principles overriding Democratic Functionalism. For example, income from property may be defended where it permits a man who has earned some income by his effort to save some of it and enjoy the interest on his savings, which he can do without diminishing anyone else's income, in complete accordance with the principle of freedom. In such a case the justification is that the protection of such property income is a corollary of Democratic Functionalism. Income which is not justifiable on the principles of Democratic Functionalism may, on the other hand, be justified on other principles, such as the satisfaction of established expectations or the special rights of selected sections of the population.

The principles of freedom, functionalism, and democracy are very closely related.

It should be noticed that the principle of freedom is hardly distinguishable from the principle of functionalism, so that Democratic Functionalism may also be considered as consisting of the principle of freedom and the principle of democracy. Furthermore the principle of freedom can also be considered as the limiting case of the principle of democracy, where the smaller freedom that is sacrificed to the greater freedom has the limiting value of zero. The closeness of these principles to each other means that Democratic Functionalism is an integrated and closely woven system. It is not given its proper due as such by those who have called it the mixed economy just because they cannot resist attaching labels to its different institutions and the only labels they have available are old ones marked "capitalism" and "socialism."

Functional Finance can achieve political acceptance as common sense.

Functional Finance is most likely to be put into regular practice not as the distinguishing policy of a particular party but as the obvious thing to do, irrespective of party, and therefore not of any interest to the writers of political pamphlets. Functional Finance is not likely to become the center of a religious movement like communism or fascism. There was perhaps a possibility of its becoming that a few years ago when it was easier to hope that world peace could be guaranteed by a demonstration, over several decades, that it is possible for capitalist countries to maintain prosperity without going to war with Russia or even with each other. The atomic armaments race and the sharpening of the international situation as a result of the demonstration by Russia that she is not likely to allow concern for world peace to frustrate her missionary-imperialist ambitions have taken away the time needed for the demonstration of capitalist full employment as well as much of the meaning of such a demonstration to the communist world. But the greatest obstacle to the development of Functional Finance into a religion is the fact that it relies on a rational element in the conduct of human affairs.

Reformers naturally underestimate social rationality.

To reformers and radicals who normally have not the great patience necessary to see the gradual adoption of many of their projects, the irrationalities of society loom larger than they are. The rational activities go on smoothly in the production and the distribution of goods and services that constitute the great bulk of human activity. It is the interruptions in rational activities that absorb our attention and it is the failure to adopt the new and better procedures that occupies our field of vision. This leads the critics of our society to a most uncritical exaggeration of the degree of irrationality in our social life and the difficulties of bringing about acceptance of a rational program like Functional Finance.

In fact the principles of Functional Finance have already been accepted to a very high degree. In practice administrators and legislators, who would certainly not recognize themselves as "Keynesians" or as "Functional Financiers," find themselves justifying government deficits as necessary to prevent depression and maintain prosperity, or refusing to reduce taxes, even though the budget is in surplus, because they see that the country is in an inflationary condition and that the tax reduction would make total spending too great. And in the academic field, it is now very fashionable to support all sorts of "Keynesian" measures after making solemn declaration of an anti-Keynesian faith.

Functional Finance has in fact been partially adopted already.

No matter what government is in power in the United States, it is quite certain that *severe* depression will be prevented by government deficits if necessary. The complexion of the party in power will only show itself in the number of anti-Keynesian speeches that will accompany it. The prevention of *moderate* depression has not yet been generally accepted as simple common sense, but the gradual extension of the same principle from more severe to less severe depression is inevitable as our skill in the use of the corrective measures develops in the course of its practical application.

The reason for the relatively rapid acceptance of this part of Functional Finance is to be seen in the absence of any real interests that are opposed to the maintenance of prosperity. Without the support of important interests the dogmas of sound finance cannot last very long.

It will be more difficult with the measures that need to be developed to prevent the great bargaining power of labor to cause inflation when there is a high employment. But here too there is reason for restrained optimism. Some labor leaders have caught glimpses of the problem. They are aware of the dangers to the labor movement from a coalition of other elements in the society against them if in the course of the race of each union to keep its wages abreast of the others they should turn prosperity into inflation. They will therefore be prepared to listen to reason and to cooperate in techniques, like the principle of wage determination suggested in this book, which would yield stability to society without working injustice on labor. In the establishment of this stability it will probably be necessary to make use of the normal procedure in political democracy of mobilizing the political pressures of other groups to overcome the power of such labor organizations as would resist them. Liberals will learn and are now learning to overcome their tendency to identify the interests of labor organizations with the interests of labor or even with the interests of society or of humanity.

Of great importance in the integration of Functional Finance into our society is the possibility of adopting the different measures slowly and piecemeal. There is no necessity for a sudden and complete adoption of the whole program. The different parts of it can work and do good even when alone, experience can improve on them, and time can lead to the whole being gradually adopted as it is seen to fit into the natural order of things. Future statesmen will then discover that they have been practicing Functional Finance just as they have been talking prose. It will be adopted not as liberal or as progressive but as common sense.

Special-interest pressures are not made more dangerous by Functional Finance.

By the politics of Functional Finance is frequently meant not only the task of getting it accepted by the authorities who can put it into practice, but the difficulties of applying it in practice because of pressures by particular groups that would work toward perverting its proper application in the general interest. Of special interest is the suggestion that the resistance to such pressures must lead to dictatorship.

Many of these suggestions that Functional Finance must lead to dictatorship are based on misunderstandings—and sometimes one is even tempted to believe deliberate misunderstandings—of the essential nature of Functional Finance. The creation of employment by the government through deficit financing is sometimes denounced as a kind of bribery by which a political party buys votes with jobs and in this way destroys the democratic society. This kind of condemnation, if valid, would constitute a condemnation of the whole democratic principle whereby politicians are tempted to do what is best for the people not out of the goodness of their hearts but out of a desire for reelection. It is a criticism which fails to distinguish between democracy and bribery. Or perhaps one should say that democracy is nothing but the bribing of the voters with good government. Would that there were much more of that kind of bribery.

Another confusion is more reminiscent of the kind of "amalgam" that is produced by the governments of Russia and its satellite nations for their show trials when they energetically and almost inextricably tie up suspected political deviationists with spies, traitors, mass murderers, and hydrophobic snakes. In the amalgam produced by the prolific "Fighters for Freedom" (of the Committee for Constitutional Government) deficit financing is identified with socialism and socialism is identified with communist totalitarianism and the slave labor camps of Siberia. This disgraceful device of condemnation by association, with the association invented by the condemning judge and jury, would not be worth mentioning were it not that perhaps the greater part of the propaganda of the "Fighters for Freedom" is highly commendable and really would help the freedom and the efficiency of our society. It is a pity that these excellent parts of its work should be vitiated by the association with the shameful distortions in its campaign against any suggested departures from the most rudimentary forms of sound finance.

Much more deserving of respect are the genuine fears of liberal-minded men concerning the dangers to liberty that may result from the government's being freed from the necessity of keeping its budget balanced at all times. It seems to many that if the government could not defend itself by declaring that it must balance the budget, only the establishment of a dictatorship would enable the government to resist the perennial pressures for more expenditures and tax reductions. Functional Finance is supposed to give the government a degree of discretion that fatally weakens its defense against the lobbyists.

Preventing inflation is a stronger maxim than balancing the budget.

This view is based on the error of supposing that the substitution of Functional Finance for sound finance constitutes the substitution of unfettered discretion for a firm rule. But Functional Finance is rather the substitution of one rule for another rule. Instead of keeping government spending at a level where it is equal to tax receipts, the government is enjoined to keep its spending at a level where total demand in the economy results in neither depression nor inflation. There may have been a time when the necessity of balancing the budget was a more effective counter to excessive demands on the government than the necessity for preventing inflation. But the wolf-crying of the budget balancers has so much damaged the effectiveness of the cry that even the most regular lip servers of sound finance are now ready to grant temporary exceptions at the drop of a hat. The prevention of inflation is not only a more important matter in reality, it is even recognized as such in dealing with practical issues by government officials, by legislators, and even by columnists and newspaper editorial writers who, when they are not considering any concrete situation, automatically proffer verbal obeisance to sound finance. With the substitution of the Functional Finance's rule of reason for the budget-balancing dogma, there is not more but *less* call for the development of dictatorial methods to resist the lobbies of special interests.

The real dangers to liberty are reactionary authoritarianism and revolutionary ignorance.

The real dangers to free society are two, neither of which is related to Functional Finance or Democratic Functionalism. The first danger comes from those who simply do not believe in democracy and would prefer to live in an authoritarian society, such as existed in olden days, although nowadays it would be streamlined with the much more efficient modern techniques of totalitarian suppression of all dissension. In this conflict clarity demands that the issue not be clouded and that it be recognized that those who want to maintain and extend human freedom should concentrate on the fight for the maintenance and the extension of human freedom and not let their energies be dissipated in irrelevant crusades against imaginary bogies invented by the enemies of freedom for this very purpose.

The second danger comes from those reformers who are blind to the degree to which the freedoms already achieved are based on the use of the market and price mechanism in implementing efficiency, decentralization, and freedom of choice. Attempts to improve the economy by throwing out the price mechanism instead of developing and perfecting it can result in breakdowns unexpected by ignorant revolutionaries and in a cancer of more and more administrative emergency measures which keep on aggravating the disorders they are intended to remedy. Functional Finance is based on a complete recognition of the necessity and of the possibilities of the price mechanism on which modern economy is built so that it is in no danger of the paralysis that would follow a policy of dispensing with the price mechanism. Functional Finance is often charged with constituting just this threat to democratic society, but the charge can only be the illegitimate offspring of the indefensible identification of Functional Finance with doctrinaire socialism and totalitarian communism.

Functional Finance leaves the world full of problems.

There remains a class of objections to the institution of Functional Finance that are much more sober than any of those discussed so far in this chapter. Objections to Functional Finance may be divided into those which are brought up by people who are looking for objections and those which really would make the life of the administrators of Functional Finance difficult. The former objections, while claiming to be part of the political problems of the *operation* of Functional Finance, really belong to the political problem, discussed earlier in the chapter, of overcoming the resistances to the *establishment* of Functional Finance. The latter are really problems of the administration of Functional Finance when it has been politically accepted.

Here we have such problems as choosing between the many different methods of maintaining an adequate level of total spending, deciding on the division of the national resources between consumption and investment, balancing the interests of the different segments of the economy which will be applying pressures for government expenditures or subsidies to be directed in ways which would benefit them rather than some other segment of the society, overcoming particular pressures for more spending or lower taxes where these would result in too much total spending and inflation, and so on and so on.

Then there is another set of problems such as the difficulty of forecasting future expenditures by other parts of the economy so as to have just the right degree of compensatory spending arranged beforehand or the difficulty of figuring out all the repercussions of any government act of spending throughout following future periods so that future compensatory plans will not be disrupted by the remaining repercussion of old activities of the same kind.

Yet another set of problems is provided by the necessity of obtaining agreement to such plans as the scheme for prevention of inflation through the operation of wage bargaining in times of full employment when the "reserve army of unemployed" is no longer available as a stabilizer of the general level of wages.

And throughout all these different kinds of problems there are purely administrative tasks like the collection of index numbers of various kinds to help determine the trends of prices and wages and output and employment or the collection of the basic statistics for determining the "indices of relative attractiveness" of the different occupations.

Reactionaries and revolutionaries both treat problems as objections.

All these different sets of problems are genuine. They will make life difficult for the administrators of the economy under Functional Finance. But there is no reason for supposing that life will be any more difficult than in any other financial system which does not give the society the benefits of Functional Finance. We have considered some of these tasks in earlier chapters in this book. We have seen that much of the concern about, say, the difficulty of forecasting the future expenditures of the different sections of the economy or of the future repercussions of government contributions to total spending (or for that matter the future repercussions of *any* contributions to total spending) arises from the mistake of supposing that it is necessary to know the future course of spending with great accuracy in order to be able to stabilize total spending. We used the analogy of the bicycle which can be ridden successfully without any accurate calculation of what would happen to it in the next minute in the absence of corrective action by the rider.

This example is typical of the general tendency to treat administrative problems as if they were administrative impossibilities. The introduction of a new element like Functional Finance seems to create an atmosphere in which familiar problems which are dealt with daily and with adequate success suddenly seems to assume the proportions of unscalable obstacles. Our economy has all along been providing some solution or other to conflicting interests and will continue to do so whether we have Functional Finance or not. The solutions have not always been the wisest in the past and they will not always be the wisest in the future. A kind of failure of nerve leads to a hysterical perfectionism in which the extremes of conservatism and revolution meet. To the conservative the fact that a proposed change will not cure all ills is a reason for rejecting the proposal in favor of changing nothing. To the revolutionary the fact that a proposed change will not cure all ills is a reason for rejecting the proposal in favor of changing everything. The sane view recognizes that perfection is not for the world of actuality, that we may improve forever without reaching perfection, that we will always have problems with us. The sane view considers the continued existence of problems not as an objection to any proposal for betterment but as a reassuring sign that we are talking of the world of actuality and not of some never-never land of irresponsible dreams.

The only security is in making haste slowly.

Functional Finance will not inaugurate a problemless world. Life will not be effortless. There will still be struggles and conflicts and difficulties and defeats. But it is an important step forward. It is a disturbing step to the conservative who sees only the difficulties remaining even if they are nothing but the old difficulties we have with us all the time magnified and made terrible by their association with something new. It is an unsatisfying step to the revolutionary with his vision of dissolving all problems by a sufficiently bold rejection of everything we have painfully acquired over the centuries in a blind jump into the unknown. But for those who see the future as a continuation of the dynamic development of the past, with a learning from our past experience and the expectation of the further continuation of the painful process of learning, Functional Finance is a step which society is now engaged in making. It has already been made in part and will be completed when it ceases to be somebody's theory but is seen by almost everybody as the simple common sense of avoiding the upside-down economy of depression or the dizzy fever of inflation.

The progress must be gradual, for only gradually can a new theory become obvious common sense. But this gradualness is the fastest way of sure progress, providing always that we do indeed "make haste slowly" and avoid the opposite danger of making "gradualness" a pretense for standing still. For the one thing we cannot do in this world of ours is to stand still. If we do not go forward in the further development of the free society but permit depressions and inflations to torment and harry the lives of millions, the eagerly waiting totalitarians will inherit the earth and wipe out all the remaining freedoms.

Fortunately there is not the slightest need for such a failure of freedom by default if only the immediate dangers of planetary destruction by modern war can be held off for several decades. The strengthening of the democracies and the demonstration to the people in the totalitarian countries (who also would rather live than die) that democracy can yield both peace and prosperity will make the earth safe for the practitioners of human freedom. But a basic element in the strategy of freedom is the establishment, as rapidly as possible, of stable prosperity in the free countries of the world.

Summary.

In lieu of a summary of this chapter and indeed as a means of bringing into closer focus the scope of the whole book, the reader who has been persevering enough to read to this point is asked to read again the first chapter of the book "The Economic Steering Wheel, or the Parable of the People's New Clothes."

B. Post-Keynesian Economics

[1]

REVIEW ARTICLES

Some Swedish Stepping Stones in Economic Theory

Monetary Equilibrium. By G. Myrdal. London, Edinburgh, Glasgow: William Hodge and Company. 1939. Pp. xii, 214. (12s. 6d.)

Studies in the Theory of Money and Capital. By E. Lindahl. (Library of Economics, section 2.) London: George Allen and Unwin [Toronto: Thomas Nelson and Sons Ltd.]. 1939. Pp. 391. ($3.25)

The two volumes whose perusal is the occasion for the following remarks consist for the most part of writings of a decade ago. In these ten years economic theory has moved forward so rapidly—much more rapidly than in any previous period of comparable length—that even the revisions of five or six years ago are very clearly dated. Professor Myrdal's *Monetary Equilibrium* was first published in 1931, and revised for a German translation in 1933 (in the *Beiträge zur Geld theorie*, edited by Professor Hayek at Vienna). "As now published in English," the preface says, "the essay is a translation of the German text without consequential modifications." Professor Lindahl's book contains an essay on "The Place of Capital in the Theory of Price" (1929); an essay on "The Rate of Interest and the Price Level" (1930), with an additional note (1939); an appendix on "The Problem of Balancing the Budget" (1935), with a note on Swedish Budgetary Reform (1939) and, finally (though printed at the beginning of the book), an essay on "The Dynamic Approach to Economic Theory" which is now (i.e., 1939) published for the first time.

Such a procedure is unfair. It is unfair to the English and American economist who cannot read Swedish (and doesn't read German) and who has been tantalized for many years with tales of how far ahead the Swedes are of all other economists. It is much more seriously unfair to the authors to have their wares shown only after their essence has already reached the public by indirect routes so that the originals look second-hand and rather faded. This unfortunate result is especially apparent in the present case because of the great advance made by Mr. J. M. Keynes, to whose genius in moulding the vague reverberations of Swedish thought into a systematic scheme these republications pay unintended but impressive homage.

The fountain of Swedish thought is, of course, Wicksell; and although all his pupils regard it as their first duty to their master to criticize his work, their preoccupation with his ideas still cramps their style. This is shown very well in Professor Myrdal's book, although he is more emancipated—perhaps more eclectic—than Professor Lindahl. Professor Myrdal's book is an "immanent" criticism of Wicksell's theory of the

574

"Natural Rate of Interest." In Professor Myrdal's own words: "I shall develop my own arguments under the assumption of the fundamental correctness of his (Wicksell's) explanation" (p. 30). We shall have more to say below about the method of immanent criticism. I, myself, shall follow a procedure directly opposite to Professor Myrdal's. I shall first outline quite freely what I consider to be the current theory, and then look back to the Swedish contributions from the new standpoint to reach which they may have been indispensable stepping stones.

From "the new standpoint" the basic principles may be sketched as follows: The number of people who find employment in a modern capitalistic society depends upon the profitability to business men of providing employment for them. The profitability depends on the money demand for the goods and services that the people seeking employment are able to produce. We may say, therefore, that the level of employment depends on the total demand for goods and services of all kinds.

The total income of society is equal to the total demand for goods and services, or the amount of money spent on them. This is simply because income cannot be received by anybody unless someone else is paying it out. Total payments and total receipts are merely different names for the same transactions, distinguishing merely whether they are viewed from the paying or the receiving end.[1] We may say, therefore, that employment is determined by total expenditure or by total income.

A certain total income can be (and must be) earned, therefore, because expenditure of the same amount is being made. The income is created by the expenditure. Where does this expenditure come from? The greater part of it comes from the habit people have of spending most of their income in the normal course of buying the goods and services that they consume. But because people do not normally consume all their income—unless they are very poor—this cannot account for the creation of *all* the income. The rest of the income, the

[1]A slight amplification may be in order here. While it is clear that total payments must equal total receipts, not all receipts can be called income. Some of the proceeds from the sale of goods and services may constitute not *income* for the seller but *costs* to him incurred in producing the goods and services; only the excess of the proceeds over his costs being his income. But in that case these costs are paid out to others and constitute *their* income, or are paid out by them as costs to a third or fourth party, so that ultimately all the payment for the first-mentioned finished goods and services must finish up as *somebody's* income. Starting with the total payments and total receipts (which must be equal), if on the one hand we do not count such receipts as are not income because they merely cover costs, and on the other hand we leave out the payments that constitute these same costs, we must be left with a net total of payment for goods and services which is necessarily equal to total income.

excess of total income over total consumption, must be created by some expenditure of another kind. This, naturally, must be expenditure that is *not* for current consumption. (That has already been counted in the first kind of expenditure which we may call *consumption.*) Expenditure that is not for current consumption is usually for the purchase of goods that are kept and added to one's wealth (possibly to increase consumption in the *future*) and is called *investment.* But *any* expenditure in addition to consumption will have the same immediate effect of creating income (though it may affect future consumption differently) so that it will be convenient, when we speak of investment, to include any other non-consumption expenditures—such as government expenditure on relief projects.

Consumption and *investment,* therefore, between them create total *income.* If the investment were to cease while consumption remained at the same level, income would immediately be diminished by that part of it that was created by (and was equal to) the investment. But if that happened and income fell, consumption would fall too as soon as the decrease in income was felt. This would mean a further reduction in income and again another reduction in consumption. Income and consumption would keep on declining until income had fallen so low that the whole of the income earned in the society had to be consumed. If some were still rich enough to be able to live on less than their whole income, others must be consuming more than their income. There would no longer be any attempt to consume less than total income and so income (and consumption) would not fall any further.

This low stable level of income and consumption could be reached by a slow movement if the people reduced their expenditure slowly because they were not fully aware of the extent to which their income had fallen or was falling. Or it could be reached very rapidly if consumption were reduced rapidly because the decline in income was anticipated. The *path* by which the stable level of income would be reached is a much more difficult thing to analyse because it depends so much upon expectations in a state of change. But in speaking of the stable level of income which tends to be reached we are on relatively firm ground.

When net investment is equal to zero the stable or *equilibrium* level of income, as we have seen, is that at which the members of society found it necessary, on the whole, to spend 100 per cent of their income. There is a corresponding level of income for every other level of investment. This is because every level of income leads to a corresponding equilibrium level of consumption when the income level has been stable long enough for people to realize what their income actually is. At a certain low income level the corresponding equilibrium level of consumption will be equal to the whole income. At lower income levels equilibrium consumption would be greater than total income. At higher levels it would be less. The greater the level of income, the greater will be equilibrium consumption; but, as income increases, equilibrium consumption will increase by a smaller amount. A table for the United States might be constructed something like the following:

(In billions of dollars)

Income	Equilibrium Consumption	Investment
100	80	20
90	72	18
80	68	12
70	63	7
60	57	3
50	50	0
40	45	−5

The third column shows the amount of investment that is just sufficient, together with the consumption, to create the level of income that will sustain this level of consumption (and income). For example, if investment is undertaken at the rate of 7 billions per annum, this together with 63 billions of consumption will make up an income of 70 billions, out of which 63 billions will be consumed and these together with the 7 billions of investment will continue to create 70 billions of income per annum, out of which 63 billions will be consumed, etc. But 7 billions of investment could not maintain an income level of 80 billions because of such an income 68 billions would be consumed and this together with the 7 billions of investment would create only 75 billions of income. Of such an income less than 68 billions would be consumed and so less than 75 billions of income would be created and income and consumption would tend to fall until the 70-billion level was reached. On the other hand, an investment of 7 billions would not be compatible with an income of less than 70 billions. If income were 60 billions, 57 would be spent, which together with the 7 billions of investment would create 64 billions of income, out of which more than 57 billions would be consumed so that more than 64 billions of income would be created. Income would go up again until the 70-billion level was reached. Given this relationship between income and consumption (the propensity to consume) the level of income is determined by the level of investment.

The equilibrium level of income is that for which the gap between income and equilibrium consumption is exactly filled by the investment.

From this it follows that any desired level of income in the society—and therefore also of employment—can be attained if it is possible to control either the consumption or the investment. Employment, when it is too low, can be increased either by increasing the level of investment, or by increasing the propensity to consume—say by redistributing income from the rich to the poor who spend a larger part of their income; or, more simply, by just giving some income to pensioners, or others, who will spend it.

Just as employment can be too low, it can be too high. If it reaches a level so high that there is a scarcity of labour all round—which may be reached perhaps with an income of 90 billion dollars in the United States—wages (and the price of all other fixed resources) would rise, because the workers would feel strong enough to demand increases, and the employers would be doing well enough not to resist them too strongly because they would be able in turn to raise the prices of their products and even gain something on the change. With prices raised workers find that their real wages have not increased—perhaps even decreased—so they would demand, and obtain, further increases which would be equally fruitless. This would lead to a cumulative rise in prices at an increasing rate—an inflation that would disorganize the economy. Money incomes would go up, but not real incomes, since with a scarcity of all kinds of productive services it is impossible to produce more goods. That is indicated in our figures (p. 577) which show the ratio of consumption to income continually diminishing as income increases up to 90 billions, but in the increase from 90 to 100 billions the ratio remains the same, for there is now only a rise in prices in the proportion 9:10, with real income, real consumption, and real investment the same as for the 90 billion dollar income.

In keeping employment from going too low or too high, it is possible to operate on the level of private investment through the rate of interest. If the rate of interest is low, many investments are worth while which would not pay at a higher rate of interest. Investment may therefore be increased by lowering the rate of interest or cut down by raising it, and in this way the authorities may be able to avoid both excessive unemployment and inflation.

The rate of interest is the rate of exchange between a sum of money in the present and a debt or obligation to pay a sum of money in the future. If a present sum of $100 exchanges for an obligation to pay (back) $105 in a year's time, the rate of interest is 5 per cent per annum. To change the rate of interest means to change the ratio in which cash changes for debt. This can only be done by affecting either the *supply* of cash and/or debts (in the sense of the total amount of them available), or else the *demand* for them (in the sense of the attitude of wealth holders as to the proportions they wish to keep their wealth in cash or in debts at different rates of exchange between them). The supply would seem simpler to manipulate.

An increase in the supply of cash will raise the relative value of debts. As individuals find that their holdings of cash have increased relatively to their holdings of debts, they will bid up the price of debts so that $100 in cash will buy only, say, $103 of obligation to pay cash in a year's time, and the rate of interest will have fallen from 5 to 3 per cent. The same effect could be brought about by diminishing the supply of debt—if, say, the government (or anybody else) repaid debts and withdrew the cash paid out by increasing taxes (or other revenues) or decreasing other expenditures. The rate of interest would be raised by the converse acts of diminishing the supply of cash or increasing the supply of debts.

Now it may be that changing the rate of interest is difficult because wealth owners will allow very large changes in their relative holdings of cash and debt without changing their relative valuation very much. (The elasticity of substitution between cash and debts is very high over a large range.) Or it may be that the rate of investment is not very responsive to changes in the rate of interest, (the schedule of the marginal efficiency of investment is very inelastic), so that it is difficult to change investment, and income and employment can be affected only by changing consumption. Or it may simply be that the authorities think it better to affect income by changing consumption rather than by changing investment. In such cases it is necessary to change the propensity to consume.

The propensity to consume can be changed by a system of redistributive taxation—as suggested above (p. 578)—but such purely redistribution possibilities are cumbersome and severely limited. In order to change consumption by 1 billion by shifting income from a section of the population whose average propensity to consume was 60 per cent (varying perhaps from a few very rich with a zero marginal propensity to a great body whose propensity is around 70 per cent) to another section of the population with an average propensity of 90 per cent (varying from 70 per cent to 100 per cent or more) it would be necessary to raise $3\frac{1}{3}$ billions as taxes from one group and use it in relieving taxation on the other group or paying it out to them in one way or another. A much simpler way is just to increase income by reducing taxation, or giving pensions, etc., when it is desired to increase consumption and, conversely, to decrease consumption by reducing incomes through taxation or otherwise.

The government, or whatever is the authority responsible for maintaining a satisfactory level of income, is thus able, like an airplane pilot, to guide the progress of the economy in two different dimensions. Consumption can be increased or diminished by increasing or diminishing expenditure that creates income, or by diminishing or increasing taxation that diminishes it. Private investment can be controlled, to some extent, by dishoarding or providing newly printed cash in exchange for debt when it is desired to lower the rate of interest, and by hoarding or destroying cash obtained in exchange for increased debt newly incurred when it is desired to raise the rate of interest.

Such a policy entails a complete liberation from the ancient belief in the virtues of keeping a balanced budget as an emblem of sound finance, and a recognition that the principles of sound finance, while they constitute valid rules of private prudence and were even wise maxims for the comptroller of the prince's purse, are entirely out of place in governing the economic activity of a modern society. They can be defended only as a concession to the prejudices of the ignorant, or as a means of securing good behaviour from the superstitious. (Though it is only a *pretence* of sound finance that is necessary for these purposes.)

* * *

In this sketch of the modern view of the problems of employment and stability and of its implications for policy, the reader will surely miss a number of concepts and expressions which are usually to be found in such discussions. These are the stepping stones that have led to the new position, but once the new position has been reached their significance is of interest only to the historian of economic thought. While they may occasionally lead to useful new ideas—as indeed may any intellectual activity—preoccupation with them will generally confuse rather than clarify the understanding of economic processes. This is true even though it is sometimes possible, with an effort, to express the modern view in terms of the old concepts. The most important of these outworn concepts are the "quantity equation," and especially its component, the "velocity of circulation," the "natural rate of interest" and (connected with this) the concept of "saving," and the distinction between *ex ante* and *ex post*.

Wicksell opened the door through which modern economists have escaped from the traditional classical approach that prevented any straightforward attack on the problems connected with employment and stability. He did this by ignoring the quantity equation—after paying his proper respects to it—and considering the connection between the amount of money and not, directly, the price level, but *the rate of interest.* This served as an introduction between general economic theory and monetary theory and led to their recent union.

Wicksell's other great service was to take the supply and demand approach that had only been applied to small sections of the economy in partial analysis and to apply it to the economy as a whole in putting the demand for goods in general against their total supply. This was novel even if it does seem, after the event, a fairly obvious thing to try. One inhibition against doing this lay in the classical dogma that total supply was its own demand—a dictum in which the tautological truth, that a general increase in output cannot make all prices fall relatively to each other, is confused with the error that a general increase in output cannot make all prices fall below costs (as is shown in our example on p. 577 when, if investment is 7 billions, an output of consumption goods that cost 73 billions, making a total income of 80 billions, could be sold for only 68 billions). Another inhibition against applying the supply and demand mechanism to the whole economy lay in the impressive Walrasian system of equations which seemed to claim the whole field of general analysis as its own even though it could say nothing particularly useful.[2] Wicksell overcame these inhibitions and thereby put the Swedish school of economics ahead of the rest of the world.

Like Wicksell, who was very conservative in many ways, his disciples hold on to concepts that they have outgrown. Thus Wicksell shows great outward respect for the "quantity theory of money" and Lindahl too says that "the quantity theory will always remain a significant part of the theory of money" (p. 141).

From the modern point of view the quantity theory has only historical interest. The use of the quantity equation (whether $MV = PT$, or $M = PKR$, or any other variant) is harmful as an exercise for elementary students. They inevitably assume that V (or K) and T (or R) can be taken as constant and then they have to try to unlearn that. It is only natural that they should do so, however much they are warned,

[2]All it could say was that everything depended upon everything else, that (because the number of equations was equal to the number of unknowns) there were a finite number of solutions that could conceivably be worked out in an indefinitely long period if the contents of all the indefinitely large number of equations were known, and that one of these solutions would describe the actual state of affairs that would be reached if the content of the equations (distribution of income, available resources, technical knowledge, and consumers' tastes) remained stationary during the unknown period that it would take for equilibrium to be reached.

for if V and T cannot be taken as independent, there is no sense in separating them out in the equations. Avoiding this misleading segregation we are left with the still simpler truism that total payments (MV) equals total receipts (PT), which we used in our sketch and so dispensed with any discussion of V, the velocity of circulation.

The concept for which Wicksell is most famous, which forms the subject of Myrdal's *Monetary Equilibrium* and is considered in some detail in Lindahl's *Money and Capital* is the natural rate of interest. We shall go into this more fully later in this article. All we need say here is that it conceives of some critical level of the rate of interest that is necessary if the economy is to function peacefully. A rate of interest below the critical level would produce a cumulative rise in prices and/or in economic activity. A rate of interest above the critical level would lead to cumulative contraction. In our account this is not so. Various rates of interest would give various levels of investment and correspondingly different levels of income and employment. Only if there is full employment would a reduction of the rate of interest lead to a cumulative process of inflation.

Strangest of all, perhaps, is the possibility, in this modern statement of the theory of employment, of dispensing with any expression for *saving* without—it is believed—any discomfort. This is possible because saving is not a positive act and so plays no real part in the game. It is merely a difference between income and consumption which may perhaps never even be calculated. If it is calculated, it is inevitably equal to investment (for the society as a whole), since it is only to the degree that investment is going on that total income (created) is greater than (income created by) consumption.

Most writers have felt, quite correctly, that changes in the desire to save are important for the course of economic events and have concluded—not so correctly—that it is therefore necessary to speak about saving and its influences. These influences are completely dealt with in the propensity to consume where they show themselves in concrete positive acts of spending more, or spending less, with the effects on income, etc. This cannot be done without grave difficulties if the function is turned inside out and observed as a propensity to save. For the amount saved, unlike the amount spent, is *not* free to increase or decrease at the will of the "savers." It is already firmly tied in its total amount by the level of investment.

To get over this unnecessary difficulty many queer definitions of income have been invented, and therefore also of saving (which is income minus consumption), which would free saving from its bondage to investment. Perhaps the queerest is saving *ex ante*, or the amount that individuals expect, or intend, at the beginning of a period, to save during the period. The difference between saving and investment *ex ante* is then considered to be a quantity of importance for the further development—a causal factor in the economic process. This is basically correct, but a frightfully awkward and mystifying way of dealing with the issue. When all the complications have been unravelled and many difficulties have been overcome, it turns out that all that is meant is that, when actual revenues diverge from what has been expected, the producers-sellers will do something about it. I do not think this is a very unfair account of the net results so far attained by the use of *ex ante*, and so *ex ante* was dispensed with as one of the stepping stones that may have been useful in reaching the present position but was no longer needed. It will be examined more fully below when we come to examine Professor Lindahl's account of it.

* * *

The same conservatism of manner that made Wicksell pay tribute to the quantity theory while undermining its sovereignty is displayed by Myrdal in his essay *Monetary Equilibrium* when he says "My analysis will be of an *immanent* nature in so far as I shall take over in the beginning the fundamental features of Wicksell's monetary theory and shall develop my own arguments under the assumption of the fundamental correctness of his explanation." Modestly adding "The Wicksellian formulation, we shall find, will need modification in several directions" (p. 31), he goes on to modify until nothing recognizable remains. Professor Myrdal defends the procedure partly as a means of more fully expounding Wicksell's historically interesting theories and partly as a protest against unnecessary novelty in economic terminology which threatens to submerge our literature in "Babylonic barbarism."

Subjected to the process of "immanent criticism" are the three criteria suggested by Wicksell which would distinguish the *natural* or *normal* level of the rate of interest from any other level. He shows that the first criterion—equality with the physical yield of real capital goods in kind—has to be modified until it becomes equality with the expected money earnings of money invested in new capital goods. Then the application of the criterion is changed so that a difference between these—a margin of profit—has to be allowed so as to make the modified first criterion comparable with the second.

The second criterion is an equilibrium on the capital market and this is interpreted to mean that the supply of funds which equals (gross) saving is equal to the demand for funds which equals (gross) investment. Clearly aware (as nobody seemed to be in 1931 outside Scandinavia) that on the normal definitions of saving and investment they were identically equal for the whole economy, he was forced to invent new concepts for these terms, and in the author's words, "Probably the chief contribution of this essay, if any, is to have originated the concepts *ex post* and *ex ante*; and to have emphasized the importance of clearly recognizing the period implicit in monetary analysis" (p. 47). The first criterion is combined with the second by saying in effect that profit margins must be such (i.e., the rate of interest must be so much below the expected return on new investment) that the investment will be equal to saving (*ex ante*). Apart from this Professor Myrdal points out many difficulties about the application of the theory. Interesting among these is the necessity of weighting different profit margins in accordance with their significance for inducing new investment. But far too little stress is laid upon the consideration that rates of interest, somewhat above and below the level thus worked out, would only in very exceptional conditions give rise to a Wicksellian cumulative process of expansion or contraction.

Wicksell's third criterion was the stability of the price level. Professor Myrdal nicely solves the quarrel between Wicksell and Davidson whether it is the price level of consumption goods or the price level of factors of production that is stabilized by the natural, or normal, or neutral, or equilibrium rate of interest that gives monetary equilibrium. He does this by demonstrating that any movement of prices is just as compatible with monetary equilibrium as any other as long as it is in conformity with expectations. Here the rigidity of certain prices becomes important, inasmuch as expectations that they will change much are likely to be falsified, and in so far as profit margins are affected when other prices move relatively to these. Professor Myrdal develops some novel ideas in connection with using the general price level as a partial criterion for policy, and weighting prices somehow by their *inflexibility* in addition to weighting them according to their effect on profit margins and the varying elasticity of investment with respect to profit margins in different parts of the economy. Quite apart from the practical difficulties of doing all this—of which Professor Myrdal shows adequate awareness—this part of the book seems particularly unreal inasmuch as, if all this were worked out, it would merely be an extraordinarily cumbrous way of expressing the relationship between the rate of interest on the one hand, by way of all the relative flexibilities, profit margins, and elasticities of investment, and the level of investment (and so of employment) on the other. Apart from its usefulness as an exercise in economic acrobatics and its historical interest, it has nothing to add to the simplified modern proposition in our sketch that the rate of interest may sometimes be used to affect investment, and so income and employment.

With Wicksell's three criteria thus either rejected or liberally transformed by immanent criticism but with a very faint ghost of monetary equilibrium still remaining, there follows an interesting chapter (VII) on "The Indifference Field of Monetary Equilibrium." In this chapter the ghost is extended to cover so many more different possible kinds of monetary equilibrium that it reaches a new record in tenuity.

Interesting is the emancipation of monetary equilibrium from prices. "If equilibrium price relations are fulfilled any movement of the absolute money prices consistent with them will leave monetary equilibrium undisturbed" (p. 132). On the other hand, it would appear that the level of employment has not much to do with monetary equilibrium since at various levels of employment there can be stability with *ex ante* savings equal to *ex ante* investment. At this stage I lose interest completely in monetary equilibrium—as is perhaps natural for one who does not believe in ghosts anyway.

But Professor Myrdal nowhere puts this last point and perhaps would disagree with it. There is another consideration that plays this part and that is the degree of monopoly in the labour market. According to Professor Myrdal there is always one level of unemployment that corresponds to the degree of monopoly strength of the workers. If unemployment were less than this there would be a tendency for wages to rise, while if unemployment were more there would be a tendency for wages to fall. "Monetary policy would have to be based upon this unemployment or else the result would be either a constant monetary equilibrium with an uninterrupted upward parallel movement of the whole price system, or a Wicksellian process which deviates from equilibrium in a downward direction" (p. 151).

The reason for the asymmetry is obscure, but this touches a very important problem and is the basis for Professor Myrdal's disagreement with those who, like myself, would take the level of employment as a more direct norm for policy. It is probably true that there is a level of employment, less than full employment (on almost any definition) such that if it is surpassed, labour will be able to demand and obtain wage increases at a rate that would disorganize the economy (and, I should think, disrupt monetary equilibrium too), and Professor Myrdal is right in supposing that attempts to increase employment beyond this level could avoid inflation only by an undemocratic holding down of wages. But he appears to be wrong in the implication that a level of employment immediately below this would bring about a cumulative *fall* in wages and prices. It is probable that that would happen if employment were low enough for long enough, but between this and the upper level of stable employment there is a great distance. As an "indifference field" for monetary equilibrium this would appear to be incomparably more significant than any of those considered by Professor Myrdal, and it is certainly far from indifferent to society near which end of this field it finds itself.

The book concludes with an eminently sensible chapter on scientific method and commonsense, and in looking at it one feels that criticisms like those made here are very unfair. It is possible that similar criticisms would be made by Professor Myrdal himself today. Economic theory, like many another field of activity, is suffering from an unprecedented rate of obsolescence.

* * *

For closer examination the four main items in Professor Lindahl's book may be taken in chronological order. First, there is "The Place of Capital in the Theory of Price" (Part III, pp. 271-350, published in Swedish, 1929). This is an elaboration of the Walrasian system of equations to take into account time taken in production, and so of the degree of roundaboutness, or the extent to which production is capital-using. The scheme is generalized from one original factor (as in Böhm Bawerk) or two (as in Wicksell) to any number, and an attempt is made to bring in imperfect foresight, but only a few very general remarks are made about uncertainty. The influences of this work can be seen in Dr. Hick's recent *Value and Capital.* In the attempt to bring in imperfect foresight the period analysis, which we shall discuss below, is suggested. An inadequate distinction between the marginal productivity of capital and the marginal efficiency of investment[3] is only natural in 1929, since even in 1934, and even Mr. Keynes in *The General Theory of Employment, Interest and Money,* when considering the schedule that relates the rate of investment to the rate of interest, called it "the marginal efficiency of *capital.*" Thus Professor Lindahl says ". . . the third ground[4] is . . . of decisive importance for the concrete level of the interest rate as a determining factor on the demand side. Owing to the importance of saving for production, the demand for saving is elastic to a considerable degree, whereas the supply . . . is relatively inelastic" (p. 291). The point here is that since saving refers to a *flow* of so much per period of time, it is comparable with different rates of investment which are similar *flows* and not with different *stocks* of capital. This is

[3]See A. P. Lerner, "Capital, Investment and Interest" (*Proceedings of the Manchester Statistical Society,* 1936-7).

[4]Given by Böhm Bawerk for the existence of a positive rate of interest, namely the greater productivity of (some) roundabout (time-using) methods of production.

quite apart from the other question whether even the marginal efficiency of investment has any direct effect on the rate of interest—a proposition that is denied in the modern theory of interest.[5]

The second item in Professor Lindahl's book is Part II, "The Rate of Interest and the Price Level," pp. 139-198, 1930. This is an extremely interesting work and it is keenly to be regretted that it was not available in English ten years ago. It is much beyond Mr. Keynes's *Treatise on Money*, and it is only when one has got a good understanding of Mr. Keynes's *General Theory* that it begins to date. There is here an analysis of cumulative processes *à la* Wicksell, an examination of possible and developing meanings of natural, normal, real, neutral, and equilibrium rates of interest, and a decision that it is best not to use any of these terms. The discussion of the differences made to analysis and policy by the existence of unemployment cannot be matched by anything before the *General Theory*. The quantity equation is honoured but only in a relatively harmless form, $E-S=PQ$, which merely says that income minus saving (i.e. the part of income that is spent) must buy up the consumption goods that are sold, and avoids any entanglements with V. The section on the differentiation of different kinds of interest rates is probably surpassed only in Dr. Hicks's *Value and Capital*, and the treatment of the effects of changing expectation on the rate of interest is very similar. Some interesting questions are raised by the insistence that a Wicksellian cumulative process necessarily involves a lengthening (or shortening) of the period of production, and that its cumulative nature is conditional upon a lag between the income streams of capitalists and *entrepreneurs* (p. 168, foot-note). Intriguing is the distinction between *primary* and *secondary* effects in working out the line of causality of the items in his quantity equation.

But most interesting of all and continually cropping up, is the insistence on period analysis, and *ex ante* as the only way for dynamic analysis; reference is made to Part I which we are to discuss next. In this work *ex ante* comes in with "A New Definition of Income" as "the current interest in every short period on the capital value then prevailing, as estimated by the owners at the moment of time in question. The income for a longer period can be regarded as the sum of these current interest streams" (p. 144): a foot-note added to the present translation reads: "It should be noted that this view, according to which income is measured *ex ante* as it arises at each moment, reduces the deviations between *ex ante* and *ex post* calculations and the difficulties connected

[5]See A. P. Lerner, "Alternative Formulations of the Theory of Interest" (*Economic Journal*, June, 1938).

with them to a minimum" (p. 144, foot-note). This foot-note thus refers to Part I. An additional note written in 1939 has nothing striking to add to Part II.

The third item is Part I, "The Dynamic Approach to Economic Theory," pp. 21-138, and is published for the first time in this volume. This is by far the most fully developed account of the *ex ante* process analysis that has appeared to date, about half of the space (pp. 74-138) being devoted to a very thorough algebraic discussion and system of notation.

After some introductory methodological remarks there are a few comments on the relationship between statics and dynamics. There is some confusion between static, which is more abstract than dynamic theory because it abstracts from changes over time, and the examination of a stationary society, which is less abstract than, and only a special case in, dynamics. Change is not abstracted from but conditions are such that the rates of change happen to have a zero value. The confusion is probably due to the use of the term "static theory," for both statics and stationary dynamics. However, Professor Lindahl does not appear to have been led into any actual errors by this identification.

Then follows the account of the "Dynamic Approach" in the scheme for period analysis to which we have continually been referring as *ex ante*. The flow of time is divided into periods so short that nobody's plans have time to change within the period. Psychological quagmires are avoided by asking no questions about the reasons for the plans for action that individuals have at the beginning of each period. The active part of the plans is always carried out. Within one period purchases (consumption or investment) always take place as planned. But planned, or expected, sales and earnings can only be fulfilled if the expectations of sales fit in with the customers' plan for purchasing. Because these do not coincide, there is discovered, at the end of each period, a divergence between actual and planned (or *ex ante*) income, saving, and stock accumulation; so a new set of plans is constructed, the active part carried out in the next period, and again there is a discrepancy between expectation and realities and a revision of plans, and so on. In this way the whole course of events can be mapped out, the state of each period depending on what went before. The fact that different individuals revise their plans at different times and at different intervals can be overcome by supposing the period so small that within the period no significant change in plan takes place anywhere.

Such a scheme is contrasted with "static" analysis, and is declared to be free from the difficulties connected with the concepts of equilibrium and really to describe the actual process of change in the real world.

But a scheme like this is even more abstract than the equilibrium approach, since it is impossible to give it concrete content by discovering the changing data of the world moment by moment and to know exactly how anybody's disappointments lead him to revise his plans. Put baldly as I have done here, this is nothing but another prayer for La Place's equation of the universe. For practical purposes, compromises and simplifications have to be made, and when this has been done, it seems to me that little if anything has been gained as compared with the simplifications and compromises of equilibrium analysis—at least until somebody invents some more useful compromise.

Professor Lindahl points to the work of Dr. Hicks's *Value and Capital* and to Dr. Lundberg's *Studies in the Theory of Economic Expansion* as examples of the use of dynamic process analysis, but my own feeling is that Dr. Lundberg's admirable ingenuity and industry have demonstrated the impossible complexities to which the process method leads before it can be applied to any practical problem, while Dr. Hicks, as Professor Lindahl points out (p. 68), makes use of the equilibrium mechanism, treating the dynamic process as a series of equilibrium positions. This is the only way so far discovered of conducting real dynamic analysis. It must be assumed that market equilibrium is continuously maintained, and it is almost imperative to assume also that there is no serious departure from short period equilibrium. The determinants of the short period equilibrium can then be considered to vary either independently or as a result of the short period equilibrium being where it is, and so one can get an account of the process of events through time.

It is, of course, virtually certain that complete short period equilibrium is rarely, if ever, reached in the actual world, but any observable regularity in economic matters must rest upon the degree to which it is persistently approximated. The assumption that it is actually reached may contain even less error than that of the data with which it is necessary to work.

The assumption of short period equilibrium is basic in Mr. Keynes's work, and in the modern theory stated above it is explicit in the reference to "equilibrium" consumption which is that found where there is the short period equilibrium adjustment of consumption to the level of income. Then there remains the question of fact. If in the real world short period equilibrium is approximately reached, then analysis like that of Mr. Keynes can usefully be applied and there is no need for the complexities of non-equilibrium process analysis. If short period equilibrium is not approximated closely enough for the assumption to be of use, economics will be fruitless until someone has invented a way of using non-equilibrium *ex ante* process analysis.

Meanwhile, premature attempts to apply the scheme before the invention has come, are tempting but dangerous. It is worth while, in view of the extreme importance of this danger, to quote a paragraph:

> In view of the fact that the scientific treatment of a macro-economic development must, for reasons already put forward, be based on a subdivision of the development into fairly short periods, it is of course impossible for the economist to follow it in detail from period to period. In spite of this, it is quite feasible to give a picture of the course of events during a fairly long stretch of time. If by the analysis of certain selected typical periods, one can determine the directions of movement during these stretches, the character of the intervening periods may also be understood. It may sometimes be necessary to modify the actual character of the periods selected so that they may adequately represent the active tendencies during the phase in question (p. 59).

It requires no great stretch of the imagination to reach from this to the most arbitrary of extrapolation of trends to say nothing of even more reprehensible statistical legerdemain.

While the reader is fascinated by the shiny mechanisms of the algebraic stratosphere, wondering what it can all be used for, and perhaps a little apprehensive of such parachuting as the quoted paragraph would indicate, he may perhaps be comforted by a conservative maxim, brought out hesitatingly after a careful demonstration of the contrary. "We must nevertheless admit the quintessential truth of the common opinion that savings on the whole are primary in relation to investment" (p. 133); and "But in the long run a certain tendency for the rate of interest to adapt itself to the amount of planned saving could probably be noticed" (p. 133). Perhaps it is unfair to cull such throwbacks, but they are very reminiscent of Wicksell's devotion to some of the ideas that he is engaged in undermining.

The fourth item in Professor Lindahl's book is a very interesting Appendix on the "Problem of Balancing the Budget," written in 1935, with a "Note on Swedish Budgetary Reform," written in 1939. Here, more than anywhere else in this book, or in Professor Myrdal's, one feels that something begun has not been completed. The Appendix is an account of Swedish theory and practice in the matter of balancing the budget, and it is impossible here to consider the issues at the length they deserve. I can merely hint that the theory seems to lag behind the practice as if it were afraid to say all that it knew. As I have indicated earlier, I believe the whole business of "sound finance" in balancing budgets is either superstition or humbug. The Swedish theory seems to have been that sound finance implies a steady increase in the net value of government owned net profit bearing assets (net after deducting government debt). But it appears that whenever this policy would interfere with the policy of maintaining employment, subsidiary devices are brought into play which open the way for the fiscal policy that is needed for maintaining employment. There are annual budgets, and capital budgets, and extraordinary budgets, and budget equalization funds. And when all these devices are insufficient the budgetary principles are revised (as in 1935). Perhaps it is politically necessary to have a façade of sound finance, and it is splendid if this is not allowed to get in the way of sensible policy.

* * *

This article seems a very ungrateful one after all the Swedes have done for economics, yet the more I read them now the more am I convinced that they have been "caught up with and overtaken" by Mr. Keynes. Perhaps I have become a hopeless "Keynesian." Perhaps the Swedes are again secretly ahead of the Anglo-Saxons, and maybe somebody in Sweden has discovered how to apply process analysis to real problems. If so it is to be hoped that this time their discoveries will be made available before they begin to stale, and that in this way they will circumvent that "attractive Anglo-Saxon kind of unnecessary originality"[6] that has led to the modern economics. But even though they have been "caught up with and overtaken" these are indispensable books for all advanced students who have any interest in the history of economic thought and they are full of fruitful suggestions for further research.

A. P. Lerner

The University of Virginia.

[6]Myrdal, *Monetary Equilibrium*, p. 8.

[2]

ON GENERALIZING THE GENERAL THEORY

A Review Article

By ABBA P. LERNER*

Ever since Keynes' *General Theory of Employment Interest and Money* appeared in 1936, economists have been tempted to show that it is not quite so general and to fit it into a *really* general theory. The latest attempt, and the most grandiose, is one by Professor Sidney Weintraub [5].

The practical problem sparking Weintraub's work appears to be the very important one of sellers' inflation (although he does not use this term). While buyers' inflation is caused by too much spending, i.e., by buyers trying to buy more goods than are available and thereby bidding up prices, sellers' inflation is caused by sellers raising prices even in the face of a deficiency of spending. A failure to distinguish between the two types of inflation aggravates a problem which has become a serious threat to democratic society.

The appropriate treatment for buyers' inflation is to cut down the excessive spending that causes it. This may be done by a restrictive monetary or fiscal policy. But if restrictive monetary or fiscal policy is used against sellers' inflation, spending is reduced when it is *not* excessive, so that we get a deficiency of demand, depression and unemployment. The inflation will continue, however, unless the induced depression is severe enough to destroy the power of sellers to raise their prices. This may call for more depression than the authorities are prepared to impose or the public willing to suffer. We then get insufficient depression to stop the inflation and we suffer from both evils at the same time. In 1958 we seem to have had sufficient depression to stop the inflation, at least temporarily, but this remedy involved a loss of output estimated at some $30 billion per annum and it severely reduced our rate of economic growth.

Galbraith has suggested [1, Ch. 13, 21] that we are rich enough to pay this price for price stability. But it is not simply a matter of a reduction in our standard of living; we are involved in a competition with communism for the planet. The failure to provide full employment is a serious handicap in this race. The loss of the $30 billion may be responsible for a fatal economizing in our expenditure on defense. We have a good chance of winning the uncommitted nations to the democratic side by contributing a major share of the cost of a development program which could make their economic development relatively painless; but the loss of the $30 billion may make us feel we cannot afford it. And the reduction in our rate of growth can make it relatively easy for the communists to realize their dream of "catching up with and surpassing" the U.S. economy.

* The author is professor of economics at Michigan State University.

The immedate practical lesson of Weintraub's book is the futility of treating sellers' inflation with the measures appropriate for buyers' inflation, and his hopes of getting this lesson across are probably heightened by his feeling that he has stumbled on a revolutionary reformulation of economics. The flamboyant publishers' blurb, vying with the all-embracing title of the book, promises "A Sensational Break-Through for the Economics of Price Theory" and announces: "A New Conceptualization of Major Importance Finally Solves the Riddle of the Price Level and Wage Costs . . . Where Keynes' Theory Failed . . . A New Perspective . . . Makes Economics a Predictive Science." And this is modest in comparison with the chapter headings in the book itself.

One hesitates to put the pin to this bubble for fear of interrupting the salutary lesson on sellers' inflation, but it is important to show that Weintraub's revolutionary claims and the justifiable scepticism they engender do not diminish the validity of his lesson.

I. *Weintraub's Model and His Proposals*

Weintraub's starting point is the observed stability of the ratio of the value of the social product or output or income to the wage bill, which ratio he calls k or the "magic constant." This k is the same as Kalecki's degree of monopoly [5, p. 41], or Marx's rate of exploitation, or the ratio between the exponents in the Cobb-Douglas production function. The constancy has been widely observed. Keynes has referred to it as "a bit of a miracle"; and it is regularly used to show that Marx's prophecy of the "immiseration" of the workers cannot be rescued even by supposing it to refer to the relative share of the workers rather than their absolute income. But nobody has ever become as infatuated with this relationship as Weintraub or as fascinated with the tricks that can be played by combining it with the rules of arithmetic in exercises reminiscent of the game of "think of a number"[1] or of H. G. Wells' attribution of the fascination of card games to people's not having learned to count properly up to 13.

The key trick is to transmute the value of the social output into the price level and the wage bill into the average wage by the appropriate multiplications or divisions. This yields a formula which has much in common with the equation of exchange of economic theory, but which is more useful because it deals with relationships that are much more stable. Unfortunately this is not too much of a recommendation, and unfortunately the new formula can confuse truisms with substantive statements just as much as the old one.

The basic relationship is:

$$Z = kW \tag{1}$$

where Z is the value of output, W is the wage bill and $k \equiv Z/W$.[2] Z is trans-

[1] "Think of a number, multiply by 2, add 10, divide by 2, subtract 5, and presto you have the number you started with!"

[2] I am following Weintraub's notation except that I am keeping capital letters exclusively for observable quantities and lower-case letters for the relationships between these derived by the arithmetical operations, and I have renumbered the equations.

muted into P, the price level, by dividing both sides of the equation by the quantity of output q ($\equiv Z/P$), while the average wage w ($\equiv W/N$, where N is the number of employees) appears in the formula because Weintraub always uses wN for W. We thus get [5, p. 9]:

$$\frac{Z}{q} = \frac{Z}{Z/P} = P = kwN/q. \tag{2}$$

Introducing output per employee, a ($\equiv q/N$), and substituting we get:

$$P = kw/a, \tag{3}$$

and introducing unit wage cost, r ($\equiv w/a$), and substituting we get:

$$P = kr. \tag{4}$$

The price level is k times the unit wage cost.

Equations (2), (3) and (4) are the main forms, and (3) the one most frequently used, of the Wage-Cost Mark-up equation (WCM) that Weintraub puts up against the equation of exchange (EOE) [5, p. 7]:

$$Mv = Pq; \quad \text{or} \quad P = Mv/q \tag{5}$$

where M is the quantity of money and v ($\equiv Z/M$) is the velocity of circulation of money. His claim is that the use of truism (3) instead of truism (5) would turn economics onto the right path and transform it into a predictive science, because k is much more stable (and therefore also much more predictable) than v, w is more predictable than M, and a is much more predictable than q, so that the MCM equation would enable us to predict P more successfully.

Weintraub then goes on to derive an empirical value for k by dividing the Department of Commerce figures for business product (Z) by compensation of employees (W), and shows that between 1929 and 1957 k stayed between a high of 2.16 at the beginning of the period and a low of 1.87 at the end of the period [5, p. 14]. Indeed the figures show much greater stability still if we break up the period so as to separate out periods of war and of depression and to make some allowance for a downward trend.[3]

After deriving empirical values for the other variables in the WCM equations and hammering home the constancy of k by repeating the evidence in the form of index numbers and charts, Weintraub has an astonishing section [5, pp. 26-29] entitled "The Detection of the Price Level: Checking the Formula," in which he proves that between 1929 and 1957 the truism was almost

[3] From 1929 through 1941 k stayed between 2.16 and 2.13, except for the depression years 1930-1934 and 1937-1939, when it stayed between 2.11 and 2.07. Through the war years 1942-1945 it stayed between 2.02 and 2.08. In the 12 years of prosperity, 1946-1957, it shows a declining trend, keeping between 2.00 and 1.97 through the first half, 1946-1951, and between 1.94 and 1.87 in the second half, 1952-1957. As against a range for 1929-1957 of 15 per cent, the subperiods show ranges between 1½ and 3½ per cent.

exactly true! P' the price level computed from the annual figures for k, w, and a, is shown to be very close to P the "actual price level" (the implicit price deflator for business gross product). This is actually plotted on a chart [5, p. 28] where the closeness of the two curves must greatly impress the impressionable.

The "remarkable confluence" of P' and P is not perfect primarily because the computed w is not really w and computed a is not really a. Data for w or W/N are unattainable because there are no figures for N, the number of people engaged in producing the business gross product and earning W, so Weintraub uses substitute figures (which I will mark with a prime). These are total employment, N', which includes employment in government enterprise, and the corresponding wage bill W'. From these we can get W'/N' or w' which is a good approximation to w. Similarly, computed a is obtained by dividing q not by N but by N'. We may call this a' and we therefore have:

$$P' = kw'/a'; \tag{6}$$

and spelling this out in the capital letters used for the actual data we have:

$$P' = \frac{Z}{W}\cdot\frac{W}{N'}\cdot\frac{N'}{Z/P}, \tag{7}$$

which reduces to:

$$P' = P\cdot\frac{W'}{W}\cdot \tag{8}$$

The "remarkable confluence" of P' and P is nothing but the similarity of the index number of W' to that of W. Weintraub's recognition of this [5, p. 29, top] does not prevent him from expressing his elation at this "confluence" as a demonstration that "our method checks out" [5, p. 29, middle].

The next chapter (4) is entitled "The Law of k" and is devoted to stressing the constancy of k as "probably the most important economic law, in the true sense, that economists have to work with" [5, p. 33, in italics]. Greater and greater excitement is worked up by reducing k to index numbers, by making charts of k as well as of index numbers of k, by comparing it with more volatile series, by tabulating year-to-year changes in k, and by referring to similar phenomena at other times and in other countries. Weintraub expresses surprise at the high value of k in the depression years as compared to the 1950's [5, p. 36, where "1930's" is presumably a misprint for "1950's"], as well as at the postwar sag in k: "For this heaviness in k has traversed a period in which 'demand-pull' inflation has been widely described, an era in which consumer goods were in short supply, and a series of years in which a sellers' market has prevailed" [5, p. 42]. The main emphasis of this chapter however is not on the *movements* in k but on k being "perhaps as close as we are ever likely to come to finding a constant in the world of economic phenomena" [5, p. 43].

Chapter 5 is on "The Law of the Price Level" which is described as "another interesting relationship," namely that "the price level will rise only if r rises" [5, p. 45]; and its introduction is celebrated by an impressive fanfare of tables, charts and correlations. But the law of the price level is *not* "another interesting relationship" at all. It is none other than the same k as it appears in equation (4), $P = kr$.

Chapter 6 "On Predicting the Price Level" describes how we can predict P ($=kw/a$) as accurately as we can predict k, w and a. If k is stable (or falls slowly at a known rate), if w is determined by known union policy, and if a grows at a known and steady rate, we are all set to predict P. Furthermore, Weintraub argues, if we want to know the effects on P of a particular wage increase, say in steel, we have only to figure how much this will increase the *average* wage in the whole economy and "magic constant" k will do the rest!

Chapter 7, "The Wedding Ceremony: Price Level and Aggregate Output," combines the four items of (3), P, k, w and a, with consumption, investment, interest rates, liquidity preference and money, the five items in the simplest Keynesian aggregate output model, to make a model with 9 equations and 9 unknowns. "Money enters into the model only through the interest rate" [5, p. 73] and can affect money wages (and therefore prices) only "through the effect on q and N" [5, p 73]. Novelty is claimed for making the demand for money "dependent not only on real output but also on the level of prices" [5, p. 72].

Chapter 8, "The Eclipse of the Equation of Exchange," is primarily a renewal of the attack on EOE, this time with charts that dramatize k's great stability in comparison with v, after quoting some rhapsodies on the stability of the latter by Milton Friedman. In this chapter Weintraub also attacks the "Strange Denial of a Wage-Price Spiral" by certain EOE theorists and insists that WCM is superior to EOE because changes in w influence P directly, while changes in M (even if they are successful in increasing total expenditures Mv or Z) affect P only indirectly through their effects on w.

Chapter 9, "A Miscast Federal Reserve," demonstrates briefly but very forcefully that the Federal Reserve Board, armed only with the power to vary the money supply, can check sellers' inflation only by bringing about severe unemployment. Weintraub goes on to argue that even this does not check inflation *in the long run,* because the retardation of investment by the induced depression must raise P, because it slows down a, the increase in output per man, and as we have seen:

$$P = kw/a \tag{3}$$

In Chapter 10, "Wage Policy: A Way Out," Weintraub rejects any kind of regulation of wages or prices and proposes "watch-tower control" by research agencies publishing their findings as to the probable effects of projected wage increases on w, the average wage level, and so on P. He believes that such appeals to reason will work because when union leaders realize that k is constant they "can never again evade price level responsibility for any immoderate wage change exactions" [5, p. 92].

The rest of the book is devoted to refining k and developing the predictive application of the new theory. Chapter 11, "Decomposing k" deals with the nonwage part of total output or income (which is equal to $k - 1$ times employee compensation), breaks this down into 8 segments and calculates the ratio of each of these segments to employee compensation for each year from 1929 to 1957. Weintraub then goes into ecstasies over the stabilities uncovered by the analysis, or resulting from "small numbers being compared to large" [5, p. 102], or created by the rounding of small ratios to the nearest percentage point, or appearing in the later part of the series. For example, net interest originating in business as a ratio of employee compensation ranges from .18 to .02 (so that the maximum is 900 per cent of the minimum). But from 1944 to 1957 it stays at .02 or .03 and Weintraub exclaims, "Can a series possibly hold more firmly than this?" [5, p. 95], although the rounding may conceal a range within this stable period reaching almost from 1½ to 3½ per cent with the top of the range 233 per cent of the bottom. Nevertheless, despite the nature of parts to be less stable than their sum, information about how they are expected to behave could improve estimates of k.

Chapter 12, "An Empirical Macroeconomic Theory of Income Distribution," although announced as "large steps toward" this, turns out to be nothing but the reconstitution of $k - 1$ from the parts into which it is split up in Chapter 11. Chapter 13 "A Final Price Level Generalization" is a repetition of the observation that k is about 2, so that if P can be expected to stay around twice r (the unit wage cost), P will fall 2 cents for every 1 cent fall in r. We are told that: "This is a result never reached or even suggested by the EOE. It indicates the wide range and deep penetrative power of the WCM-formulation" [5, p. 110].

This however is not yet the climax. The last chapter "The Price Level Over Time: The Final Synthesis for a Growing Economy" provides a still higher power of the "think of a number" game. Here Weintraub combines:

$$P = kw/a \tag{3}$$

with a growth truism taken from Harrod:

$$g = s/c \tag{9}$$

where g ($\equiv \Delta q/q$) is the rate of growth of output or increase-in-output per (unit of) output, s ($\equiv S/Z$) is the saving ratio, S standing for absolute money saving, and c ($\equiv i/\Delta q$) is the marginal capital-output ratio, i ($\equiv S/P$) standing for real saving or real investment or marginal capital.

Harrod's truism says that the rate of growth is equal to the saving ratio divided by the marginal capital-output ratio. It is true because the saving ratio divided by the marginal capital-output ratio means saving (or investment) over income (or output) divided by investment (or saving) over the increase in output. The saving (or investment) cancels the investment (or saving) so that we are left with "over output" divided by "over the increase in output," and this is only an unusual way of saying "increase in output divided by output," which is the definition of the rate of growth. In symbols:

$$s \equiv S/Z = \frac{S/P}{Z/P} = i/q \quad \text{and} \quad c \equiv i/\Delta q,$$

so that:

(9)
$$s/c = \frac{i/q}{i/\Delta q} = \frac{1/q}{1/\Delta q} = \Delta q/q \equiv g.$$

This is all right as long as we remember that the marginal capital-output ratio c is *not* the marginal efficiency of investment and does *not* mean that an additional \$$c$ saved and invested would result in an additional \$1 of output per annum. The truism says no more than that, in the period observed, investment was c times the increase in output. The increase in output was due not only to the investment but also to increase in population, increase in skill, increase in technical and scientific knowledge, discovery of new resources, depletion of old resources, and acts of God like the size of the harvest or changes in the terms of trade or the behavior of the Board of Governors of the Federal Reserve System. It is very hard to remember all this all the time and that is why capital-output ratios and truisms like Harrod's are even more conducive to error than the EOE.

So far Weintraub's guilt is only by association, but in combining (3) with (9) Weintraub [5, p. 112] arrives at:

(10)
$$p = kw \cdot \frac{s}{c\Delta q/N}$$

and substituting b ($\equiv \Delta q/N$, the increase-in-output per man),[4] he achieves [5, pp. 113-14]:

(11)
$$P = kw \frac{s}{cb}, \text{ or:}$$

(12)
$$P = kw \frac{g}{b},$$

"the final synthesis between the price level and the phenomena that are responsible for economic growth" [5, p. 113].

What these formulae tell us is that instead of saying "output per man" we can say "increase-in-output per man divided by increase-in-output per (unit of) output" because the "increase-in-output" 's cancel out leaving us with "per man" divided by "per (unit of) output" which means output per man.

[4] It must be noted that b is the increase-in-output per man and not the increase in output-per-man as is suggested by Weintraub's "per employee output growth rate" [5, pp. 112-13]. These two are equal only if N, the number of men, does not change. If q and N both increased by say 10 per cent, increase-in-output per man is 9 or 10 per cent, depending on whether we take the final or the initial N, while there is no increase in output-per-man.

In symbols this means that in the WCM equation:

$$P = kw/a, \tag{3}$$

instead of writing a, which stands for output per man or q/N, we can write $\frac{\Delta q/N}{\Delta q/q}$, because the Δq's cancel out leaving us with $\frac{1/N}{1/q} = q/N \equiv a$. If we do this we get:

$$P = kw \cdot \frac{\Delta q/q}{\Delta q/N} \cdot \tag{13}$$

If we now write g (increase in output per unit of output) for $\Delta q/q$ and b (increase in output per man) for $\Delta q/N$, we get:

$$P = kw \cdot \frac{g}{b} \cdot \tag{12}$$

If, in accordance with equation (9), we write s/c for g we get:

$$P = kw \cdot \frac{s}{cb}, \tag{11}$$

and if we now restore $\Delta q/N$ for b we get:

$$P = kw \cdot \frac{s}{c\Delta q/N} \cdot \tag{10}$$

It is possible to do the same trick with "investment" as with "increase-in-output." Thus instead of output per man we can say investment per man divided by investment per unit of output. Instead of a (or q/N) we can write $\frac{i/N}{i/q}$. Weintraub does just this and [5, p. 115] comes out with:

$$P = kw \cdot \frac{i/q}{i/N} \cdot \tag{14}$$

In exactly the same manner we could say horsepower per man divided by horsepower per unit of output, or the number of filter-tip cigarettes per man divided by the number of filter-tip cigarettes per unit of output. All of these are only queer ways of saying output per man; and the queerer the irrelevant (canceling) items the less the danger of forgetting its irrelevance and supposing that the equation "conveys some new information" [5, p. 115]. But "increase-in-output" is not sufficiently queer to make its irrelevance apparent, so that it leads Weintraub to suppose that the statement "So long as equipment per head grows faster than equipment per unit of output . . ." [5, p. 115] means something more than "So long as output per head increases. . . ."

In an arithmetical example of "the predictive application" of the final synthesis, Weintraub uses language that might be interpreted as assuming that c, the marginal capital-output ratio, is indeed the marginal efficiency of investment,[5] but this does not touch the validity of his conclusions because the i's (real saving or real investment or marginal capital) cancel out and the Δq's (increases-in-output) also cancel out, so that c, which $\equiv i/\Delta q$, also cancels out.

In equations (10), (11), (12), (13), and (14) we have five different expressions, each in turn taking the place of the last item in equation (3)—$1/a$ and all meaning exactly the same—men per (unit of) output or the inverse of output per man. If output per man (a) is constant (in which case $1/a$ and all its synonyms will be constant too), P will vary with w, growth or no growth. If we put some growth elements into the equation, sound or unsound, and then take them out again we will always be left with the relationship we started with.

Some even more fanciful developments of this game, breaking up b, the increase-in-output per man, into investment and consumption, lead to "profound implications which are significant for economic development" [5, p. 118], such as that "high savings are thus capable of raising *future* real wages" [5, p. 117]. Reference in connection with this is made however not to Adam Smith or even to Ricardo, but to some puzzling propositions in Joan Robinson's *Accumulation of Capital* [5, p. 118n].

II. *Evaluation*

Notwithstanding all these extravagances, Weintraub has his finger on a matter of the utmost practical importance—the need for anti-inflationary measures more acceptable than bleeding the economy with depression. It will be a pity if this valuable insight should fail to help develop such measures either because of the extreme conservatism of his practical proposals or because of the rather revolutionary claims in which the theoretical analysis is wrapped. Yet, it is necessary, having recognized the value and validity of the insight, to evaluate both the practical proposals and the economic-theoretical claims.

1. The practical proposals for checking inflation without resorting to depression to keep wages and prices from rising are most disappointing. Although his analysis concentrates (or even overconcentrates) on the wage rate as the crucial element that forces prices up, and although he observes that exhortation "blows quick and wears short" [5, p. 89], Weintraub pins his faith on giving publicity to estimated effects of proposed wage increases on the price level. But union leaders, rather than accepting responsibility for the effects wage increases have on the price level and endeavoring to practice restraint, may just as well turn the edge of the "magic constant," charging the monopolists with increasing P and blaming the implacable k for the inevitable increase in w forced on helpless union leaders who cannot buck the Law of k! At any rate it seems more than likely that particular prices will continue to be raised by businesses and that particular wages will continue to be raised by

[5] "Suppose that the amount of equipment needed to produce one unit of output—or $1 worth—is $5" [5, p. 113].

unions, neither the former nor the latter being ready to sacrifice particular interests for the sake of relatively small effects on abstractions like the general price level or the average wage level.

Furthermore, even if "watch-tower control" [5, p. 89] should indeed be effective in checking particular wage and price increases that threatened to raise the general price level (i.e., if businessmen and union leaders were persuaded to sacrifice their particular interests for the sake of the general good or for the sake of public applause) this would disrupt the proper price relationships since it would not provide for the relative movements of prices that are necessary in an economy subject to change.

2. The claim that changes in M or Mv can affect P only indirectly through the effect on w, amounts to a denial of the possibility of buyers' inflation. In this Weintraub is just as one-sided as those who deny the possibility of a wage-price spiral generated on the supply side by sellers.

3. Weintraub's proposals are all for stabilizing P by preventing w from rising more rapidly than a and never for holding down w by checking increases in P. This is a consequence of his one-sidedly seeing k as operating only from w to P and never from P to w. But the Law of k is perfectly symmetrical between w and P, and is no better for predicting P from w than for predicting w from P. If there is no excess demand and we know that w will rise in a certain manner, the Law of k tells us that P will rise proportionately. But if excess demand is bidding up P, the Law of k tells us that w will move up proportionately. They may both be pulled up by the market force of excess demand or pulled down by the market force of insufficient demand. Or they may both be pushed up administratively by powerful sellers, or pushed down administratively by powerful buyers. And yet all the time they stay in the same proportion k, so that if we know what will happen to either one of them, we can figure out what will happen to the other. The problem is to predict how *both* will move while held together in the stable relationship k or $1/k$.

4. One wonders why Weintraub should be surprised at k being lower in 1930-34 than in the years immediately before and after, or at the postwar decline in k. A lower k should be expected in depressions because profits fall more in depression than wages do. And it is natural that a long period of continuing prosperity should reduce k.[6] Prosperity makes entrepreneurs more optimistic, so that they push forward their break-even point and lower their mark-up; it increases their readiness to expand and compete; and it lessens the degree of monopoly and the "rate of exploitation" by reducing the reserve army of unemployed workers. (All of these expressions are after all nothing but different jargon for a reduction in k.)

While the *expectation* of continuing prosperity has the effect of gradually lowering k by lowering the *planned* mark-up, an *actual* depression or recession also lowers k, though it does this suddenly by an unplanned fall in profits. However, it also strengthens the expectation of depressions as part of the natural order of good and bad years, and this has the opposite effect, raising

[6] "But if the bad times should not be expected to come, the continued high, boom time profits being made would tempt more competition to come in and participate. This increase in competition would result in lower rates of price markup" [2, p. 179].

k. On these grounds I would predict that the (engineered) interruption of prosperity by the depression of 1958, by upsetting expectations of continuing prosperity, will have the effect of reversing the trend and *increasing k* in 1959 and 1960.

5. There is no novelty in making the demand for liquidity depend on the price level. Keynes did not need to make this explicit because it is clearly implicit in his measuring everything in terms of the wage unit instead of the dollar. Indeed the only purpose of this rather troublesome procedure was to take care of the need for more dollars when prices and wages are higher.

6. The stability of *k* is an essential ingredient of the whole Keynesian revolution. It alone makes it possible for the wage unit to be used as a kind of index number of prices. In an early popularization of Keynes' *General Theory* I spelled out why a change in *w* (in the short run in which *a* is given) would lead to a *proportional* change in *P* [3, esp. pp. 116-20].

7. Weintraub's well-taken and important criticism of the futility of treating sellers' inflation by a restrictive Federal Reserve *monetary* policy, fails to point out that the alternative that comes to mind immediately—a restrictive *fiscal* policy (which reduces *v* rather than *M*)—is subject to exactly the same criticisms. This gap is another indicator of the way Weintraub is often really thinking of the falsity of the quantity theory of money while criticizing the irrelevance of the equation of exchange.

8. There seems to be an unresolved conflict between the academic and the trade titles of the book. The academic title is concerned with a theory that would lead to appropriate governmental or social *policy*, in particular for dealing with sellers' inflation when a restrictive monetary policy is futile or harmful and when *P* can be controlled only through *w*. Weintraub recognizes that monetary policy is under the control of the authorities while wage policy is not, and attempts to deal with this in his proposals for "watch-tower control." But the trade title emphasizes *forecasting* and declares that *M* (monetary policy) is harder to forecast than *w* (wage policy). Here the policy problem of regulating, controlling, or influencing *w* seems to have been abandoned or forgotten in favor of the forecasting problem of guessing what the government and everyone else will do or fail to do. A more careful working out is needed of the relationship between the internal problem of telling the government what to do and the external problem of guessing what in fact will happen.

9. The "trade" assumption that the course of *w* is *given*, in combination with the assumption that the direction of influence is always from *w* to *P* and never from *P* to *w*, leads Weinbraub to argue that a demand or buyers' inflation would be recognized by an increase in *k*, and if that is not observed we cannot be said to have a buyers' inflation [5, p. 72n]. But if *w can* increase in response to an increase in *P*, observation of the behavior of *k* tells us nothing as to whether any inflation is a buyers' or a sellers' inflation.

10. Weintraub argues that even if a sellers' inflation is checked in the short run by an engineered depression, this only aggravates inflation in the long run because the set-back to investment reduces the growth of *a*, output per man. This argument implies that the time-shape of *w* is unaffected by the depres-

sion—which is contrary to the assumption that the depression is sufficient to check the inflation in the short run.

The argument is not really needed since the damage done by loss of output is reason enough for not using depression as the treatment for sellers' inflation. It is, however, possible to salvage two less drastic but still significant results: (a) If a, the increase-in-output per employee has been, and is expected to remain at, 2 per cent per annum it may require a 6 per cent level of unemployment to provide price stability by keeping w from rising at no more than 2 per cent. But if depression, by checking investment, reduces a below 2 per cent, it will take more unemployment to stop the inflation. w can no longer be permitted to rise at 2 per cent and unemployment must be increased to 7 per cent if that is the unemployment needed to stop w from rising relatively to a. The reduction in the increase in a necessitates a more severe depression to stop the inflation. (b) If the induced depression reduces a by more than it reduces w it will raise unit costs and aggravate the inflation even in the short run. If the effects on w are rapid while the effects on a are slow (which may be the case because the latter are cumulative results of the diminished rate of investment), the depression may be anti-inflationary in the short period but inflationary in the longer period. This is a truly dynamic effect and it may be what Weintraub has in mind, but he does not make is clear that it depends on the continuing depression reducing a by more than it reduces w.

11. Weintraub claims that his WCM approach integrates the microeconomics of the firm with the macroeconomics of the economy as a whole by applying to the latter the principle of the unit wage cost mark-up that determines the price of the product of the individual firm. This can be very misleading because the unit wage cost mark-up of the firm, k', is very different from k (or Z/W), when production is split into a series of stages operated by different firms. In general k' will be very much larger than k because direct wages are only a part of the cost. On the other hand the unit *total* cost mark-up of the firm will in general be much less than k since it covers only one element in $k - 1$, namely the profits of the firm. The difference between the individual firm's mark-up and k is only another aspect of the unclosed gap between micro- and macroeconomics.

12. Weintraub's "wedding" of the theory of the price level to the theory of aggregate output is a kind of "silver wedding" or the marriage of a long-wedded couple; but it carries with it a nuptial air because of a mistaken identity. The wedding that economists have been looking forward to for a very long time is between the theory of the determination of the *general* or *absolute* price level and the theory of the determination of *particular* or *relative* prices. The analysis of the general or absolute price level has been integrated with the analysis of aggregate output ever since the Keynesian revolution, and both are part of macroeconomics. The analysis of particular or relative prices has been inseparable from the analysis of the output of the firm or the industry for a much longer period and both are part of microeconomics. The union we are still waiting for is one between micro- and macroeconomics, and not one between the price and output aspects of macroeconomics. That is now in its third decade.

III. *Another Approach to a General Theory*

In my own attempts to generalize Keynes—and nobody seems to be immune from this ambition—I have been led to believe that instead of arranging a marriage by combining macroeconomics and microeconomics in a single set of equations, it would be more fruitful to heed Marshall's warning that *natura non facit saltum* and to see whether "macro" and "micro" cannot be treated as limiting cases at the extremes of a continuum or spectrum. This is the way in which competition and monopoly have been brought into relation with each other. Long-term and short-term analysis are also best bridged in such a manner. There is plenty of precedent; and indeed it is just because such continuity can be utilized throughout economics that Marshall was led to his motto.

To be able to use this method one needs a measure by which one can locate the place of the observed phenomenon in the continuum. In the case of the competition-monopoly spectrum, for example, we may use the "degree of monopoly," or we may use the inverse of the elasticity of demand, but the more general measure is the degree to which one may safely neglect repercussions. A small seller in a large market may neglect the effect of his sales on the market price; this is perfect competition. The larger the seller in relation to the market the less defensible is such neglect, and so we pass through various degrees of imperfect competition to monopoly as some undefined limit. Going in a slightly different direction we observe that a small seller in a large market can disregard the reaction of his competitors to his price policy. The larger he is in relation to the market the more must he take into consideration the reaction of his competitors; and in the interweaving of his policy with the expected policies of his rivals we have the strategies of oligopoly. We may continue further along the same line and consider that when the seller is not only very large in relation to a particular market but of importance for the economy as a whole, he must take into account not only the reactions of competitors but those of other groups in the economy, his suppliers or his customers, who may find it worth while to organize a "countervailing power" against his. Beyond that, a powerful seller must take into account the reaction of the government, and we find ourselves gliding from economics through political economy into the realm of politics.

In the same way a small buyer may neglect the effects on *income* of his decisions to spend or not to spend. Although someone else's income must be reduced by a dollar when he spends a dollar less, he is not concerned with this. It will have no discernible effect on his own income. But as the buyer, or the group of buyers we are considering, becomes larger in relation to the economy, it becomes less and less appropriate to neglect the repercussion on income, because spending by the members of the group will significantly consist of purchases from other members of the same group. If the group consists of a quarter of the economy, then, in the absence of some special information that tells us otherwise, we would expect about a quarter of the spending to consist of buying from other members of the group. If the group wants to increase its saving by a dollar and expects to achieve this by consuming a dollar less, it will be disappointed. Its income will fall by a quarter so that its saving will increase by only 75 cents. If a group consisting of half of the economy tries to save a dollar by consuming a dollar less, it will find itself saving only 50 cents. And finally, if we take the group that is the economy as a whole, we find that when it spends a dollar less, its income falls by the whole dollar and there is no increase in saving at all. The repercussion which could be entirely neglected for a small seller has now, in the other limiting case, become absolute. This is because there is now nobody else to absorb any part of the repercussion.

It is the inability of many to pay attention to the repercussions that leads them to balk at the bridge from "micro" to "macro" and to insist on the "self-evidence" of the proposition that a cut in prices would cure a depression, because a cut in the price charged by a small seller increases his sales. Such crude anti-Keynesianism is rescued by a more sophisticated and more valid argument in terms of the effect of price reductions on the value of cash balances. It is here that a more careful examination of a spectrum of price flexibility can clarify the issues even if the result is not exactly a wedding between Keynesian and classical positions, but merely their location on a spectrum that goes farther than these positions in both directions.

If there were perfect price flexibility, so that any deficiency in demand would make prices fall so rapidly and excess demand would make prices rise so rapidly that we would not have to worry about what happens while the adjustment is going on, there would be no room for "Keynesian economics," or indeed for any policy at all with regard to effective demand. No policy would be necessary to prevent depression as long as there were some floor under the supply of hard money in existence; and no policy would be necessary to prevent inflation as long as the quantity of money did not increase indefinitely. Any excess of demand would be cured by the reduction in the real value of the money stock as prices rose. Any deficiency of demand would be cured by the increase in the real value of the money stock as prices fell.

Policy is necessary because we do not have, and never can have, this kind of price flexibility. This is why those economists, like Pigou and Patinkin, who have explored the way in which perfect flexibility would work, have been careful to point out that they are not recommending reliance on price flexibility, or even on any available measures for increasing price flexibility, as an adequate public policy. With different degrees of imperfection in price flexibility different policies become appropriate, and it is these differences in the supposed position of the economy on a spectrum of price flexibility that explain the different policy recommendations rather than any subjective attachments of economists to different philosophies.

If there is imperfect flexibility downward of prices, the cure of a deficiency of demand by price deflation involves a protracted period of depression aggravated by continuing expectations of further reduction in prices which are still resisting the downward pressures. It then becomes appropriate to bring about the increase in the real value of the money stock by less painful methods, namely by increasing the money stock in nominal terms. The mechanism of recovery and the attainment of equilibrium and price stability then proceeds in exactly the same way as if the increase in the real value of the money stock had come about without benefit of policy—namely through perfect price flexibility. This is the Keynesian general case of an increase in the money stock—in terms of "wage units" so as to include the case where it is brought about by deflation.

The next position on our spectrum is where the inflexibility has invaded the money market and the rate of interest fails to fall in response to the increase in the real value of cash balances (the Keynesian special case with the liquidity trap) or where investment and consumption fail to increase in response to a fall in the rate of interest. The secondary inflexibilities would not matter if prices in general were perfectly flexible, since an unlimited fall in prices would constitute an unlimited increase in the wealth of the owners of the cash and this would induce the necessary increase in spending anyway. In the absence of unlimited price flexibility, the same cure could be obtained by an unlimited increase in the nominal quantity of money. But where this is unpractical (and even where it might be practical) resort to a more direct method of increasing demand might still be desirable. The government can increase its own spending or induce more spending by others by reducing taxes (or use a combination of these measures, including a larger budget with its net positive effect on total spending). If monetary policy is inadequate it can be supplemented by fiscal policy.

Farther along the same spectrum we have the situation where prices not only refuse to fall when there is a deficiency of demand, but tend to *rise* if there is a level of demand that provides a satisfactory level of employment. Prices will then be stable only if there is considerable unemployment. In the absence of this degree of depression, wages and prices will be rising in a sellers' inflation, with labor blaming the wage increases on price increases, and business blaming the price increases on wage increases.

In this case, monetary and fiscal policy cannot provide full employment with price stability. If monetary and fiscal policy is applied so as to achieve price stability, it causes depression. If it is directed at achieving full employment, is causes inflation. Full employment together with price stability can be attained now only by providing an artificial market to replace the missing competitive market that would have prevented such price behavior. The administered prices and wages that rise as soon as unemployment is less than, say, 6 per cent (when 2 or 3 per cent is all that the genuine frictions make necessary) must be so administered, in the general interest, that the general price level is constant as long as there is no excess demand. Such price regulation, like the regulation of the prices charged by public utilities, would not be interfering with the free market. It would rather be interfering with the *interferences* with that administration of prices which destroys the free market and makes sellers' inflation possible. Sellers' inflation does not fit into the Keynesian scheme any more than into the classical scheme, because Keynes, like the "classical" economists, assumed that although prices might be reluctant to fall in spite of unemployment, they would not rise unless there was excess demand. Sellers' inflation is possible because prices are raised even at less than full employment as long as the unemployment is not severe enough to hamstring the price and wage administrators

Another and closely related spectrum may be envisaged in the degree to which money is incorporated in models of the economy. At one end of this spectrum is the barter economy where monetary complications are absent. Moving along the spectrum, we come to models where money is spoken of but not brought into close relationship with the "real" economy, and money is supposed to affect only the absolute level of prices; the relations between prices, including the rate of interest, are determined in the barter department. Here the rate of interest stands for either the marginal efficiency of capital (when stationary states are considered) or the marginal efficiency of investment (where growth and decay are permitted to enter the analysis). Farther along the spectrum are models where changes in the quantity of money are not immediately sterilized by changes in the price level, because price flexibility is less than perfect, so that employment is not always full. This is the Keynesian analysis (including the modern anti-Keynesians) that stresses real-balance effects. Still farther along the spectrum is the region I would like to explore, where money is *completely* integrated in the model, where the enjoyment of liquidity is not considered any different from the enjoyment of any other good or service, and where the cash balance is perfectly at home with all other assets yielding liquidity as part of the income flow while constituting part of the assets of the household, just as houses yield house-room as part of the income flow while constituting a part of the assets of the household. It then becomes unnecessary to bring in real-balance effects as a complicating afterthought and it is much easier to deal with the problems of price levels and employment. In such models it would be convenient to speak of wealth as a vector containing both assets and income, so that an increase in either, the other being constant (as when there is a change in the rate of interest) would constitute an increase in wealth.

Perhaps a more interesting spectrum would be that of the degrees of equilibrium. This might dispose of the tiresome arguments as to whether unemployment equilibrium is not a contradiction in terms. Here we might start with the most equilibrial kind of equilibrium, where there is no excess or deficiency of demand whatever that might sooner or later result in some change in the price even with perfect price flexibility. Such an equilibrium by definition rules out any involuntary unemployment.

Farther along the spectrum we find an equilibrium in which there is involuntary unemployment and it does not disappear—either because there is a rigidity of wages and prices so that the situation is frozen, or because prices and wages are both falling so that there is no incentive for employment to be increased. This may be because the increase in the real value of the money unit is being canceled by decreases in the supply of nominal cash or is being offset by increases in the desire to hold cash, so that the rate of interest does not fall; or because investment and consumption are unresponsive to the rate of interest, while the effects of the increase in the real value of the money stock on the propensity to consume (the Pigou effect) is small in the period we are considering. This is the Keynesian unemployment equilibrium. Any increase in output would result in losses that would push output back to the previous level.

In describing this equilibrium, Keynes tells us that while he has rejected the classical postulate that the wage is equal to the marginal disutility of work, he still maintains the other classical postulate that the wage is equal to the value of the marginal product. (We may extend this to include imperfect competition by changing this to say that the marginal cost of labor is equal to the marginal value product of labor). Workers would be happy to do more work at the same rate of pay, so that labor is off its supply function. This is why this equilibrium is not as equilibrial as the first one on this spectrum. Nevertheless we are justified in calling it an equilibrium because there is a certain stability about the situation. Keynes opened himself unnecessarily to criticism by supposing that an increase in employment would necessarily lead to a fall in real wages (though he later recognized that this was not essential to his model) saying that labor was not in a position to reduce the real wage,

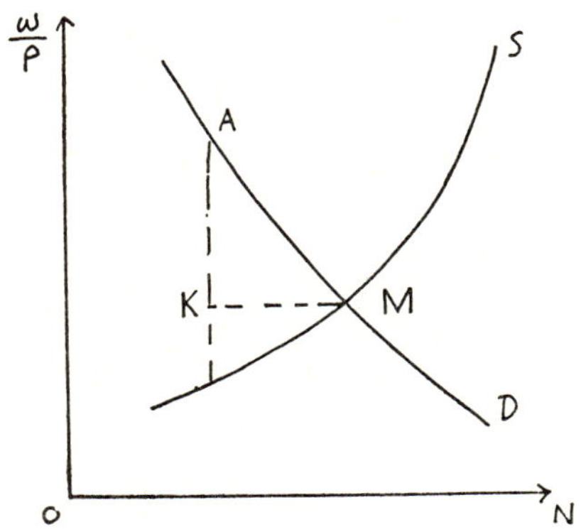

FIGURE 1

because a reduction in the money wage makes prices fall proportionately so that the real wage stayed the same. What is relevant is not the inability of labor to reduce the real wage but its inability to bring about an increase in demand which increases employment—whether this would lower the real wage or *raise* it.

We can deal with this better if we move farther along the spectrum to an even less equilibrial equilibrium, which is at the same time closer to the realities of a depression. At this point on the spectrum, the *second* classical postulate is rejected,[7] namely that the wage is equal to the marginal product of labor (or the marginal cost of labor is equal to its marginal value product).

In a depression business is no less eager to sell more products at the current price than labor is eager to do more work at the same wage. In Figure 1 (following Patinkin) the actual situation is represented by the point K. The S curve shows how much labor would be supplied at various real wage rates (w/p is the wage-price ratio—w is the wage and p is the price level). The D curve shows how much labor the employers would demand *if they could sell*

[7] This is done by Patinkin referring to a suggestion by Liviatan [4, p. 218 ff] but Patinkin seems to underestimate the importance of his and Liviatan's innovation.

the corresponding amount of product at each wage-price ratio. But they are unable to sell that much product so they only demand the quantity of labor indicated by *K*. Full equilibrium with full employment would be at *M* where workers would find all the work they want and employers would sell all the goods they want to sell at the prevailing wage-price ratio. Since *K* is off both curves it shows that *neither* of the classical postulates holds. If we were to follow Keynes and reject only the equality between the wage and the marginal disutility of work, we would be at *A*, and the real wage would be higher than at full employment. If we rejected both postulates we might argue, as Patinkin does, that, starting at *M*, a fall in demand would result not only in involuntary unemployment (we would be off the supply curve) but also in business depression (we would be off the demand curve too), and both wages and prices would fall. If they both fell at the same rate, we would be at *K*, with the same real wages as at *M*. If prices fell faster than wages, real wages would rise and we would be above *K*; and if wages were to fall faster than prices we would be below *K*. What happened to real wages therefore would depend on the relative flexibility of wages and prices; and there is no necessity for the negative relationship between real wages and employment indicated by Keynes.

There is however no need to assume, as Patinkin does, that at any point to the left of *M* wages and prices must be tending to *fall*. This assumption is itself the result of declaring a dichotomy between full employment and unemployment when we can do better by supposing a spectrum. If we succumb to the temptation to assume a simple dichotomy between pure unemployment, when an increase in demand increases only output, prices staying unchanged, and pure full employment when an increase in demand increases only prices, because output cannot increase, we get a curve of the supply price of output in relation to the wage level that consists of a left-handed *L*, as in Figure 2—a horizontal line *AF* showing a constant supply price up to full employment at *F* when the curve suddenly becomes vertical. No matter how high the price goes (relatively to the wage) the quantity supplied cannot be increased. (The vertical measure in this diagram is the *inverse* of the real wage, which is measured vertically in Figure 1. It is p/w instead of w/p.)

This curve can also be read as showing (the inverse of) the real wage for any level of employment. Up to full employment the real wage is constant. At full employment the real wage is indefinite, depending on how the race goes between rising prices and rising wages in the inflation. Where one would be on the curve would depend on what business is able to sell as determined by the state of business or over-all demand.

With this model one is tempted to identify full employment with price stability because the corner point, *F*, seems to indicate both. If demand increases above *F* output cannot increase but prices rise. There will then be abnormal profits and a competitive increase in the demand for labor. Wages will be bid up until the same real wage is restored and the demand curve once more passes through *F*. If demand decreases there is a reduction in output but the price-wage ratio is unchanged. There are now unemployed workers, business is slack, and there is pressure on wages and prices to fall. If prices and wages fall rapidly without limit, demand will increase and the demand curve will rise until it cuts at *F* again. If wages and prices are sticky, or if they fall but it takes a long time before the resulting increase in the value of the money stock raises demand so as to restore full employment, we have underemployment equilibrium. This, however, is temporary, even though it may be temporary for a very long time if nothing else is done about it. We still have prices rising whenever the demand is above *F* and prices falling or tending to fall whenever the demand falls below *F*. *F* therefore seems to represent both full employment and price-level equilibrium.

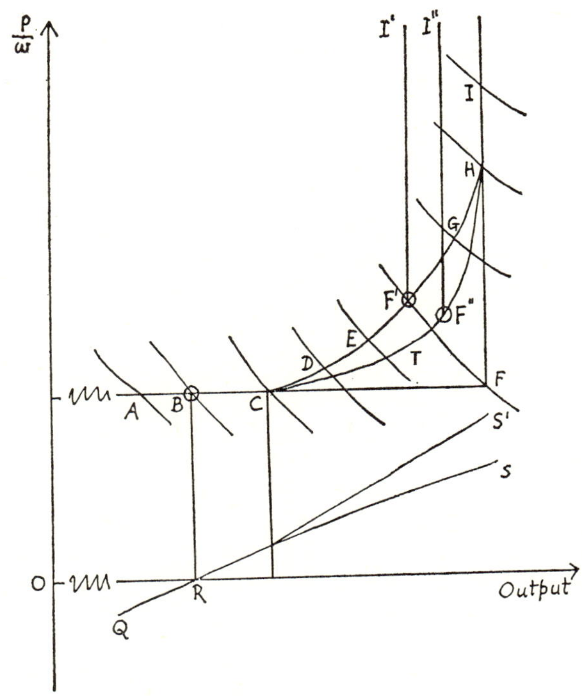

FIGURE 2

But this need not be the case at all. It is quite possible to have less than full employment—to be on the horizontal arm of the supply curve—and for prices and wages to be rising. Of course this cannot be due to excess demand. The increase in prices and in wages cannot be a market response. It can occur only if prices and wages are being pushed up administratively by sellers. We then have a sellers' inflation. Buyers' inflation can be cured only by removing the excess demand that causes it. Sellers' inflation can be cured only by measures that remove the power of sellers to raise prices. Reducing the level of demand may do this, but only by creating a depression severe enough to break down the administrative power of sellers to push up their prices. If we do not want to suffer this degree of depression, which may be quite severe, we must either continue to suffer from the inflation or we must clip the power of sellers by other means—namely by a regulation of administered prices so as to make these behave the way they would in a competitive market.

As long as sellers retain the power to raise prices administratively, we can mark off on the horizontal arm of the supply curve the point *B* where the degree of unemployment and depression is just sufficient to check sellers' ability or willingness to raise prices. This is the level of employment at which wages rise no more rapidly than productivity so that we have price-level equilibrium. We may call it *price-level equilibrium employment*. To the left of *B* prices will fall and we will have deflation, and to the right of *B* prices will rise and we will have inflation. But it is not buyers' inflation but sellers' inflation. Only when we get above *F* will the inflation be a buyers' or demand inflation. Keynes assumed that the point of full employment is also necessarily the point of price-level equilibrium employment, so that only buyers' inflation is possible.

In my *Economics of Employment* I spoke of price-level equilibrium employment, but I called it "Low Full Employment," and I treated the power of labor to raise wages as one of various frictions that prevented unemployed factors from moving to where they could be used. Because of all these frictions, any further increase in demand could only raise prices. It now seems to me to be misleading to call *B* any kind of full employment; and misleading to lump together the power of sellers to raise prices and genuine frictions that prevent factors of production from moving from one area or one occupation to another.

Through the point *R*, directly below *B*, we can draw a line *QRS* indicating the rate of movement of prices that would accompany any given level of output and employment. To the left of *R* the line lies below the axis showing that prices would fall, and the further to the left, i.e., the lower the volume of output and employment, the lower the point on *QRS* and the greater the rate at which prices would fall. At *R* wages rise just rapidly enough to balance the rate of increase of productivity so that prices are stable. To the right of *R* the line lies above the axis indicating that the price level would rise, and that the greater the volume of employment the greater would be the rate of price rise because of the greater power of the price administrators to raise prices. At *F*, or full employment, the power of sellers to raise prices becomes irrelevant because beyond this point there is excess demand. The market itself then raises prices whether there exists any administrative power to raise them or not. Sellers' inflation then bows out of the picture and buyers' inflation takes over.[8]

A closer look blurs this clear distinction between sellers' inflation and buyers' inflation. Full employment is not reached suddenly; it also is a matter of degree. As we move up the level of employment, long before resources everywhere are fully utilized we will come across bottlenecks and increasing marginal costs as capacity is approached.

[8] If any level of employment other than *R* persists for some time, the rate of change of prices (whether upwards or downwards) comes to be anticipated, the movement is accelerated, and the rate of price rise or of price fall will be greater. The line *QRS* would swing round *R* in an anticlockwise direction, becoming steeper in the process. The longer the movement persists the steeper will the curve become and the inflation or deflation will develop into hyperinflation or hyperdeflation.

If we were to consider the increase in employment as requiring the application of increasing quantities of labor to a given supply of capital, we might expect to find increasing marginal cost almost from the beginning of the curve, but this would be so only if we were considering a very long run in which capital was properly adjusted for permanent operation with each volume of employment measured along the horizontal axis. If, on the other hand, we were concerned with short-run problems of output and employment varying with an industrial equipment designed for some normal level of employment of the current labor force, then the supply curve would be fairly horizontal for some time before we got into problems of crowding the capacity. We would then have a curve of supply price like that marked in Figure 2 by the alphabet from *A* to *I* at the points where a series of demand curves cut it.

As before, *B* is the point of price-level equilibrium employment, with wages rising no faster than can be matched by rising productivity. At *C* there would be a pure sellers' inflation with prices rising at a rate indicated by the height of the *QRS* curve above the horizontal axis directly below *C*. But now we have increasing costs and bottlenecks before we get to perfectly full employment; and prices rise more than wages, so that the real wage falls as we move along the supply curve up the alphabet. If wages did not change at all, prices would rise as shown by this curve and real wages would fall in that proportion. We now have an additional reason why wages would rise: Not only is the bargaining power of labor raised by the higher level of employment, the pressure for wage increases is intensified by the attempt to make up at least what is lost in real wages by the price rise, and the resistance to wage increases is diminished by the feeling that workers have just cause for complaint. This is indicated by the replacement of *RS* by *RS′* with a greater rate of wage and price increase for each level of output and employment above *C*. At some point, say *F′*, the combined pressure for wage increase becomes so great that any further increase in employment is prevented. A further increase in demand would make wages rise as rapidly as prices, so that p/w would stay the same and we would only get inflation (not visible in Figure 2). We may therefore call *F′* "full employment."

A higher level of employment could be reached only by measures that succeeded in reducing the genuine frictions so that more of the unemployed factors might be moved to where they could be used. This would lower the curve of supply price to a position like *ABCTF″HI*. (The complete removal of all frictions would bring us back to the reverse *L* curve *AFI* that we started with, *CF′H* coinciding with *CFH*. There would then be no bottlenecks or increasing costs until there was perfectly full employment at *F*.) The diminution in frictions would give us *T* as the level of output and employment reached with the same demand conditions, with a higher real wage (lower price-wage ratio), and a greater volume of employment. It would make possible a still further increase in output and employment in response to a further increase in demand to a new full employment level *F″* where wages would once more rise so rapidly as to prevent any further increase in demand from increasing employment any more.

Possible positions are then bounded on the right by a vertical line through the full-employment level F' or F'' so that the effective curve of supply price is $AF'I'$ or $AF''I''$. But the economy may very well find itself off the supply price curve anywhere *above* and *to the left of* it as long as the point is not so high as to show a real wage reduced below the level at which workers are able and willing to work. Such points would be like K in Figure 1 where, in a depression, both workers and employers would be happy if demand were greater and output and employment were greater at the existing price-wage ratio. Prices would meanwhile be rising if the point were to the right of B (price-level equilibrium employment), and they would be falling if the point were to the left of B. The point would be moving up if prices were rising relatively to wages, and down if the converse were true; and this movement might be increasing or decreasing the level of demand and thereby the level of output and employment. These would be short-run effects which could affect output and employment in either direction. The long-run tendency, if the quantity of money had any stability, would be for the value of the money stock to increase if the point was to the left of B and for the value of the money stock to fall if the point was to the right of B. The long-run equilibrium toward which the economy would be tending would therefore not be full employment at F, F' or F'', but price-level equilibrium employment at B, or anywhere above B as long as it was below the height in Figure 2 at which the real wage is so low that workers are unable or unwilling to work).[9]

At points like F' or F'' it becomes very difficult to say whether we have buyers' inflation or sellers' inflation. I would be inclined to say that F' and F'', like F, are points where sellers' inflation yields to buyers' inflation. But strictly speaking, at such points there is no over-all attempt to buy more goods than are available, and if sellers were not able to exert any influence on prices there would be no inflation at F' or F'', or anywhere short of H. The real wage would indeed fall very low, but in the perfectly competitive market where sellers' inflation is impossible nothing could be done about this as long as labor was available, and there might be even more labor available as a result of the low real wage. On the other hand, at any point to the right of C at least a part of the pressure for increased wages, and for increased prices to cover increased wages and other costs, would be the result of increases in *demand.*

It may be that further development of this analysis will turn out to be fatal to the concept of sellers' inflation, of which I have become quite fond, but it seems to me that the unification and clarification of economic theory will be better served by the Marshallian approach of searching for continuities than by the dialectical or ceremonial union of opposites.

[9] This limit is not a reflection of the supply curve of voluntary employment, since the lower the real wage (in the economy as a whole) the *greater* would be the supply of labor by workers sacrificing leisure for minimum subsistence. It would be a reflection of the conditions of the supply of labor only in the sense that it would be affected by the diminished survival of healthy workers; and this would be better represented by redrawing the whole supply curve to show the changed nature and size of the working population.

References

1. J. K. Galbraith, *The Affluent Society*. Boston 1958.
2. A. P. Lerner, *Economics of Employment*. New York 1951.
3. ———, "Mr. Keynes' General Theory," *ILO Rev.*, Oct. 1936; reprinted in S. E. Harris, ed., *The New Economics*, New York 1947, pp. 113-32.
4. Don Patinkin, *Money, Interest and Prices*. Evanston, Ill. 1957.
5. Sidney Weintraub, *A General Theory of the Price Level, Output, Income Distribution and Economic Growth*. Trade title, *Forecasting the Price Level, Income Distribution and Economic Growth*. Philadelphia 1959.

[3]

RICHARD T. ELY LECTURE

EMPLOYMENT THEORY AND EMPLOYMENT POLICY

By Abba P. Lerner
University of California, Berkeley

In the early years of the Keynesian era, before all the anti-Keynesians became Keynesian anti-Keynesians, we knew that we could maintain full employment while avoiding inflation by having a rate of effective demand that was neither too small nor too large. All that remained was to get the authorities to do the right thing. Those who spoke of inflationary dangers either were prisoners of the inappropriate assumption of full employment or saw in the expansion of demand an infernal "sorcerer's apprentice" machine with no "stop" button.

Now, in the fourth decade of the Keynesian era, we have graduated from a state of innocence of the inflationary dangers from full employment policies to a state of obsession with them.

This is not due to a lack of theories of inflation. We even have models with price levels rising or falling in any degree but identical in real terms, the different price changes being offset by different money rates of interest and adjustments in monetary obligations. But we generally make price stability a basic objective, so that degrees of inflation are automatically degrees of evil. We have blamed the evil on too much money, on too much spending, on increases in these, on such increases relative to the volume of goods to be bought, and on an excess of investment over saving. But all of these have about the same intent, for which I shall use the term "excess demand." This has the additional convenience that it can also be blamed for "repressed inflation" when prices do not rise.

We have also blamed excess demand on expectations of rising prices, and blamed these expectations on expectations of increases in incomes and so on, but our problem today is not in the search for causes of causes. It is the breakdown of the simple Keynesian formula for preventing both inflation and unemployment by avoiding both excess demand and deficient demand.

This breakdown comes from an underestimation of the Keynesian revolution. The key element in the revolution was the official recognition of a downward rigidity of the money wage. Its significance was obscured at first by Keynes's focusing on the inability of workers to reduce the real wage. The confusion was compounded by Keynes's denial that downward wage flexibility would cure the unemployment and a great debate between neoclassical economists arguing that with sufficient wage flexibility falling prices would cure any unemployment by increasing the real value of claims to wealth, and Keynesians pointing out that Keynes spoke only of degrees of flexibility achievable in the real world, which would be swamped by deflationary dynamic expectations. Both sides were right and both failed to see that the recognition of "downward rigidity" involved nothing less than the dethronement of the market as the determinant of price!

If supply exceeds demand, the market is telling the price to fall. If the price does not fall, it is obeying a more powerful master—a price administrator who can just as well tell the wage to go up when the market is telling it to go down. And this is exactly what we see in the un-Keynesian coexistence of unemployment with inflation—un-Keynesian because Keynes not only did not see this possibility himself but even succeeded in banishing it from the vision of others.

In 1935 or 1936, Robert Bryce and I asked Keynes whether the maintenance of sufficient effective demand for full employment could not result in perpetuating inflation. Keynes could not understand our question, although we persisted until we exhausted his patience—and apparently also my own, for the question of administered inflation seems to have been washed from my brain for a decade or two by this episode.

Cost inflation or administered inflation or markup inflation is now receiving much attention. As wages rise, prices rise too by virtue of the markup of price over cost by the price administrators of business. The wage administrators then raise the wage again to restore its real value or its markup over the minimum basic cost of living. The two sets of markup administrators, trying to get round each other, provide the twist or couple that drives the inflation.

Just like demand inflation, administered inflation persists by virtue of ever renewed attempts at the impossible. In demand inflation the attempt is to buy more than 100 percent of the supply. In administered inflation it is the attempt of labor and business, by their respective markups, to get, between them, more than 100 percent of the joint product.

Special credit should go to Professor Sidney Weintraub for his attempts to direct the attention of economists to this crucial markup of price over wage or ratio of the national product to the wage bill, instead of debating the relative inadequacies of the liquidity-preference half and the time-preference half of the theory of effective demand—a debate not indeed on the famous question as to which blade of the scissors does the cutting, but which blade would make a worse razor.

Noting that the price-wage ratio was more stable than either the velocity of circulation or the propensity to consume, Weintraub unfortunately could not resist the temptation to provide it with its own truistic "basic formula" to rival the quantity equation and the multiplier that are in the service of the other ratios.

There are, however, those who are so impressed by the efficiency of the whole scissors, even though neither blade makes a good razor, that they are unable to put it down even when a different instrument is called for. They try to cure administered inflation by reducing effective demand because that works for demand inflation, and then they try to cure the resulting unemployment by increasing effective demand, back and forth, in what the British have dubbed "Stop and Go." Disappointed, frustrated, and disgusted with the inevitable failure, they declare that Keynes is all wet and functional finance a mirage.

In my first encounter with the indecent entrance of the inflation dragon on the stage before his cue was called, i.e., before full employment was reached, some remnant of the brainwashing made me give the name "full employment" (albeit "low full employment") to the point where the dragon first appeared—whispering the cue, as it were, to legitimize the dragon's prematurity. But I nevertheless still find this a convenient expression, leaving the term "high full employment" for real full employment. The Phillips curve was a refinement of this idea —suggesting that one can do business with the dragon—buying some reduction in the degree of inflation by feeding him a certain number of jobs (I almost said a certain number of unemployed, but that would make the metaphor too vivid), seeking the optimum position on the curve where the gain from this dragon trade is maximized.

There is a tendency to suppose that the optimum position is where the number of unfilled jobs is equal to the number of unemployed workers. This assumes that an unmanned job is somehow the equivalent counterpart of a jobless man, but a jobless man is a human tragedy, while an unfilled job is merely an indication that output could be greater if more productive resources were available; i.e., that output is limited only by the availability of productive resources and not by an insufficiency of demand. This would call for congratulation rather than for complaint. The complaint, when contrasted with concern about jobless men, only reflects the fear that unfilled jobs lead to inflation. The real trade-off is between employment and inflation.

Since it is marginal equivalence which gives us an optimum, we should strive for the point between low and high full employment where the harm from additional inflation is just equal to the good from the accompanying increase in employment.

To recognize such an optimum we must first decide what would be acceptable terms of trade—how much additional inflation would be worth suffering for the sake of a 1 percent increase in employment. In the range between 2 percent and 6 percent unemployment it seems that a 1 percent increase in employment carries with it about a 2 or 3 percent increase in the national product. This is a measure of the economic gain.

The distributive harm from having an inflation higher by 1 percent per annum consists of the transfer of income from those who buy to those who sell at the higher prices (including the sale of their services for income). This transfer amounts to 1 percent of the national product (during the first two years).

In a hyperinflation there is a further loss from disorganization of cost and profit calculations. But an economy that had become accustomed to a considerable rate of inflation—even as great as 25 percent per annum—would have developed automatic and regular adjustments to wages, rents, etc., and a correspondingly high money rate of interest. The disorganization would not be very serious, or in any case not very different as between a 24 percent and a 25 percent rate of inflation. These adjustments would not correct the urge to minimize cash balances, which involves a wasteful shift of time and energy from production (or from enjoying consumption) into more frequent shopping. The remedy for this—a subsidy to holders of cash to bring the private cost of liquidity closer to the zero social cost of providing it—is probably too unorthodox to be applied, but this element of damage from the rate of inflation being greater by 1 percent per annum would clearly be minor.

The first thing to consider in estimating the distributive harm—the harm from the transfer of 1 percent of the national product from buyers to sellers—is that most members of society are both buyers and sellers. In an inflation people pay higher prices but they also earn more money. In an economy which has adjusted itself to a continuing inflation, a very large part of the transfer will cancel out in this way, and in the model of ideal adjustment there is complete cancellation and no transfer.

But in an unprepared-for increase in inflation in the real world there will be considerable transfer to others from those whose selling prices have risen less than their buying prices—basically those with incomes fixed in money terms like pensions, rents, interest, and the salaries of nonmilitant employees like university professors. But these could not cover more than say a quarter of the total payments and therefore could not amount to more than one quarter of 1 percent of the national product.

While the greater part of these redistributions cannot be disentangled from the large element of chance that pervades our economy in any case, some may be welcomed and others deplored. There will, however, be serious injustices to recipients of modest fixed pensions, alimony, relief, or health insurance payments, or interest on modest savings. Where these cannot be corrected directly by collection from the seller-beneficiary, they can (and should) be compensated out of the general funds of society. Such compensation could not amount to more than a quarter of the quarter of 1 percent of the national product which covered all the uncanceled payments, or one-sixteenth of 1 percent of the national product.

The second point to remember is that compensation is not a social loss, but only a transfer to the victims from those who have to pay additional taxes raised, or suffer the reduction in benefits from government expenditures curtailed, to provide the compensation money. Much of this would even be a transfer from those who have gained in the inflation what the victims have lost. In any case, the only real loss would be from the increase in administration in collecting taxes and distributing the compensations and from the disturbance to the price mechanism by the additional taxes. We may estimate this loss at not more than one-quarter of the compensation or one-sixty-fourth of 1 percent of the national product. This is the figure that should be compared with the 2 or 3 percent of the national product gained from a 1 percent increase in employment. The acceptable trade-off ratio is therefore more than 100:1. One-tenth of 1 percent increase in employment more than cancels the harm from 10 percent inflation! The moral is that the optimum point must be very close to high full employment.

I would apologize for so much elementary arithmetic were it not that many policy suggestions seem to be based on the assumption that 1 percent of additional inflation is worse than 1 percent of additional unemployment. Proposals to restrict effective demand so as to guarantee price stability imply that inflation is an absolute evil, so that 1 percent of additional inflation is worse than any degree of unemployment; while those who would restrict effective demand to the point where wages would be stabilized and increased productivity showed itself in falling prices, must subscribe to an arithmetic that shows zero inflation as infinitely worse than any degree of unemployment.

Such weird arithmetics are usually obscured by colorful pronouncements such as that even incipient price increases show that the economy is "overheated," or that a high level of unemployment constitutes a boom that is bound to be punished by a "bust"—metaphors that suggest either the perils of primitive steam engines or the angry fates of Greek tragedy. Fortunately practice has not followed these preachings since the Great Depression. This is because unemployment is very unpopular and political pressures and the desire for reelection cause the authorities almost always to fail in their declared intention to prevent inflation at all costs. But compromise policies have adopted points close to low full employment where an additional 1 percent of unemployment is accepted to avoid less than 1 percent of additional inflation.

There is, of course, also concern about the balance of payments, and for this a decrease in employment is just as good as or even better than a checking of the inflation. Whereas price disinflation can only gradually build up more export trade, an increase in domestic unemployment brings about an immediate and reliable improvement by a reduction in the quantity of imports we can afford to buy.

This is not the place to discuss sacrifices that many countries are making for the sake of an imaginary "stability of the exchange rates" demanded by the international gold standard and its successors. But I cannot refrain from pointing out that they have developed a more friendly face for economic warfare. Instead of "exporting unemployment" by each restricting others' exports, they peacefully increase their own unemployment. That this results in a decrease of imports, which happen to be the other countries' exports is just tough luck. "Beggar my neighbor" has been replaced by "beggar myself."

A parallel proposal in the political field was made a few years ago to save the United States and the Soviet Union the great expense and the dangerous uncertainties of developing and maintaining effective Intercontinental Ballistic Missiles. It was proposed that H-bombs be buried in the principal cities of both countries, and that each government be given by the other a reliable electronic capability of detonating the bombs in the cities of the other country. Perhaps it is an indication of the lagging of the other social sciences behind economics that the proposal was dismissed as "too logical."

There are yet other arguments brought against moving to the optimum trade-off point near high full employment. The structural unemployment argument claimed that even when we had 5 to 6 percent unemployed, we were very close to full employment, the unemployed having been made unemployable by automation. The evidence for this —a negative correlation between years of education and percentage unemployed—may, however, only show that counting the years of schooling is an easy way of deciding how to allocate scarce jobs.

Then there is the fear of "accumulated" inflation. A 1 percent increase in the rate of inflation will make prices higher (than they otherwise would have been) by an average of one-half of 1 percent during the first year, and by 1½ percent during the second year (hence the

1 percent transfer from buyer to seller in the first two years). In the following years it will be 2½ percent, 3½ percent, etc., above the previous trend line. Soon the compound interest factor becomes significant and it might be thought that with such a growing shift of income from buyers to sellers the burden of compensation would become intolerable. But if the inflation continues at the higher rate the whole necessity of compensation fades away. As the economy gets used to the inflation, it develops the appropriate automatic adjustments of wages, rents, pensions, etc., between the buyers and sellers so that the need for public compensation diminishes rather than increases.

The related consideration of the danger of disorganization is much more cogent. The markups may also adjust to the inflation. Larger and larger markups may be called for as the adjustments which correct the inequities to the buyers simultaneously neutralize the benefits to the sellers from the previous markups. It might then be rational to suffer the current loss from a low level of employment as the price of preventing hyperinflation in the future.

I would now give less weight to this consideration than I once did. Inflation may not accelerate. We have seen inflations continuing for a long time at about the same rate and even slowing down. But still there is the danger.

The economic cost of holding the economy down to low full employment so as to avoid this danger—some $50 billions per annum—seems far too large an insurance premium against the risk of sliding into hyperinflation in the future, especially since the payment, instead of guaranteeing our future wisdom, would even increase the danger if popular resentment at the unemployment should bring support to irresponsible inflationists.

But to plead for a more rational choice of the optimum point on a given unemployment-inflation spectrum is only a secondary and interim issue. My primary purpose is to argue that we do not have to accept the spectrum. We can arrange to enjoy the benefits of high full employment and price stability.

I am referring of course to incomes policy and the wage and price guideposts. These have not been too successful up till now, but my thesis is that greater success will follow a better understanding of the guideposts, not as a substitute for monetary and fiscal regulation of effective demand, or even as a parallel support to these, but as a replacement for a part of the competitive price mechanism that has broken down (or perhaps never worked properly).

In a strictly market governed economy, i.e., where prices always rise or fall so as to make supply equal to demand, full employment does not require any monetary or fiscal policy. We are in a neoclassical world in which price levels adjust the real value of any nominal money supply to fit the demand for real cash balances.

Monopolies and monopsonies do not interfere with this. They only raise the prices obtained by the monopolists, or lower those paid by the monopsonists, relatively to other prices, thereby raising their real incomes relatively to the incomes of others.

But if we have a "double monopoly" when monopolists sell to each other, no others are there to be exploited, so that both together cannot gain anything. As they raise their selling prices they see their buying prices rise, and while their margins rise in absolute terms these cannot rise relatively to each other and a price race ensues. If the authorities do not increase the total rate of spending, there is a deficiency of demand. But the prices, instead of being pushed down by the market, continue to be raised by the monopolists. Sales and output fall as much as may be required to induce the monopolists to give up the race. This is the point of low full employment.

With a double monopsony instead of a double monopoly, all this is in reverse. Each reduces his buying price to increase his share and is frustrated by the fall in his selling price which is the other monopsonist's buying price. The margins fall absolutely but not relatively, and unless the authorities reduce the level of spending there is excess demand. Each wants to buy more than is available. But the prices, instead of being bid up by the market, continue to be pushed down by the monopsonists until the pressure of excess demand is great enough to induce them to give up the downward race and they merely prevent prices from rising.

This condition is familiar to us as "repressed inflation" (when it is usually the government who keeps prices down). The opposite case, at low full employment, when sellers would like to sell more but the prices do not come down, is, however, not called repressed deflation but recession or depression. Perhaps depression is a compression of the two words repressed deflation. Our problem is one of "overrepressed" deflation. The monopolists do not merely stop the deflation from reducing prices; they continue to raise them. Or perhaps it is better to put this the other way round. There is not enough deflation (and unemployment) to stop the double monopoly completely from raising prices. We are above "low full employment."

Our monopolists are the suppliers of labor power, whom I shall call labor, and the suppliers of the goods produced with the labor power, whom I shall call industry. Labor sells labor power to industry, and industry sells goods to labor. Labor and industry are of course not monopolists in the usual sense of the word, in the sense related to the elasticity of demand for the output of the firm, but their behavior is what counts to us behavioral scientists.

Labor maintains at least a constant ratio of the wage to the cost of living (the price of goods) unless unemployment is severe. This is equivalent to a degree of monopoly or a rate of markup. (Markup is the excess of price over marginal cost, here the excess of the wage over some basic cost of living. Degree of monopoly is markup over price, rate of markup is markup over marginal cost, and the average variable cost is a proxy for marginal cost.) Industry competes vigorously, at least in its own language; but insofar as it operates with rates of markup we economists have a measure of its degree of monopoly.

The task of the guideposts is to enable the appropriate level of effective demand to yield us full employment with price stability, as in the "innocent" Keynesian theory. To achieve this the guideposts must get wages and prices to behave as if they were market determined. Fortunately we do not need to carry this to the extreme "neoclassical" degree that would make both monetary and fiscal policy unnecessary (by giving us automatic full employment via wage and price deflation). Since we can maintain adequate demand by monetary and fiscal policy it will suffice to make wages and prices behave as if market determined only within the narrow range that is compatible with our other objective—price stability. But even for this we must overcome the double monopoly.

This has of course been recognized by the administrators of the guideposts, but an overemphasis on average wage and price levels has led to the neglect of the relations among the different wage rates and among the different prices.

The emphasis was on stabilizing the price level by getting wages to rise in proportion to the increase in productivity. This is a loose expression generally taken to mean the average product of labor. But what is necessary for price level stability for a given rate of industry markup is that marginal costs should on the average remain stable, and that means that wages should rise with the average of the marginal productivities of labor.

The formula that wages must rise in proportion to productivity was naturally seized upon by workers in industries (or even firms) with a large increase in average product to claim a correspondingly large wage increase. The misinterpretation is reminiscent of the equally disingenous way Colin Clark's taxable capacity guidepost—that raising in taxes more than 25 percent of the national income leads to inflation —was perverted by businessmen into a warning against taxing any individual more than 25 percent. Like the businessmen's perversion, the perversion here was also properly denounced. But the correction usually took the form of insisting that the proper criterion for the wage increase is the increase in productivity not of the industry but of the economy as a whole.

This is the wrong correction. It does not indicate what the wage in the industry should be because it is the guidepost only for the average wage in the whole economy, and as we all know the average does not really exist. It is only a figment of the arithmetic. The wrong correction was taken to mean that no wage increase that exceeds the national average increase in productivity is in conformity with the guideposts and that any wage increase that does not exceed this average is in conformity. But this in strict logic implies that price level stability requires an absolute freeze in relative wages. The case is the exact opposite of the famous hotel porter, who when given what he had said was his average tip, gratefully told the guest that it was the first time he got as much as the average.

Guideposts for particular wage rates cannot be developed without considering the functions of differences in relative wages. One of these is to induce workers to go where they are needed more. Bringing this in makes it possible to give a reasoned answer to the workers in the high productivity gain industries. They can then be shown that if the reduction in the price of the industry's product made possible by the high productivity gain leads to an increase in demand greater than the increase in output per man, then more workers should be drawn into that industry from other industries and an above-average wage increase is appropriate. But if the increase in demand is less than the increase in output per man, then workers have to be drawn away from this industry into others, and the wage increase, if any, must be below average.

All this comes out even more clearly if we look at industries with below-average increases in productivity. If the wage rises at the guidepost rate for the average wage, the price of the product will have to be raised by the increase in the marginal cost, which is equal to the excess of the wage increase over the low increase in the marginal product. If with this price increase the demand falls or increases less than output per man, labor must be shifted from this industry to others, and a below-average particular wage increase is indicated. But if the product is a noninferior good on which a larger part of income tends to be spent as total income increases, and this tendency more than overcomes the rise in price so that there is an increase in demand, and the increase in demand is greater than the low increase in output per man (a combination that is quite normal, especially in the growing service industries), then more workers should be drawn into this industry, and for this purpose the wage must rise more than the average although the increase in productivity is less than the average.

Clearly what is creeping in is supply and demand, or rather the need for an artificial replacement for the malfunctioning market organ disorganized by the double monopoly.

The guideposts for particular wage rates must be expressed as rules governing departures from the central guidepost for the average wage. These departures can be based only on indicators of the conditions of supply and demand for labor in each labor market. Productivity gains can influence the guideposts only via their effect on supply and demand in the labor market. The wage increase should be greater than the average where the demand is greater relative to the supply than on the average, and it should be less where the reverse is the case. The departures must furthermore be such as will keep the average of all the wage increases in conformity with the central guidepost. Insofar as the upward pressures of the double monopoly can be relied on, the guideposts may be expressed as maximum increases. If we had double monopsony, they would be better expressed as minima. But they are really the desirable changes, and departures from them are no better in one direction than the other.

Until such rules are worked out and applied at least to the important labor markets, the guideposts can have only limited and temporary influence and are liable to be disobeyed, discredited, and destroyed as the pressures and temperatures of supply and demand inequalities accumulate beneath the procrustean freeze of relative wages.

This metaphor is not as mixed as it sounds. The guidepost practitioners, not unaware of the issues I have raised, have in fact been depending on unofficial departures from the guideposts, in both directions, in response to supply and demand pressures, to let some of the accumulated steam escape—thus thawing some of the freeze. But such departures are more likely to reflect organized power of pressure groups and relative lack of social responsibility rather than the social need for moving people between the different labor markets.

They have also depended on the mobility of workers in response to the relative ease of finding employment in different labor markets. But this is an effective adjustment mechanism only when there is severe unemployment and men are trying hard to find any job whatever. And even if there were such high mobility in response to the relative ease of finding jobs, a frozen set of relative wage rates would result in relatively large numbers of unemployed workers in the markets where the wages and the job conditions are relatively attractive, waiting and hoping to be hired, while the markets where conditions are relatively unattractive would be frozen with a scarcity of workers, a small output, high prices, and enormous profits protected from competition. In short, the prices and wages would fail to perform their social functions.

The reliance on such very poor substitutes for a real set of guideposts (which itself would only be a poor substitute for the missing piece of market mechanism) seems to me to be due less to the difficulties of developing the rules than to a powerful series of objections that would certainly be raised and the political difficulties that would emerge.

Perhaps the most powerful objection is the cry of "price control." This is not a logical objection, because price control prevents, or tries to prevent, a price from increasing when demand exceeds supply. It compels the price to disobey the market which is telling it to rise. The particular guideposts would do just the opposite. They would be reflecting the market forces of supply and demand and telling the wage to obey these—to rise more where there is a relatively greater excess of demand and to rise less where there is a relatively greater excess of supply—instead of serving the double monopoly. The guideposts would be interfering not with the market mechanism but only with the interferers with the market mechanism.

Another powerful objection is the cry that collective bargaining would be weakened by losing its primary task. the setting of wage rates. This is a more logical objection and no argument can shake those for whom collective bargaining has become an absolute good—an end in itself. But those who view collective bargaining only as an instrument for improving the condition of the people could perhaps be made to see that the guideposts would serve this purpose much better where the collective bargaining of a trade union has become one side of the double monopoly.

Closely related to this is the cry that government regulation of wages and prices constitutes a totalitarian denial of individual liberty. It is not easy to get the singers of such slogans to look and see if anybody's liberty to work or buy or sell is really being interfered with, or indeed any liberty other than the liberty of the double monopoly to hamstring the price mechanism.

Subject to severe criticism would be the apparent concentration on the regulation of wages, with the regulation of prices all but forgotten. This apparent one-sidedness is inevitable because average wages have to rise with average marginal productivity if average prices are to be stable. This means that there must be enough price reduction to balance the increases; otherwise the employer monopolists would be taking advantage of the wage regulation to increase their relative markup —an injustice which if not promptly removed would certainly destroy the whole guidepost attempt. The price guideposts cannot, however, be based on the relatively simple indicators of supply-demand relationships possible for wages—such as the percentage of unemployed or of unfilled vacancies. In general there will have to be reliance on competition to prevent any general increase in the rate of markup with investigation of complaints of prices rising more than costs or failing to fall as much as costs. This is the general problem of antitrust or antimonopoly with its various measures for increasing competition by outlawing restraints of trade, reducing or removing protective tariffs, unloading government stockpiles, applying more direct government influence as a large purchaser, and many other such devices, including as a last resort a greater activation of competition or threats of competition by government "yardsticks" or by government "counterspeculation" wherever competitors are being discouraged in spite of apparently high profit opportunities.

In this I would give more credit than I once did to the effectiveness of sermons by the administration, perhaps accompanied by hints of other measures up its sleeve to deal with sinning monopolists. The denunciation of a proposed steel price increase by President Kennedy seems to have been a prime factor in raising the level of low full employment.

In the regulation of prices and wages there has to be a symbiosis of legal with moral pressures. Laws which are not accepted as morally valid are not successful—as we have seen with prohibition—but the enforcement of appropriate laws can help to establish the customs from which the moral support can develop—as we are seeing in some fields of racial integration. In the matter of guideposts, the development of public opinion pressure can strengthen and in turn be strengthened by the use of sanctions to develop habits of compliance; and the crude wage regulations and competitive stimulants can grow into a more and more efficient substitute for the missing piece of the price mechanism.

We must remember that this is the way in which the familiar basic institutions of the free market were evolved. Richard T. Ely, for whom this lecture is named, first taught me that markets and money, prices and contracts did not drop from heaven but grew out of painstaking and daring innovation and experiment.

A sanction frequently proposed, both as a means of strengthening the guideposts and as an alternative to them, is for the authorities to declare that though they will provide all the effective demand needed for full employment, they will sternly refuse to provide any more under any circumstances, so that if prices rise there will be insufficient demand for full employment.

The argument is that if this threat is believed, both labor and industry will obey the guideposts, or refrain even in the absence of guideposts from raising wages and prices to levels that would result in inflation and unemployment.

This is not good advice because even if the unemployment succeeded in containing the inflationary pressures, these would only emerge with greater force whenever an attempt was made to permit higher employment again in the future. Second, the authorities would never be able to carry out the promised cruel and unusual punishment, and this being foreseen, the threat would not be believed. Third, even if it were believed, each particular trade union or industrial monopoly would feel that the future depression was coming anyway because of the wickedness of everybody else, so that its own restraint would only increase the ill-gotten gains of the others. And finally the use of unemployment or the threat of unemployment to fight inflation may work the wrong way. Just as in foreign policy, it is unsafe to assume that while we will agree to negotiate only from strength, the enemy, unlike ourselves, can be pressured into reasonableness. We may find him as determined as we are.

However, if the authorities made good their threats and remained in power and gained credence for their threat for the next time the low employment threshold was crossed, this would strengthen support for the development of sanctions for more complete guideposts to force everybody to behave in ways that would be better for all.

A particularly interesting variant of the "stern refusal" policy was recently provided by Israel. A sharp increase in concern for the balance-of-payments position led the Minister of Trade and Industry to propose a uniform subsidy on all exports, to be financed by a uniform tax on all imports. This was opposed by the Minister of Finance, who proposed instead to give subsidies only where really needed. A closer examination showed that the counterproposal was based not on economic illiteracy but on a recognition that a partial devaluation would quickly become a complete one, which would soon thereafter be nullified by a wage increase induced by "unneeded" profits. Behind this was the further calculation that it would take a long time before the bureaucracy would negotiate the discriminatory subsidies. Meanwhile economic recession, created by restrictive monetary and fiscal measures and unalleviated by any significant growth of exports, could greatly increase the efficiency of the economy by inducing labor to give up many featherbedding, job-protecting practices like "last in, first out" in jobs (which prevented useless workers from being fired). The leaders of the Association of Manufacturers were persuaded to support the counterproposal by astonishment at the labor organizations' agreeing for the first time to waive an increase in cost-of-living allowances and hope of being able to negotiate export subsidies for their own businesses.

The benefit from depreciation probably would be shortlived, there being no effective guidepost system, but it seems to me that continued depressions would strengthen rather than weaken the cost-increasing (and thereby employment-reducing) job-protection practices and do serious longer-term harm to the economy by reducing investment and the technical progress that goes with it. Nevertheless I sadly expect to see this experiment repeated in other countries. The British price-cool-off and wage-freeze seems to me to be one such case.

On the other hand persistent and successful maintenance of high full employment would yield a long-term benefit in reducing the average rate of markup. There would in the first place emerge high profit rates. The markups, adjusted by competition to yield normal rates on the average over good times and bad times, would yield superior profits on the larger outputs of the continuing good times. We can see this result in the sharp rise in profits during the recent increase in the level of output; and you must all have been getting literature from the labor unions which plays up this result of higher output as the root cause of inflation. But whatever we may think of its economic analysis, this literature reflects a pressure for higher wages in response to the higher profit rates.

Any increase in money wage rates induced by such profits by themselves only result in further increases in prices and a sharpening of the double monopoly inflationary pressure. But the high profits are visible also to entrepreneurs and would-be entrepreneurs. As they acquire confidence in continuing good times, some seek to exploit the prospects of adequate profit rates from lower markups. Such optimistic new competitors now escape the normal decimation that was their fate in the past during the recurring bad times, and their continuing competition brings about a reduction in the average rate of markup, lowering profits to normal. This gives labor a larger share of the total product (accompanied by false claims to credit for this by the organizers of pressure for higher money wages).

In the longer period, a more complete adjustment to continuing prosperity permits both real wages and profits to be raised by a reduction of expenditure on relatively inefficient but cheaper standby equipment for use only at peak output periods and by easier maintenance of continuous technological research. A greater supply of the less demanding kind of entrepreneurship that does not have to worry about depressions or recessions leads to a further, and this time parallel, reduction in both markups and profit rates. This increases the relative as well as the absolute share of labor and permits the average wage to rise more than the average marginal product.

We have a different natural hisory if administered inflations are combated by administered recessions. The short period effect of a disinflationary cut in demand is a cut in profits, from a fall in sales followed by distress price cuts. When adjustment had been made to the lower level of demand, the bankruptcy of weaker competitors permits somewhat higher markups to restore almost normal rates of profit with lower sales. And in the long run both markup and profit rate would return to the old norm.

We may speculate briefly on the general shape of our future in the absence of a more complete guidepost system. As the economy becomes more affluent, it is able to maintain an increasing proportion of unemployed at rising standards of normal decency. This increase in the "demand for unemployed" is accompanied by a parallel increase in the supply. Labor, scared by the growing unemployment, concentrates more and more on protecting jobs against technological progress, while the affluence makes them increasingly able to sabotage "automation" while demanding higher pay for fewer hours. This lowers the level of low full employment. It takes a larger percentage of unemployment to keep inflation down to any specific rate.

But how important is it that we succeed, by a completed guidepost system, to reach and maintain high full employment without inflation?

There is first the direct increase in the national product from having some 3 percent more of the labor force at work. This would mean a bonus of 6 to 9 percent of national product or some $50 billion worth of additional output. The bonus is the gap between low full employment national product and high full employment national product—an increasing fraction of the growing national income if, as I shall argue, the low full employment level (percent employed) is likely to fall over time. These figures are debatable, but even if they came to $100 billion, the mere increase in output would not add much to the happiness or well-being of the people of the United States. A Parkinsonian law of Veblenian conspicuous consumption makes men's urgent needs grow to absorb the available means to satisfy them. Perhaps the most significant direct result of greater growth and greater consumption at current American levels (of both affluence and poverty) is only the more rapid exhaustion of the mineral resources of the planet.

The second and much more important result is the indirect effect on the image of the West in the eyes of the challenging East and the uncommitted South. It would remove the remnants of belief in the Marxian theory that capitalism is inferior to communism because it must maintain a "reserve army of unemployed" to keep the exploited workers in increasing misery. It does not matter that the argument has been transmogrified to say that a totalitarian society is superior to a democratic society because it alone is able to regulate wages and prices for full employment without inflation. A successful guidepost system would vaporize the grain of truth in this, demonstrate the combination of these two objectives with two other great objectives, greater efficiency and freedom, strengthen (or perhaps one should say rescue) the esteem of the South for the West, and weaken the belief of the East, and even of the Further East, that the West is hypnotically moving toward its Marx-ordained doom. It would be an important step in the integration of order with freedom, which with the slow and intermittent growth of freedom within the order of the East constitutes the convergence on which the future of civilization depends.

The third result, possibly even more important than the second, is the social hygiene of full employment. The list of important social benefits is so long that it strains the credulity—but only until one sees them as the fruits of the removal of a miasma in which a multitude of diseases flourish. Among these diseases are the feelings of uselessness and failure, the unsatisfied need of being needed, with all the resentments and the further injustices that are set in motion by these frustrations, the fear of and resistance to innovation as a destroyer, the concentration on monopolistic, legislative, and other protections against competition, the unjust condemnation of the unemployed as unemployables, and worse still the conversion of some of them into genuine unemployables. Most important of all is the vicious and apparently inevitable concentration of the unemployment on underprivileged and alienated minorities, fostering undiscriminating hatreds as these develop their own subcultures of poverty and race in which they see themselves as victims of the "system" which owes them a living without work until they can get employment at fair rates of pay, which comes to mean the rates of pay of workers with skills and experience they do not share.

The fourth and crowning result is the way the first three cooperate with and magnify each other. The alleviation of the unemployment-nurtured diseases increases potential output, improves our image in the South, and fosters the acceptability in the East of coexistence over collision. The greater output makes possible an easier carrying out of the tasks, imposed on us by both morality and prudence, of helping the South break out of its poverty, and rehabilitating the domestic minorities so badly damaged by past injustice. Meanwhile the improvement of our image in the South and in the East, by increasing the prospects of peace, promises to set free still more resources for this spiraling cornucopia.

To enjoy these blessings from high full employment we must move on from having learned how to avoid severe depression. We must develop an operating set of wage and price guideposts to replace the element in the price mechanism paralyzed by the double monopoly—if only the threatening atom but give us the time to deal wisely with this our second most important problem.

[4]

From *The treatise on money* to *The general theory*

By ABBA LERNER
Queens College, CUNY

IN this discussion of the development of Keynes's thought from the *Treatise on money* of 1931 to his *General theory of employment interest and money* of 1936, I shall be concerned not with the actual comments, criticisms, and correspondence that took place but with the resulting contribution to a better understanding of the way our economy works.

Almost forty years of Keynesian economics have made it hard to understand why it was so difficult for all except some "cranks" to see (1) that the volume of output and employment depends on the demand for the products, (2) that the existence of serious unemployment a great part of the time must mean that demand is not automatically sufficient to absorb the potential supply, and (3) that an economic policy is therefore required to maintain a sufficiency of demand for prosperity.

It now seems to me that the difficulty can largely be traced to the multifold confusions of thought arising from ambiguities in the concept of "saving" or "savings" (*S*). This blessed word and symbol exuded thick fogs of mystical mischief in much the way that the concept of "value" has in Marxian economics. There, "value" is conceived of as a fluid (aptly called "sweat" by Champernowne in an old unpublished essay on Marxian economics) which is absorbed into the product from the laborers who worked at it, in proportion to the number of hours of labor applied. This "value" is carried forward from intermediate product to intermediate product up through to the final product. Each commodity thus has a quantity of "value" incorporated in it, proportional to the quantity of labor used up, directly and indirectly, throughout all the stages of its production.

Basic to the pre-Keynesian economics was the generalization to the economy as a whole, of the equalization of supply and demand for a particular commodity by the appropriate movement of the price in a free exchange market. By analogy, it was supposed that a similar adjustment would equalize overall supply and demand by an automatic movement of the general price level to a point where it would produce full employment. This was elaborated in Walrasian general equilibrium systems and celebrated in Say's law.

Various underconsumptionist cranks thought they saw a huge hole in the system, in that consumers did not spend the whole of their income. They saved some of it. Since anyone's income can come only from the spending by others in buying his product, the saved income failed to be recreated. Unless the underconsumptionist's remedy was applied, income would thus fall—perhaps even to the severe level of depression where there would be no net saving.

The economists naturally responded by pointing out that the underconsumptionists had forgotten about *investment* expenditures which could fill the gap. As long as the savings were all used for investment, there would be no underconsumptionist "hole."

This rebuttal was too easy. All that it proved was that income and employment were whatever they were, since the underconsumptionists' argument indeed implied that income and employment were less than what they actually were—that the total spending (which was creating the current income and was therefore equal to it) was less than the current income. But the response generally took the form of saying that the saving or savings provided the (physical) resources or the (monetary) funds required for the investment, and the two were not very clearly distinguished from each other. Like the "value" flowing from labor into commodities, saving was treated as an entity that flowed into and was needed for the investment.

The idea of saving as an entity or substance that had to be converted into investment, or incorporated in the investment, gave rise to the thought that perhaps the underconsumptionists had some-

38

thing. Perhaps here might be the source of the troubles of business cycles, of booms and slumps, of depression and inflation. With investment less than saving, the uninvested saving could perhaps become a kind of poison to the economy—"aborted savings" causing depression. Conversely, investment exceeding saving (miraculous bricks without straw?) could cause inflation or booms that had to be followed by busts. Thus Professor Hayek, for example, insisted that one must start by assuming a state of full employment—something that the established theory has already explained—and not from a state of underemployment which still had to be explained. A difference between investment and saving could perhaps be the clue to a departure from the full employment equilibrium position.

If saving (S) is to mean resources available for investment, it must stand for the available productive resources *minus* the resources used up in consumption. But S was also defined as *income minus consumption* ($S = Y - C$). Consequently the conception of S as resources available and necessary for investment had buried within it the assumption of full employment. The economists' response to the underconsumptionists proved not merely that income was what it actually was, but that actual income was full employment income, created by the full use of all the productive resources. Only in full employment did S stand both for the excess of income over consumption and for the resources available for investment.

The confusion could most easily be prevented by avoiding the use of the symbol S, and thus avoiding the danger of supposing that there has to be an entity—saving—because there exists a symbol. The word saving could, if necessary, be represented by "$Y - C$." This would have kept it clear that only C (consumption) and I (investment) are the actual phenomena to be considered, and there would be nothing to distract one from asking whether the sum of the two, Y (total spending), is more than or less than or just equal to what is needed for full employment without inflation.

A number of economists tried to escape from the ambiguities of S by changing definitions, while retaining $I - S$ as a possible clue to the determination of the level of employment or of changes in the level of employment. Denis Robertson defined Y as *the previous period's income*. He soon learned that the resulting $I - S$ was no clue to what would happen but only an unusual way of describing the excess of current income over the previous period's income. Swedish economists spoke of *expected* or *ex-ante* I and S and found that the resulting $I - S$ provided no clue but only an unusual expression for the excess of actual over expected income. Keynes, in the *Treatise*, redefined Y as "normal" income, but the resulting $I - S$ was only an unusual way of referring to an excess of actual over "normal" income or abnormal profits. But only abnormally high *expected* future profits (or abnormally low ones) could provide a clue to what would happen, and no simple formula can tell us what those expected profits are.

In the *General theory*, Keynes took an important step towards eliminating the pernicious effects of seeing S as a "substance" (and seeking astrological virtues in $I - S$). With rigid consistency he defined I and C as *actual* investment and consumption, Y as their sum, and S as $Y - C$. S was thus always equal to $I + C - C$ and could never differ from I. $S - C$ being thus always equal to zero, it could therefore be a clue, like double entry book-keeping, only to confusions of thought or mistakes in arithmetic.

There was incredible resistance to this logical consistency, and pained outcries from those who felt deprived of $I - S$ as a potential instrument of economic prognosis. But the virulence of the S-engendered confusions is demonstrated by its ability to infect even Keynes himself, although perhaps only when he was overworked and very tired. In a meeting at the Federal Reserve in Washington in 1944, Keynes expressed concern lest, after the war, an excess of saving might result in depression and stagnation. I suggested that any such depression could be prevented by increasing disposable income (*e.g.*, by deficit financing). Keynes retorted that this would only make matters worse since it would *increase* the saving. (This led Evsey Domar to whisper to me that Keynes ought to read the *General theory*.)

With S thus almost completely sterilized (as nothing but a conceptual arithmetic difference between actual income and actual consumption) it became easier to concentrate on analyzing only the actual constituents of income and sources of employment, C and I. For the former, Keynes, in the *General theory*, developed the consumption function and the multiplier, and for the latter he developed the marginal efficiency of investment (which he called the marginal efficiency of capital) and the determination of the rate of interest by the supply of money and the liquidity preference. This enabled him to have great fun at the expense of pre-Keynesian economists who, corrupted by spending much time in considering barter economies, used the expression "rate of interest" for the marginal efficiency of investment in a barter economy and then used if for both the rate of interest *and* the marginal efficiency of investment in a money economy.

By transforming the marginal *productivities* (of capital and of investment) into marginal *efficiencies,* he changed them into pure numbers that could be compared with rates of interest. The "bearishness" of the *Treatise* was refined in the *General theory* by separating out the time preference involved in eagerness to sell long term assets for short term assets from the liquidity preference involved in the eagerness to sell less liquid assets for more liquid assets. This made it easier to understand the possibilities and the limitations of fiscal policy in influencing consumption and of monetary policy in influencing the volume of investment. Taking all the risks and uncertainties surrounding investment decisions and concentrating them on the expectations that constitute the marginal efficiency of investment, leaving it to be compared with unambiguous current rates of interest, was a great help to clearer analysis. Another advance was the shift from considering the different *forms* of liquid assets to examining the different *motives* that contribute to the demand for liquidity. With such aids to economic analysis, Keynes, in the *General theory,* laid bare the forces that could generate an "equilibrium" with involuntary unemployment, if $C + I$ were insufficient to create the aggregate "effective" demand that would result in full employment.

A different conclusion having been reached, it remained to be seen just what were the differences in the theory that led to the difference in the conclusions. The underconsumptionists' "hole" had been plugged, and "$I - S$" had been sterilized by the consistency of Keynes's definitions. There began a search for the new element in the new theory that resulted in the new conclusion. This search turned out to be more baffling than the search for the flaw in the economic system that permitted serious involuntary unemployment. The search predated the publication of the *General theory,* and many clues to this search can be found in the *General theory* itself. The reason for the hunt being so baffling is that *there is no new element* representing a discarded old element in the old theory. There is no theoretical flaw, no logical error or inconsistency in the classical theory—at least not in the neo-classical versions that spelled out the part played by the increased value of the money stock in lowering interest rates and stimulating investment.

The Keynesian conclusion differs from the classical conclusion only because of a difference in empirical assumption. "Stickiness downward" of wages prevents the unemployment from reducing wages, and thus costs and prices, which would have increased the real value on purchasing power of the money stock, which would have lowered the rate of interest, which would have increased investment, income, and consumption until equilibrium would have been reached at full employment. "Stickiness downward" of wages is what prevents automatic movement to full employment.

To this, the classical economist naturally and bitterly cries "No Fair." He always knew that the automatic mechanism for reaching full employment would not work if wage rigidity, or anything else, stopped it from working. But Keynes denied that wage rigidity was to be blamed.

The trouble here is also semantic. Keynes explicitly agreed that a degree of wage flexibility (flexibility I) that sufficiently increased the value of the money stock would automatically yield full employment. He only insisted that the degree of wage flexibility that could reasonably be expected to be achieved in practice (flexibility II) would do more harm than good. It would not only be too late and too little, but would establish expectations of further wage and price reductions in the future with *perverse* results on employment. This was taken as an exoneration of wage inflexibility, lumping inflexibility I with inflexibility II. And so the hunt was on for the crucial contribution to economic theory, hidden somewhere in the *General theory,* that must be given credit for the crucial difference in the conclusion.

Quite a number of candidates were nominated for the honor of responsibility for the new insight, but all of them turned out to be either irrelevant or merely results of the recognition of the "stickiness downward" of wages. Some were even suggested by Keynes himself in the *General theory.* Among these were:

1. The inability of workers to bargain about their *real wages.* Accepting lower money wages only resulted in lower prices, leaving the same real wage, which was too high to permit full employment. This

candidate failed on both counts. With flexibility I, the classical automatic process would reach full employment via the increased value of the money stock from the reduction in wages costs and prices. Furthermore, this would be so whether the real wages rose or fell in the process.

2. A *liquidity trap.* This could prevent the rate of interest from falling enough to induce the volume of investment needed for full employment. But with flexibility I, the unlimited increase in the value of the money stock would fill any finite liquidity trap.

3. A *collapse of confidence.* This could inhibit investment even if interest rates fell to zero. But with flexibility I, the unlimited increase in the wealth of the owners of the money (and of the government bonds) would induce increases in consumption (and in gifts to friends and to good causes). These would provide sufficient demand to yield full employment even if it did not restore confidence in investment opportunities.

(A liquidity trap and a collapse of confidence would hamper a Keynesian expansionist monetary policy in the same way. But this would matter only as long as timidity limited the degree to which such expansionary monetary policy was undertaken. Professor Mintz pointed out long ago that no liquidity trap could absorb the monetization of the whole national debt, and if it did it could be fed the whole of the still greater private debt. But in some extreme situations a modest Keynesianism II might have to be replaced by a more daring Keynesianism I.)

4. The peculiarity of money in that it cannot be freely manufactured. It has a *low or zero elasticity of supply.* A demand for more money cannot be satisfied (except by a Keynesian expansionary monetary policy). But with flexibility I, unemployment induced by an increase in the demand for money would set in motion the mechanism that leads to full employment via the increase in the real value of the money stock. (If newly mined gold or silver increased the money supply, flexibility I, by making mining more profitable, would also increase the supply of money in nominal terms.)

This argument led Keynes to the conjecture that eagerness for ownership of *land,* which also cannot be manufactured, was responsible for depressions in the past. But there is no limit to increases in the price of land, so that wages can fall indefinitely relative to the price of land. The money wage in terms of land does have flexibility I.

5. The peculiarity of money in that even where it can be manufactured it has a *low elasticity of employment.* Printing money, and even digging for gold and silver, does not provide much employment. This is true of very many goods and is not so very peculiar. The significance of this element depends on:

6. The peculiarity of money in that it has a *zero elasticity of substitution.* "[I]ts utility is solely derived from its exchange-value, so that as the exchange-value rises, there is no motive or tendency to substitute some other factor for it." And "money is a bottomless sink for purchasing power, when the demand for it increases since there is no value of it at which the demand for it is diverted . . . so as to slop over into a demand for other things" [1, 1936, p. 231].

But these peculiarities of money have just the opposite result. If prices fall for reasons other than an increase in the demand for money, there is an automatic and proportional increase in the *real* quantity of money—in its purchasing power—even if the elasticity of supply is zero. The elasticity of employment is irrelevant because no more money is produced, and the elasticity of substitution is irrelevant because there is no change in the relative price of liquidity, a unit of which never changes in terms of goods in general (for the reasons quoted from Keynes above). If there *is* an increase in the demand for money, the supply of money *in real terms* will increase in proportion to the increase in demand. Until this situation is reached, the demand for more money continues to raise interest rates, increase unemployment and (with flexibility I) lower prices and increase the value of the money stock. Instead of a bottomless sink, money is rather a bottomless purse or "widow's cruse" that can satisfy fully any increase in the demand for money so that there would be no withdrawal of demand from other things. (This seems to be remembered by Keynes a few pages later where he says (it seems rather grudgingly) "The only relief . . . can come . . . from . . . a rise in the value of money which enables a given quantity to provide increased money services" [1, 1936, p. 234].

An increased demand for money is not an increased *flow* of labor or commodities offered for money at lower prices. It is a demand for a larger *stock* of money. It shows itself in a diminished readiness to *lend* money, an increased eagerness to *borrow* money, and an increased offering of securities and other *assets* in exchange for money. It does not directly lower prices. What it does is raise interest rates. This reduces investment and employment, and with flexibility I, this lowers prices and starts the movement toward full employment. Again it is only because we do not have flexibility I that any of these elasticities are of relevance.

A recurrent riddle is whether the Keynesian or the classical position deserves to be called the more general theory. Keynesianism can be said to be more general because it includes consideration of "stickiness downward" of wages and prices and the consequent steady condition of involuntary unemployment. On the other hand, Keynesianism can be said to be the narrower, because it denies serious attention to flexibility I. I would prefer to say that the classical position (as restated with greater care in response to the Keynesian challenge) is the more general theoretical construction, while Keynesianism is the more practical application of the same theory.

A more serious narrowness must however be charged to Keynesian economics when compared with the post-Keynesian generalization. The Keynesian integration of "stickiness downwards" into economic analysis made possible a better understanding and a better practical treatment of depression. But the formulation of the analysis in terms of the "wage unit" (the money price of the labor unit), hampered the analysis of inflation and the recognition of autonomous increases in the wage unit, *i.e.*, increases in prices not due to excess demand. When prices (in general) increase and the wage unit increases in the same proportion, there is no inflation "in terms of the wage unit."

The classical formula: "Increased demand causes inflation of prices and decreased demand causes deflation of prices" was changed by Keynes (and in my functional finance) to: "Excess demand causes inflation of prices and deficient demand causes depression" (deflation of output and employment). This is because of "stickiness downward." But "stickiness downward" is no explanation of why we do not have flexibility I. It merely states that we do not have it. The coexistence of depression and inflation, since it cannot be due to the coexistence of excess demand and deficient demand, indicates that there must be a cause of inflation other than excess demand, since the existence of depression is clear enough evidence that demand is deficient. This discovery weakened the acceptance of Keynesianism and set economists to look behind the "stickiness downward" and the "perverse" upward movement of wages and prices when there clearly was a deficiency of demand. This led to the recognition that *the market was not in charge.* It had been shown some time ago by Patinkin, in *Money, interest and prices* [3, 1956, p. 213] that while *the real wage* could not be below the marginal disutility of work and could not be above the marginal product, there was no necessity for it to be equal to either of these; and the further the economy was below full employment, the greater the possible range of the real wage between the two limits. It now became clear that *the nominal wage*—the wage unit—also had a greater freedom. It could move autonomously in response to such things as the expectation of inflation. The autonomy of the wage unit destroyed the autonomy of monetary and fiscal policy. A new ball game had been established in which only direct influence on the wage unit by an incomes policy, as a kind of splint on the fractured price mechanism, can restore a free economy working at a satisfactory level of employment.

Without an incomes policy to rein the inflation of the wage unit, we are doomed to suffer both engineered depressions from misguided attempts to check inflation by restrictionary monetary and fiscal measures, as well as continuing inflation as the authorities find that even while inflation is continuing unabated and even accelerating, they have to relax the restrictions if they are to avoid intolerable depression.

But this belongs to the sequel—the development of economic theory *beyond* the *General theory of employment, interest and money* as that book is understood by most Keynesians. The most persistent exponent of this development is Sidney Weintraub, who can find sentences in Keynes that indicate Keynes was often ahead even of himself.

References

1. Keynes, J. M. *The general theory of employment, interest and money.* New York: Harcourt, Brace, 1936.
2. ———, *Treatise on money.* New York: Harcourt, Brace, 1930.
3. Patinkin, D. *Money, interest and prices; an integration of monetary and value theory.* Evanston, Ill.: Row, 1956.

[5]

Reprinted from SOCIAL RESEARCH, AUTUMN 1977, VOL. 44 No. 3

From Pre-Keynes to Post-Keynes

BY ABBA P. LERNER

Pre-Keynes: With a stable money supply, economic prosperity and price stability require only that wages (and thus prices) behave themselves and adjust to the money supply.

Keynes: With sticky wages (and thus stable prices), prosperity requires only that the money supply behave itself and adjust to the wage (and price) level.

Post-Keynes: Both money supply and wages must behave themselves. For prosperity money must adjust to wages. For price stability average wages must rise only with productivity.

STAGFLATION, the simultaneous inflation and depression from which we are now suffering, is seen by many as a "paradox" that demonstrates the bankruptcy of economic science. I see it rather as a confirmation of the deeper economic understanding developed in the last half-century. This development has been from a pre-Keynesian overconcentration on microeconomics (which deals with the automatic market mechanism), through a Keynesian overconcentration on macroeconomics (which deals with government policy), to a post-Keynesian integration of macroeconomics with microeconomics to deal with the combination of depression with inflation.

The pre-Keynesian economics which, following Keynes, I shall call "classical" was basically microeconomics and had not integrated *money* into the theoretical system. It took prices seriously only as *relative* prices—as the rate of exchange of goods for goods in the "real" economy. The "money veil," which had led to mercantilist confusion of money with real wealth, was so perfectly transparent to the classicals that they could look right through it and see only the "real" or barter economy where the only prices are *relative* prices. The quantity of money in the economy was considered relevant only for the absolute price level.

When unorthodox amateur economists suggested that depression might be due to insufficint *total* (macroeconomic) demand for all the goods and services, because of "oversaving" or "underinvestment," they were confronted by the established economists with examination questions in microeconomics like: "Would not an excess supply of savings lower the rate of interest and thereby cure the excess of supply over demand?" The amateur economists, of course, always flunked.

In the classical scheme, there was no need for government concern about either inflation or depression. There was no danger of inflation as long as the quantity of money was kept relatively stable by the constancy imposed by nature on the total quantity of gold that had been mined over the ages. With the invention of paper and credit money this natural limitation to the quantity of money was replaced by legal limitations to the creation of money by private bankers (the reserve requirements) and by constitutional limits to the creation of money by the government. There was no danger of depression because of the (microeconomic) laws of supply and demand. An excess of the supply of anything over the demand for it would cause the price to fall until it brought the two into equality, and the market would be cleared. Involuntary unemployment was an excess supply of labor. It would cause the price of labor to fall relative to prices. At the lower real wage the market would be cleared and full employment automatically restored.

Keynesian Classicalism

Keynes's 1936 book, *The General Theory of Employment, Interest, and Money,* which inaugurated the Keynesian revolution in economic thought, began by pointing out that in the classical argument the reduction in wages was a reduction in the *real* wage in a barter economy. It meant that less of the product went to the workers and more was left for the employer. That was what made it profitable to employ more workers. But in a money economy it is only the *money* wage, not the real wage, that is subject to negotiation between workers and employers.

This does not matter in microeconomics. A money wage cut in a small (micro-) part of the economy would have no significant effect on the demand for and the price of the product. More profit would be left for the employer and it would pay him to hire more men and expand his output. But with a *general* reduction of money wages one cannot expect prices in *general* to remain unchanged. Competition would reduce prices in proportion to the reduction in costs. The prices of other productive factors competing with the cheaper labor would also be reduced. All costs, all prices, and all income could be reduced in the same proportion as the money wages. There would then be no reduction in the *real* wage and no increase in employment.

This did not destroy the classical conclusion. It called only for a further development of the argument in macroeconomic terms. Keynes provided this by turning from the supposed effects on *real wages* to the effects on *real spending.* The reduction in money wages leads to reductions in prices. As this does not cure the unemployment, wages and prices continue to fall. When they have fallen far enough to make the purchasing power of the existing money stock great enough, the owners of the money stock, now flush enough with money (as less and less is needed with the lower prices), will spend enough (or lend enough to others who will spend enough) to buy enough more goods and services to call for enough additional workers to restore full employment.

Keynes thus turns out to be not only the supreme classical economist,[1] who put the finishing touches on the classical edifice, but also the supreme monetarist in showing that the

[1] This seems to have been vaguely recognized by those classical economists who (insensitive to the sarcasm in the "enoughs") declared, "We are all Keynesians now."

completed classical theory is indeed essentially monetary. What happens to real wages plays no part in the completed Keynesian-classical argument.

Keynes's purpose in completing the classical micro- argument was of course not to praise it but to bury it. Spelling it out made it clear that the conclusion rested essentially on the increase in the real value of the money stock, and that the practical policy choice was between two ways of achieving this. One way was to suffer depression severe enough and long enough to bring about enough microeconomic reductions of money wages and money prices to bring about the required macroeconomic increase in the value of the money stock. The other way was to provide the same increase in the value of the money stock by increasing the number of dollars. The choice was between adjusting the prices to the money and adjusting the money to the prices. The latter method would achieve all the beneficial results of the former while avoiding both the depression and the injustices of the increased burden of all existing monetary obligations. The fundamental Keynesian revolution was essentially a *policy* revolution. It consisted of choosing the second method and calling on government to provide the additional money.

The Keynesian revolution thus pushed discussion from microeconomics to macroeconomics, and policy from waiting for automatic (micro-) market cures for depression to exercising governmental (macro-) policy to regulate the overall quantity of money (with an assist, in emergencies, from fiscal measures).[2]

[2] The highly fashionable contrasting of "Keynesianism" with "monetarism" arises from a misuse of the term "Keynesianism" for the *special* fiscal measures prescribed by Keynes (and by no means only by Keynes) in the depths of the depression when investors were afraid to invest. There was such a collapse of confidence that neither method of increasing the real value of the money stock would have helped. Only increased spending by the government, or by the beneficiaries of tax reductions, could have been effective in increasing spending and employment until investors' confidence was restored. Hence the call for *fiscal* measures.

This concentration on macroeconomics is even more obvious in my own formulation of the Keynesian revolution as "functional finance" with its three pairs of governmental instruments for regulating the overall volume of spending in the economy—borrowing and lending, buying and selling, and taxing and subsidizing.

The classical method of increasing the real value of the money stock is spoiled only by the rigidity of money wages. This is what makes the required depression too costly. Nostalgic classical economists are therefore intrigued with the possibilities of reducing the rigidity and letting supply and demand take care of the problem.

Unfortunately, the measures that could in practice be applied to diminish the wage rigidity, instead of making things better, make things worse. Weakening the trade unions, penalizing strikers, reducing unemployment pay, hampering credit to unemployed workers, cutting off school lunches, and other such measures for inducing workers to agree to (money) wage reductions work slowly and unevenly. The wage and price reductions are scattered and gradual. Instead of the lower prices which would cure the unemployment, we get falling prices. Buyers postpone their purchases in the expectation of bigger bargains later, reducing the spending and aggravating the depression. Keynes therefore approved of workers' resistance to these measures for lowering wages in general.

Much sport has been made of Keynes's inconsistency in blaming wage inflexibility for the failure of the classical automatic cure for depression, even while blaming wage flexibility for aggravating depression. But the two flexibilities are completely different concepts. *Ideal* flexibility would indeed yield prices low enough to validate the classical theory, but Keynes used it in his completion of the classical argument only to show its unpracticality. *Practical* flexibility, the kind that one could reasonably hope to reach in practice, was opposed by him because it could result only in the falling prices which aggravate depression.

For upward movements in wages and prices, Keynesianism remained perfectly classical. The laws of supply and demand did not work for a general deficiency of demand, but the law of excess demand lost none of its power to cause wages to rise in response to excess demand—that is, to an increase in total spending when there already was full employment. This asymmetry—wage and price flexibility upward but inflexibility downward—indicates that something was missing in the Keynesian revolution.

Missing was a microanalysis of how the determination of *particular* wages (and prices) is affected by the downward abrogation of the market laws of supply and demand. The answer is that wages are determined not by the market but by wage administrators—by the wage negotiators representing workers and employers, who have the power to command wages to stay up even when the market is telling them that they should be going down because supply is greater than demand.

Keynesian economic policy to avoid severe depression was beginning to be applied with some success in the '50s and '60s. Then the wage administrators discovered that their power to defy the market was not limited to keeping money wages from falling in the face of depression. They discovered that they could also use their power in the upward direction and get money wages to rise. And so stagflation was born—rising prices together with depression or recession.

What gave the wage administrators this power was something about the laws of supply and demand that had not been fully understood. Like the physical laws of Newton, the traditional formulation of the laws of supply and demand turns out to be not quite correct. They also have a "relativity" that had been overlooked.

In the traditional formulation, excess demand causes the price to rise and excess supply causes the price to fall, while equality of supply and demand keeps the price where it is. But this is correct only if the initial expectation is one of price stability. If the price has been rising at, say, 10 percent per annum and is expected to continue to rise at that rate, an excess of demand—a shortage of supply—will raise the expectation, replacing it by a higher expectation of price rise, perhaps 12 percent. A deficiency of demand will reduce the expectation, perhaps to 7 percent; while a clearing of the market, equality of supply and demand, would merely confirm and strengthen the previous 10-percent expectation. The price will not stay where it is. It will continue to rise at the previous 10-percent rate. It is only an understanding of this "relativity" that has made it possible for many countries to keep on functioning in the face of continuing inflation.

By the early 1970s extraneous events had brought about a rate of inflation in the United States of about 6 percent per annum which was generally expected to continue. It was kept going by the wages rising to keep up with prices, and the prices rising to keep up with costs. The same wage administrators who, with stable prices, had prevented wages from *falling,* now did exactly the same thing in real terms by preventing wages from *falling behind* the expected 6-percent rise in prices. And so the stagflation could continue.

Criticism and Modification

There were three different responses to the phenomenon of stagflation. The "Keynesian classical" economists, who had absorbed Keynes's completion of the classical argument but were reluctant to accept the Keynesian policy revolution, responded by hailing stagflation as a paradox with which the Keynesian revolution could be vanquished. The asymmetrical Keynesian theorem, that excess demand always caused inflation and deficiency of demand always caused depression, they read backward. They read it as saying that inflation is always caused by too much spending and depression is always caused by too little spending. From this it followed that the coexistence of depression and inflation meant that there was too much spending and too little spending at the same time. This is of course nonsense, so Keynesianism must be rejected as a mistake. In due deference to the departed, Lord Keynes was declared not really guilty of Keynesianism.

The government, also reading backward that inflation is always caused by too much spending (too much money chasing few goods), responded by trying to check the inflation by holding down the level of spending. But they were also partially influenced by the practical political wisdom that government spending and easier money create jobs. Under the combined pressures of desire to be reelected, some glimmerings of Keynesian economics, concern for the unemployed, and fear of ruinous business depression, they switched (temporarily) to (Keynesian) expansionary policies and increased total spending in the economy whenever the rate of unemployment threatened to reach double digits.

Keynesians, seeing wages and prices rising even though there was much less than full employment, realized that functional finance was not enough. Their response was to turn again to governmental macroeconomic policy, which had been so successful in dealing with depression, for a solution to the new problem of "premature inflation"—inflation setting in *before* increased spending had brought about full employment.

I was one of those Keynesians. In the middle 1940s I suggested that prices could be kept stable by certain regulations to stop wages from rising more rapidly than productivity.[3] In a series of lectures throughout the country I proposed some rules for differential wage adjustments based on the different degree of unemployment in different segments

[3] In a seminar at the New School for Social Research on "The Integration of the Social Sciences," later in more detail in my *Economics of Employment* (New York: McGraw-Hill, 1951) and with some further elaboration in my *Flation* (New York: Quadrangle, 1972).

of the country. However, the most frequent reaction was the "joke" that appointing all the administrators required for making the wage adjustments would by itself solve the unemployment problem, forgetting that these were already employed by business and by labor as wage negotiators.

My *Economics of Employment,* published in 1951, distinguished between "low full employment" when the unemployment, although too severe to be socially acceptable, was severe enough to prevent wages from rising more than productivity, and "high full employment" with only the "frictional" 4 percent or so of unemployment that could be reduced only by improvements in the structure of the labor market.

"Low full employment" surfaced again much later in Milton Friedman's "natural level of employment." However, I did not consider "nature" to be so omnipotent. I provided some suggestions for wage regulations with two objectives: (1) to stabilize the price level by awarding wage increases equal, on the average, to the expected average rate of increase of productivity in the economy (say 3 percent per annum) and (2) to bring about appropriate *relative* movements of wages by awarding higher wage increases in sectors where there was a less-than-average oversupply of labor (unemployment relatively low) and lower wage increases (or no wage increases) where there was a more-than-average oversupply of labor (unemployment relatively high). These ideas also surfaced later in theoretical discussions of "incomes policy" and in practical policies of "wage-price guideposts" under Kennedy and as "wage-price guidelines" under Nixon.

These policies were unsuccessful. There are a number of obvious reasons. The incomes policies were applied unimaginatively and reluctantly by administrators who did not believe in them and who had consistently declared that they could not work. So much emphasis was put on objective (1), the desired *average* increase in wages, that it came to be regarded as the universally legitimate, fair, and just rate of increase to which everyone was entitled. Objective (2), the adjustments in *relative* wages, was lost sight of. When a severe shortage of some special skill called for an above-average increase in a wage, this was resisted. The regulation, instead of working as a (crude) substitute for the price mechanism, became a price control—an interference with the price mechanism. It interfered with the mobilization of the scarce skills. When the resistance was finally overcome by a bureaucratic recognition of the necessity of an "exception" (or was evaded by the development of a black market), workers everywhere else demanded equal treatment. The regulation then broke down and incomes policy was abandoned.

But there is a more fundamental reason underlying the breakdown of incomes policy. This was the Keynesian neglect of micro- or market analysis in turning to macropolicy—to governmental regulations—to solve the new problem of stagflation.

The macroeconomic task of adjusting the level of money spending to the wage and price level by monetary and fiscal policy could be taken over by government because that does not interfere with the market determination of wages and prices. But incomes policy does. *Uniform* adjustment of all wages freezes *relative* wages and prices, and the market mechanism is immobilized. Continually changing conditions generate shortages and surpluses which remain uncorrected, and the regulation must break down. *Differential* wage adjustments for different levels of unemployment in different sectors does tend to correct the shortages and surpluses. But it is still an incomparably crude artificial substitute for the market. It mobilizes neither the specialized knowledge nor the personal interest of the man on the spot. The rules inevitably become much too complicated for general use long before they become sophisticated enough to be able to deal with all the different conditions which are effectively handled, in a market system, by the decentralized decision makers—the men on the various spots.

The need for mobilizing the incentives and the initiatives of the decision makers throughout the economy in the operation of an incomes policy was recognized by Wallich and Weintraub in their "Tax Incentive Incomes Policy" (TIP).[4] While maintaining the same *average* corporation income tax rate, this would impose higher corporation tax rates on different corporations based on the degree to which the corporation raised the wages it pays. Its tax rate would be higher the more its wage increase is above a national norm established by the government.

TIP constitutes a movement toward mobilizing the market micromechanisms. The corporations would weigh the benefits from granting higher wage increases against the costs of the higher tax rates incurred. The higher wage increases would be granted only by corporations which could pass on the cost (of the higher tax as well as of the increased wage) to their customers, and this would properly be where their products are more urgently demanded.

Inflation Pollution

A supplement to this scheme, suggested by Lawrence S. Seidman,[5] would impose differential payroll tax rates for different wage-rate increases *below* the norm (in the form of rebates on the payroll tax for more moderate wage-rate increases). This modification makes the scheme somewhat more like the proposal suggested by Professor Machlup, and put forward in my *Economics of Employment* (p. 239) "to make the excess wage payments nondeductible as legitimate business expenses" so that they "would come out of the employers' own pockets." It would increase the efficiency of TIP by equalizing the (payroll tax) cost of equal wage increases (for wage in-

[4] Henry C. Wallich and Sidney Weintraub, "A Tax-Based Incomes Policy," *Journal of Economic Issues* 5 (June 1971): 1–19; Sidney Weintraub, "An Incomes Policy to Stop Inflation," *Lloyds Bank Review*, no. 99 (January 1971): 1–12 and *Keynes and the Monetarists* (New Brunswick: Rutgers University Press, 1973).

[5] Letter to *The New York Times*, December 22, 1976.

creases below the norm). But I find myself more deeply indebted to Seidman for another contribution. He threw a sudden bright light on the whole issue by an astonishing statement of the obvious. He pointed out that raising average wages by more than the average increase in productivity is a pollutive activity bringing about the harmful environmental externality of inflation.[6] Inflation pollution is thus comparable to oil-spill pollution or noise pollution, but much more serious.

This applies only to *cost inflation* or *wage-push* inflation—the kind of inflation that is compatible with less than full employment. Where the inflation is due to excess spending—to attempts to buy more than the economy can produce—there is no externality to be internalized, no inflation-inducing behavior by individuals or firms to be discouraged. The obvious solution is for the government to eliminate the excess spending. On this the classicals and the Keynesians see eye to eye.

The same is true for depression. Keynesians and classicals agree that the cure lies in increased *real* spending, attainable through an increase in the real value of the money stock (except in time of economic prostration, with a liquidity trap or a collapse of investor confidence, when increasing the real value of the money stock does not help). They differ only on the *method* for achieving the increase in the real value of the money stock. Only when inflation is caused not by excess demand but by wage increases greater, on the average, than the average increase in productivity does pollution theory have to be brought in. *Raising wages by more than productivity is the inflation-generating activity.*

The recent innovation of turning to market mechanisms for protecting the environment from pollution permits a much more efficient and much more far-reaching mobilization of incentives than is possible with the differential tax rates just mentioned. It allows a finer graduation of the incentives in accordance with the urgency of the behavior they are to pro-

[6] Laurence S. Seidman, "A New Approach to the Control of Inflation," *Challenge* 19 (July–August 1976): 39–43.

mote, and it properly affects *all* potential polluters and not only those who pollute above some "norm." This should not be surprising because the development of the theory and practice of environmental protection is nothing more than a harking back to the prehistory of the market mechanism when freely available natural phenomena first became scarce resources. Exactly the same novelty must have been experienced when not pure air but land first became scarce. It was then that we departed from "that early and rude state of society" of Adam Smith's famous deer and beaver parable "which preceded . . . the appropriation of land." The imposition of a charge for the use of land constituted a shocking revolutionary innovation that violated what had been taken for granted as an inalienable natural right.

At the heart of environmental-protection theory is the social-efficiency principle that any act that damages anyone is justifiable *only if the benefit is greater than the damage.*

This condition is brought about automatically if the party who would be damaged by the act is in a position to veto it. The beneficiary from the act (A) will then have to compensate fully the veto holder (B). He will do this only if the benefit to himself is greater than the damage to B, so that even after paying B enough to persuade him not to exercise his veto—that is, enough to compensate him fully for the damage—A will still have some gain left over. The veto guarantees that the act will take place only if the benefit is greater than the damage.

But B's veto itself damages someone else. It damages A. By the same principle it too should be exercised only if the benefit is greater than the damage. Fortunately, this is also achieved automatically. The situation is symmetrical. The benefit (to B) from the veto is the avoidance of his damage from the act in question. The damage (to A) from the veto is the loss of his benefit from the act. The veto will be used only if the minimum compensation demanded by B is greater than what A is willing to pay, and that will be because B's benefit from exercising his veto is greater than A's damage from the veto.

Social efficiency is achieved even if B does not have veto power, provided A has the full power to decide whether the act should be undertaken or not. If the damage (to B) from the act is greater than the benefit (to A), the act will still be prevented because B can then fully compensate A for refraining from the act and still be better off than if the act were undertaken. If the benefit (to A) is greater than the loss (to B), B will not be willing to pay enough to get A to abandon the act. The symmetry is complete.

What is necessary for the socially desirable result, for social efficiency, is only that the one or the other should have complete power to decide whether the act should take place or not. The rest is done by mutually beneficial agreement between the parties. Whether it is A or B who has the power to decide does not affect the achievement of socially efficient *allocation* of resources among different *uses.* It is important only for the socially efficient *distribution* of income and wealth among *persons.*

Efficient allocation of resources by mutual agreement is also achieved automatically where an act by A benefits B while it damages himself. The act will nevertheless take place if the benefit is greater than the damage. B will induce A to perform the act by fully compensating him. B will still have some gain left. In all cases, those to whom the decision matters most get their way, either by adequately compensating the opposing side, to whom it matters less, or by rejecting the (necessarily inadequate) compensations offered.

By now it should be obvious that we have covered not merely what is usually called "pollution" but the market system as a whole. Just as pollution is just one more case of using up some part of a scarce resource, so is the using up of part of *any* scarce resource a case of pollution, a despoiling of the environment, by leaving less of the scarce resource for other uses. The purchaser of any good in a free market, just like the

B in our last example, has to compensate either the producer who would rather not have to work at making it or the alternative user of the good (or of other goods that could have been made instead). The purchaser is able to buy the good because it matters more to him. That is why he is willing to pay enough to get the other side, to whom the decision matters less, to make the good available.

Government and Market

This brings us nearer to our Keynesian-classical problem of determining when the government is responsible for the proper working of the economy and when the free market does the job, so that there is no need for government concern. But before we can deal properly with this we have to go back still further to the still wider question: When is government needed at all?

There is no call for government concern when a person does something for himself which does not affect anyone else, anyone *external* to himself. Indeed, any such interference by government is generally regarded as a violation of individual freedom. The same is true whenever two or more individuals engage in a mutually beneficial agreement by a free exchange of goods or services or other benefits, and nobody else is affected thereby. Again there are no externalities and no call for governmental concern.

Of course, government must first provide the conditions for the possibility of free exchange, but this too turns out to be a case of the correction of an externality, perhaps the most important of all bad externalities—namely, that involved in anyone "taking" something without due consideration of the deprivation of those for whom less is left over. In more usual language, the first responsibility of government is to establish security of property (private or public) and outlaw the use of force or fraud, including the force inherent in monopolistic and monopsonistic power over price. Anyone who wants to "take" anything will then have to obtain the consent of those harmed by the "taking." He gains the consent by giving something in exchange. In a money economy he pays money. He has to *buy* instead of *take*.

Protection of the environment has received more attention than improvement of the environment. Economists, faced with the popular notion that pollution should simply be prohibited, have pointed out that there is an appropriate degree of discouragement that would result in an optimum quantity of pollution. This is where the marginal social benefit from the activities which result in pollution is just equal to the marginal social harm from the pollution. Further restriction of pollution would do more harm than good. The optimum degree of discouragement would be achieved by the optimum charge per unit of pollution committed. The optimum charge is one that is just equal to the damage done to others by an additional unit of pollution.

In many cases bringing about the optimum charge for a pollutive activity calls only for extensions of the market mechanism to previously unconsidered scarcities. This means recognizing new rights of those affected, rights which enable them to participate in the deals. They can then bargain for possible benefits or for compensation for damages. What had been externalities are thus "internalized." The optimal degree of pollution has been agreed upon, and government can retire from the field.

But there are important cases where it is not possible to have all the beneficiaries, or all the victims, participate in the bargaining. It then remains for the government to act on their behalf and correct for the externality by applying appropriate degrees of discouragement to activities with bad externalities and of encouragement to activities with good externalities. Where there remain bad externalities which are not internalized by improved market mechanisms, government is called for to *impose* the optimum charge. Fixing the optimum charge will bring about the optimum quantity of pollution.

We are now ready to deal with inflation as a pollution. It is not possible for all those damaged by such inflation to get together to bargain with those responsible for bringing it about. It cannot therefore be cured by an extension of the market mechanism through the creation of individual property rights of "freedom from inflation damage." It is necessary for the government to step in and provide the discouragement of inflation-generating acts.

The Weintraub-Wallich TIP proposals and the Machlup-Lerner proposal move in this direction, but they compare unfavorably with the devices that have been developed in the theory and practice of environmental protection. They provide for higher taxes (to discourage excessive wage increases) only on firms whose wage increases exceed the wage-increase norm. But the norm is not applicable to the *firm's* wage increase. It is only the *average* wage increase in the economy as a whole which has to be kept to the average productivity increase in the economy as a whole. If the average wage increase is excessive, social efficiency requires that *all* wage increases be equally discouraged. The Seidman addendum does apply differential taxes for different wage increases *less* than the norm, but that still does not make the discouragement equal for all wage increases. Even for wage increases above the national norm, TIP would make the same wage increase much more expensive for a corporation whose profits are high relative to its wage bill.

Furthermore, all these proposals leave open the question whether the charge provides the optimum degree of discouragement. Its authors seem to have been concerned only with objections that the charges, set by government decree, would not be powerful enough. What is required is a discouragement of wage increases (when otherwise wages would rise more than productivity) which applies with equal intensity to all wage increases and which is equal to the marginal damage caused per unit of wage increase.

It is, of course, very difficult, if not impossible, to figure the marginal social damage from a unit of inflation-generating excessive wage increase, but this problem too has been solved by the environmental protectionists. If it is hard to figure the marginal damage from a pollutive act, which must determine the optimum charge, the *total quantity* of pollution to be permitted may be set instead. But the optimum *allocation* of the pollution still requires each polluter to have to pay the optimum charge. This problem is solved by issuing a number of "pollution permits" which, in total, permit the chosen quantity of pollution to take place; and having the different polluters bid for the permits. The result is that the pollution is concentrated in the firms where it makes possible the greatest saving of other factors of production or the greatest increase in valuable output. That is why those firms are able to outbid the others for the permits.

Fortunately, it is very easy to determine the optimum quantity or degree of inflation. By far the most common view is that the optimum degree of inflation is *no inflation.* This calls for the stabilization of that price level index which is of importance to most people, namely, the cost of living of the great majority, say, the 50 or 80 percent of the population in the middle with regard to income level (those between the lower and the upper quartile or between the highest and lowest decile). There are some other candidates for the choice of optimal degree of inflation, but the same procedure can equally be applied to any one of them.

With no expected change in the degree of monopoly (or its inverse, the degree of competition), average wages have to rise at the same rate as productivity to keep average costs and the price level constant. If productivity is expected to increase at 3 percent per annum, average wages must be made to increase at 3 percent too. Inflation or deflation of prices will then be limited to the degree of error in estimating the average rate of increase of productivity—a degree of error which is quite innocuous in this context.

Wage-Increase Permits

The government can achieve this price-level stability by issuing wage-increase permits equal to 3 percent of the annual wage bill, distributing them to the employers in proportion to their wage bill, and requiring every employer to hold a number of permits equal to the wage increase that he pays. The permits would have to be legally tradeable or hireable on a free market. Those employers who want to raise wages by more than 3 percent would have to buy or rent the corresponding additional permits. They would be able to get them only from employers who raise wages by less than 3 percent and are left with surplus permits. (Any employer who *lowered* wages would be entitled to correspondingly additional allowances of wage-increase permits, which he would sell.) The result would be that while wages could rise only 3 percent per annum overall, the freely operating market in the permits would enable the man on the spot to decide how much to increase particular money wages in accordance with the infinite complications of demand and supply on the different markets.[7]

With such a plan in operation the market price of the permits will depend on the degree of pressure for increased wages above the average 3 percent per annum provided by the available number of permits. With the fixed supply of permits the price will rise just as high as may be required to overcome

[7] The idea first came to me as a rumor that some such scheme had been proposed by Dr. Von Weizsäcker of Bonn. I was immediately reminded of Kenneth Boulding's green stamp plan for effective yet impersonal population growth regulation. But only when I got Seidman's illuminating suggestion of treating inflation as pollution did all the elements suddenly begin to fit together, like the excruciatingly easy last few pieces of a jigsaw puzzle.

this pressure. If there is little pressure the price will be low. If there is no pressure at all they will have no value.[8]

It might seem that the permits could become frighteningly valuable, since a permit for a $100 wage increase above the norm would last indefinitely. The higher wage would be an increase only in the first year. The permits could constitute enormous subsidies to employers who raise wages by less than the norm. This looks like a perverse subsidy to industries with low marginal need for their products. But the subsidies would not be perverse because they do not induce increased production. They *decrease* the output of these less urgently needed products by decreasing the wages there, driving workers to where the more urgent demand induces higher wage increases in spite of the added cost of the required permits.

The year is, indeed, an arbitrary period for our purpose. It seems, however, to be a reasonable time for the stabilized average costs to have stabilized average prices and removed the inflationary pressure for wage increases greater than productivity. The continuation of the higher wage would then not be so valuable. If the higher wage would call for a less-than-norm wage increase in the future, the firm would get some spare permits it could sell. But these would not be very valuable either.

With cost-push inflation thus treated as a pollution, once the administration and the policing of the wage-increase-permit market have been worked out (and there is no reason for supposing any insuperable difficulty), the problem properly returns to microeconomics.

The wage-increase-permit plan would, of course, be unacceptable if it led to an increase in the ratio of markups over

[8] If the pressures should go the other way—that is, if wages tended to rise less than productivity, or even to decrease absolutely—the scheme would have to be worked in reverse. *Deflation* of wages would then be the pollution to be combatted, and there would have to be permits for paying *less* than 103 percent of last year's wages. These permits too would have to be freely marketable. Such a scheme would have helped to prevent the falling prices that aggravated the great depression of the 1930s. However, it is almost certain that those conditions will never be permitted to return.

costs (which would increase profits relatively to wages). But there is little reason for expecting this to happen, even though it might appear unfair to have an incomes policy which holds down wage increases without a similar mechanism for holding down profit increases. But the latter is unnecessary because the markup is a *ratio* which automatically keeps profits in line with wages. The actual degree of competition, with all its imperfections, has succeeded in keeping the markup ratio, or the average degree of monopoly, remarkably constant. Any stepping up of the measures against monopoly and restraint of trade would have the effect of *diminishing* the profit share and increasing labor's share of the national product. But much more effective in increasing labor's share would be the intensification of competition when the cure of both inflation and depression makes business enterprise much less risky and a smaller profit per unit will be needed to make enterprise rewarding. The government will therefore be able to leave the problem of depressionary inflation to be solved automatically by the extended market mechanism—including the market in wage-increase permits—and concentrate on the correction of other social inefficiencies.

Social Distribution Efficiency

Among the social inefficiencies calling for government action are not only the social inefficiencies of *allocation* of resources among different uses but also social inefficiencies of *distribution* of income and wealth among different persons. Extreme inequalities of distribution make equal access of all to the market, and even the most perfect efficiency of allocation, more of a mockery than an engine for overall social efficiency. Where the benefit from the alleviation of extreme poverty is greater than the damage from the same dollar reduction in the taxpayer's income, the difference is the measure of the gain in social efficiency of distribution.

Such improvements in the social efficiency of distribution point in the direction of equalization of income and wealth. This must be limited by the need for inequalities as incentives for producing what is to be available for distribution. But the reduction, or in richer countries the elimination, of real poverty can be achieved without prohibitive loss of output. Output may even be increased by the alleviation of ill-health and production-reducing resentments. Improvements in efficiency of distribution cannot, however, be reached by the internalizing of externalities. There is no way in which the beneficiary can compensate the loser. The internationalization of externalities, whether through more sophisticated market mechanisms or whether through government charges or subsidies on activities producing good or bad externalities, work only for efficiency of allocation.

The effects of increased allocative efficiency on the social efficiency of distribution are unpredictable. There have indeed been some philosophers, and even some economists, who have assumed, without any basis, that the distribution that results from allocative efficiency, even if not a socially efficient distribution, is somehow "just"! Almost all economists have denounced this strange judgment, but that has not prevented economists in general from being unjustly charged, in leftist circles, with teaching it.

The institutions which increase social efficiency are the fruits of millennia of social engineering and the natural selection of the communities which were most successful in developing them. They range from the establishment of security of property, private and public, to the infinitely complex extensions and limitations of individual, group, and national property rights to encourage industry, inventiveness, and the accumulation of instruments of production and to measures to minimize nonfunctional inequalities of income and wealth. Extreme familiarity with these instruments often causes men to take them for granted, to attribute the benefits to the gratuitous benevolence of an "invisible hand" in contrast with current further development of the institutions as a different "visible hand" of public policy.

Micro-Macro

We have separated stagflation into its component parts: stagnation and inflation. The stagnation component (inadequate total spending at the current wage and price level to yield full employment) calls for macroeconomic governmental measures for increasing total spending. The inflation component, which cannot be excess-demand inflation, calls for microeconomic market adjustments of wages and prices, with the government only internalizing an externality by administering the wage-increase permits.

With the demarcation of the borders between macroeconomics and microeconomics, in theory and in policy, a peace settlement becomes possible between Keynesian and classical economics, between fiscalism and monetarism, and between functional finance and "sound finance." The peace treaty calls for a restatement of the functional-finance formulation of Keynesianism. The Keynesian objection to monetarism is only that it seems to be reading the world backwards in expecting a stable rate of increase in the money stock to succeed in inducing wages and prices to adjust automatically to the money—to behave in the way that would make that rate of increase in the money stock the appropriate one for full employment. But once the desired rate of increase in wages has been brought about by the wage-increase-permit market, and an adequate level of spending has been reached, prosperity with price stability can be preserved by—and indeed requires—a regular growth of the money stock equal to the rate of increase in output, with minor adjustment for secular changes in liquidity preference. The monetarist formula for the rate of increase of the money stock then becomes as Keynesian as it is classical.

From this it follows that the national budget does not have to be concerned with the total level of demand in the economy. Of functional finance's three pairs of instruments—borrowing and lending, buying and selling, and taxing and subsidizing—the first, borrowing and lending, can usefully be segregated and put in charge of the monetary authority—the Federal Reserve System's open-market operations. These can regulate the size of the money stock and thereby maintain adequate but not excessive total spending. The government can then concentrate entirely on its use of the remaining two pairs of instruments, returning to its fundamental role of promoting social efficiency, internalizing externalities for allocative efficiency, and alleviating poverty for distributive efficiency. Taxing and subsidizing are the means by which it increases both parts of social efficiency. Buying and selling are means for achieving the same objectives where direct government enterprise appears to be more efficient than subsidizing (bribing?) private enterprise to do the job.

The government must then consider that when it increases (or decreases) its spending this can disturb the monetary authority's task of regulating total spending. To avoid such disruption it must offset any change in its spending by bringing about an opposite change in spending in the rest of the economy so as to keep total spending where it should be. The obvious way is to increase taxes when it spends more and decrease taxes when it spends less.

This looks rather like the resuscitation of the traditional principle of balancing the government's budget. This principle was explicitly rejected by functional finance, which considered the maintenance of the desirable total level of spending in the economy a primary responsibility of the government. It followed strictly that the government could not let itself be diverted from this objective by consideration of the equality or inequality of the government's spending to its tax revenues. But that is no longer the case where the stabilization of the price level by the wage-increase-permit mechanism permits the regulation of total spending to be delegated to the monetary authority. Nevertheless, the *principle* that the government should balance its budget, if not annually then over some other time period, is *not* restored.

In the first place, even if the government feels that it must not in the slightest complicate the task of the monetary authority, it will not have to increase (or decrease) its tax collection by an amount just equal to any increase (or decrease) in its spending. When it increases its spending it will have to increase taxes by *more* than its increase in spending, taking account of how much of the increased taxes would come out of people's savings and not out of their spending; and similarly for decreases.

In the second place, the government does not really have to consider this at all. The monetary authority is capable of keeping *total* spending at the proper level in any case, bringing about the necessary opposite movement in private spending.

In the third place, it would rather seem desirable for the offsetting reduction (or increase) in spending to be met in part by taxpayers and in part by the borrowers of the money made available by the monetary authority. This would call for conscious collaboration between the Bureau of the Budget and the monetary authority in determining how much should be fiscal and how much should be monetary.

These three considerations, while rather upsetting to any *principle* of balancing the government budget, do not rule out the possibility of the budget being nevertheless balanced. But a growing economy needs a substantially increasing quantity of money and probably also of government bonds. The additional money and government bonds can be created only by government spending *newly created* money or incurring *newly created* government debt. This can come only from a continuing substantial *deficit* in the government budget.

The monetary authority, in taking over the lending-and-borrowing pair of functional-finance instruments in its open-market operations, can only increase the money in the economy by decreasing the quantity of bonds or increase the bonds by decreasing the money, keeping constant the sum of the two.

Part of the need for increased money and government bonds could be met by the expansion of bank money through bank credits. But this is only a reflection of the government's bountifulness in permitting the banks to run deficits themselves (when reserve requirements are reduced) or to appropriate for themselves the major part of a government deficit (when it is financed by borrowing from the Federal Reserve System, by virtue of the fractional reserve money-creation multiplier) and to enjoy privately the command which a deficit yields over a part of the national resources.

Only when price stability is being guaranteed by wage rigidity in a depression, and neither monetary policy nor classical wage and price flexibility can bring about enough total real spending for full employment, must government divert its spending and taxing and its buying and selling instruments from their proper task of increasing social efficiency and have them pinch hit for the impotent lending and borrowing instrument.

The fiscal measures are indeed very blunt instruments for this moonlighting, but that matters little in the "upside down" economy of severe unemployment. Labor and other idle resources are not really scarce from the social point of view (no matter how scarce they are for the victims of the depression), and this turns "the science of scarcity" topsy-turvy. In the upside-down economy *any* additional spending does much more good than harm. But the establishment of price stability by the wage-increase permits makes possible a monetary policy for full employment that can turn the economy right side up again; and Keynesians and classicals will no longer appear upside down to each other.

A More Practical Postscript

Although an additional 1 percent of unemployment is incomparably more damaging than an additional 1 percent of inflation, there is an important sense in which inflation is nevertheless the number one problem. This is because we are not in a position to choose between the evils. As long as inflation continues, governments will continue to treat it as due to excess demand, and they will hold down the rate of spending in the economy. This medicine will not cure the inflation but it will continue to give us high unemployment and the "paradox" of stagflation. That is why we must cure the inflation first.

In this essay I have attempted to indicate the most logical and most efficient means for offsetting the excessive pressure for rising wages (and thus prices). But the wage-increase-permit scheme is too rational, too simple and too obvious, and therefore too suspect, a device. It helps us to understand the issues, but there will have to be decades of debate before the practical problems of its application even begin to be seriously considered. The urgency of the problem therefore calls for an acceptable, if cruder, device that will fit in with our habitual procedures. The Weintraub-Wallich-Seidman TIP proposal is such a device. It would yield a large part of the benefits from a wage-increase-permit scheme. Limited initially to, say, the thousand largest corporations, its administration would cost no more than a few *million* dollars while the gain in national product would run in the *tens of billions* of dollars.

Any suggestion for an improvement does more harm than good if it unduly prolongs debate before action is taken; but I believe the following two modifications of TIP contain that modicum of rationality which would make the proposal *more* acceptable:

(1) I would consolidate Seidman's increasing tax rebate (for wages restrained below a norm) with Weintraub-Wallich's in-

creasing tax penalty (for wages increased above a norm). The increasing tax rebate (like all subsidies to combat pollution) consists of a lump-sum grant plus a tax per unit of pollution (here, unit of wage increase). Consolidation means giving each of the corporations included in the plan a lump-sum grant (which may take the form of a tax reduction) and imposing a charge on its average wage increase whether this is above or below "the norm." This means, of course, that there is no norm for the *firm's* wage increase. The intention would still be to achieve the *social norm* of wages rising in proportion to productivity and to make the sum of the grants equal to the sum of the charges.

(2) I would base the grant (or tax relief), as well as the charge, not on the *profit* of the firm but (as in Seidman's addendum) on a previous wage bill (adjusted for changes in employment). The charge paid by the firm would then be proportional to its average wage-rate increase times the base figure. This will prevent unjustified differences in the charge per unit of wage increase because of differences in the profitability of firms or because of differences in the wage share in a firm's total costs.

Such a modified TIP, unlike the wage-increase-permit scheme, would have no market indication of how high the charge would have to be to offset the excess pressure for wage increases. The charge, as well as the grants, would have to be set by trial and error, and there would be no room for possible fine adjustment of the number of permits for a *gradual* reduction of the rate of inflation, if that should be considered desirable.[9] With the high unemployment of our stagflation this cannot be very serious, but if it should be serious the device could be extended to apply to the largest 10,000 or 100,000 firms.

To many it will seem an advantage of the modified TIP over the wage-increase-permit scheme that the government could

[9] As suggested in my *Flation*, chap. 11, "Disinflation."

set the charge for wage increases for, say, a year at a time. This would make it easier for firms and labor unions to bargain about wage rates, having to worry only about what the charge will be next year.

However, the differences between the benefits from the "ideal" wage-increase-permit scheme, the modified TIP, and the original TIP, even without the Seidman supplement, are minuscule compared with the benefits from any one of them as compared with allowing the stagflation to continue. A suggested improvement that has the effect of delaying the application of some form of incomes policy would become a classic instance of the better as the enemy of the good.

[6]

4. KEYNESIANISM: ALIVE, IF NOT SO WELL, AT FORTY

Abba P. Lerner

Keynesianism is the *new way of thinking* about the economy which John Maynard Keynes promised to provide in his *General Theory of Employment, Interest and Money.* It was, of course, not a new kind of logic or some way of thinking "with ones blood" or anything like the mystical irrationalisms with which we are plagued today. Any genuine contribution can consist only of pointing out logical errors, of spelling out implicit assumptions or of changing the assumptions. Of these three, the first disqualifies the conclusions and the second opens up the theory to scrutiny, but only the third can lead to different conclusions. If the different conclusions suggest different policies to be followed, the contribution can be important in determining what those in authority should be not only *thinking* but *doing* about the economy. This is what Keynes had in mind when he bragged about what he was going to do, and I do not see how anyone can doubt that he did indeed succeed in doing this. The essence of the Keynesian revolution was to establish the recognition of the *responsibility of the government* to maintain a satisfactory level of employment in the economy – by showing that there is no effective automatic market mechanism for achieving this.

The recognition of this responsibility is frequently denied even by those in the government who are actively engaged in carrying it out. Thus, we have our President, as well as almost all the candidates opposing him, declaring their loyalty to the principle that the government budget ought to be balanced, but nevertheless planning or demanding large deficits as necessary for adequate employment.

Keynes also contributed in the two first ways. He pointed out errors of applying micro-arguments to macro-issues, such as taking Mr. Micawber's excellent advice for David Copperfield's private budget, and applying it to the budget of a sovereign nation, or crudely generalizing an individual employer's ability to vanquish his competitors and hire more workers, if he could cut the wage he pays, to arrive at the conclusion that a general wage cut would increase *general* employment. He also spelled out the implicit assumptions which underlie the Classical Economists' conclusion that there *is* a satisfactory automatic full-employment mechanism. But there has been a confusion between these contributions and the much more important one of establishing governmental responsibility for an adequate employment policy.

One result of this confusion was a reversal of the normal response by the old guard to any revolutionary idea. The normal response goes from "what strange nonsense" to "that's what we always said – or at least what we meant to say." But in this case the same formulas, instead of being used to claim that they had always held the new doctrine, were used to *misinterpret Keynes* so as to be able to claim him as a supporter of the old doctrine (in a more up to date model – improved by his clarifications of the implicit assumptions). Those who reject this claim are charged with the heresy of "Keynesianism" of which John Maynard Keynes himself is absolved.

As a consequence I am frequently asked by eager students, in hushed tones and with raised eyebrows, whether it is really true that I am still a "Keynesian." This bothers me and other Keynesians and this is what could make Keynes feel not so well.

But it is not a serious sickness. It is only a minor unpleasantness in the realm of theoretical disputations in the history of economic thought. In the world of practical policy, the basic Keynesian principle – governmental responsibility for an acceptable level of employment – is very much alive and flourishing. This is what must be credited for the unprecedented government budget deficits (for peacetime), thanks to which we are being spared the much more serious depressions that otherwise would be upon us. The more vigorous high-employment policy that would be possible is, however, in part held back by the aid and comfort which the shanghai-ing of Keynes gives to the crude micro-to-macro economic generalizations that are so natural to the businessman.

The situation reminds me of Mark Twain's report, in his "letters from the Earth," of Adam's first great contribution to science. He refers not to the Adam whose book is now enjoying its bicentenial, but to the Adam of Adam and Eve, and tells of how he discovered the Principle of Fluidic Precipitation – the law that water flows downhill, not up; and how the discovery of the law later got into dispute and the credit was given to a more recent person. Keynes' principle of governmental responsibility seems to be about as firmly accepted as Adam's law. I sometimes wonder whether it will have to be rediscovered all over again by a "more recent person" before it will be applied in full force.

To clarify these perhaps cryptic remarks, I will consider four steps in the development of the Neo-Classical Model. It was apparently built on, or at least constructed in response to, a part of the Keynesian analysis. First is a "crude Keynesianism" of the introductory chapters in macro-economic text books. It explains the level of income as determined by the investment and the propensity to save (alias the multiplier).

This is not Keynes' "General Theory" (which, we should remember, he called the general theory of *Employment, Interest, and Money*). It is a simplification of the General Theory that leaves out money. It was put forward by Keynes only for the special case of a deep depression when providing more money would not help. But so admirably did it fit the depression of the 1930s that it stuck in the minds of many who forgot the rest of the General Theory. Or perhaps they never learned it. As my mother used to say: "If you never knew, and you forgot, it is very hard to remember." Sometimes the term "Keynesians" refers to those who got stuck at this stage.

The second step brings in the supply and demand for money in the form of an LM curve to complement the IS curve implied in stage 1. Equilibrium now requires that for any combination of income and interest levels, not only must desired saving (S) be equal to actual saving and a desired investment (I) equal to actual investment (and thus I = S, since actual I and actual S are always equal), but the desired stock of money (L) must be equal to the actual stock (M) supplied by the authorities.

At this stage the model could properly be considered a synthesis of parts of the Keynesian and parts of the classical analysis. It is not really Keynesian since it says nothing about full employment or about governmental responsibility for it. It is certainly not classical since it is compatible with any level of involuntary unemployment and says nothing about full employment or about any automatic mechanism for achieving it.

The third step consists of repeating the classical declaration that unemployment will cause wages to fall, and that this will restore full employment. It also, incidentally, rehabilitates the classical conditions of full employment: equality of the wage to the marginal disutility of work and equality of the wage to the marginal (value) product of labor.

Keynes called these the two classical axioms. He rejected the first because his "General Theory" included less-than-full employment, and unemployed workers looking for work have a marginal disutility of work which is *less* than the marginal utility to them of the wage. But he failed to reject the second axiom, although it too applies only in full employment. Less than full employment occurs only in a depression when employers would love to employ more workers if only they found the extra customers to buy the extra product. It would increase their profits. But it would do so only if the marginal (value) product is *greater* than the wage.

At this stage the model is perfectly classical. But it does not show how the fall in wages would restore full employment. In fact the argument looks very much like the individual employer's crude generalization to the economy as a whole about wage cuts in his factory.

The fourth step, which completes the neo-classical model, consists of filling in the assumptions under which the fall in wages would indeed bring about full employment. The missing assumptions were provided by Keynes – or perhaps they were always there, implicit in what the classical economists "always meant to say." As spelled out they are as follows: Wages and prices and money income will fall, while the quantity of money does not fall (or at least falls less) until prices have fallen far enough to make the real value of the money stock great enough to make the rate of interest low enough to make the investment big enough to raise consumption and income high enough to result in full employment. In Keynes' words "it is therefore on the effect of a falling wage – and price-level on the demand for money that those who believe in the self-adjusting quality of the economic system must rest the weight of their argument; though I am not aware that they have done so."[1] And "If, indeed, labor were . . . to reduce its money demand . . . to whatever point was required to make money so abundant relatively to the wage-unit that the rate of interest would fall to a level compatible full employment, we should, in effect, have monetary management by the Trade Unions, aimed at full employment, instead of by the banking system."[2]

The explicit recognition of the necessity of these assumptions and their general acceptance is what led to the widespread announcements of a few years ago that "we are all Keynesians now" and to the Neo-Classical Model being billed as a Neo-Classical *synthesis* of Keynes and the Classics.

This leaves us with a puzzle. The "Neo-Classical Synthesis," with its assumptions as spelled out by Keynes, shows how flexibility of wages leads to full employment. Only an *inflexibility* would prevent the automatic mechanism from bringing about full employment. Why then did Keynes repeatedly insist that inflexibility downward of wages (and consequently of prices) was *not* the issue and why did he persistently assert that flexible wages would make depressions worse rather than better?

The answer to the puzzle is to be found in distinguishing between two different meanings of "flexibility." The flexibility required for the Neo-Classical model is an *ideal* flexibility that Keynes considered of no relevance for any problem of the real world. The spelling out of the implicit assumptions was undertaken by Keynes only in order to show up the ideal and impractical nature of the implied inflexibility, and all the more effectively to *reject* the assumptions and to dismiss any reliance on that kind of flexibility. Indeed he did not even find it possible to take it seriously. This is shown – though apparently not clearly enough – in the language he used when he tried to envisage its operation. He had to assume some non-existing institution like the "monetary management by the Trade Unions" in the quotation above from page 267, or to declare explicitly that "the assumption (of the maintenance of income in the face of a shift in "the demand for capital" or "the amounts saved out of given income) could only be saved by a *complicated assumption providing for an automatic change in the*

1. John Maynard Keynes, *The General Theory of Employment, Interest, and Money* (New York: Harcourt, Brace, 1936), p. 266.
2. *Ibid.*, p. 267.

wage-unit of an amount just sufficient in its effects on the liquidity preference to establish a rate of interest which would just offset the supposed shift, so as to leave output at the same level as before."[3] And even when, for the sake of an argument, he did assume ideal flexibility, he did not see it leading to full employment. Thus when he says "if . . . money wages were to fall without limit whenever there was a tendency for less than full employment . . . there would be no resting place below full employment," he does not pause at "full employment" even to put a comma, but continues with "until either the rate of interest was incapable of falling further or wages were zero,"[4] in the course of an argument on the necessity of some price rigidity for monetary stability.

The flexibility that Keynes objected to was not the unrealistic *ideal* flexibility implied or assumed in the neo-classical model. It was another kind of flexibility altogether. It was the *practical* degree of wage flexibility one could reasonably expect to be achieved by governmental policy. This kind of flexibility would be slow and uneven, with *falling* prices and expectations of further price reduction. It would only postpone spending and intensify the depression; and the policy would be abandoned long before prices were *low* enough and the value of the money stock big enough to start the movement towards full employment.

What I am saying here appears to many as a denigration of Keynes. I am in fact declaring that there is no new theory at all in the General Theory. Rather than finding the classical theory wrong, Keynes only fixed it up by filling in the tacit (or missing) assumptions. What kind of revolution is that? Not even any broken eggs for the omelet!

The answer is that it was a *practical* revolution – not a revolution in economic theory. It was more like the English than the Russian Revolution, killing fewer people and keeping the Royal Family with limited functions. The classical economists, just like Keynes, held that if wages did not fall, unemployment would not be automatically cured. The revolution was in thinking *what to do* – in the judgment that trying to create the ideal flexibility is impractical and that government action is required to increase *demand at the current prices.*

This makes many theoretical economists unhappy. Teaching

3. *Ibid.*, pp. 179–180, emphasis supplied.
4. *Ibid.*, p. 303.

economics consists so much of correcting logical errors that a fixation on logic becomes an occupational hazard. It leads economists to expect, nay to demand, some *logical* innovation in any respectable revolution. Because of this there has developed an active sport, among admirers of Keynes, of seeking out truly original theoretical contributions in the "General Theory" to lend authenticity to the Keynesian revolution. And among these Keynes himself was not missing. The hunt has turned up a number of unconvincing candidates for the prize for theoretical originality. Among these are: expectations in economic decisions, the demand for cash balances, the liquidity trap, the centrality of uncertainty in investment decisions, the equality of saving and investment, the propensity to consume and the multiplier. Occasionally incidental asides are offered, such as the euthanasia of the rentier, the desirability of more socialization of investment and the dangers of false liquidity creation and of destabilizing speculation on the stock exchange.

And then there are over-enthusiastic Keynesians – perhaps I should rather say over-enthusiastic anti-classicals – who are not satisfied with merely noting the non-existence of the foundations on which both the classical and the neo-classical edifices stand. They waste their energies in attacking the impregnable logic of the super-structure. This leads them to such exercises as denying the tautologies of Say's Law and Walras's Law; playing with fixed coefficients of production so as to escape contamination with marginal analysis (supposed guilty of improper and indefensible moral implication or of the improper philosophical sins of assuming perfect knowledge and perfectly competitive equilibrium); exaggerating the uncertainties of life, the vagaries of group psychosis and the flexibility of the monetary and market mechanism, so as to throw out the baby of rational public *policy for full employment* together with the dirty bath-water of the foundationless *automatic full employment*; declaring that all economics has been rendered obsolete by joint stock companies becoming multi-national corporations; or even outlawing all attempts at rational thought, by demanding that "everything be taken into account – dialectically."

At the same time a different game is being enjoyed by those who feel that Keynes had been given too big a hand. In attempts to solve the problem by denying the facts, some declare that the "involuntarily unemployed" are really employed in searching for better jobs, or that the unemployed are only supplying the demand for customers by the welfare- and unemployment compensation-industries. Others question the comparability of our statistics with those of countries with far lower unemployment figures. Some, mistaking symptoms of unemployment for causes, take employers' requests for diplomas (so as to reduce the crush of job applicants) as showing a genuine need for unavailable skills, while others cloud the issues by developing unusual terminologies for Keynes' concepts. Thus, Leijonhufvud elaborates an analysis of "quantity responses" (rather than price responses) to disequilibrium. I take this to mean that inadequate demand results in depression and unemployment instead of price and wage deflation, while Clower explains depression as due to "constrained demand" (because of reduced income) – a new name for depression.

Perhaps the "most unkindest cut of all" is the development, in Keynes' own Cambridge, of a "post-Keynesian" school which, in ideological or political revulsion against marginal analysis, finds in Keynes a (perhaps posthumous) intent quite different from both the Neo-Classical doctrine and "pre-post-Keynes" views like my own. Postulating that consumption (C) is approximately equal to the wage bill (W), they find that investment (I, the other component of the income created) must be approximately equal to profits (P, the other component of the income received). They then claim that this equation (I = P) tells us that the share of profits in income is determined by how much the capitalists decide to invest – as if the equations can not be read backwards to read that the level of investment is determined by the share of profits in income, or as if investment has no effect on consumption (C, which = W), or vice versa.

To these disturbances that tend to reduce respect for, and the influence of, the Keynesian Revolution, must be added a number of slips made by Keynes himself in the course of clarifying his thought while writing the book. One slip, mentioned above, was to retain the second classical axiom of the equality of the wage to the marginal (value) product of labor, which is required only for full-employment equilibrium. He also joined the fruitless hunt for a theoretically more exciting basis for the Revolution than the absence of ideal flexibility and the perverseness of practical flexibility. This led to an excursion (ch. 17) into "the essential properties of interest and money" where he makes the "own rate of interest" stand for the marginal efficiency (or rate of return) of *lending* an asset, for the marginal efficiency of *holding* it, as well as for the marginal efficiency of *producing* it. This results in a tangle worthy of Keynes' own sarcasm as displayed in his picture of Hayek as Ibsen's wild duck (p. 183) and in the crushing quotation which shows Hansen confusing the marginal efficiency of investment with the rate of interest in the course of warning his readers against this very confusion. (p. 193)

Another contribution to Keynes' current low Neilson rating is a quality that it is rather rash of me to pronounce. I refer to Keynes' timidity. He did not carry his conclusions all the way. I first was hit by this quality – to my great astonishment – when, at a lecture to the Federal Reserve in Washington in 1944, he showed concern that there might be "too much saving" after the war. When I pointed out that the government could always induce enough spending by incurring deficits to increase incomes, he at first objected that this would only cause "even more saving" and then denounced as "humbug" my suggestion that the deficits required to induce enough total spending could always be financed by increasing the national debt. (I must add here that Evsey Domar, at my side, whispered "He ought to read the *General Theory*" and that a month later Keynes withdrew his denunciation).

In Washington, where he was engaged in difficult international economic negotiations, Keynes was unquestionably overworked and tired. But in the *General Theory* the same timidity shows itself in his comparison of the Neo-Classical with his own recipe for increasing the real value of the money stock. Thus "just as a moderate increase in the quantity of money may exert an inadequate influence over the long term rate of interest, while an immoderate increase may offset its other advantages by its disturbing effect on confidence; so a moderate reduction in money wages may prove inadequate, while an immoderate reduction might shatter confidence even if it were practical."[5] The "Pigou effect," hewing unmercifully to the neo-classical logic, showed how a sufficient reduction in prices must bring about enough spending for full employment, but this is, of course, just as applicable to a sufficient increase in the quantity of money. But perhaps the "moderation" is not really timidity but a practical adjustment to

5. *Ibid.*, pp. 266–267.

the general public's allergy to logical extremes.

By far the most important source of the decline in respectability of Keynesianism is the emergence of "stagflation." This is not, as the name suggests, a kind of inflation – it is a kind of *stagnation.* Prices are rising but this is not due to excess demand being pumped in to inflate the economy – in the way gas is pumped in to inflate a balloon. What we have is a growth of the wage-unit; and in terms of the wage-unit any general rise of prices and wages is invisible. The wage unit – the money wage rate – rises together with the prices. To be applied to our present situation Keynes' analysis must be adjusted, or rather *translated*, from the *wage-unit standard* to the *money standard.*

It is not that Keynes was unaware of the importance of changes in the wage-unit. He spells this out very clearly. "Thus we can cometimes consider our ultimate independent variables as consisting of (1) the three fundamental psychological variables . . . (2) the wage-unit as determined by bargains reached between employers and employees and (3) the quantity of money . . ."[6] In speaking of the mercantilists he declares (perhaps over-generously, but that is another story) that "there was wisdom in their intensive preoccupation with keeping down the rate of interest . . . by maintaining the domestic stock of money and by discouraging rises in the wage-unit; and in their readiness in the last resort to restore the stock of money by devaluation if it had become plainly deficient through a rise in the wage-unit or any other cause." And he adds the footnote: "Experience . . . indicates . . . that there is a steady tendency for the wage-unit to rise and that it can be reduced only admidst a decay and dissolution of economic society . . . thus . . . a gradually increasing stock of money has proved imperative."[7] Yet when addressing current issues he naturally (in 1935) did not seem concerned about escalation of the wage-unit. "In the long run . . . we are still left with a choice between a policy of allowing prices to fall slowly with the progress of technique and equipment whilst keeping wages stable, or of allowing wages to rise slowly whilst keeping prices stable."[8]

This option does not seem to be available now. We have not been successful in preventing the wage-unit from rising faster than

6. *Ibid.*, pp. 246–247.
7. *Ibid.*, p. 340.
8. *Ibid.*, p. 271.

"economic progress" – the increase in output per man. As we use up our planet we may indeed be approaching a period of "economic regress" with *diminishing* output per man.

In our present situation an important Keynesian policy lesson that seemed to have been absorbed by almost all economists – that the quantity of money should not be reduced in a depression – is apparently being "unlearned." This policy lesson, properly understood, must be read in the wage-unit language. It is the reduction of the quantity of money, and consequently the accompanying reduction of spending and of income, in *wage-units*, that results in the reduction of the wage-bill in wage-units – which means a reduction of "labor-units" or employment. Yet we read every day in newspapers, magazines, and especially in the economic education provided as a public service by the large commercial banks and by the Federal Reserve Banks, that the wise and prudent policy is to increase the quantity of *money* by no more than some 5 percent per annum. At the current rate of price increase this is a *decrease in wage-units.*

It is such "unlearning" of a significant Keynesian lesson rather than any failure to have made a "theoretical break-through," or any failure to have found a flaw in the neo-classical logic, that would make Keynes feel not so well today. By the time he got to the end of his book Keynes seems to be giving up the idea that he has earned, or indeed that he needs, any diploma certifying a theoretical break-through or some logical innovation. His conclusion is: "Our criticism of the accepted classical theory of economics has consisted not so much in finding logical flaws in the analysis as in pointing out that its tacit assumptions are seldom or never satisfied, with the result that it cannot solve the economic problems of the actual world."[9]

Exposing the "tacit" classical assumptions to the open air leads almost automatically to their being discarded, and thus to the corollory that there is no satisfactory automatic mechanism for reaching and maintaining full employment. The practical conclusion is that the government has the responsibility, because only the government has the means, for a full employment economic policy. This lesson, though not as consistently applied, seems to be as firmly established as Adam's Law.

9. *Ibid.*, p. 378.

[7]

On Keynes, Policy, and Theory— A Grumble*

BY ABBA P. LERNER

In the Summer 1979 issue of *Social Research* three essays[1] are devoted to showing that in a recent article[2] I had completely misunderstood and misinterpreted Keynes's basic economic theory—in common with most modern economists, such as Hicks, Hansen, Samuelson, and Modigliani. Yet all three writers seem to be in agreement, almost all the time, with my main thesis. This is that Keynes's most important *practical* contributions lay in showing how unreasonable was the policy of waiting for the natural working of the laws of supply and demand to cure general unemployment.

Keynes had shown that the normal supply-and-demand argument was a microeconomic one which rested on the existence of many substitutes for any item. A fall in its price (indicating excess supply) would induce consumers to increase their demand for it by substituting it for uncheapened alternatives, and would cause producers to reduce their supply of it by shifting to the production of uncheapened alternative products, thus restoring equilibrium. But this argument is completely inapplicable to a decline in *overall* employment and

[1] Edward Nell, "Keynes as New Dawn," J. A. Kregel, "From Post-Keynes to Pre-Keynes," and Joseph Halevi, "Comment on Professor Lerner's Paper: A Marxist View," *Social Research* 46 (Summer 1979): 207–254.

[2] Abba P. Lerner, "From Pre-Keynes to Post-Keynes," *Social Research* 44 (Autumn 1977): 387–415.

economic activity because there is no alternative to "everything," either in consumption or production.[3]

Keynes went on to show that there is an alternative and logical argument that "theoretically" could yield the classical conclusion. If unemployment caused wages to fall, this would reduce prices and incomes; and if this went far enough, it would automatically increase the value of the money stock enough and reduce the need for money enough to make the economy liquid enough to increase investment and consumption enough to restore full employment. This logical argument of the theoretical automatic restoration of full employment came to be called "the cash balance effect."

Contrary to repeated charges by all three writers, I had neither assumed nor attributed to Keynes the hypothesis that wages are absolutely rigid downward.[4] I do assume, and also attribute to Keynes, the belief that the resistance of workers to wage cuts would lead to long periods of possibly increasing depression, unrest, and other troubles; and I accept his conclusion that a much superior method of increasing the value of the money stock is to create more dollars (or pounds.)

All three articles refer to statements by Keynes that *neither* deflation of wages *nor* increasing the quantity of money can cure depression, and we shall have to explain those statements, but it is only fair that Keynes be given the last word on the choice between the two practical policies.

[3] This is also clearly recognized by Kregel, who writes: "Keynes, in fact, believed that he had adopted, with minor modifications, the orthodox theory of price determination, while rejecting that its results could be extended uncritically to the economy as a whole" (p. 213, n. 8). This makes me wonder, both at his loud complaint to heaven, "How can it be claimed [apparently by me] that Keynes's theory creates an inviolate division between macro- and microeconomics?" and at his gentle rebuke, "Nor does it seem correct to intimate that the problems of prices and wages, individual and aggregate, were completely rejected by Keynes" (p. 213).

[4] I did indeed summarize Keynesian policy as "With sticky wages . . . prosperity requires only that the money supply . . . adjust to the wage . . . level" (p. 357) but my article makes it abundantly clear that "sticky" means "not flexible enough downward for the Pre-Keynesian policy to work."

We must remember that in his summary practical judgment Keynes's "flexible wage policy" means such policy as might in practice be carried out in England or the United States, not in some theoretical model which could reduce wages instantly and to an infinitesimal fraction of the initial level.

This is what Keynes says:

> While a flexible wage policy and a flexible money policy come, analytically, to the same thing, inasmuch as they are alternative means of changing the quantity of money in terms of wage-units, in other respects there is, of course, a world of difference between them.[5]
>
> Having regard to human nature and our institutions, it can only be a foolish person who would prefer a flexible wage policy to a flexible money policy, unless he can point to advantages from the former which are not obtainable from the latter. Moreover, other things being equal, a method which it is comparatively easy to apply should be deemed preferable to a method which is probably so difficult as to be impracticable.[6]
>
> Having regard to the large groups of incomes which are comparatively inflexible in terms of money, it can only be an unjust person who would prefer a flexible wage policy to a flexible money policy, unless he can point to advantages from the former which are not obtainable from the latter.[7]
>
> Having regard to the excessive burden of many types of debt, it can only be an inexperienced person who would prefer the former.[8]

And to make sure the reader realizes that all these disadvantages of the former—the disinflationary "flexible wage"—policy are due to the resistance to wage reduction in a democracy, Keynes warns us again on the very same page that:

> It is only in a highly authoritarian society, where sudden, substantial, all-around changes could be decreed that a flexible wage-policy could function with success.[9]

[5] J. M. Keynes, *The General Theory of Employment, Interest and Money* (London: Macmillan, 1936), p. 267.

[6] *Ibid.*, p. 268.

[7] *Ibid.*

[8] *Ibid.*, pp. 268–269.

[9] *Ibid.*, p. 269.

It is important to note that here Keynes unfortunately uses the same expression "flexible wage policy" both for the perfect flexibility in the power of an absolute dictator—or the manipulator of a mathematical model in which the wage is a free variable—as well as for the very limited flexibility which the government of the United States or of Great Britain could rationally hope to be able to carry into effect. This has given some critics of Keynes the pleasures of charging him with blaming inflexibility (i.e., lack of infinite flexibility) for *causing* unemployment and blaming flexibility (the existence of limited flexibility) for *worsening* it.

This brings me to my basic grumble. My argument—and indeed also Keynes's—is that the resistance of workers to wage cuts makes the "flexible wage policy" unviable. A democratic government that was foolish enough, unjust enough, as well as inexperienced enough to try the "flexible wage policy" would not be long-lived enough to conclude the experiment. Whether indeed other troubles would result from the "flexible wage policy" thus becomes irrelevant. The resistance by workers to wage cuts deep enough and soon enough for the policy to work is sufficient to kill the policy. But the three knights do not consider it sufficient to kill the "flexible wage policy" only once. They have to kill it twice more. They try to show that even with more wage flexibility the unemployment would still not be cured if the money stock is reduced, and then to kill it a third time by showing that even a large increase in the value of the money stock would not help if investors' confidence collapsed: "The content is a discussion of alternative policies, but *the point itself is theoretical*—primarily a difference in analysis" (my italics).

I am reminded of one of my mother's stories. The marriage broker instructs a tongue-tied boy on how to conduct a conversation when introduced to a prospective bride and her family: first you talk about family, then about likes and dislikes, and then one can expand into philosophy. After some hesitation, the boy says to the girl: "Do you have a brother?"

An abrupt "No" ends the attempt. "Do you like noodles?" tries the boy again. "No." A longer pause, and the boy turns to philosophy: "If you had a brother, would he like noodles?"

Whether the nonexistent deeper and sooner reduction in wages and prices would or would not have succeeded in restoring full employment seems to be "the point" in the same way as the preference of the nonexistent brother is "the point" of significance for "theoretical analysis."

My basic grumble is with the alleged contrast between theory and policy. I do not see how anyone can doubt that Keynes strongly advocated a policy of adjusting money to wages rather than the "flexible wage policy" of government trying to get the wages to adjust to the money supply. He gives very persuasive reasons for his advocacy, and this is what I take to be the meaning of theory.

Of similar basic irrelevance to the charge that I do not understand Keynes's theory are the three quotations from Keynes and Joan Robinson at the beginning of Kregel's article. These show that Keynes and Robinson had indeed heard of and not forgotten that there have been inflations, that they understood that a commonsense definition of full employment must refer to a level of employment short of the absolute maximum possible level of output (when the marginal product of labor and the competitive real wage would have fallen to zero), and that according to "some people" (not Keynes) capitalism is doomed because only severe slumps can hold efficiency wages within a reasonably stable range.

What still remains to be explained in dealing with the major theme of the "trilogy" are why Keynes can be quoted as saying that *neither* "flexible money policy" *nor* "flexible wage policy" can cure depression, what Keynes had in mind in referring to the possible co-existence of unemployment and inflation, and what are the urges that drive the three authors to such intense concentration on the "true theoretical revolution" in Keynes that makes practical full-employment policy seem insignificant.

The first puzzle clearly vanishes as soon as one remembers that Keynes was writing in the 1930s and not in the 1970s. The great financial crash and liquidity crisis of the very beginning of the Great Depression were clearly due to the Federal Reserve, in disregard of its basic duty as "lender of last resort," permitting a vast reduction of the money stock. The fall in wages and prices was thus doubly "not enough" to increase the value of the money stock enough to provide enough liquidity to restore prosperity. The actual fall in wages and prices created an expectation of further wage and price reductions, and the expectations of *falling* prices swamped the effects of the degree that they were already *lower* than in 1929 and led to further deepening of the depression. In the resulting collapse of confidence by investors, the increase in the real money stock which had meanwhile taken place became irrelevant. There was no *demand* for money to invest so that any politically acceptable increase in the supply would merely be added to the idle balances. Just like any politically acceptable decrease in the money wage, it would be "too little and too late."

Indeed, all the further troubles from the "flexible wages policy" turn out to be nothing but more and more of the "not enoughs." Any decrease in the quantity of money—which can never fall below the "hard money" or "outside money" in the economy, only calls for *enough* further wage and price reduction. The same is true of "flexible money policy" if, as seems to have been the case in the United States, the largest number the government could come up with for deficit financing for economic revival was $3 billion. This too was "not enough" until the war spending brought prosperity. Professor Lloyd Mintz's suggestions that the whole National Debt could be monetized was disregarded out of kindness, and when it was considered that even if indeed nothing whatever could be done to increase investment Professor Pigou reminded us that *enough* wage and price reduction would turn every owner of $1.00 into a millionaire in real terms and surely provide enough demand for goods and services for full employment. But enough of the "not enoughs." We will do well enough with Keynes's "last word" on this issue.

Keynes then turned to the only immediately available instrument in the special case of the liquidity trap—expansionary government *fiscal* policy. As we all know, this special emergency treatment came to be called "Keynesianism." This identification deserves the special title of "Bastard Keynesianism" and gave rise to the monstrous canard that for Keynes "money doesn't matter." What was true was that "flexible wage policy" and "flexible money policy" both failed because they were "not enough," as is clear from his dramatic condemnation of "flexible wage policy" in the quotations above. But his rather backwardly framed declaration—"There is, therefore, no ground for the belief that a flexible wage policy is capable of maintaining a state of continuous full employment, any more than for the belief that an open-market monetary policy is capable, unaided, of achieving this result"[10]—is not at all relevant to our present discussion. The key word is "unaided," which refers to the impotence of merely increasing the real value of the value stock, by either method, in the special case of the liquidity trap.

The second puzzle dissolves when we look at what Keynes had in mind when he spoke of the coexistence of unemployment with inflation. He was referring to what he called bottlenecks—"a succession of earlier semicritical points at which an increasing effective demand tends to raise money wages though not fully in proportion to the rise in the price of wage goods."[11] This is the unemployment that is part of any reasonable definition of *full employment* with no *involuntary* unemployment. These "unemployed" are the "voluntarily unemployed" who are not willing to work for their marginal value product and can be lured into employment only as long

[10] *Ibid.*, p. 267.

[11] *Ibid.*, p. 301, quoted by Kregel, p. 212.

as they can be bamboozled, by accelerating inflation, into believing their real wage to be greater than it actually is. This is described at length in Friedman's explanation of the nature of reductions below the "normal" level of unemployment. There is, naturally, no indication that Keynes, writing in the 1930s, had in mind anything like the coexistence of inflation with genuine, involuntary unemployment in an expectational inflation with total employment far below Keynes's "semi-inflation" of "bottleneck points" from overhigh use of capacity. In Keynes, "semi-inflation" increased employment required not only lower real wages but also increases in prices and in absolute as well as in relative profits in a theoretical movement toward "full inflation" where further increase in real output is impossible and the marginal product of labor and the real wage would have fallen to zero. Pace Kregel's declaration (footnote 17, p. 219), it is not expectational stagflation—as he claims—but supernormal full employment that is the "semi-inflation" of the General Theory.

I find it very hard to conceive that Keynes, who, in a regime of stable prices, saw so clearly how workers' resistance prevents wages from *falling enough* below expected stable prices to cure unemployment, would not have seen just as clearly, in a regime of *rising* prices, how workers' resistance would prevent wage increases from *falling enough behind* the expected price increases to check an ongoing expectational inflation. But Keynes did not live in a period in which such expectations were likely to arise. The nearest to his recognition of the problem that I am aware of is in the statement: "Some people argue that a capitalist country is doomed to failure because it will be found impossible in conditions of full employment to prevent a progressive increase of wages. . . . Whether this is so remains to be seen. The more conscious we are of this problem the likelier we shall be to surmount it."[12] Unfortunately, the problem appears to be seen by Keynes only as a problem

[12] J. M. Keynes, "The Objective of International Price Stability," *Economic Journal* 53 (June-September 1943), also quoted by Kregel.

of full employment or overfull employment—with none of the involuntary unemployment of "stagflation." Keynes refers only to the *voluntary* unemployment of those who are unwilling to work at the lower real wage required by a further movement past more and more severe bottlenecks toward the "perfect" full employment where the marginal product of labor would have fallen to zero. This is the region in which Friedman's inexorable "natural level of unemployment" rules.

I must resist the temptation of trying to solve the third puzzle—of trying to explain the powerful urges that lead to what seems to me such a bizarre misreading of Keynes. Nell merely hints at Keynes's "true intent" or "basic theory" that capitalism "won't work nohow." Kregel carries this considerably further while Halevi carries this far beyond my ability to see the relevance of his arguments. Perhaps the excitements of killing the "flexible wage policy" a second time because of a possible decrease in the money supply and the increase in real debt, and killing it yet a third time because of harmful effects on expectations and on investor confidence, make it difficult to remember that all the killings are directed only against an illegitimate *application* of microanalysis to macropolicy and in no way damages microeconomics itself. This causes them to conjure up "a complete abrogation of the market laws of supply and demand in determining the level of employment" and to replace these laws by a mysterious "theory of effective demand" which makes no use of markets or of money. In this, strangely enough, they are helped by Friedman's impeccable logic, even when deducing the most catastrophic policy conclusions from the most incredible assumptions, and the loan of his greatly simplifying axiom that changes in the *nominal* quantity of money (or in spending) have no effect on the *real* quantity of money (or on the volume of *real* purchasing). These arguments are, of course, perfectly appropriate in a "semi-inflation" accompanying any reasonable definition of full employment and leave the "revolutionaries" neatly, if somewhat uncomfortably, ensconced in a Friedmanian classical or neoclassical pre-Keynesian universe. But to go further into this would, I fear, drag my pen away from economic analysis to political ideologies and their fascinating way of meeting in extremes.

Another "must." I must commend Kregel for a sound criticism of the incipient anti-inflation policy hinted at in my article. He points out the inadequacy of directing the plan only at wages. In the two years that have elapsed since my article was published I have changed my plan from "WIPP" (a Wage Increase Permit Plan) to coauthor, with David Colander, a book called *"MAP"—A Market Mechanism Anti-inflation Plan.* "MAP" applies in completely symmetrical fashion to the earnings of capital and labor, to government and nonprofit enterprises as well as to private enterprise, and it permits adequate treatment of changes in capital-labor ratios. The book is to be published soon by Harcourt Brace Jovanovich.

In science there is always the possibility of being wrong, and incredible as it seems to me, perhaps Keynes was, after all, really a cryptocommunist who believed that the true essence of his basic theory was that an efficient economy could be reached only by the abolition of capitalism and the central planning of investment and the distribution of income, as the basic nonmarket determinants of effective demand. This "complete abrogation of the market laws of supply and demand in determining the level of employment" would seem also to leave the determination of individual prices to some unspecified device (like detailed central decision or Lange-Lerner socialized markets with no material incentives for effort or for enterprise that would affect anybody's income).

Whether or not this is really what "Keynes really meant" will not be known until the technology of psychoanalyzing the departed has become much more reliable than that of psychoanalyzing the living, but the importance of Keynes, as indeed of any contributor to understanding in any field, is not "what he really meant." It is what he has contributed to our understanding of the issues. I once had a professor of English literature who greatly enlightened me by his motto: "The important thing is not what Shakespeare *meant* but what Shakespeare *means.*" The great advances in the understanding of the operation of our economy that my Keynesian colleagues and I have derived from Keynes's teaching and its subsequent further developments I call "post-Keynesian," but it pleases some Marxoid Cantabrians and some New School economists to call it "Bastard Keynesianism."

*I am indebted to my colleague Professor Ervin Sobel for a number of improvements and clarifications.

C. Inflation, Money and Incomes Policies

[1]

MONEY AS A CREATURE OF THE STATE

By ABBA P. LERNER
New School for Social Research

A favorite pastime at the London School of Economics, where I was first introduced to the subject of economics, was the cruel baiting and tearing to pieces of Professor Knapp's *State Theory of Money*. The chief performer in this sport was Professor Gregory who spent several lectures at the beginning of his course on money in ridiculing Knapp's notions that the value of money derives in some metaphysical manner from the sovereign authority of the state. Gregory held with the classics that the value of money derives from the scarcity of gold and that this scarcity is impervious to declarations by government officials.

Later in the course the state managed to creep back quietly and unobtrusively through its power, via the banking system which it could control, to mitigate the scarcity of gold by economizing in the monetary demand for it. This was done by the substitution of currency and bank credit for gold thus reducing the demand for gold in relation to the supply. There was considerable development of the devices for such economies. Fiduciary issues of currency in addition to that which was backed 100 per cent by gold; fractional backing of currency which stretched gold further; the development of the banking system with the pyramiding of bank money on fractional currency reserves which were in turn backed less than 100 per cent by gold; the use of foreign exchange standards which permitted currency to be used instead of gold as reserves for central banks; and so on through a long list culminating with the temporary issue of "fiat" money, without proper backing, to deal with crises involving an urgent need for liquidity.

But the lesson of the first lectures on Knapp was never entirely forgotten. The money created or expanded by state action was made to recognize its inferiority to gold. It was merely a substitute for gold. Its value depended in the last resort on the gold backing or at least on the ability of the authorities to keep their promises to redeem the notes in good solid gold.

Since then we have been emancipated theoretically from the fetishism of gold. Nearly everybody who defends the use of gold in modern currency systems guards himself by saying that he is doing so only in order to be kind to somebody else's unreasonable prejudices. It is no longer a paradox to declare that the value of gold depends on the possibility of getting dollars for it rather than the other way round. And it is only from inferior textbooks that students are still getting the impression of some mysterious influence that gold exercises at a distance on the value of the currency backed by it. Even for those who have got no further from gold than to rest their emphasis on the quantity of money, it seems hardly more essential to explain the value of currency in terms of gold backing than to explain the value of gold in terms of its being backed by some still more primitive form of money, such as cattle or fish.

Money, as I have said in an article of that name in the *Encyclopaedia Brittanica,* is what we use to pay for things. The basic condition for its effectiveness is that it should be generally acceptable. Its transformability into gold and the guarantee of this possibility of gold backing (or any other kind of backing) are nothing but historical accounts of how acceptability came to be established in certain cases. These were possibly the only ways in which general acceptability could be established prior to the development of the well-organized sovereign national states of modern times. General acceptability had to be transferred in some such way from something which had already acquired it in the course of history. But if general acceptability could be established in any other way these historical methods would no longer be necessary or relevant.

This is just what has happened. The modern state can make anything it chooses generally acceptable as money and thus establish its value quite apart from any connection, even of the most formal kind, with gold or with backing of any kind. It is true that a simple declaration that such and such is money will not do, even if backed by the most convincing constitutional evidence of the state's absolute sovereignty. But if the state is willing to accept the proposed money in payment of taxes and other obligations to itself the trick is done. Everyone who has obligations to the state will be willing to accept the pieces of paper with which he can settle the obligations, and all other people will be willing to accept these pieces of paper because they know that the taxpayers, etc., will accept them in turn. On the other hand if the state should decline to accept some kind of money in payment of obligations to itself, it is difficult to believe that it would retain much of its general acceptability. Cigarette money and foreign money can come into wide use only when the normal money and the economy in general is in a state of chaos. What this means is that whatever may have been the history of gold, at the present time, in a normally well-working economy, money is a creature of the state. Its general acceptability, which is its all-important attribute, stands or falls by its acceptability by the state.

But there is another and much more serious sense in which the state is the responsible creator of money. The second most important problem that modern civilization has to solve if it is to survive the totalitarian threats to its existence is the prevention of severe inflations and depressions. (The first problem is, of course, the establishment of world peace before we slip into an atomic war by way of appeasement and/or preparedness.)

Depression occurs only if the amount of money spent is insufficient. Inflation occurs only if the amount of money spent is excessive. The government—which is what the state means in practice—by virtue of its power to create or destroy money by fiat and its power to take money away from people by taxation, is in a position to keep the rate of spending in the economy at the level required to fill its two great responsibilities, the prevention of depression, and the maintenance of the value of money.

Up till now governments have shirked these responsibilities, seeking refuge in an alibi of helplessness. The extraordinary complacency both of the government and of its critics in the face of the recent rise in prices can be appreciated only if one imagines what would have been the reaction to a government declaration that it was going to default on say 30 per cent of its interest and repayments to holders of war bonds and other government obligations. An equal despoiling of patriotic subscribers to war loans through the price increases does not prevent the treasury from still advertising government bonds as giving back $4.00 for $3.00. Nobody seems to find this dishonest. And even this denial of responsibility is as nothing compared with the way in which nearly all states have nearly all the time permitted depressions to begin, to grow, and to establish themselves without calling into play their power to create the money demand which would have made the depression impossible.

Before the tax collectors were strong enough to earn for the state the title of creator of the money, the best the state could do was to tie its currency to gold or silver which had a stability of their own that antedated the appearance of the state. By that policy extreme inflations were made impossible, and in a small country even small inflations (relatively to other countries) would be checked by the disappearance of the money in an outward flow of gold. By the same policy a limit was set to depressions. For the world as a whole they could not go below the point at which the available and fairly steady supply of gold-money became so redundant on account of the small volume of business (or possibly because of lower prices) that it spilled out into increased spending by somebody who was supersatiated with liquidity. For individual countries special conditions of foreign trading and lending might lead to much worse depressions, but on the other hand any further depression beyond that determined by these special conditions would be quickly corrected by an inflow of gold-money from the rest of the world.

The return to such methods now can only be proposed by exuberant Republicans who have not yet given a second thought to their meaning. The "margin of adjustment" involved in so crude a mechanism—which stretches from the limits of price rises within a gold standard to the level of depression that corresponds to zero net investment—have become wider still. The United States can carry much more inflation than we have so far had without running out of gold, while the level of unemployment that would be possible before a redundance in the supply of hard money came to the rescue grows greater with our growing productive competence and is now far beyond the limit set by the political conditions for the maintenance of a free society.

No government will be able to sit back and wait for the degree of unemployment which will result in the degree of price fall that will create enough idle money to induce sufficient private investment to start a movement back to prosperity. The New Deal and the war prosperity will have shown enough people that serious depression is dispensable. Some form of functional finance will in fact be practiced by whatever government we have. The only danger is that it will be too little and too late.

Less well worked out is a technique of dealing with the other responsibility of the creator of money—the responsibility for maintaining its value. The key points here are not in the direct supply of money, or even in the regulation of the level of spending. The key points are in the determination of wage rates and in the determination of rates of markup of selling prices over costs.

Wage determination by collective bargaining brought an improvement over the condition of the unorganized worker bargaining with a large employer in time of depression. With the abandonment of severe depression as part of the technique of influencing the determination of wage rates, and with the growth of trade unions to national and international size, the power of the trade unions has become too great for the purpose of determining wages by collective bargaining. Each union is forced to use its power to try to increase the share going to its members even though its more intelligent leaders know that what it gains is not from the employer, who can and will pass any wage increase on in higher prices, but from the population as a whole—which means in the main from other workers and their families. They also know that the other trade unions will have to do the same so that there is nothing left but a general inflation. For any particular trade union to restrain itself in the scramble may merely mean that it is left behind while the inflation continues. So that unless some alternative mechanism of wage determination is developed, a full employment policy will mean inflation. The acceptance by the government of its responsibility for preventing depression would seem to make it impossible for it to carry out its second responsibility for maintaining the value of money.

On the other hand it seems to be very likely that the Nathan report is right in believing that after the restocking boom the maintenance of adequate spending will be impossible without an increase in real wages; that is, in the ratio of money wages to the prices of finished goods. This is the same dilemma in a different form. Higher wages relatively to prices are necessary for long-run prosperity but raising wages will do no good because they will only lead to higher prices and inflation.

The dilemma can be resolved only by the government going to work on both money wage determination and on markup rates. Both are problems of monopoly and as such are inevitably destructive of a free economy. Markup rates must be reduced by antimonopoly measures of the kind that the government was working on when interrupted by the war. The most important help to the government in this will be the policy of maintaining full employment which will make it profitable for business to work with smaller markups. The effects can be speeded up by the government making the benefits of the full employment more immediately evident to producers by costlessly guaranteeing adequate (or even unlimited) sales of standard goods at moderate prices, releasing the energies and initiative of businessmen from the worries of selling to the concentration on efficiency in production.

The trade union monopolies must be tackled by establishing an artificial free market with compulsory arbitration for wage determination in which both the worker and the employer get a fair deal. Starting from some initial set of wage rates, such as the prevailing rates, wages in general can be raised by 1 per cent about every four months (on account of the secular growth in labor productivity) without the general level of cost and prices having to rise. This would be the basic money wage movement. In areas and industries where the level of unemployment is more than twice the national average the wage increase would not take place. Where the level of unemployment is less than half the national average the wage would be increased 2 per cent instead of 1 per cent.

This would have to be accompanied by measures to maximize the mobility of labor, removing all restrictions on entry to any occupations. The appearance of twice the national average of unemployment would then be evidence that workers consider the existing conditions in the area of industry more attractive than elsewhere, so that it would be fair for the increase to be forgone. Workers who insisted on the increase would in effect be claiming the retention of an advantage over workers in general.

Less than half the average of unemployment would be evidence that workers in general considered the conditions less attractive than elsewhere. A refusal of employers to raise wages by the required 2 per cent would then be seen as an attempt to maintain substandard conditions. In the end there would emerge a set of wage rates which would correspond to the workers' own estimates of the necessary compensation for differences in net advantages.

I have no time to defend these proposals. They are only intended as an indication of the direction in which solutions to these most pressing problems might be found. I will only make two remarks.

The side-stepping of collective bargaining will undoubtedly be denounced as an attack on labor. It is important to note that it will appear so only to those who in their thinking have completely substituted the labor unions for the workers, raising these instruments for improving the economic welfare of labor to the status of ends in themselves. We should remember that an end in itself is nearly always a means for some end which one does not like to mention aloud, such as the maintenance of the position, prestige, and salary of a union bureaucrat.

The second remark is addressed to another professional group—monetary theorists. I have gone quite a way from the traditional field of monetary theory. I find that this is inevitable if we are to begin to take seriously a slogan which we have been repeating for quite a while now. The problem of money cannot be separated from the problems of economics generally just as the problems of economics cannot be separated from the larger problems of human prosperity, peace, and survival.

[2]

THE INFLATIONARY PROCESS[1]

1. SOME THEORETICAL ASPECTS

Abba P. Lerner

I PROPOSE to attempt short answers to four questions:

What is inflation?
Why is it bad?
Why do we have it?
What should be done about it?

I

You will observe at once the hardly hidden assumption that inflation *is* bad, but this implication is not simply a way of insinuating my own prejudice. It will help in the development of the definition of inflation. For we want to take some action about the inflation, and that means that we think there is something that we would like to have otherwise — something that is bad.

In working toward the definition of "inflation" I shall proceed by the tailor's method of trying several on for fit, not because I think they will be satisfactory, but in order to diminish criticism of the final product. First there is the definition of inflation as an increase in the amount of money, but this definition was not able to survive the 1930's. The amount of money was then increasing very rapidly, but hardly anybody could be persuaded by Carl Snyder that we were suffering from inflation.

The second definition makes inflation an increase in the rate of spending and therefore of income, and nearly everybody is liable to say that anything that increases the rate of spending is *inflationary*. Yet we would not say that we are suffering from inflation as soon as we begin to recover from the lowest depths of a depression. Any influence is called inflationary if it tends to increase demand and deflationary if it does the reverse. These two words refer to the effects of any *event* within the economy in increasing or decreasing demand. They do not refer to the economy as a whole, and whether it is suffering from inflation or deflation. Inflationary events can take place during a state of deflation, and deflationary events can take place during a state of inflation, and in general we hope they will. Enough of them may even turn a state of deflation into a state of inflation. But if there is an increase in money demand that is accompanied by an increase of employment and output, without any general increase in prices, we do not say that we are suffering from, or even enjoying, inflation. We must not confuse a step in the direction of Jerusalem with the condition of being there.

According to the third definition, which is much more common, inflation is an increase in money demand in relation to the supply of goods and services so that the price level has to rise. But this is not really satisfactory either. We can imagine a state of affairs in which there is a continuous increase in money demand in relation to supply, and a continuous rise in prices but which is generally foreseen. We could then have rising prices without any of the evils that we dislike in inflation. The rising price level would be just offset by a correspondingly higher rate of interest. If prices were rising, say, at a constant rate of 10 per cent per annum, all the real economic relationships could be just the same as with a constant price level, provided the rate of interest were 15½ per cent instead of 5 per cent per annum. The relationships between debtors and creditors would be the same since the $115½ received in settlement for the loan of $100 for a year would be able to buy just as much, with a 10 percent price rise, as $105 would have been able to buy with a constant price level. The lender would know that if he wants to keep his real capital intact he must reinvest not merely the $100 returned but also $10 out of the interest and could consume $5½ with which he can

[1] Symposium at meeting of the American Economic Association, December 29, 1948.

buy neither more nor less than with $5 at the prices of a year ago.

Nor is it even necessary that prices rise at a constant rate, as in the example. No matter what the pattern of movement of the general price level, as long as it is roughly anticipated and the rate of interest is correspondingly adjusted, there will be no disturbance in the real relationships between debtors and creditors, no distortion of the economic processes and none of the evils that we are concerned about in connection with inflation.[2]

What is harmful about inflation is not the rise in prices but the failure to anticipate and offset them. Because of this failure there are upsets, disappointments, and surprises, undesirable distortions in production, waste of resources, injustices between creditors and debtors, and all the other objectionable features of inflation. The essential element that Hayek has seized upon as that hallmark of disequilibrium is the disappointment of expectations. This is what takes the matter out of the purely monetary world of changes in the price level, and results in *real* changes in production and consumption not anticipated and not intended by the people who suffer them. *People are induced to do things other than what they really intend.*

Workers may be induced by high or by rising money wages to work harder than they would if they were clearly aware of the shrinking purchasing power of money; consumers may be forced by higher prices to reduce their consumption and set free resources for other purposes; business men may be tricked into failing to make adequate provision for the replacement of their stock of capital goods. In all these cases the instrument for diverting people from carrying out their real intentions is an excess of demand over supply. This is the definition of inflation I wish to use — *an excess of demand over supply.*

In the case of the foreseen price rise there is no excess of demand. People expect to spend more money in the future, but they also expect to pay the higher prices. The expected demand can be equal to the expected supply. The essence of inflation is the excess of demand, the expectation or intention of buying more than will be available to be bought, that must result in disappointment and the disruption of plans.

Furthermore, rising prices are not only insufficient to indicate inflation; they are also unnecessary. We can not only have rising prices without inflation (as in the example above of a foreseen rise in prices) but we can have inflation without rising prices. Prices may fail to rise even though there is excess demand, and in that case it is even much easier to see the excess demand.

The price may stay down because the sellers decide not to raise the price, as in the case of automobiles, or because the buyers refuse to pay more than a "fair" price, as has been alleged to be the case sometimes in the demand for labor, or because the price is kept down by a third party, as when price ceilings are imposed by the government. In all such cases there is an excess demand which results in some people being disappointed and forced to act contrary to their intentions. This has been called "suppressed" inflation by Röpke and others, as distinct from "open" inflation when prices are not prevented from rising.

In the case of "open" inflation the excess demand is not seen so clearly as in the case of "suppressed" inflation. Current demand is equal to the current supply, prices rising as much as may be needed to clear the market. Yet this clearing of the market is not an equilibrium except in the empty sense in which the supply is always equal to the demand because it is nothing but the same transaction seen from the other side. There is no real equilibrium because the buyer's expectations are not fulfilled. The higher prices that clear the market are not those anticipated by the buyer,

[2] Symmetry demands that falling prices would not imply deflation or deficiency of demand if the price fall is accurately anticipated so that there are no surprises. This is, however, even more difficult to imagine or to hope to arrange because the rate of interest has to be correspondingly *lowered* and this means an impossibly low or a negative rate of interest even for moderate rates of fall of prices. If prices are falling at 10 per cent per annum and the appropriate rate of interest for a stable price level is 5 per cent, the required rate of interest would have to be about *minus* 5½ per cent. $100 borrowed a year ago could be settled, including interest, for $94½ which, with the 10 per cent price fall, would be able to buy as much as $105 a year ago. However, if the appropriate negative rate of interest could be established, say, by a tax on holding money, falling prices, if anticipated, would not mean there was deficiency of demand or deflation.

and he buys less than he expected to be able to buy when he was working for the money he now spends. There is a gap between expected prices and the higher actual prices, and between expected purchases and the lower actual purchases.

The gap is sometimes said to be due to a lag. The lag, however, is not in the price rise but in the *expectation* of the price rise. The expectation always lags behind the reality so that the purchasing power, the power to obtain goods, lags behind the spending power, the power to spend dollars. The disappointment at the purchasing power of the dollars results in demands for higher earnings, which are again doomed to disappointment when the increased spending power is still unable to purchase more goods than are available. The expectations lag performs the same function as stabilized prices in keeping demand in excess of supply.

The cumulative spiralling rise in prices and incomes is merely a result of the attempt to overcome the lag in expectations. During the course of the inflation there is a kind of equilibrium in which the rate at which prices and income are rising is determined by the expectations lag. If the lag were constant, prices and income would rise at a constant rate. The response increases in rapidity and magnitude. The acceleration grows at ever increasing rates; and the expectations are always pushing the actual prices ahead of themselves, even if the inflation is allowed to develop into hyperinflation of the kind experienced in Germany and Hungary.

The fundamental difference between "open" and "repressed" inflation is that the former maintains the excess demand by fraud while the latter maintains the excess demand by force; the former utilizes the optical illusion of expectations unable to keep up with reality, while the latter firmly holds down the price in the face of excess demand. (A stable black market, where prices are neither controlled nor rising, is just where there is *no* inflation.) Both controlled prices and rising prices maintain an excess demand so that in neither case is the rational classical price mechanism permitted to govern the distribution of scarce goods among the applicants. Instead the distribution is decided by the skill or good fortune of individuals in happening to get ahead of the others in their expectations of price rises or in getting to the head of the line, or in finding favor with whatever substitute rationing device takes the place of the price mechanism.

I am encouraged in suggesting this definition of inflation by the observation that it removes a disturbing asymmetry. I refer to the limping contrast between inflation and depression. Now we no longer have to consider unemployment as the opposite of rising prices. Inflation as an excess of demand corresponds perfectly to deflation as a deficiency of demand. Deflation may lead to falling prices just as inflation may lead to rising prices. In the absence of rigidities, falling prices might lead to a hyperdeflation which would be as much more devastating than a hyperinflation, as a mild deflation with a twenty per cent deficiency of demand is more devastating than a mild inflation with a twenty-five per cent excess demand. We should remember that the deflation of the thirties was of the same order of magnitude as the inflation we have been experiencing since the end of the war. When rigidities prevent prices from falling in spite of deficient demand, this does not of itself cure the deflation, which can show itself with even greater clarity in the lack of demand that causes the unemployment depression with stable prices. When price rigidities or price controls prevent prices from rising in spite of excess demand, this does not cure the inflation, which shows itself even more clearly in the unsatisfied demand for scarce goods and in the development of rationing or other means of determining how they are to be allocated. Depression is the name for deflation with prices prevented from falling. Inflation with prices prevented from rising has been called suppressed inflation. Perhaps the symmetry could be expressed by giving the name of *suppression* to this opposite of depression, for it is not the inflation that is suppressed any more than deflation is absent in depression with stable prices. It is only the rise in prices that is suppressed, the underlying inflation or excess demand remaining as strong as ever. Suppression is merely a particular kind of inflation just as depression is a particular kind of deflation. Inflation is excess demand. Suppression is inflation in which the excess demand is prevented from raising prices.[3]

II

The second question, "Why is inflation bad?", has already been answered in part. By force or by fraud it frustrates the choice of consumers in the distribution of their income between its various uses. By sabotaging the price mechanism it clouds the judgement of all users of resources and frustrates their socially valuable tendency to be more economical of resources that are more useful in other parts of the economy. Such resources are no longer necessarily more costly to use. Inflation is unjust. Open inflation is unjust to creditors. Suppression is unjust to those who are excluded by the substitute rationing mechanism. Open inflation endangers democracy by ruining the middle class. Suppression threatens democracy by the development of bureaucracies. Inflation is bad because it sabotages one of the most valuable instruments of modern society — the price mechanism. The injustices, the inefficiency and the dangers to democracy are only some of the results of this sabotage.

The most popular argument against inflation is that it harbors the germs of deflation and depression. Inflation, it is said, has always been followed by depression. If we permit a boom we will have to suffer the bust. I cannot see any validity in this argument, however excellent its objective. If we can have a policy of preventing or checking inflation, we can with no more difficulty have a policy of preventing deflation when we have stopped the inflation. The very same machinery does the trick if switched to reverse.

It is true that if an open inflation is stopped in its tracks by a determined refusal to increase the amount of money, the removal of the expectation of further price increases stops the flight from money into goods and the attempt to rebuild money stocks to normal will cause a *reduction* in spending and the possibility of a very serious deflation. But this only proves that a simple halting of the monetary printing press is not a good way of stopping an open inflation that has raised the velocity above normal. What has to be stabilized is the rate of spending, perhaps by stabilizing the level of money income. The difficulty arises only from the primitive failure to distinguish income from money which has been preserved to plague us to this day by the concept of the velocity of circulation. Our quaint use of the complex symbol, MV, for the unitary concept of income, inevitably gives students and politicians, who have learned that M stands for money, the false impression that V is an independent multiplicand. Actually, V is nothing but a symbol saying that we should speak of income and not of money, but by "correcting" it preserves the idea it was intended to destroy — the idea that income is the same thing as money. And then the observation that stabilizing money may not stabilize income makes the stabilizing of income look almost impossible. To avoid this confusion it is necessary only to remember that the objective is the stabilization of *income* or more accurately of *outgo* or *spending*, and anything that is done about money should be entirely incidental.

There is more validity to the idea that open inflation, by reducing the value in real terms of the stock of money and of monetary claims on the government, "uses up" this stock of wealth and liquidity so that when the inflation comes to an end the community, feeling itself poorer, will have a lower propensity to consume. In this way, as Woytinsky has argued, inflation would make subsequent depressions more

[3] Dr. Machlup reminds me that Röpke preferred the term "repressed inflation" to "suppressed inflation" because he was not content to argue, as I do, that holding the prices down does not solve the problem. He wanted to argue further that the prices could not for long be kept down — that the excess demand must break out again in open inflation. Although this is often quite likely, I do not see any necessity for the price control to break down. The excess demand can do enough harm even if the price control is completely successful.

Dr. Villard has pointed out that my suggested change in terminology would lead to my supporting the proposition that depression could be prevented by removing resistances to price reductions. But I would object to this proposition only if used without the change in terminology that would make it acceptable. I would still be opposed to attempts to cure an insufficiency of demand by permitting prices to fall without doing anything to correct the basic insufficiency of demand. This would be just as bad as attempting to cure an excess of demand by merely permitting prices to rise without doing anything about the excess demand. Permitting prices to fall would prevent depression, only in the sense that depression means deflation without price reductions. What it would leave is deflation *with* price reductions which may be worse than deflation without price reductions because of their self-reinforcing effects on expectations.

likely. But such a difficulty can so easily be corrected, by creating more government deficits as soon as deflation threatens, that the argument is suitable only for those who think it worth while developing the most complicated policies in the hope of achieving a state of affairs in which policy would no longer be necessary. We may be satisfied to say that inflation is bad because it sabotages the price mechanism.

III

The third question is "Why do we have Inflation?". Sometimes it is because the government, like the present Chinese government, has to print and spend more and more money in order to be able to meet its essential expenses. We then have hyperinflations as only one among many other symptoms of a larger social disorder with which we cannot deal here.

Sometimes it is because a mistimed fear of deflation leads to measures that create or increase excess demand, and an exaggerated fear of causing deflation paralyzes the action necessary for stopping the inflation. If this is accompanied by an unreasoning allegiance to cheap money, an unwillingness to impose sufficient taxation to eliminate excess demand and the suppression of price increases by the government (as in housing) or by private producers (as in automobiles), we have the outlines of a situation much nearer home.

Yet stupidity is rarely a complete explanation of what we do. We must not fail to consider the possibility that the cure for inflation may sometimes turn out to be worse than the disease. Or, putting the matter more positively, we must not forget that inflation can perform important functions.

It is argued with great plausibility that sudden and large shifts of resources, as in the shift from peace to war production, cannot be induced rapidly enough through the price mechanism. During the war, the price mechanism was abrogated by general price ceilings, and resources were allocated by authority with the help of an excess demand which greedily attracted all available resources wherever they were not restricted by the controls. This is elevated by Galbraith into a "disequilibrium system" which worked marvels in our war production. Yet it may be that the price mechanism is inadequate only if we will not permit the large price changes that would be necessary for the large readjustments, and that devices could have been worked out that would have overcome without compulsion such obstacles as the automobile manufacturers' preference for making automobiles rather than tanks or the inelasticity of demand for essential raw materials. And it may be that with these devices the price mechanism would have made the war economy even more productive than it was. But the devices were not available for practical application, and so the inflation performed an invaluable function in the miracle of our war production.

Another function of inflation in wartime is to bring about the necessary reduction in consumption. Sometimes this is done by an open inflation which transfers real income to entrepreneurs who cannot help making exorbitant profits which for the most part they save. Such saving is brought about by an aggravation of the inequality of income, and the anger of the frustrated consumers is diverted to the "profiteers." In the last war the savings were induced in the U. S. by suppression rather than by open inflation, the saving being done, not by profiteers but by the public at large, which saved a very large part of its income because the goods on which they would have spent their money were available, if at all, only in limited amounts at low prices. This method had the advantage that instead of aggravating the inequality of real income it diminished it very much — and in England it did this to a degree that interfered with other (incentive) functions of inequality of income.

The effects on the inequality of income are as relevant for peace as for war. The price mechanism attacks a special scarcity of any commodity by raising its price so as to discourage demand and encourage supply. But if supply is not responsive to price and the commodity is an important and essential commodity for people with low incomes, the higher price does not really mean that the good goes to those who have a greater need for it, which would be the best thing for the allocation of the scarce item. It rather means that poorer people are further impoverished by having to spend a larger proportion of their income on the scarce and expensive item. Just as the rise in the price of a rich man's luxury reduces real inequality, so a rise in the price of a poor man's necessity increases it.

It is possible to devise measures for keeping the benefits of the price mechanism without permitting such undesirable aggravations of inequality. Modigliani has proposed one for the meat shortage which offsets the inequality by equal money payments to all and offsets the inflationary effect of the monetary distribution by a special tax which incidentally checks the functionless windfall profits. Housing would probably be the field where such a device could most usefully be applied. But until the compensatory devices are properly worked out and made acceptable to a society which has an unholy horror of subsidies outside certain sacred regions, a good case may be made out for some kind of rationing rather than using the price mechanism, especially where attempts to correct the inequalities would strengthen the spiral of open inflation, while a certain degree of inequality is needed to maintain the incentives that keep our economy working efficiently. While it is possible for suppression to reduce the incentives below the social optimum, it is also possible for free prices of scarce necessities to exaggerate the inequalities beyond all reason. If England is a serious example of the former, China is certainly a horrible example of the latter.

Finally we must come to the connection between inflation and full employment. Under full employment strong trade unions can continually raise wages more rapidly than productivity increases. This results in higher prices, further wage increases, inevitable disappointments at the failure to raise real wages, the expectations lag, and the spiral of open inflation. No degree of understanding of the problem by responsible trade union leaders can help very much since each trade union owes it to its members to make sure that it is not left behind in the general rush. The vicious circle can best be broken by developing an artificial free market, on the lines I suggested to this meeting two years ago,[4] to adjust relative wages for relative scarcities while letting their general level rise just as much as the over-all increase in productivity.

To many it seems unfair to hold down wages if the circle can be broken by holding down the price level instead. The inflationary spiral can be broken this way too, but only by means of a rise in wages and a volume of unemployment sufficient to prevent any further pressure on wages. This would be more harmful than even a pretty severe inflation. On the other hand, the stabilization of the money wage level would stabilize prices at the normal mark-up (given by the degree of monopoly in the organization of business) with no threat to full employment and production. It would then be possible for all sorts of measures to be taken to increase the degree of competition and, indeed, there is good reason to believe that the maintenance of full employment itself, by raising the break-even points, would automatically reduce the rate of mark-up. There is no disadvantage to labor, rather the reverse, in stabilizing wages rather than prices.

All this is on the assumption that the total demand is kept high enough to provide full employment but not high enough to create excess demand. Excess demand can always be reduced in a normally well administered society by imposing taxes high enough to stop people from spending more than enough to buy the whole product that the economy is able to produce. But we must not forget the bad effects of taxes. A tax on the purchase of a commodity or on the earning of income may divert the citizen from purchasing the taxed commodity to buying other things that constitute less effective use of resources, or may divert him from earning some income into relatively less desired leisure. This is even more likely to be the case because of our reluctance to tax the ordinary working man, which is what is necessary for preventing inflation, and our tendency to use the tax power to equalize income by very high income taxation especially at the margin, where it is so harmful in its effect on the use of resources. It may be that the only taxes which are popular enough to be enacted are those which would do more harm than the inflation which they would prevent. It is even possible for a tax with a very high marginal rate to re-

[4] "Money as a Creature of the State," *A.E.A. Proceedings*, May 1947, pp. 312–17.

duce the supply of goods more than it reduces the demand for them, so that it would aggravate rather than relieve the inflation while adding its own damages to the destruction wrought by the inflation. We may have inflation because the cure would be worse than the disease.

IV

Our fourth and last question is "What should be done about it?" Our first comfort is that we need have no fear of the hyperinflations that threaten countries whose governments are unable to collect taxes regularly. Nor need we fear any severe depressions, which can always be prevented by government deficits. On the other hand we must realize that the maintenance of full employment without inflation depends on the acquiescence and cooperation of labor organizations in permitting collective bargaining to be superseded by other techniques for determining wage rates that would prevent the general wage level from rising faster than productivity. The most hopeful procedure would probably be to give the trade union national organizations the responsibility for running the new machinery. There is a ticklish problem here of initiation, since the cooperation of labor will depend on the success in obtaining full employment without inflation just as much as the success will depend on the cooperation. Nor should we disregard Singer's warning [5] against the British optimism regarding the solution of this problem by the unification of the trade unions.

One lesson that comes most clearly out of our analysis is that *it is no solution to change from open inflation to Suppression or from Suppression to open inflation.* Economists have on the whole been stressing the inadequacy of hoping to cure inflation by clamping down on prices. But there is still much too general an assumption that the removal of price ceilings will correct the excess demand and restore the benevolent rule of the price system. Sometimes this is based on the assumption of a given total rate of spending that would be unaffected by the removal of the ceilings. There would then result only a once for all rise in price to an equilibrium level. But without rather powerful evidence to the contrary, one should expect the increase in price to call forth a successful demand for higher wages and start a spiral of open inflation which might very well be more disruptive than the suppression. Nor can one argue that this would be prevented by the limited money supply. That, as we have seen, threatens to stop the spiral in a way that would justify the otherwise idle fears that every inflation must be atoned for in a depression. Rising prices and suppression are both symptoms of excess demand. Only by working for the elimination of the primary cause, the excess demand, can one hope for satisfactory results.

The economic devices for checking excess demand are very simple. They include higher taxes, but not where they would destroy incentives too much, and not merely on the rich who would not cut their spending much, but on the lower middle class and in the main on ordinary workers. Intransigeant equalitarians may be soothed perhaps by the thought that the taxes would not reduce the workers' real income but merely safeguard them from losing in higher prices the money that the tax prevents them from spending. Next there are economies in expenditure by the government itself or by business or by private individuals. Such saving might be encouraged by taxes which exempted saved income. Then there is the discouragement of investment if consumption cannot be reduced sufficiently. And finally there is the encouragement of imports, when these become available in greater quantities, on which excess demand can be dissipated.

The economic devices for checking excess demand are very simple. The unsolved economic problems are largely terminological rather than substantial, as in the debate between fiscal policy and monetary policy as to which is the Real Thing and which is merely the window dressing, when it is perfectly clear that a faulty exercise of either can wreck an excellent program in the other. The really difficult problems are political, although there are some quite respectable administrative ones.

A fundamental political problem stems from the fact that inflation of the kind we have been having here is very popular. It is popular because it is associated with full employment and an unprecedented prosperity. There is a re-

[5] H. W. Singer, "Wage Policy in Full Employment," *Economic Journal*, December 1947.

luctance to undertake responsibility for measures which might possibly set off a depression if someone else in another position should bungle his part of the job.

Perhaps we will continue to be as lucky as in the past, but if increasing defense demands should shatter this delightful dream, we will have to choose between a policy which puts all the problems straight before the public and a policy of obtaining the cooperation of the public by the fraud of open inflation or by the force of suppression. It may be that the public will insist on being fooled part of the time, that we can get their cooperation in difficult ventures only by manipulating them with money payments of deceptive value, by giving them imaginary rewards for which they cannot get any real goods. But I would want to refrain from such trickery until it is demonstrated that more honest measures, more worthy of a society that swears by democracy, could not do a better job by taking people into the confidence of the managers, clearly telling them what they can have and what they cannot have, what is possible and what is not possible, that they cannot have their cake and eat it. Perhaps I am too romantic but I think the public can be told that there is no Santa Claus.

[3]

CHAPTER XI

SELLERS' INFLATION AND INFLATIONARY DEPRESSION*

In Chapter X, which deals with inflation and depression, these are treated in the more or less traditional way which assumes that inflation is caused by excess demand—by buyers trying to buy more goods and services than the economy can supply even when everybody can find all the work he wants. In the last few years a new kind of inflation has been attracting attention that seems to be able to flourish without excess demand.

In 1957, the United Automobile Workers International Union (UAW) invited the three big automobile corporations to lower the 1958 automobile prices as a first step in checking the inflationary process from which our economy was suffering. Not unnaturally, the corporations in effect replied, "After you, my dear Alphonse." Yet the proposals and counterproposals were something more than sparrings for better future bargaining positions. They clearly demonstrated three phenomena of the first importance: (1) a genuine concern, on both sides, with the dangers of inflation, (2) a readiness to cooperate in checking the inflation (provided that such cooperation was not exploited and diverted for the benefit of the other side), and (3) perhaps the most important, a recognition that the inflation was caused not by *buyers* trying to buy more of everything than could be supplied—by "too much money chasing too few goods"—but by *sellers* pressing for higher prices.

President Eisenhower recognized this when he made his appeal to labor and to business to help the fight against inflation by exercising restraint and refraining from demanding higher wages or prices. If inflation in general could be caused only by excess demand for goods by *buyers,* restraint by *sellers* (of products or of labor)

* This chapter is based on a paper delivered to the Johns Hopkins Political Economy Seminar on November 6, 1957, and condensed in an article in *Commentary,* February 1958, entitled "Halting the Current Recession."

would always be irrelevant and the President's appeal would be pointless. In the presence of excess demand by buyers, restraint by sellers would be ineffective, and in the absence of excess demand by buyers it would be unnecessary.

But excess demand by buyers is *not* the only possible cause of inflation. This is shown by the experience of rising prices while output was failing to keep up with our growing productive capacity, when we were perfectly capable of supplying much more than the current overall demand for goods and services, and when efforts by sellers to persuade the public to buy were as strenuous as ever. In such conditions price increases cannot be due to the pressure of *buyers* who are finding it difficult to buy. Prices are rising because of pressures by *sellers* who insist on increasing prices (even though they are finding it not so easy to sell). The inflation is not *buyer-induced* but *seller-induced.* We have not a *buyers' inflation* but *sellers' inflation.*

The authorities, in endeavoring to stop the inflation by applying budgetary retraint and tight money, have been very effective in removing excess demand, but have not completely removed the upward pressure on prices from the sellers' side. They have, however, been so effective in reducing demand that they have overdone this and removed some demand that was *not* in excess. They have brought about a condition of *deficient demand*—not enough demand to enable us to make full use of our productive potential. Nevertheless prices keep on rising. The net result is that we are now suffering at the same time from both inflation *and* depression —prices are rising and at the same time we are not fully utilizing our available labor force and productive potential.

This appears paradoxical only because of our habit of assuming that inflation, or rising prices, is always caused by excess demand, and many people still argue as if the only kind of inflation possible is demand inflation or buyers' inflation. Although they cannot deny that they see excesses of potential supply much more often than they see excesses of buyers' demand, they insist that "there ain't no such animal" as sellers' inflation. They declare that "inflation is inflation" and they sternly dismiss all talk about a new kind of inflation that does not respond to the orthodox treatment of monetary and fiscal restrictions as diversionary tricks by naughty children who are trying to dodge their medicine.

Unfortunately, such sternness is only too understandable. Some of the economists who were early to recognize the nature of sellers' inflation were so impressed by the impossibility of dealing with it by the orthodox instruments of monetary and fiscal policy that they capitulated to the temptation of dallying with "mild" or "moderate" inflation as part of an acceptable policy. The orthodox economists quite rightly point out that such a capitulation is indefensible either on moral or on practical grounds. Even a "mild" inflation accumulates, at "compound interest" and robs pensioners, fixed income receivers, and many other unfortunate victims, while it sabotages the proper calculations and accountings necessary for wise economic decisions. In time many of these faults could be corrected by institutional adjustments, but to keep the inflation "mild" is more difficult than to prevent the inflation from starting in the first place. The very same excuses for accepting "creeping" inflation instead of maintaining price stability would be even more seductive for permitting a "creeping" inflation to become a "walking" one. Stronger still would be the pressures for changing from a "walking" to a "running" inflation and for permitting a "running" inflation to break into a "gallop." Retreat only induces further retreat.

But the objections to appeasement do not in the least diminish the importance of recognizing the existence of sellers' inflation, for it is not the *recognition* of the existence of sellers' inflation but rather its *denial* that is dangerous. It is the belief that the medicines appropriate for buyers' inflation are the only medicines available, when joined with the discovery that these do not work, which give rise to defeatism and appeasement.

Another reason for reluctance to recognize sellers' inflation is that it has often been called "cost inflation" or "cost-push inflation" or "wage-cost inflation," giving the impression that the whole of the blame for it falls on labor or on trade unions. When trade unions raise wages by more than can be absorbed by increasing productivity, costs rise. The employer then seems to be completely innocent of "profit inflation" in passing on the increase in costs as long as he does not raise his markup, i.e., as long as he does not increase the prices he charges for the product in a greater proportion than his costs have increased. But a sellers' inflation could just as well be started by an increase not in the wages but in the markup. Prices would rise and wages would then be raised by workers in attempts to maintain (or restore) their original buying power. Business would then "innocently" raise their prices again only in proportion to the increase in their costs, and we would have the inflation upon us as well as endless dispute about who started it first—the famous chicken and egg.

The "who started it first" debate is a complete waste of time because there *is* no original situation in which there was a "just" or "normal" distribution of the product between wages and profits. Any change can be seen either as a disturbance of equilibrium or as the correction of an inequity—all depending on the point of view. The term "sellers' inflation," by treating wages and profits on exactly the same footing, avoids the mutual recrimination. Sellers' inflation takes place whenever wage-earners and profit-takers together attempt to get shares that amount to more than 100% of the selling price. It is futile to ask whether this is because the wages demanded are too high or whether it is because the profits insisted on are too great.

It is of course impossible for the sellers to get more than 100% of the proceeds but it is precisely on such an impossibility that any continuing process depends. Buyers' inflation is similarly built on trying for the impossible. In that case it is buyers trying *to buy more than 100%* of the goods available. Their attempt bids up prices. They do not (and cannot) succeed in buying more than 100% of the available goods, but they keep on trying and so we have the continuing process of buyers' inflation. In sellers' inflation it is the sellers who keep trying to get more than 100%, so they keep on raising wages and prices and we have the continuing process of sellers' inflation.

The resistance to recognizing sellers' inflation takes many forms. One argument is that there must have been some excess buyers' demand or prices could not have risen. This begs the whole question since it assumes what it wants to prove, namely, that the only possible cause of rising prices is excess buyers' demand.

A more sophisticated argument points out that as long as output shrinks less than prices increase (and this is usually the case), there must have been an increase in the total amount spent by the buyers. This is indisputable, but an *increase in expenditure* is not the same thing as *excess demand.* An excess of demand by buyers is the *cause* of the price increase. An increase in expenditure could be the *result* of attempts by the authorities to keep down the unemployment induced by price increases imposed by sellers.

A still more sophisticated argument along the same lines is that if the authorities would only be resolute and not permit an increase in expenditure, the depression and unemployment resulting from a wage or price increase would stop the sellers from increasing prices. The question then is how much unemployment would be required and whether it is morally desirable or politically possible for the authorities to induce or permit unemployment of the required volume and duration.

Before considering this question it would be desirable to review briefly the main approaches to the general problem of inflation and depression.

First, there is the classical approach. This assumes perfectly flexible prices and wages, so that any excess of demand makes prices and wages rise, and any deficiency of demand makes prices and wages fall, until price stability and full employment are restored. Monetary and fiscal policy are unimportant. As long as the quantity of money is kept fairly stable by some automatic device such as the gold standard, the price level will automatically adjust itself so as to yield full employment with price stability and without inflation. The corresponding policy is *laissez faire*—do nothing.

The second is the Keynesian approach, developed by Keynes in the early 1930's, to take account of the fact that we do not have the degree of *downward* price and wage flexibility that is needed to make *laissez faire* a satisfactory policy. We have seen in Chapter X that the automatic cure depends not on wages falling relatively to prices or on wages and prices falling relatively to incomes but on wages, prices and incomes all falling relatively to the quantity of money. This process may take years of severe depression, so that the appropriate policy is to abandon *laissez faire*—not to wait for the price level to adjust itself to the quantity of money but to adjust the quantity of money to the price level.

This switch from *laissez faire* to an active monetary and fiscal policy also applies in the opposite direction to prevent *excess* demand or buyers' inflation. Instead of waiting for the price increase to *absorb* the excess demand it calls for monetary or fiscal policy to *remove* it, adjusting demand downward to the price level instead of waiting for the price level to rise until it has adjusted itself to the high level of demand.

The third approach takes account of the fact that an insufficiency of demand, even when causing considerable unemployment, may not only fail to make prices and wages fall quickly enough to provide the automatic (classical) cure, but may even be unable to prevent them from continuing to rise. When we have strong trade unions with the power to raise wages, strong corporations with the power to set prices administratively, and a general atmosphere in which it is considered normal, natural and only fair for wages to be increased regularly by more than the increase in productivity in the economy (plus or minus any increase or decrease in labor's share of the product), prices must increase and we have sellers' inflation. The widespread and generous feeling that workers are entitled to the increases in wages that they get is made much easier by a recognition that any raise need not be taken out of profits, since it is possible, as well as proper, to "pass it along" to the ultimate purchaser in higher prices. Indeed it is usually considered only right that profits, in dollars, should be *increased* so as to protect *real* profits from the declining value of the dollar.

We have already mentioned the argument that a really firm refusal on the part of the monetary authorities to permit the volume of expenditure to increase, no matter what happened, would bring the sellers to their senses. Realizing, or discovering, that they will not be able to sell so much if they raise their prices, they will refrain from raising prices and they will not grant, or ask for, wage increases that raise costs by more than can be squeezed out of profits. But the question is will they? Or rather how severe a state of depression and unemployment would have to be maintained in order to induce sellers not to use their power to raise prices, and how able and willing would the authorities be to bring about and maintain this degree of depression and unemployment?

An interesting indication of the strength of the most important element in the setup—the general feeling of the propriety and inevitability of continuing wage and cost increases (to be "passed on" in increased prices) was provided in the very debate about automobile prices and wages referred to earlier. The U.A.W. had asked the automobile corporations to reduce automobile prices by $100 in 1958, promising to take this into consideration when presenting their 1958 demands for wage increases. The counter-suggestion, clearly put forward as an extreme bargaining position, was deeply concerned with the danger of inflation. This counter-suggestion included the continuation of the previous contract which offered a regular wage increase of 2½% per annum in addition to a cost of living adjustment. But 2½% per annum is more than the average increase in output per head in the American economy, so that there was a significant piece of sellers' inflation right at the lower end of the range subject to negotiation. Another indication is provided by the outcome of the protracted steel strike of 1959 which the steel company fought under the flag of preventing inflation. The settlement was such that the main question remaining was whether or not the companies would be able to postpone the price increase until after the November 1960 elections.

In such an atmosphere it would require, one would think, a quite severe depression to change people's notions of what is the proper development of wage rates and of the corresponding prices (since the right of wages to increase goes together with the right of profits at least not to fall).

At the same time the avoidance of severe depressions seems to have won a firm place in the country's economic policy. With such a setup there is no need to worry whether the cure is worse than the disease —whether the depression would be more harmful than the inflation that it would prevent. This cure is not one that any government would seriously attempt to carry out.

All this brings us to the perhaps only too obvious conclusion that sellers' inflation cannot be cured or prevented by measures directed against excess demand by *buyers*. It can be successfully treated only by attacking the pressure on prices by sellers.[1]

In a perfectly competitive market the institutions and mores that

[1] In an outstanding article which concentrated on showing the inadequacy and superficiality of proposals to prevent inflation by monetary and fiscal policies and declarations, Professor Sumner H. Slichter seemed to suggest that the distinction between buyers' inflation and sellers' inflation is a futile fantasy. Thus he said (using somewhat different terminology) "Much time has been wasted in recent years in discussing whether inflation is demand-inspired or

give sellers the power to push prices up cannot exist. Prices cannot rise unless there is excess demand. If there is a deficient demand prices must fall. We cannot have inflation and depression at the same time.

But where prices are administered by decrees of large firms, and wages are administered by joint decrees of powerful unions together with powerful employers or employer groups, the situation is different. Sellers' inflation is a by-product of the process, and together with sellers' inflation we can also have depression—indeed we *will* have depression with our sellers' inflation if the authorities try to cure the inflation by reducing ("excess") demand.

These by-products of administered wages and prices have important similarities to, and are no less socially harmful than, the monopolistic exploitation that would result from unregulated administration of prices by private owners of public utilities. We have gone a long way towards eliminating the latter evil by *regulating* the prices set by public utilities. A similar device can be used to eliminate sellers' inflation. Just as public utility prices can be and are being regulated so as to prevent monopolistic exploitation, so administered prices and wages can and should be regulated so as to prevent sellers' inflation and the depression it may bring with it.

The regulation of administered prices and wages to prevent sellers' inflation would have to follow somewhat different lines. It would not be concerned with the rate of return on investments, nor would it regulate anything other than *price*. The purpose of the regulation would be only to prevent *restrictive prices* or *restrictive wages* from

---

cost-inspired. (Some 70 or 80 years ago the Austrian theory of value produced a similar debate as to whether demand or cost determines value; the argument ended suddenly when it dawned on the economists that each blade in a pair of scissors cuts.)" ("On the Side of Inflation," *Harvard Business Review*, Sept./Oct. 1957, p. 32.)

However, the inapplicability of this analogy jumps to the eye in his very next sentence which shows that it *can* make sense to distinguish between the "blades," since he went on to say, "Thus changes in the price level may originate either with shifts in the demand schedules or with shifts in the supply schedules." And in another article, Professor Slichter definitely aligned himself with the "sellers' inflation" blade in declaring that, "There is no evidence that prices are rising ahead of costs and are pulling costs up. The evidence is all the other way: that prices are being sluggishly adjusted to slowly rising costs." ("Government Spending Can Reduce Taxes," *Harvard Business Review*, July/Aug. 1957, p. 106.)

being administered. A restrictive price is one that results in the demand for a product falling below capacity output. A restrictive wage is one that results in less than full employment in the specific labor market to which it applies. With monetary and fiscal policy concentrating on maintaining adequate buyers' demand for full employment while preventing buyers' inflation, it would be possible to maintain a stable price level while wages rose on the average at the same rate as productivity.

To achieve this, the regulatory body, following a set of rules, would have to do the following things:

(1) Permit an administered price increase only when production and sales are at capacity. Such price increases should not be withheld on account of profits being high.

(2) Enforce decreases in administered prices whenever production and sales are significantly below capacity. A price decrease should not be waived on account of profits being low (or even negative) as long as the price more than covers current operating costs (more exactly, short period marginal costs).

(3) Permit increases in wages in general at a rate equal to the average trend of increase in national productivity.

(4) Permit increases in administered wages greater than this only where the labor market is significantly tighter than on the average—e.g., where unemployment is less than half the national average.

(5) Permit only smaller increases in administered wages, or no increases at all, wherever the labor market is significantly slacker than on the average—e.g., where unemployment is more than twice the national average. (Some prices must fall if others rise if there is to be price level stability but it is possible to avoid reductions in money wages because of increasing productivity.)

This is of course not a fully worked out solution ready for immediate application. Much remains to be developed—such as generally acceptable criteria of capacity of different firms and industries and generally acceptable measures of slackness or tightness in particular labor markets. The regulations could be enforced by treating as nondeductible for income tax any unauthorized part of wages or of other costs paid out. The regulations would enforce more intense price competition. While making prices more "correct" they would also eliminate high cost firms (now sheltered by their more efficient competitors keeping prices above the "correct" level). While the public would benefit from the increased efficiency of the economy, such elimination of "competition by the inefficient" would conflict with special interests and with certain so-called anti-trust polices that are in effect anti-competition policies and need to be reconsidered.

There remain important problems of organization and administration of the regulatory body as well as the need for widespread and intensive public discussion to bring about the familiarity with, and the understanding of, the nature and purpose of the proposed regulation that is essential for its effective operation in a democracy. And in the course of such examination and debate important developments, changes and improvements are to be expected. Nevertheless the general lines indicated seem inevitable if sellers' inflation is to be attacked at its roots.

It is to be expected that one of the most powerful debating points against the proposed price (and wage) regulation will be the charge that it means *price control*. But price regulation is not price control —it is almost the exact opposite. Price control consists of an attempt by authority to *interfere* with the price mechanism by establishing a price below that which clears the market, i.e., below the "genuine" price, discussed in Chapters III, IV and V. Price regulation on the other hand rather *restores* the price mechanisms. It interferes only with interferences, preventing the monopolist or cartel or trade union or whoever else determines an administered price or wage, from setting it above the "correct" level.

The regulation of public utilities prices, by moving the actual price closer to the "correct" price without making them any less "genuine," increases output and leads to a more efficient use of the resources of the economy. The owners of the public utility are indeed deprived of monopoly profits, but the gain to consumers is much greater than the loss to the monopolists.

The regulation of administered prices and wages to prevent sellers' inflation would similarly establish prices that are both "genuine" and "correct" and compatible with full employment and price level stability. The cry of "price control" would be entirely without justification.

The restriction of output in the whole economy that results from attempts to curb sellers' inflation by reducing total spending, is more damaging than restriction of output by monopolistic public utilities. The latter shifts resources from producing more useful products to producing less useful products, while the former shifts resources from the production of useful products to producing nothing at all—except the human frustrations and suffering from unemployment. The regulation of prices and wages to prevent sellers' inflation is therefore more important than the regulation of monopolistic public utilities, and no more repugnant to the basic principles of the free, competitive society.

The full utilization of existing capacity may sometimes lead to inadequate profits, or even to losses, but that is the nature of the competitive *profit and loss* system. It shows that an error was made in the past in producing too much capacity in the industry, but that is no reason why society should not benefit from the use of the capacity once it has been produced. The low profits or the losses are then performing their proper function of discouraging further investment in such industries. In other cases the "genuine" prices—those that clear the market at full capacity output—will yield very large profits. The prices are nevertheless "correct" and the large profits are performing their proper function of encouraging more investment in such industries.

Just as low profits are no excuse for monopolistic restriction of output, so high profits are no excuse for enforcing price reductions below the "genuine" level. That *would* be price control and is to be equally condemned whether it is imposed by government or whether it is due to "restraint" on the part of producers who are powerful enough, and rich enough, to be able to do this. The existence of excess capacity in steel and in automobiles means that current prices are too high (to be "correct"). The emergence of gray and black market prices during and after World War II meant that prices were then too low (to be "genuine"). The generosity of the corporations at that time in selling too cheap (in part to privileged suppliers of the black market) is no justification for their selling too dear now. A defender of the free market or profit and loss system should not be appalled at the emergence either of profits or of losses.

It is possible that the trade unions would easily see all the social benefits from keeping the prices of products down to the level needed for capacity production and full employment, but would denounce the regulation of wages as an intolerable interference with the fundamental right of collective bargaining. It is possible that employers would quickly appreciate the desirability of curbing excessive wage demands but would reject the regulation of prices as an alien and unthinkable interference with the free economy and an impious infringement of the sacred rights of management in setting prices.

Such responses would indicate that "after you, my dear Alphonse" really means "include me out" or "let George do it," and that we would not have the cooperation that is necessary for success. But the true interests of labor would not be damaged by the trade unions' relinquishing the right to institute a sellers' inflation, nor would true interests of capital be betrayed by the loss of the same right. The justification of the free economy and its institutions rests ultimately not on any ancient divine rights but on their efficiency in satisfying the needs and the desires of a free people.

It has been very fashionable for some time to *deplore* inflation and to quote Lenin's declaration that inflation is the Achilles' heel or the Trojan Horse of capitalism. Recently it has become even more fashionable to *preach* restraint as a remedy for inflation to parties who cannot be expected to respond because they have no assurance that the others will play their part. The preaching seems to have stimulated many public declarations of conversion by Labor and Management to a readiness to *promise* restraint, provided the other parties cooperate. It is unlikely that the *deploring,* the *preaching,* the *declarations of conversion* or the *promises* will lead to any genuine results. The regulation of administered prices and wages would *provide* the restraint needed to protect the free economy from sellers' inflation and inflationary depression.

[4]

Chapter 15

PHASE THREE

EVEN a completely successful incomes policy with the proper flexibility, undisturbed by pressure groups, is only a crude imitation of a properly working competitive market system. It cannot deal with different conditions in millions of points in the economy where the market mechanism would have served very much better to reflect changes in local conditions of demand, supply or technology. But the waste from such crudity of the substitute market mechanism is much less than the waste of unemployment, and maybe even less than the waste from continuing inflation, provided some protection is given to those who are hurt most severely by inflation. The justification of an incomes policy is essentially that it permits the elimination of administered depression and makes possible a functional finance policy of high or full employment.

The application of incomes policy is, of course, most inefficient in the beginning, but as the incomes policy continues to be applied—whether it is suddenly rechristened Phase Three or given any other name—it can do better and better. It develops into something somewhat closer to the market mechanism of classical economics.

This is due only in part to the development of criteria for determining when wages should rise more and when they should rise less than the average, and to the development of protection of the markup from exploitation by firms or industries which may find their monopoly power increased. As the expectation of inflation diminishes, the pressures which the incomes policy has to combat become weaker and weaker. More and more prices and wage rates are set by the market mechanism or by the wage and price administrators at levels which are not in conflict with the incomes policy. Phase Two becomes less and less active because it becomes less and less needed. What I am now describing is a kind of fading away of Phase Two with the elimination of the expectation of inflation on which Inflation III was based.

There are those who exaggerate the advantages of a truly free market by saying that it is infinitely better. Infinity, however, is a very large number. Suffice it to say that a free market is very much to be preferred, wherever it would work properly, to the administrative mechanisms of incomes policy in Phase Two. If the expectation of inflation should be replaced by an expectation of stable prices, Phase Two would atrophy. There would remain only the rudiments, the empty regulations which would not need to be put into action unless there should be a resurgence of a new inflation to be followed by a new freeze and a new incomes policy under a new Phase Two, which might once more fade away as it succeeded in removing the expectation of inflation.

There could thus be established a kind of psychological-political-economic cycle. This cycle, like all other cycles, can be made unnecessary if it is understood. The proper steps can be taken to prevent it rather than to cure it by avoiding the policies which would start it. In many cases this would merely mean the application of functional finance to prevent the excess demand of Inflation I. There are, of course, other possible igniters of expectations of rising prices. But whatever it was that started an Inflation III, the removal of the expectation of rising prices by an incomes policy would lead to a return to the much more efficient and much more satisfactory free market mechanism. This is what I am calling Phase Three.

There has been much opposition to Phase Two by economists and even more by moralists with a completely different argument. They refer to the damage done to society by having laws to regulate wages and prices, declaring that such laws are bound to break down, to fail to be respected, and this will lead to the decay of respect for law and great damage to the whole moral climate of society. There can be no question that for all sorts of reasons which we can not go into here, there has been a deterioration in the respect for law, and an increase in crime. But to blame Phase Two, or incomes policy, for significantly contributing to the loss of a respect for law rests on a mistaken identity—exactly the opposite of the mistaken identity discussed in an earlier chapter. There we spoke of the evils which resulted from treating Inflation II as if it were Inflation I, trying to stop inflation caused by wage and price administrators as if it were inflation due to too much spending. We saw that this mistaken identity led to holding down total spending as a cure for Inflation II or Inflation III. This, being the wrong remedy, did not cure inflation, but instead presented us with administered depression. The mistake in the present case is exactly the reverse. The cure for Inflation III is declared to be inappropriate because of the harm it would do if used as a cure for Inflation I. The mistake here is not in applying the wrong remedy. Based on the same confusion, it consists of *refusing to use the right remedy.* It is, of course, not possible to cure Inflation I by an incomes policy. If there is too much spending any attempt at regulating prices or wages could lead only to repressed inflation with all its moral evils. But since the regulations of incomes policy are to be applied only as long as there is *not* too much spending, and only when the wage and price administrators are pushing up prices *against* the market, none of these horrors are real. They are fantasies born of the same mistaken identity when approached from the other side.

If incomes policy succeeds in stopping rising prices and, after a time, removing the *expectation* of rising prices, the managers of Phase Two find themselves with less and less to do as we move toward Phase Three. This is the turn from Inflation III to Inflation 0—the situation where prices are not rising, and are not expected to be rising. The defensive expectational Inflation III loses the basis on which it stands. We can have price stability with full employment and without any further active operation of Phase Two's incomes policy. In Phase Three we are back again in the natural healthy situation of prosperity without any administered inflation or wage and price administrators that need regulating. There would only be the frame-work of the incomes policy for re-activation if it should ever become necessary.

This happy ending to the story, however, will not emerge if it should turn out that we had to deal not with Inflation III but with Inflation II. As long as the different parties to production are insisting on getting more than 100% of the product between them, this will not work. Inflation II can be stopped only by bringing about sufficient depression to crush the insistence of the parties on shares adding up to more than the whole product.

It was with such a theoretical "solution" in mind that I distinguished between high full employment and low full employment when I wrote *The Economics of Employment* back in 1951. High full employment was what one would naturally call full employment, when all who wanted to work were able to work as much as they wished to at the current wages. Unemployment would be only of the frictional type, involving people who were on their way from one job to another, or who were temporarily unemployed because their skills were inappropriate or they were in the wrong part of the country. Low full employment would be that level of employment at which prices were stable. But this would mean that Inflation II pressures for increasing wages and prices had been liquidated by a long, severe and continuing depression.

The only excuse I can give for calling this any kind of full employment, is that I had not at the time realized that this was a basic departure from the Keynesian view in which both of these "full employments" were regarded as identical. It had assumed that the right amount of spending is all that is needed for "flation"—neither inflation nor depression. In this language this would mean that low full employment, which is required for price stability, and which I at that time described as corresponding to 6 million unemployed in the United States, is identical with high full employment, with only frictional type unemployment, which I described as corresponding to 2 million unemployed in the United States. It is the failure to see the existence, or even the possibility, of this gap which constitutes the inadequacy of the Keynesian theory of inflation and depression and of the functional finance policies for dealing with these problems.

The Phillips curve, of which we have been hearing a great deal in recent years, is a refinement of what seems to be the same idea as the distinction between high full employment and low full employment. It is a much more sophisticated idea since it consists not of two points but of a curve which contains all the combinations of degrees of employment (or unemployment) and corresponding degrees of inflation between high full employment and low full employment. Each possible combination of unemployment and inflation is represented by a point on a curve anchored on the two limiting positions: high full employment with the highest level of inflation considered and only frictional unemployment, and low full employment with the highest level of unemployment considered and no inflation at all.

The Phillips curve suggests that we have the possibility of choosing where we would like to be on that curve; whether we would rather have more unemployment and less inflation, or less unemployment and more inflation. As indicated above, the evil from 1% more unemployment is so much greater than the evil from 1% more inflation that if one has a choice in this trade off one should always choose a point nearer high full employment, the upper end of the Phillips' curve, where there is less unemployment even if this means more inflation.

It is, however, questionable whether we really can obtain higher levels of employment at the cost of higher levels of inflation, or lower levels of inflation at the cost of lower levels of employment. We can get higher or lower levels of *employment* by providing higher or lower levels of spending, but between the politically and morally impermissible catastrophic depression that crushes Inflation II, and the excessive demand of Inflation I, the effects on *prices* and inflation are questionable. Neither a lower nor a higher level of employment makes it possible for the sellers to get more than 100% of the product. But in the absence of an incomes policy, *any* level of employment, in conjunction with Inflation II, will be accompanied by continuing and accelerating administered inflation of wages and prices. The resistance to the greater inflation, taking the form of monetary restraint, will restore the previous politically determined level of administered depression.

The argument (which will be recognized as similar to Professor Milton Friedman's "natural level of employment") is stronger than might seem from this formulation. It applies not only to any attempt to *increase* the level of employment at the cost of an *increase in the rate* of inflation, but also to attempts to *maintain,* at any *level of* inflation, any level of employment greater than the politically determined inflationary recession. Even with much unemployment, however, as long as there is any inflation going on, rising prices will be blamed by labor and capital for the failure of attempts to obtain more than 100% of the product, and the same escalation of inflation will result. Only at the level of low full employment—the zero point on the Phillips curve—will we be able to achieve Milton Friedman's natural level of employment. This means a degree of unemployment and of business depression severe enough (and long-lasting enough) to have destroyed the power of the wage administrators to raise wages by more than the increase in productivity.

In Professor Friedman's formulation, any rate of employment greater than his natural rate of employment results in inflation, and any rate of employment below his natural rate leads to deflation. The result is that total money spending at any given level will lose purchasing power in the inflation case, and will gain purchasing power in the deflation case, automatically restoring employment to his natural level, no matter what the level of total spending. If total spending is increased in proportion to the increase in output, the 4 per cent or so a year that shows the combination of the increase in output per worker and the increase in the number of workers, we will have neither inflation nor deflation, but price stability—with, of course, his "natural" level of employment. This looks somewhat like Functional Finance or Keynesian economics, but it is only the price level that is controlled by this "right amount of spending" and not the level of employment.

Professor Friedman's analysis also looks very much like the classical analysis in his system's inability to provide more than a natural rate of employment (except for temporary periods when workers are misled by inflation into believing that they are getting more than they really are). The analysis suggests that the additional workers (those employed only when the level of employment is above his natural rate) do not really want to work for the real wage they can get. They are *voluntarily* unemployed (except during the inflations when they are *involuntarily employed;* they are enslaved—not indeed by force, but by the fraud of the inflation).

This fits in with Professor Friedman's known adherence to the "objective" methodology that considers only "revealed preferences." The workers who are unemployed at the natural level of employment (my "low full employment") are seen as acting "as if" they did not want to work at the prevailing real wage.

Whenever they are employed (which is only when employment is above the "natural" level) money wages rise. It is "as if" instead of being pleased at having found work they felt cheated and were insisting on a higher rate of pay if they are to continue to come to work. But there are those who, like myself, find it possible to distinguish between the wage administrators (even if these reflect a policy supported by a majority vote of the workers) and the newly employed and unemployed men and women. The decisions of the wage administrators (which are the revelations from which the "revealed preferences" are derived) are not necessarily the true preferences of the newly employed men and women who usually do not say that they are sorry they went to work, or of the unemployed who would be willing to take jobs at the current wage (or even less), but have not been able to find them. To these the "natural" level of employment is still a "low full employment" which does not really deserve to be called full employment. It is only the depression position that would be reached by the consistent treatment of Inflation II with the remedy appropriate for Inflation I, if any government were callous enough, fanatical enough, and suicidal enough to persist in such a policy to the bitter end.

But the zero point on the Phillips curve (which is identical with my "low full employment") still does not really mean no inflation. It only means no *unexpected* inflation. Any excess of inflation over and above that expected would cause capital and labor to respond by increasing their claims. If there is no unexpected inflation, the claims for higher wages or higher prices remain unchanged, and the expected degree of inflation or of acceleration of inflation comes about as anticipated. The expectation of stable prices, namely, an expectation of a zero rate of inflation, is only a special case. The zero point on the Phillips curve, or "low full employment," represents a situation in which the expectations, whatever they might be, could be realized. A higher level of employment would bring about higher inflation than that anticipated or expected. And a lower level of employment would result in a rate of inflation (or of acceleration of inflation) lower than that anticipated. Even "low full employment" is no unfailing specific against Inflation III.

This is a misleading symmetry, however. It is not the symmetry between excess demand and deficient demand. Deficiency of demand is operative when there is less than *low* full employment, but above this level it is not excess demand but pressure by sellers that raises prices and price expectations. Only when there is more than *high* full employment does excess demand come into play, and then incomes policy cannot work. Attempts to apply it would result only in price control, with all its evils and inevitable breakdown.

In the range between high full employment (say 3% unemployment) and low full employment (say 10 or 15% unemployment) it is possible for incomes policy to stabilize the degree of actual, and thereby of expected, inflation, making the two equal. This *flattens out this portion of the Phillips curve*, as shown in the accompanying simple diagram. The level of unemployment (U) measures, from left to right, how low the economy is running. Vertically is measured the excess of actual inflation (AI) over expected inflation (EI). H indicates high full employment, and L low full employment.

To the left of H we have excess demand, overfull employment, and Inflation I. The farther to the left, the greater the excess demand, the overemployment, the excess of actual over expected inflation, and the inflationary pressure. In this region dwells the dragon of hyperinflation. To the right of L we have so severe a deficiency of demand that unemployment and depression have broken the power of workers and of business to press for higher wages and prices. There is no Inflation II or Inflation III to counter the downward market pressure on wages and prices, and we have deflation. Perhaps we should call this Deflation I, it being the obverse of Inflation I. In this region dwell the wild beasts of hyperdeflation.

The two tails of the diagram—the backward rising curve to

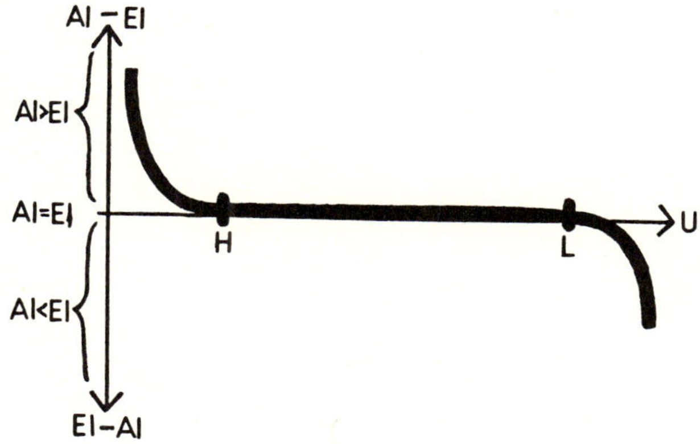

the left of H and the forward falling curve to the right of L—if put together, leaving out the middle range, exactly represent the classical theory of the price level, which failed to deal with depression. It failed because there is no "point" or knife-edge of a single "natural" or equilibrium level of employment at which the tails meet. Between the tails at the extremes there is the wide range that encompasses various degrees of depression or recession from high full employment to low full employment. Within this range much or little unemployment is compatible with much or little inflation, so that incomes policy can change the inflation rate, and aggregate spending policy (functional finance) can change the unemployment rate.

Some countries have for brief periods found themselves in hyperinflations of excess demand to which the tail on the left refers. So far no economy has found itself in a hyperdeflation (the right-hand tail) with prices falling more and more rapidly while the total quantity of money in the economy is continually being decreased the way it is continually increased in hyperinflations. The nearest approach to this was during the great depression of the thirties, when prices, employment, and the quantity of money were all diminishing, but there is no reason for believing that such a catastrophe will ever be permitted again.

Our present and future troubles are all concentrated in the middle range. Inflation I prevents us from going above H, and Deflation I prevents us from going below L. Within the middle range attempts during the 1960's to reduce Inflation I or II by holding down demand (for fear of slipping over to the left of H into hyperinflation) increased unemployment from 4 to 6%. Incomes policy then reduced the rate of inflation from 6 to 3½% per annum even while unemployment was reduced from 6 to 5%. If the unfulfillable ambitions of Inflation II can be stilled and the expectations that give rise to Inflation III can be eliminated by an uninhibited use of incomes policy, we will be able to apply the principles of functional finance in accordance with Keynes's economic policy to establish and maintain an optimal level of employment at a stable or even a zero rate of inflation.

[5]

MAP: A Cure for Inflation

ABBA LERNER AND DAVID C. COLANDER

A PARADOX?

To cure inflation and stagflation, we must first understand them. For the orthodox economic theory, stagflation presents a logical paradox. In that theory, inflation is always due to too much total spending. Since unemployment is due to too little (total) spending, stagflation seems to tell us, paradoxically, that we have too much spending and too little spending at the same time!

A paradox appears only when a failure of the facts to fit the theory is interpreted as a contradiction or an impossibility. But "the actual *is* possible," and when reality and theory conflict, it is the theory that must give way. The paradox disappears as soon as we escape from the dogma that inflation must be due to too much spending.

Stagflation is caused not by too much spending, but by self-fulfilling expectations. Prices rise to keep up with the cost of production. Wages rise to keep up with the increasing cost of living and with increasing output. Government, to avoid catastrophic depression, expands total spending in the economy to keep up with wages and prices. But to be able to counter charges that it is "ultimately"[1] responsible for the inflation, it puts an "anti-inflationary" *restraint* on the expansion as soon as the unemployment is not too catastrophic. This *restraint* is what turns inflation into stagflation.

A FLAW!

In this vicious circle of prices, wages, and spending chasing one another, each of the three actors continues the dance because he has to keep up with the others. The result is a continuing *expectational inflation-unemployment equilibrium*. The stagflation is a result of a *flaw* in the market mechanism that prevents it from working properly.

The flaw is a mutation of the older flaw that was responsible for the Great Depression of the 1930s. That flaw was diagnosed, and its cure prescribed, by Keynes in 1936. It consisted of the failure of prices and wages to fall far enough and fast enough to cure the unemployment (given the level of spending in the economy). The cure, since the prices would not adjust to the spending, was—a la Mohammed and the mountain—to adjust the spending to the prices. The

[1]"Ultimately," on the ground that "basically" the inflation must be due to too much spending. "Ultimately" and "basically" here mean "shut up and stop questioning the orthodox dogma."

mutation of the flaw is that prices and wages do not merely refuse to fall (as is necessary to cure a depression if spending does not rise); they keep rising, caught in the vicious circle of the spending, the prices and the wages all chasing one another. The simple Keynesian cure for the original flaw—providing adequate but not excessive total spending—cannot deal with the mutation.

PREVIOUS PLANS

It might seem that if any one of the three participants in the dance stopped running, the inflation would have to stop. But this turns out not to be so. *Spending* is the item that has most consistently been chosen as the one to be stopped. The weapon used for this is "sound finance," which relies on restrictionary monetary and fiscal policy to stop the inflationary increase in spending. But this works quickly enough only through catastrophic depression and unemployment. If the unemployment is severe but less than catastrophic, it works too slowly and is still too painful.

A few plans have been devised to work on *price increases*. However, these plans do not overcome the administrative problems stemming from the ease with which quality changes can be used to obscure, or to be disguised as, price changes.

It is also possible to work on *wage increases*. Limiting the average increase in wages to the average increase in output per person would stabilize average cost and average price. A number of plans on these lines are currently receiving wide attention. (They mostly propose only to *reduce* wage increases slightly so as to moderate the inflation slightly.) But all such plans give the impression of discriminating against labor by holding down wage increases while leaving profits unchecked. This is bound to make them unacceptable to labor and thus impossible to implement in a democratic society.

What we learn from this is that it is not enough to stop only one of the three inflationary elements in the tripartite expectational inflation. It turns out to be necessary to deal with wages and profits together. Once this is done the government will no longer have to keep expanding total spending to keep up with any rising prises. Since it will not have to prove it is not responsible for an ongoing inflation, the government will also feel free to give up the "anti-inflationary" restraint on the expansion that is responsible for the *stag* in the stagflation.

FAULTY SOCIAL ACCOUNTING

The mutated flaw which makes the wages and prices keep rising in the futile inflationary race to keep up with one another is a *social* flaw in the *private* accounting of firms. The inflationary impacts of wage and price decisions are not taken into account, just as environmental impacts, health impacts, and other socially important consequences are often not taken fully into account in the decisions of individuals or firms.

Individuals and firms can be made, and are being made, to take these environmental impacts into account through the imposition of incentives (usually taxes or subsidies) to correct the accounting, so as to have the private decisions made responsibly from a social point of view. The inflation cure must similarly apply such an incentive to stop the excessive (i.e., inflationary) wage and price increases.

Total spending in the economy must still be kept increasing enough to be able to buy the output of full employment, though not more than enough (which would bring excess demand inflation). Functional finance is still essential. But the cure for inflation is now faced with an additional *two-fold task*.

1. It must stabilize the *average* price (the price level), and at the same time

2. It must leave *actual* prices and wages free to be adjusted individually, by the market and by free bargaining, to the continuing changes in tastes, techniques, and availabilities. It must also be *fair* in its effects on the relations between wages and profits, and it must *not take too long* to achieve these objectives.

WHY PREVIOUS PLANS FAILED

Attempts to cure the inflation have failed so far because they have not satisfied all the necessary conditions. The same also seems to be true of the anti-inflation proposals now being considered.

Wage and price controls, when applied in the crudest possible way (sometimes as a preparatory step only) as a freeze of all wages and prices, immediately achieve objective (1), but they do nothing at all for objective (2). As the controls develop, they attempt to adjust the wages and prices to the changing tastes, techniques, and availabilities, but they do this not by using market and bargaining methods but by centralized administration. The task is too much for this method and the attempt regularly breaks down in an "administrative nightmare." Wage and price guidelines and guideposts have been greatly discredited, but they are proposed again from time to time only because nothing better has come up.

Similarly desperate (which means without hope) are attempts to stop the inflation by "jawboning"—attempts to persuade the public, even while they are experiencing the inflation going on, that the inflation is ending—so that they will stop raising wages and prices. This attacks the problem precisely the wrong way 'round. We must first stop the inflation. Only when the public sees that the inflation has stopped will it stop expecting the inflation to continue.

The necessity of dealing with both wages and prices was recognized in the wage and price guidelines and guideposts, but these failed because they attempted to handle administratively a task that requires the flexibility and the resistance to political pressure of a decentralized market mechanism.

MAP—THE MARKET ANTI-INFLATION PLAN

The market mechanism is needed to transmit the appropriate incentive against inflationary wage and price increases. Such incentives could be imposed by the government, as in most of the wage-oriented proposals. But the market mechanism is also required for *setting the appropriate level* of the incentive and for continually *adjusting the level* to changing conditions. This is what we believe is provided by the Market Mechanism Anti-Inflation Accounting Credit Plan. We have abbreviated this to Market Anti-Inflation Plan, or MAP, to indicate that it shows the way we have to go to cure our inflation and its stagflation offspring.

The basic idea of MAP is to correct the accounting flaw by translating the *social harm* from the inflationary element in price and wage increases into a *private cost* that the firm will try to avoid, and to do this through the market mechanism so as to avoid all administrative control or regulation of wages or prices. MAP leaves these free for determination by the market or by bargaining, as they are now, directing the market influences only on the (dollar) *Net Sales* or factor payments of the firm (gross sales minus purchases from other firms). Since Net Sales consists of the *combined* profits and wages, this clears MAP of any suspicion of bias between the two.

Prices in general rise, which is what we mean by inflation, when total national Dollar Net Sales is increasing faster than the total national (net) real output. This also means that national Net Sales per unit of input is increasing faster than national average output per unit of input—"productivity." A device that prevented every firm from increasing its Net Sales per unit of input by more than the national (average) increase in productivity would stop the inflation. But this would achieve only objective (1). It would *freeze* the economy, preventing the adjustments of *relative* Net Sales (the relative wages and profits) that are essential for the efficient working of a free and unregimented economy.

FUNCTIONAL RELATIVE AND NON-FUNCTIONAL INFLATIONARY INCREASES

To achieve objective (2) MAP must eliminate the non-functional inflationary part of the increases, which is *proportional*, without interfering with the functional *relative* changes.

The excess of a firm's increase in *Net Sales* per unit of input over the national average increase in *output* per unit of input may be called its "*inflationary impact*." It constitutes the firm's contribution to the inflation—in the sense that if this excess is added up for all the firms, it comes to the excess of the increase in national Net Sales over the increase in national net output, which is the inflation.

One might therefore be tempted to say that the greater a firm's "inflationary impact," the more it is to blame for the inflation (as seems to be assumed in some of the anti-inflation plans), and that a firm with a "deflationary impact" (Net Sales *decreasing* relative to national output per man) is to be praised.

This is not the case at all. The *differences* in various firms' "inflationary impact" reflect the functional *relative* changes and not the inflationary *proportional* changes. A firm's greater-than-average increase in Net Sales may be the completely warranted necessary changes in relative price, reflecting a greater-than-average scarcity of its product. Nevertheless we will find the "inflationary impact," cleared of all connection with blame or praise, of great use in achieving objective (2). If general inflation is to be prevented, every *greater-than-average* scarcity of a product must still be balanced by a *less-than-average* scarcity elsewhere, with a *less-than-average* increase (or an absolute decrease) in price and in Net Sales. Neither blame nor praise is deserved in either case, but the accounting flaw must be corrected in all cases.

A COUNTER-INFLATIONARY INCENTIVE

To correct the accounting flaw, which is the failure of firms to take into account the inflationary part of the increases in their Net Sales for which the inflationary pressure is responsible, a counterinflationary incentive must be imposed that is just equal to the inflationary pressure that it has to offset. Since an inflation affects *all* Net Sales, the counterinflationary incentive must also be applied to all Net Sales. It will then not interfere with the relative changes in Net Sales.

The appropriate counterinflationary incentive is that which is just sufficient to make *total* national Net Sales increase at the same rate as total national output. Average Net Sales per unit of input will then also be increasing at the same rate. This means that the rate of inflation will be zero, so that the total of the "inflationary impacts" of all the firms will add up to zero. The sum of positive "inflationary impacts" will be just equal to the sum of *negative* "inflationary impacts" (the "deflationary impacts"). This gives MAP the weapon needed to achieve objective (2).

ANTI-INFLATION ACCOUNTING CREDIT

Only the market can tell us what is the appropriate size of the counterinflationary incentive, but MAP can harness the market mechanism for this task. MAP creates *a new commodity* to be traded on the market—"Anti-Inflation Accounting Credit." It requires each firm to *buy* Anti-Inflation Accounting Credit in an amount equal to its "inflationary impacts," or enables it to *sell* such "credit" in an amount equal to its "deflationary impact," and it lets the market set the equilibrium price.

The free market price of the "credit," in discouraging demand and encouraging supply (which is what all prices always do) until they are equal in the market equilibrium, *ipso facto* discourages "inflationary impacts" and encourages "deflationary impacts" until *these* are equal. The inflationary and deflationary impacts then just cancel each other, and there is no inflation. The free market price of Anti-Inflation Accounting Credit *is* the incentive we need, is of just the strength we need, and is continuously adjusted by the market as conditions change.

All firms remain free to set their individual Net Sales as high or as low as they wish, after taking into account what they will have to pay or receive for the "credit" they buy or sell. This is how the social flaw in the private accounting is corrected. The firms are induced by the price of the "credit" freely to set their Net Sales, and thereby also the wages and prices, at the levels required for an inflation-free economy.

(In an *expectational deflation*, such as we had in the 1930s, all this would be reversed. The equilibrium price of "credit" would be negative and the price of "deficit" positive. Firms with deflationary impacts would be *required* to sell their "surplus credit" at the negative price. A generalized MAP would symmetrically require firms with deflationary impact to buy ADD (Anti-Deflationary Debits) to cancel their deflationary surplus "credit.")

A SELF-DEFLATING INFLATION DEFLATOR

Extra "credit" permits a firm to enjoy greater Net Sales. The higher the inflationary expectations, the more will firms be willing to pay for additional "credit" (or insist on getting paid for their spare "credit"), the higher will be the price of "credit," and the stronger will be the counterinflationary incentive—the price of "credit." MAP thus turns the inflationary pressure against itself, jujitsu fashion.

An important result is that as the inflationary pressure is weakened by the counterinflationary pressure, the price of "credit" falls and the counterinflationary pressure also weakens. As MAP deflates the inflation it is also itself deflated. When both the inflation and the expectation of inflation stop, the price of "credit" falls to zero or to whatever counterinflationary pressure may stil be required to offset any remaining upward pressures on prices and wages other than inflationary expectations.

There are many ways in which these principles can be applied. What follows is a very concrete picture of one way in which MAP could work. This might be called "model A."

MAP'S RULES

1. The responsibility for curing the inflation is given by Congress to the Federal Reserve. Its current responsibility for maintaining a sound money supply is interpreted as one *compatible* with prosperity and price stability (functional finance). Under MAP, the Federal Reserve had its responsibility extended by Congress to include responsibility for the *maintenance of price stability* through MAP.

MAP alone cannot prevent too much spending from causing excess demand or too little spending from causing depression and unemployment, while a functional finance spending policy alone cannot prevent expectational inflation. For prosperity, total spending must be enough to buy the output of full employment at the current prices. But that could leave us with inflation. For price stability, Net Sales (i.e., wages-plus-profit) must rise at the same rate as national output. But that could leave us with severe unemployment or with scarcities and black markets. With both functional finance *and* MAP we can have both prosperity and price stability.

MAP also provides better signals to indicate when total spending is too much or too little. An excess of total spending above that required for full employment, not being able to raise the average price or to increase employment and output, immediately shows itself in a rise in the price of Anti-Inflation Credit (AIC) and in shortages and black markets. Any deficiency of demand, having no way of reducing average price, immediately shows itself in swollen inventories or reduced employment and output (and in a negative price of "credit" and a positive price of "debit").

2. The Federal Reserve sets up an Anti-Inflation Credit (AIC) Office which monitors the Anti-Inflation Accounting position of each firm. At the initiation of MAP the AIC Office credits each firm with free AIC equal to 102 percent of its annual, pre-MAP (dollar) Net Sales (2 percent being the estimated national annual increase in productivity).

A firm is any employer who is subject to income tax. Net Sales consists of gross sales (including "internal sales," i.e., inventory increases at cost) *minus* purchases from other firms, and it is therefore equal to the firm's Profit *plus* its Wage Bill. Profit includes interest payments, rents, fees and other purchases from, and sales by, those firms. The Wage Bill includes all the costs of employment—wages, salaries, and the cost of all fringe benefits.

3. A firm's AIC (its Anti-Inflation Credit with the AIC Office) is the measure of its noninflationary Net Sales. Net Sales in excess of the firm's AIC constitutes an "inflationary impact" because it raises the average price level (unless offset by firms with Net Sales below their AIC). It can therefore be said to incur an Anti-Inflation Accounting *Deficit* and must cancel the deficit by buying additional AIC equal to this "deficit." Net Sales below a firm's AIC constitutes a "deflationary impact" because it lowers the average price level (unless offset by firms with Net Sales above their AIC) and can be said to earn Anti-Inflationary Accounting Credit "surplus," which is available for the "deficit" firms to buy.

The AIC Office maintains a market in AIC, buying and selling AIC freely to all comers, adjusting the price as may be necessary to bring supply and demand into equality. No AIC is created or destroyed in this trading, so that total AIC and total Net Sales are unchanged.

(In an *expectational deflation*, the price of "credit" would be *negative*. "Deflationary impact" firms would be required to buy ADD (Anti-Deflation Debits) to cancel the "surpluses" from their Net Sales growth falling below national average productivity.)

The money paid for additional AIC comes out of the Net Sales (i.e., the income or wages plus profit) of the buying firms and adds the same amount to the income of the selling firms. MAP can thus be said to consist of exactly equal amounts of "stick" and "carrot" incentives. MAP is also completely neutral in the sharing of such increases or decreases between profit and wages as it is in the sharing of income in general.

4. A newly hired employee (including all the employees of a new firm) entitles the firm to additional free AIC equal to his Wage (including fringe benefits) in his previous employment. Conversely, on the separation of an employee from a firm (which includes all the employees of a firm that closes down) the firm's AIC is reduced by the corresponding amount, calculated the same way.

Additional capital investment—whether financed by stocks, bonds, or reinvested (declared) profits (including all the investment of a new firm)—entitles the firm to AIC equal to interest on the additional investment at the prime rate of interest. Conversely, on the retirement of capital invested (which includes all the capital of a firm that closes down), the firm has its AIC reduced correspondingly.

5. The AIC Office keeps a continuous record of each firm's AIC as adjusted by hirings and separations of employees, by increases and reductions in capital invested, and by its purchases and sales of AIC. With this updated record of each firm's AIC, it is able to check whether the Net Sales corresponds to its total AIC.

6. Soon after the beginning of MAP the AIC Office starts off the trade in AIC by setting a price of AIC at which it expects to generate demand and supply in about equal quantities, guaranteeing to buy and sell AIC at this price up to an amount estimated as needed for a month's use. Beyond that limited guarantee it leaves the price entirely to the free market. Firms will then have two further months in which to adjust their total AIC to their Net Sales, or their Net Sales to their AIC. Check audits will be made at the end of a year when each firm's AIC is automatically increased by 2 percent to allow for increasing productivity. The national total AIC and Net Sales thus keeps up with both components of total national output: the output per unit of input and the volume of inputs. Net Sales stays proportional to output, so that the price level cannot change.

7. Government agencies and other institutions financed by government and private nonprofit corporations are subject to MAP just like private firms, but instead of "Net Sales" they would use "Net Income Generated—the cost of the labor and capital services or, namely, what is left of Net Sales if profit is eliminated. This may be considered the "price" paid for the service rendered, and it is most convenient to treat it as "Net Sales." Labor and capital, business and government, are thus all treated the same way.

HOW LONG WOULD MAP TAKE?

If MAP is imposed when an expectational inflation is going on, with prices rising at 6 percent, labor and capital inputs increasing at 2 percent, and productivity increasing at 2 percent per annum, total Net Sales will have been increasing at 10 percent. Suddenly Net Sales is reduced to 4 percent (the 102 percent basic AIC credited, increased a further 2 percent by the increase in labor and capital inputs). This is just enough to buy the increased output *at last year's prices*. Since prices have been rising, and are expected to continue to rise, there will be a demand for additional AIC to legitimize the increase in Net Sales from the *expected* increase in prices. The price of "credit" will be correspondingly high. But as it becomes apparent that the *actual* average increase is only 4 percent, the 10 percent expectation will diminish and with it also the demand for extra AIC. The price of "credit" will consequently fall.

Any continuing expectation of *any* inflation at all (which depends on Net Sales increasing at something *more* than 4 percent) is bound to be disappointed and revised downward. When the inflationary expectations have been completely eliminated by the disappointments, the expectational inflation will be completely cured. There would then be no "expectational inflation" demand for "credit," and its price would fall to zero or to what is required to offset any upward pressures on prices and wages due to causes other than expectations of continuing inflation.

As with all anti-inflation plans, there is a temptation to beat the gun by establishing higher base prices and wages for incorporation into the plan before it is jelled, and if the design of the plan permits this, it could result in a pre-plan spurt in the inflation. But such a possible development ends as soon as the base Net Sales are fixed. Once MAP is installed, the (initial) goal would be reached as soon as the rules are understood and obeyed. If, as seems pretty certain, there is a lively prior discussion, the cure could take very little time, or no time at all, or even *less than no time!*

Unless there is a general expectation of the inflation stopping or being significantly reduced soon after the imposition of MAP, there is no danger of MAP being imposed. Such an expectation would lead, after the base Net Sales of firms had been set, to anticipation of smaller future price increases and a greater willingness of sellers to accept lower price increases now rather than wait, as well as a greater readiness of buyers to wait rather than buy now. *This would result in at least a slowdown even if not a pre-emptive complete cessation of the inflation before MAP comes into effect.* But as soon as MAP *is* imposed, any remaining expectation of any average price increase will meet quick disappointment and reconsideration.

MAP IS A NEW USE OF AN OLD TRICK

MAP will indeed seem to many people a wild-eyed revoluntionary dream too good to be true. But it is, on the contrary, a well-established device that is operating under our eyes all the time. So familiar is it that it has become invisible—like Sherlock Holmes' invisible postman. This device regularly achieves the same two-fold task of keeping the *average* of a large number of quantities of some item fixed, while each *actual* quantity remains unregulated, for free determination by one of a large number of people. *MAP is no new invention.* MAP is just a plagiarism—a copy of this ancient device. What makes MAP seem strange is only that the item to which MAP is applied has not been treated in this normal way in the past.

One example of the only too familiar miracle will suffice. The price of oranges is adjusted by the market to make the demand equal to the supply. It achieves our objective (1) by making the *average* number demanded per consumer equal to the average number available per consumer, even while achieving our objective (2) by permitting the *actual* number of oranges demanded by each consumer to be chosen freely by the consumer when taking the price into consideration.

For this miracle to work, society at one time had to decide to make the ownership of oranges a legal property right of individuals. This undoubtedly was a shocking, impious, revolutionary, and "antisocial" idea when first suggested to the head of an unindividualized tribe. We expect some of the same resistance to MAP even if it is not accompanied by the claim that it could cure the inflation so quickly.

This bare-bone description of the operation of model A MAP, of course, leaves much to be filled in. We have heard hundreds of objections, nearly all of which have turned out to be either misunderstandings or problems for which we have been able to find satisfactory solutions. Some of the solutions, we hope, will be improved on, and other problems for which there are no satisfactory solutions could come to light. So far we have not met any fatal objections, and we feel that MAP *does* indicate the way we will have to go if we are to cure our inflation-stagflation.

This is not to say that we think we have a finished blueprint. The sketch of model A does, we hope, give a good idea of the general way in which MAP works. But many, if not most, of the actual numbers or time periods we have baldly pronounced may well be changed and improved.

COMPLICATIONS AND VARIATIONS

One possible variation of MAP is the extension of "the previous year" (for the determination of the grants of free AIC) to an average of several years, so as to diminish distortions from specially favorable or unfavorable years. Another is the restriction of MAP to firms above a certain size. This would be very important if some bureaucratic administration of wages or prices were involved, but it does not seem a very serious matter since MAP calls for only the *monitoring* of the truthfulness of the reports. This task is not different in kind from the monitoring and auditing of income tax and social security tax. There will, of course, be some cheating, but the incentives for cheating will be very much less than with income tax. The actual accounting task is comparable to what is being done by organizations like Master Charge.

There are many secondary problems, such as the determination of the amount of free AIC for new entrants to the labor force with no previous Wage. There might be some minimum wage before an employee is included in MAP. There is the possible hiring of retirees only for the sake of large, free AIC based on their last Wage. Some adjustment will have to be made to prevent shrinkage of a firm's Wage Bill, and its free AIC, from the retirement of high-Wage senior employees and from the recruitment of low-Wage beginners. This adjustment could provide for the up-grading of the Wage with seniority.

EFFECT ON THE DOLLAR

One effect of the end of inflation in the United States, until such time as the other countries stop their inflations too, will be a *rising* value of the dollar in terms of the other country's currency, equal (with lags and anticipation) to that country's inflation rate. The United States would gain about as much from the cheapening, in dollars, of its imports as it would lose from the cheapening, in dollars, of its exports. But the stabilization of the dollar in purchasing power would make it a much more desirable store of value and reserve currency for the rest of the world than it has ever been. If the Federal Reserve supplies all such foreign demand for U.S. dollars without permitting a tightening of liquidity and depression at home, this would develop an unprecedented scope for exchanging U.S. dollars for real imports or for philanthropic or political expenditures abroad.

A SLOW OR QUICK MAP?

Among the variations in the application of MAP is the issue of *slowing* the disinflation. Many people would be hurt by a sudden end to the inflation. Assets, such as houses, bought at superinflated prices based on the anticipation of further inflation will fall in value if the further inflation does not come about. There will also be other serious inequities. Workers with contracts for wage increases for several years at the high rates appropriate in continuing inflation will benefit from being able to spend their inflation-powered future wages on goods with stable prices, while those with contracts due for renewal soon after the imposition of MAP will have to get *less* than the 2 percent average rate of increase to balance the others' gains. Conversely, a quick MAP would be very hard on those with contractual monetary obligations undertaken in the expectation that they would be paid in more easily earned depreciating dollars. To soften such inequities a *gradual* disinflation has been suggested.

This could be done very simply by setting a higher initial Net Sales Increase Norm (beyond which additional AIC is required). This could be set not at 4 percent but at, say, 9 percent for one year (instead of the pre-MAP 10 percent), 8 percent for the next year, and so on, taking, say, six years to reach 4 percent and complete price stability.

It can be argued that such a slowing of MAP only spreads out the inequities of the disinflation over a longer period, during which it partially continues the inequities of the inflation. Another way of avoiding these inequities is a legal adjustment, at the beginning of MAP, which would deflate the monetary obligations so as to keep their value constant in *real* terms. This is a kind of indexation in reverse and would apply only to *pre-MAP* contracts, as contrasted with suggested *permanent* indexation to correct the inequities from continuing inflation. But such interfering with "the sacredness of contracts" is a matter for very serious consideration.

A quick MAP, or a fully anticipated slow MAP, if it could quickly reduce the price of AIC to zero, would have the great advantage that it would not give time for the development of a host of troubles that arise if we have positively priced AIC for a considerable time. But unless there is a successful legal deflation of inflation-powered contracts, the pressure for "catching up" by those left out by such contracts will necessitate high AIC prices for a considerable time.

In a slow MAP the gradual disinflation could be obscured by random changes in domestic or world conditions, so that for some time it may not be obvious that MAP is really stopping the inflation. To break the inflationary expectations a really dramatic demonstration may be desirable.

It is also possible that eliminating inflation quickly does not require a significantly higher price of AIC than does reducing the inflation gradually. If this is so, the case for a quick MAP is stronger.

A further difficulty for a quick MAP is the possibility that there is an inherent upward pressure on wages and prices even at less than full employment, and even in the absence of any expectations of inflation. Further study may be able to discover whether this is so. If it is, a quick MAP is an illusion and price stability will require a permanent positive price of AIC.

However, even if a careful weighting of the pros and cons should come out definitely in favor of a quick MAP, a gradual disinflation may be dictated by the political need to reduce resistance to MAP from those who would lose, or who think they might lose, as well as from those to whom all quick measures seem dangerous.

We believe we have explained the nature of our inflation-stagflation and derived from this a logical treatment. It is time we stopped repeating the doleful dirge, "Nobody knows what to do about the Great Paradox," and set about undertaking a look at the political and legislative procedures, at the border of which our MAP ends. *There is a cure* for Inflation-Stagflation. We should not limit our plans and our hopes to moderating their escalation, nor should we allow debate about possible improvements in a plan to postpone action indefinitely.

D. Capital and Interest Rate Theory

[1]

ALTERNATIVE FORMULATIONS OF THE THEORY OF INTEREST

THE first part of this article develops a technique for analysing the more recent developments of interest theory. This is used in the second part to show that several apparently different theories of the rate of interest really say the same thing. In the third part the different formulations of interest theory are examined for hidden implications concerning the relative importance of elements they all recognise.

I

From the " classical " [1] view that the rate of interest is the price that equates saving to investment, to the " modern " view that it is the price that equates the demand for holding cash to the supply of cash,[2] there are two steps. The first step—a fairly easy one—is to recognise that " hoarding," " dishoarding " and changes in the amount of money also have something to do with the supply of " credit " and the rate of interest—in the short period, at any rate. The second step—one that for most trained economists is a terrifying and long-postponed departure into uncharted waters—is to recognise that, by simple arithmetic, saving and investment are always equal to each other (for the whole economy) whatever the level of the rate of interest or anything else.

[1] I have put the word " classical " in inverted commas throughout this article because I believe that the theory of the rate of interest referred to by that label here and in Mr. Keynes' writings was not clearly held by many economists who have right to that title. In the writing, if not in the mind, of the classical economists the total stock of capital played a more important rôle than the rate of investment, and some long-period time preference was more significant than the actual rate of current saving. It is only when applying some unclarified notions as to what the rate of interest would be in a stationary state with full employment (where, of course, there can be no saving or investment) and trying, in an elementary text-book, to present these as a theory of the current rate of interest, that some orthodox economists have been forced, in attempting to avoid some much cruder confusions, to present something like the " classical " theory of the rate of interest. Some economists who have been manœuvred into defending such lightly proposed formulations have discovered a strong attachment, born of chivalry, for their newly adopted charges. A study of the development of classical theories of interest as a result of such a situation, would, however, form the subject of another article.

[2] This is, of course, one particular formulation of the " modern " theory of interest (namely the " Keynesian "). That other " modern " formulations come to practically the same thing is the thesis of Part II of this article.

When these two steps have been taken, the rest is merely a matter of re-establishing one's equilibrium in the new position and of taking one's bearings. There remains only some arbitrariness in the language in which the new position is described.

An obvious way of bringing in the complications connected with " hoarding," " dishoarding " and changes in the quantity of money (*i.e.*, of taking the first step from the "classical" to the " modern " position) is simply to add these elements to (or subtract them from) the " classical " supply and demand curves for saving. The rate of interest is the price paid for loans or " credit." If the only suppliers of loans on the loan market in any period were people who saved some of their income in the period and every one of these supplied exactly the amount he had saved, then the supply of loans would be equal to the amount of saving. Similarly on the other side of the market; if the only people to demand loans were investors and no investor borrowed either more or less than he invested, then the demand for loans would be equal to the amount of investment. The rate of interest, then, in equating the supply and demand for loans (or " credit ") would thereby equate saving to investment.

To some extent these conditions may be relaxed without impairing the purely " classical " argument that the rate of interest equates saving to investment. If some savers " hoard " or lend less than they save, but this is exactly compensated by others who " dishoard " or lend more than they save, the total amount saved is still equal to the amount loaned on the market. Similarly, if some investors " hoard " or borrow more than they invest but this is exactly offset by other borrowers who " dishoard " or invest more than they borrow, then the total amount invested is still equal to the total amount borrowed. Or again, if there is a balance of net " hoarding " (or " dishoarding ") by savers, but there is an equal balance of " dishoarding " (or " hoarding ") by investors, the pure " classical " theorem would still hold. Saving would no longer be equal to lending or the supply of " credit," nor would investment be equal to borrowing, or the demand for " credit," but saving would be greater (or less) than lending by the same amount as investment is greater (or less) than borrowing, so that the rate of interest that made lending equal to borrowing would also equate saving and investment. In general, any one of the conditions given above may be relaxed if there is another compensating deviation in the opposite direction from the same or any other condition.

If there is no such exact equality between " hoarding " by some and " dishoarding " by others, and there is a balance of net " hoarding " in the whole economy (net " hoarding " will be a negative quantity if there is a net balance of " dishoarding "), then net " hoarding " is the measure of that amount of saving that does not get invested but is " hoarded " either by the savers themselves or by people who borrow from them. The rate of interest which must always equate lending to borrowing then fails to equate saving to investment but makes saving equal to investment *plus* net " hoarding." To get the equilibrium, net " hoarding " must be added to the investment curve to give the net demand for " credit."

An increase in the amount of money has an effect opposite to that of net " hoarding," and therefore identical with that of net " dishoarding." The borrowers of the new money may invest it, in which case the creation of the new money, like " dishoarding," has permitted an increase of investment *not* balanced by any increase in saving. The borrowers of the new money may spend it on consumption goods, and in this case, again like " dishoarding," it has permitted a diminution of saving (or an increase in dissaving) not balanced by any decline in investment. Or, finally, the borrowers of the new money may neither invest it nor spend it, but just " hoard " it, and in this case the creation of the new money, once more just like an act of " dishoarding," has permitted an equal and opposite volume of " hoarding " to take place and to cancel the effect that the increase in the amount of money might have had on the relationship between saving and investment. In the absence of any net " hoarding " the rate of interest that equates lending to borrowing does not equate saving to investment because some of the lending is provided not by savers, but by the monetary authorities who loan out the new money. What the rate of interest does is to equate investment, which is equal to the demand for " credit," to the supply of " credit " which is equal to saving *plus* the increase in the amount of money. Of course the opposite is true for a decrease in the amount of money.

Taking into account the effect both of *net* " hoarding " and of net changes in the amount of money, we can restate the position as it appears after the " first step " has been taken. The formula would now run : The rate of interest is the price that equates the supply of " credit," or saving *plus* the net increase in the amount of money in a period, to the demand for " credit," or investment *plus* net " hoarding " in the period. Our argument up to this point is illustrated by Fig. 1.

S is the supply schedule of saving, showing how much would be saved (measured horizontally) at each rate of interest (measured vertically). I is the schedule of investment showing how much would be invested (measured horizontally) at each rate of interest. These two schedules intersect at P_c, the "classical" point of equilibrium, which shows the rate of interest being determined at that level (AP_c) at which saving equals investment, both being equal to OA. L is the schedule showing the amount of net "hoarding" that would take place at each rate of interest. In the figure this is shown as a *positive* amount (*i.e.*, at all the rates of interest considered there would be a net balance of "hoarding" and not a net balance of "dishoarding") which is greater for lower

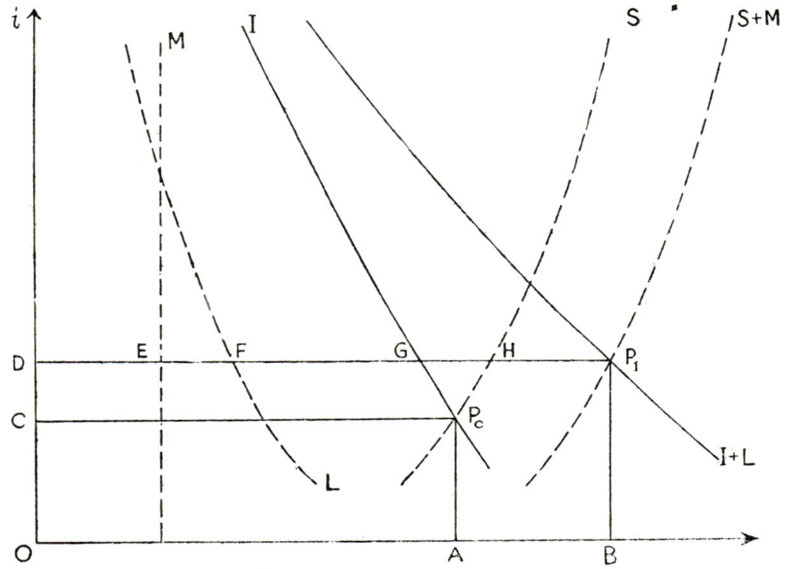

FIG. 1.

rates of interest. There is no reason for expecting "hoarding" always to outbalance "dishoarding" in the economy, and this is taken to be so in the figure merely for the purpose of simplifying the diagram. "Hoarding" could be taken as a negative quantity at some or at all rates of interest (and shown by the L curve falling to the left of the vertical axis) without affecting the argument in any way. There is, however, a good reason for net "hoarding" to be greater (or net "dishoarding" to be less) the lower the rate of interest, so that the L curve slopes down to the right. This is because the higher the rate of interest the greater the benefit lost by "hoarding" money instead of lending it out at interest, and the greater the temptation to "dishoard" and benefit by the receipt of interest.

The M curve shows the increase in the amount of money in the period, and is here shown as a positive amount and independent of the rate of interest. Both of these conditions are postulated merely for the purpose of simplifying the diagram. A *decrease* in the amount of money could be shown by drawing the M curve to the *left* of the vertical axis, signifying a *negative increase* in the amount of money. It might be the policy of the monetary authorities to take the rate of interest into account when deciding by how much to increase (or decrease) the amount of money. Thus if they increase the amount of money more (or diminish it by less) the higher is the rate of interest, then the M curve will slope *upward* to the right. But all such differences in assumptions would merely complicate the diagram without affecting our argument in any way.

The M curve is now added horizontally to the S curve, giving the total net supply schedule of loans (or " credit ") marked $S + M$. The L curve is added to the I curve, giving the total net demand schedule for loans (or " credit ") marked $I + L$. The two new curves intersect at P_1, giving an equilibrium into which the complications due to " hoarding " and to changes in the amount of money appear to have been incorporated. This is the position as it appears when the " first step " has been taken.

It is at once apparent that Fig. 1 contains a good deal of muddle, and in this it reflects the state of mind of voyagers in the middle of our two-stage trip. In the apparent equilibrium indicated by P_1 saving is not necessarily equal to investment (in the figure it is greater by GH), while the amount of money hoarded is not necessarily equal to the increase in the amount of money (in the figure it is greater by EF, which is equal to GH). This exactly portrays the disturbed state of mind of people who declare that saving can be greater than investment if the difference is hoarded.

The second step clears up the muddle. As soon as it is recognised that saving must always equal investment,[1] we get Fig. 2, where the S and I curves coincide, giving the new curve SI. For each scale of investment there is a corresponding level of income. This is determined by the propensity to consume. For each level of income there is a corresponding supply schedule of saving (with respect to the rate of interest) just like the S curve in Fig. 1. Thus for any particular rate of interest there is a particular scale of

[1] Any reader who still feels uneasy on this point might read one of my articles —" Mr. Keynes' General Theory of Employment," *I.L.O. Review*, October 1936, or " Savings Equals Investment," *Quarterly Journal of Economics*, February 1938.

investment, measured by the abscissa of the point corresponding to that rate of interest on the investment curve, and a particular supply schedule of saving showing how much would be saved at different rates of interest if income were at the level corresponding to the particular scale of investment. This supply schedule of saving will pass through the investment schedule at the point on the latter corresponding to the particular rate of interest, so that the two curves will have this point in common. All other points on the particular supply schedule of saving are illegitimate, and may be left out of the picture, because they contradict themselves in assuming a rate of interest other than that which forms the

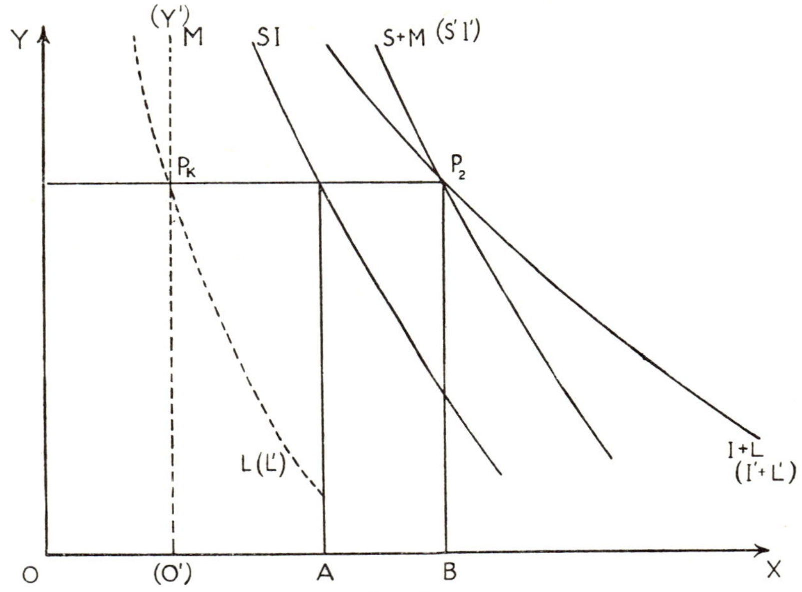

FIG. 2.

postulate on which the whole curve is constructed. Such a point would indicate how much would be saved at a rate of interest of 5 per cent. if the level of income were such as could exist only if the rate of interest were 4 per cent. The only legitimate point on the supply curve of saving is the one which falls on the investment curve and shows that at that particular rate of interest the amount saved will be equal to the amount invested. The locus of such legitimate point for different rates of interest must coincide with the *I* curve, making it an *SI* curve.

The *SI* curve is added to the *M* and *L* curves as in Fig. 1 to give the supply of "credit" $(S + M)$ and the demand for "credit" $(I + L)$. Equilibrium is reached at P_2, where the supply of " credit " is equal to the demand for it. There can now be no divergence between saving and investment such as was possible in the equilibrium visualised after the first step had been taken (*GH* in Fig. 1), nor can there now arise a difference between the increase in the supply of money in the period and the amount " hoarded " (*EF* in Fig. 1). P_2 must always be of the same height as P_k (the intersection of *M* and *L* which shows " hoarding " equal to the increase in the supply of money).

We must now examine a little more closely the nature of the items we have been handling: *S* (saving), *I* (investment), *L* (" hoarding ") and *M* (changes in the amount of money). *S* and *I* are essentially and naturally of the nature of *flows*. They must be measured as " so much per unit of time " or as " so much in a given period." In the absence of any change in the running of the whole economy it is reasonable to suppose that their values will be proportional to the period taken. At the same rate of interest, if we consider a period twice as long, we would expect to find that twice as much is invested and saved. It is not so clear in the case of *L* and *M*.

Let us first consider *L* or " hoarding." " Hoarding " by any individual was used to indicate an excess of *S* over *l* (lending) or an excess of *b* (borrowing) over *I*. $S = Y$ (income) $- C$ (expenditure or consumption). " Hoarding " therefore $= (Y - C - l) + (b - I) = (Y + b) - (C + I + l)$. Now, $(Y + b)$ is equal to total money receipts and $(C + I + l)$ is equal to the total money outlays. The excess of the former over the latter, which is what we have called " hoarding," is *the increase in the amount of money held*. This item can indeed be measured as " so much in a given period," but there is no reason for supposing that at each rate of interest, everything else remaining unchanged, an individual will continue to " hoard " (or " dishoard ") the same amount in successive periods in the way in which he may be expected to continue to save at the same rate. If the rate of interest has been the same for some time, an individual will neither " hoard " nor " dishoard." Only when there is a *change* in the rate of interest (and for a short period after the change) will " hoarding " or " dishoarding " take place.

The reason for this difference between the ways in which *S* and *I* respond to the rate of interest and the way in which *L* (" hoarding ") responds to the rate of interest is as follows. Saving, investing and " hoarding " all take place only when there is some kind of maladjustment. Saving takes place when the capital value of an individual's assets (representing future yields) is

Q 2

considered by the individual to be too small as compared with his current income, so that he uses some of his income to increase the stock (and value) of his assets. The rate at which he saves is equal to that rate of saving which equates the marginal utility of income forgone to the utility of the marginal increment of assets acquired (or that of the future consumption that it may represent). Investment takes place whenever the capital stock of society is too small as compared with the rate of interest, in the sense that if the capital stock were just maintained, the marginal rate of return on the activity of maintaining it would be greater than the rate of interest. In such circumstances the capital stock is augmented. The rate of investment that takes place is the rate that makes the marginal rate of return on investment equal to the rate of interest.

In both of these cases, the acts of saving and of investment have some tendency to wipe out the maladjustment that calls them forth, in so far as saving tends to increase the value of assets held by an individual, thus rendering further saving less urgent, while investment tends to increase the stock of capital, and thus to lower the marginal rate of return on maintaining it. Both of these tendencies, however, are very weak in the short run, because the amount that can be saved or invested in a short period, limited in the way indicated above, is small compared with the total value of assets or the total stock of capital, so that many periods must elapse before there is any noticeable effect on these and on the rate of saving or investment that corresponds to a given rate of interest.

The maladjustment which calls forth "hoarding" is an inequality between the marginal utility of the stock of money held initially by any individual and the rate of interest which is the price that has to be paid (or the reward that has to be forgone) for the sake of enjoying this marginal utility. It does *not* take a long time to eliminate such a maladjustment which arises when there is a change in the rate of interest, since there is no increasing cost of "hoarding," as there is of saving (because of the diminished marginal utility of income) or of investment (because of the diminished marginal efficiency of investment). It is possible for an individual to borrow or lend (or withdraw or repay loans) and thereby very quickly to adjust the marginal utility of his stock of money to the rate of interest. As soon as these transactions are completed, no more "hoarding" or "dishoarding" takes place until the rate of interest (or something else) changes again.

What all this means is that while I and S, the *levels* of investment and saving, depend on the *level* of the rate of interest,

" hoarding " depends on a *change* in the rate of interest. In this it is more like a *change* in I or S, which would also depend upon a change in the rate of interest. This is quite natural, for " hoarding," as we have seen, is nothing but a *change* in the amount of money held. From this it follows that the true parallel to I and S would be not " hoarding " or the *change* in the amount of money held, but the total *amount* of money people wish to hold, for that, just like I and S, could be expected to stay put as long as the rate of interest (and other influences) remained unchanged.

If the period under consideration is taken to be long enough for the amount of money held to be completely adjusted to the change in the rate of interest, it is a simple matter to adjust our argument and reinterpret our diagram in accordance with this consideration. " Hoarding," or the *increase* in the amount of money held in the period at each rate of interest (L in Fig. 2), is the excess of the amount of money people wish to hold at each rate of interest over the amount of money they held at the beginning of the period. We can therefore obtain the curve showing the *total amount* of money people wish to hold, by simply *adding* this initial amount of money held to the L curve—*i.e.*, by moving the whole curve to the right, by a distance representing the amount of money held at the beginning of the period. We can suppose the L curve in Fig. 2 to have been treated in this way, so that it now represents the total amount of money people will wish to hold at each rate of interest. This curve is now recognisable as the demand curve for money to hold. It will naturally have a positive value for all rates of interest as it is shown to have in the figure.

An analogous treatment can be applied to the M curve which represented the *increase* in the supply of money. This can be turned into a curve showing the total amount of money available in the new position (at the new interest rate) by adding to the *increase* in the supply of money the initial supply of money or the amount of money available at the beginning of the period. On the new interpretation the M curve will be the supply curve of money.[1]

Now, the total *supply* of money, or the total amount in existence or available at the beginning of the period, must necessarily be equal to the total amount of money *held* at the beginning of the period, because all money in existence must be held by somebody, and all money held by anybody must be in

[1] For some suggestions which I have found useful in the preceding paragraphs I am indebted to Dr. L. M. Lachman, at the London School of Economics, who must not, however, be held responsible for anything I say in this article.

existence. This means that the M curve and the L curve will both have been shifted to the right by *exactly the same amount.* It follows that the relationship between the two curves and the ordinate or height of their point of intersection P_k will not have been affected by this change. The ordinate of P_2 will also be unaffected, since the $S + M$ and the $I + L$ curves will also have been shifted to the right by exactly equal distances.

We must now observe that in substituting the supply of money for the change in the amount of money and substituting the demand for money to hold or liquidity preference for " hoarding," we would appear to have involved ourselves in a greater difficulty than the one from which we wished to escape by this measure. We now find that to get the $S + M$ and the $I + L$ curves we have to add the M and I curves, which now measure *definite* amounts of money, independent of the length of any period, to the SI curve, which measures an amount of saving and investment which is *indefinite* unless some arbitrary length of period is postulated.[1]

This difficulty disappears as soon as it is observed that the arbitrariness of the SI curve does not matter at all. We get exactly the same result whatever the length of the period considered. If the period is longer we add equally larger amounts to both M and L (the supply and demand curves for money), and so the height BP_2 (which gives us the rate of interest) is unaffected; and however small the period, the height of BP_2 is unaffected. When we see this we also see that the whole business of adding the SI curve to the M and L curves is quite unnecessary. We can get the answer to our question more directly by just looking at the M and L curves (the amount of money and the liquidity preference schedule) and their intersection P_k. This is nothing but the diagrammatical representation of the formulation of the modern interest theory favoured by Mr. Keynes.

When one has reached the new position and adjusted oneself to its implications, a backward glance at the two steps that led from the " classical " to the " modern " theory of interest (at any rate in its " Keynesian " formulation) shows them to be as Machiavellian, as they seem terrifying to a " classical " economist who is

[1] The addition appears even more strange, indeed quite impossible, if we consider the S and I curves to represent not *amounts* saved or invested in some arbitrarily chosen *period*, but as *rates* (or *intensities*) of saving and investment. However, it is always possible to consider some finite *period* in which saving and investment are *amounts*, instead of concentrating on the limiting *ratio* between saving (or investment) and the period of time which constitutes the *flow*, so that our difficulty is seen to consist only in the arbitrariness of the period chosen.

making up his mind to venture on them. For the first, easy step is the insinuation of Liquidity Preference as a junior partner in the old-established one-man firm in the business of interest-determination, and the second, much more nasty, step is to put Saving-Investment, the senior partner, to sleep, as a preliminary to kicking him out.

While the tougher economists, like Mr. Keynes, are not impressed by the wickedness of such a procedure, and the slightly less tough salve their consciences with a shrug of the shoulder and a murmured plea that in science the end justifies the means, other economists who have ceased to be " classical," but are still somewhat "romantic,"[1] will be very loth to dispose of the " Old Man " so summarily, and will prefer to keep him on in the firm as a sleeping-partner with suitable honours and harmless occupations. In this way we find other formulations of the modern theory of interest, differing from Mr. Keynes' in the letter rather than in the spirit. The analysis of these formulations by means of the apparatus used above will enable us first to see the differences, if any, in this logical form, and then to examine the pros and cons of the differences in their emphasis on, or implications concerning, the various objective factors involved.

II

The clearest of such modern formulations of interest theory seems to be that of Prof. Bertil Ohlin.[2] According to Prof. Ohlin, the rate of interest is the price that equates the supply and demand for " credit " which may be measured *Gross* or *Net*. The *net* supply of credit (or the supply of *new* credit) is the amount saved *plus* any net dishoarding (or *minus* any net hoarding) by lenders, since it is this sum that they lend on the credit market. The net demand for credit (or the demand for *new* credit) is the amount invested *plus* any net hoarding (or *minus* any net dishoarding) by borrowers, that being the sum borrowed on the credit market. These supplies and demands are both considered not as simple quantities, but as schedules relating the various quantities of new credit that would be supplied or demanded at the different rates of interest. Since Prof. Ohlin—as this account of his theory shows—has not only taken the first step from the " classical " towards the " modern " theory of

[1] See D. H. Robertson, ECONOMIC JOURNAL, September 1937, p. 436, n. 2.

[2] "Some Notes on the Stockholm Theory of Saving and Investment," II, ECONOMIC JOURNAL, June 1937, and his rejoinder to Mr. Keynes in " Alternative Theories of the Rate of Interest," ECONOMIC JOURNAL, September 1937.

interest, but has emphatically stated that saving must always be equal to investment, thereby making the second step, it is possible to explain and illuminate his theory by means of our Fig. 2. We will consider first his *net* formulation in terms of the supply and demand for *new* credit. There are two different ways of doing this.

The simple way is to interpret the M curve as showing dishoarding by lenders and the L curve as showing hoarding by borrowers, both being schedules showing the different amounts that would be hoarded or dishoarded at different rates of interest. The SI curve shows investment (and therefore also saving) as a function of the rate of interest just as before. The addition of this curve to the M curve gives us the total supply schedule of new credit $S + M$. Its addition to the L curve gives us the total demand schedule for new credit $I + L$. The intersection of these supply and demand schedules for new credit at P_2 gives us the rate of interest BP_2. Again we see that we could have saved ourselves the trouble of adding the SI curve and gone direct to P_k as the equilibrium point showing the rate of interest $O'P_k$.

This interpretation of Fig. 2 has the disadvantages: (*a*) that it suggests that the lenders will always dishoard a fixed amount, irrespective of the rate of interest (unless we re-draw the M curve, making it slope upward to the right to show that they would be induced to dishoard more at higher rates of interest), and (*b*) that it implies that at all rates of interest it is the lenders on the whole who dishoard and the borrowers who hoard. There is no reason for supposing this to be the case, since it is possible for lenders to hoard by lending something less than their total saving, and for borrowers to dishoard by investing (or spending on consumption) more than they borrow. These are not fundamental objections, since they boil down to nothing more than the unavoidable arbitrariness of a base line for our measurements. It is nevertheless worth while, for the sake of dispelling any uneasiness that may remain, to go on to the slightly more complicated second interpretation (or rather adaptation) of our Fig. 2 as an illustration of Professor Ohlin's argument.

Since hoarding is not peculiar to borrowers and dishoarding is not restricted to lenders, and since it is only the net balance of hoarding and dishoarding that matters to us, we can use one curve to measure the *net* hoarding or dishoarding by the whole economy, in a schedule showing this as a function of the rate of interest. This is the new meaning of the L curve. The M curve then becomes a new Y axis (which we mark $O'Y'$), since at the rate of interest OP_k hoarding equals dishoarding, so that net hoarding equals zero. At higher rates of interest net hoarding is negative (dishoarding is greater than hoarding or net dishoarding is positive), and at lower rates of interest net hoarding is positive. We therefore rename our L curve L', to remind us that it is now considered with respect to the vertical axis $O'Y'$, which it cuts at P_k. With the shifting of our vertical axis a distance OO' to the right, the saving-investment curve must also be shifted the same distance to the right to show the same schedule of saving-investment. This merely means re-naming, as $S'I'$, the previous $S + M$ curve. This curve (in its investment aspect, I') is then added to the L' curve of *net* hoarding (positive for rates of interest less than $O'P_k$ and negative for higher rates of interest) to give $I' + L'$, which is the same as the previous curve, $I + L$. The intersection of these two curves at P_2 gives us the rate of interest at which the supply of credit (which consists of saving plus net dishoarding by savers) is equal to the demand for credit (which consists of amounts borrowed and used for investment plus net hoarding by people other than savers), the various items being rearranged somewhat so that all uncancelled (or *net*) hoarding or dishoarding is included in the second curve.

Once more we get the same answer, and we see again that the incorporation of saving and investment is completely unnecessary for the purpose of getting the answer to our question. P_2 gives the point where saving is equal to investment *plus* net hoarding. Since we know that saving is always equal to investment, we can remove these from both sides of our equation without losing anything, and we see that P_2 gives us the rate of interest at which net hoarding equals zero. By going directly for this we, and Professor Ohlin, would have saved ourselves a lot of trouble. Our only comfort is that all this empty ceremony about saving and investment may have done something to preserve the dignity of our ancient monarch, deprived of all influence in the real affairs of state. The effects of such ceremonial activities will be dealt with in the third section of this article, when we consider the importance of differing formulation with the same logical content.

We can now consider Prof. Ohlin's *Gross* formulation. Mr. Keynes says that the rate of interest is the price that equates the supply and demand for *cash*. Prof. Ohlin says that it is the price that equates the supply and demand for *credit*. The identity of meaning of these two propositions is shown in Fig. 3.

Along the vertical axis is measured the rate of interest. The M curve shows the amount of money available in an economy. If the amount of money is fixed independently of the rate of interest, this curve will be perpendicular, as it is drawn in our diagram. If the supply of money is governed by the rate of interest (as it may be if the monetary authorities are influenced by the rate of interest in determining the amount of money), the *M* curve will have a corresponding shape. The horizontal distance between the *M* curve and the *A* curve shows the value, at each rate of interest, of all the other assets in the economy. The lower the rate of interest the greater the value of these assets, because then the expected future incomes which these assets represent will lose less in being discounted to give the present value of the assets.

At each rate of interest—and the corresponding value of the assets—people will wish to distribute their wealth in a certain proportion between cash and other assets. At a higher rate of interest people will wish to hold less cash, partly because of the higher reward for holding other assets, partly because the value of

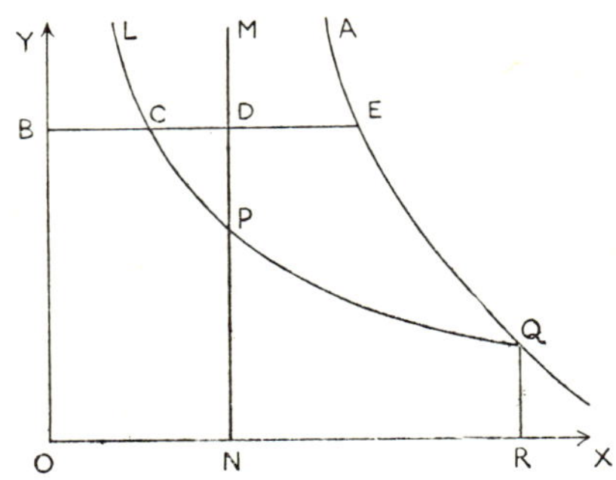

FIG. 3.

other assets shrinks relatively to the value of a given amount of money, and partly because at the higher rate of interest investment and incomes will be less. The *L* curve shows the way in which at each rate of interest people desire to distribute their wealth between cash and other assets. Thus if the rate of interest is *OB*, the amount of cash (here shown fixed independently of the rate of interest) being *BD*, the value of other assets is *DE*, so that the total value of assets including cash is *BE*. At this rate of interest (and the corresponding value of other assets) the owners of wealth wish to hold in cash not *BD*, the amount of cash actually available for them to hold, but *BC* (*i.e.*, *BD minus CD*); and they wish to hold in the form of other assets not *DE*, the value of the existing other assets, but *CE* (*i.e.*, *DE plus CD*).

At the rate of interest *OB*, then, all property-owners together will try to exchange *CD* of cash for the same cash value of other assets by exchanging with each other. Of course they cannot succeed in doing this, because whatever the extent to which cash and other assets change hands, the total of cash remains at *BD*, which is *CD* too much—and the total of other assets remains at *DE*, which is *CD* too little. But the attempt to get rid of cash and to acquire other assets has the effect of raising the price of these assets, and thus of lowering the rate of interest.

This process continues, the line *BE* moving down, *DE*, the value of other assets, increasing, and *CD*, the excess of cash or the deficit of other assets, diminishing until it disappears, *C* and *D* meeting in *P*. *P* is the point of equilibrium, there being no further incentive for the value of assets and the rate of interest to change. *NP* is the equilibrium rate of interest.

Mr. Keynes calls the *L* curve the demand for money and the *M* curve the supply of money, measuring both of these in the familiar way from the *Y* axis towards the right. The rate of interest is determined by the equilibrium shown at *P*, where the demand for cash *BC* is equal to the supply *BD*. Professor Ohlin looks at the picture from the other side, measures his quantities from the *A* curve towards the left. The *M* curve then measures the supply of assets which is the demand for credit and the *L* curve measures the demand for assets which is the supply of credit.[1] The equilibrium giving us the rate of interest is shown at *P*, where the supply of credit *ED* is equal to the demand for credit *EC*, and it is thus that the rate of interest is determined. Our figure shows very simply that the equation of *BC* to *BD* is the same thing as the equation of *EC* to *ED*.

As Fig. 3 is drawn, one might get the impression that the Keynesian argument is more reasonable because it is represented by the more normal procedure of measuring supply and demand

[1] We may assume that when Prof. Ohlin says that the supply and demand for assets " govern " the demand and supply of credit, he means that the former are the *schedules* which determine both the *quantity* of credit supplied (and demanded) on the market and the *price* or rate of interest in which alone we are here interested. Such an interpretation is supported by a passage in Prof. Ohlin's article in the ECONOMIC JOURNAL, September 1937, p. 423, where he says : " When it is said in pure theory that the price of a commodity is governed by supply and demand, the meaning is that it is determined by the demand and supply *curves*, which express the planned sales and purchases at different possible prices during a certain future period." It must be presumed that by the quantity of credit supplied (and demanded, since supply must equal demand) Prof. Ohlin means not the amount of credit that actually changes hands on the market, for that belongs to the *net* rather than to the *gross* analysis, but the total value of assets in existence (which is the actual demand for credit or capital-disposal) and the value of assets people wish to hold (which is the actual supply of credit or capital-disposal). Prof. Ohlin's somewhat obscure expression for this familiar form of showing an equilibrium by the intersection of supply and demand schedules is related to his use of the *ex ante* concept.

from the Y axis towards the right, while Prof. Ohlin's argument is very peculiar because it entails measurement from some strange-looking curve and towards the left. This, however, is entirely arbitrary, since the figure could quite easily be re-drawn the other way round and show the supply and demand for assets (the demand and supply of credit) measured from the Y axis towards the right, and the supply and demand for cash measured towards the left, and from a curve of exactly the same shape as the A curve in our figure. Any reason for preferring one of these formulations to the other must be based on quite different grounds.

In concluding this analysis of the logical content of Prof. Ohlin's *net* and *gross* formulations of the theory of interest I would like to mention two points.

First, in the *gross* formulation, even as given by Prof. Ohlin himself, there is no mention whatever of saving or of investment. Poor senior partner has been completely forgotten. Secondly, although Prof. Ohlin insists that the distinctions between *ex ante* and *ex post* analysis is essential for dealing with these problems, I have been able, I think, to present the whole of his interest theory without making any use of that mechanism.

The differences between Professor Ohlin's formulation of the theory of interest and that of other "modern" but not quite "Keynesian" economists, like Dr. Hicks and Mr. Robertson, are very slight and need not occupy much space. Dr. Hicks speaks of the rate of interest being determined by the supply and demand for *loans* in place of Ohlin's *credit*, but any difference between these can only be in the nature of some arbitrary variation of the base line for measurements which affect supply and demand equally and give the same rate of interest as the answer. Dr. Hicks' supply and demand for loans can be illustrated in our Fig. 2 in exactly the same way as Professor Ohlin's supply and demand for credit. Dr. Hicks emphasises the arbitrary nature of the choice between speaking in terms of *loans* or of *cash*, declaring that if we equate the supply and demand for money, the equation of the supply and demand for loans follows automatically, and if we equate the latter the former equation is otiose. This is shown very clearly in our Fig. 3.

The kernel of Mr. Robertson's theory of interest is also the same, although it is not so easy to disentangle it, on the one hand from his peculiar terminology and on the other hand from the numerous side issues that he delights to bring in. In his last rejoinder to Mr. Keynes,[1] however, he consents, under protest, to

[1] ECONOMIC JOURNAL, September 1937, p. 428.

use Mr. Keynes' terminology for a while, so that saving is always equal to investment, and this enables the reader to see that his "loanable funds," the supply and demand for which determine the rate of interest, is parallel with Professor Ohlin's "credit" and Dr. Hicks' "loans," so that Mr. Robertson is right when he says that his apparatus and Mr. Keynes' are "but alternative pieces of machinery," from which it follows that the vigorous attacks made so frequently by Mr. Robertson on Mr. Keynes' formulation must rest either on minor terminological quibbles which we cannot discuss here, or on differences in implicit assumption about the data which determine the relative convenience of the different formulation. These we can discuss in the next section.

III

Just as in the examination of the different formulations of interest theory we found it convenient to use Professor Ohlin's largely as representative of the others, so we shall find it convenient here to compare his formulæ with that of Mr. Keynes, now looking not for similarities in their analytical content, but for differences in their empirical implications and suggestions. On this we may come to a judgment as to these relative merits as tools for economic investigation.

Professor Ohlin's *gross* formulation has the advantage (as compared with Mr. Keynes') of making it harder for the student to forget that there is a different rate of interest for every different kind of "credit" determined by the supply and demand for that kind of "credit" (or the demand and supply of the corresponding assets). The emphasis in the *asset* side also diminishes the danger, which is quite considerable, if, like Mr. Keynes, we look only on the money side, of overlooking the effect on the rate of interest of changes in the total value of other assets. There is then a shift of the L curve to the right, but there is no change in purely psychological propensities to draw our attention to this shift.

Professor Ohlin's *gross* formulation, or a simple variant of it, is also a more useful method for the discussion of the intricate complementarities that arise when there are several different kinds of assets. It enables us, for example, to deal more easily with the question : How will an increase in the desire to hold equities due to an expectation of increased yields, affect the (bond) rate of interest ? The answer is that if equities are complementary with bonds against money, the rate of interest will fall, while if equities are complementary with money against bonds, the rate of interest will rise. Or the same results can be put, not quite so simply, in terms of the different elasticities of substitution between bonds, equities and money. In any case this analysis [1] presupposes an awareness of the problem in terms of the demand for holding different values of various assets. The same treatment is suitable for all questions, like those concerning the relationship between long- and short-period interest rates, which concern the demand for different kinds of assets. (In this case bonds and bills.)

Against these advantages must be set the danger in Professor Ohlin's formulæ of forgetting that the ceremonies performed in honour of saving and investment are quite empty. Although it is clear that they play no real part in either of his formulations, Professor Ohlin is extraordinarily and suspiciously emphatic in declaring that they really do affect the result. Thus : " Does this mean that [the height of the] rate of interest has no connection with the disposition of individuals and firms to save . . . ? Of course not. But it has such connections only indirectly." [2] And even more emphatically at the end of his last article : " The quantity of claims . . . *provides a direct link with saving, investment and the whole economic process.*" [3] Our analysis has shown that the real connections between saving and investment and the rate of interest (for, of course, everything in an economy is connected with everything else) are of a far more indirect nature than would be suggested by their simple and purposeless addition to both the supply and demand schedules for cash or credit.

This leads to another disadvantage, from which Professor Ohlin's *net* formulation suffers more than his *gross* formulation, that readers may easily take the attentions paid to savings and investments too seriously and suppose it to be very little removed from the " classical" theory of the supply and demand for savings. Mr. Keynes himself has fallen into this trap.[4]

Dr. Hicks seems to have been successful in keeping all of these in what seems to me to be a right perspective. Essentially he has put in a more mathematical manner what I have endeavoured to show in my curves.

Mr. Robertson, on the other hand, seems to be more to blame than Professor Ohlin, and gives one the impression that his very deep pseudo-classical formulations really contain more than empty ceremony. His concession, in this last article,[5] in employ-

[1] Based on the general lines laid down by Hicks and Allen in " A Reconsideration of the Theory of Value," *Economica*, 1934.

[2] Economic Journal, June 1937, p. 221.

[3] *Ibid.*, September 1937, p. 427 (his italics).

[4] " Alternative Theories of the Rate of Interest," Economic Journal, January 1937, p. 245.

[5] *Ibid.*, September 1937, p. 428.

ing Keynesian language shows him quite definitely to have taken the two steps from the " classical " to the modern view, and his ancient trappings are justified, when challenged, by quite new and very ingenious arguments in terms of the modern theory. Yet one still feels that there is behind all this a harking back to the old system that provides the energy for his cunning. I wish to consider here only one of his points—namely, that the marginal efficiency of capital " can exercise a direct influence on the rate of interest." A closer examination of this shows that Mr. Robertson is assuming that if there is an increase in investment, there is an increase in the demand for cash to hold to finance the investment, or else a tendency for the increase in income, formed by the increase in investment, to be hoarded.[1] This may be so to some extent if we consider a very short period, but it cannot be generalised, so that it is better to consider such effects as changes in the demand for money rather than as " direct " effects of the increase in investment to be measured by the schedule of the marginal efficiency of capital.

Certainly there is no very simple relationship between such increases in the demand for holding cash, which are most directly related to the *rate of increase* of the rate of investment (or the level of incomes), and the *level* of the rate of investment on which the unsophisticated " classical " argument is based.

This effect, which fits without any difficulty into the simplest Keynesian formula of the supply and demand for money, should be distinguished from another which does not fit so easily into that scheme. An increase in the marginal efficiency of capital may be accompanied by an increase in share values, and this may affect the rate of substitution between bonds and cash,[2] and in this way the rate of interest. To consider this as an effect (direct or indirect) of an increase in the marginal efficiency of capital on the rate of interest is not correct, for it is not the change in the marginal efficiency of capital that has the effect, but the change in the total value of shares. An increase in the marginal efficiency of capital, while increasing the profitability of *new* investments, can lower as well as raise the value of *existing* investments, and may leave it unchanged. There is, of course, the consideration that the new investment, by adding to the total of assets, may tend to increase their value, and thus to have some effect, of the nature here discussed, on the rate of interest, but this effect is certainly negligible in the short-period determination of the rate of interest to which all this argument refers.

[1] I am indebted on this point to a discussion with Dr. M. Kalecki.

[2] See page 227 above.

We see, then, that against the very simplified form of the Keynesian system, which speaks as if there were only one kind of asset and only one rate of interest, the other formulations have an advantage against which several disadvantages have to be put. We are saved from the task of weighing these advantages and disadvantages by the consideration that a more sympathetic interpretation of both systems, bringing in both cash and assets, as in our Fig. 3, gives us the advantages of both.

A. P. LERNER

Berkeley, California.

[2]

INTEREST THEORY–SUPPLY AND DEMAND FOR LOANS OR SUPPLY AND DEMAND FOR CASH

ABBA P. LERNER

New School for Social Research

WHEN I, as a Keynesian, say that the rate of interest is determined by the supply and demand for cash, i.e. the *stock* of cash and the quantity of cash that the public wishes to *hold* at various rates of interest, I do not, of course, mean to deny that in the economic universe everything is to a greater or less degree dependent on everything else. The whole system of Walrasian equations is necessary to describe the determination of the equilibrium of the economic system as a whole. Nevertheless, it seems to me that there is more meaning in my statement than is admitted by critics like Dr. Fellner and Dr. Somers,[1] who prefer to say that the rate of interest is determined by the supply and demand for loans and who declare that my statement is correct only on the assumption that all the other prices and quantities in the Walrasian scheme are given. This means that "the rate of interest equates the demand and supply of cash only in the sense in which the shoe price can also be said to perform this function if all other prices are given." [2]

It cannot be denied that the rate of interest, being the price paid for a loan, must be at the level where the demand for loans is equal to the supply of loans. But to say that the rate of interest is determined by the supply and demand for loans is unsatisfactory, because such a formulation, unlike most partial analyses of this kind, does not even give the first approximation provided by a statement like "the price of shoes is determined by the supply and demand for shoes." [3]

In the case of shoes, such a simplification from the Walrasian formulation of general equilibrium is permissible because an increase in the demand for shoes (say because a shortage of rubber makes people walk more) does not as a rule have a very important effect on the supply of shoes. In the case of *loans* this relative independence does not hold. When there is an increase in the demand for loans, say because business men want to borrow more money in order to spend it, there is likely to result from this an increase in the supply of loans. The increased spending on the construction of new factories or in the purchase of additional consumption goods will increase incomes, and part of these incomes will be saved and offered on the loan market. The part of these incomes that is not saved but spent will increase incomes still further and part of these further additions to income will be saved and offered on the loan market. Such induced increases in the supply of loans may partly or wholly offset the effect of the increase in the demand for loans. (Similarly, if there is a decrease in the supply of loans because some lenders decide to spend their money instead of lending it, this will increase the amount of money in the hands of those from whom the purchases are made, and these may directly or indirectly increase the supply of loans; or the money spent by the erstwhile lenders may flow into the hands of erstwhile borrowers who will now decrease their demand for loans.)

There may be delays in the working out of these effects. Some may argue that any increase in demand for loans can increase the supply only in a degree smaller than the increase in demand. Others may argue that the supply would increase in an equal degree and in some circumstances in a greater degree. These complications, important as they are for other purposes, are not significant for the present issue. As long as the change in demand for loans *may* have an important effect on the supply of loans (or a change in the supply of loans may have an important effect on the demand for loans, or a change in demand or supply by some can have an important effect on the demand or supply by others), we cannot use this partial analysis. We are then faced with the

[1] "Alternative Monetary Approaches to Interest Theory," this REVIEW, XXIII (1941), pp. 43–48.

[2] *Ibid.*, p. 48.

[3] The proposition that the rate of interest is determined by the supply and demand for loans is often called the "Loanable Funds" theory of interest. This phrase seems to be ideally suited to cloud the distinction between the supply and demand for *loans* and the supply and demand for the *cash* (funds) in which the loans are made.

question of whether we can find some way of correcting this fault in the partial analysis or whether we must give it up and go back to the correct but not very illuminating statement of general analysis that the rate of interest, like any other price, depends on everything in the entire economy.

One solution is to construct simplified Walrasian or general equilibrium schemes in which there are a small number of variables representing composite quantities, such as output of consumption goods in general or output of investments goods in general. Perhaps the most enlightening of these schemes and the easiest for the non-mathematical economist to understand is that constructed by Professor Oscar Lange.[4] The schemes, although they raise difficulties of their own in the unavoidable implications of some sort of homogeneity in the really non-homogeneous entities to which they refer (like the output of consumption goods or the output of investment goods or even the output of goods in general), are of great value in elucidating some of the more complex interrelationships between the different variables. But they are much more difficult to understand than the simple supply and demand partial analyses to which all of us are accustomed.

Many economists and all non-economists still do not feel quite satisfied when they are shown that there are *n* equations to determine *n* unknowns, and are not much happier when they are shown a simplified account which they do not fully understand and which they suspect of all kinds of skulduggery even though there are only six unknowns and six equations. Is it not possible to apply something like the familiar supply and demand analysis and yet give not too inaccurate an account of the determination of the rate of interest?

The partial supply and demand analysis can be salvaged. The clue to this lies in noticing that the disturbing effects of a change in demand on the supply (and vice versa) arise only in those cases where the increase in demand for loans is not for the purpose of holding the extra cash but for the purpose of spending it. To the extent that the borrower increases his own holding of cash his borrowing cannot indirectly increase the supply of loans. And even when he does spend the money he borrows, there can be no increase in the supply of loans if the person who receives the money from him keeps it and adds it to *his* previous stock of cash. In fact, if we consider all such increases of cash in the hands of all the members of society who receive any of this money in the course of its wanderings through the economy, we can say that the money which people in general wish to add to their stores of cash cannot come on to the loan market again as an additional supply of loans resulting from the original increase in demand for loans, but that the money which nobody wishes to add to his store of cash keeps on moving until it is offered again on the market for loans.[5]

Thus by bringing in the demand for cash to hold (and in parallel fashion the supply of cash), we can eliminate the effects of demand on supply (and of supply on demand) which threatened to frustrate the attempt at partial analysis. In the demand for loans we must count only that part of the demand which the borrowers, or the other people who indirectly receive the borrowed money, wish to add to their stock of cash. Similarly, in the supply of loans we must count only those loans which come from new issues of money or which the lenders are able to supply because they wish to decrease their holdings of cash. Any other loans indicate a withdrawal of cash by the lenders from other parts of the economy (where the lenders would have spent it if they had not loaned it out) and the withdrawals have the effect of increasing the demand for loans or decreasing the supply of loans in these other parts of the economy. When this is done, the corrected demand for loans consists of the demand for additional cash to be held by the borrower or by those who directly or indirectly receive the money from the borrowers when they spend their borrowings. The corrected supply of loans consists of newly created cash *plus* the cash set free by the lenders (who may

[4] "The Rate of Interest and the Optimum Propensity to Consume," *Economica*, v (N. S., 1938), pp. 12–32.

[5] It is not necessary for this to attempt to follow the adventures of the identical dollars that start the train of additional spendings and receipts. This is impossible anyway, even theoretically, unless all the money in the economy is hard cash and there is no credit whatever. We merely mean the increases in anybody's payments (and therefore in every case in somebody's receipts) which are induced directly or indirectly by the initial increase in spending by the borrowers of the new loans or by the erstwhile lenders who spend the money instead of lending it.

be lending only indirectly, spending the spare cash which eventually finds its way into the hands of the actual lenders). The demand for loans is nothing but the demand for additional cash and the supply of loans is nothing but the supply of additional or spare cash. If we add the stock of cash actually in existence to both sides of this supply and demand, and subtract the decrease in demand for cash from both sides (i.e. the cash set free and loaned out, directly or indirectly), we have the demand for loans translated into the demand for cash and the supply of loans translated into the supply of cash.

We are then tempted to deny that we have a supply-and-demand-for-loans theory of interest and to say that the rate of interest is determined by the supply and demand for the stock of cash, since it is this supply and demand for cash which determines the equilibrium of the supply and demand for loans. It is only when the supply or stock of cash is equal to the demand for it that the supply of loans is equal to the demand for them.

It cannot be overemphasized that the supply and demand for cash refers to the *stock* of cash while the supply and demand for loans refers to the *flow* of lending and borrowing which is measured as so much *per period of time*. If the stock of cash in existence is in accord with the stock that people wish to hold, there will be no attempt by individuals to increase their holdings of cash by increasing the rate of borrowing (or reducing the rate of lending) and there will be no attempt by individuals to decrease their holdings of cash by increasing the rate of lending (or decreasing the rate of borrowing). The equilibrium of the supply and demand for the stock of cash is therefore a necessary and sufficient condition for the equilibrium of the supply and demand for the flow of loans. The actual rate of borrowing must be equal to the actual rate of lending (since these are merely different aspects of the same phenomenon), and there is no desire on the part of borrowers or lenders to vary these rates of borrowing or lending.

In saying that the "cash" theory of interest is preferable to the "loans" theory, I do not deny that the actual rate of interest is in fact agreed upon by the suppliers and demanders for loans. I only mean to assert that in estimating the effect of any event on the rate of interest we are likely to be misled unless we take into account the effects of the event on the supply and demand for the stock of cash. For example, the simple "loans" theory might lead to the conclusion that an increase in the profitability of investment in new capital goods, by increasing the demand for loans, must raise the rate of interest. But if the investors and others are led by the same increase in the profitability of investment to reduce their own holdings of saving by investing or spending out of their previous stocks of cash, the supply of loans will increase more than the demand for loans and the rate of interest will fall. This is liable to be overlooked if we concentrate on the effect on the demand for loans, but is seen at once if attention is directed to the effects of the initial event on the supply and demand for the stock of cash.

It might be argued that the "loans" analysis is adequate if we consider a short period in which there is no time for the increased spending by the borrowers to bring about the increase in lending by those whose income will be increased.[6] It is true that in this case an increase in the demand for loans will have the effect of raising the rate of interest, but even then we cannot say that the rate of interest is a function of the supply and demand for loans. Rather is it a function of the *rate of change* in the supply (or demand) for loans. If there is a once for all increase in the demand for loans of this nature, there will at first be an increase in the demand for loans without any increase in the supply. After some delay, the increased spending by the lenders will increase incomes and savings. The part of the increased income which is not saved will be spent and will increase other incomes. In this way saving *immediately* increases by the amount of increase in investment (since that is the amount by

[6] For this it is necessary to assume that the increase in the profitability of investment or in the attractiveness of consumption which brings about the increase in the demand for loans (or the decrease in the supply of loans) does not induce the borrowers (or the erstwhile lenders) to increase their expenditure out of their previous holdings of cash in anticipation of the forthcoming borrowings (or reduced lendings out of their income). If there should be such an anticipatory increase in spending, the increased lending to which it gives rise may come about even before the increased demand for loans, leading to a (temporary) *fall* in the rate of interest.

which income increases in relation to consumption), and the supply of loans *gradually* expands (as the increased rate of investment raises income to the corresponding higher level) until it has increased as much as the demand for loans. After this both the supply and the demand for loans will be greater than before in the same degree and there is no reason why the rate of interest will be maintained at the higher level only if the *rate at which the demand for loans increases* continues at the higher level. The rate of interest in this case is raised not by the greater *demand* for loans but by the greater rate of increase in the demand for loans.[7]

Of course, a higher level of economic activity will probably bring with it a need for more cash to be held in connection with the greater volume of transactions, and the increase in the demand for cash will tend to raise the rate of interest. This looks something like the proposition criticized in the preceding paragraph, but there is no reason for believing that the greater need for cash that accompanies the greater volume of transactions is the same as the cash temporarily absorbed by the borrowing (which may initiate an increased volume of transactions) in the interval between the initial borrowing and the time when it results in increased income saving and lending. The increased *transactions* demand for cash may be greater or less than this transitional increase in the demand for cash, and in any case it fits perfectly into the formula that the rate of interest is determined by the supply and demand for cash.

Methodologically, Lord Keynes' contribution was to point out that partial analysis can be made a little more complicated, bringing in three or four variables instead of the Marshallian two, and yet remain manageable. For some economists who are accustomed to black and white of either the very simplest kind of partial analysis with only two variables, or else the complete Walrasian general equilibrium with everything depending on everything else, this point of Lord Keynes seems difficult to grasp. The liquidity preference theory of interest is an example of this kind of more complicated partial analysis, bringing in the supply and demand for cash to support the supply and demand for loans. Perhaps some difficulty has been caused by the shorthand method of expressing it which may seem to imply that borrowing and lending have nothing to do with the rate of interest.[8]

[7] If the demand had previously been constant, the rate of increase in the demand for loans was zero, and now during the change it is positive. When the demand for loans is stabilized at the higher level, the rate of increase in the demand for loans is again zero and the rate of interest falls to the previous level.

[8] In the article referred to above, Fellner and Somers conceive of the supply of cash as consisting of (a) the cash demand for securities, (b) the cash demand for goods, and (c) the stock of cash (considered as the supply by the owners of the cash to themselves). In parallel fashion, the demand for cash is conceived as consisting of (a) the supply of securities against cash, (b) the supply of goods against cash, and (c) the stock of cash (considered as the owners' demand of cash from themselves). In equating this supply and demand for cash the items (c) can be eliminated because being identical they are always equal to each other. The items (b) can be eliminated if we assume that the supply of each commodity is equal to its demand. This leaves only the items (a) which may indifferently be called the supply and demand for loans or the supply and demand for cash. On this interpretation it is true that the rate of interest can be considered as determined by the supply and demand for cash only if all the other prices are given,— namely in items (a).

Unfortunately the same criticism applies to the proposition that the rate of interest is determined by the supply and demand for loans. This is inevitable where the supply and demand for cash is defined so as to mean the same thing as the supply and demand for loans.

It should be observed that this account of the "loans" theory is not subject to the criticism made above of the partial or simple supply and demand analysis which was upset because the supply and the demand were not independent. Here the interdependences are taken account of only too well. It should further be observed that this account of the "cash" theory is also quite different from the partial Keynesian "cash" theory (which is defended in the present article) and indeed misses its essential feature. In the Keynesian theory, the supply and demand for cash refers to the *stock* of cash and to the desire to *hold* cash, sometimes called liquidity preference. In Fellner and Somers' article, the supply and demand for cash refers to the *flows* of cash currently offered and demanded for goods and securities. Even the existing stock of cash seems to be translated into a flow by supposing it to be offered by its owners to themselves each period. Fellner and Somers' strictures are applicable only to this "flow" account of the "cash" theory of interest. It is fitting that their strictures should be equally applicable to the theory they favor.

[3]

Reprinted for private circulation from
THE JOURNAL OF POLITICAL ECONOMY
Vol. LXI, No. 1, February 1953
PRINTED IN U.S.A.

ON THE MARGINAL PRODUCT OF CAPITAL AND THE MARGINAL EFFICIENCY OF INVESTMENT

ABBA P. LERNER
Roosevelt College

I

ATTEMPTS to apply the principles of marginal analysis to the theory of capital lead to many difficulties. While a good many of the difficulties are traceable to the heterogeneity of the many different things that are included in "capital," the more basic and more baffling of the difficulties would still be encountered even if capital were completely homogeneous. A more basic difficulty, which is obscured by the "index-number" problem raised by the heterogeneity of capital, comes to the surface if the heterogeneity of capital is taken out of the picture by one device or another. Perhaps the most tempting of such devices is the device of measuring the quantity of capital by its "dollar volume" or, in other words, by its *value*.[1]

II

How unsatisfactory it is to measure the *quantity* of a factor of production by its *value* may be brought out most clearly by supposing the same procedure to be followed for any other factor of production. Let us suppose that we used this procedure in analyzing the effect of an increase in the supply of labor on its marginal product. The resulting fall in the wage (in the long-period equilibrium) would reduce the value of the previous supply of labor, and this reduction in the value of the previous supply of labor would have to be subtracted from the value of the additional labor which is the denominator of the fraction measuring the marginal product of labor. This would make the "corrected" marginal product of labor greater than it appeared before. If the decrease in the value of the

[1] An interesting example of this procedure is to be found in Lloyd Metzler's "The Rate of Interest and the Marginal Product of Capital," *Journal of Political Economy*, LVIII (1950), 289–306, and "The Rate of Interest and the Marginal Product of Capital: A Correction," *ibid.*, LIV (1951), 67–68, where it logically leads to confusing conclusions such as that the benefit to society from an increase in capital is not measured by "the marginal product of social capital"; that the *social* marginal substitution between present and future consumption is measured not by the "marginal product of social capital" but by the "*private* marginal product of capital": and that in long-period equilibrium the marginal product of capital would be equal to the rate of interest only by accident.

previous supply of labor were equal to the value of the additional labor, the denominator would fall to zero and the "corrected" marginal product of labor would be infinite! And if the value of the total supply of labor should fall, that is, if the elasticity of demand for it were less than unity, the marginal productivity would be—should we say—greater than infinity or—should we say—negative? It clearly does not make any sense to proceed in this way.

Yet in the case of capital this procedure is most tempting. It may be defended as *natural,* since everybody measures his capital in dollars. It may be defended as *appropriate,* since the equilibrium (which is the long-term stationary equilibrium) is one in which everybody is just satisfied with the *value* of his capital stock in relation to his income so that he does not try to convert some of his income into capital or vice versa. It may be defended as *unavoidable,* since there is no other homogeneous measure for the heterogeneous collection of items that make up the capital goods that constitute the social capital. And most of all it can be defended as *essential* if the marginal product of capital is to be compared with the rate of interest. Only if capital is measured in the same units as the income yield is it possible to declare the marginal product to be so many points per cent per annum and see whether it is equal to, greater than, or less than the rate of interest. And yet the results of measuring capital by its value never turns out to be of any use for solving any problem.

III

The essential trouble is clearly connected with the problem, or perhaps rather the conundrum, of measuring the quantity of capital in an economy and of comparing this measure for different stationary states. It has been stated that the difficulty arises from "the fact that it is impossible to find an invariant unit in which to measure the social quantity of capital" but that the "problem of measuring the quantity of capital is not an index-number problem . . . the problem . . . would exist even in the simplest economy in which all output consisted of a single type of consumers' goods."[2]

Nevertheless, in a profounder sense the problem *is* an index-number problem. An index-number problem arises whenever two (or more) different kinds of things have to be combined in a single measure. It is true that there is no index-number problem involved in measuring the quantity of capital if there is only one kind of capital good, but our problem would still be with us if there were only one kind of capital good and only one kind of consumption good. The measurement of the marginal product of capital still would involve measuring the capital and the consumption goods in the same units so as to obtain a pure number for the marginal product of capital that could be compared with the rate of interest. Unless this is done, the closest we could get to an expression of the marginal product of capital to compare with a rate of interest would be to say that "the marginal product of a hundred more units of capital would be five units of consumption goods per annum." But this would *not* mean a marginal product of capital of 5 per cent per annum, because the statement depends on the units that are used in measuring capital and on the units used in measuring consumption goods. We can get a measure to compare with a rate of interest only if there is a *single* unit for measuring both the capital goods and the consumption goods, and

[2] Metzler, "The Rate of Interest and the Marginal Product of Capital," *op. cit.*, p. 292.

this is essentially an index-number problem. The problem is *evaded* by measuring both capital and consumption in dollars, and it is evaded only with disastrous consequences for the validity of the analysis. The easy way out of taking the value of capital as the measure of its quantity is really no way out.

It is possible to eliminate the problem by sufficiently extreme abstraction. This is done most effectively by Professor Knight in his account of "Crusonia," which is conceived as "living on the natural growth of some perennial which grows indefinitely at a constant (geometric) rate, except as new tissue is cut away for consumption."[3] Here both the capital and the consumption are of the same kind of thing, so that there is a marginal product of capital of so many percentage points per annum which is comparable to a rate of interest and, in equilibrium, equal to the rate of interest. There can be no appreciation or depreciation of capital in terms of consumption, since they are both the same thing. There are no factors of production other than the stock of the perennial. The valuation of this as capital is nothing but the capitalization of the expected future income, discounted at the rate of interest. This comes to the same as the current flow of new growth on the perennial divided by the rate of interest. Thus if the rate of growth is 5 per cent per annum, so that 100 tons of the perennial becomes 105 tons in a year if none of it is cut away, and the accretion of new growth is at the rate of a million tons a year (so that this would be the total accretion if there were none cut away for a whole year), then the capital is twenty times the annual growth or income, or twenty million tons, and its value is twenty times the value of the annual income.

[3] Frank H. Knight, "Diminishing Returns from Investment," *Journal of Political Economy*, LIV (1944), 26–47; see *ibid.*, p. 30.

If, then, there is an increase in capital, capital and income increase in exact proportion, while the rate of interest stays the same—remaining equal to the constant rate of growth. There being no change in the rate of interest, which in the system cannot change, there is no problem of any possible change in the valuation of the capital in terms of consumption goods.

IV

In the more common but less heroic abstractions that follow the Austrian fashion this method of avoiding the problem is not available. Labor is applied to a productive process illustrated by the maturing of timber, the quantity of capital corresponding to the period of time that elapses from the application of labor in planting the trees to the time when they are ready for the ax. With diminishing returns from lengthening the period, an increase in capital per worker, which goes with a longer period of production, must also be accompanied by a lower rate of interest in the new equilibrium equal to the lower *marginal* rate of growth. The existing capital (which consists of the standing trees) increases in value in terms of the product, timber, because its value is nothing but the discounted value of the timber it is going to yield, and the rate at which it is discounted is lower.[4] At the same time the capital *falls* in value relatively to the value of labor (or the

[4] It is true that the discounting will be over a longer period now, but this is more than offset by the greater yield of timber to be discounted, since the rate of growth diminishes continuously over the time by which the period of production is lengthened. The average rate of growth over this period must therefore be greater than the rate of discount because the latter is equal to that lowest rate of growth which is found at the end of the longer period.

wage) which must be higher in the new equilibrium to remain equal to the discounted value of its marginal product, the marginal product of labor being greater and the rate of discount less.[5]

The previously existing capital therefore increases in value in terms of the *output*, timber, and falls in value in terms of the *input*, labor. Should we consider this a capital gain or a capital loss? If we use consumption goods (here represented by the output of timber) as the measure of value, we must say that there is a capital *gain*. But, if we use *labor* as the measure of value, we must say that there is a capital *loss*. Where the final product is not timber but some further product made by timber in co-operation with direct labor, it is possible for the price of timber to fall so much in terms of the final product that the capital (which must increase in value in terms of timber) will fall in terms of the final product, so that there is a capital loss not only in terms of the input (labor) but also in terms of the final output (though not in terms of timber).

The classical economists, like the Austrians, used models in which labor is used to produce final products which are different from both the labor and the capital instruments, so that they, too, were unable to avoid the problem in the very neat manner available to Knight. But they had another way out. They would not reach the new long-period equilibrium as long as the wage remained above the subsistence level. The supply of labor would increase until the marginal product of labor was no higher than in the original equilibrium. The additional capital would then all be used up in employing the addition to the laboring population in the same manner as before. There would be the same wage, the same rate of interest, the same period of production, and no appreciation or depreciation of the existing capital either in terms of consumption goods or in terms of labor or in terms of any intermediate product. Except for the scale of operations, and other possible complications caused by increasing scarcity of land which are not directly relevant to our immediate problem, everything is exactly the same.

The classical solution, however, does not succeed, as Knight's does, in showing equality between the marginal product of capital and the rate of interest; except in those formulations which seem to assume that the capital does in fact consist of consumption goods in some mystical "wages fund."

V

It is of interest to see how Knight's model and the classical model fit in with the notion of a period of production corresponding to the quantity of capital or the degree of capital intensity.

These concepts have no place in Knight's scheme. An increase in the quantity of the perennial plant, brought about by failing to consume the whole of the growth, does not change the manner of production in any way whatever. Nothing is changed but the scale. The growth of the perennial plant being at a constant (geometric) rate, proportional to the quantity of it in existence, and the only input (in the stationary state) consisting of a decision not to consume more than the current accretion, the period of

[5] Again the discounting will be over a longer period, but, as was pointed out in the previous note, the additional growth over the extra period is at an average rate somewhere between the old rate of interest and the new lower rate of interest, so that it is greater than the new lower rate of interest, and the lengthening of the period *adds* to the increase in the discounted value of labor's marginal product that would result from a simple reduction of the rate of discounting.

production is completely arbitrary. The current growth may just as well be considered as due to the stock not being consumed five years ago as to its not being consumed a hundred years ago or to its not being consumed one second ago, so that the period of production concept is quite meaningless.

Another way of looking at this is to imagine the exponential curve that would correspond to the constant geometric rate of growth. At the rate of interest which is equal to this rate of growth (both being, say, 5 per cent per annum), it makes no difference which length of period one is supposed to use. It is as though we had a forest in which it made no difference what was the age of the trees cut down. Whether we cut down seedlings or mature trees or trees thousands of years old, as long as we did not remove more than a certain number of tons of timber each year, the forest would continue to give the same yield forever. In terms of Figure 1 it is as if the productivity curve $\varphi(t)$ (which shows the amount of timber that can be produced per year by each worker as a function of the length of time the trees are permitted to grow) were an exponential curve like the interest curve v_0u_c and coincided with it. Instead of there being an optimum period of production (or optimum age of trees for cutting) equal to Ot_0, where the discounted value of the timber is at a maximum, any period of production (that is, any age of tree for cutting) would be just as good as any other.

But as soon as we leave Knight's perennial and consider forests where it *does* make a difference at what age the trees are cut, the period of production does become relevant. And the same kind of thing, that is, the existence of many methods of production with different time dimensions and having different efficiencies, is true of all production outside of "Crusonia."

The essential difference between "Crusonia" and the Austrian model is that in "Crusonia" the miraculous perennial constitutes the *whole* of the productive resources. If *all* the factors of production were increased, there would be no reason for diminishing productivity or for any optimum quantity of capital (like that corresponding to Ot_0 in Fig. 1).

In the Austrian model there is a sharp dichotomy between services whose

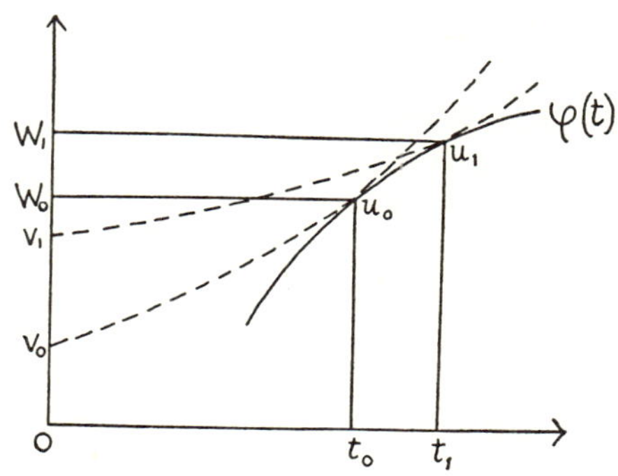

FIG. 1

sources of supply are fixed (the services of land) and services whose sources of supply may be increased or decreased (the services of capital). Land, being fixed in supply by definition, yields a fixed flow of services. The supply of laborers being determined by forces outside the province of pure economics (the classical assumption of perfectly elastic supply of labor at subsistence level having been abandoned), the supply of the services of labor is also a given flow. The relevant economic magnitudes are then the *flows* of these services of land and labor, on the one hand, and the *stocks* of accumulated instruments of production and other forms of capital, on the other hand. The flows of services are called "original factors" and are conceived of as initiating production at the left of diagrams like Figure 1, while all the existing stocks of instruments, goods in process, inventories, and everything else, are nothing but the material incorporation of services provided in the past by the flow of original factors and destined to yield consumption services in the future just as the trees in the forest model consist, for economists, of the accumulated or congealed labor which has not yet yielded the final service represented by the consumption of timber.

In this model the capital is quite different from the land and the working population that between them yield the flow of original factors. Capital exists only because it is worth while to use productive processes which take time. The quantity of capital in existence corresponds strictly to the average period of production, a longer period of production meaning that there are more instruments, equipment, and inventories, all of them being essentially goods in process which are needed only because of the time delay that the technical process imposes between the application of the services of the "original factors" and the final consumption of the product.

If it were possible to increase in proportion and with equal ease all the sources of productive services—land and men as well as machines and stocks and equipment of all kinds—there would be no point in the distinction between capital and the sources of the "original factors of production." There would be no significance in the idea of a period of production and no place for any theory or, indeed, any consideration of capital. "Crusonia" would be a very satisfactory model. But in the real world, in contrast with "Crusonia," this is not possible.

On the other hand, the sharp distinction in the Austrian model between *stocks* of capital goods and *flows* of original factors of production, with the stocks all freely producible and all needing continual replacement and the flows provided by a sphinx-like Nature which must be asked no questions, is also far from reality. Many things can be produced, which are then for all practical purposes permanent yielders of a service just like the purest form of pure land. There are services and stocks provided by "Nature" whose exhaustion is of the utmost importance. Most kinds of land are economically indistinguishable from produced capital of the purest "forest" type. "Crusonia" and the Austrian model are *both* extreme abstractions, in opposite directions, from the actual world in which we live.

VI

What about the relationship between the rate of interest and the marginal product of capital in the different models we have considered? In "Crusonia" the question cannot even be asked, since there is no distinction between capital and other factors of production. All we have is the rate of growth, and this must be equal to the rate of interest. Nobody would give a higher rate of interest for a loan of the "economic substance" (which is both consumption good and source of future consumption goods) than he would suffer in reduced future yield from the perennial if he cut his present need from it; and nobody would accept a lower rate of interest than he could get by leaving the potential loan to increase on the vine.

But this is not really the marginal product of capital as we have been supposing it to be so far. It is the *marginal efficiency of investment*. What is involved is the sacrifice of present consumption for the sake of yield of income in the future (which in turn may be consumed or left on the vine as further investment, indefinitely). If the perennial source of all good things were to be called "capital," and if there should be a miraculous increase in the quantity of the perennial, and if the rate of growth were unaffected, it would be appropriate to say that the marginal product of the additional capital was 5 per cent (or whatever was the rate of growth). But such supplemental miracles are not the normal order of events even in "Crusonia." The only and the continuing economic problem is to decide how much of the perennial to consume and how much to leave to grow for the future. This decision is one of *investment* or *disinvestment* and *never* one about capital.

In the Austrian scheme there is something that looks much more like an issue concerning capital. Given a production curve like $\varphi(t)$ in Figure 1, there is at any rate of interest, say that represented by the exponential curve v_0u_0, a period of production like Ot_0, which is most appropriate and which maximizes the discounted marginal product of labor. If one is at such a point and the rate of interest is changed, say it is reduced to that represented by the exponential curve v_1u_1, the appropriate period of production is no longer Ot_0 but Ot_1. But it is only in a long-period equilibrium that this point will be reached.

If the quantity of capital were miraculously increased to correspond to this longer period of production, the new equilibrium would be reached immediately. In the absence of such a miracle there can be no question of increasing the quantity of capital by the difference between the quantity in the first equilibrium and the quantity in the second equilibrium. There is simply no way of doing this.

If Ot_0 is thirty-five years and Ot_1 is forty years, the minimum period in which the new equilibrium could be reached would be five years. But that would require miracle enough, for it would mean having the planting continue as usual with no cutting taking place at all for five years. During these five years the number of trees would be increased. Their age distribution would be raised from a range between zero and thirty-five years to a range between zero and forty years, the average age therefore increasing from half of thirty-five to half of forty. Since the crop of timber represents the total supply of consumption goods available for the society, this is impossible unless someone else is ready to maintain the economy for these five years of input without any output.

All that the economy can do is to *invest* a part of its income each year in increasing the stock of capital, the rate at which it *invests* not being indicated at all by the kind of analysis provided by the Austrian models.

Furthermore, there is no way of comparing the marginal product of capital with any rate of interest. We may know that having so many more trees of various ages in the forests permits the output of timber to be greater by so many board feet, but the additional stock of trees of different ages and the additional flow of board feet of timber are not of the same unit. So the relationship between them cannot be expressed in terms of a rate of return per annum that can be compared with a rate of interest. We can have a measure of the *marginal efficiency of investment*, since we can know by how much the sacrifice of so many board feet this year, by permitting the trees to be increased in number and age, will yield an additional future flow of board feet. This can be expressed as so many board feet per annum per hundred board feet currently sacrificed and so can be compared with a rate of interest. But there is no way of comparing a rate of interest with the marginal product of board feet yielded by additional trees.

VII

In the real world, of which both "Crusonia" and the Austrian model are simplified abstractions in different directions, there can only be additional difficulties in the way of finding a marginal product of capital to be compared with any rate of interest. We may therefore say that in general there can never be any clear meaning in the comparison of the marginal product of capital with the rate of interest. What then becomes of our initial problem? Is the marginal product of capital equal or not equal to the rate of interest in long-run stationary equilibrium? This question cannot be answered and should not be asked. It is essentially meaningless, because no problems about capital can ever arise. All the problems that look like capital problems turn out to be investment problems.

The real problem is indeed the one that remains in Knight's "Crusonia" abstraction—namely, that of investment (and disinvestment)—and it is a solid advantage of that model that it abstracts away entirely from the pseudo-problems of capital. The Austrian model looks as though it shows a marginal product of capital, but a close inspection, say, of Figure 1, shows that the rate of interest does not apply at all to any relationship between trees and board feet but is applicable only at the margin at t_0 or at t_1, where there is only a question of the sacrifice of board feet in the present for board feet in the future, that is, only a question of *investment*.

Even if we take the case of a shift from t_0 to t_1 by means of external help from someone else, a Marshall Plan which increases the amount of capital, we are not helped. If we are *given* the additional trees of varying age, we have no measure of the marginal productivity of the additional capital that we can compare with any rate of interest. We have so many more trees of certain ages, and, as a result, we have a greater annual crop of timber, but we have nothing to compare with a rate of interest.

Even if we suppose that the Marshall Plan takes the form of someone from outside supplying us with the timber we need (that is, with our consumption goods), so that we are able for the five-year period to continue planting trees without cutting any timber, this will still not enable us to measure the marginal product of capital as a percentage per annum. The Marshall Plan benefits will have enabled us to *invest* the potential income or output day after day by refraining from cutting it down. But the denominator in the fraction is always timber or consumption and never trees or capital goods. So what we have is always a marginal efficiency of investment and never a marginal product of capital.

VIII

In the *Economics of Control*[6] and in an earlier article on this subject[7] I suggested giving an exact meaning to the phrase "marginal product of capital," namely, the marginal efficiency of investment in long-period equilibrium when net investment is equal to zero. This seems to fit in with the Austrian usage and with diagrams like Figure 1, but I am not so sure now whether it was a good thing for the understanding and development of eco-

[6] (New York: Macmillan Co., 1944), chap. xxv

[7] "Capital Investment and Interest," *Proceeding of the Manchester Statistical Society, 1936–37*, pp 26–31.

nomic theory. It might be better to write off completely our investment in this phrase and to speak only of the marginal efficiency of investment.

IX

In "Crusonia" there is never any change in the marginal efficiency of investment because the single economic substance, the magical perennial, has a constant geometric rate of growth. If all productive resources could be increased with equal ease, so that there would be no reason for changing their proportions, there would be no reason for expecting any departure from the constant marginal efficiency of investment that we find in Crusonia. Since there is reason to suppose that in the real world there *are* differences in the ease of producing the sources of different productive services, Knight, in the article referred to above, recognizes the reasonableness of expecting a diminishing marginal efficiency of investment or "diminishing returns from investment" if we assume a given state of knowledge and that investment is investment in "things." Knight, however, goes on to consider that, since all investment is for the future, a large part of it must be of an exploratory nature so that it might be considered an investment not in "things" but in knowledge. The knowledge so discovered will increase productivity, and this, he argues, may offset or more than offset the declining marginal efficiency of investment in "things" that would emerge if there were no new knowledge. There is therefore no presumption of a declining marginal efficiency of investment.

To clarify this, it is useful to consider more closely the meaning of the schedule of the marginal efficiency of investment. We may imagine it as a curve on a chart where the vertical axis measures the rate of interest and the horizontal axis measures the rate of investment that would be undertaken at each rate of interest. In any given situation, with a certain existing constellation of the different capital goods in the economy and with a given knowledge of technical possibilities of production, the curve will slope downward from left to right because of the heterogeneity of factors of production which results in increasing costs of additional provision for the future in terms of sacrifice of the output of goods for current consumption. This phenomenon would be with us even if it were possible to produce every kind of source of productive factors, including land and people, with equal ease, or rather with equally increasing cost in terms of consumption goods sacrificed.

The negative slope would apply not only to the curve of marginal efficiency of investment in "things" but also to the curve of marginal efficiency of investment in "research," taking this in the widest sense of all expenditure that increases our knowledge of productive possibilities even if they are of the roughest kind that emerge from undertaking any risky investment and discovering whether it works or not. This does not mean that we can have any kind of reliable knowledge of the results that will come out of "research." It merely means that some "research" *seems* more promising than other "research" and that, because of the omnipresent heterogeneity, the allocation of resources for research runs up against increasing costs as resources have to be used whose apparent efficiency for research diminishes relatively to their apparent efficiency for the production of current output of consumption goods.

The effect of the increase in the quantities of the different kinds of capital goods (which accumulate as investment continues) is to *lower the curve* of the marginal efficiency of investment. This is because the kinds of capital goods that can be produced more easily (relatively to those that can be produced only with greater difficulty or only in smaller quantities or which cannot be produced at all) come to be available in greater quantity, and so their usefulness diminishes. Further investment must therefore be applied either to making more of the things that are less useful or to making more of the things that are harder to make. For each *rate* of investment (measured on the horizontal axis) there is therefore a smaller rate of return, so that that rate of investment will be undertaken only if there is a lower rate of interest. This lowering of the curve of the marginal efficiency of investment is what is often meant by "diminishing marginal product of capital." The way in which the whole curve falls as a result of an increase in different proportions of most kinds of capital goods is not, however, anything that can be given a simple measure or number that can be compared wih a rate of interest.

The acquisition of new knowledge by "research" (which includes, we must remember, all that is learned in the course of undertaking risky investments of all kinds) can never *diminish* our possibilities of getting future income out of any rate of present application of productive services for this purpose. But new knowledge can also increase our possibilities of producing current income (which always means income in the relatively near future) out of the same productive services. A given sacrifice of current income may therefore release *less productive services*, and their efficiency in producing more income in the (more distant) future may not have increased as much as their efficiency in producing current income. In such a case new knowledge *will* have reduced the schedule of the marginal efficiency of investment by reducing the amount of future income made possible by a given sacrifice of current income.

Even if this never happened and new knowledge always increased the possibility of producing future income relatively to the possibility of producing current income, it would not follow that it would always raise the marginal efficiency of investment.

In the first place, the new knowledge may show that what looked like worthwhile investments are really not worth while. Such discoveries have the effect of *lowering* the curve of the marginal efficiency of investment. They may increase the *actual* return on investments, but they reduce the *supposed* or *expected* returns on which the schedule of the marginal efficiency of investment is inevitably based.

Second, we must consider *gross* investment rather than *net* investment. That is to say, we must include all replacement as part of investment. Even if all "research" were "positive," that is, uncovered new possibilities of producing for the future, and none of it merely deflated false expectations, this would merely mean that the *area* under the curve of the marginal efficiency of investment is increased.

If the new knowledge consists of finding better and easier ways of doing the old things, so that, instead of the old kinds of capital goods being replaced as they wear out, much better ones can be produced instead, the curve of the marginal efficiency of investment will be raised near the origin. There will be a very high rate of return on the replacement of old equipment by better new equipment. But there is likely to be a sharp limit to the rate at which this particular kind of investment can be carried on, especially if it is not felt desirable to increase very much the capacity of the industries affected. The very saving in resources which makes the new equipment better than the old may consist of reducing the amount of investment necessary. The curve would then drop very rapidly, so that the current rate of investment could be reached only by resorting to investments with a *lower* marginal efficiency of investment (*meI*) which would be undertaken only at a *lower* rate of interest. Such a possibility is shown in Figure 2, and it does not seem to be very far fetched. Indeed, it seems to me that this is implicit in Knight's remark that "it does not seem unreasonable to believe that . . . the only form of investment which has finally yielded any real return, to society or to the average individual, is the growth of knowledge, that the multiplication of things has not, on the whole, been profitable."[8]

X

The marginal efficiency of investment is then a declining function of the rate of investment, which is indicated by its being drawn sloping down from left to right in Figure 2. Furthermore, the curve as a whole will tend to be lowered over time as the result of the accumulation of capital goods by continuing net investment. New knowledge may either raise or lower the curve, so that, although this *may* raise the curve enough to offset the effects of the accumulation of capital goods, there remains a general presumption that the schedule of the marginal efficiency of investment will fall over time. This implies a falling rate of interest if a given rate of investment and employment (such as full employment) is to be maintained in the short-period equilibria which we must assume to be approximated over time. This, in turn, raises the question of how the decline in the rate of interest affects the values of capital assets and whether it might not thereby bring about a divergence of social benefit from private benefit in the investment activity that gives rise to the whole process; so that, in the absence of a counteracting public policy, there might not be more investment or less investment being undertaken than is socially desirable.

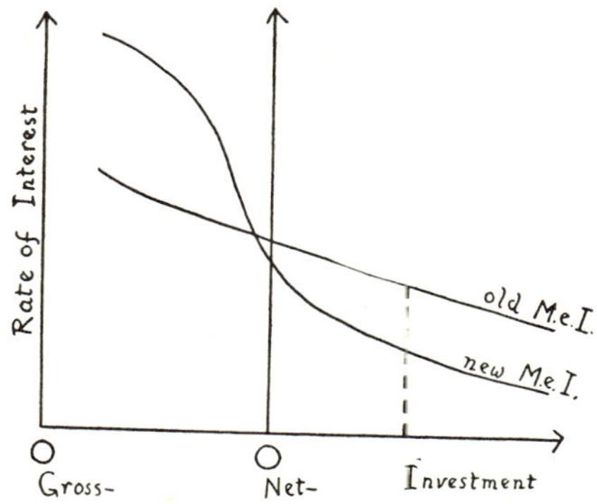

FIG. 2

[8] *Op. cit.*, p. 41.

XI

At lower rates of interest the sources of productive factors will tend to be more valuable relatively to the final or consumption goods, since the value of the former is given by the discounted value of the final consumption goods that the services they provide are expected to produce; and the rate of discount is less. The value of the total supply of *all* the sources of productive services *must* be greater, because it is simply the discounted value of the total output of consumption in the future. It is obtained by simply dividing the current income of the economy by the rate of interest, and we now have a larger current income to be divided by a smaller rate of interest. There is an inevitable capital gain.

In the real world, however, the most important source of productive services is not supposed to be subject to pecuniary calculation of capital gain or loss, because it consists of human workers, the calculation of whose value in terms of expected earning power is considered impious. It is therefore possible that the remaining sources of productive services, the existing nonhuman productive equipment, the capital and the land, could suffer a capital loss rather than a capital gain if they were increased sharply relatively to the human resources, and had a very low substitutability for them, so that the fall in the value of their services would more than overcome the benefit from the reduction in the rate of interest at which their services were discounted. This is easy to suppose for some special kinds of capital equipment which are displaced by other kinds of equipment as a result of the investment. Although it is not impossible, it seems most unlikely that this could happen to the total of all capital goods and land. But even if this should happen, it would not be relevant for our purpose.

We are here concerned with the possible benefits or damages that investors may bring to other members of society through their investment. In the cases where calculations of capital value are socially respectable, that is, in the cases of land and of capital equipment, expected earnings are capitalized, and capital gains or losses are seen to emerge. In the case of human beings expected earnings are not capitalized, and we do not speak of capital gains or losses in the value of the human beings concerned or of the families that are going to produce income-earning human beings in the future. But the benefits or damages are just as real whether the capitalizations are calculated or not. We must really consider the effect on *all* the sources of all the productive services in the economy, and so we must say that there is a net social benefit from the investment that would show itself as a capital *gain* if we did capitalize all the future earnings at the lower rate of interest. This seems to show that there is a divergence between private and social benefit from private investment, the social benefit being greater than the private benefit.

XII

It may be worthwhile to consider in another way the effects of the reduction in the rate of interest. As far as actual loans are concerned, there is no net gain. The lenders lose on account of receiving a lower rate of interest just as much as the borrowers gain from having to pay less interest. The benefit to all owners of property whose value has increased because the future earnings are discounted at a smaller interest rate lies in their knowledge that they can borrow more and more easily if they want to and in the satisfaction and the additional feelings of security that this knowledge gives them. In the case of land and of marketable capital equipment this benefit shows itself in an increased valuation of the capital—in a capital gain. In general, however, the capital gain cannot be consumed, since there is no corresponding increase in consumption goods available. One man can consume his capital gain only to the extent that he can pursuade another to sacrifice consumption in exchange for some of his capital. But everybody can enjoy the additional feeling of security, good luck, or even an illusion of good judgment in putting himself in a position where he was able to win the capital gain. This kind of benefit is also available to the worker who is now able to borrow more money and more easily on the basis of his expected future earnings; and, as long as workers in general do not try to exercise that possibility they can enjoy the benefit in the same way that the capitalist can enjoy his capital gain, although the imperfection of the credit market seriously curtails his additional powers of borrowing, just as they curtailed his original powers of borrowing.

My conclusion is that investment, in so far as it lowers the rate of interest, gives rise to a social benefit that is not taken into account by the investor, and to that extent the social benefit is greater than the private benefit. It would therefore be socially desirable to provide some additional inducement to get the investor to invest more than he does.

XIII

But why should the act of investment be credited with the *reduction* in the rate of interest that increases the value of capital resources? Does not rather an increased eagerness to invest result in a *higher* rate of interest that is necessary to prevent the increase of investment from bringing about inflation?

What we have here is the difference between the increase in schedule of the marginal investment or the *desire* to invest and an increase in actual investment. An increased desire to invest results in a higher rate of interest being necessary if there is a satisfactory level of effective demand to begin with, and the inflationary pressure that would be caused by the increased investment is checked by the method of raising the rate of interest. In this case there will be practically no increase in investment, since the way the higher rate of interest prevents the inflationary effect is by preventing the additional investment from taking place.

But in so far as some additional investment does take place, this lowers the curve of the marginal efficiency of investment in succeeding periods and makes it necessary for a lower rate of interest to rule if the same level of effective demand is to be maintained. What we can say, therefore, is that an increase in the schedule of the marginal efficiency of investment has the effect of raising the rate of interest and therefore of lowering the values of capital assets. Any activity therefore which has the effect of raising the schedule of the marginal efficiency of investment, such as research leading to capital-using inventions or discoveries, has a side effect that is socially harmful in its causing the value of capital assets to be reduced by the increase in the rate of interest necessary for the prevention of excessive effective demand. To the extent that this effect is not taken into consideration by those engaged in such activities, it is in the social interest to discourage activities that tend to raise the schedule of the marginal efficiency of investment.

But, with any given set of opportunities for investment, additional investment can take place only if there is a decrease in consumption that sets free the resources needed for the investment. It is therefore an increase in thriftiness that must take place if there is to be an increase in investment. Such an increase in thriftiness will *lower* the rate of interest in the short period in which the increase in thriftiness actually operates, for without such a reduction in the rate of interest there would be nothing to induce the additional investment to take the place of the reduced consumption in maintaining the level of income. The extra investment uses up some of the opportunities for investment in following periods, so that a lower rate of interest is needed to maintain the level of investment. If the propensity to consume remains low in the following periods, there is an additional reason for a lower rate of interest; and, if there has been a continuing increase in the level of productivity and the level of income that corresponds to full employment (or the other level of effective demand that is being maintained), still more investment is needed to correspond to the greater volume of saving that would be called forth, and there is still another reason for having a lower rate of interest. All these indications then point in the same direction: to a lower rate of interest being made necessary by an increase in thrift. It is therefore to the increase of *thrift* that our corrective measures should be directed rather than to the activity of investment. An increase in thrift makes it necessary for the rate of interest to be lowered. This increases the value of capital assets, and that is a benefit to the owners of the capital assets—a benefit that the exercisers of the thrift have not taken into account. It is therefore desirable, in the social interest, that *thrift* should be encouraged beyond the point to which the private interests of the savers would lead them.

It is perhaps desirable to end this article by stressing once more that this conclusion has validity only in an economy where full employment (or some other given level of employment) is being maintained. (It does not matter whether it is maintained by conscious government activity or in any other manner.) Only if the level of economic activity is somehow being maintained does greater thrift necessarily result in more investment, so that the effects of the additional investment, the reduction in the rate of interest and the appreciation of capital assets, can be properly attributed to the increase in thrift. If the level of economic activity is not being maintained and we have unemployment or the danger of unemployment, we are in the "upside-down" economy where thrift is socially harmful; and if we are in an inflation there are other reasons, much more important than those we have been considering, for reducing effective demand—by increasing thrift or in any other way.

[4]

A NOTE ON THE RATE OF INTEREST AND THE VALUE OF ASSETS [1]

In the accompanying figure the rate of interest is measured along the vertical axis, while the value of a given stock of assets is measured along the horizontal axis. *ON* measures the money stock, and the distance between the *M* curve and the *A* curve measures the value, at each rate of interest, of the given stock of assets other than money. It is clear that the value of the assets [2] will be greater if the rate of interest is lower, since the value of an asset is obtained by discounting the expected future yield from which its value springs, and the lower the rate of interest, the less of this value will be lost in the process of discounting. But can we say any more about the relationship of this value and the rate of interest?

If we consider the *M* curve to be the vertical axis, disregarding the part of the figure that lies to the left of it, we can describe the way in which the value of assets increases as the rate of interest diminishes in terms of the *elasticity* of the *A* curve. The *A* curve can then be considered as the horizontal sum of a series of *b* curves (not shown in figure), one for each asset, each *b* curve showing the value of the particular asset for each rate of interest. The elasticity of the *A* curve at any rate of interest will be equal to the arithmetic average of the elasticities of the *b* curves at that rate of interest, weighted by the corresponding current or discounted values of the assets. In the same way the *b* curve for any particular asset can be considered as the sum of a series of *z* curves, one for each item of future income or each future income payment that the asset is expected to yield at a particular future date. From the shape and distribution of these *z* curves (not shown in the figure) we can build up the *b* curves and then the *A* curve, and if we know something about the former we may be able to discover something about the shape of the latter.

The shape of any *z* curve is given if we know the *size* of the future income payment to which it refers and the *time* at which this payment is expected to accrue; from these two we can calculate the present (discounted) value for each rate of interest. Changes in the size of the future income payment would change all the abscissæ of the curve in the same proportion, moving the curve "iso-elastically." The elasticity of the *z* curve, at each rate of interest, is therefore uniquely determined by the date of the payment alone.

Given the date of the payment, the greater the rate of interest, the more

[1] This note was originally written as an appendix to my article "Alternative Formulations of the Theory of Interest," published in the ECONOMIC JOURNAL in June 1937 and reprinted in *Essays in Economic Analysis* (Macmillan, 1953) (where the figure appears as Fig. 3). It was apparently never submitted for publication. It is now published with some slight editing as a result of my discovering the manuscript among my papers while preparing to enjoy a fellowship at the Center for Advanced Study in the Behavioral Sciences at Stanford, California.

[2] Throughout the rest of this note assets stand for assets other than money.

is the present value affected by any change in the rate of interest, and the change in present value is exactly in proportion to the change in the rate of interest. In other words, the elasticity of each z curve diminishes as the rate of interest falls, and in the same proportion as the fall in the rate of interest, reaching zero when the rate of interest reaches zero.[1]

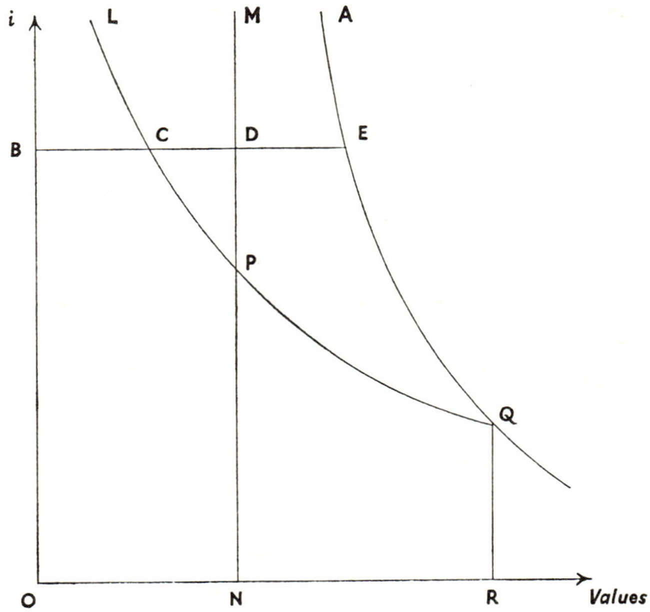

In exactly the same way, given the rate of interest, the farther in the future is the date of the payment, the more is the present value affected by any change in the rate of interest and the greater is the elasticity, and this increase will also be exactly in proportion to the postponement of the payment.

This is because a postponement of the date of the payment is analytically equivalent to an increase of the (instantaneous) rate of interest in the same proportion. Either change would reduce the present value of the future payment in the same degree. The analytical equivalence becomes transparent if we take the case of an increase in the rate of interest and reduce the unit period in the same proportion as the rate of interest is increased. We then have exactly as many more periods as in the case of the postponement of the date of payment with the same interest or discount rate per period as before. Alternatively, we could take the case of a postponement of the payment and increase the unit period in the same proportion as the date of

[1] The z curves will be of the form $z = ae^{-it}$, where z is the present value, a is the future income payment, i is the instantaneous rate of interest, t is the time distance of the payment in the future and e is the " natural " logarithmic base.

the payment is postponed. We then have no change in the number of periods but an (instantaneous) rate of interest per new period raised exactly in proportion to the postponement of the date of the income payment.

The *b* curve showing the values of an asset expected to give rise to several income payments at different dates in the future will consist of the horizontal sum of the several *z* curves corresponding to these expected future income payments. Although each separate *z* curve shows a declining elasticity, it does not follow that the *b* curve will do the same.

In the first place a change in the rate of interest may cause some assets to be substituted for others, so that the values of the future income payments on which the *z* curves are built will be changed. But wherever this happens there will always be movements in opposite directions, with a displaced asset decreasing in value while the value of the displacing asset increases. Since we are interested only in the final summation of all the *z* and *b* curves in the *A* curve, we may disregard this complication.

In the second place, as the rate of interest falls, the weights of the *z* curves with greater elasticities corresponding to more distant yields must increase *more than proportionately* because their greater elasticities reflect a greater increase in their present values from the fall in the rate of interest. This change in weights may be sufficient to offset the diminution in the elasticity of each of the *z* curves as the rate of interest is reduced.

Where an asset is expected to produce equal income payments at regular periods for ever, the shifting in the weights in favour of the more elastic *z* curves, corresponding to more remote income payments, is exactly sufficient to offset the decline in the elasticity of each *z* curve. In that case, as can more easily be shown in a more direct fashion, the value of the asset moves in exactly inverse ratio to the rate of interest, and the elasticity of the *b* curve is equal to unity throughout its length.

If we suppose that there is a myopia in the evaluation of future incomes, so that equal incomes in the more distant future are given less and less weight (or, more simply, that incomes accruing after some point in the future lie beyond a horizon and are not counted at all), it becomes much more difficult for the diminishing elasticity of the *z* curves to be offset by the high elasticities of the *z* curves of the very distant income payments. The influence of the latter is curbed by the lower (or zero) weights given to the income payment, as well as by the exponential increase in their discounting with their distance.

At high rates of interests it is still possible for *b* curves to have a high elasticity. Income payments that are sufficiently far in the future to be sufficiently subject to discounting to make their present values very elastic with respect to changes in the rate of interest, may still be sufficiently free from myopia to retain enough weight to be able to confer a high elasticity to the *a* curve. But at a lower interest rate an income payment has to be proportionately farther in the future for its *z* curve to have the same elasticity.

It then becomes more and more subject to myopia, or the danger of falling beyond the horizon, so that its influence is attenuated or lost.

Even if we deny myopia as well as the limiting " horizon," an asset that is expected to yield a constant income for ever will have a *b* curve with a constant elasticity of unity. If we allow our horizon to cut off *any part* even of the most remote future, the *b* curve will be inelastic and will show a declining elasticity as the rate of interest falls; and the same will be true for any asset yielding a constant income that is expected to come to an end some time in the future. It is only an asset yielding a *rising* income that can have a *b* curve with an elasticity greater than unity, and then only if the bulk of the expected future income, even after discounting, lies beyond that rather distant point in the future where the discounting becomes heavy enough to make the present value of the asset vary more than in proportion to changes in the rate of interest. As the interest rate is reduced the critical point moves farther into the future, so that this condition is less and less likely to be satisfied by any asset. We can therefore say that there is a very strong presumption that the *b* curves have elasticities that are less than unity and are lower for lower rates of interest.

In adding the *b* curves for the different assets to get the *A* curve of our figure showing the values of all the assets together (other than money) the very strong presumption that the elasticities of the *b* curves are low remains in the form of a very strong presumption that the elasticity of the *A* curve is low for ordinary rates of interest. The very strong presumption that the elasticities of the *b* curves are falling cannot as safely be transferred to the *A* curve because of the possibility that a decline of the rate of interest may sufficiently increase the weights of the relatively more elastic *b* curves so to raise the average. But the considerations of myopia and of the " horizon," and the frequency of assets with finite lives, can be applied again at this stage of the argument in exactly the same way. We thus retain a very strong presumption that the *A* curve is inelastic and a strong presumption that its elasticity diminishes with the rate of interest.

This analysis of the behaviour of the *A* curve with respect to changes in the rate of interest becomes significant when we contrast it with the behaviour of the *L* curve in the figure, which shows (in its distance from the vertical axis *Oi*) how much of their total wealth (including money) people wish to hold in the form of money. At very high rates of interest people will want to hold very little money above the minimum that is necessary for carrying out transactions given the technical and institutional environment. There will be very little consideration of the rate of interest, and the elasticity of the *L* curve will be very low. At lower rates of interest money which might be earning interest will be used for providing additional convenience in transactions and the other liquidity benefits. The money essential for the transactions motive diminishes relatively to the money now held for precautionary and speculative motives. These needs for money are much less urgent, so that in determining how much should be held there will be greater consideration of cost. This cost is none other than the rate of interest foregone when the wealth is held in the form of money. The elasticity of the *L* curve will therefore be higher at a lower rate of interest.

It may be the case—as Keynes has suggested—that this increasing elasticity reaches infinity at some positive rate of interest. But even if this is not so, it seems likely that the *L* curve (which becomes more elastic as the rate of interest falls) will meet the *A* curve (which becomes less elastic as the rate of interest falls) at some positive rate of interest. This is shown at *Q* in our figure. Below *Q* the *L* and the *A* curves coincide indicating the public's wanting to hold *all* their wealth in the form of money.[1] This means that the money authorities will not be able to reduce the rate of interest below *RQ* unless they are prepared to acquire *all* the assets in the economy other than money.

Abba P. Lerner

Michigan State University,
E. Lansing, Michigan.

[1] They cannot hold more than this, even if they should want to, unless the banking authorities, after having bought up all the non-monetary assets in the economy, allow the public to borrow still more money to hold on the security of the expected future earnings of their non-transferable personal skills, etc.

[5]

ON SOME RECENT DEVELOPMENTS IN CAPITAL THEORY*

By ABBA P. LERNER
Michigan State University

I

In 1936 Keynes introduced the term "marginal efficiency of capital," substituting the word "efficiency" for the word "productivity." His declared purpose was to obtain a measure that could be compared with the rate of interest, *i*. He did this by considering values rather than physical quantities [4].

At least as important was the undeclared shift from considering the stock of capital to considering the flow of investment and its influence on the level of employment. This led me to substitute "marginal efficiency of investment" for his marginal efficiency of capital, leaving the term "marginal productivity of capital" to represent the effects on output of having a greater stock of capital [5]. I would now like to suggest a slight change in terminology which would clearly show both distinctions, using four terms instead of two: the marginal productivity of capital (*mpK*), the marginal productivity of investing (*mpI*), the marginal efficiency of capital (*meK*) and the marginal efficiency of investing (*meI*).

MpK is the extra flow of output resulting from a unit increase in the stock of capital. But this is not comparable with *i* because the units of output may not be the same as the units of capital. It is possible to make *mpK* commensurable with *i* by measuring both the capital and the output by their value either in dollars or in output, which we can call apples, but this would obscure the distinction between the effects of a change in the size of the capital stock (K) and a change in the rate of investing (I).

We can isolate these different influences by distinguishing between apples and apple trees, so that *mpK* stands for the extra potential apples per annum from one extra tree. This diminishes with K, the number of trees already in existence, because the more trees there are the less favorable is the best site remaining available for planting yet another tree.

* Comments and questions by Jack Hirshleifer, Dale Jorgenson, Arthur Lerner, and Robert Solow are responsible for some significant clarifications.

284

MpI is the extra capital produced by diverting resources from making one unit of consumption goods to making capital goods. It is also not comparable with *i*. The greater is *I*, investment, the rate at which trees are being planted (or *S*, saving, the rate at which apples are being sacrificed) the smaller will be *MpI* because more use will have to be made of resources that are relatively less efficient at planting new trees than at coaxing apples out of the already existing trees. *MpK*, too, will diminish as *I* increases because fewer resources are left to help trees produce more apples.

We get a rate of return to compare with *i* by multiplying together the two marginal productivities. If a tree yields 100 apples per annum (net), *mpK* is $\frac{\text{100 apples per annum}}{\text{1 tree}}$. If it takes the sacrifice of 1,000 potential apples to plant an additional tree, *mpI* is $\frac{\text{1 tree}}{\text{1,000 apples}}$.

The product is $\frac{\text{100 per annum}}{\text{1,000}}$ or 10 percent per annum.

MeI is this rate of return which in (perfectly competitive) equilibrium will be equal to *i*. A positive *I* will then indicate that *K* is less than that appropriate to *i;* namely, that *meK* is greater than *i*. In long-period equilibrium *K* would be adjusted, *meK* would be equal to *i*, and *I* would be zero. *MeK* may, therefore, be defined as *meI* when $I = 0$.

These relationships are illustrated in Figure 1 and Table 1, in which position (1) represents an initial long-period equilibrium, position (2) a new short-period equilibrium following a reduction in *i*, (3) a long-period equilibrium corresponding to that lower *i*, and (4) a new short-period equilibrium following a further reduction of *i*. The *meI* curves are downward sloping because $meI = mpI \times mpK$ and both of these diminish as *I* increases.

The downward slope of the *meK* curve may seem to be more questionable. While *mpK* may be expected to fall as the ratio of capital to other factors increases, *mpI* is as likely to rise as to fall in response to an increase in *K*. If *mpK* falls less in making capital goods than in making consumption goods, giving up a unit of consumption sets free enough resources to make more extra capital goods than it did before the increase in *K*. *MpI* will have increased!

But the new capital goods will suffer exactly the same decline in their *mpK* in making consumption goods. The greater number of trees that can be planted when 1,000 potential apples are sacrificed is exactly offset by the greater decline in yield of potential apples per annum per extra tree. As long as there is any decline in *mpK* in making capital goods, as *K* increases, *meK* will be downward sloping.

II

The peculiar nature of capital in relation to time in the productive process and how this applies just as much to the services of capital as to land or labor services is shown in Figure 2. Time is measured along *AB*. The increasing distance from *AB* of a point moving along the line *AC* represents the cumulative application of "original" or "noncapital" factors of production—land-labor services (hereafter called "labor"), beginning at *A* and concluding at *B*. The line *BC* represents the emergence of the product at time *B*. The total length of the process is *AB* and the average time between the application of the factor and the

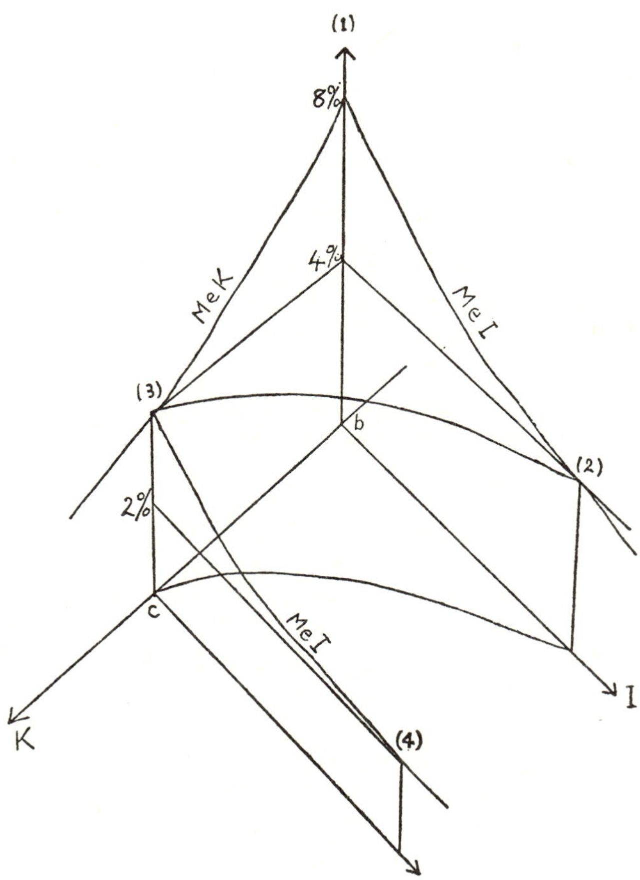

FIGURE 1

TABLE 1

		(1)	(2)	(3)	(4)
i	Rate of interest	8%	4%	4%	2%
K	Capital stock (number of trees)	2,000	2,000	6,000	6,000
O	Output (potential apples per annum)	1,000,000	1,000,000	2,100,000	2,100,000
C	Consumption (apples produced and consumed per annum)	1,000,000	700,000	2,100,000	1,500,000
S	Saving (O–C) (potential apples sacrificed per annum to produce trees)	0	300,000	0	600,000
I	Investing (trees produced per annum, net)	0	40	0	48
O/K	Average productivity of capital (potential apples per annum per tree)	500	500	350	350
mpK	Marginal productivity of capital (extra potential apples per annum per extra tree)	400	400	240	240
I/S	Average productivity of investing (trees planted [per annum] per apple sacrificed [per annum])	—	1/7,500	—	1/12,500
mpI	Marginal productivity of investing (extra trees planted [per annum] per extra apple sacrificed [per annum])	1/5,000	1/10,000	1/6,000	1/12,000
p_k	Price of capital goods ($=1/mpI$ in short period equilibrium) (price of a tree in apples)	5,000	10,000	6,000	12,000
meI	Marginal efficiency of investing or rate of return ($\equiv mpK \times mpI$) ($=i$ in short period equilibrium) (extra apples per annum per extra apple sacrificed from consumption)	8%	4%	4%	2%
meK	Marginal efficiency of capital or rate of return in long period equilibrium ($\equiv meI$ when $I=0$)	8%	8%	4%	4%
K'	Value of the capital stock (value of the trees in apples)	10,000,000	20,000,000	36,000,000	72,000,000
K'/O	"Capital-Output Ratio"	10	20	$17\frac{1}{7}$	$34\frac{2}{7}$
$\Delta K'/\Delta O$	"Marginal Capital-Output Ratio"		∞	$14\frac{6}{11}$	∞

emergence of the product is LB. If AC is a straight line, LB will be half of AB. The total quantity of capital, measured by its labor content, will be represented by the area of the triangle ABC or the rectangle $LMCB$.

If $i > 0$, the values of the flow of consumption goods and of the stock of capital goods will exceed the values of the labor services incorporated in them. If we represent the value of a unit of land-labor by the vertical distance AA' we can show its growth as, with the passage of time, it turns into a unit of output. In equilibrium this growth in value must correspond to the rate of interest or discount. The unit of labor applied at time A has an initial value AA' which grows at a rate equal to i, reaching B'' at the end of the process. The other units of labor, since they are applied later, do not reach so high a value. The values they do reach are traced out by the curve $B''C'$. The growth in value may be conceived of as due to inputs of capital services; i.e., as resulting from the reinvesting from moment to moment of the continuous increase in the value of the goods in process during the production period. The causal influence is, of course, the other way around. All inputs are put in only because of the expectation of a greater value of future outputs.)

The total value of output is represented by the area $BB''C'C$ at the further end of the figure, of which the rectangle $BB'CC'$ represents the payment for land-labor, the remainder $B'B''C'$ being the return to capital. The value of the capital stock is represented by the complete solid figure $ABCB''$. $AA'BB'CC'$, the lower slice of this figure, represents the land-labor incorporated in the stock of capital. It may be considered as corresponding to the "wages fund," or "rent and wages fund," and we may call this "land-labor capital." The rest of the figure, the upper part $A'B'C'B''$, represents capital that must be invested in addition to the initial payment for the land-labor because it is impossible for the capital providers to start consuming all the interest on these (wages and rent) payments from the moment they make them. We may call this part of the capital the "interest fund" or "capital capital."

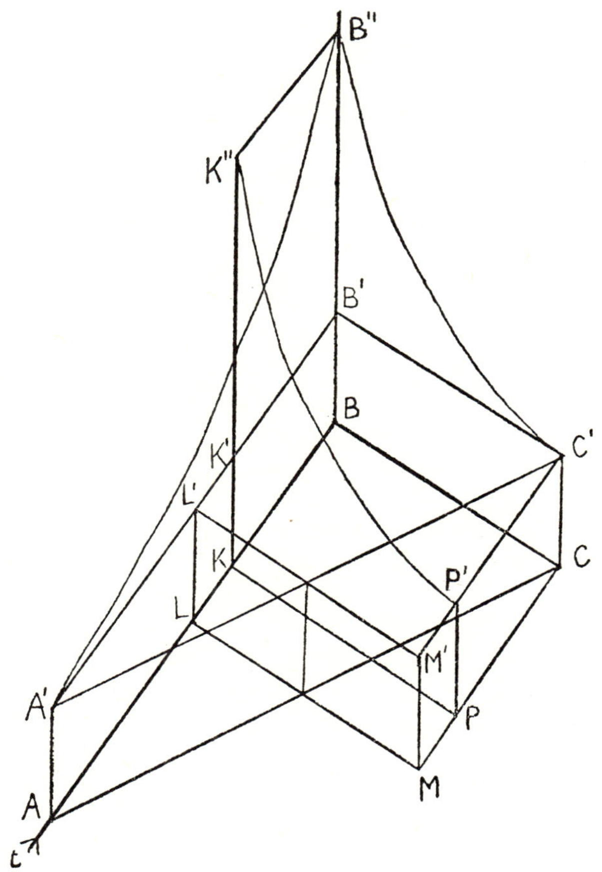

FIGURE 2

The average period of production is now represented by *KB*. The point *K* is obtained by moving the plane figure at the end of the diagram back along *BA* towards *A* up to *K*, where the volume it will have moved through, the slice between the congruent parallel planes *BB″C* and *KK″P*, will be just equal to *ABCB″*. KB will be less than *LB* because the greater weight of capital services comes closer to the end of the process when there are more capital earnings that must be reinvested as capital services.

It should be noted that the average period of production, which is also the capital-output ratio and the measure of capital intensity, is not independent of the rate of interest or the price of waiting, just as it is not independent of the relative prices of land and of labor. Without the relative prices it would be impossible to have a single measure of input.

III

I now turn to "post-Keynesian" capital theory—the development, mostly in Cambridge, England, of models of economic growth centering largely, in its present presumably introductory efforts, on steady states, often called "golden ages," in which everything grows at the same rate so that all the current ratios are steady. The "Keynesian" element is the direction of influence from investing to saving rather than the other way around, as in Keynes's insistence on this direction of influence via employment and the multiplier. The difference which makes it post-Keynesian is that full employment is usually assumed. *I* influences *S* by increasing not employment but profits. The additional spending that constitutes the investing is received and saved by the capitalists. If they spend some of this, no less is saved, because that only increases their income enough to make the *S* seem appropriate.

As one who certainly has spilled not too little ink in the "saving equals investment" spree of the 1930's and 1940's, I should have had no difficulty with this kind of argument. But I experienced severe discomfort which I traced to an unreadiness to accept the implied reduction in real wages. The rather startling response to my expression of these difficulties in Cambridge was "of course, if you bring in the inflation barrier the whole process is stopped and we just have inflation." The trouble was clearly that my own post-Keynesianism rests essentially on the belief that most economies today are at or beyond the inflation barrier. Nevertheless, it seemed incumbent on me to try to overcome my provincialism and make the assumptions necessary to follow the analysis.

This was not easy. One difficulty was the reversal of the roles of capital and investment. I tend to consider as natural a short-period model in which the quantity of capital is given by history. Together with the current techniques it governs the current investment opportunities. The problem is to achieve the desired level of employment, perhaps with some consideration, among other social objectives, of a desired rate of growth.

Post-Keynesian capital theory does all this the other way around. The rate of growth of everything is set by the rate of growth of population and the technical progress, since it is only when everything else has been completely adjusted to these that a steady state can be achieved. A greater degree of thrift—meaning that a larger fraction of the output is saved and invested—thus does not show itself in a more rapid rate of accumulation of capital or of economic growth. It shows itself only in a higher level of capital stock in relation to output which just absorbs the higher rate of saving and investing in growing at the predetermined steady rate of growth of everything.

But after many painful exercises have got one into the swing of thinking in terms of states of steady growth, some interesting things begin to emerge. It now makes sense to isolate the effects of an increase in K from the effects of an increase in I by holding I, or rather I/K, constant not at zero but at g the rate of growth of a steady state. In particular, what may justify the pains is that technical progress can be incorporated in the main structure of the model instead of being dragged in as an afterthought.

IV

If technical progress is neutral as between the use of capital and the use of labor, it fits into g, the steady state rate of growth, in exactly the same way as an increase in labor. A 1 percent per annum rate of such neutral technical progress means that each succeeding year the same number of men working with 1 percent more machinery can produce 1 percent more output including the 1 percent greater output of machines required by the 1 percent increase in the number of machines operated per working man. It is just as if the working population grew at an additional 1 percent per annum, except that per capita wages and incomes now rise.

However, some interesting questions arise as to how it is appropriate to define neutrality of technical progress—the line between capital-using and capital-saving technical progress. Here the field has been narrowed to competition between J. R. Hicks and R. F. Harrod.

Hicks's definition is enticingly neat, "equiproportional increases in the marginal productivities of capital and labor" [1] and works ideally for an individual producer who can freely change the number of men he hires or the number of machines he rents or buys and will not be induced by Hicks-neutral technical progress to change the ratio in which he combines them.

But society as a whole cannot vary the ratio between the quantities of capital and labor. It can only vary the uses to which they are put. If the marginal productivities of labor and of machines both increase by 10 percent, an additional unit of labor used in the production of machines produces 10 percent more of these, and each machine in turn produces 10 percent more of its product. The marginal product of labor used indirectly is then increased twice by 10 percent; i.e., by 21 percent. Labor will, therefore, be shifted from direct use, where its marginal product increases by only 10 percent, to indirect use, where the technical progress—the increase in marginal productivity—is "multiplied" by the number of stages in the economic process. Similarly, labor will be shifted from indirect uses to still more indirect uses. This is what constitutes the substitution of capital for labor.[1]

Harrod's definition of neutral technical progress—"technical progress that results in no change in the capital-output ratio for the same rate of interest"[2]—gives us neutrality with respect to the substitution between direct and indirect labor. By avoiding any reference either to the marginal productivity of capital or to physical quantities of capital, it avoids the traps that surround these concepts. If the marginal productivity of direct labor increases by 10 percent, Harrod-neutrality would be satisfied by a 10 percent increase in the productivity of men making machines with no increase in the marginal productivity of machines; by an unchanged marginal productivity of men or machines in making machines with a 10 percent increase in the marginal productivity of machines making final goods, or by some intermediate changes that add up to a 10 percent increase of productivity in the indirect manufacture of final goods just as in the first two cases.

In all three cases, K' the value of the capital stock K (measured in terms of output) will increase in the same proportion as output. In the first case, each batch of 100 retired machines is replaced by 110 of the new kind, each new machine having the same capacity and the same marginal cost as one of the old machines. In the second case, the number of machines does not change, but each new machine has a 10 percent greater capacity and a 10 percent greater marginal cost. The third case is intermediate between these two. The only difference between the three cases is in the degree to which the 10 percent increase in the value of the stock of capital goods is due to a change in the number of machines and the degree to which it is due to a change in the value of

[1] Hicks may not have intended to identify the marginal productivity of capital with the marginal productivity of capital goods, but only on this interpretation is Hick's neutrality different in content from Harrod-neutrality.

each machine. The increase, decrease, or stationariness of the capital output ratio—the Harrod criterion—will correctly indicate capital-using, capital-saving, or neutral technical progress.

V

Harrod, feeling that a measure of technical progress should hold "the quantity of capital in some sense" constant if it is not to "ascribe to technical progress some element of the increase of output which is better ascribed to capital accumulation," suggests that the proper measure of the quantity of capital for this purpose is not its value in terms of consumption goods but "the length of the productive process" defined as "the average time of waiting multiplied by the number of man hours (or other non-capital factors of production as currently valued in terms of man hours) in respect of which there is waiting"[3]. This means the average period of production of our "labor."

But technical progress can also affect the productivity of capital services, changing the structure of production and altering the value of the capital stock, the average period of production and the capital output ratio, even though the average period of production of labor has not changed.

This is shown in Figure 3 (which reproduces part of Figure 2). The broken lines show a shift in the input stream from the middle to both ends of the production process, the added area Q being just equal to the subtracted area R, and $BB'CC'$, the labor content of the output, and $AA'BB'CC'$, that of the capital stock, are unchanged and so is LB labor's average period of production. But the value of the output is increased because the addition S (the accumulated value of Q) must exceed the subtraction T (the accumulated value of R), while the value of the whole capital stock, including the "capital capital," must increase still more since it must grow in the same proportion as $B'B''C'$, the interest on it. Since that increases by the same absolute amount as total output $BB''C'C$, it will increase in a greater proportion. The overall average period of production and the capital output ratio will therefore increase from KB to say K^*B. Harrod's restriction of "the average time of waiting" to "noncapital" factors of production is unjustified. We must recognize that at any moment the capital goods and their services are just as "given" as the labor force and the land and their services.

VI

I have so far followed the convention of treating capital as a stock and labor as a flow. But the legitimization of capital services on a par with labor opens the way to a more pleasingly general approach which treats every flow of a productive service as yielded by a stock of the source of that flow, and also reduces the differences between the Hicks and Harrod neutrality to a difference between the private and the social points of view that lie behind them.

In microeconomics we consider a producer who buys or hires his factors of production on the market. If he uses only flows of services to produce a flow of output, he simply gets the difference between the two flows of payments for these as the payment for the flow of his personal services. He requires no capital to run such a business.

Capital comes into the picture only if the producer wants to own some of the sources of the flows of services. Even if he lets others own all the buildings and machines, etc., and buys their services (or rents the sources) he will normally find it necessary to own some goods in process which incorporate past services which will contribute to future output. They constitute working capital and must also be considered

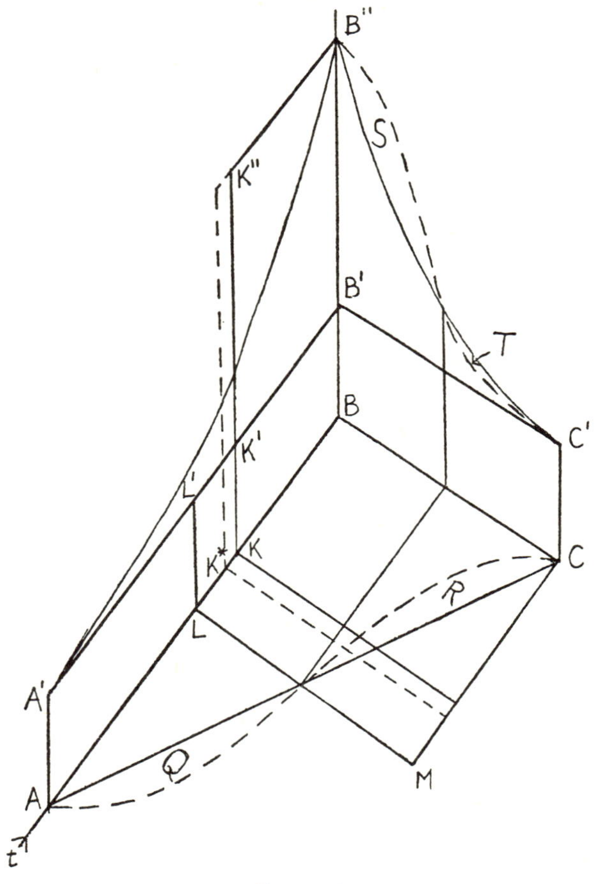

FIGURE 3

as sources of flows of productive services. We may then define private capital as sources owned.

The more of the sources he is to own, the greater the amount of capital he must have or borrow. A capital-using invention from his point of view is one that induces him to shift from the use of services that he buys to the use of services from sources that he owns, for which he needs capital. This will happen whenever the marginal productivities of the services of owned sources rise relatively to those of bought services. This fits Hicks's formula that a capital-using invention raises the marginal productivity of capital relatively to the marginal productivity of labor, etc., remembering that by capital we mean any sources that the producer owns and that by labor we mean any productive services that he buys.

But the economy as a whole cannot change the proportions between sources owned and sources rented. It can only change the uses to which the given flows of services from the given stock of sources are directed. In particular, it can and will shift them away from the manufacture of producible sources whose marginal productivity relatively to their marginal cost has fallen and toward the manufacture of producible sources where this has risen.

From the macroeconomic point of view, the significant distinction is not between services flowing from sources owned and services bought from others but between sources that are producible and sources that are not. Producible sources may then be called "social capital." From the social point of view a technical improvement is capital using if it diverts current services from producing current consumption goods to increasing the stock of producible sources, capital saving if it diverts current services in the opposite direction, and neutral if it does neither. Harrod's device—his use of the capital-output ratio (for a given *i*) as an indicator of the bias in technical progress—accurately reflects the initial direction of movement of the marginal productivity of indirect relative to that of direct use of resources.

VII

There is, however, a third and more natural because more direct indicator of the bias in technical progress. This is none other than a change in our *meI*, the marginal efficiency of investing.

MeI has been defined in terms of potential consumption goods: the future flow of consumption goods made possible per unit reduction of current consumption via the shifting of current services from making current consumption goods to making (producible) sources. A change in *meI* is, therefore, a change in the relative marginal productivity of indirect as compared to direct use of services flowing from all kinds of sources: labor, land or capital, producible or nonproducible. It may even be read as the marginal efficiency of indirectness in the use of productive services of all kinds.

An increase in *meI* (which = *mpK* × *mpI*) may be the result of an increase in *mpK,* the marginal productivity of (the services of) producible sources in making consumption goods. But it may also come about from an increase in *mpI* by virtue of an increase in the *mp* of services in general (including nonproducible sources) in making producible sources relatively to their productivity in making consumption goods. In the first case, *meI* takes the form of an increase in the prices of producible sources: the tree is worth more because it produces more apples. In the second case it takes the form of a reduction in their marginal cost: it takes a smaller sacrifice in apples to get an extra tree. Combinations of these are, of course, also possible. In all cases an increase, decrease, or absence of change in *meI* (for a given ratio of *I* to *C*) is a proper indicator of whether an improvement is capital using, capital saving, or neutral in the fundamental sense of how it affects the marginal efficiency of indirectness in the use of the currently available flow of services yielded by the currently existing stock of sources of all kinds.

REFERENCES

1. J. R. Hicks, *The Theory of Wages* (London: Macmillan, 1935), p. 123.
2. R. F. Harrod, *Towards a Dynamic Economics* (London: Macmillan, 1948), p. 23.
3. ———, "The Neutrality of Improvements," *Econ. J.,* June, 1961.
4. J. M. Keynes, *The General Theory of Employment, Interest and Money* (London: Macmillan, 1936), p. 138.
5. A. P. Lerner, "Capital, Investment and Interest," *Proceedings, Manchester Statistical Society,* 1936-37.
6. ———, "Alternative Formulations of the Theory of Interest," *Econ. J.,* June, 1938.
7. ———, "Equilibrium and Dynamic Concepts in the Theory of Employment," *Economica,* Apr., 1939.
8. ———, *The Economics of Control* (London: Macmillan, 1944), Chaps. 20 and 25.
9. ———, "Money," *Encyclopaedia Britannica,* 1946.
10. ———, "Investment, Economic Aspects," *Encyclopaedia Britannica,* 1947.
11. ———, *The Economics of Employment* (McGraw-Hill, 1951), Chap. 6.
12. ———, "The Essential Properties of Interest and Money," *Q.J.E.,* May, 1952.
13. ———, "On the Marginal Product of Capital and the Marginal Efficiency of Investment," *J.P.E.,* Feb., 1953.

[6]

PALEO-AUSTRIAN CAPITAL THEORY

Abba P. Lerner
Florida State University

June 1980

This article attempts to show how two very simple adjustments[1] *to the diagrammatical representation of the old Austrian "average period of production" as a measure of capital intensity can protect it from the objections raised against it by Frank Knight, John R. Hicks, and many others, that led to Hicks' development of a Neo-Austrian theory.*

1. The Average Period of Production

Although many far more elaborate models illustrating the concept of the average period of production were developed in Hayek's *Prices and Production* (1931) and his *The Pure Theory of Capital* (1939) the basic known diagrams are the following:

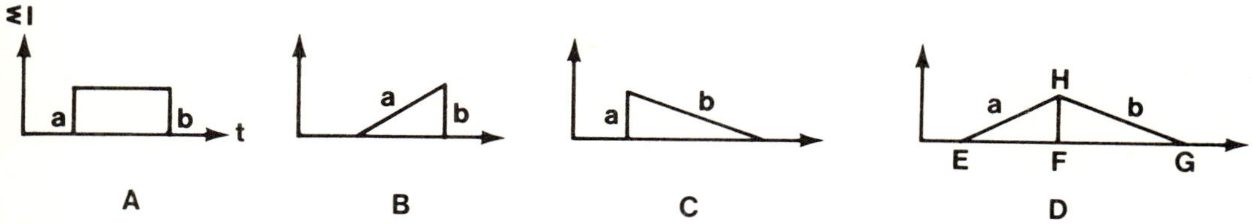

Figure 1

In these diagrams the horizontal axis measures time (t), from left to right, and the vertical axis measures accumulated net input (inputs minus outputs, ΣI).

From the point of view of an individual investor the inputs are services, materials or equipment of any kind that he buys. The outputs are what he sells. These are represented in the diagrams as the emergence of units of input that have been transformed into units of output during the process of production.

From the point of view of the economy as a whole, which cannot buy inputs from anybody, and cannot sell outputs to anybody, the inputs are the supposedly permanent flows of labor and land services into the economy. The outputs consist of the products which are consumed. Any instrument or intermediate product that has been produced and is not yet worn out or used up is considered as inputs that have not yet been transformed into outputs and are still *within* the process (which is represented by one of the diagrams of figure I) and are due to emerge, in time, as outputs which will then be consumed.

Diagram A, with vertical input and output lines at points in time a and b, illustrates a point input-point output process. B shows a continuing input throughout a with the output emerging all at once at b. Here we have flow input-point-point output. C shows point input-flow output, while D (which had been used by Jevons) shows a combination of B and C, flow input-flow output, input from E to F and output from F to G.

The horizontal *distance* from a point on the input line to a point on the output line represents the time elapsing—the waiting period—from input to output. A horizontal line of *input-unit* thickness represents the *amount of waiting* involved in this: one unit of input multiplied by the waiting period—so many *input-unit-days* of waiting.

The total number of such horizontal lines of input-unit thickness that can be drawn in the diagram and fill it completely is given by the maximum height of the figure (FH in diagram D) which shows the combined thickness of all the horizontal lines.

Each of the four diagrams could be filled by a set of such input-unit-thick horizontal lines. The *average* length of the set of such horizontal lines would measure the *average* waiting period, in the whole process, for the inputs to yield the outputs. This is the *average period of production*. This average is the sum of the lengths of all the lines divided by the number of lines, which is the same as the *area* of each figure divided by its *maximum height*.

A *vertical* line of *time-unit* thickness, drawn in the diagrams all the way from the base to the top, represents the quantity of input that has been applied to the process up to the date corresponding to the position of the line on the horizontal axis *minus* the quantity of input that has emerged from the process (as output) by that date. It therefore measures the accumulated net input or the *quantity of capital* that is incorporated in the process *at* that date. The *average* height of all the lines that completely fill the diagram is the *average* of the varying quantity of capital incorporated throughout the total period from the beginning of the progress to its end, when there is no capital left.

In a stationary economy, with a constant permanent stream of inputs and a corresponding constant permanent stream of outputs, there would have to be at least one "set" of processes of each type, consisting of one process of each age, a new one being started in each time-unit and an old one ending in each time-unit.

The quantity of capital incorporated in a process at any date is shown by the height of the particular vertical line that corresponds to the age of the process at that date. The quantity of capital incorporated in the whole set of processes is shown by the whole set of such lines, one in each of the processes in the set. This set of vertical lines is identical with the set of vertical lines that can be drawn in the diagram of that process. The sum of such vertical lines of time-unit thickness (just like the sum of horizontal lines of input-unit thickness) gives us the *area* of the diagram. The area of the diagram thus represents the total amount of capital in the whole set of processes.

The total current flow of inputs into the whole set of processes consists of one unit for each process, represented in each process by the horizontal line that begins at the current date. The whole set of horizontal lines, one for each process in the set, is identical with the set of horizontal lines of input unit thickness that would completely fill the diagram, while the *number* of such lines is given by the *height* of the diagram.

The ratio of the area of the diagram to its height is the ratio of all the capital in the whole set of processes to the current flow of all the inputs. It is thus a measure of *the capital intensity* of the process, which is also the capital intensity of the whole set of processes.

Applying this analysis to every set of all the different processes in a stationary economy, and averaging their capital intensities, gives us the capital intensity of the whole economy.

At the same time, as we have seen, the ratio of the area of each diagram to its height is also the measure of the average period of production of each process and of each set of processes in the whole economy. It thus follows that the average period of production is identical with, and can be considered a measure of, the capital intensity of a process, of a set of processes and of the whole economy.

This identification of capital intensity, or the ratio of the capital *stock* to the *flows* of input or output, with the average period of production is implicit in very old capital conceptions such as the "wages fund." Refined, clarified and emphasized by the Austrians, it is one of the most illuminating concepts in economic theory. It appeals immediately to anyone in charge of production decisions, whether in a capitalist or socialist society, who realizes that he needs a supply of resources to start up any production, only because there is a time interval between the application of the inputs and the emergence of the output. If there were no such interval, he would need no capital. He would be able to acquire all his inputs in exchange for some of the instantaneous flow of output, and could immediately start enjoying, as profit or surplus, any part of the output that is left over.

Nor would it take very long for him to recognize that the longer it is necessary to wait for the output, the more would be the quantity of capital required—the quantity of inputs he must obtain before he can start paying for them out of the output. It seems to follow naturally, that the longer the average period of production, i.e. the longer it is necessary to wait for the outputs to begin to pay for the then current inputs, the greater would be the amount of capital required to establish an ongoing set of production processes. It follows that the rate of interest would have to be lower for such a longer production process to be undertaken. A lower rate of interest would make processes with longer average periods of production (more capital intensive processes) relatively more profitable, and would induce a shift from shorter period to longer period processes.

2. The Criticisms

At this point one is tempted to write QED, but some of our most eminent economists, even while paying tribute to the economic illumination provided by the concept of the average period of production, have expressed serious criticisms of the concept.

These criticisms range from general condemnations to the pointing out of particular limitations. But, with one fundamental exception, they all seem to be inappropriate.

In *Capital and Time* (1974) John Hicks says: ". . . the only kind of capital-using production which will fit into the old Austrian scheme is production without fixed capital, production that uses working capital (or circulating capital) only. Fixed capital (plant and machinery) will not fit in" (p. 8).

Strangely enough, Hicks himself provides, in anticipation, as it were, an adequate rebuttal to this criticism. In his 1939 *Value and Capital* he says:

"In the simple cases they (Bohm-Bawerk and his followers) dealt with, it seemed natural to think of a particular unit of current input giving rise to a finite stream of future outputs at determinate dates in the future.[2] After a certain time the 'intermediate products' (or, as we might say, equipment) which result directly from the initial input will be worn right out or have passed finally into finished output. By averaging the lengths of time for which it is necessary to wait for the finished outputs due to the initial input, we get the Austrian 'average period of production' " (p. 218). Here Hicks follows the Austrian line in arguing that fixed capital is only circulating capital that is being used up more slowly.

However he goes on to ask: "But what sort of average is it? What are the weights? . . . So far as one can judge, the weights appear to be taken as quantities of output, or, at the furthest, values of output.

When the 'average period' is understood in either of these senses it has to meet crushing objections. Professor Knight has shown how impossible it is to identify a finite series of outputs of this sort, which can be imputed to any particular current input. It is ordinarily intended that current input shall be succeeded by an indefinite stream of future outputs. It is not possible to distinguish particular outputs out of this stream as being 'due' to current input . . .

Therefore the Austrian 'period' will not do; nevertheless, Bohm-Bawerk was not talking complete nonsense. His theory was valid enough for the cases he was considering; it ought to be possible to find a generalized concept which will meet Professor Knight's objections, and will yet include Bohm-Bawerk's argument as a special case." (p. 219) and: We can now see just where it was that Bohm-Bawerk went wrong . . .

"It was too tempting to jump to the conclusion: that because, in the first case considered (point input-point output, our case A), the effect of a change in interest was to change the actual length of time elapsing between input and output, so something of the same kind must be generally true . . ." (pp. 222–223), but ". . . when we generalize the process, making a stream of inputs produce a stream of outputs,[3] the whole notion collapses. This is most obvious if we take the case of an unterminating process, a process that goes on forever . . .[4] For the determination of a Period of Production, we must be able to associate particular inputs with particular outputs; and it is in the very nature of the use of durable instruments that this cannot be done" (*Capital and Time,* 1974, p. 9).

Hicks asked what weights are used in calculating the average period of production—quantities of output or values of output or what? As we have seen, there are no weights at all, or perhaps one should say, there are identical unit weights which we would have called input-units. We shall have to come back to this below.

One of Knight's "crushing objections" is that it is not possible to distinguish "which particular future outputs are 'due' to current input." This is because in his complete concentration on the "synchronized" current flows of inputs and outputs, he can see no technical processes which take time.

What looks like a repetition of Knights' "crushing objection" under which "the whole notion collapses," is Hicks' declaration, quoted above, that "for the determination of a Period of Production, we must be able to associate particular inputs with particular outputs and it is in the nature of the use of durable instruments that this cannot be done" (*Capital and Time,* p. 9). However, this may refer not to the synchronized total flows of inputs and outputs in a stationary economy, but to a flow input-flow output process—our case D.

This argument, if it were valid, would be much too strong. It is impossible to associate particular inputs with particular outputs in every one of the four cases except for case A, and then only if there is only one unit of input and only one unit of output.

In my explanation of the diagrams, I spoke of horizontal lines whose average length is the average period of production. This might suggest the association of the particular unit of input at the beginning of the horizontal line with the particular unit of output at its end. But there is no need (except for simplicity of exposition) for the lines to be horizontal or even straight. In any one of the four cases, as long as there is only one line, no matter how complex its gyrations in between, that connects each unit of input with one unit of output, the sum and the *average* of the *horizontal distances* between the beginning and the end of each line would be unaffected, and would still measure the same average period of production. There is no more need to associate particular inputs with particular outputs to obtain the *average* period between them than there is a need to associate a particular transaction of each dollar with the next transaction of that dollar to obtain the *average* velocity of circulation of money.

Immediately preceding the last quotation from *Capital and Time*, Hicks said that ". . . The stream of inputs must begin before the stream of outputs; nothing is produced from nothing. But the initial deferment, which may include a long period of pure experiment, has nothing to do with the capital-intensity of the process as a whole" (p. 8). An initial deferment of the output, if it is due to a period of experiment that is part of the nature of the process—so that it is experienced in every process—it is an essential part of the process and would show itself in a longer time dimension of every one of the four types of processes. If however, it is some research whose results would be available to others, this brings about a technological change and has no place in the stationary state where we have only "given processes."

Hicks thus concedes that Bohm-Bawerk's theory was valid enough for the cases he was considering, but "it will not do" because it is illegitimate to generalize "the effect of a change in the rate of interest on the actual length of time elapsing between input and output" from the first case (our case A) to the other cases. This touches on the only valid item in all the criticisms, the failure of the diagrams to take into account the rate of interest.

Although I have tried to show that all except one of the criticisms of the period of production concept fail, I am surprised less by the criticisms than I am by the continual acceptance of the concept as "illuminating" and as valid in some cases. A closer look at the diagrams will show that until we make the adjustments referred to at the beginning of this article, the proven identity of the average period of production with the capital intensity of a process is not applicable at all to any practically useful capital theory.

The first thing to notice about the four diagrams is that they all show total input equal to total output. Both are represented by the height of the diagram. If the inputs and the outputs are taken as quantities, this implies not only that there is only one homogeneous input and only one homogeneous output, but, furthermore, that the quantity of input has been made equal to the quantity of output by a peculiar definition. This could be arranged by choosing as the unit of output the total quantity of *output* divided by the number of units in the total *input* (or conversely, to define the unit of *input* as the total input divided by the total number of units of *output* yielded by the process). Since this would have to be done separately for every different process, this definitional trick would make it impossible to compare the productivities of different processes and to judge whether one is more efficient than another.

Such equating of total input to total output is reminiscent of the simplest labor theory of value in which the value of an output is *defined* as the labor (power) input poured into it. This is especially surprising coming from a school whose other most well known passion was the destruction of the labor theory of the value of products (unless the purpose was to show the equal validity of the converse—a product theory of the value of labor!). It is possible, however, by making the two adjustments referred to above, to interpret the Austrian analysis in a form that makes it more applicable to the actual economy.

3. The Adjustments

The first adjustment consists of three parts: 1. interpreting the diagrams as measuring all the different labor and land service inputs and all the outputs by their market value, say in dollars, at the time of their input or output, 2. remembering that the diagrams can only represent equilibrium conditions in a stationary state with a given period of production or capital intensity that rewards management with a "normal profit" which is included in the inputs, and 3. recognizing that the diagrams, in consistently leaving out all reference to the rate of interest assume a *zero* rate of interest equal in the stationary equilibrium to a *zero* marginal efficiency of investment in each process. This means that the value of the outputs must be equal to the value of the inputs.

The second adjustment is to bring in a positive rate of interest by adding a third dimension to our diagram D.

It is convenient to begin by turning our diagram D upside down so that the "height" of the process is measured *downwards* from the base line EG. The whole triangle EGH will now form the *base* of a 3-dimensional structure.

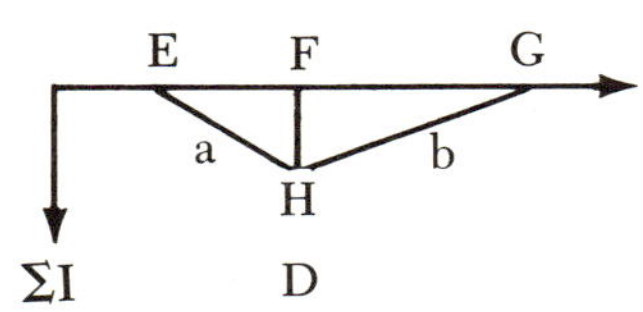

Figure 2

To make it easier to see the more complicated diagram we turn the base around a little, counterclockwise. We now add a constant vertical height on this base, measuring one unit of value, say one dollar, in the third or truly vertical dimension.[5] This gives us the 3-dimensional "ground floor," EE′HH′GG′, of the building we have begun to construct on the base EGH. The flow of inputs of land and labor services is now represented not by the line EH (previously *a*) but by the area EE′HH′. Similarly the flow of output is now represented not by *b* or HG but by the area HH′GG′. There is no change in meaning since the area is the base line (EH or HG) multiplied by the height, and the height is *one value-unit* (one dollar) and so does not change the measure.

Time continues to be measured in the direction marked *t*. So far we are still assuming a stationary equilibrium with the rate of interest and the marginal efficiency of investment at zero. The direction marked I still measures the aggregate *net input* in the process (aggregate input *minus* aggregate output). This too is measured not by a line (line FH) but by an *area*, like FF′HH′, at the appropriate date, and parallel to FF′HH′. In the third direction—the truly vertical—direction—we measure the *value* (V).

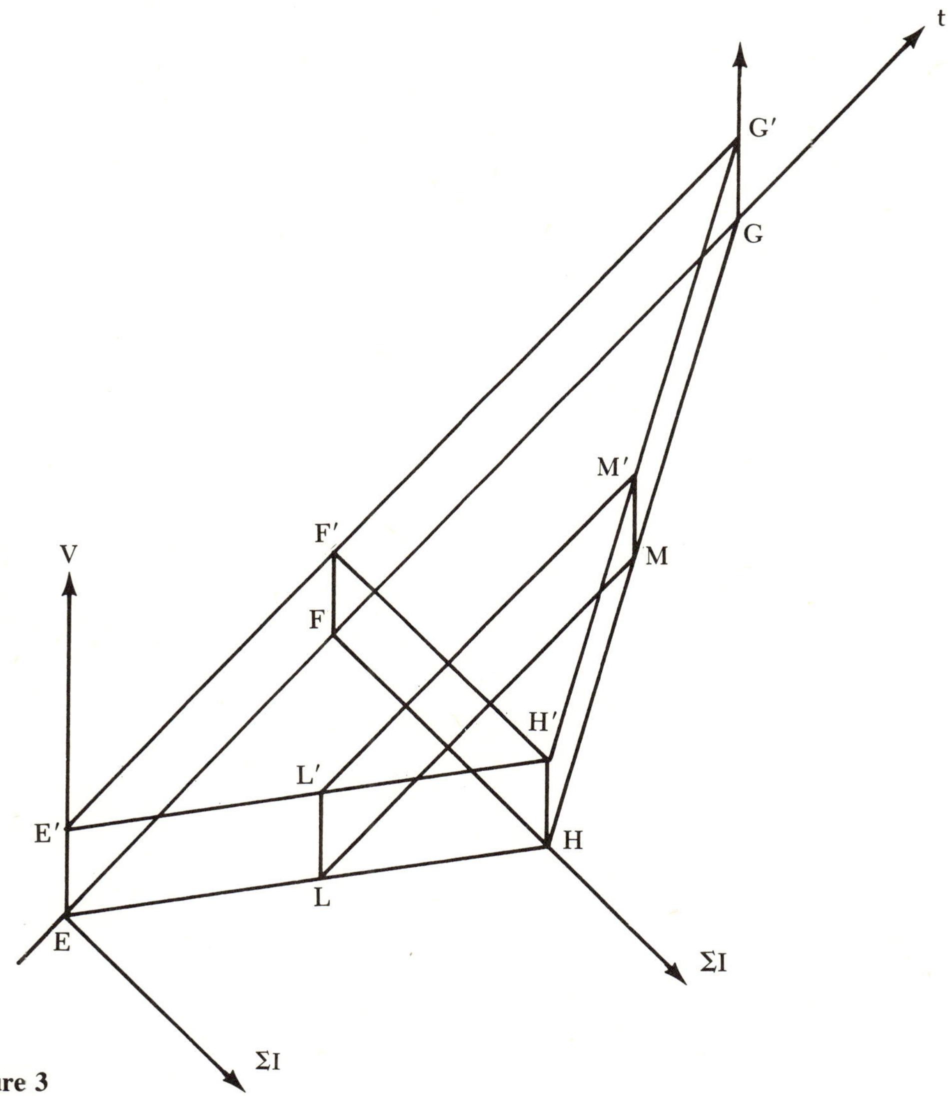

Figure 3

As before, the net total incorporated capital (the aggregate net input) increases as one moves forward along the time axis from E toward F and then diminishes from F to G as the inputs emerge as outputs, until, at time G, the process comes to an end. But now the waiting of each unit of input until its emergence as output instead of being represented by a horizontal *line* in the EG (or time) direction, is now represented by a vertical *slice* in the EG (or time) direction. The slice has a thickness of one input-unit, a height of one value-unit (EE′ or one dollar), and the same length as the unit-thick horizontal line on which it stands. One such slice (the longest) is EE′GG′. Another such slice, parallel to EE′GG′, is shown here as LL′MM′ drawn from LL′ (about halfway between EE′ and HH′) to MM′ (about halfway between HH′ and GG′).

In diagram D the sum of all the horizontal lines added up to the area EHG and represented the total capital incorporated in all the processes in a set of processes, and the ratio of the *area* EGH to the *line* FH measured the average period of production. Now the sum of all the vertical slices constitute the whole volume of the figure. Now it is the ratio of the *volume* of the figure EE′HH′GG′ to the *area* FF′HH′ which measures the average period of production and the capital intensity of the process.

But now we must give a different interpretation to the continuing equality between the total value of inputs and the total value of outputs. Now it is not due to any trick of definition. It is due to assuming a stationary equilibrium and a zero rate of interest. Equilibrium requires that the value of the total output of goods and services *exceed* the value of the total input of land and labor services hired by the interest cost of waiting for the inputs to yield the outputs. At a zero rate of interest the inputs and the outputs must be *equal* in value. The marginal efficiency of the investment must be zero, equal to the zero rate of interest. If the value of the total output were greater there could be no stationary equilibrium. There would be a positive rate of return, a profit to be made and a disequilibrating force for rate of return, a profit to be made and a disequilibrating force for expansion. Conversely, if the value of the output were less, there would be a disequilibrating force for contraction.

We can now bring in a positive rate of interest and recalculate the average period of production and the capital intensity of the process with a positive rate of interest. This measure depends of course on the rate of interest as well as on the prices of the labor and land services on which it depended when we were assuming a zero rate of interest.

For equilibrium it is now necessary for the marginal efficiency of the investment to be equal to the positive rate of interest. If the positive rate of interest is constant over time, the value of the land and labor inputs must increase over time at a constant (proportional) rate just equal to the rate of interest. The horizontal slices of figure 3 (the ground floor EE′GG′HH′) are no longer appropriate. Their constant height only shows what the inputs of the land and labor services would be worth throughout the process at the unchanging values which are appropriate to a zero rate of interest.

But with the values increasing over time at the constant rate of interest, the vertical slices increase in height, with the increase proportional to the height already attained, as shown in figure 4 by the exponentially rising curve. E′G″ traced by the top of EE′GG″ the longest of the vertical slices in the time direction. All the other slices will be rising at the same rate, and their tops will be tracing out the same exponential curve but, like LL′MM″, starting later and stopping sooner, they cannot grow as high as GG″.

Turning to the purpose of this whole exercise, we can now integrate the input of, and the payment for, the *capital* services with the input of and the payment for the land and labor services. These enter into the process along the area EE′HH′. But the total paid for them is measured by the area of the rectangle FF′HH′.

The capital services also begin along the line EH or E′H′ but, unlike the land and labor inputs, the capital services do not stop with the initial input at the beginning of the slice. They continue along the whole slice and consist of the ploughing back of all

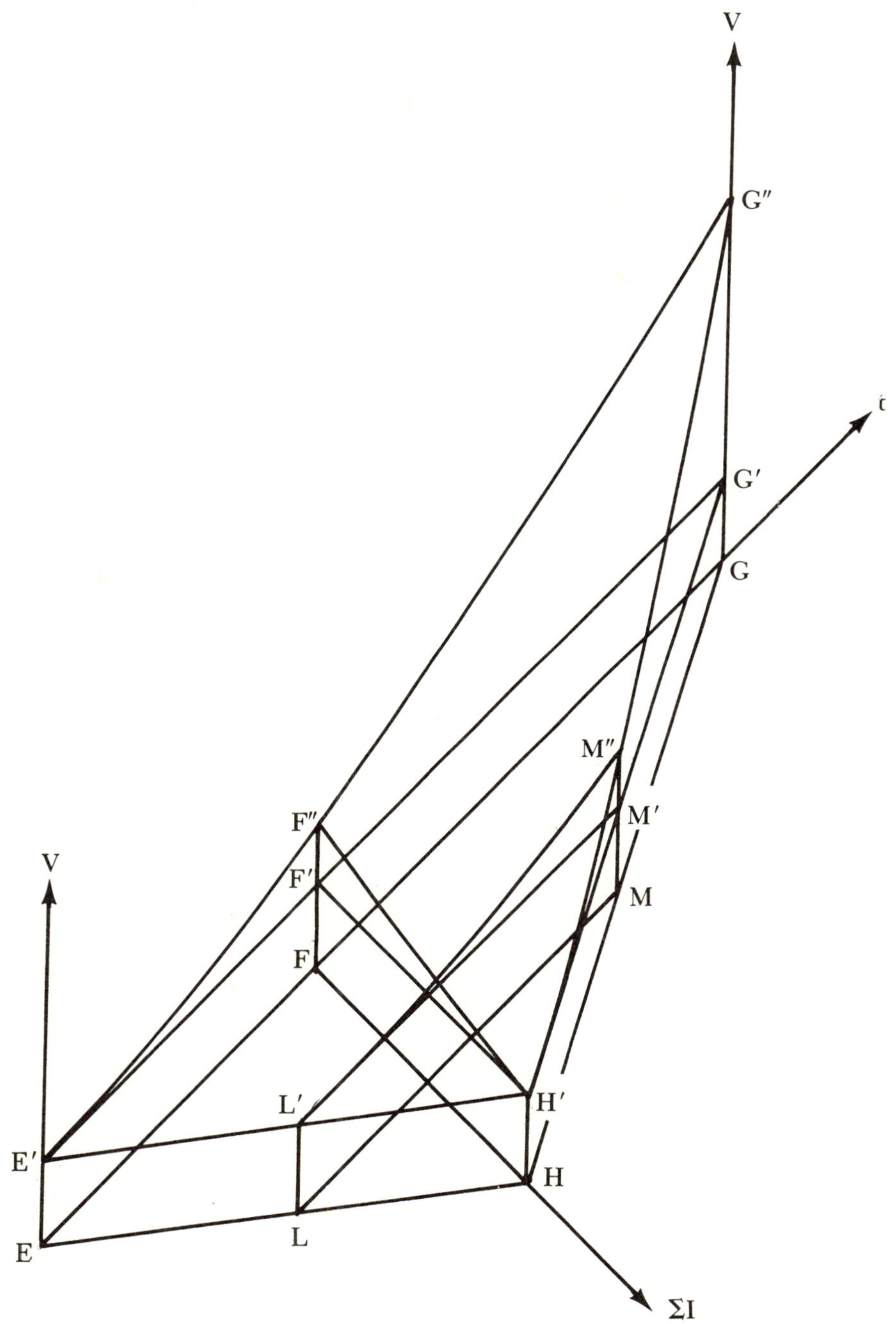

Figure 4

the increases in value shown by the increasing height of the slice, *above* the "ground floor," as it extends in the time (EG) direction, ending only when the slice reaches the output line HG. The investor, after paying for the land and labor services along EE′HH′, has to *reinvest* every increase in the value of each slice over time, while waiting for the outputs of the process to emerge. It is only this *reinvestment* of the accumulating increases in value while waiting throughout the process, which constitute the capital service inputs. If there were no need to wait, the payments to the factors could be paid for out of the instantaneous proceeds and no capital services would be necessary.

To see the inputs and outputs of these additional units of capital services we must complete the construction above the "ground floor" of figure 3. All the exponential curves like E′G″ and L′M′ in figure 4 (the tops of the slices) form a surface, E′H′G″. This surface (the "roof" of the building) is everywhere rising in the time direction at a rate equal to the rate of interest.

Every point on the surface E′H′G″ shows in its rise (as it extends in the time direction) the increase in the value of the land or labor service input represented by the slices as it passes through that time unit. Each slice begins with the unit value EE′ but now it increases in value over time, until it ends along HG, the further edge of the base of the figure, by which time it will have grown up to the height of a point on H′G″, the further edge of the "roof" of the structure. This growth consists of interest being earned and not taken out but reinvested. This reinvested increase in value is the capital service input. It now can be seen as just as essential an input as the input of land and labor.

The longest vertical slice in the time direction is the slice EE′GG″. The volume of this slice divided by its height GG″ will be equal to its average length in time. This can be more easily seen by supposing the slice itself to be sliced horizontally into strips one value-unit high, and of course one input-unit wide. The length of any one of these strips will represent an actual period of production—the time elapsing from a unit of input to a unit of output.

The longest strip in the longest slice is the bottom strip which begins at E. Higher strips begin later and later until the last one is reduced to zero length since it begins and ends at G″. The average length of all these strips is the average period of waiting from inputs to outputs of that slice, or its average period of production, so that the volume of the slice (which is the *sum* of the volumes of the strips), divided by its height GG″ (which is the measure of the *number* of strips in the slice) gives us the average period of production of that slice.

The same is true of all the other parallel slices which (together with the longest slice) make up the whole volume of our three-dimensional figure. The average of the average periods of production of all the slices in the figure is the average period of production of the process represented by the figure, as well as of all the sets of this process in the economy. A similar figure can be drawn for every other kind of process in the economy as well as for all the processes in the whole economy.

We now slice the total volume of our figure 3 *in the I direction* into parallel vertical slices corresponding to the "northward" lines parallel to FH in diagram D. Corresponding to FH we now have the slice of time-unit thickness FF′HH′. All the similar slices parallel with this slice make up the whole of the volume we have built up. Each of *these* slices represents the volume of capital, the aggregated net inputs of labor services, land services, and capital services incorporated in the process at one point in the lifetime of the process. Each slice also measures the capital incorporated in one of the processes in the set. The sum of these slices constitutes the total volume of the whole three-dimensional diagram (just as the "northward" lines filled the area of diagram D), and represents the total value of the capital that must exist in a whole *set* of such processes. It can therefore represent the total capital value of all the sets of all the processes in the whole economy.

Figure 4, just like diagram D, can be interpreted as representing a *single* productive process as it proceeds through time, a complete *set* of such processes as must exist in a stationary state, and the set of all the sets of the different processes in the whole economy in stationary equilibrium. In all of these possibilities the capital intensity—the ratio of the value of the capital to the value of the flow of inputs or of outputs (which two are equal to each other if we include the capital services in the inputs) is identical with the average period of production. This is the old (Paleo) Austrian Theory of Capital and does not suffer from any of the difficulties that led Hicks to the development of a Neo-Austrian Theory of Capital. The surface area E′G″H′—the "roof" of our construction—would then indicate the total flow of capital service inputs in all the different processes in all the different sets of processes in the economy. EG would represent the average of the *total* lengths of all the processes, and volume of the three-dimensional figure would represent the total value of all the capital in the whole economy.

Figure 4 does not show anywhere geometrically an area that would represent the total current flow of inputs or of outputs which must be related to the total value of capital to give directly the degree of capital intensity. We were able to show that this must still be equal to the average period of production because this relationship is clearly visible in each of the vertical slices (in the time directions) that together make up the whole figure. However, the relationship can be made visible by a fairly simple manipulation of the figure.

Since it is only the total capital value and the total value of the flow of inputs (or of outputs) that are required to show the average period of production and the capital intensity, it does not matter if we slide all the different time-longitudinal slices forward in the time direction (except for the longest one EE′GG″) until they all end at the same point in time, at G. The forward edges of all the slices would then constitute a plane surface in the V and I dimensions. Its height or value dimension will range from GG″ at its highest point to HH′ at its lowest point at a distance FH from G in the I direction.

The base of the figure will then look like diagram B instead of like diagram D as is shown in the three-dimensional figure 5.

The plane GG″HH′ (facing forward in time) will then represent the current flow of output in the stationary economy. The figure will also *indicate* the input of the total flow of land and labor services along the surface EE′HH″, but the value of this input flow, which is also the value of the output flow "due" to them is measured by the area GG′HH′—the lower part of the total output area GG″HH′. Similarly the input of the capital services is *indicated* by the vertical upward movement along the curved exponential surface (the "roof") E′G″H′ which faces "backwards" in time and consists of the tops of the same (shifted) slices. But the value of the flow of capital service inputs, which is also the value of the output "due to" the capital services, is *measured* only by the upper area G′G″H′.

In this article I have tried to show that, in a stationary economy the average period of production, with the capital services properly integrated, is identical with the capital intensity measured as the capital-output ratio or the capital-input ratio, and that this stands up untouched by Knight's and Hicks' criticisms of the average period of produc-

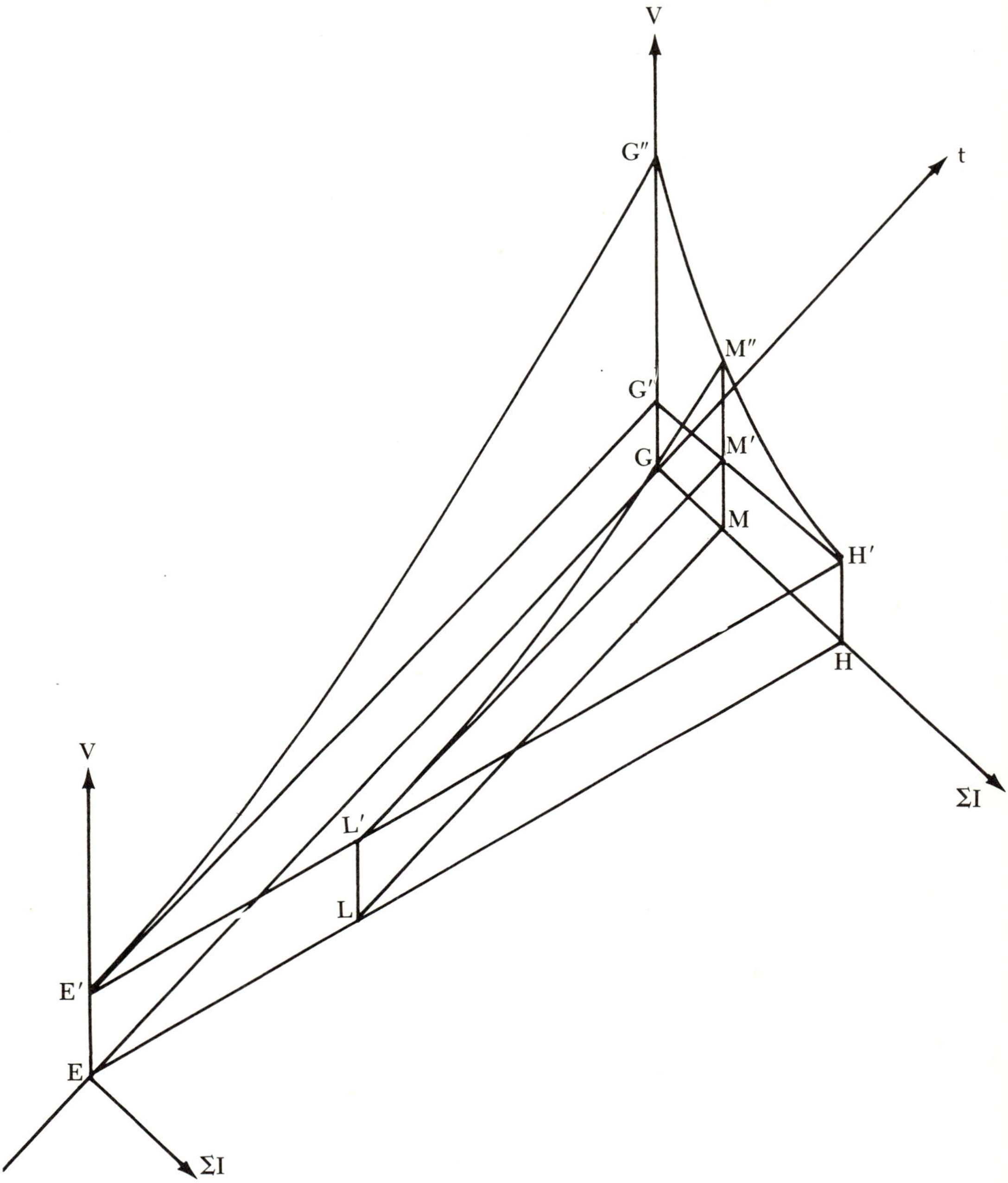

Figure 5[6]

tion. It was the failure of the simple diagrams like our A, B, C and D, to show the inputs of the capital services, and their value, that gave rise to the legitimate complaints about the average period of production as a *general* measure of capital intensity, and of its ability to show how a lower rate of interest would lengthen the average period of production.

A reduction in the rate of interest will induce investors to shift from shorter to longer production processes (which will require a shifting from the production of current consumption goods to the production of additions to the stock of capital), until the prices of inputs and outputs have changed as a result of these shifts to the point where further shifting is no longer profitable. In the new stationary equilibrium (if it should be reached), with the lower rate of interest, it will not necessarily be true that the new capital intensity (and the new average period of production) will be greater than in the original equilibrium. The increased stock of real capital goods, as well as the less than proportionally increased real output and the increase in the ratio of the former to the latter, cannot be measured by the change in their *values* at the new, changed, relative prices.

In his *Value and Capital* Hicks looks for "a numerical index to the character of the plan which can be relied on to change in a given direction when the rate of interest varies" (pp. 217–218), and would do what the Austrian theory claims for the average period of production. It would show the response of capital intensity to changes in the rate of interest. It would not be subject to the objections discussed above against the validity of the Austrian average period of production and it would also not be limited to the economics of stationary states which Hicks regards as "in the end nothing but an evasion" (*Value and Capital,* p. 117). He claims that in "the elasticity of this capital value [of a planned income stream] with respect to the discount ratio [1/1 plus the rate of interest]" (*Value and Capital,* p. 186), he has finally found the "True Period of Production" that the Austrians were looking for.

That this formula should give us the response of the value of capital to changes in the rate of interest is not surprising since that is what it is by definition. But that it should be called the average period of production—let alone the *true* average period of production—comes only from its turning out to be *"average length of time for which the various payments are deferred from the present, when the times of deferrment are weighted by the discounted values of the payments"* (p. 186).

This looks very much like the Paleo-Austrian average period of production of a stabilized technology at the appropriate stabilized rate of interest in a stationary economy, which is represented in our figure 6. This figure differs from figure 5 in that the slices are shifted backward in time, instead of forward, so as to make them all *begin* at the same time, namely at E, instead of *ending* at the same time, G. But now all the horizontal strips of each slice are also shifted back in time to the "front" of the building so that they also all begin at time E. Their one input-unit-width and their one value-unit-heights, all beginning at time E, make up the area EE″HH′ just as in figure 5 their *ends* made up the area GG″HH′. The base of the figure now looks like diagram C.

The "True Period of Production" does not have the flaws with which Hicks and Knight charge the old Austrian Theory but, as we have seen, the old Austrian theory is also innocent of these charges. Figure 6 seems to show that the Neo- and the Paleo-Austrian periods of production are identical. EE′HH′ in figure 6 is identical with GG′HH′ in figure 5 (both representing the value of the input or output of land and labor services) and E′E″H′ (the value of the input of capital services) in figure 6 is identical with G′G″H′ in figure 5. The total *volume* is the same in both figures.

In both figures the areas can be considered, with Knight, as the current "synchronized" flows of inputs and outputs, disregarding, as he does, the content of the rest of the figures.

If we look at these figures in terms of a stationary state, we can interpret figure 5 as

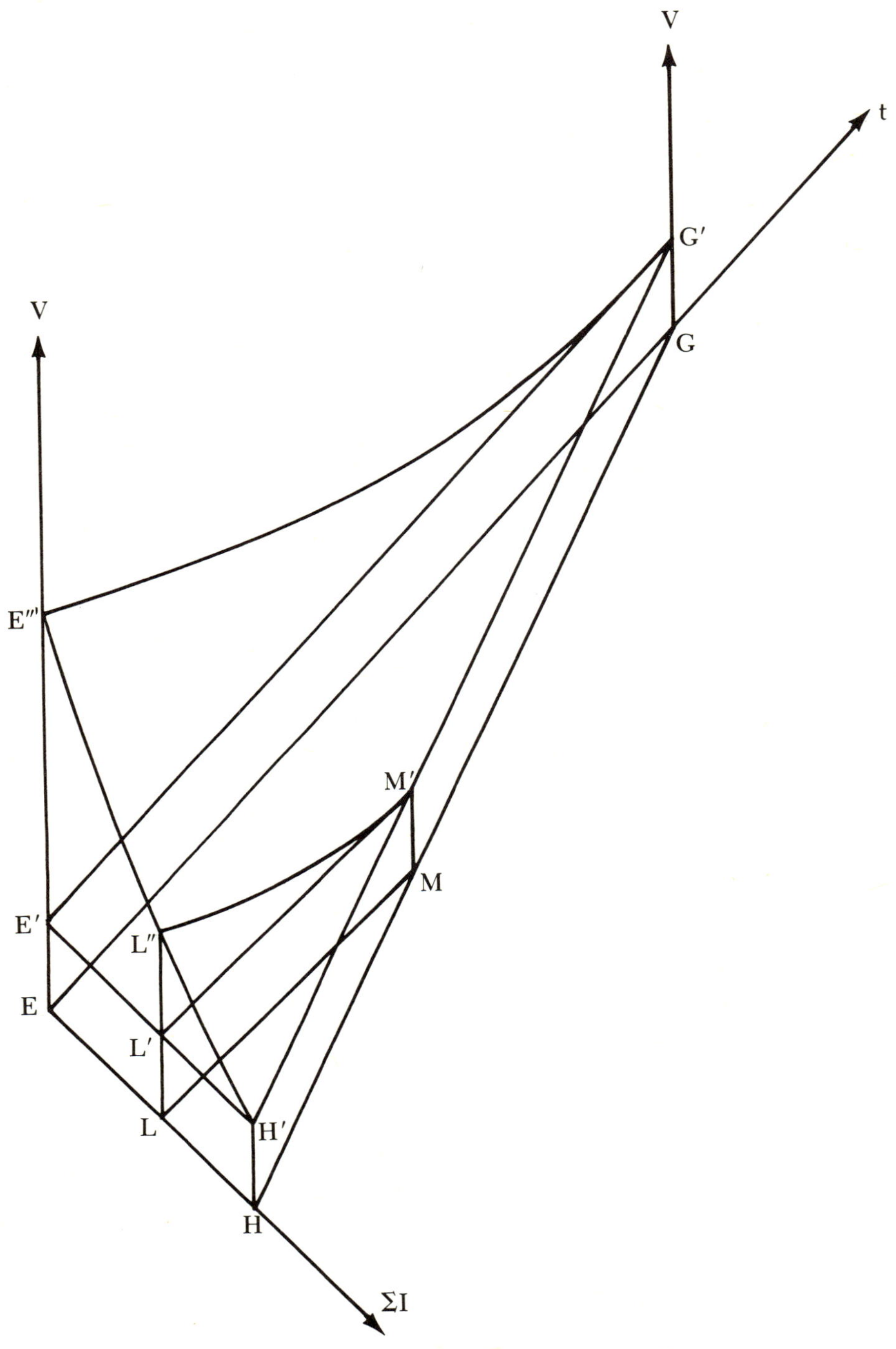

Figure 6

"backward looking" showing the past inputs to which the current output at time G is "due;" while figure 6 can be interpreted as "forward looking" showing the future of outputs which are "due" to the current inputs at time E.

But there still seems to be a fundamental difference between the Neo-Austrian and the old Austrian theory. The Neo–Austrian theory does not involve the "evasions" of assuming a stationary economy. Can it then succeed, where the old theory fails, in showing the response of the capital intensity of a non-stationary economy to changes in the rate of interest?

All that we can extract from the old theory is that if the rate of interest is reduced, this will create an incentive to investors to shift from the current processes to longer period processes (if there are any such) which were available but less profitable at the old rate of interest but which are more profitable at the new rate of interest. This proposition is, however, not applicable to the economy as a whole. It is applicable only to the individual investor who naturally disregards the effects of his decisions on the economy as a whole and who properly neglects the miniscule feedback on himself. He can reasonably assume that all other prices are unaffected by the change in the rate of interest at which he can borrow money.

But when we turn from the investor's micro-economic view to the economist's macro-economic view of the economy as a whole, *everything* has changed and we find ourselves helplessly involved in the "evasion" of trying to compare stationary states with all the prices different. We cannot say whether the new stationary state (if we should ever get there), with the lower rate of interest and the same technical possibilities, will have a higher or a lower *value* capital-output ratio. We are also confronted with the questions: What made the rate of interest fall? and (what may be only other aspects of the same question, on which Wicksell and Hayek did much work) if we start from an equilibrium with full employment where will the extra resources come from which would be needed for the shifting to longer period, more capital intensive, processes?

The Neo-Austrian formula for the average period of production of a stream of planned net outputs, even though it is not contaminated in any way by association with stationary economies, can be represented by figure 6. It is purely "forward looking," built only on the current plans or expectations of future net outputs from all the processes that are currently in operation (none that may be planned but have not yet been started). But it is just as limited as the old Austrian theory to the micro-economics to the individual investor. The changes in his plan in response to the rate of interest also rest on his assumption that all prices remin unchanged; and this cannot be fitted into any macro-economic analysis of what would happen to the economy as a whole, exactly as in the old Austrian theory.

The situation is even slightly worse. In the old Austrian analysis of stationary economies, we can at least say that what will happen if the rate of interest does *not* change. Nothing will happen. Everything will stay the same. But with the Neo-Austrian approach there can also be net investment or net disinvestment and then we cannot even say that if there is no change in the rate of interest, nothing will change. The Neo-Austrian "True Period of Production"—the average period of all the planned future net outputs from the processes currently in operation—does not assume a stationary state, but it is in a sense even more stationary. The old Austrian diagrams can be seen as moving pictures of a condition which does not change—the continuation of the phenomenon of a stationary economy. The new Austrian theory is not such a moving picture. It is rather like a single frame in a movie of a state which is changing over time, with investment or disinvestment contributing to changing the whole structure. The single frame or "still" gives us the expectations as of a single moment but tells us nothing about what succeeding frames would show us. In this sense the Neo-Austrian period of production is even more static than the stationary economies of the old Austrian average period of production.

NOTES

1. These simple adjustments were devised and written up by me during the academic year 1931–32, the third year of my undergraduate study at the London School of Economics. I had just learned about the average period of production from Professor Friedrich von Hayek's first course at the London School of Economics on capital theory. At the time, a group of my fellow students (who were avid discussants of economic theory in the third year undergraduate study room) were very excited about my essay and its three-dimensional diagram. We persuaded the editor of *The Clare Market Review,* the LSE student magazine, to print it in that magazine. But we realized in time that this would be a most inappropriate item in a magazine primarily devoted to student humor. It was only about a year later that I dared to submit an article to a professional economic journal ("The Diagrammatical Representation of Cost Conditions in International Trade," *Economica,* August 1932).

Over the years I had thought that these adjustments to the diagrammatical representation of the Austrian Theory of Capital had been included in my 1944 *Economics of Control* but sometime in March 1980 I discovered that I had confused the basic diagram in that essay with another three-dimensional diagram (p. 336) which, instead, showed the relationship between the marginal productivity of capital and the marginal efficiency of investment and renamed the marginal productivity of capital the marginal *efficiency* of capital.

My 1931 diagram clearly showed that the concept of the average period of production, as I had learned it from Hayek, had the rate of interest fully integrated in it. But some simplifying diagrams, which omitted the rate of interest, have led to misrepresentations of the concept and make me believe that my diagram can be useful even after all these years. I do not know whether a copy of my original essay still exists anywhere—it was mimeographed at the time—but I have a vivid memory of the diagram from which I find it easy to reconstruct the content of the essay in the present article.

2. This looks like our case C, point input-flow output. But in *Capital and Time* (1974), Hicks says that "The elementary process of the older Austrian theory, was of a simple, too simple, type. There was associated with a unit of output, forthcoming at a particular date, a sequence of units of input at particular previous dates. The sequence of inputs, and the single output, constituted the process" (p. 7). This is our case B. But, as we shall argue, all the four cases fit equally well into the Austrian theory—and all are equally inadequate as descriptions of the complete Austrian concept of the average period of production.

3. Our case D.

4. Processes that yield a *permanent* output are ruled out here because any such process is incompatible with a stationary economy, they would be increasing the size of the economy so that it would have to be not stationary but growing.

5. What we called "vertical" lines before were really lying down on the paper and perhaps should rather have been called "northward," rather than vertical, in figure 1, and "southward" in figure 2.

6. This was the form of the diagram in my lost 1931 essay. A closely related diagram appears (with inadequate explanation) in my 1965 article "Recent Developments in Capital Theory," *American Economic Review,* May 1965, Figure 2, p. 288.

PART THREE
METHODOLOGY, IDEOLOGY, AND POLITICS

[1]

Reprinted for private circulation from
The Journal of Political Economy, Vol. XLVII, No. 4, August, 1939
PRINTED IN THE U.S.A.

FROM VULGAR POLITICAL ECONOMY TO VULGAR MARXISM[1]

A. P. LERNER
London School of Economics and Political Science

BEFORE the rise of marginal analysis the classical political economists had failed to give a complete explanation of the mutual determination of all prices and, therefore, also of the incomes of the owners of the various factors of production. By simplifying the factors into the three items—land, labor, and capital; by assuming a given subsistence level of wages (via pressure of population); by positing a constant proportion throughout the economy between capital and labor; and by eliminating land from their picture in considering only the rentless margin of cultivation, the inadequacy of the premarginal theories was considerably cloaked, but it could not be prevented from showing itself in the necessity of pretending to explain the unexplained share of one or more of these factors as a residual or surplus. The indeterminacy which left it free to decide which factor or factors were to be treated as recipients of residuals provided the opportunity for scholastic disputation, while the fact that the income accruing to the owners of each of the three factors of production corresponded very closely to the three social classes of landlords, capitalists, and workers provided the energy for the insistence that some particular factor was rewarded only by the surplus and the implication that the owners of that factor were social parasites or worse.

It would appear to be difficult to consider the workers as functionless residual claimants in this sense; but the physiocrats, in their obsession with the fundamental fruitfulness of land, almost succeeded in doing so. Ricardo much more convincingly stressed the surplus nature of rent and as a capitalist (and a sympathizer with the laborer) was distressed at the prospect of the landlord's passively absorbing all the fruits of technical progress and of the capitalists' accumulation. Malthus, as a defender of the landed interests, was more concerned with the evils of a high profit (interest) rate as a brake upon economic ac-

[1] A review of Maurice Dobb's *Political Economy and Capitalism: Some Essays in Economic Tradition.* London: George Routledge & Sons, Ltd., 1937. Pp. viii+360. 10*s*. 6*d*.

tivity and found a useful function for the landlords in their propensity to spend.

As a result of these disputes it was impossible for classical political economy to avoid occupying itself with problems of the class structure of society and its class conflicts. Because of this, Marx was able to consider the development of society as a whole, to simplify it into a manageable shape by the concept of the class struggle, and to build up his great contribution to the "laws of motion" of social organization without departing very considerably from the topics commonly dealt with by the classical political economists. It required very little shifting of the basis of the argument to enable him to lump land and capital together as instruments for providing surplus value for their owners by means of the exploitation of labor.

With the development of marginal analysis the gap in the theory was closed and political influences had to seek some other confusions whereby the advocacy of particular interests might contrive to acquire the respectability of impartial scientific doctrine. In the meantime the landlord and capitalist classes had more or less resolved their differences in a marriage settlement, and the great remaining social conflict was between capital (in the wider sense, including the landed interests) and labor on the issue of capitalism *versus* socialism.

The influence of capitalist propaganda occasionally showed itself in a completely unwarranted identification of the marginal product of a factor—which is what the owner of the factor would be paid in a perfectly competitive capitalist society—with the deserts of the owner of the factor. In this way the capitalist system was shown to be just.

But such barefaced apologetics was rather rare among competent economists. (Though many who are quite innocent give the impression to the majority of their students that they are using this apologistical argument, and they can be blamed for using a terminology—like Professor Pigou's "exploitation"—that suggests that it is only departures from the distribution which would result from perfect competition that can give rise to injustice.) Much more common and very useful from the point of view of capitalist apologetics was the withdrawal of the pure economist from the consideration of social structures and the class basis of society. It became fashionable to regard such items as the distribution of income or of property and the tendency of inventions to be labor saving as "data"—even when these items were clearly not "given" independently of the economic processes considered, but were influenced or even determined by them—

wherever the examination of the determination of these data would lead to significant sociological considerations. This prevented the economists from prosecuting the "process analysis" of the "laws of motion" of society as a whole and restricted them to what Marx called "vulgar political economy"—the contemplation of static equilibria subsequently refined into the pure logic of choice in which there were no social classes, nor even men and women, but only an indefinite number of factors of production all applied in a symmetrical manner in accordance with given production functions to provide the products demanded by given scales of preference and receiving awards related to their marginal productivities. Such asceticism enabled them to construct beautiful and harmonious systems that could, on occasion, be identified by the careless or the unscrupulous with existing capitalist economy and permitted any criticism of the actual society, which naturally had to go outside of these imaginary systems, to be dismissed as "unscientific."

Mr. Maurice Dobb's book consists of eight essays, the main theme of which is this degeneration of classical political economy, which was intimately concerned with social structure and class relationships, to modern pure economics to which such matters are foreign. In bringing this issue clearly before the English reading public—and the English reading economist—Mr. Dobb has rendered a valuable service. This service is no less valuable for America where an unclarified sense of the same inadequacy of economic theory provided the motive for those institutionalists who were not merely seeking an excuse for their ignorance of economic theory. This is the burden of chapter ii, "Classical Political Economy"; chapter iii, "Classical Political Economy and Marx"; and in particular chapter v, "The Trend of Modern Economics"; while chapter vii, "Imperialism," perhaps the best chapter in the book, is an excellent example of a more profound treatment of a real and historical phenomenon, transcending the limits of pure economics and partaking of the virtues of the tradition of political economy.

There is, however, a subsidiary theme running through the book which is, in my opinion, false and which so much irritates a reader who is acquainted with modern economic theory that he is likely to miss the main theme and reject the whole book as a scholastic apologetic for an exploded theory of value. In the oversimplified account of the development of fashions in economic theory given at the beginning of this article the development of marginal analysis in place of the labor theory of value is seen as a fundamental improvement in theory which closed a gap and so forced class ideologies to search for other chinks in the logical armor of economic theory, or, failing at that, to try to restrict economic theory to harmless abstractions. The effective reply to such apologetics—beautifully illustrated in Mr. Dobb's own excellent essay on imperialism—is to override the restrictions and to consider all the relevant social implications, even if that is considered to be in bad taste. But Mr. Dobb's practice (in this and in other respects as will be shown below) is better than his theory, for he seems to regard the labor theory of value as an instrument far superior to marginal analysis, which is a kind of Trojan horse insinuated by bourgeois apologists into the citadel of political economy for the purpose of emasculating a discipline rendered dangerous by the Marxian corollaries. This secondary theme is all the more likely to submerge the primary one as it appears right at the beginning of the book in a very poor first chapter, "The Requirements of a Theory of Value."

Mr. Dobb is too good an economist to attempt to defend the labor theory of value in its crude form which says that in capitalist society commodities tend to exchange in proportion to the average socially necessary labor time incorporated in them, which is simply false. He supports a more refined form of the labor theory of value (as elaborated in Ricardo's footnotes and Marx's Vol. III) which makes allowance for differences in the ratio of capital to labor in different commodities and refers to the amount of labor incorporated at the rentless margin. In this form it is not false, but neither is it a theory of value. Without modern marginal analysis the position of the rentless margin is unexplained and the relative importance of capital and labor in affecting price, as well as the proportions in which they will be combined in different commodities, are all undetermined. That the author should overlook such inevitable, and indeed well-known, objections is a phenomenon that requires further explanation.

Some further plausibility is given to Mr. Dobb's case by his speaking of marginal analysis most of the time as if it were a one-sided utility theory that did not take into account the cost or resistance side—let alone give it symmetrical consideration—and so was entirely too subjective, the whole edifice resting on utility, whose very existence is open to question. Against this the labor theory of value is supposed to be grounded on the solid rock of objective cost—anchored to the bedrock of observable effort expended—providing a constant that determines the system, etc.; minor variants of these metaphors abound throughout the book.

It seems to be necessary, though not very obviously so, to acquit Mr. Dobb of using some variant of the essentially ridiculous and metaphysical Aristotelian dogma used by Marx (though Dobb would deny even this) that commodities must have some quality or attribute or "substance" in common that enables their exchange values to be compared, and that this common element, which Aristotle as a result of living in a slave economy was unable to see, is none other than the socially necessary abstract human labor congealed within them. Mr. Dobb does believe, however, that only in terms of a cost theory of value (and the labor theory of value is considered to be a defensible, and the only defensible, cost theory of value) "can the concept of surplus acquire a meaning; while without it (or something akin to it) no criterion of the differentiation between class incomes seems able to exist" (p. 30). It is this sociological consideration that is the real reason for holding on to the labor theory of value rather than any methodological concern for a constant that would anchor the theory of value to bedrock. Mr. Dobb would say that the two arguments really mean the same, but that is merely because he has substituted the sociological argument for the Aristotelian dogma which has had the inconvenient habit of vanishing whenever anyone had the temerity to question its self-evident nature.

The theory of surplus value, including the labor theory of value, was very much worth while when it was put forward by Marx. If, in its fundamental (and tautological) statement that property-owners appropriated to themselves that part of the product that did not go to the workers, it failed to explain satisfactorily what determined either the values of the commodities or the distribution of the product among the various factors and the social classes, it was in this no worse than any of the contemporary premarginal theories. Sociologically it had the advantage of bringing the fact of social classes into the picture so that its effect on values through demand, and thus on prices and distribution again, is less easily overlooked. Politically it served the purpose of harnessing to the revolutionary cause the workers' petty bourgeois reverence for private property by presenting the whole output as their product and therefore justly their property, so that the part of the social income going to the capitalists and landlords appears to have been filched from its rightful owners. But now that marginal analysis has solved the value problem, it is not only illegitimate to persist in repeating the Marxian *riposte* in that unscientific debate—it is quite unnecessary. For Mr. Dobb is quite mistaken in supposing that the concept of surplus and consequently the "criteria of differentiation between class incomes" can have no meaning except on the basis of a cost—i.e., labor—theory of value. On the contrary, only with the development of marginal analysis has the concept of surplus been sufficiently refined to enable it to be used in rigorous argument. The retention of the labor theory of value and the theory of surplus value is now as useless to the socialist movement, and probably more harmful, than would be the compulsory perpetuation of Marx's tonsorial habits.

In modern economic theory *surplus* represents that part of the income accruing to the owner of a factor of production that is *not necessary* for the purpose of making available the productive service that the factor yields. What part of any income is in this sense a surplus or "unnecessary payment" is thus seen to depend upon the width or narrowness of the point of view considered. From the narrow point of view of the section of the economy controlled by the individual who has to make any payment—i.e., the firm—none of the payment is surplus since it is absolutely necessary for the firm to make the payment in order to obtain the service of the factor. From the point of view of a somewhat larger section of the economy—say, a group of firms arbitrarily defined as an "industry"—all that has to be paid in order to get any particular factor service into the industry and keep it there is (slightly more than) what it can earn outside the industry, plus or minus any adjustment for different "net advantages" in the two fields of employment. An amount larger than this is likely to be paid because of competition between the firms within the industry.[2] This difference in the factor's remuneration is a surplus from the point of view of the industry.

The wider the point of view taken (the larger the section or area of the economy considered) the more restricted will be the alternatives available, the smaller the amount necessary to pay to keep any unit of productive service within the economic area considered, and the greater the difference between this and what is in fact paid for the use of the service—the surplus. If the widest point of view of all is

[2] The equalization of price for similar services will result in all the inframarginal units being paid at the same rate as the marginal unit, even though their efficiency (and the relative preferences of the owners) as between use within and without the industry is such that they would have stayed in the industry even if their remuneration were less.

taken—that of the whole economy—and is combined with the correspondingly exhaustive temporal horizon that is often called the short-period point of view,[3] alternative occupations are wiped out altogether and the surplus is at a maximum. Payment for the services yielded by property of any kind is unnecessary because the property is in existence and its services are available for the economy, however small the reward it will pay; all the income that people get as owners of property is surplus. Furthermore, of the income that people get for their work, only the minimum necessary to enable them to do their work is a necessary payment—the rest is surplus just as much as income from property.

[3] The phrase "short period" as contrasted with "long period" suggests a narrower point of view so that one would expect it to make a smaller part of income appear as surplus, but the opposite is the case.

The true temporal analogy of the narrow point of view would consist of segregating for particular attention some limited period of time and considering as surplus the excess of what a factor yields when used *within* this period over what it would yield if it had to be used *outside* the period. Corresponding to a widening of the point of view would be an extension of the period in time. This would reduce the alternative employments available to the factor outside the period and increase the part of its income that appears as surplus. Corresponding to the point of view of the whole economy would be the view that embraced the whole of the (relevant) future within the period of particular attention so that, just as in the one case there remains no use for the factor outside the area considered, so in the other case there remains no use for it outside the period considered.

The short-period point of view, however, does not pick out a short period for particular attention—a procedure which would indeed enable us to consider the alternatives of using factors inside and outside the short period. It supposes, instead, that a short period exhausts the whole of the future that has to be considered so that there is nothing outside it. It might perhaps better be called the short-sighted point of view, which so narrows the horizon that no possible uses of a factor outside the short period can be seen. It is thus really a "wide" point of view which, by completely abolishing alternative earnings of the factors, maximizes the part of their earnings which appears as surplus.

The long-period point of view is a longer-sighted point of view with a horizon that permits one to consider the possibility of factors being used outside the short period. In allowing these possibilities it is less exhaustive, and so "narrower," and diminishes the part of income that appears as surplus.

It is, of course, possible to combine a long horizon with a wide temporal point of view where the period that is given special attention is very long. This, like the short-period point of view, would also eliminate alternative uses of factors in other periods, but instead of by shortsightedness it would be by considering a plan for the whole of the future period that is seen. This, however, is not what is usually called a long-period point of view.

If a longer-period point of view is taken, some of the payment for the use of property in the short period appears to be necessary even from the point of view of the society as a whole; namely, when the use of the factor in the short period uses up some or all of the factor so that some alternative use outside the period has to be sacrificed. That part of the payment for the use of the factor which has to be paid to the owner to compensate him for the loss of this alternative use is necessary and not surplus.

All the payments that are necessary from the point of view of society, even when they appear to be so only from a long-period point of view, represent considerations of real importance for any economy, whether there is any private property in it or not, and this is so even if they appear as payments to property-owners for the use of their property. The sacrifice of a future use for a present one is just as real and necessary a social cost as the amount of the product that has to go to the worker to enable him to do his work.

This notion of surplus can be recognized as nothing but a more precise form of the Marxian concept of the surplus value which arises as soon as society is able to produce a surplus over and above what is necessary to maintain its working population and which is capable of being absorbed by exploiters. The advantage of this over the cruder concept, apart from its independence of any obsolete theory of value, is that it enables us to deal not only with income from property but also with that deriving from strategic professional opportunities, from bureaucratic caste systems, or from any other instrument for the appropriation of social surplus in accordance with any social or class structure. The class structure is thus seen as the complicated thing it is rather than as an elementary dichotomy of "the relation of individuals to the structure of production" as either capitalists or workers. Using modern theory, the complexities of the concepts both of surplus and of class are seen more clearly and more realistically. This brings us again to the question why Mr. Dobb, who gives many indications of being a very good economist, and who lives in Cambridge where the modern theory of surplus has been developed,[4] should want to stay with the old premarginal and question-begging theory of surplus value.

The explanation of this secondary theme of Mr. Dobb's would seem to follow the same pattern as his own explanation of bourgeois "vulgar political economy."

[4] See Joan Robinson, *Economics of Imperfect Competition*, chapter entitled "A Digression on Rent."

The "vulgar political economists" were so much impressed by the elimination, in the bourgeois revolutions, of precapitalist forms of exploitation proper to slave or feudal economies that they identified this with the complete abolition of all forms of exploitation of man by man and saw in liberal capitalist economy the final form of liberated human co-operation, awaiting only the polishing-away of some frictions to be revealed as the practical answer to all the utopias.

Mr. Dobb is probably the ablest representative of the communists and of the many socialists who are so much impressed by the elimination, in the Russian Revolution (via the abolition of private property in the means of production), of the capitalist forms of exploitation that they identify this with the complete abolition of all forms of exploitation of man by man and see in Soviet Russia the final form of liberated human co-operation, etc., etc.

Once a belief such as this is acquired, whether in the early years of the Revolution because of its original promise or whether later as a result of ignorance, Soviet propaganda, and panic from fascism, it comes emotionally tied up with all one's hopes for the future of mankind and, as such, is maintained with a tenacity that is all but impervious to disillusioning facts. The evidence of the establishment in Russia of an oppressive and reactionary bureaucracy has, however, been such as to shake all but the most fanatical believers in Soviet democracy, while even more damaging to the faith is the re-establishment in Russia of just such an inequality of incomes and other privileges as provided one of the bitterest plaints in the socialist indictment of capitalism.

As is always the case when an ideology finds itself sick, the scholastics are called in—in this case to prove that socialism has nothing to do with equality of income which is discovered to be a "bourgeois" ideal or even a counterrevolutionary trick. Passages from Marx that were directed against a foolish notion of socialism as an equalitarian rationing of every item in the individual's consumption are reinterpreted as attacks on the ideal of equality of income. But this is not enough. It is necessary to divorce the notion of exploitation under capitalism from the inequality of income that establishes classes and exploitation and class struggle, for this might raise suspicions as to the truly socialist nature of the inequalities that are being intrenched in Russia. Or, at the very least, the connection has to be pushed into the background where it will not disturb the faithful.

An excellent instrument for this purpose is the theory of surplus value. In its magnificent simplification it *defines* exploitation as the appropriation of surplus value by the owners of private property. With the abolition of private property exploitation thus automatically disappears and justice is supreme in Russia. Of course, in the transition "exploitation" has lost the limitations imposed by the convenient definition which would indeed equally well have allowed one to argue that there was no exploitation in a precapitalist society where the slaves belonged to the state or to the priesthood and there was no private ownership of means of production; so the definition is conveniently forgotten. But the purpose is served. There is by this legerdemain extracted an "objective" notion of surplus, uncontaminated by any connection with considerations of the distribution of income among individuals, a notion ideally suited for the apologetic purposes of the friends of the Soviet Union. The appropriate name for this kind of literature would seem to be "vulgar Marxism," standing in exactly the same relation to Marx and Soviet Russia as "vulgar political economy" stands in relation to the classical economists and nineteenth-century capitalism.

As might be expected, such a procedure leads to scientific retrogression as well as to political reaction. This is seen most clearly in Mr. Dobb's attitude to the economics of socialism—a field in which nothing can be done without the marginal analysis that is rejected by him for the political reasons indicated. In chapter viii, "The Question of Economic Law in a Socialist Economy," he occasionally forgets the "bourgeois" nature of marginal analysis and uses it to some effect, but he does not get farther than might be expected from such absent-minded excursions. Possibly as a compensation for these improper backslidings a good deal of ingenuity is devoted to minimizing the possibility as well as the advisability of satisfying the tastes of consumers in the socialist society. This is done by means of arguments which are reminiscent of the antisocialist economists who tried to prove socialism to be impossible but whose arguments have lost almost all influence since marginal analysis was successfully applied to the problems of socialist economics. The same reactionary effect is observable in chapter iv, "Economic Crises," where the main argument is invalidated by illegitimate shifting between profits which include interest and profits which exclude it, while Mr. Keynes's recent developments in the theory of employment are rejected, one feels, mainly because of their unwelcome minimizing of the real effects of changes of money wages and because of an unwarranted fear that the theory might be used to weaken the case for socialism; so that here, too, Mr. Dobb finds himself allied with the extreme right wing of anti-New Dealers.

But all these shortcomings are only secondary consequences of Mr. Dobb's secondary theme. If they are not allowed to obscure the main topic the book can be read with great benefit by every economist. It is extremely well written, full of suggestive ideas, and everywhere brings in all sorts of important sociological considerations that are habitually overlooked. In short, economists have so much to learn from the comprehensive sociological approach of Marx that even this "vulgar Marxism," when put forward with the clarity and penetration of which Mr. Dobb is capable, makes a very valuable book.

[2]

PLANNING AND FREEDOM

By ABBA P. LERNER

WE ALL KNOW the naive planner who in his enthusiasm thinks that everything in our society ought to be planned. He sees nothing but complete chaos in our economy as a whole because nobody plans what things should be produced for the citizens to consume, or who is to produce them and where and with what resources, or who is to consume each item which is produced. He is fond of imagining travellers from another planet visiting our irrational Earth and being shocked beyond belief to discover that the production of goods and services indispensable to the life and welfare of the people is left to the whim of private, irresponsible seekers after profit. His great concern is for the establishment of a general plan which would bring order in the place of this incredible chaos.

Such naive planners often speak as if they had never noticed that the economy in which we live, whatever its grievous faults, does succeed in getting millions of things produced from raw materials shipped from the far corners of the earth and sent to every village where the consumers want them. They fail to see anything surprising in what they call complete chaos being able to provide a larger population than ever existed in the past with higher standards of living than were ever imagined possible in the past. It never occurs to them that the visitor from the strange planet would never believe that all this could happen without there being some sort of order in the society.

If such naive planners were taken seriously by many people they would be very dangerous. They have observed many things which are unsatisfactory about our society, and because they do not understand the nature of the economy in which they live they would destroy the instruments which they do not understand, and of whose very existence they are often not aware, before they had anything better or even anything else at all to put in their place. Their eagerness to abolish the profit motive puts them into the same category as the primitive socialists who wanted to abolish the use of money or the romantics who wanted to abolish the use of machinery. They fail to see that the profit incentive is an integral part of the instrument which has been the ordering principle of our "chaotic" society in the past and can be improved upon so that it will be even more effective in the future in inducing individuals to perform the manifold activities that have to be performed in the general social interest.

In place of the existing institutions, which are chiefly aimed at utilizing human self-interest by constructing situations in which activities which are socially desirable are made profitable to the business man, the naive planners would establish extremely crude alternatives. These would suffer from the kind of inadequacy experienced in the first years of the Russian Revolution, when a partial return to the institutions of private enterprise became necessary to save the economy from complete breakdown.

There is not much direct danger from such naive planning because its inadequacies are pretty generally understood. Its readiness to abolish private property, the price system and the profit motive without recognizing these as instruments that have in the large worked for the general social benefit and without any adequately worked out substitutes for them is recognized by enough people as being not much more reasonable than, say, to refuse to use electricity because it was used by capitalism.

THE REACTION TO THE NAIVE PLANNER

But there is a danger to human progress from an exaggerated reaction to such naive planning. This reaction has made many people object to *any* proposals for improving the working of the economy as if they were part of such a naive plan and based on a failure to understand the first principles of the operation of a modern economy.

The reaction to the naive planner who sees in the word planning a magic answer to all problems has been the growth of an opposite disorder which sees in planning the end of individual liberty. This itself would not be quite so bad were it not that the same people who see dictatorship in all planning see planning in almost every important proposal for an improvement in the operation of our society.

The immediate effect of all this is that in place of a reasoned consideration of the advantages and disadvantages of any specific proposal for change we continually find ourselves involved in a general debate whether any extension of governmental responsibility is not a step in the direction of the establishment of a totalitarian society. The threat of totalitarianism becomes a bogey to frighten away all progressive suggestions, and a welcome instrument in the hands of the opponents of any progressive measures. The actual benefits or actual objections are thus lost in continuing speculation about the general connections between government responsibility, planning and totalitarianism.

Incidentally, this means that economic problems are not examined for what they are. Instead, the discussion is immediately shifted to the sociological question of the drive to totalitarianism. That sociological considerations are brought in is no objection. These are very often fundamental and must be taken into account. But the procedure is uncomfortably reminiscent of another debate which has passed into history. During the 1920's anti-socialist economists brought up the argument that a socialist society could not be anything like as efficient as a capitalist society because it could not have the guidance of the price mechanism. They admitted that a socialist society might be able to develop incentives other than that of profit, but insisted that the price mechanism was imperative for the performance of the important functions of indicating what were the activities which would best serve the general social interest and of measuring the relative efficiency of different ways of performing the socially useful tasks.

In the early 1930's several economists pointed out that it would be perfectly possible for a socialist society to make use of the price mechanism for these purposes and showed, moreover, that a socialist society could use the price mechanism more consistently and make it serve the social interest more thoroughly than is possible in a capitalist society. This is because in a socialist society the price system would not be distorted by extreme inequalities of income, by restrictions in output by monopolies, or by the necessity for permitting each enterprise to be able to expect a profit, even if this meant producing less than was socially desirable.

This demonstration was so successful that very few economists nowadays would dispute it. But the effect was not to convert the opponents of socialism into socialists. They merely shifted their ground, and now give other reasons for the same opinions. They could no longer declare that a socialist society would not be able to make use of the price mechanism, but they shifted to sociological arguments.

THE ROAD TO SERFDOM

They declared that there were sociological and political reasons why socialist societies would fail to make use of the price mechanism, but they put more emphasis on another argument, also sociological, which claimed that in any case the liberties of the individual would be lost. They said that even if the government of a collectivist society had at its disposal the price mechanism and other instruments for maintaining the freedom of the individual, or even developing it still further, it would not be able to resist temptations to simplify its problems by ignoring the rights and wishes of the individuals. They claimed that even if the members of the government were deeply concerned for the freedom of the individual, the pressures and difficulties of managing a complex modern economy would not permit them to indulge in such luxuries, and that in any case the people who were most ready to throw individual liberty overboard would have a great advantage over their competitors for positions of influence.

The same argument is now being applied not only to socialistic proposals for far-reaching collectivism but also to proposals which do not aim at all at supplanting private enterprise by public enterprise. It is directed against proposals that government undertake the responsibility for maintaining a money outlay on goods and services at a level sufficient to maintain full employment at all times. Every extension of government responsibility is attacked as a step on the road to serfdom—to quote the title of the recent book by Dr. Hayek of the London School of Economics, which is enjoying a tremendous vogue in America largely among those who have always been looking eagerly for any stick with which to beat progressive suggestions.

Much more serious than the welcoming of arguments like these by the natural enemies of progress is the effect they have had on socially minded people. Many progressives have really been frightened away from progressive measures by the warning that even the most well-intended proposals for extending government responsibilities in the economic sphere are full of deadly totalitarian danger. They have been impressed by the claim that seemingly harmless proposals for government action to remedy some evil will automatically lead to the need for still more government action; that any intervention with the automatic working of the economic system will lead to the necessity for still more intervention and that in this way gradually and quietly the totalitarian society in which everything is regulated will have crept up on us before we know what has been happening.

There are two fundamental flaws in this argument which has so unnecessarily frightened many good liberals into the arms of reaction. In the first place it is not true that government intervention by its nature tends to call for more government intervention, and in the second place even where there is a proliferation of government intervention and regulation it is completely false to identify such a development with the emergence of the totalitarian state.

THE PROGRESSION OF STATE INTERVENTION

The first of the two fallacies derives its plausibility from the fact that such a progression of government intervention growing on itself does frequently come about. It is the result of government intervention in a manner which reflects a failure to understand the mechanics of the economy so that the intervention has unexpected effects which are themselves undesirable. Similarly uninformed attempts to remedy these secondary evils will result in still other evils, and so the intervention can grow.

We have seen such a growth in the attempts by the government to prevent prices from rising even while it was itself causing the prices to rise by failing to levy sufficient taxation to offset the excessive distribution of income by the war expenditures. Attempts to stop this price rise by simply ordering prices not to rise (namely, by setting price ceilings) naturally led to a shortage of goods. This has to be remedied by rationing, which results in many cases in black markets and in an unwillingness of producers to make the goods whose prices are limited when the same resources can be applied to other goods or to what could be passed off as better qualities of the same goods. The next step is a minute surveillance of production so as to ensure that the intent of the law is not evaded by such shifts from producing rationed and low priced goods to goods which can be sold at higher prices.

Such a course of development is the effect not of *any* extension of government responsibility or planning, but only of bad planning—that is of planning by people who do not understand the mechanism of the economy, who are therefore always surprised by the unexpected effects of their foolish measures, and who go on to apply additional unintelligent planning with still more unexpected and unwelcome effects. Proliferation of regulation is the effect of what Carl Landauer has called "planless planning."

This is not to say that planners will always be wise. Many foolish plans will no doubt continue to be advocated and applied. Government intervention will often grow in places where we would be better off without it and where it appears to become necessary because of previous imperfections of government intervention as well as because of other imperfections in our imperfect world. There can be no guarantee that we will know exactly how any proposal will work out and that no further patching will be necessary. The moral is only that in considering any proposal we should examine it as carefully as we can in the light of what we know about how it would work. We should recognize that to reject it purely on the basis of a general sociological principle that any extension of government responsibility starts us on the slippery path to totalitarianism is no wiser than to embrace any and every extension of government action, without examining its particular merits, as a step out of chaos toward a consciously planned rational society.

TOTALITARIANISM AND PLANNING

The more important of the two flaws is the second, which identifies the proliferation of regulation with the clandestine emergence of the totalitarian society. No matter how far "planless planning" may lead to the extension of regulation and the growth of red tape, and no matter how much the regulations may interfere with the free actions of individuals, it is *not* totalitarianism. It is unfair to totalitarianism to suggest that it is so meaningless and passive a thing that it can come about by accident, as it were, without anybody working for it or even noticing that it was coming. That is not the nature of the beast.

One might not be worried by the immorality of being unfair to totalitarianism, but such unfairness is dangerous because it involves an underestimation of the totalitarian danger. It makes us look in the wrong direction and can seriously weaken our defense against the quarter from which we really are being threatened.

We must recognize that there are people who believe in a totalitarian society, who do not merely suffer the suppression of the individual because of the exigencies of administrating a complex economy but who believe that it is right and proper and desirable that the individual be subjected to the purposes of some mystical larger interest of the State or the Folk or the Race or what not. These people are prepared to fight for their ideals with a loyalty and a heroism to which our hatred of their ideals must not blind us. We have found that it is impossible to live peaceably with them and we have been lucky in defeating their attempt to dominate the world. We know, nearly all of us, that we cannot get them to come over to our side by any processes of logical demonstration of the error of their ways. Our only hope for the prevention of similar totalitarian attacks in the future is to remove the basis on which the totalitarians can build their power.

Totalitarianism can be established in a democratic country only by the violent destruction of the institutions which serve to maintain the dignity of the individual and of the men who protect such institutions. To perform this act of violence the totalitarians must win to their cause a large number of men and women who have come to believe in totalitarianism and who are willing to sacrifice themselves for that cause. This first step is possible only where the democratic society has failed so completely in providing a good life and a meaningful place in society for these men and women that they can be persuaded that democracy has nothing to give them.

Hundreds of reasons have been given for the rise of totalitarianism in Germany, and most of them have some truth in them. But there can hardly be any doubt that by far the most important single item was the failure of pre-Hitler Germany to provide its workers with work. The feeling of rejection and abandonment, even more than the material suffering of unemployment, is what made these men and women ready to listen to Hitler. Whatever other forces may have contributed to his rise to power, it is certain that they would not have been sufficient to bring it about if Germany had experienced some moderately successful planning for full employment.

Although we have defeated Nazism on the field of battle we may still lose the peace to totalitarianism under some other name if we are not successful in removing the bases on which it can be built. The first battle in the larger struggle is the battle against mass unemployment. If the fear of extending governmental responsibilities hinders us from taking the necessary steps to prevent the emergence of serious and prolonged unemployment after the war, it will have delivered us to the very danger from which it promises to guard us.

GOVERNMENT REGULATION AND THE INDIVIDUAL

Although the proliferation of regulation is by no means to be identified with totalitarianism and the destruction of the rights and dignity of the individual there are some connections between the two which give plausibility to the illegitimate identification and which are significant in other ways. In the first place, the totalitarian society is also full of regulations of the individual's behavior. But the difference is that the restrictions of the individual in the totalitarian society are deliberate measures for subjecting the individual to the purposes of the leader or the leading clique. They are not the results of inefficiency. In the democratic economy, overgrown with red tape because of unintelligent legislation, an increase in efficiency as the government learns how to simplify its procedures would reduce the amount of red tape. As a totalitarian society becomes more efficient with experience, the subjection of the individual to the state would be increased rather than diminished. The similarity because of abundant regulation is only a superficial one.

Abundant regulation, even if it is not directed by an ideology of the subjection of the individual, can nevertheless be very unpleasant. If everything has to be governed by rules and regulations the strangulation of the individual spirit and of business enterprise by red tape can be a great evil. If it goes to very great extremes it can cause a very high degree of dissatisfaction with the inefficiency of the system. People who are extremely discontented with the democratic but regulated system will be converted more easily to a totalitarian ideology.

A great deal of the red tape will be connected with measures directed toward protecting the rights of the individual, such as lengthy legal procedures based on meticulous attention to due process of law. The totalitarian will be able to promise to cut through all such "inefficiencies" in his society where the will of the leader is above the law, and in other such ways will be able to utilize the discontent with red tape just as he utilizes the discontent with unemployment. By diminishing the efficiency of society and imposing inconveniences and hardships on many people, proliferation of red tape renders the democratic society less attractive in comparison with its rivals. However, it is difficult to imagine this evil ever growing as important in this respect as the failure to provide security of livelihood and self-respect in satisfactory opportunities for employment.

The basic difference between the red tape from unintelligent government intervention and the deliberate subjection of the individual in a totalitarian society is that the former kind of regulation is subject to correction. It comes from a failure to understand how the regulation operates in the working of the economy. With time understanding can come and with it improvement in the measures, so that unintended effects are avoided. The individual will then find himself approaching the ideal situation, where the regulations are such as to maximize the total of individual freedom of action in choosing his way of life. A further diminution of government responsibility and of the concomitant regulation would diminish and not increase the total of individual freedom. The remaining regulations will be those which are necessary to check license rather than liberty. By restricting some individual activities they will be increasing the freedom of all the individuals together.

Such an ideal is of course impossible of complete realization, but it provides a general yardstick to help us in judging each suggested extension or limitation of government on its own merits. This principle does not *solve* the problems facing a democratic society either in its defensive action against totalitarian dangers or in its positive program for improving on itself. But it makes it clear that every proposal must be considered on its direct merits. It shows that any general rule of avoiding governmental responsibility at all costs is a pseudo-solution. And it reminds us that the greatest responsibility falls on him who would avoid responsibility by failing to act.

FULL EMPLOYMENT AND THE LABOR MARKET

With the extension of government responsibility many new problems will arise that have not yet been solved. Some of these are now apparent in the matter of the extension of governmental responsibility for the maintenance of full employment. A successful full employment policy, with the resultant establishment of a sellers' market for labor, will strengthen the bargaining power of the trade unions to the point where they will be able to get any increase in wages they ask for, the employer always finding it possible to pass on the wage increase (and perhaps a little extra) by raising the price of the product. What this means is that we would be in serious danger of a cumulative inflation of all prices and wages, with no gain to labor as a whole and probably a loss to everybody from the disorganization that inflation brings about in the operation of a complex economy.

It is true that this is the result not peculiarly of *governmental* action, say by deficit financing, in bringing about full employment. It is rather the result of full employment itself, even if it is brought about by any other means or even if it comes about by pure chance. The problems are the problems of full employment. Yet since it seems to be very unlikely that full employment could be maintained by chance and since in any case there is no justification for relying on such good luck, the government must undertake responsibility for solving this problem if it is going to establish a full employment policy.

In the past we have been guarded from inflation by a large volume of unemployed labor. We need to find a more economical and a more reasonable means of performing this function. This means that one of the most important functions of trade unions was to redress the weak bargaining power of the isolated worker in a buyers' market for labor. With the establishment of a sellers' market for labor in a full employment economy, the trade unions lose this particular function. The worker's bargaining power is maintained more effectively by the competition of the employers for his labor. A shortage of labor will mean that the employer will have to divert some of his ingenuity from satisfying the whims of customers to improving the conditions of work so as to attract scarce workers. We have seen some of these things happening during the war, when workers in many places have been able to choose hours of work and so on. With experience in finding out what are the things which will keep workers on the job, their conditions will be improved more effectively and more in accordance with the real preferences of the workers themselves than they could be even by the most powerful trade unions and the most laborious governmental regulation in times when labor is plentiful, and the worker will help the employer to circumvent the regulations in order to increase his chances of keeping his job.

While full employment contributes in these and other ways to serving the freedom of the individual in choosing his conditions of work, there will have to be some regulations to prevent inflation. But these are not objections to the provision of full employment. They are merely indications that there will continue to be problems. There is no reason why these problems should not be solved or why, except for correctible mistakes, their solution need diminish the amount of individual freedom rather than increase it.

The exaggeration of new problems, which will always be with us, into blanket objections to any extension of government responsibility betrays a lack of faith in the possibility of developing institutions to give us the freedom that we need. It shows an unhealthy deference to the existing institutions, as if these were the only ones that can give us the individual freedom that we have. It fails to see that in the past our institutions have to a considerable extent been molded to give us what we want from them and that this will be even more true of the future. Whether we will be free will depend on whether we want to be free and not upon the accident of what functions seem to call for governmental activity rather than for private enterprise. A society in which public enterprise is completely taboo can be run by a Gestapo, with the complete destruction of individual freedom, and an economy in which the government runs all economic activities can provide and maintain the liberty of the individual if this is recognized as a sufficiently desirable objective.

[3]

די לעגענדע וועגן פּאַראַזיטישן מיטלקלאַס*

פֿון ד״ר אַבאַ פּ. לערנער

פֿאַראַן אַ פֿאַרשפּרייטע נטיה צונויפֿצומישן צוויי באַגריפֿן: מיטלקלאַס און פֿאַרמיטלערס: דער מיטלקלאַס — ווי עס ווײַזט דער נאָמען אַליין — באַשטייט פֿון מענטשן וואָס געפֿינען זיך נישט אויפֿן שפּיץ און נישט אויפֿן דעק פֿון דער סאָציאַלער היעראַרכיע פֿון רײַכקייט, פּרעסטיזש און השפּעה, נאָר ערגעץ ווו אין מיטן. פֿאַרמיטלערס זײַנען די וואָס שפּילן די ראָלע פֿון פֿאַרבינדערס צווישן פּראָדוצענטן און קאָנסומענטן פֿון גיטער און דינסטוונגען וואָס ווערן פּראָדוצירט אין דער געזעלשאַפֿט; דאָס זײַנען הענדלערס וואָס פּראָדוצירן נישט אַליין די גיטער, נאָר קויפֿן זיי פֿון די פּראָדוצענטן און פֿאַרקויפֿן זיי צו די קאָנסומענטן, באַקומענדיק דערבײַ רווח. דער צונויפֿמיש פֿון בײדע באַגריפֿן איז אָבער נישט קיין איבעריק געפֿערלעכער, ווײַל די הענדלערס, וואָס זײַנען די פֿאַרמיטלערס צווישן די פּראָדוצענטן און די קאָנסומענטן, זײַנען טאַקע אינעם רובֿ פֿאַלן מיטגלידער פֿון מיטלקלאַס אין זינען פֿון פֿאַרנעמען אַן אָרט אויף די מיטעלע שטאַפּלען פֿון דער סאָציאַלער היעראַרכיע.

איך וויל רעדן קודם־כּל און מערסטנס וועגן דעם פֿאַרמיטלער, הגם דאָס מיינט נישט, אַז דאָס וואָס איך האָב צו זאָגן וועגן דעם מיטלקלאַס איז ווייניקער וויכטיק.

אין אַ סך טיילן פֿון דער וועלט זײַנען ייִדן — אין פֿאַרגלײַך מיט אַרומיקע פֿעלקער — מער ווי פּראָפּאָרציאָנעל פֿאַרטראָטן אינעם מיטלקלאַס. אַחוץ אַנדערע סיבות איז דאָס געשען צוליב דעם וואָס עס האָבן עקסיסטירט ממשותדיקע באַגרענעצונגען פֿאַר זייער אָנטייל אין אַנדערע באַשעפֿטיקונגען. די נטיה צו שאַצן גרינג די סאָציאַלע נוצלעכקייט פֿון פֿאַרמיטלערס אין פֿאַרגלײַך מיט אַנדערע מיטגלידער פֿון דער געזעלשאַפֿט איז דעריבער באַזונדער שטאַרק נוגע ייִדן. אין אַ סך פֿאַלן זײַנען די אַטאַקן אויף דער נוצלעכקייט פֿון פֿאַרמיטלערײַ געווען נישט מער ווי אַ פֿאַרשטעלטע פֿאָרעם פֿון אַנטיסעמיטיזם. מוז מען דעריבער באַזונדער שטאַרק באַדויערן, וואָס ייִדן האָבן אין אַ גרויסער מאָס איבערגענומען די מיינונג, אַז די פֿאַרמיטלערס זײַנען רעלאַטיוו נוצלאָזע מיטגלידער פֿון דער געזעלשאַפֿט אָדער גאָר פּאַראַזיטן, וואָס נישט בלויז טוען זיי ניט זייער חלק אין דער נוצלעכער אַרבעט, נאָר זיי ברענגען גאָר אַ בפֿירושן

* גערלייענט אויף דער 21סטער יאָריקער קאָנפֿערענץ פֿון ייִוואָ דעם 19טן יאַנואַר 1947.

65

שאָדן דער געזעלשאַפֿט מיט זייער טעטיקייט. דאָס קאָן מען למשל זען פֿון דעם באַזונדערן שטאָלץ, מיט וועלכן טייל ציוניסטן ריידן וועגן זייערע דערגרייכונגען בײַם סטימולירן דעם וווּקס פֿון ייִדישע פֿיזישע אַרבעטערס און ייִדישע פֿאַרמערס. איך האָף, אַז מען וועט מיך ניט חושד זײַן אין וועלן פֿאַרקלענערן דעם באַטײַט פֿון די דאָזיקע גאַנץ נוצלעכע טעטיקייטן. איך באַדויער בלויז די ראָמאַנטישע גוזמאות וואָס נעמען זיך פֿון דעם דאָזיקן קוקן אויפֿן פֿאַרמיטלער פֿון אויבן אַראָפּ: ווײַל דאָס איז דאָך דער זינען פֿון האַלטן, אַז ווען אַ הענדלער ווערט אַ פֿאַרמער איז דאָס תּמיד פּראָגרעס. מען קאָן אפֿשר אויסטײַטשן אַזאַ אײַנשטעלונג מיטן פֿאַקט, אַז יעדער איינער איז נוטה צו קוקן מיט קינאה אויף יענע געביטן, צו וועלכע מען לאָזט אים ניט צו. אָבער דאָס באַרעכטיקט ניט דעם מיסטיציזם וואָס בינדט זיך מיטן געדאַנק, אַז עס איז דאָ עפּעס אַ באַזונדערע שיינקייט אין דער אמתדיק „פּראָדוקטיווער” אַרבעט אין פֿאַבריק און אויפֿן פֿעלד.

נישטאָ קיין שום באַרעכטיקונג פֿאַר אַזאַ קוק אויף די הענדלערישע טעטיקייטן פֿונעם פֿאַרמיטלער. ס'איז ניטאָ קיין שום גרונד צו מאַכן אַ חילוק צווישן פּראָדוקטיווקייט פֿון דירעקטער אַרבעט און ניט־פּראָדוקטיווקייט פֿון האַנדל. די טעטיקייט פֿונעם הענדלער איז אין אמתן אויך אַ מין אַרבעט וואָס האָט אַ גאַנץ באַשטימטע נוצלעכקייט. זײַן אַרבעט באַשטייט אין העלפֿן באַוועגן זאַכן פֿון איין אָרט צום אַנדערן. דער הענדלער געפֿינט אויס, אַז ער קאָן קויפֿן פֿאַר אַ קלענערן פּרײַז אין איין אָרט און פֿאַרקויפֿן פֿאַר אַ העכערן פּרײַז אויף אַ צווייטן אָרט. די זאַך וועלכע ער קויפֿט און פֿאַרקויפֿט איז טײַערער אין דעם צווייטן אָרט בלויז דערפֿאַר, וואָס מען נייטיקט זיך אין איר דאָרטן שטאַרקער איידער אין דעם אָרט, ווו ער קויפֿט זי. זײַן טעטיקייט באַשטייט אַזוי אַרום אין באַוועגן זאַכן פֿון די ערטער ווו מען נייטיקט זיך אין זיי ווייניקער צו ערטער ווו מען נייטיקט זיך אין זיי מער, פֿון ערטער ווו זיי זײַנען ווייניקער נוצלעך צו ערטער ווו זיי זײַנען מער נוצלעך.

אָבער די טעטיקייט פֿון באַוועגן זאַכן פֿון איין אָרט צום צווייטן איז לחלוטין ניט ספּעציפֿיש פֿאַר דעם פֿאַרמיטלער. דאָס איז דער תּוך פֿון מענטשלעכער טעטיקייט בכלל און פֿון דער גאַנצער „עכטער” אָדער דירעקטער פּראָדוקציע בפֿרט. דאָס אייניציקע וואָס מענטשן קענען טאָן איז באַוועגן זאַכן פֿון איין אָרט צום צווייטן, און די סאָציאַלע באַרעכטיקונג פֿאַר אַזאַ טעטיקייט קאָן באַשטיין בלויז אין דעם וואָס עס איז בעסער, די זאַך זאָל זיך געפֿינען אויף דעם נײַעם אָרט איידער אויפֿן אַלטן.

דאָס איז חל אויף יעדער מיגלעכן מין אַרבעט. די אַרבעטערס קאָנען ניט שאַפֿן קיין מאַטעריעלע אָביעקטן. זיי קאָנען בלויז מאַניפּולירן מיט מאַטעריאַלן וואָס עקסיסטירן אויף דער ערד. אַן אַרבעטער קאָן באַוועגן קוילן פֿון דער וואַנט פֿון אַ קוילנגרוב צו דער באַן וואָס פֿירט זיי אַוועק. ער קאָן זיי באַוועגן פֿון אונטער דער ערד צום אייבערפֿלאַך, פֿון ראַיאָנען וואָס פּראָדוצירן קוילן צו די וווינהײַזער און פֿאַבריקן ווו מען דאַרף זיי האָבן. דער פֿאַרמער טוט גאָרנישט

אַחוץ באַוועגן שטיקער ערד מיט זײַן לאָפּעטע און אַקער־אײַזן, אָדער באַוועגן באַגיטיקונג (קונסטמיסט) פֿון די זעק צו דעם פֿעלד ווו זיי זײַנען נייטיק פֿאַר דערנערן די געוויקסן, אָדער באַוועגן די זריעה צו שטיקער לאַנד ווו זי קען צום בעסטן אויפֿגיין. דער פֿאַבריק־אַרבעטער באַוועגט מאַשינען, כּדי צו ברענגען זיי אין באַרירונג מיט מאַטעריאַלן, און באַוועגט די שרויפֿן כּדי זיי זאָלן זיך האַלטן פֿעסט; ער ציט פֿאָדעם פֿון באַוול אָדער פֿון וואָל אָדער אַראַנזשירט זיי אַזוי זיי זאָלן זיך צונויפֿפֿלעכטן, כּדי זיך צו פֿאַרוואַנדלען אין שטאָף, אָדער זיך פֿאַרבינדן מיט אַנדערע פֿעדעם, כּדי זיך צו פֿאַרוואַנדלען אין אָנצוגן, קליידער און העמדער. אַפֿילו די פֿיזישע אַרבעט פֿון פּאָעט באַשטייט אין באַוועגן קליינע סכומען טינט פֿונעם טינטער צו געוויסע ערטער אויפֿן פּאַפּיר. די מאָלערײַ האָט מען אַ מאָל באַצייכנט ווי לייגן די ריכטיקע קאָלירן אויף די ריכטיקע ערטער אויפֿן לײַוונט. און אין איצטיקן מאָמענט בין איך פֿאַרנומען מיט באַוועגן טיילעכלעך לופֿט, כּדי געוויסע כוואַליעס זאָלן אָנרירן אײַערע אויערן.

אַזוי ווי אַלע טעטיקייטן קאָנען באַצייכנט ווערן ווי „באַוועגן גיטער פֿון איין אָרט אויפֿן צווייטן", איז נישטאָ קיין פֿיזישער סימן מובֿהק וואָס זאָל דערלויבן צו מאַכן אַ חילוק צווישן פּראָדוקטיווע און ניט־פּראָדוקטיווע באַשעפֿטיקונגען. דער איינציקער פּרוּוושטיין פֿאַרן באַטײַט פֿון די דאָזיקע טעטיקייטן איז די מאָס, אין וועלכער זיי זײַנען נוצלעך פֿאַר מענטשן, דורך העלפֿן זיי טאָן דאָס וואָס זיי ווילן, דורך מיגלעך מאַכן אַ פֿולער און בעסער לעבן פֿאַר די יחידים, פֿון וועלכע עס באַשטייט די געזעלשאַפֿט.

דאָס מאַכן דעם חילוק צווישן די טעטיקייטן פֿון פֿאַרמיטלערס און טעטיקייטן פֿון אַנדערע אַרבעטערס איז בלויז איינער פֿון אַ גאַנצער סדרה פּרוּוון צו מאַכן אַ חילוק צווישן פּראָדוקטיווע און ניט־פּראָדוקטיווע באַשעפֿטיקונגען.

מיט צוויי יאָרהונדערטער צוריק האָבן די פֿראַנצייזישע פֿיזיאָקראַטן, די זיידעס פֿון דער מאָדערנער עקאָנאָמישער וויסנשאַפֿט, געהאַלטן, אַז בלויז דאָס לאַנד און די מענטשן וואָס אַרבעטן אויפֿן לאַנד זײַנען באמת פּראָדוקטיוו. די אַגריקולטור, האָבן זיי געטענהט, ברענגט אַרויס פּרוכט, בעת די מאַנופֿאַקטור איז אין דער אמתן ניט פּראָדוקטיוו, ווײַל זי בײַט בלויז איבער די פֿאָרעם פֿון דעם וואָס דאָס לאַנד האָט אַרויסגעבערענגט. די מאַנופֿאַקטור האָט — פֿיזיש גענומען — ניט צוגעגעבן קיין שום נײַס: זי האָט בסך־הכּל טראַנספֿאָרמירט וואָל אין שטאָף, ציגל אין הײַזער, ווייץ אין ברויט. בלויז די ערד האָט געגעבן דאָס וואָס פֿיזיאָקראַטן האָבן אָנגערופֿן „ריינער פּראָדוקט".

דער פֿאָטער פֿון דער מאָדערנער עקאָנאָמישער טעאָריע, אַדאַם סמיט, האָט געמאַכט אַן אַנדער חילוק. לויט אים קאָנען בעלי־מלאָכות זײַן פּונקט אַזוי פּראָדוקטיוו ווי די פֿאַרמערס, בתּנאַי אַז זיי פּראָדוצירן אַ מאַטעריעלע סחורה, אַ זאַך וואָס לאָזט זיך אָנטאַפּן. דער בויאַרבעטער, דער שנײַדער, דער אינזשעניר זײַנען אַזוי אַרום פּראָדוקטיווע אַרבעטערס, ווײַל נאָך דעם ווי זיי האָבן אָפּגעטאָן זייערס, קאָנען הײַזער, קליידער אָדער בריקן זאָגן עדות וועגן זייער פּראָדוקטיווקייט. אין דער זעלביקער צײַט וואָלט אַ מוזיקאַנט, אַן אַדוואָקאַט, אַ זינגער אָדער אַ פּראָפֿעסאָר געדאַרפֿט פֿאַררעכנט ווערן צו „נישט־פּראָדוקטיווע".

אין בײדע פֿאַלן איז דער חילוק געמאַכט געוואָרן צוליב גאָר אַנדערע טעמים ווי וועלן לויבן די פּראָדוקטיווע אַרבעט להיפּוך צו דער נישט־פּראָדוקטיווער. די כּוונה איז ניט געווען צו געבן אָנצוהערן, אַז די ניט־פּראָדוקטיווע אַרבעט איז ווייניקער נוצלעך, ווייניקער ווערטפֿול אָדער ווייניקער בכּבֿודיק. די פֿיזיאָקראַטן האָבן געשטעלט דעם טראָפּ אויף דער פּראָדוקטיווקייט פֿון דער ערד, ווײַל זיי זײַנען געווען פֿאַראינטערעסירט אין אַ באַשטימטער שטײַער־פּאָליטיק. זיי האָבן געוואָלט אַרויפֿלייגן אַלע שטײַערן אויף די ערדבאַזיצערס, כּדי אין גאַנצן צו אַבסאָרבירן זייער רענטע.

אַדאַם סמיט ווידער האָט בפֿירוש אונטערגעשטראָכן, אַז די אַרבעט וואָס ער האָט באַצייכנט ווי „ניט־פּראָדוקטיוו“ קאָן אַ מאָל זײַן פֿון דער גרעסטער וויכטיקייט פֿאַר דער געזעלשאַפֿט. ער איז אויסן געווען אויסצוטיילן יענע טעטיקייטן וואָס שאַפֿן צוגאָבן צו דעם אַקומולירטן רײַכטום פֿון דער געזעלשאַפֿט, ווי הײַזער, פֿאַבריקן, מעבל אאַז״וו. אַזעלכע צוגאָבן קאָנען געמאָלט זײַן בלויז ווי אַ רעזולטאַט פֿון טעטיקייטן וואָס ברענגען אַרויס אַ דויערדיקן מאַטעריעלן פּראָדוקט. דער מענטש וואָס האָט געטאָן אַ דינסט וואָס מוז קאָנסומירט ווערן תּיכּף ומיד (ווי דער געזאַנג פֿון אַ זינגער אָדער די דינסט פֿון דער פּאָליציי) קאָן טאַקע דערמיט האָבן געטאָן אַ ניט אַן ערך נוצלעכערע און וויכטיקערע זאַך. ער קען הייבן דעם לעבנס־מצבֿ אָדער העלפֿן אײַנשטעלן עלעמענטאַרע זיכערקייט, וואָס אָן איר וואָלט דאָס לעבן ניט געווען מיגלעך; אָבער ער וואָלט ניט געשאַפֿן ד י ר ע ק ט קיין שום צוגאָב צו דעם רײַכטום פֿון דער געזעלשאַפֿט, וואָס זאָל זיך לאָזן אָנטאַפּן. דאָס איז די איינציקע סיבה, פֿאַר וואָס אַדאַם סמיט האָט אויסגעטיילט די דאָזיקע אַרבעט ווי אַ „ניט־פּראָדוקטיווע“.

אַ חילוק צווישן דעם אַרבעטער און פֿאַרמיטלער ווערט אַ מאָל געמאַכט אויף דעם סמך, וואָס דער אַרבעטער אַרבעט פֿאַר לוין בעת דער פֿאַרמיטלער שטרעבט צו רווח. דאָס באַקומען לוין באַטראַכט מען ווי אַ בכּבֿודיקע זאַך און אויך ווי אַ סימן פֿון ווערן עקספּלואַטירט דורכן קאַפּיטאַליסט וואָס צאָלט די לוינען. אין דער זעלביקער צײַט ליגט אויף דער רווח־מאַכערײַ אַ פּגם, און דאָס בינדט זיך מיט דער אידעע, אַז דאָ האָט מען צו טאָן מיטן עקספּלואַטירן אַנדערע. אַ טייל פֿון דעם דאָזיקן אומחן אויף רווחים שטאַמט פֿון עטישע קאָנצעפּציעס וואָס פּסלען דאָס שטרעבן צו רווחים, ווײַל ס׳איז אייגננוציקייט, און וואָס פֿאַרלאַנגען אַ פּראָדוקציע „פֿאַר נוצן און ניט פֿאַר רווח“. עס איז אָבער ניט מיגלעך צו זאָגן, מיט וואָס איז דאָס אַרבעטן צוליב רווח מער אייגננוציק אײדער דאָס אַרבעטן פֿאַר לוין. אין בײדע פֿאַלן איז דער פּערזענלעכער געווינס דער סטימול צו נעמען אויף זיך די טירחא, און אין קיין איינעם פֿון זיי ווערט די אַרבעט ניט געטאָן לשם פּאַטריאָטיזם אָדער מענטשן־ליבע. מאָראַליש געהערן זיי צו דער זעלבער קאַטעגאָריע. ווײל מען קומען צו אַן אויספֿיר בנוגע דעם דאָזיקן ענין, בלײַבט איבער בלויז איין וועג: מען מוז זען, צי די דינסטטוונגען, וועגן וועלכע עס האַנדלט זיך, זײַנען סאָציאַל נוצלעך, און ווי שטאַרק נוצלעך זיי זײַנען; מען דאַרף פֿעסטשטעלן, צי דאָס וואָס עס ווערט געצאָלט פֿאַר

די דאָזיקע דינסטטוּונגען איז טאַקע אומבאַדינגט נייטיק כּדי צו מאַכן זיי מיגלעך. אַזוי אַרום קומען מיר כּסדר צוריק צו די יסודותדיקע קריטעריעס פֿון סאָציאָלער נוצלעכקייט.

אַזאַ צוגאַנג ווערט אָפֿט מאָל אָפּגעפֿרעגט דורך מאַרקסיסטן און דורך אַנדערע וואָס האַלטן די דאָזיקע קריטעריעס פֿאַר צו סוביעקטיוו. זיי מיינען, אַז עס איז אַ סך בעסער צו האָבן אַן אָביעקטיוון מעסטער פֿון ווערט. זיי זעען אַזאַ אָביעקטיוון מעסטער אין טעאָריעס פֿון ווערט, וואָס זײַנען באַזירט אויף קאָסטן, בעיקר — אויף אַרבעטקאָסטן. אָבער יעדער *מענטשלעכער* פּרוּוו־שטיין פֿאַרן באַטײַט פֿון יעדער טעטיקייט מוז זיך אין לעצטן סך־הכּל פֿאַרט באַזירן אויף איר נוצלעכקייט פֿאַר מענטשלעכע באַדערפֿענישן, און מענטשלעכע באַדערפֿענישן מוזן ממילא זײַן סוביעקטיוו. אָנקומען צו אַנדערע קריטעריעס הייסט — ניט וועלן זען די אמתע פּראָבלעם.

דער פּרוּוו צוצושרײַבן דעם גאַנצן ווערט צו דער אַרבעט פֿירט צו פֿאַרשווענדערישקייט אין דעם באַנוץ פֿון לאַנד און פֿון קאַפּיטאַל און איז דורך דעם גורם נידעריקע עפֿעקטיווקייט פֿון דער ווירטשאַפֿט און אַ נידעריקן לעבנס־מצבֿ. דאָס ניט וועלן נעמען ווי געהעריק אין באַטראַכט דעם אָרט פֿון לאַנד און קאַפּיטאַל אין עקאָנאָמישער קאַלקולאַציע איז געווען איינע פֿון די סיבות פֿאַר דער מוראדיקער ירידה פֿון פּראָדוקטיווקייט אין רוסלאַנד אין די ערשטע יאָרן נאָך דער רעוואָלוציע פֿון 1917. די רעסטאַווראַציע — הגם אין אַ באַגרענעצטן פֿאַרנעם — פֿון דעם פֿרײַען מאַרק און דערמיט פֿון סוביעקטיווע שאַצונגען אונטער דער אַזוי גערופֿענער נײַער עקאָנאָמישער פּאָליטיק (דער נעפּ) אין 1921 האָט געפֿירט צו אַ ראַשיקן באַרג־אַרויף. דאָס יאָר 1928 איז געוואָרן דאָס בעסטע יאָר פֿאַר די רוסישע קאָנסומענטן זינט דער רעוואָלוציע. נאָך 1928 איז דער מאַרק ווידער אַרײַנגעלייגט געוואָרן אין חרם. די אומפֿעיִקייט פֿון די מלוכישע פּלאַניר־אָרגאַנען אויסצוחשבונען ווי עס געהער צו זײַן די פּראָדוקטיווקייט פֿון לאַנד און קאַפּיטאַל און צו באַנוצן זיך מיט מעכאַניזמען פֿון מאַרק האָט בײַגעטראָגן אין אַ גרויסער מאָס צום פֿאַלן פֿון לעבנס־מצבֿ וואָס האָט זיך דעמאָלט אָנגעהויבן. דעם באַטײַט פֿון די דאָזיקע היזקות קאָן מען זען צום טייל דערפֿון, וואָס אין סאָוועטישע דיסקוסיעס איז מען זיך גאַנץ אָפֿט מודה אין אַזאַ פֿאַרשווענדערישקייט, אין פֿאַלן ווו אירע סימנים זײַנען באַזונדער בולט. אָבער ניט אַן ערך שטאַרקער רעדט דערפֿאַר דער פֿאַקט, אַז אַפֿילו די שטרענגסטע פֿאַרבאָטן צו פֿירן האַנדל דורך פֿאַרמיטלערס וואָס מען באַצייכנט זיי ווי „ספּעקולאַנטן", זײַנען ניט אין שטאַנד צו מאַכן אַ סוף צו דער דאָזיקער אומלעגאַלער טעטיקייט. צו דער זעלביקער קאַטעגאָריע געהערן די גוט באַקאַנטע „קאָמבינאַציעס" פֿון די אַדמיניסטראַטאָרן פֿון סאָוועטישע פֿאַבריקן, אַ דאַנק וועלכע זיי פֿירן צווישן זיך אַן אומלעגאַלן אויסבײַט מיט די סחורות, ווײַל זיי פֿילן, אַז דאָס איז אַן אומבאַדינגטער תּנאַי פֿאַר דער עפֿעקטיווער פֿונקציאָנירונג פֿון אונטערנעמונגען; מען טאָר טאַקע ניט — אָבער אויף אַזאַ אופֿן מײַדן זיי אויס די ביוראָקראַטישע פֿאָרמאַליטעטן וואָס וואָלטן אָפֿט שטאַרק פֿאַרשלעפּט

דאָס אײַנשאַפֿן זיך אומצאָליקע קליינע אָבער אומבאַדינגט נייטיקע טעכנישע דעטאַלן.

דאָס ברענגט אונדז צוריק צו דער וויכטיקייט פֿון פֿאַרמיטלער וואָס גע־פֿינט אויס די מיגלעכקייט פֿון רווח דורך אַריבערפֿירן גיטער פֿון ערטער וווּ מען נייטיקט זיך אין זיי ווייניקער, צו יענע ערטער וווּ מען נייטיקט זיך אין זיי מער. מיר האָבן שוין פֿריִער פֿעסטגעשטעלט, אַז די דאָזיקע אָפּעראַציעס זײַנען אין תּוך גענומען אידענטיש מיט דער פּראָדוקציע אין ענגערן זינען. אָבער פֿאַקטיש קאָן מען גיין נאָך ווײַטער. ווען אַ פֿאַרמיטלער קאָן האָבן רווח דורך אַריבערפֿירן געוויסע גיטער פֿון איין אָרט צום צווייטן אָדער דורך מאַכן זאַ־פּאַסן פֿון גיטער אין צײַטן פֿון רעלאַטיוועך שפֿע, כּדי צו פֿאַרקויפֿן זיי אין אַ צײַט פֿון רעלאַטיוון דוחק, טוט ער אַלע מאָל אַ דינסט פֿאַר דער געזעלשאַפֿט. די מאָס פֿון דעם דאָזיקן דינסט ווערט געגעבן דורך דעם עודף פֿון פּרײַז, פֿאַר וועלכן ער פֿאַרקויפֿט, איבערן פּרײַז פֿאַר וועלכן ער קויפֿט. וואָס גרעסער עס איז דער חילוק, אַלץ גרעסער איז ניט בלויז זײַן רווח, נאָר אויך די מדרגה, אין וועלכער די געזעלשאַפֿט געניסט דערפֿון. די שער צווישן בײדע פּרײַזן ווײַזט די מאָס, אין וועלכער דער פֿאַרמיטלער פֿאַרגרעסערט די „ריינע" פּראָדוקציע פֿון דער געזעלשאַפֿט דורך פֿאַרוואַנדלען רעלאַטיוו נוצלאָזע זאַכן אין רעלאַטיוו נוצלעכע.

דאָס אינטערעסאַנטע דערבײַ איז, וואָס די סאָציאַלע נוצלעכקייט פֿון דער טעטיקייט פֿון אַזאַ „ספּעקולאַנט" איז ווינציקער ספֿקדיק איידער די סאָציאַלע נוצלעכקייט פֿון דער טעטיקייט פֿון אַ פּשוטן אַרבעטער. אויך דער אַרבעטער קאָן טראַנספֿאָרמירן אַ זאַך וואָס איז ווייניקער נוצלעך, ווי למשל שטאָל, אין אַ זאַך וואָס איז מער נוצלעך, ווי למשל אַן אויטאָמאָביל. אָבער ס'איז ניטאָ קיין גאַראַנטיע, אַז די שטאָל וועלכע ער טראַנספֿאָרמירט אין אויטאָמאָבילן וואָלט ניט געקאָנט מיט מער נוצן פֿאַרניצט ווערן אין אַן אַנדערער באַשעפֿטיקונג. לאָמיר זיך פֿאָרשטעלן, אַז די פּראָדוקציע פֿון לאָקאָמאָטיוון איז צוליב מאָנאָ־פּאָליסטישע באַגרענעצונגען אָדער צוליב פֿאַלשער פּלאַנירונג קלענער איידער עס וואָלט געווען סאָציאַל געוווּנטשן. הייסט עס ניצן די שטאָל וואָס וואָלט על־פּי שׂכל געדאַרפֿט גיין פֿאַר לאָקאָמאָטיוון אויף אויסצואַרבעטן אויטאָמאָבילן איז בײַ אַזעלכע באַדינגונגען אַ פֿאַרשווענדערישע טעטיקייט, אין וועלכער אויך דער אויטאָמאָביל־אַרבעטער שפּילט אַ שעדלעכע ראָלע, הגם ער פּערזענלעך איז דאָ גאָט די נשמה שולדיק. דער אַרבעטער קאָן ניט זײַן זיכער, אַז דאָס וואָס ער טוט איז באמת נוצלעך פֿאַר דער געזעלשאַפֿט. דער אויטאָמאָביל־אַרבעטער קאָן ניט וויסן, צי דורך אויסאַרבעטן אויטאָמאָבילן באַטייליקט ער זיך ניט אַ מאָל אין אָפּציִען רויוואַרג און אויך זײַן אייגענע אַרבעט פֿון עפּעס אַנדערש וואָס וואָלט געווען וויכטיקער פֿאַר דער געזעלשאַפֿט.

דער פֿאַרמיטלער איז ניט אויסגעשטעלט אויף אַזאַ ריזיקע. אויב ער קויפֿט געוויסע פֿאַרטיקע גיטער אין איין שטאָט, ווײַל ער קאָן זיי פֿאַרקויפֿן פֿאַר אַ העכערן פּרײַז אין דער צווייטער שטאָט, קאָן ניט זײַן קיין ספֿק, אַז די דאָזיקע

גיטער זײַנען מער נייטיק אינעם אָרט ווו ער ברענגט זיי, איידער דאָרטן פֿון וואַנען ער האָט זיי גענומען. דאָס וואָס ער טוט איז אַלע מאָל סאָציאַל נוצלעך. אַנדערש וואָלט ער ניט געווען בכּוח צו האָבן רווח. וועגן דער דאָזיקער אויסערגעוויינטלעך הויכער פּראָדוקטיוויקייט און נוצלעכקייט פֿון די פֿאַרמיטלערס זאָגט עדות זייער פֿעיִקייט זיך דורכצושלאָגן ניט געקוקט אויף אַלע מינים באַגרענעצונגען פֿון זייערע טעטיקייטן. קיינער ווייסט ניט בעסער פֿון קליינע ייִדישע הענדלערס וואָס פֿלעגן וואַנדערן פֿון דאָרף צו דאָרף און פֿון שטאָט צו שטאָט אין משך פֿון יאָרהונדערטער, ווי פֿאַרשיידן און ווי ראַפֿינירט ס׳זײַנען געווען די באַגרענעצונגען וועלכע מען פֿלעגט אויף זיי אַרויפֿלייגן און וועלכע זיי האָבן אַלע מאָל באַוויזן גובֿר צו זײַן. פֿאַראַן אַפֿילו אַ מיינונג, אַז דווקא דאָס אַרײַנדרינגען פֿון די דאָזיקע הענדלערס אין דער מיטל־עלטערישערווירטשאַפֿט האָט מיגלעך געמאַכט דעם אויפֿקום פֿון מאָדערנעם קאַפּיטאַליזם און די אַנטוויקלונג פֿון מאָדערנער אינדוסטריע און מאָדערנעם לעבנס־מצבֿ.

ניט געקוקט אויף דעם איז פֿאַראַן אַ ווײַט פֿאַרשפּרייטער ווידערווילן לגבי דעם הענדלער און אַ גרינגשאַצונג פֿון זײַן טעטיקייט. דער הענדלער וואָס האָט רווח פֿון קויפֿן שרויפֿן אָדער טשוועקעס אָדער ענלעכע קליינע אַרטיקלען אין איין רוסישער שטאָט און פֿאַרקויפֿן זיי אין אַן אַנדערער, איז עובֿר אויף דעם סאָוועטישן געזעץ קעגן ספּעקולאַציע און קאָן פֿאַרמישפּט ווערן צום טויט. און פֿון דעסט וועגן איז אַ סבֿרא, אַז זײַן אַרבעט איז די פּראָדוקטיווסטע פֿון אַלע אַרבעטן אין גאַנץ רוסלאַנד. אַ סך רוסישע ריזן־פֿאַבריקן האָבן געמוזט באַגרענעצן זייערע אָפּעראַציעס, ווײַל עס האָבן זיי געפֿעלט געוויסע טעכנישע קלייניקייטן און עס וואָלט גענומען אַ לאַנגע צײַט צו באַקומען זיי דורך נאָרמאַלע ביוראָקראַטישע וועגן. דער הענדלער וואָס שטעלט צו עטלעכע אַזעלכע קלייניקייטן פֿון אַן אַנדער אָרט העלפֿט אײַנהאַלטן די אינדוסטריע אין גאַנג און טוט דערמיט אַ דינסט פֿון גרעסטן באַטײַט. טאָ פֿון וואַנען נעמט זיך די טענה, אַז ער עקספּלואַטירט כּלומרשט די אַרבעטערס? דאָס נעמט זיך פֿון צונויפֿמישן צוויי פֿאַרשיידענע מינים טעטיקייטן, וואָס זיי טראָגן לײדער דעם זעלביקן נאָמען — ספּעקולאַציע. איך האָב ביז איצט גערעדט וועגן ספּעקולאַציע אין באַדינגונגען פֿון קאָנקורענץ להיפּוך צו דעם אַנדערן מין, וואָס מען קאָן אים אָנרופֿן מאָנאָפּאָליסטישע ספּעקולאַציע. די מאָנאָפּאָליסטישע ספּעקולאַציע באַשטייט אין מאַכן די גיטער בכּיוון קנאַפּ: דאָס פֿירט צו אַ וווּקס פֿון פּרײַזן און ברענגט אַזוי אַרום אַ רווח דעם מאָנאָפּאָליסטישן ספּעקולאַנט. זײַן טעטיקייט איז אין אַלגעמיין גענומען אַ שעדלעכע פֿון סאָציאַלן שטאַנדפּונקט. אַ מאָל טוט מען אַפֿילו פֿאַרניכטן גיטער, כּדי קענען נעמען העכערע פּרײַזן פֿאַרן רעשט. אין מער אָפֿטע פֿאַלן איז דער דעסטרוקטיווער כאַראַקטער פֿאַרשטעלט: ניט די פּראָדוצירטע גיטער ווערן צעשטערט, נאָר עס ווערט באַגרענעצט זייער פּראָדוקציע.

די פּשוטע פֿאַרמיטלערס זײַנען ניט בכּוח אונטערצונעמען אַזאַ מין ספּעקולאַציע. זיי מוזן זיך באַנוגענען מיט ספּעקולאַציע וואָס קומט פֿאָר אין באַדינגונגען פֿון קאָנקורענץ און וואָס באַשטייט אין אויסגעפֿינען סחורות מיט פֿאַר־

שיידענע פּרײַזן אין פֿאַרשידענע ערטער; דאָס דערלויבט צו מאַכן אַ רווח בײַם טראַנספּאָרטירן זיי פֿון איין אָרט צום צווייטן. מאָנאָפּאָליסטישע ספּעקולאַציע פֿאַרלאַנגט אַ ווײַטע מאָס קאָנטראָל איבער פּראָדוקטיווע רעסורסן: אַנדערש וואָלט געווען ניט מיגלעך צו מאַכן די גיטער קינסטלעך קנאַפּ, כּדי אַרויפֿצושרויפֿן דעם פּרײַז. דער שאָדן וועלכן עס ברענגט דער מאָנאָפּאָליסטישער ספּעקולאַנט ווערט געמאָסטן נישט בלויז דורך דעם טייל פֿון סאָציאַלן פּראָדוקט, וועלכן ער נעמט צו פֿאַר זיך, נאָר קודם־כּל דורך יענעם טייל וועלכן ער פֿאַרניכט כּדי צו קאָנען נעמען פֿאַר זיך אַ גרעסערן חלק פֿון דעם וואָס בלײַבט איבער. דער רעשט פֿון דער געזעלשאַפֿט ווערט אַזוי אַרום געטראָפֿן אין צווייען. דער נישט־מאָנאָפּאָליסטישער, ד״ה דער קאָנקורירנדיקער ספּעקולאַנט — און דאָס איז דער פֿאַרמיטלער, וועגן וועלכן מיר ריידן — האָט ניט אַזעלכע מיגלעכקייטן צו פֿאַרקריפּלען די סאָציאַלע פּראָדוקציע. ער קאָן מיט גאָרנישט מאַניפּולירן די פּרײַזן, ווײַל ער איז צו קליין לגבי דעם מאַרק. ער מוז אָננעמען ווי געגעבן די פּרײַזן, פֿאַר וועלכע ער קאָן קויפֿן און פֿאַר וועלכע ער קאָן פֿאַרקויפֿן. די רעזולטאַטן פֿון זײַן טעטיקייט קאָנען דעריבער באַשטיין אין אַריבערפֿירן גיטער פֿון ערטער וווּ זיי זײַנען ביליק צו ערטער וווּ זיי זײַנען טײַער, אַנדערש גערעדט — פֿון ערטער וווּ מען דאַרף זיי ווייניקער צו ערטער וווּ מען דאַרף זיי מער. דעם ריינעם געווינס דערפֿון האָט די געזעלשאַפֿט.

און דער דאָזיקער געווינס פֿון דער געזעלשאַפֿט איז מער געזיכערט אײדער אין פֿאַל פֿון דעם פּשוטן אַרבעטער, ווי שווער ער זאָל ניט האָרעווען. בלויז דער קאָנקורירנדיקער ספּעקולאַנט קאָן זײַן זיכער, אַז ער איז ניט געצוווּנגען — צוליב מאָנאָפּאָליסטישער ספּעקולאַציע ערגעץ וווּ אין דער עקאָנאָמישער סיסטעם, אָדער ווי אַ רעזולטאַט פֿון ביוראָקראַטישער אומגעלומפּערטקייט, און אפֿשר אַפֿילו באמת צוליב סאַבאָטאַזש — צו פֿאַרניצן זײַנע רעסורסן פֿאַר רעלאַטיוו ווייניקער נוצלעכער, און ממילא סאָציאַל פֿאַרשווענדערישער, טעטיקייט. בלויז אַזאַ ספּעקולאַנט קאָן זײַן זיכער, אַז ער ברענגט באמת נוצן דער געזעלשאַפֿט דורך העלפֿן בעסער צו באַדינען דעם קאָנסומענט.

עס איז פֿאַרשטייט זיך אמת, אַז דיווירטשאַפֿט וואָלט ניט געקאָנט עקסיסטירן, אויב יעדערער וואָלט געווען אַ פֿאַרמיטלער און אויב קיינער וואָלט ניט געווען באַשעפֿטיקט אין דירעקטער פּראָדוקציע. עס איז אַפֿילו אמת, אַז וואָס ווייניקער פֿאַרמיטלערס, אַלץ מער מענטשן וואָלטן געווען פֿרײַ פֿאַר אַנדערע פּראָדוקטיווע טעטיקייטן. די איינציקע סיבה פֿאַר וואָס ניט יעדערער קאָן ווערן אַ פֿאַרמיטלער אָדער אַ הענדלער, איז דאָס וואָס אין אַ געזעלשאַפֿט מוז מען טאָן אַ סך זאַכן און ניט בלויז איינע. עס וואָלט געווען פּונקט אַזוי שלעכט, אויב יעדערער וואָלט געדאַרפֿט ווערן אַ קוילן־גרעבער אָדער אַ לאַנדאַרבעטער אָדער אַ שטיינהאַקער. אַלע מינים אַרבעט זײַנען וויכטיק, כּדי די געזעלשאַפֿט זאָל קאָנען פֿונקציאָנירן, און עס איז פּונקט אַזוי אמת בנוגע יעדער באַשעפֿטיקונג, אַז אויב די אַרבעט וואָלט געטאָן געוואָרן דורך אַ קלענערער צאָל מענטשן וואָלט פֿאַרבליבן מער מענטשן פֿאַר אַנדערע באַשעפֿטיקונגען.

אײך איז אמת, אַז אויב עס וואָלט געווען זייער אַ גוטע פֿונאַנדערטיילונג פֿון גיטער און דינסטטוונגען צווישן פֿאַרשיידענע ערטער און פֿאַרשיידענע צײַטן, און אויב דאָס וואָלט אַדורכגעפֿירט געוואָרן דורך אַ געזעלשאַפֿטלעכן מאַכטאָרגאַן, וואָלט פֿאַר פֿאַרמיטלערס ניט פֿאַרבליבן קיין סך צו טאָן און זיי וואָלטן געדאַרפֿט זוכן אַנדערע פּרנסות. אָבער דער אויספֿיר דערפֿון איז ניט, אַז מען דאַרף אויף וועלכע ניט איז אופֿנים באַגרענעצן די פֿאַרמיטלערס און צונעמען בײַ זיי דעם חשק צו זייער טעטיקייט, נאָר אַז די מאַכטאָרגאַנען דאַרפֿן זיך באַמיִען אײַנצושטעלן אַזאַ פֿולקומע פֿונאַנדערטיילונג, אַז מען זאָל קיין פֿאַרמיטלערס ניט דאַרפֿן. דער דערפֿאָלג פֿון די מאַכטאָרגאַנען בײַם פֿאַרבעסערן די פֿונאַנדערטיילונג וואָלט דערפֿירט צו אַזאַ גלײַכמאָסיקער צעשפּרייטונג פֿון גיטער איבער דער גאַנצערווירטשאַפֿט, אַז די פּרײַזן פֿון גיטער אין פֿאַרשיידענע ערטער און אין פֿאַרשיידענע צײַטן וואָלטן געווען אויסגעבאַלאַנסירט, און די פֿאַרמיטלערס וואָלטן נישט געפֿונען קיין ערטער ווו די גיטער וואָלטן געווען בנימצא אין רעלאַטיווער שפֿע און ממילא וואָלוול, אָדער ערטער ווו די גיטער וואָלטן געווען קנאַפּ און ממילא טײַער. עס איז בכלל גוט צו האָבן אַזאַ פֿולקומע פֿונאַנדערטיילונג פֿון גיטער, לחלוטין אומאָפּהענגיק פֿון אירע רעזולטאַטן אין פּרט פֿון פֿאַרקלענערן די נייטיקע צאָל פֿאַרמיטלערס. אָבער כּל־זמן פֿאַרמיטלערס קאָנען מאַכן אַ לעבן פֿון אַזאַ ספּעקולאַציע, איז דאָס אַ סימן, אַז די פֿונאַנדערטיילונג איז נאָך ניט גענוג פֿולקום, כּדי צו מאַכן זיי איבעריק.

אַ פֿולקומע פֿונאַנדערטיילונג וואָלט טאַקע געמאַכט די פֿאַרמיטלערס איבעריק. פּונקט ווי שלאָסערס וואָלטן געווען איבעריק, ווען מיר וואָלטן געווען האָבן אַ פֿולקומע סיסטעם פֿון רערן פֿאַר וואַסער און גאַז, וואָס וואָלטן קיין מאָל ניט קאַליע געוואָרן. אָבער דער צושטאַנד פֿון די רערן וואָלט ניט געוואָרן בעסער דורך דעם וואָס מיר וואָלטן געלייקנט די נוצלעכקייט פֿון שלאָסערס און באַגרענעצט זייער טעטיקייט בײַם פֿאַרריכטן רערן וואָס ווערן יאָ קאַליע. דער ריכטיקער מעטאָד וואָלט געווען צו הייבן סײַ די קוואַליטעט פֿון די רערן, סײַ די עפֿעקטיווקייט פֿון דירעקטער פֿונאַנדערטיילונג, אַזוי אַז סײַ שלאָסערס, סײַ פֿאַרמיטלערס זאָלן האָבן ווייניק צו טאָן. און ס׳איז ניטאָ קיין שום סיבה, פֿאַר וואָס מען וואָלט ניט געדאַרפֿט שטרעבן צום וווּקס פֿון פּראָדוקטיווקייט אויף י ע ד ע ר אָפּשניט פֿון דער ווירטשאַפֿט. ווידער אַ מאָל: ס׳איז ניטאָ אין דעם פּרט קיין שום חילוק צווישן דער טעטיקייט פֿון פֿאַרמיטלער און דער טעטיקייט פֿון אַנדערע נוצלעכע מיטגלידער פֿון דער געזעלשאַפֿט, אַחוץ דער גרעסערער זיכערקייט, אַז דאָס וואָס די פֿאַרמיטלערס טוען איז באמת סאָציאַל געוווּנטשן.

און איצט אַ פּאָר ווערטער וועגן דעם מיטלקלאַס אין ברייטערן זינען, וואָס נעמט אַרום ניט בלויז פֿאַרמיטלערס, נאָר אויך מענטשן פֿון פֿרײַע פּראָפֿעסיעס, אָנגעשטעלטע, הויך קוואַליפֿיצירטע אַרבעטערס, אַדמיניסטראַטאָרן און ספּעציאַליסטן מכּל המינים.

די פֿונקציע פֿון פֿאַרמיטלער באַשטייט אין פֿאַרבינדן דעם פּראָדוצענט און דעם קאָנסומענט פֿון פּראָדוקטן. די וואָס פֿאַרשטייען ניט זייער נוצלעכקייט

טענהן אָפּט מאָל, אַז דער פֿאַרמיטלער טיילט אָפּ דעם פּראָדוצענט פֿון קאָנסומענט אַנשטאָט זיי צו פֿאַרבינדן. פּונקט אַזוי וואָלט מען געקאָנט זיך חקירהנען, צי די וואַפּנע טיילט פֿונאַנדער די ציגל אָדער זי נעמט זיי צונויף. דער מיטלקלאַס, וואָס טיילט אָפּ מענטשן אונטער אים דורך מענטשן איבער אים, טוט פֿאַקטיש די פֿונקציע פֿון פֿאַרבינדן ביידע.

די עקסיסטענץ פֿון אַ מיטלקלאַס באַטײַט, אַז ס'איז דאָ אַ געוויסע מיגלעכקייט — ווי ניט גענוג ידי דאָזיקע מיגלעכקייט זאָל ניט זײַן — פֿאַר מענטשן מיט פֿעיִקייטן און ענערגיע צו דערהייבן זיך אַפֿילו פֿון רעלאַטיוו נידעריקן עקאָנאָמישן אָפּשטאַם צו וויכטיקע פּאָזיציעס אין דער געזעלשאַפֿט. די וואָס האָבן ניט קיין געהעריקן חלק אין פּריווילעגיעס און בעסערע שאַנסן אין דער געזעלשאַפֿט קאָנען האָפֿן אויף פֿאַרבעסערונג און אויסברייטערונג פֿון אַזעלכע מיגלעכקייטן מיט דעם ווײַטערדיקן וווקס פֿון מיטלקלאַס. זיי זײַנען דערפֿאַר גענוג פֿאַראינטערעסירט אין דער פֿונקציאָנירונג פֿון ווירטשאַפֿט און אין דער אָרגאַניזאַציע פֿון געזעלשאַפֿט בכלל, אַז זיי זאָלן האָבן אַ געפֿיל פֿון אַחריות פֿאַר יענע טיילן פֿון איר, וואָס דינען דעם אַלגעמיינעם וווּיל און זײַנען ניט בלויז מיטלען פֿאַר זיכערן די פּריווילעגיעס פֿאַר אויסדערוויילטע מינאָריטעטן. די דאָזיקע שיכטן האָבן הייסט עס אַ שטיקל חלק אין דער געזעלשאַפֿט. עס איז ניט אמת, אַז זיי האָבן צו פֿאַרלירן בלויז זייערע קייטן. זיי פֿילן זיך ניט אין גאַנצן אָרויסגעשטויסן, ס'איז זיי ניט אַלץ איינס. זייער אומצופֿרידנקייט קאָן באַנוצט ווערן גיכער אויף צו פֿאַרבעסערן די געזעלשאַפֿט און ניט אויף צו צעשטערן זי. אַזעלכע שינויים וועלן גיכער זײַן פֿון אַזאַ מין, אַז דאָס וועט באמת ברענגען נוצן פֿאַר דער גרויסער מאַסע פֿון פֿאָלק. די דאָזיקע שינויים וועלן באַטײַטן אַ פּראָגרעס וואָס וועט זיך באמת באַרעכטיקן אין לעבן, ווײַל זיי וועלן איבערלאָזן טיילן פֿון אונדזער געזעלשאַפֿט, וואָס האָבן זיך אַנטוויקלט אין משך פֿון יאָרהונדערטער און וואָס זײַנען וויכטיק פֿאַר איר ווײַטערדיקער עקסיסטענץ. גלײַכצײַטיק וועלן עלימינירט ווערן יענע טיילן וואָס זײַנען שעדלעך און וואָס קאָנען באַזײַטיקט ווערן אָן אַ סכנה, אַז דער גאַנצער מעכאַניזם זאָל אײַנגעבראָכן ווערן. די שינויים וואָס וועלן קומען אויף אַזאַ אופֿן וועלן זײַן גיכער ענלעך צו די וואָס זײַנען לעצטנס פֿאָרגעקומען אין די פֿאַראייניקטע שטאַטן און אין ענגלאַנד און וואָס האָבן אַזוי פֿיל געטאָן אויף צו פֿאַרשפּרייטן וווילשטאַנד און זיכערקייט ניט צעשטערנדיק די פֿרײַהייט.

דער מיטלקלאַס שאַפֿט אַ המשכדיקע ליניע פֿון מיגלעכן פּראָגרעס פֿונעם דעק צו די שפּיצן. פֿאַרקלענערט ער דערמיט דעם קאָנטראַסט צווישן די עקסטרעמען דורך לײַכטער מאַכן די באַוועגונג צווישן פֿאַרשיידענע שיכטן. בעת יעדערער וועט זען מער געלעגנהייט פֿאַר פּראָגרעס און אַנטוויקלונג סײַ פֿאַר זיך גופֿא סײַ פֿאַר די מיטגלידער פֿון דער געזעלשאַפֿט ווי אַ גאַנצע, וועט זײַן ווייניקער אָרט פֿאַר דער בלינדער אַקציע וואָס לאָזט איבער די צוקונפֿט אין גאַנצן אויפֿן באַראָט פֿון עפּעס מיסטישע מטושטשדיקע גליקן וואָס דאַרפֿן קומען ווי אַ מין אויטאָמאַטישער רעזולטאַט פֿון צעשטערן אַן עקסיסטירנדיקע, אַבסאָלוט

שלעכטע אָרדענונג. די פּראַקטיק האָט געוויזן, אַז אַזאַ בלינדע אַקציע פֿירט געוויינטלעך אין איר לעצטן סך־הכּל צו אַ סיטואַציע וואָס איז ערגער ווי די סיטואַציע בײַם אָנהייב. אַ שטאַרקער און וואַקסנדיקער מיטלקלאַס איז נייטיק פֿאַר דער מדרגה פֿון סאָציאַלער מאָבילקייט און סאָציאַלער אַחריות וואָס איז אַ תּנאַי פֿאַר דעם אמתדיקן פּראָגרעס. די באַזונדערע שוואַכקייט פֿון מיטעלע קלאַסן אין אַ סך טיילן פֿון דער וועלט איז געווען אַ היפּשער פֿאַקטאָר בײַם העלפֿן דעמאַגאָגן צו היפּנאָטיזירן מיט פֿאַרפֿירערישע לאָזונגען די האָפֿענונגסלאָז אויסגעוואָרצלטע. דאָרטן ווו עס עקסיסטירט אַ שטאַרקער מיטלקלאַס מיט סאָציאַלער באַוועגלעכקייט, סאָציאַלער אַחריות און ממילא מיט אינעווייניקסטער סאָציאַלער צונויפֿגעבונדנקייט — דאָרטן זײַנען דאָ ניט אַן ערך גרעסערע שאַנסן פֿאַר אַ סאָציאַלן פּראָגרעס וואָס וועט געבן אַלץ מער און מער פֿרײַהייט און זיכערקייט אַלע מיטגלידער פֿון דער געזעלשאַפֿט.

[4]

Offprinted from the AMERICAN SCHOLAR, Volume 29, Number 3, Summer, 1960.

Economics and the Control of Man

ABBA P. LERNER

How can economics serve to control human behavior? Should it do so? For what purpose? These are the questions I would like to consider here.

In one sense economics neither has nor can have a purpose of its own: it is the study of ways in which people can succeed in achieving their purposes. The economist does not ask what these purposes may be; he is concerned only with the means and methods. Economics has been defined as the study of the allocation of scarce means among alternative ends, and it is not an accident that no mention is made of what the alternative ends might be. The economist as economist can never criticize the ends: he can only criticize means for achieving them; and he can criticize these only by the criterion of their efficiency in achieving the given ends.

But in another sense, in refusing to take any position as to the ends themselves, and leaving it entirely to the individual to choose what he wants to get, or to the group which has somehow arranged to work together as an individual, the economist is silently accepting a most important end—the end of letting individuals decide freely for themselves what they want. The economist then devotes himself to considering how this end can be achieved most efficiently. This idea has been expressed by saying that the economist is basically interested in the maximization of freedom.

The economist is, of course, interested in achieving the greatest possible production of the goods and services the individual would like to have. This is in itself a matter of increasing a man's freedom, in the sense that he is free to enjoy more of the things that

ABBA P. LERNER is professor of economics at Michigan State University. He is the author of *The Economics of Control, The Economics of Employment*, numerous articles, and a forthcoming book entitled *Everybody's Business*.

This article is derived from a paper presented at a conference on Modern Knowledge and the Control of Man held at the New School for Social Research.

he wants instead of suffering the oppression of doing without them. But the economist is concerned with freedom in a more basic sense. He is concerned with discovering to what extent it is possible to let one individual have more of what he wants *without taking anything away from anyone else.* This is the kind of efficiency that really can be said to work toward increasing human freedom to the highest degree.

If the end of economics is the maximization of human freedom, it would be something of a paradox if it used "controls" to do this, for the essence of freedom is the absence of controls. I have been in trouble with this paradox a number of times ever since I wrote a book called *The Economics of Control.* Many readers of this book have been disappointed because I do not discuss controls in the most obvious sense of restrictions on men's freedom to choose their occupations, their residences, the prices they are permitted to pay or to receive for goods and services, or the quantities they are permitted to buy or to sell. There are, of course, those who are concerned not with the freedom or even the welfare of the people affected, but with the freedom of the controller, or of a controlling group or elite, to use controls to fashion society, or even humanity, in accordance with certain ideals or messianic objectives. More often there is nothing more sinister about the interest in controls than the feeling that some special situation calls for controls instead of the normal uncontrolled procedures of free markets, or a dislike for the market system, or a failure to understand it. Whatever current dilemma we find ourselves in always seems to be in some way different, so that there is always an excuse for imposing controls in the name of some emergency.

It is hard for me to remember, but it is possible that in 1932, when I first thought of writing *The Economics of Control,* I too had a prejudice favoring regulation by authorities. Or there may be other explanations of my having chosen the word "control." Anyway, over many years, in the course of learning more economics and writing the book, the meaning of the word changed subtly and it was softened. "Control" came to mean to me not commands to people to act in a certain way, but institutions that caused men to behave in a desired way without feeling that they were being deprived of their freedom, and indeed, without their really *being* deprived of it. The great paradox is rather that the economist was concerned with understanding the operation of institutions that caused men *freely* to behave in such ways as to achieve the end of increasing every individual's opportunities for doing what he preferred or getting what he wanted. There are situations in which people can be forced to be free, such as those in which laws command them to keep to the right of the road so that they are free to drive with much more safety. The *economic* institutions are those by which people are not forced but induced to do of their own free will what is needed to guarantee freedom in general.

The high prestige that economics enjoys among the social sciences is a result of its success in discovering and explaining the dynamics of several vital processes: how the market mechanism can work to induce the resources of the world to be harnessed to the production and distribution of the goods and services that consumers want; how this is achieved through the unintended collaboration toward this purpose of millions of people who are directly concerned for the most part only with earning a living for themselves and their families; how these millions of people find they can achieve their private ends by doing just the things that are useful for the "social purpose" of helping to provide complete strangers in distant parts of the world with the goods and services that they desire.

Many of the most celebrated economic principles prove to be tautologies whose real contents do not match their external splendor. And this can also be applied to some of the reasons cited for the success of economics as compared with her sister social sciences. The real reason for this success is to be found in the nature of social problems that are counted as "economic." Many times some social action is proposed that is in the general interest, or at least in the interest of what appears to be the majority, but there are some who do not like the results and will not agree to it. To coerce them is considered to be immoral, or too expensive, or dangerous, and so the social action is held up until some way is discovered, or invented, to make it possible for the general consent to be achieved. This means that some device must be developed for compensating the objectors, while retaining some of the net benefit all around. When such a device is not found possible, there remains a conflict of interest, and the problem is a political one. Where it *has* been found possible to develop such a device, and a set of institutions has been built up for the regular achievement of such compensation, the problem is declared to be an economic one. Economics is the successful social science because those problems which have been solved successfully are declared to be economic problems. The conflicting interests have been reduced to some common measure, usually money, and full compensation can be paid wherever the benefits from the proposed action are greater than the damages. The solved problem then falls naturally into the realm of social problems to which the measuring rod of money is applicable, namely the realm of economics.

Money and the market are the institutions by which people are induced, or tempted, or bribed, to do what is in the social interest. If this is control, it is a subtle, a gentle, even if very effective, form of control in which the controllees have the illusion of not being controlled but free. One may argue that the donkey who follows the carrot (and who regularly gets one) only *feels* more free than the donkey who flees the stick (and who regularly gets that). But could it not be that this is all that is meant by saying he *is* more free? Is not freedom, after all, essentially an illusion?

The true heroes of the maximization of freedom in our economy were not the classical economists. These merely discovered the nature of the operations of the price mechanism in harnessing the private interests of the enterpriser and the worker to the social interests of producing and providing things that people wanted and getting them to the places where they wanted them. The true heroes were the preclassical *political economists* who developed the institutions that made it possible for the system to work, going back to the ancient solons who developed the institution of private property and then corporate property, who established the rule of law that gave security to property and the freedom of individuals to move and to trade. The classical economists, although they were also political economists in concerning themselves with governmental economic policies for the further development and refinement of economic institutions for maximizing freedom, were primarily concentrating on explaining the "natural" working of the system thus developed. This was especially true around the end of the nineteenth century and the beginning of the twentieth, when the system seemed to be working pretty well and required little tampering. That is why it seemed appropriate for the name of the discipline to be changed from "political economy" to "economics." The implication was that economists were basically concerned with studying some fundamental or universal aspects of the nature of the world and of men, a study that had more in common with physics than with politics.

In part this was a natural reaction to the annoying stupidities of sentimental socialists or anticapitalists who had no understanding of the complex and subtle machinery that made modern life possible, and who had eyes only for flaws in the operation of the economy of the present and wished only to contrast it with idealized utopias of the future. In part it was a natural reaction to the even more annoying vaporings of opponents of unromantic industrialism and calculating rationalism who believed in imaginary golden ages of the past. But the resulting over-concentration of economists on the aesthetic perfections of perfect competition led to the elevation of the absence of any sort of control, of *laissez faire*, from an extraordinarily effective instrument that was a part of the whole economic system, to a sacred principle of social organization—from a piece of machinery that must be judged by its efficacy in achieving the desired ends of society, to a moral imperative.

In recent decades such pious worship of *laissez faire* has become less and less possible as the responsibility of government for more and more social objectives has come to be taken for granted. The alleviation of poverty, the provision of public health services, the furnishing of education for all on higher and higher levels, the responsibility for the availability of more elaborate and more essential communication services, and the massive equalization of income and of wealth by progressive taxation—all go to make up what might be called the revolution of our time, were not the word usually reserved for more spectacular but less important changes in the life of man in society. And now so vast has become the government's necessary expenditures for defense, in addition to all these other activities, that it is almost impossible, but alas not quite impossible, for people in authority to be unaware of the way in which the financial activities of the government impinge on the economy. The government cannot evade the responsibility for so directing these programs as to keep the totality of economic activities in the country from generating the evils of inflation on the one hand, and of depression, or perhaps I should say recession, on the other.

It is almost a quarter of a century since the Great Depression and Lord Keynes clarified the role that the government of a modern state must play in keeping total expenditure in the economy, private and governmental, at the level required for full employment without inflation, by appropriate monetary and fiscal policies. When there is too little spending, with consequent unemployment, the monetary authorities can encourage business to spend more on investment and the public to spend more on consumption by an expansionary monetary policy. Such a policy increases the money supply and makes credit easier (by lowering interest rates), thus increasing total spending and employment. When too much spending causes an inflation, the monetary authorities can check or prevent this by a restrictive monetary policy. This policy decreases the money supply and makes credit tighter (by raising interest rates), thereby inducing business to spend less on investment and the public to spend less on consumption.

The government can also reduce total spending by a restrictive fiscal policy, that is, by spending less itself or by increasing taxes so that taxpayers will have less left to spend after taxes; it can increase total spending by an expansionary fiscal policy, by spending more itself or reducing taxes so that taxpayers will have more left to spend.

In choosing between these different instruments for regulating total spending, the government would naturally take account of the condition of the economy, which sometimes makes one of these instruments more effective and sometimes another. The government's choice would also be influenced by its preference as to which of the different kinds of spending to change, using monetary policy when it preferred to influence private investment more, and varying certain taxes if it preferred to change private consumption, unless it preferred to modify its own spending program. But despite the way these secondary considerations determined the details of its monetary and fiscal policies, the government could still apply its monetary and fiscal policies so as to maintain continuous prosperity.

At the present time this painfully learned lesson seems to be in great danger of being forgotten or perhaps rejected. This has made the relearning of the lesson, with some changes that will prevent the recurrence of the same crisis, a matter of the utmost importance for the persistence of free society.

I am aware that this is a strong statement, and that I am to be suspected, and properly, of exaggerating the importance of my own discipline; but I am convinced that this is not a crisis for the economics profession but for the economy at large. Indeed, the failure to solve the economic problems of society is the highroad to success for the profession of teaching economics, for in times of prosperity interest in economics drops sharply. It is when the economy is in the throes of depression or inflation that it seems important to study economics and that the profession booms—at least as long as the economy remains viable. The crisis is one of free society as a whole, and it would be wrong indeed if I allowed a professional modesty to curb my wish to speak out about it.

What has happened since the path-breaking work of Keynes is that a new element has entered the picture that he did not foresee, although it is possible now, with the benefit of hindsight, to point to some clues that could have been seen even in his time. This new element is the growth of the power of large corporations and of powerful trade unions to increase the prices of the product or of the labor that they sell, *even in times of considerable depression and incomplete utilization of capacity*. Instead of inflation being caused only by the pressure of buyers trying to buy more goods and services than the economy can produce, so that it is always a "buyers' inflation," it is now possible to have inflation even when this is not the case—even when the output of the economy is far below capacity and there is substantial unemployment. We also can have "sellers' inflation," when prices are raised by the pressure of sellers.

With this development, attempts to stop a sellers' inflation by restrictive fiscal or monetary measures, which would be the appropriate cure if it were a buyers' inflation, only brings about depression. Attempts to cure this depression by expansionary monetary or fiscal policies only restore the sellers' inflation. The resulting frustrations have induced a regression to a pre-Keynesian worship of a balanced government budget as a charm against the bedevilment of inflation in the midst of recession. Instead of the budget being used as an instrument for balancing the other expenditures in the economy so as to maintain prosperity, prosperity is sacrificed, as in ancient (pre-Keynesian) times, to the fetish of a balanced budget, and the economy continues to suffer from sellers' inflation moderated by induced depression.

In an affluent society such as ours, which could waste 10 per cent or more of its productive resources and still give the unemployed a bearable standard of living, this could be accepted with some equanimity were we not living in the crucial years of the Communist challenge for title to the planet. One can hardly call it a race, for the Free World is barely running. With a few billions of dollars, or perhaps tens of billions of dollars per annum, we could help the uncommitted millions of Asia, Africa and Latin America to raise their standards of living rapidly enough to make freedom meaningful to them, but we are told that we cannot afford it. Additional expenditures on defense might save the world from destruction by protecting the Russians from the temptation of thinking they could destroy our retaliatory power by a first blow (to which the rules of the game entitle them), but we are told we cannot afford that. And we are told this while we are complacently losing some thirty to fifty billion dollars a year from the induced depression, and spending perhaps one hundred billion dollars a year on goods that we need so little that we have to spend another ten billion in persuading ourselves to buy them. The balanced budget (or rather the declaration of intent to balance the budget) is not merely a symptom—it is a powerful tranquilizer. Widely representative of this frightening complacency, except for its unusual openness, is the response of a woman interviewed recently over television. Asked by Dave Garroway what she thought of the United States position vis à vis Russia on intercontinental and extra-planetary rockets, she said that the United States had always been and would always be first in everything. When Garroway pointed out that we were not first in outer space, he was met with, "Give us time!"

The apparent political success of such gambling with the future of free society on the chance that we *will* be given time will continue as long as we fail to realize that what we really cannot afford is to check a sellers' inflation by engineering depression. We must check the sellers' inflation directly by preventing administered prices and administered wages from being so handled that they cause sellers' inflation. This means stopping such increases in the general wage level as cannot be met out of increased productivity or reduced profit margins, and stopping such increases in prices of products as cannot be offset by price reductions elsewhere.

Even though such controls need involve no threat to the freedom of individuals and no sanctions more grievous than the elimination of certain tax privileges, there will be strong resistances. But the government cannot evade its responsibility by hiding behind a balanced budget (or the hope of an apparently balanced window-dressing of a budget). Nor can this responsibility be evaded by an unwillingness to see that while we are merely recovering some lost ground, the Russians are increasing their output rapidly and the Chinese promise to grow at an even more rapid pace if they can overcome the stresses of the introduction of a still more violent exploitation of human capacity for toil.

When I say that we may be witnessing in our lifetime the failure of the free world to withstand the totalitarian onslaught, it is not my language but the objective situation that is melodramatic. We may fail because we are unprepared to make the effort needed and because we are using the superstition of the primacy of a balanced budget to excuse the failure to make the effort. Economic knowledge, by re-exploding this reincarnation of an old fallacy, and by showing how the authorities can avoid sellers' inflation as well as buyers' inflation, can set us free to apply our vast resources for the defense of the free world and the economic development of the poor world in our fight with the totalitarian world. This is the task and this is the case for political economy.

[5]

CHAPTER IX

ECONOMIC DEMOCRACY (OR, THE MARKET AND THE BALLOT)

Many critics of democratic capitalist societies claim that political democracy is not enough—that it needs to be supplemented by economic democracy. Political democracy gives each man an equal vote concerning the conduct of government; economic democracy would give each person the same amount of power concerning the production, distribution, and consumption of wealth or income. All men would then be equal economically as well as politically. There would be neither rich nor poor, just as there would be neither powerful nor weak, neither oppressors nor oppressed.

This view of "economic democracy" is very closely related to the idea of economic equality. The absence of economic democracy in this sense is attributed to private property and private enterprise. The way to achieve economic democracy therefore seems to be to abolish private property and private enterprise.

There is a fundamental confusion in such a lumping together of economic democracy, economic equality and the abolition of private enterprise and private property. It would be quite possible to eliminate all private property and all private enterprise without getting any of the benefits hoped for by those who desire economic as well as political democracy—witness Soviet Russia and Nazi Germany where limitations in varying degrees of the rights of private property and private enterprise did not prevent unprecedented oppression.

We might better ask, "What do we fundamentally mean by democracy?" Fundamentally we mean respect for the individual—a willingness to recognize individual desires and preferences and a readiness to satisfy them except where this would interfere even more with the desires and preferences of other individuals.

Sometimes democracy is equated with majority rule. But rule by the majority, while doubtless preferable to rule by the minority, does not touch the essence. It is not democracy if a majority wantonly oppresses a minority any more than if a minority oppresses a majority. It is not democracy if a majority, for example, forces a minority to adopt and practice the majority's religion. On occasion, the absolute overruling of a minority by a majority cannot be avoided; but genuine democracy is much more than majority rule. It implies fairness, reasonableness, consideration of the sentiments and interests of special groups, and taking into account not merely the numbers of people with different preferences, but the degree to which the issues matter to different people. Minorities should not be repressed unless the only alternative is as severe a repression of the majority. Fortunately, it is rarely necessary to choose between two such stark alternatives.

These views of democracy are pretty widely held in our country. Most Americans believe, for instance, that proportional representation, whatever other shortcomings it may have, is democratic, in that it assures minorities that they will not be under-represented in legislative assemblies even if their votes are so spread that they have majorities in very few constituencies and possibly in none. We also believe it democratic, when a group of people are engaged in a common enterprise, for those who put more money or effort into it than others to have a larger number of votes in its management. (There may arise the question of whether the people who put more into an enterprise did so only because they were richer rather than more interested, and whether they were justly entitled to be richer in the first place. But let us ignore that problem for the moment. It is once more the question of justification for inequality of income or wealth which is coming up in Chapter XII.) In cases of this kind we find not the simple absolute majority rule of "one man one vote," but a system by which the degree of concern that the party has in the undertaking is given due weight in the number of votes he can cast. The most extreme form of unequal voting is to be found in the limiting case where the issues are of concern only for one person. We agree that a person has the right to do whatever he wants with his own spare time, or in his own home, or with his own property, as long as no one else is harmed. This is equivalent to giving him *all* of the votes on such activities and none to anyone else. Yet we see nothing undemocratic in such freedom of the individual. On the contrary we would maintain that interfering with his freedom would be undemocratic.

A number of people, concentrating on this aspect of democracy and dissatisfied with the ways in which modern complex civilization interferes with individuality and privacy, have built for themselves an imaginary golden age in the past in which everybody produced everything he needed or wanted all by himself in his own house or garden. He did not depend on anybody for anything and could not be interfered with by anybody. Like the Jolly Miller he could sing "I care for nobody no not I / And nobody cares for me." He could produce one thing, if he preferred it, or he could produce something else instead. He could work as long as he liked or as little as he liked and nobody cared. He could devote himself to the accumulation of material things or he could concentrate his attention on spiritual matters, and again nobody could gainsay or interfere with him. This is called the Distributist Ideal.

Whether or not anything approaching this ever happened in the past, it seems quite clear that it could not be done on a large scale today. The amount of production necessary not only to maintain modern standards of living but just to keep alive the present large population on our planet is impossible except by mass industrial production. If we were to give everybody a piece of land on which he had to produce by himself everything that he needed, everybody would starve to death. But we do have a mechanism by which the same result can be achieved, and to a certain extent is achieved, without giving up the efficiency of modern mass production. The instrument which does this is of course the *market.*

The market can be considered as an instrument for distributing goods among different people *democratically,* i.e., in accordance with their individual preferences as shown by their willingness to vote for them by spending money on them. If the goods were distributed in any other way, e.g., by a non-democratic authoritarian rationing technique, we would have an inferior distribution of goods; it would not be possible for each person's preference to be taken into consideration by whoever was in charge of the distribution.

Non-market distribution could be very much improved upon if persons were free to barter their rations with each other. Every such exchange could only benefit the people concerned, because if either party to an exchange were not benefited he would simply refuse to participate. But for each person to look for somebody else who has the things he wants to get and who happens to want what he has to give, would take up so much time that it would be extremely wasteful and inefficient.

The market, by placing the goods conveniently in stores and by providing the consumer with some money with which he can directly buy what he wants, gives us immediately the same results which could be obtained in a barter economy only after endless searching and exchanging and re-exchanging.

In doing this the market performs the democratic task of bringing about a distribution or allocation of goods that takes into consideration the preferences of all the individuals as between the different goods. It is as if it allowed each individual to vote, with dollars, as to which of the available goods and services he wanted to have, and then *fulfilled all the election promises*—giving him the things he voted for. The market also permits each individual to vote in different degrees for different items, and in different degrees for additional amounts, in a way which is much beyond the possibilities of the ballot as a modern skyscraper is beyond a simple mud hut.

But this is only the first of the results brought about by the market as a kind of super-ballot system for achieving economic democracy. This result is what was described in Chapter II as the function of "genuine" prices. But if the "genuine" prices are also "correct" prices, as described in Chapter III, the market brings about all the benefits of the imaginary ideal distributist society of self-sufficient households, because the "correct" prices constitute guides directing those things to be produced which consumers prefer. If there is an increase in the demand for any item, it yields an extra profit. Producers, seeking this profit, expand output, thereby adjusting production to demand. In this way the consumer is able to vote effectively for the *production* of the different things he wants. He votes when he puts down his dollars, and the things he votes for get produced and delivered to him.

Furthermore, the economic "voter" is not left—as in political balloting—to choose between two or three candidates, neither of whom may appeal to him very much; there are literally millions of things on which he can vote and on which he can vote for in differing *degrees* and get them in different *amounts.* Whether he wants more clothing or more housing or more holiday travel; whether he wants more underwear or more ties or socks, or whether he wants cotton or wool or nylon; whether he wants some of these for some items and some for others, whether he wants a particular kind of weave in the wool or nylon or another kind, or different proportions or combinations of mixtures between them, he can vote for these and get them to the *degrees* and in the *quantities* that he chooses. This is called *consumers' sovereignty,* and forms an essential part of economic democracy.

The "correct" prices and wages also lead to the ideal choice by workers, i.e., the perfectly free and democratic choice, as to how hard or how long to work—just as in the ideal distributist society. If the wage is a "genuine" wage, i.e., if the worker has a genuine opportunity to work as much or as little as he wants to at the wage, he will work another hour or make an extra effort only as long as he prefers the pay to the leisure or the ease that he has to give up in order to get it. This, however, does not give us the ideal degree of work or effort unless the wage is also "correct," i.e., unless the wage is equal to the value of the marginal or extra product resulting from the extra work in hours or in effort.

If the wage is less than the value of the marginal product, the worker will do less than the most desirable amount of work. He will stop at a point where the extra product is still worth more than the extra effort that would be needed to produce it. This is wasteful underproduction, and is the result of the worker not getting all that he is voting for by his expenditure of working time or effort. If the wage is greater than the value of the marginal product, the worker will do too much work. He will work up to a point where the extra product is worth *less* than the extra effort by as much as its value is less than the pay. With "correct" prices and wages, both of these forms of waste are avoided.

From another point of view this may be seen to maximize *freedom.* If the wage is just equal to the value of the marginal product, the rest of society is quite indifferent as to whether he works harder or the opposite. If he makes the extra effort, his extra pay takes away from the total product just as much as his effort adds to it, so that there is just as much left over for others as before. If he decides to take it easy, the reduction in his pay just cancels the reduction in total output and there is again just as much left over for others as before. He is not doing a favor or a disfavor to others by working harder or by working less; nobody is obligated to anybody—just as in the distributist ideal—so that, just as in the case of the Jolly Miller, there would be no social pressure on the individual to work harder (or the opposite). That is the essence of independence and freedom.

It might seem that consumers' sovereignty applies only to a small part of our economy, since most goods are bought not by consumers but by firms. But the preference of the consumer works itself way back through all the things which are sold by firm to firm. If at the current prices the consumer prefers nylon to woolen socks, the retailer and the wholesaler will demand nylon socks, and the sock manufacturers will demand nylon. This demand will be reflected in the nylon manufacturer's demand for chemicals, and so on through no matter how many steps in the enormous complexity of our economy.

But there are a number of other conditions which must be satisfied if we are to reach true economic democracy with consumers' sovereignty. These conditions have by no means yet been fully satisfied in modern societies, although they have been sufficiently met to provide a higher standard of living and greater opportunities for its members than was ever possible before.

First, there must be a free market in which people can buy or sell what they want without any restrictions and in which the prices are those that clear the market. Otherwise, they cannot freely exercise their dollar votes.

Second, there must be no restrictions, open or hidden, on anybody's going into any occupation nor may there be any special privilege. Equality of opportunity is basic to economic or any other kind of democracy. Without equality of opportunity some people cannot freely earn the dollars with which to vote and with the resulting "incorrect" prices, there is not the correct delivery of the items voted for. If people are not able to get certain jobs because they lack experience and then cannot get experience because they cannot get the jobs, they are being effectively kept out. The restriction may benefit those who are in, but it interferes with true economic democracy. The same thing is true if tradition or prejudice creates obstacles for a particular race or sex, or if it takes a lot of money or political and family connections for a person to acquire a certain skill. In modern democracies, more and more such restrictions have been removed by way of subsidized education, educational loans and scholarships, although it is by no means true that the poor man has just the same opportunities as a rich or well-connected person.

Third, there must be no monopolistic restriction of the output of any product in order to keep up its price, or any monopsonistic restriction in the input of any factor of production in order to keep its price down. As was shown in Chapters III and IV this causes a departure from "correct" prices and distorts the voting power of the dollars.

Fourth, taxes must not interfere too much with the "correct" prices and thus with the efficiency of the economy. Taxes tend to interfere with the efficiency of the economy by raising prices relatively to marginal cost and thereby above the "correct" level, but different taxes do so in different ways and some interfere very little.

A fifth condition essential to any reasonable approximation to the ideal of economic democracy is that there should be no depression or inflation—most particularly, no depression. A democracy must maintain the dignity of every individual, including that of the worker. He is now given considerable protection in our country by social legislation and by labor organizations, but there is nothing which can give him so much dignity as the knowledge that if he is not being treated well he can leave his job and get another one without much difficulty. His employer is then not doing him a particular favor by employing him, any more than he is doing his employer a favor by working for him.

The ability of a worker to leave his job easily is not the same thing as the right to strike. A decision to strike is made not by the individual worker but by a union, and the degree to which the opinions of the members of the union influences the decision, varies from union to union. The union can increase the dignity of the individual by protecting him from unfair treatment by his employers, but the union can also be an organ of oppression. By far the most effective protection of a worker against unfair treatment by his employer is his ability to quit and quickly get another good job. This he cannot do if there is a depression.

From what I have said so far it might seem that we would never need to make use of the political ballot, the market being so enormously superior. But this is not so. The political ballot is necessary to establish general rules which must be observed by everybody. If it is decided, for example, that a market system should exist, in which case it would have to apply to everybody, or that the nation needs an army that would presumably defend everybody, a minority that disagrees will have to be overruled—unless they come to outnumber the others on this matter (in which case, of course, they become the majority) or if they feel so much more strongly about the issue than the majority that the majority thinks it better to give way.

Such a decision is by nature a *public* decision, not a *private* one. A private decision is a decision by a man to do something which does not affect others. If I decide to work harder and then use the proceeds to buy more goods, there is just as much left for everybody else, as we have seen above. This is what makes my decision a private decision.

The market can in fact be correctly described as an instrument for making decisions private which would otherwise be public. (There are of course other decisions that are private in any case, like whether I will read or sleep this evening.) The "correct" price or wage is precisely the price or wage which leaves others unaffected by anyone's decision to work more or work less or to buy more or buy less of any item. That is what makes the decision private. An "incorrect" price or wage does not do this. When I decide to buy more at an "incorrect" price or to work more at an "incorrect" wage, there is either more left or less left for others. Where the price or wage can be made "correct" this is remedied and the decision is made private.

The distinction between private and public decisions turns out to be the same as the distinction between economic and political matters. If it is possible, by using devices such as private property and the market, to enable those who want something to get it without interfering with others, then the decision can be made a *private* one. In the interests of freedom it is desirable to do this wherever possible. And every time we succeed in doing this, we shift something from politics into economics. Economics can use the superior system of the super-ballot which we call the market, not because economists are smarter than political scientists, but because wherever anybody discovers or invents a method of doing this so that the issue can be handled by the market—and he may be a lawyer or an engineer, a mathematician or even a political scientist—the economists grab it and say it is part of their realm. It stops being politics and becomes economics.

The distinction between private and public, between economic and political, breaks down where people can complain that they *do* care what other people do privately in their own homes or with their own spare time. But such complaints do not fit in with a free society, even if they are made by a very large majority. In a truly free society you must be allowed to do anything you like as long as it does not interfere with anything anyone else wants to do.

[6]

Capitalism and Freedom. By MILTON FRIEDMAN. Chicago: University of Chicago Press, 1962. Pp. v, 202. $3.95.

This rewrite of lectures and articles by Milton Friedman is largely a defense of liberalism against "liberalism"—that is, (to spell it out since the quotation marks are easily transposed) of nineteenth-century European liberalism's concern for individual freedom against twentieth-century American "liberals." To these he refers (quoting Schumpeter) as "the enemies of the system of private enterprise [who] have thought it wise to appropriate its label" (p. 5), and he characterizes them by their readiness to rely on the state for the furtherance of welfare and equality.

Although Friedman is no more against welfare than the "liberals" are against freedom, he seems to have reacted so strongly against the failure of many "liberals" to understand the nature, the merits, and the potentialities of the market system, and their consequent tendency, in or out of season, to cry "there ought to be a law," that he tends to cry "never, never pass a law —well hardly ever!" In this he is buttressed by a deep political pessimism about the inevitable corruption of even the best-intentioned government action by narrow partisan interests. The result is that although he erects his system on an unimpeachable framework that all "liberals" as well as all liberals would accept—recognizing that a case may be made for government intervention whenever the market system fails to work satisfactorily by reason of monopoly or "neighborhood effects" (divergence between private and social benefits or costs)—his pessimistic antigovernmentism leads him to some strange extremes.

Thus, he is against fair employment practices legislation (FEPC) because by admitting the government into that area one opens the way to unfair employment practices legislation like the Nuremberg laws (UEPC?). (He does *not* object to government enforcing honest labeling on the grounds that this would open the way to enforcing or protecting dishonest labeling.) His treatment of racial and other discrimination as a matter of taste whose gratification is legitimate (however bad the taste) would be applicable, and not merely elegant, if the resulting supply of black, white, and mixed schools or housing had no great "neighborhood effect" in depriving Negroes of reasonable facilities. His displeasure with the Keynesian concentration on fiscal policy (a result of its development at a time when monetary policy was not working well or was being worked very badly) leads him to declare the belief that "a rise in government expenditures relative to tax receipts, even when financed by borrowing, is *necessarily* expansionist" (page 82) to be based on one or the other of two extreme assumptions; either a liquidity elasticity of infinity (the liquidity trap) or an investment elasticity of zero (collapse of confidence). But although one of these extreme assumptions is required for the belief that *monetary policy* is completely ineffective, neither is really necessary for the belief that expansionary *fiscal policy* "is *necessarily* expansionist." All that is needed is the rejection of the opposite extreme assumption of an unchangeable velocity of circulation. Friedman himself judges that "$100 increase in government expenditures can on the average be expected to add just about $100 to income" (page 84), so that, unless the government expenditures have no value whatsoever, they would bring about a significant expansion not only of employment but also of useful output. Nor would Friedman deny that in time of less than average prosperity the multiplier would be greater than unity. Nevertheless, he concludes that the belief that expansionary fiscal policy can relieve depression is "economic mythology" (*ibid.*).

And yet in spite of these and a few other extravagances, *Capitalism and Freedom* is an important and valuable book with which as a liberal "liberal" I find myself in enthusiastic agreement some 90 per cent of the time. For the book powerfully demonstrates an impressive number of ways in which both freedom and welfare could be increased by a fuller utilization of the price mechanism. In some cases this could be achieved by freeing the price mechanism from governmental or private hindrances that have outlived any justifications they may once have had; in other areas, like education, by developing new institutions (for providing security of investment in human capital) that would permit the competitive price mechanism to begin to operate in them. Annoyance with Friedman's antigovernment complex should not be permitted to obscure the legitimacy and the persuasiveness of his plea for permitting private enterprise to compete freely with government enterprise in such activities as schooling or mail delivery, or his arguments against price supports, tariffs and import restrictions, output restrictions, rent and wage controls, and the ICC's perversion from combating railroad monopolies to enforcing general transportation monopolies. He provides a beautiful analysis of the American Medical Association's self-virtuous conspiracy against the American public. Particularly welcome is his treatment of the control of money, even though it suffers from his inability to credit governmental authority with the power to learn to avoid even "inexcusable" misjudgments, and his chapter on international trade and financial arrangements, where he deserves special praise for his unflinching courage in demonstrating how any compromise on the unpopular cause of flexible exchanges endangers all the popular aspects of free trade and sentimental internationalism.

Every liberal, "liberal," or simple decent fellow interested in public affairs can gain much by reading this book and even more by rereading any part that may repel him. The antigovernment extravagances that I have perhaps overemphasized in this review are to be deplored less for the (to my mind) bad advice to which they lead than for their inhibitory effect on potential readers of an important book that will provoke much thinking and rethinking.

ABBA P. LERNER

Michigan State University

[7]

Professor Samuelson on Theory and Realism: Comment

Contradictions do not exist in nature because nature does not differ from itself. Similarly there can be no real methodological difference between economists who do not differ in the methods they use in their actual scientific work. The dispute between Professors Machlup and Samuelson on the need for realism in theories can, therefore, only reflect a semantic confusion.

Machlup identifies theory with "postulated relationships." But this is not sufficient. The postulated relationship "if pigs had wings they'd fly away" does not qualify as a scientific theory until one has shown how it can be related to experience. Machlup recognizes this when he says that "we always combine the postulated relationship (which constitutes the theory) with an assumption of some change or event" [1, p. 733] to deduce consequences that can be tested empirically. If we *always* do that, it follows that *the possibility* of such a combination is an additional necessary condition that must be satisfied before a postulated relationship qualifies as a theory. The postulated relationships must be subject to the possibility of empirical testing.

The combination of a postulated relationship with a particular set of observed changes or events in the complicated and messy world of reality necessitates recourse to "impure" conditions that involve deviations from the "pure" theory of imaginary limiting cases like perfect gases or smooth surfaces or dimensionless particles or infinite elasticities. The possibility of making adequate allowances for such deviations in the observed changes or events, or in the observations testing the deduced implications, may be said to constitute the "realism" of a theory. I do not think Machlup would question the desirability and importance of "realism" in this sense.

Any set of postulated relationships can usually be combined with many different sets of assumed changes or events, and the more there are of these, the more useful the theory. The theory is, therefore, "wider" than any particular application of it, and the wider the better. Such width makes it harder to identify the theory with any particular application of it to the real world, and may be said to constitute the "unrealism" of a theory.

"Realism" and "unrealism" are lively and attractive words, but they constitute a trap. They sound like contradictory qualities, but they mean nothing more than "applicability" and "generality"—less colorful (and less calorific) words perhaps, but guiltless of suggesting a nonexistent contradiction. "Realism" furthermore easily comes to stand not only for being *subject* to empirical testing, but also for the ability to *survive* such a test; and "unrealistic" to mean either "*not subject* to empirical testing" or "*failing* in an empirical test," (which, of course, implies that it *is* subject to empirical testing).

Samuelson's denial that a theory "is much wider than any of the consequences deduced" [2, p. 736] cannot be taken seriously unless he would claim that his factor-price equalization analysis has no applicability outside the consequences deduced about post-Marshall-Plan Europe; and his denial that theories can ever explain anything but can only describe cannot be taken seriously until he denies that his analysis even helps to explain the European economic recovery.

The logic can be saved by reading "any of the consequences deduced" as "all the consequences deduced," and defining "theory" to include all the conceivable assumed changes and events that can be combined with the postulated relationships as well as all the inferences that would follow from all the combinations, including all the adjustments that would have to be made for the "imperfections" or complications of the real world. But nobody would ever finish spelling out such a theory. Only a drastically brief abstract hint at all these relationships could ever serve as a *usable* theory. The truth of the abbreviation does imply the truth of all the implications but it is only the abbreviation that is a usable theory, and the genius of scientific advance consists precisely in the invention of such simplifying abstractions. The *realism* of the theory depends on the possibility of allowing accurately enough for the differences between the actual world and the abstract model. It does *not* mean that the abbreviated hint at the infinitely complex relationships, the model that is simple enough for human beings (or even computers) to be able to use, must consist of, or contain, an accurate description of reality. This is yet another possible meaning of "realism" and the one that Machlup so strenuously and properly objects to.

But Samuelson does not really insist that useful theories have to be "realistic" in this last sense. For him a theory is "realistic" if it passes the empirical test. This is clearly shown by Samuelson's attributing his successful prediction of European economic recovery to "the degree of realism of the model" [2, pp. 737-38], and the model he uses is an extremely abstract one, by no means intended as an accurate description of the world in which the European economic recovery took place.

The desirability of realism in this sense would not be disputed by Machlup or by any F-twister, but Samuelson's suggestion that an F-twister would have said that a theory "is even better for its inadequacy" [2, p. 737] can be explained only by the theory that men are beguiled by words, and especially when they leave their work to indulge in methodological disputation. This general theory can be applied to the particular case of Samuelson trapped (or playfully allowing himself to be caught) by a pseudo-transitivity from "width" via "unrealism" to non-"realism" to "inapplicability" to "failing" (inadequacy) in an empirical test, so that welcomers of *width* are taken to be advocates of *error*.

"Unreality" in the sense of "width" or generality of a theory is appreciated by everybody, not only by F-twisters. Non-"realism" in the sense of the failure of a theory in an empirical test, sets F-twisters, just like everybody else, to look for a better theory. Meanwhile, until the better theory is found and established, the old theory continues in fairly good standing, made use of by everybody, not only by F-twisters, on the "wider" theory that there may have been some error in the test.

My conclusion is that there is no real difference between Samuelson and Machlup and F., and that they should all go back to their work where they are "all of them right."

ABBA P. LERNER*

* The author is professor of economics at Michigan State University.

REFERENCES

1. FRITZ MACHLUP, "Professor Samuelson on Theory and Realism" *Am. Econ. Rev.*, Sept. 1964, *54*, 733-35.
2. PAUL SAMUELSON, "Theory and Realism: A Reply" *Am. Econ. Rev.*, Sept. 1964, *54*, 736-39.

[8]

THE ECONOMIST'S CAN OPENER

ABBA P. LERNER
UNIVERSITY OF CALIFORNIA, BERKELEY

Professor Milton Friedman's Presidential Address to the American Economic Association annual meeting in Washington on December 29, 1967 was admired and enjoyed as much by his opponents as by his followers and disciples.[1] All enthusiasticilly applauded his impressive demonstration of how so many economists had changed their opinions over the years. Nevertheless I am moved to make some critical remarks because there is a danger that in the extensive attention given to the address in the press, the admiration and affection for Milton by his colleagues will be taken by the wider public as an endorsement of Friedman's doctrines.

In his exercise in the history of economic thought Friedman concentrated not on the conversion of "classical" economists to Keynesianism in the 1930's and 1940's (in Friedman's own words "we are all Keynesians now"), but on the expansion of outlook in the 50's and 60's from "Special Keynesianism" or "depression economics"—the narrow application of Keynesianism to the conditions of severe depression—to the wider view covering both depression and inflation, which justified Keynes' title "The *General* Theory of Employment Interest and Money." This wider, or more complete theory includes all that was sound in pre-Keynesian or "classical" economics so that Friedman's account of the expansion from Special to General Keynesianism makes it look rather like a return to the old-time pre-Keynesian or classical religion, and it is liable to give aid and comfort to those who have never understood the Keynesian revolution at all.

Special Keynesianism, concentrating as it does on the special conditions of severe depression, notes that there is insufficient spending even though plenty of money is lying idle so that making more money available would not be of much help. It therefore plays down monetary policy in favor of expansionary fiscal policy measures to bring about the increase in spending which spells the turn to prosperity. In treating this neglect of monetary policy as if it were the essence of *General* Keynesianism instead of the special prescription (or rather of non-prescription) for the conditions of severe depression, Friedman has over the years taken the stance of insisting that "money matters."

Now that the victory of Keynesianism has eliminated severe depressions and left us only with the problem of moderate ones, a somewhat less special Keynesianism calls for making more money available. More money now *would* be effective in lowering interest rates and encouraging investment and

[1]"The Role of Monetary Policy," later published in *Am. Econ. Rev.*, March 1968, Vol. 58, No. 1.

thus bringing about more spending and more employment. In a dramatic turn Friedman now warns us that money does not matter *that much.* Only very temporarily, he tells us, can changes in money affect *real* elements in the economy like the real rate of interest or the level of employment. It can have significant effects only on the *monetary* aspects, namely, only on the price level and its movements. Any attempt to lower the rate of interest by making more money available pushes it temporarily below the "natural" rate of interest and causes inflation. The real interest rate then returns to its natural level in the form of a higher *money* rate that reflects the expected rate of reduction in the value of money because of the induced inflation. Attempts to prevent this rise in the money rate of interest (to say nothing of attempts to bring it down to the originally intended *lower* money rate) by making still more money available will only accelerate the inflation together with the rise in the money rate that corresponds to the same basic real rate. This basic real or natural rate corresponds in turn to the real economic conditions of the economy, the opportunities for real returns on investment and the willingness of the population to divert real resources from consumption. Friedman completes the argument for the converse movement. Decreasing the supply of money can only very temporarily increase the money rate of interest. It will cause prices to fall and a *lower* money rate will emerge which corresponds to the increasing value of money in the ensuing deflation, with the same underlying natural real rate of interest. In this direction too, monetary changes cannot significantly affect real items like the real rate of interest or the level of employment.

This part of Friedman's address may be seen either as a complete return to the full-blooded pre-Keynesian "classical" economics which Keynes is often charged with having invented, or as the doctrine of a "Keynesian now" who out of the General Keynesian spectrum of all possible levels of (real) effective demand, limits his view, no longer to the "Special" part that illuminates deep depression, but to both extremes of the spectrum.

One of these two extremes is the part that applies to the very low levels of effective demand that lie deeper than deep depression—to the levels where effective demand has been so low for so long that all resistances to wage and price reductions have been swept away, where all money contracts have perhaps been voided after the fashion of the voiding of "gold clauses," and where we have "true deflation"—where deflation really means falling prices because supply exceeds demand just as inflation means rising prices because demand exceeds supply.

The other extreme is the part that applies to the very high levels of effective demand beyond full employment—to the region of "true inflation" where any further increase in spending can result only in further increases in prices.

In both of these areas there is no difference whatever between Keynesian and Classical economics. The difference lies entirely in the Keynesian generalization of classical economics to cover the area between the extremes where we happen to live most of the time. Of this range Keynes considered only the part where prices and wages are so administered that they *do not fall* in spite of supply exceeding demand—i.e., where prices and wages are "sticky downward." We are currently expanding Keynesianism to cover another part of this range where prices and wages are so administered that they *rise* in spite of available supply exceeding demand.

All economists are agreed that true inflation should be combatted by restricting total money demand and true deflation by increasing money demand, because there is agreement that even in true inflation and in true deflation, even if price and wage administration are swept away by hyper-inflation or hyper-deflation, there would still remain imperfections in wage and price flexibility which would result in deplorable inefficiencies and injustices. The important unsolved problem of the developed economies, which gives scope to disagreement among economists, is precisely how to bring under social control, perhaps by some artificial market, such of the administration of wages and prices as cannot be subjected to the governance of a natural competitive market.

It is Friedman's assumption of flexibility of prices in response to changes in effective demand that distracts him from attending to the significant area of the spectrum that the Keynesian revolution opened up for our study and limits his vision to its less significant tails. In his address Friedman told of the three professors on a desert island who found a can of food but no can opener. The chemist offered to build a fire that would cause the can to burst. The physicist undertook to direct the trajectory of much of the contents to a banana leaf. The economist said "Let us assume we had a can opener." Price flexibility seems to be Professor Friedman's can opener.

[9]

HE GROWLERY

4 Keynesian on Hayek

.n article on Friedrich A. Hayek
Forbes Magazine, October 1,
979, follows a current fashion in
oing violent injustice to Keynes
ıd Keynesians, who are charged
ith a propensity to favor govern-
ental interference with the mar-
et on behalf of special interests.
ne would never guess from such
ırrent writings that Keynesians
əject to such distortions of the
arket mechanism just as strong-
as Hayek does, or that they are
st as enthusiastic as Hayek or
dam Smith about the operation
the market mechanism's "invis-
le hand" in making possible
e great increase of productivity
d of human well-being in mod-
n society.

The mess in which our econ-
ny finds itself is due to a wide-
read failure to understand what
e price mechanism can do and
ıat it cannot do. The present
y for balancing the govern-
ent budget—an inappropriate
plication to the economy as a
ıole of what is a good general
e of prudence for an individ-
l—neatly illustrates this.

Hayek does not make the mistake of applying microeconomics to macroeconomic problems. But what he does is much more damaging to scientific progress. Inappropriate application of microeconomics to macroeconomic problems can be corrected by pointing out why the particular application is inappropriate, but to declare certain investigations to be out of bounds allows no chink for the entrance of enlightenment. Hayek declares macroeconomics unclean, warning us that it is dangerous even to look at things which might lead to a theory of how you could do something about the economy as a whole. (Surprisingly this is preceded by a declaration that "only a theory can replace a theory.") He outlaws even the contemplation of any aggregated figures such as the gross national product, or the national employment or unemployment. We must use the prices provided by the market only as guides to privately profitable behavior. For the resulting social benefits, we must be thankful but ask no questions.

The market in 1980

Keynesians have no quarrel with Hayek about the proper use of the market mechanism and the evils of distorting it for intended (and often mistaken) benefits to special groups. But we differ fundamentally in our view of the origin and the perfection of the market mechanism as it exists in 1980.

The difference with Hayek is that Keynesians, and even most anti-Keynesians, see the market mechanism not as handed down from Sinai or installed by visiting extraterrestrial demi-gods. We see it as having evolved over thousands of years by ingenious Solons, establishing laws about property and the acquiring of goods by purchase in the market instead of by the strong simply taking from the weak. This is why Hayek is able to lump together Friedman and Keynes as "scientism-touched" heretics.

In the 1930s, Keynes recognized that the market mechanism—just as it cannot prevent people from starving to death if the market value of their services is very low—is not able to maintain a satisfactory level of economic activity and employment. Before Keynes' theory and policy could be generally accepted, he had to overcome two arguments.

The first was the microeconomic argument that unemployment, since it is an excess supply of labor, would automatically lower wages and be cured by the market system's supply and demand mechanism. He showed that this was a microeconomic argument that holds only for one commodity among many substitutes. Consumers can switch to a cheapened item from buying others and producers can switch from producing an item to producing other, uncheapened, products until the excess supply vanishes. Keynes showed that this microeconomic argument cannot be applied to the economy as a whole, because *there are no substitutes* for output as a whole.

The second argument to be overcome was the more sophisticated one that unemployment, by lowering wages, would result in lower costs and prices, and as prices fell, the existing quantity of money, the money stock, would increase in its purchasing power until this induced enough total spending (purchasing) to restore full employment. Keynes overcame this argument by forcing serious recognition that it does not work. Ever since we have become affluent enough to eliminate starvation as an instrument for reducing wages, wages have not fallen far enough or fast enough.

Keynes then pointed to a more practical as well as a more humane alternative to increasing the value of the money stock by the starvation method of increasing the value of each dollar. We can increase the value of the money stock by increasing the number of dollars.

A partial application of Keynesian theory and policy between 1961 and 1969 gave us the longest period of sustained economic growth in our history. But then came an era of stagflation—inflation and depression at the same time. This was considered unnatural. Inflation was taken to show that there was too much total spending in the economy, whereas recession, Keynes had taught, was the result of too little total spending. Having both together then means that we have too much and too little total spending at the same time. This contradiction was hailed as a disqualification of the Keynesian theory that depression is due to too little total spending. But the contradiction comes only from combining the Keynesian approach with the false belief that inflation can be caused only by too much total spending.

Inflation can also be caused by a general *expectation* of inflation. When prices have been rising for some time, for no matter what reason, people expect them to keep on rising. Workers insist on raising wages to meet the rising cost of living. Business then has to raise prices because its costs are rising. And so prices and wages chase each other ever upwards in the wage-price spiral of our expectational inflation.

Hayek and microeconomics

In the 1930s, the unavailability of starvation as an instrument for curing unemployment (through the lowering of wages) called for Keynes' alternative cure—the direct increase of total money spending. But for Hayek only microeconomic theory is kosher. This prevents him from distinguishing between doing something to make the economy as a whole work better (such as increasing the total spending in the economy when it is insufficient for prosperity) and distorting the market mechanism on behalf of some particular interest.

This comes out very clearly in Hayek's illustration of how an increase in total spending causes trouble. The extra spending is concentrated on dining out, and the restaurant boom collapses when the credit card bills come in.

But this is not because of the increase in total spending. It is because Hayek assumes a temporary increase in spending that is expected to be permanent and is concentrated on a particular section of the economy. An increase in total spending would normally be spread around on things in general. As long as unemployed resources are available in general the increase in total spending could be permanent and could produce a permanent increase in *production in general*. This is what we have seen in every upsurge in economic activity. But Hayek, according to the article in *Forbes*, believes that "it is [only] *relative* prices that count, not the general level of 'all' prices" and that "When the government injects *demand* into the economy . . . it must inject it at some particular point; it can't spread it evenly."

Of course if we are assuming full employment equilibrium with no unused resources, it is not possible to have any net increase in real output. An increase in demand which is "spread evenly" could only increase *prices* evenly. But this only tells us that we cannot increase overall employment if we already have full employment.

However, the question still remains: Is the Keynesian 1936 solution to depression also effective when we are suffering from inf

tion? Keynes had no explicit answer to this question because inflation was not a problem in 1936. His analysis does, however, contain a very clear implicit solution.

It is true that Keynes spoke only of wages not falling. To apply this to the present inflation problem, we have only to remember that the resistance to wages falling meant, in 1936, resistance to permitting wages to fall *relative to prices*. Since prices were stable and were expected to remain stable, the implied words "relative to (the stable) prices" did not need to be uttered. What we have now is exactly the same resistance to wages falling relative to (our rising) prices. It is by spelling out this implied phrase that a Keynesian graduates into a "Post-Keynesian."

An increase in total spending will, of course, only intensify the inflation if people are already trying to buy more than the economy can provide. But it will not do that if it only enables people to buy additional goods that can be produced by unemployed resources.

In an inflation not caused by too much total spending, there can be too little total spending to provide a satisfactory level of employment, and so we can and do have stagflation. The old Keynesian formula—an increase in the level of spending—still works perfectly well to cure the unemployment—the stagnation—element in a "stagflation." But it does nothing to cure the inflation element.

The right kind of meddling

For that, something is needed which was not needed in Keynes' time, namely a program (other than starvation) which would stop the wages and prices from rising. But one is not even allowed to think about this if one obeys Hayek's proscription of macroeconomics. What is called for is a kind of meddling with the market mechanism, but not the kind which both Keynesians and Hayekians condemn. There should be no interference with the use of the market mechanism, but rather a further development of the market mechanism—an addition which will prevent wages and prices from rising but will not interfere with the proper use of the market mechanism.

Hayek not only lumps together both kinds of "meddling with the market mechanism" but condemns them both together as the fruits of "constructivism"—of treating the economy as a "mechanism" which can be improved on (as well as messed up) instead of recognizing it as an "organism" which can only be injured by any attempt to improve its working. One almost wonders whether he has ever considered how the operation of human organisms has been improved by such "constructivist" meddlings as eyeglasses, wheelchairs, appendectomies, vaccinations, or insulin. He also lumps together protectionism, socialism, and fascism as faces of the basic sin of "constructivism," or "playing God."

To improve our market mechanism so that it will prevent the price level from rising while leaving all individual prices free to respond to supply and demand (in accordance with our well-developed microeconomy), a new commodity must be introduced.

Introducing a new commodity is nothing new. Over the millennia, more and more items that had been outside the market mechanism have been included. Before land was scarce, there was no price on land. If you wanted some land, you just burned down some trees and used the ashes for fertilizer. After a few years it was no good any more, so you cut down some more trees. In time, we couldn't allow that to go on. So we made laws which said "you have to buy the right to cut down trees." Many said this was a wicked thing because God made the trees for all to enjoy. To establish a law which makes land a marketable good is to play God. But we established the law and it saved the forests (except in some parts of the world where they didn't do this and the forests became deserts). What we now need is a property right which will not allow any seller to raise his prices unless he buys that right—in competition with others—from sellers who lower their prices, so that the average price will be stabilized.

How this can be done without price control (that is, without preventing individual prices from rising or falling in relation to other prices in a free market) is a problem on which economists have been working for some time. Such a plan, and one which even keeps strictly to Hayek's excellent prescription for government "only to make and enforce general abstract *rules*," has just been completed in a recent book by Professor David Colander and myself, *MAP—A Market Anti-Inflation Plan* (Harcourt Brace Jovanovich, 1980). But for Hayekians, any change in the rules of the market system is an impermissible interference. To make such a change is both to play Satan by perverting the market mechanism in some private interest, and to play God by attempting to improve on the laws of the economy which (like the laws of nature?) have to be "*found*, not *designed*."

ABBA LERNER
Professor of Economics
Florida State University

PART FOUR
WAR AND PEACE

[1]

How To Keep The Peace . . .
An Analysis and a Proposal . . A. P. Lerner

INTRODUCTION: A STATEMENT OF THE PROBLEM

No person who is interested in the future of human liberty can at the present moment avoid taking a definite stand concerning the threat of a third world war.

In this memorandum we have tried to show how a maximum of security against war (short of surrender to any aggressor) can be obtained with a minimum of change in social organization.

This is not because there are no things we would like to change. It is because to require more than is absolutely necessary to assure peace is harmful because it lessens the chance of the really indispensable requirements being accepted. On the other hand, to require less than is necessary diminishes the chance of peace by giving a false sense of security.

We have tried to clarify the main issues well as to propose the solution which would meet the least resistance. We would consider better than ours any solution of the problem which would meet with less resistance without losing effectiveness, or which would be more effective without encountering more resistance. But all the proposals we have so far seen are either not sufficiently effective or demand things which, however desirable otherwise, are not indispensable for international peace. We know well enough how discouraging will be the resistances to any effective peace plan. But since to our best understanding there is no easier way out, it follows that if anything can be done at all, it will have to be on the lines of our minimized requirements.

TWO POSSIBLE SOLUTIONS

Another world war could be avoided with certainty only if all the powers would be willing to forego military action in all circumstances. There are two instruments which would increase the likelihood of the powers undertaking to forego military action and keeping their word. One is a **General Disarmament Agreement** with adequate inspection. The other is a system of **Collective Security**, i.e. an organization of the powers in defense against potential aggression by any one of them, commanding such an overwhelming array of military strength that the potential aggressor, seeing the chances of success negligible, is deterred.

Both instruments have their limitations. A disarmament agreement alone may be broken by any nation and then once more war can be avoided only by surrender to the aggressor, involving the acceptance of imposed ideologies, intolerable restrictions of liberties, or wholesale exploitation.

A system of collective security, on the other hand, could be misused and could also break down. Instead of serving to insure a just peace, it might be used oppressively, namely for purposes other than the prevention of aggression. At the same time, defections or disagreements might put an end to its overwhelming power. The collective security organization could also lose its effectiveness if the military strength of the nations loyal to it were to decline in relation to that of an agressor. It must remain both **strong** and **just** if it is to succeed. Collective security prevents war only to the extent that it deters aggressors. If its deterrent effect is insufficient, we are left with an armaments race and eventually war.

For this reason every effort should be made to induce the government of the United States to propose a **disarmament agreement** in the first place and to promote it by every means short of war or surrender.

SOURCES OF RESISTANCE TO DISARMAMENT

Proposals for effective disarmament (with inspection) face three kinds of resistance. These stem from **Tradition, Fear** and **Ambition.**

Tradition: Nations are traditionally reluctant to give up any part of their sovereignty for any reason whatever. Recognition of the threat of an atomic war may help overcome this tradition. It could be further weakened by convincing the individual nations that their independence and freedom would not be threatened, either by individual nations or by international bodies, if they gave up their sovereign rights to the extent necessary for effective disamament.

Fear: Nations are reluctant to weaken their military power out of fear of impairing their relative military position, thus depriving themselves of the possibility of resisting outside pressure and laying themselves open to foreign domination. It is necessary to convince them that general disarmament need not lead to shifts of relative national power, and that the security obtained through it is greater than the protection offered by an arms race.

Ambition: Some governments may pursue a policy of aggrandizement, aiming to conquer part or all of the world for ideological, power, exploitational or other reasons. They may choose war if war is the only way to carry out their policy of aggrandizement.

How can we deal with these sources of resistance to effective disarmament?

The only thing we can do against the tradition of unlimited sovereignty and ambitions for aggrandizement is to influence our own people and our own government not to allow these obstacles to stand in the way of disarmament. Lack of freedom of communication prevents us from exercising the same influence on people in some other countries. Yet if a sincere disarmament proposal is made by us, this may itself have a great effect on other nations.

The principle obstacle we have to overcome is fear—especially each power's fear of giving up armament prematurely, thus becoming a prey to the ambition of other powers. Our first objective must be the fourth of the four freedoms of the Atlantic Charter—**freedom from fear.** The tradition of sovereignty, and even ambition, may to a great extent be interpreted in terms of fear. One of the results of universal fear is the belief that a war for world hegemony is imminent. This is now leading Britain, America and Russia to expand their spheres of influence by every means available, so as to secure a more favorable initial position in the expected war.

A **General Disarmament Agreement** as such would counteract fear and lessen the danger of war breaking out because of fear.

THE NECESSARY FEATURES OF EFFECTIVE DISARMAMENT

The fear of premature relative disarmament can be overcome by proceeding by stages, such that at each stage there is a gain in security corresponding to the armaments sacrificed **without a serious change in the relative power position at any time.** The stages worked out for atomic energy control in the Lilienthal report form a useful pattern for this kind of procedure.

Insofar as the atomic bomb is concerned, the principles and methods set forth in the Lilienthal report are admirable. But disarmament cannot be wholly effective if limited to only one or a few selected kinds of armament. Such a partial disarmament is likely to affect relative power and to increase the fear of those who think themselves relatively weakened. The disarmament agreement must be comprehensive including all weapons not needed for domestic purposes.

The disarmament agreement must cover not only technical disarmament in war weapons but also political disarmament, involving a relaxation of systems of alliances, of spheres of influence, and of such restrictions of freedom within these spheres as are imposed to insure the subservience of the occupied countries. This includes the withdrawal of occupation forces. Such withdrawals, apart from benefitting the occupied countries, would contribute to the removal of causes of conflict. Like other disarmament measures, they should not be directed at changing the relative military position of the powers in terms of potential conflict.

Disarmament should therefore begin with the atomic bomb and should then proceed rapidly, eliminating in two or three years the production of all weapons not needed for domestic use, as well as standing armies, military training and all other economic, psychological and educational war preparations.

THE ROLE OF INSPECTION

An indispensable feature of any satisfactory disarmament agreement is effective inspection to give all nations adequate assurance that no secret armament is being undertaken. The Disarmament Agreement must therefore immediately set up a **Disarmament Inspection Commission.** The Commission is not a decision-making body, hence no voting need take place and the veto question does not arise. The only task of the Commission is to check on compliance with disarmament agreements and to publish its findings. It is not concerned with sanctions. If any power breaks the agreement, the arms race and a possible war may start unless checked by a collective security organization. The Commission exists only to make sure that no power, by secretly breaking the disarmament agreement, can gain a great advantage over an unarmed world.

The Commission should have offices in every country with all the privileges attached to diplomatic agencies. It should have an adequate staff of competent inspectors recruited from all nations, especially from the small neutrals (Sweden, Switzerland, etc.) and nominated by a qualified majority of the nations. The inspectors must have free access and facilities for checking everywhere. Denial of access would constitute a clear violation of the Agreement. The reports, regular and extraordinary, of all inspectors should be published **automatically.** To substantiate the factual correctness of the reports, rechecks and reinspections should be undertaken whenever inspectors report suspicious circumstances or whenever a report issued by an inspector is contradicted.

Furthermore, the inspectors and those who may help inform them should be granted a maximum of independence. The inspectors should be able to protect their informants, and enable them to emigrate.

In general the disarmament should be dissociated from all other domestic and international issues. Its sole objective is to eliminate the danger of war by a mutual renunciation of the means of waging war. Repugnant as any social system may appear to outsiders, attempts to change it by war must be renounced and belligerent as any country's ideology, material preparations and policies may be, military action should be taken only in the case of "clear and present danger." This does not mean that an aggressor must always be given the advantage of choosing the time and place for the first overt attack—but merely that, short of virtual surrender, forcible action should be postponed with careful regard for the possibilities of favorable changes in the suspected nation's government or policy.

COLLECTIVE SECURITY—A CHECK TO POTENTIAL AGGRESSORS

As long as agreement on these lines is observed by all, war is avoided. Such a scheme however may break down. It is necessary therefore to provide for ways to prevent war in case the disarmament agreement breaks down. This implies a collective security agreement.

Under the collective security agreement all nations will pledge themselves to proceed jointly against any of their number who is guilty of violating the Disarmament Agreement or of an act of aggression. Under its present statutes, the United Nations organization cannot put such an agreement into effect because any member possessing the veto can stop action against itself or against any other nation it may wish to support. Collective security however means that **collective** military action will be taken against any aggressor.

Simultaneously with proposing the Disarmament Agreement, the United States Government should therefore invite all nations to join such a collective security organization, or to change the United Nations statutes so that they can effectively provide collective security.

If the Disarmament Agreement rapidly and effectively abolishes all warlike preparations, there will be no necessity for the collective security organization to act in any way. But if some country violates the Disarmament Agreement, war can be prevented only by surrender or by a collective security organization with sufficient power behind it to make it effective as a deterrent.

If any significant power should refuse to participate in the Disarmament Agreement, there could of course be no disarmament agreement and peace would depend right from the beginning only on the collective security organization. A collective security organization can be established even if it is not universal as long as the signatory powers are strong enough to deter potential aggressors.

If we should fail to mobilize the practical universality which is necessary for the disarmament agreement or even the overwhelming majority of power which is necessary for collective security, humanity will face a life and death struggle in which civilization may well be utterly destroyed.

The very frightfulness of this outlook may become a favorable factor in inducing all nations to agree to disarmament. If this old decision to disarm is not taken now, we will live in terror and insecurity and will have to devote ourselves to constant war preparations. But in an atmosphere free of terror, institutions for the peaceful settlement of international problems will grow. The more successful we are in building up such institutions, which constitute the essence of an effective legal world order, the less danger there will be of backsliding into an armaments race.

One bold decision now can avert the doom facing humanity.

[2]

The President Addresses the World

. . . by Abba P. Lerner

[*The following article was written soon after Hiroshima and Nagasaki, but the time seemed inauspicious for the publication of so frank a discussion of the possibility of war between the U.S. and Russia. The course of events has increased rather than lessened the timeliness of Mr. Lerner's article. The author has chosen to present his ideas in the form of a presidential proclamation.* The Editors]

FELLOW CITIZENS of the United States — fellow members of the Human Race. My responsibility as President of the United States has constrained me until this hour to keep silent on the most important matter that has ever confronted me, or indeed anybody else. But the matter can wait no longer. With the atom bomb so soon to be in the arsenals of many nations the same responsibility now drives me to speak out with complete frankness about the greatest issue before mankind.

The issue is not a new one. The atom bomb did not create it or even change it. This first of human problems has long been ,and is still, whether civilization will put an end to war before war puts an end to civilization. But the atom bomb has hastened the day of judgment. It is now to be decided whether the twentieth century will show the end of the human adventure or whether it will mark the beginning of its glorious fulfillment.

The responsibility for the fateful decision falls more heavily on the United States of America than on any other nation, and it falls more heavily on the President of the U.S. than on any other man. The full recognition of the critical nature of the present moment in the history of the whole world forces me to depart from the customary glosses of diplomacy and to speak today in plain words.

The Real Danger

We are drifting toward a war between the U.S. and Russia and we are moving toward this war with increasing speed. When the imminence of such a catastrophe first becomes apparent it is usually declared to be "unthinkable" just as the last war was declared to be "unthinkable" around 1934. The threatening conflict has passed beyond that stage and everyone is thinking about it.

There is no serious danger of any other source of world conflict. If there were any sign of a Spain or an Argentina or of one of our former enemy countries preparing to qualify as a great power by the acquisition of some atomic bombs, immediate military action by the U.S. or by Russia would clear up the matter in a few hours—unless, indeed, this were merely the incident signaling the beginning of the conflict between the U.S. and Russia. That many people speak as if the danger of world war came from a revived Germany or Japan only shows what nonsense people will talk in order to keep away from the unpleasant "unthinkable" reality.

ABBA P. LERNER, distinguished economist and author of "The Economics of Control," is Professor of Economics on the Graduate Faculty of Political and Social Science, New School for Social Research, N.Y. He is currently on leave, and teaching at Roosevelt College. He was formerly Lecturer at the London School of Economics.

A similar running away from the issue is shown in the vast exaggerations of the importance of nuclear fission for peaceful purposes and even in the concern lest extravagant military precautions should unduly interfere with the freedom of scientific inquiry. Scientific research is of great importance. The ultimate benefits from the utilization of atomic energy for peaceful purposes may be tremendous. But surely every sane man would be delighted to sacrifice the next ten or even fifty years of scientific progress if there were reason for believing that this would seriously help to prevent the next war so that there will be a world in which science can advance.

Our primary problem is not to defend scientific freedom or scientific progress, and it is not to prevent monopolistic restrictions on the peacetime application of nuclear energy. Our primary problem is to prevent the war between Russia and the U.S.

Deadly Distrust

I do not think that anyone in the U.S. fails to recognize how great was Russia's contribution as our gallant ally in the war against Germany, and Russia recognizes how great was the contribution of the U.S. to the victory. There can be little doubt that if either the U.S. or Russia, or England had not played its part, all the efforts of the other allies would not have sufficed to win the war. But this does not alter the crucial fact that at the present time we do not trust Russia, Russia does not trust us, and we and the Russians are drifting toward the calamity.

I must here stress the obvious truth that the distrust is not made inevitable by the difference in our economic systems. We were able to cooperate during the war although we made effective use of the techniques of private enterprise and the Russians had for many years outlawed it from their economy. We are not directly affected by the Russians' use of collectivist techniques of economic organization and the Russians are not harmed by our extensive use of private enterprise side by side with our public enterprises.

The degree to which any country makes use of private or collective enterprise in its economy is a private matter that need affect other nations no more than its language or its table manners. Collectivist countries can exist side by side with capitalist countries and with mixed economies, and all can gain from exchanging their products with each other in mutually beneficial trade. If there were an inherent incompatibility between collectivist and capitalist economies, our case would be even graver than it is.

Russia's distrust of the capitalist world is based in the first place on her experience of capitalist intervention in the early years of the Bolshevist Revolution. Twenty years of peace and the joint fight against Naziism might have overcome this painful memory, but the Russians are brought up on a doctrine which teaches them that it is impossible for a capitalist society to maintain economic prosperity without engaging in imperialist expansion, aggression, and war.

This means that however well intentioned the present rulers of the capitalistic countries may be, they or their successors will be forced to wage war, perhaps at first against each other, but ultimately against the U.S.S.R. The Russians therefore believe that as long as any strong capitalist countries continue to exist they must be prepared to meet aggression.

American distrust of Russia is largely based on the recognition of this Russian distrust of the capitalist world. Before the atomic bomb the obvious policy for America and the rest of the capitalist world was to prove to the Russians, by actual accomplishment over several decades, that capitalist countries can maintain prosperity through full employment policies without having to go to war. The atom bomb has taken away the time needed for such a long-period demonstration and has given point to a second American suspicion of Russia.

This is the suspicion that comes from supposing the Russians to be dedicated to the final spread of communism over the whole world and ready to support that conquest with Russian arms. Whether this is their purpose or not, I have heard no one deny that the suspicion has been strengthened by recent Russian political action in states bordering on Russian territory. And those who feel this suspicion can dramatize it by pointing at Russia's political dynamism and ruthlessness, undoubtedly greater than that of the capitalist powers, and at the fact that in a few years Russia will have the atomic bomb too.

Parallel to this there is the suspicion felt by many Russians and by their friends in capitalist countries that capitalist nations are led by ideological considerations to plan the destruction of the Union of Socialist Soviet Republics. The most important thing in both cases is not whether the suspicions are justified but that the suspicions are felt by many people. To show, no matter how logically, that these suspicions are groundless is no more useful than to follow the diplomatic custom of pretending that they do not exist. There is not the slightest doubt that the suspicions exist and that they are driving us to destruction.

The Push-button War

If we allow several years to elapse without producing anything more effective than the United Nations, as now developing, we will find ourselves in a completely hopeless situation. Many nations will have atomic V2's and all will be living under the imminent threat of the release of the other nations' V2's. Every nation will feel that its only salvation lies in destroying its enemy first and will try to be ready to push the buttons before the enemy does. Each nation will also have considered the possibility of not reaching for the buttons in time and will have atomic V2's spread in inaccessible places for punishing the enemy if her own cities should have been destroyed first.

When this state of ultimate preparedness has been reached there will be no more hope. Any rumor or accidental explosion or the act of some madman will force every nation to push its buttons. There will be no time for investigation and the destruction of civilization will take, not years or months, but minutes. Even an attempt to save the world at that time may very well start off the final wave of suspicion that leads to the pushing of the button. It is only in the few years of grace *before* we are all prepared that there is any hope.

It has frequently been suggested that we allay Russia's suspicions by "giving her the secret" of the atom bomb. If this means anything at all it means that we should send our atom bomb engineers to Russia to show her how to make the bombs in a few weeks or months instead of in the few years it will take her without this instruction. This can only make the situation worse, because the only result will be to deprive ourselves of the few years we have in which to prevent the ultimate preparedness.

It must be emphasized that this conclusion in no way rests on any assumption of aggressive intentions on the part of Russia. No matter how sincere the Russian desire for peace, it is still true that to speed up Russia's ultimate preparedness is only to hasten the advent of the same fatal situation with everybody's fingers on the deadly buttons.

The only hope that I can see is in some kind of International Police Force to keep the peace. Such an International Police Force would, of course, take over the atomic bomb with all the materials, instruments, and skill for making, using and further developing it. It would also have complete control of all other powerful weapons, such as battleships, bombers, tanks, rockets and so on; the national forces being left with only such weapons as are necessary to deal with burglars and the like.

The International Police Force would, of course, have to inspect all the world to be sure that no power was secretly preparing atomic bombs or other weapons which could threaten the rule of international law. Without thorough inspection the whole business would be a farce. Full and free inspection all over the world by the agents of the International Police Force to prevent secret armament would be an essential condition for its success.

Those who have expressed skepticism over the possibility of effective inspection for atomic armament all over our planet have usually assumed that only atomic bombs were to be subject to inspection—that nations would still be permitted to have military secrets in connection with other armaments and that private industrial secrets would continue to be hidden from the eyes of the inspectors.

On these assumptions the skeptics are probably right. But the only sensible conclusion is that the assumptions must not be permitted to stand. All other heavy armaments must be handed to the International Police Force together with the atomic bomb, while secrecy in industry must also be sacrificed, with proper compensation for those who would bear more than their fair share of the burden, wherever such secrecy would impede adequate inspection. This may be considered a high price by some (while others might even welcome it) but who can say that it is too high a price to pay for survival?

Three Fundamental Freedoms

Merely hiring inspectors is not enough. There are three freedoms which are fundamental for world peace. These freedoms are very desirable on their own account, but this is not why I bring them up in the present connection. It is vital not to jeopardize peace by insisting on anything, no matter how desirable, which is not absolutely essential for peace. Many conditions, whose universal establishment is greatly to be desired, must be ignored here. I list the three fundamental freedoms not because of their direct contribution to the dignity of man but because without them peace cannot be secured. Any effective plan for world peace must inisist on them with absolute inflexibility.

The first fundamental freedom is *Freedom of Speech.* This includes the various specific prerequisites for making it effective, like freedom of the press, freedom to listen to the radio and see the press of other countries, freedom of travel for newspaper reporters and the like. Without such Freedom of Speech, it would be possible for a national government effectively to sabotage the inspectors.

The second fundamental freedom is *Freedom of Movement.* People must be free to move in and out of all countries, together with their families, or others who might be held as hostages to prevent them from saying abroad what they may be afraid to say in their own countries. Freedom of movement is a necessary condition for real freedom of speech. In its absence authoritarian governments can give their populations quite false notions of what the outside world is like and in this way prepare them to support movements dangerous to world peace. It is to be hoped, of course, that there is no basis for such suspicions, but even if they were completely groundless, the removal of the restrictions on movements are essential for the elimination of the suspicions and the elimination of the suspicions is essential for world peace.

Freedom of movement does not necessarily involve unlimited freedom of *immigration.* But restrictions on *emigration* must be removed if there is to be any confidence that there is freedom of speech.

The third fundamental freedom is *Freedom from Discrimination,* on a basis of Race, Creed, Caste, or other non-functional distinctions. This freedom is not absolutely necessary for peace in the immediate future because in most cases oppressed religious and racial minorities are not strong enough to wage war. But racial discrimination is going to become more and more dangerous for peace in the future and no permanent stability can be built unless the resentments of myriads of oppressed racial groups are eliminated.

Everything else can be left to each country to arrange according to its preferences. But the fundamental freedoms and the right of unlimited investigation by its inspectors, together with its monopoly of heavy armaments, are what the International Police Force must obtain from every nation if it is to fulfill its functions of preventing the atomic war.

The UN is Not Enough

At present there exists no International Police Force. It must, therefore, be immediately created. The United Nations is not such an International Police Force and at present shows no signs of becoming one.

The UN is based on the maintenance of national sovereignties which by definition must be impaired by an International Police Force. It is built on the unanimity Rule, or Veto principle, which prevents it from the beginning from dealing with any conflicts between the great powers from which alone the world war can come about.

Up to the present moment the International conferences have signally failed in every important task. When they were not engaged in dividing the world into spheres of interest as if to set the stage neatly for a coming conflict, they have engaged in sacrificing the democratic principles of the Atlantic Charter in appeasing increasing demands for more favorable strategic handicaps in such a coming conflict.

Peace is Still Possible

This completes the black side of the picture. It is our good fortune that on the other side there are three brighter facts on the basis of which it is possible to build world peace.

The first basic fact is that for several years the U.S. will be the only possessor of atomic bombs and, therefore, for that period, will not be forced to push the fatal buttons by the fear that an enemy might push its buttons first. We have several years of grace.

The second basic fact is that the U.S. is not tempted to use its great power to subject the world to itself for the sake of exploiting it for economic gain. We do not dream of using our power to lower the standard of living in the rest of the world for the sake of raising the standard of living for our own inhabitants. This has been demonstrated by the behavior of the U.S. since the end of the war. If we had any such ambitions we were then in a position to make the planet our own.

With the atom bomb to back our other forces, with our fully mobilized Army, Navy, and Air Force, and with the industrial armaments machine which had supplied not only ourselves but our allies in great measure, no one could have disputed any regime which we might have wanted to dictate to the world. Our demobilization at an unprecedented rate has demonstrated our peaceful intent to all. To all, that is, but those who see American imperialism in our not "giving the bomb" to Russia and who seem to think that peace would be served by our throwing away the years of grace.

The third basic fact is that the U.S. is by far the richest country in the world. We can afford to invest in the establishment of a permanent peace as much as we spent on the last war, and we can do this while maintaining and further raising the highest standard of living in the world.

The Solution

In the light of these three basic facts and in the light of the perilous international situation, I feel that I can discharge the responsibility that rests upon me as President of the United States of America at this most critical point in history, only by pressing with all the power at my disposal for the following policy:

1) I hereby propose that the United Nations constitute itself as an International Police Force with the minimum conditions for its effective operation as I have here outlined them.

This means removing the veto power from the UN and making such further changes in its constitution as are necessary to enable it to bring every nation under its authority. It means the transfer to the International Police Force of all heavy armament, including the atom bomb and complete control over their manufacture, their storage and the materials necessary for their manufacture. It also means that every nation must provide the fullest freedom of inspection to the agents of the UN and undertakes responsibilty for the establishment of the three fundamental freedoms throughout its territory.

(2) I propose that Russia be invited to draft a constitution for the International Police Force (as was originally suggested by Professor Einstein) which would satisfy these minimum requirements and which would give her any further safeguards she may desire, and that the U.S. delegation be instructed to accept all such safeguards unless they impede the working of the organization or are incompatible with the safety of other nations.

A World Peace Loan

As a further safeguard to Russia, and primarily in order to remove her suspicion that the capitalist world might combine to use the International Police Force to attack collectivist Russia, I propose the floating in the U.S. of a World Peace Loan of $250 billions over the next ten years, to finance the industrial development of all the backward and devastated areas of the world, up to $100 billions of this sum to be available for the peaceful development of Russia.

These loans would, of course, be conditional on the successful establishment of the International Police Force. They would be made only where they could earn interest at the rate of 3 per cent per annum. This means that they would materialize only where they would increase the productivity of the region where they are invested by more than enough to pay the interest and where there is a reasonable prospect of the country's being able to provide exports in the future sufficient to service at least the interest on the loan. No doubt many countries would want to borrow only if they saw a prospect of repaying the principal too within, say, fifty years, and in that case they would not borrow unless they saw a reasonable prospect of servicing the repayments as well as the interest.

In Russia, and in all parts of the world which are relatively poor in capital equipment, enormous amounts of capital can be invested to yield, in terms of the increase in output which the capital will make possible, vastly more than 3 per cent. The economic gain to the borrowing countries is measured by the excess of these yields over the 3 per cent they will have to pay to America.

Of course the whole scheme would be wrecked if we did not permit the borrowing countries to earn the dollars they will need for the interest payments and the capital repayments. The only way they can earn these dollars is by selling exports to us. We must, therefore, pledge ourselves not to impose any new restrictions on our imports direct or indirect; for only future large import surpluses can constitute the real repayments for our great export surpluses during the ten years or so of lending.

These interest payments and repayment of capital require no apologies here. They are of the essence of the plan. For however beneficial such a plan for the industrialization of the world would be for the populations which it would lift out of the misery of the ages, we must here consider it only from the point of view of its contribution toward dispelling the suspicions which are now hampering the establishment of peace.

What is relevant here is the recognition by the borrowing countries, and especially by Russia, that we will have a great stake in their continued prosperity. A large part of the standard of living of the American people will consist of our import surpluses from these countries. These countries would then know that America does not want to conspire with other capitalist countries to pervert the International Police Force into an anti-Russian instrument. The relevant purpose of the World Peace Loan is to show the Russians by this great investment in their economic reconstruction that we have no aggressive intentions but on the contrary are prepared to build up an enormous stake in the peaceful development of Russia and the rest of the world.

If UN Fails

But this is not the end of our troubles. For there can be no assurance that the United Nations will even agree to discuss such an establishment of the International Police Force. Or the United Nations may meet and various countries may deliberately prolong discussion while feverishly working on the manufacture of atomic bombs, planning to use these bombs to strengthen their bargaining power. If this happens the United Nations will indeed have performed the fatal function of hypnotizing us during the period of grace and delivering us to the fatal buttons of atomic preparedness.

I therefore propose further that if UN has not reached agreement on all the basic conditions within one hundred days, the U.S. shall proceed to join together with such other countries as will agree on a Peace Plan with the same basic conditions and fundamental freedoms and with the same plan for a World Peace Loan.

I do not think it would be many days before the greater part of the world will have come in. The plan can be put in motion as soon as another important country has joined with the U.S. Only in the case of Russia and the countries now being welded into the Russian sphere of influence is there likely to be any delay. But as soon as it is seen that the World Peace Loan promises rapid development and prosperity for those who join in the Peace Plan many countries now in the Russian sphere of interest will move over as soon as they can into the orbit of the American sponsored peace area.

Russia can be expected to hold out and perhaps to denounce the Peace Plan as an anti-Russian bloc. The only answer to this is to keep asking Russia to join on the same terms as the others.

The Ultimate Responsibility

If Russia or any other power should stay out of the Plan for as long as a year after its inauguration, which means not later than one year and a hundred days from now, this will have to be taken as *prima facie* evidence of aggressive intentions which would be thwarted by the inspection or other conditions of the Peace Plan. For if meanwhile the deadline is passed the world will once more be faced by the nightmare of the push-button war.

The International Police Force of those nations who are in the Plan must then be prepared to act. Every effort should be made to get the remaining countries to come in by non-military means. Intensive attempts should be made, for example, to reach the populations of such countries and to let them know the true nature of the proposals in case they are being misled by their governments, and this should be done in spite of any protest against such action by the recalcitrant governments. But in the last resort we must be prepared to use force. Once the situation is clearly seen there is no way of avoiding the steps I have indicated.

Even if recalcitrants should press us to this extremity, this does not mean an immediate all-out attack with atomic bombs. The nature of the force to be used against a recalcitrant country becomes a matter of strategy and tactics, directed toward getting the country to join the World Peace Plan on the same conditions as the other countries and the United States, while keeping to a minimum the destruction and suffering and the consequent bitterness. But humanity must not be allowed to become an excuse for cowardice. It must not be allowed to force us to accept the only alternative policy which is to wait until the recalcitrants have accumulated enough atomic bombs to destroy the whole world.

I have described the terrible nature of our situation and have indicated a way to safety. I am confident that once the first step is taken the others will follow smoothly and quickly and that even though we must be prepared for all eventualities, there would be no need to use force against recalcitrants. But the most difficult step is the first step—to get the American people and their representatives to agree quickly on the adoption of the Peace Plan and to forget their small differences, for all our differences are small in comparison with the question of war or peace.

Decentralization

If we should fail to do this the atomic war will come in a few years, and we must grimly devote ourselves to the task of trying to save what can be saved out of the world destruction. For this it will be necessary to decentralize our whole economy, relocating our cities in ribbons spread evenly over the whole country, putting vital defense elements deep underground, mobilizing everything with an intensity that has not been equalled anywhere on the earth and involving a detailed central control over the occupation, location, and habits of every man, woman and child in the country, squandering on this at least as much as we would have invested in the World Peace Loan. The fundamental freedoms will have gone by the board. Our only consideration will be that enough of us survive the disaster—if indeed the atomic poisoning of the atmosphere shall not render our planet completely uninhabitable—to begin life again when we emerge from a darker dark age.

Four Commissions

To carry out the proposals I hereby appoint four commissions. The first commission will draw up details of a plan for the constitutions of the International Police Force and the World Court (which some may wish to call the World Government) which will take the place of war in settling disputes between nations.

The primary objectives of the constitution will be (1) to see that the machinery for settling disputes is fair and unprejudiced and (2) to prevent the International Police Force from interfering in the domestic matters of any country, other than the inspection to prevent armament and the establishment and maintenance of the three fundamental freedoms. The Commission will submit the constitution to the UN for approval or amendment while inviting the Russians to propose alternative plans. This commission will also prepare the alternative peace plan that would be made necessary by the failure of UN to form itself into the International Police Force.

The second commission will work out plans for the World Peace Loan. It will have to find out as far as possible how much each country or region would like to borrow, what would be the nature of the excess imports it would obtain in the years it was borrowing to build up its capital equipment, and what would be the nature of its exports in the fifty years or so of interest payment and capital repayment. It will also have to check whether the plans of the various countries are consistent, both internally and with each other.

The third commission will study the available productive resources both of the U.S. and of the rest of the world to obtain the necessary background information which the second commission will need for preparing the World Peace Loan. This study of resources will also be helpful for other plans for development and effective utilization of resources both in the U.S. and in the rest of the world.

The fourth commission will study decentralization in the U.S., what it would cost both in material terms and in terms of interferences with the freedom of the individual, and will prepare a plan for decentralization to be ready to be put into action one year from today, the commission to give interim reports monthly.

We Must Act Now

If we in this country start the Peace Plan there is every reason to believe we will have peace and we will not have to forget our civilization and burrow underground to save some of us alive. I, therefore, hope and pray that the American people will through their representatives support and implement this policy so that it can be carried out during our period of grace. By so doing we will transform the atom bomb from an instrument of annihilation into the harbinger of peace.

[3]

[Reprinted from SOCIAL RESEARCH, Vol. 31, No. 2, Summer, 1964]

NUCLEAR SYMMETRY AS A FRAMEWORK FOR COEXISTENCE

BY ABBA P. LERNER

THE ultimate security of world peace lies with the eventual establishment of world law, yet the author does not wish to engage in the fascinating game of constructing models of world governments, world courts or world constitutions. The purpose of this study is to examine the interim problem of coexistence by means of the non-utopian procedure of "starting from here."

Karl Marx, for one, made a clear distinction between his own "scientific socialism," the examination of facts as given, or starting from here, and the "utopianism" of other thinkers. He was, it is true, more utopian than other socialists in his failure to apply his principle to anything but the political problem of the seizure of power by the revolutionary party. Yet that he was completely correct in making the distinction between scientific socialism and utopianism is shown by the contrast between the conspicuous success of the communists in seizing power and their failure to achieve the better life and the greater individual freedoms that they hoped would come naturally once they had seized power. In concentrating on the seizure of power the communists made effective use of non-utopianism. But it was the reformers who, non-utopian in their approach to economic and social problems, "starting from here" have improved the condition of the people, bringing what were considered to be the economic and social fruits of socialism to the inhabitants of the so-called capitalist countries. Such experience indicates that the scientific or non-utopian approach to the long-run problem of establishing world law is to go by way of the relatively short-run, here and now problems. It is to start from here with the immediate task of assuring the continuation of peaceful competitive coexistence growing into a co-operative coexistence that we hope may lead to the long-run objective of peace under world law.

The problem of prolonging competitive coexistence so as to give it a chance of developing into a true peace under world law does require that distasteful subjects be dealt with, and indeed one may be tempted to abandon this approach in favor of the aesthetically more pleasing exercise of building utopian models of a peaceful world order. Prolonged competitive coexistence must reckon with armaments and arms control, with nuclear strategies, with civil defense and bomb shelters, with the nature of wars that are less than fatal to civilization, with conditions that increase or decrease the probability of the outbreak of war, with how a conflict is ended in what might look more like surrender than victory, and with problems of recovery from nuclear wars. Yet it is precisely what is done in the short-run treatment of these unpleasant problems that will determine whether or not a peaceful world order will ever get established.

From the new thinking that has been made necessary by the new situation posed by nuclear weapons, some definite conclusions seem to be emerging. The dangers of nuclear weapons have altered the general situation by so changing the rules that nobody can hope to win a war. The damage suffered even by the "winning" side will be so great that neither side will go into an all-out war with the thought that it could gain from the war, even if victorious. Each side will fight an all-out war only if it seems unavoidable, and will initiate one only if it feels that if it does not do so the other side will "pre-empt" or attack first, with even more disastrous results.

Occasionally it is suggested that the adequate mutual deterrents implied in this situation, which would make it certain that neither side can ever hope to gain from an all-out war, do not yet exist, though it is likely that they will exist in the near future; and that even then there would be a constant danger of disruption by technical break-throughs resulting in even newer weapons that would give one side the temporary possibility of launching an all-out attack on the other with relative safety. But it seems to this author that our escape from nuclear holocaust up to now is an indication that the belief in any such temporary advantage has not been held with sufficient confidence to make it significant. There remain however four different kinds of danger of war against which preventive measures must be taken: (1) a pre-emptive all-out attack (*i.e.,* hitting first when the other side is expected to attack,) (2) the emergence of disputes that could develop into violent conflict, (3) the escalation of a "small" war into a big one, and (4) an accidental explosion that would look like an attack and would result in war.

The essence of the new thinking that comes out of the new situation is a recognition that the impossibility of winning in any real sense makes the situation *symmetrical.* Any policy that would be good for either side must also be good for the other side. Any policy that one side can adopt can also be adopted by the other side. Any policy that can be denied to one side by the other can also be denied to the other side by the first. Only symmetrical policies are viable. The impossibility of winning is only one example of this. "Winning" is ruled out as an objective only because it is not a symmetrical policy: it is impossible for both sides to win.

Similarly ruled out by the principle of symmetry is a policy of a "first strike" (*i.e.,* of destroying the other side's power of retaliation by striking first). This is denied to each side by the invulnerable deterrent of the other side. What follows next is that the *capability* of a first strike is also ruled out in the same way as are also the *appearance* of the capability of a first strike, the *intent* to build a first strike capability, the appearance of an intent to build a first strike capability, and so on. Any of these would destroy the symmetry or the appearance of symmetry and force the other side to engage in preparation for a first strike of its own and the explosion of a pre-emption—one side or the other hitting out in an attempt to diminish the destructive power of an expected attack by the other side.

Also ruled out by the principle of symmetry would be a policy of having more power than the other. Since it is impossible for both to succeed in this, it would result in a senseless and dangerous race. Since the invulnerable deterrent must be adequate to deter, there is no meaning left in comparisons of the degrees of adequacy of the mutual deterrents.

The question then that must be answered is: What is the objective both of diplomacy and of the use of force in any dispute if attempting to win in any real sense is ruled out? That is, what is the alternative to victory? As soon as this is seen as a question rather than a slogan, the answer becomes apparent. The objective is to discourage aggression by making it too costly. The objective is to take the profit out of war.

These words used to be applied to the profits of munition makers and war profiteers, on the theory that wars were fomented by such people for the sake of the money they could make. Whether or not there was ever any truth to such suspicions, this is not the definition of the term with which we are here concerned. Here the term refers to the gain that a government engaged in aggression hopes to get for its country. The objective of resistance to such aggression is to make the cost so great that no gain remains for the aggressor, and if this could be made clear in the beginning, the aggression would be discouraged and no fighting would be necessary.

There are further corollaries. If escalation is to be prevented, the response to aggression must not go too far beyond the objective of making the aggression unprofitable. For example, if the threat of the response should fail to deter and the aggression should actually take place, and the response is also put into effect, no attempt must be made to pursue the further objective of making the aggressor suffer more than the victim. This would again be asymmetrical and could therefore result in escalation. In the absence of an effective system of international law, it is difficult to establish independently and objectively that aggression is really aggression; and in any case, the aggressor country would deny that its action was aggressive (and indeed very likely succeed in convincing its citizens that it really was not the aggressor). There is no room, until world order is established, for seeking revenge or punishment or even justice. The *only* purpose of the use of force must be to make aggression unprofitable, thus establishing a deterrent which might affect in advance the decision of a would-be aggressor. Only if the use of force is limited by both sides to this objective can coexistence be stable. But the interest of both sides in the stability of coexistence should be sufficient to lead to the voluntary acceptance of this limitation if its necessity is clearly seen.

The symmetry principle goes further. It cannot distinguish between aggression and resistance to aggression, and must treat them as equal or symmetrical. The aggressor country will call its act legitimate and will see in the response of the other an act of aggression. With the same concern for avoiding nuclear war and the same recognition of the principle of symmetry as seen by a victim, the aggressor will proceed to threaten a counter-response to the response, also on a scale just sufficient to make the response unprofitable. If it succeeds in this, it deters the deterrent and suffers no undesirable consequences of its aggression. The aggressor country might in effect say: "Look, we have done, or we are going to do something that you call an act of aggression. You had better accept this and do nothing, because if you attack us, we shall respond in a manner that will leave you worse off than if you had not attacked us. We will not try to punish you for your attack (which you call a response to what you call our aggression) but we will hurt you only just enough to make you suffer more than you would suffer if you passively accept the so-called aggression."

Since the purpose of the response to an aggressive act, or rather of the threat of the response to such an act, is to deter it, the response can function only if it is not subject to being prevented by the threat of a counter-response. The threat to counter the feared aggression must, therefore, be a "committed" threat. That is to say, the side that fears the aggression must be able to state that it is committed to the response. If the aggression occurs the response (which would make the aggression unprofitable) will take place automatically—the response could not be withheld even if the victim wished to withhold it. One should recognize that this is just the kind of reasoning used by Khrushchev when he said that if certain things were done by the West, the Soviet rockets would fly "automatically."

Exactly the same argument applies to the counter-threat and to the counter-counter-threat, and so on indefinitely. All of these must be "committed," in the same sense and for the same reason. We must therefore look at the total result of all these responses and counter-responses.

If each response is greater than the preceding one that gave rise to it, or even just as great, we would once more have an unlimited escalation into total annihilation. But if each response is limited to making the previous response unprofitable, it can be a smaller response and the process is then self-limiting.

The basic condition for the series of responses and counter-responses being self-limiting is essentially that each side should be more concerned with reducing its own losses than with imposing losses on the other side. In other words, self-interest must exceed hatred for the other. If the hatred is greater than the self-interest (which we may express by an HQ or "hatred quotient" greater than 100 per cent) an attack is hard to discourage. To render it unprofitable would call for a response that imposed more damage than had been inflicted by the preceding aggression or response. There would then have to be an explosive escalation and no possibility of stability. If men are more eager to destroy one another than to save themselves, there is little hope for peace or even for coexistence.

If the HQ, the hatred quotient, is less than 100 per cent, that is, if self-interest is greater than hate, each response can be smaller than the preceding response (or aggression) and still make the preceding response (or aggression) unprofitable. Thus, if self-interest is more than twice as great as hatred of the other, a response that did as much as half the damage done by the preceding response (or aggression) would be sufficient to make the latter unprofitable. Each step in a series of committed responses would then be half the size of the preceding response. Thus, if the threatened response should fail to deter the original aggression, and the whole series of responses, counter-responses, etc., are set in motion, the total damage that would result would be limited to no more than twice the damage done by the first response to the aggression.

If A fears an aggression by B, A threatens to respond with a limited attack on B (if the aggression should take place) such as will impose one unit of damage to B, which is judged sufficient to make the aggression unprofitable. If that threat deters the aggression, all is solved. But B will want to deter A's response by making it, also, unprofitable. To achieve this, B has to threaten a counter-response that will impose a damage of one-half a unit, in order to make the response unprofitable to A (since the HQ is less than 50 per cent). A considers the damage to itself, consisting of one-half a unit, to be greater than the benefit to itself resulting from imposing a whole unit of damage on B. The following chart illustrates this:

	Damage threatened by		
	A	B	Both
	1	1/2	3/2
	1/4	1/8	3/8
	1/16	1/32	3/32
	...	...	...
	...	...	...
Total damage	4/3	2/3	2

If both sides have made their retaliatory responses automatic (so as to avoid the deterring of the deterrence) and could see what the final outcome would be, A could reduce its first response to three-quarters instead of one, since the (limited) escalation would raise that to 4/3 x 3/4, that is, 1, which is the amount of damage that would make the initial aggression unprofitable. If the threat failed and the aggression did take place (perhaps because A had underestimated the value to B of the aggression) then A would suffer an additional damage of 1/2 (*i.e.*, 2/3 x 3/4) from the series of automatic responses. This risk is the very much worthwhile cost of a system that deters aggression and settles disputes (one way or the other, with aggression either deterred, by being made unprofitable, or condoned) while the danger of escalation into all-out war is completely removed.

If HQ, the hatred quotient, were greater than this, so that the counter-deterrence had to be three-quarters instead of one-half of the initial deterrence, total possible damage would amount to 4, as shown in the chart below:

	Damage threatened by		
	A	B	Both
	1	3/4	7/4
	9/16	27/64	63/64
	. . .	. . .	. . .
	. . .	. . .	. . .
Total damage	16/7	12/7	4

A could then still limit the total damage to B to one unit by starting with a smaller initial deterrence that would escalate to 1 for B and to 3/4 for A. If the HQ were much less than this, say ten per cent, so that one-tenth of a unit of damage to a country was more than that country would want to suffer for the sake of imposing one unit of loss on the other country, then the escalation would develop as shown in the following chart:

Damage threatened by

	A	B	Both
	1.00	0.1	1.1
	.01	.001	.011
	.0001	.00001	.00011
	. . .	. . .	. . .
	. . .	. . .	. . .
Total	1.010101	.101010	1.111111 or $1\frac{1}{9}$

A could then reduce its initial deterrence to only very slightly below one.

But if hatred became almost equal to self-interest and the HQ approached 100 per cent, the result would be as follows:

Damage threatened by

	A	B	Both
	1	1	2
	1	1	2
	. . .	. . .	. . .
	. . .	. . .	. . .
Total	∞	∞	∞

In this last case, as in the case where hatred outstrips self-interest, the escalation seems unlimited.

In all the types of cases discussed, the procedure would be simplified once it became familiar and more clearly understood. The total amount of damage calculated for the entire series of responses would be undertaken in the first step taken by each side. In our first example, A would impose a cost or damage of one unit on B in response to the aggression, and B would impose a damage of one-half a unit on A, which would be sufficient to make the response (which B would probably call aggression) unprofitable. In our second example, the damage imposed by A and by B would be 1 and $\frac{3}{4}$ respectively. In our third example, it would be 1 and .1. In our last example the escalation seems unlimited; nevertheless the damage could be reduced to 1 and 1.

This last example, which is the limiting case just before excess of hatred over self-interest makes settlement impossible, turns out to be closely related to Professor Szilard's proposal (which was what first drew the attention of the present author to this problem), sometimes described as the trading of evacuated cities as a means of settling international disputes. Put in this form, the proposal seems to be subject to the fatal criticism that an unlimited escalation could result from the two countries trying to impose different trading ratios on each other. If one country tried to apply the 1:1 ratio but the other insisted on destroying two cities for each one of its own that was destroyed, destruction would escalate indefinitely until one side or the other gave in. This criticism would not apply if the procedure rested on an understanding and acceptance of the principle of symmetry, and of the limitation of responses to the objective of making the other's aggressions or responses unprofitable. For it would then be seen that any response greater than 1:1 cannot be applied symmetrically without an explosion.

Indeed, it is this limiting case, corresponding to the maximum possible HQ compatible with stability, truncated to its first pair of steps so that it stops at 1 and 1 units of damage (where one unit is the amount of damage believed to be just enough to make the initial aggression unprofitable), that would become the general case. Even if the HQ is much less, so that a counter-response of one-half or less would suffice to make the response itself unprofitable, it would be best for the convention to be established of making the damage the same for A as for B. Ideally, it would be sufficient for the country responding to aggression to be able to say truthfully, "Our response hurts us *as well as* you. We do not get any benefit out of it." But it would be psychologically easier for the aggressor to accept the response if the responding country could say, "It hurts us *as much as* it hurts you." Although this would have the moral disadvantage of constituting a concession to the notion that the response is a punishment rather than merely a device for taking the profit out of aggression, it has the overwhelming practical advantage that it completely avoids disputes as to the correct measurement of the HQs of the two countries, assuming only that they are less than 100 per cent.

We have thus far dealt with (a) pre-emption, (b) disputes, and (c) escalation. The danger of pre-emption would be eliminated by the removal of first strike potentialities and of apparent intentions of providing first strike potentialities. The settling of disputes—and disputes are bound to arise—would be achieved by the development of the type of policy or device just examined. This would either deter unwelcome unilateral acts (aggressions) by making them unprofitable, or it would permit them if the cost of the necessary responses is deemed more onerous than the aggression. Escalation of disputes or conflicts not settled by the threat of response is checked by the self-limiting nature of the responses. There remains the fourth danger, the danger of accidental war.

But an accidental explosion that looked like a nuclear strike would start a nuclear war only if there were existing or suspected first strike capabilities. If each side had for the sake of its own safety done everything it could to convince the other side, and had indeed convinced the other side, that it did not have and was not preparing any first strike potential, then any accidental explosion would be believed to be an accidental explosion. To make a country more careful, it could very well be treated as if it had committed a deliberate aggression, namely, by a response that would elicit a counter-response, etc. Even if the accident was firmly believed to be a deliberately imposed injury, the kind of policy or device suggested here would lead only to limited additional damage to each side, and would avert the danger of nuclear holocaust.

We can now consider whether the development of the devices and policies that are necessary if competitive coexistence is to be stabilized helps or hinders the development of the long-run objective of a state of peace under world law, which alone could put an end to the wastes, the costs, the uncertainties of the stabilizing devices, and to the possibilities of their breaking down for technical, political or psychological reasons.

It appears that the new ways of thinking that result in these unorthodox devices have a strongly positive relation to the development of the frames of mind that would make the attainment of a world order under law more probable. First, there is a symmetry as the basic principle which will have to be accepted by both parties for the same reason—the desire for survival. This moves in the direction of the acceptance of equal treatment under law. Second, the calculations necessary for the development of the techniques outlined here necessitate the comparison only of "our" gains with "our" costs, and the comparison of "their" gains with "their" costs. These are the calculations needed to discover what damage done, what cost or price imposed on an aggression, will suffice to make the aggression unprofitable. Such calculations will help us to get away from the most dangerous of traditional practices, the "zero-sum game" habit of identifying the loss of one side as a gain for the other.

It will be very hard to get away from this kind of "zero-sum game" thinking, which ceased to be appropriate when the world changed and wars could no longer be won by the side with the greater number of battalions. The ambition to win is now appropriate not on the battlefield but only on the football field—and there only as long as it is acceptable to lose games. We can aim at winning at football only because it is agreed that if our team does not win with the usual instruments, it will not resort to knives and machine guns. We can try to win at football only because we do not escalate.

In the third place, the settling of disputes by the procedure of threatening and sometimes perhaps actually imposing losses on both sides is very much like the primitive trial by ordeal. The verdict goes not to the one who has justice on his side but to the one who cares more about the issue, in the sense that he is willing to endure more for the sake of having the outcome his way. This is of course far less satisfying than justice under law, but it maintains the stability of coexistence, and thereby provides the opportunity for its own development into the institution of world justice between states, just as trial by ordeal developed into the administration of justice between citizens.

Fourth, if we maintain stability of coexistence by the kind of procedures indicated, and this involves occasional destruction of cities or other valuable objects, there will inevitably develop a system of ransoming such objects by paying money fines, either to the other country or to "charity boxes," like projects in economic development, or scientific research, or outer space ventures. This would mean that the initial sublimation of war into demolition of evacuated cities would be further sublimated into fines. The next steps would include the arbitration of the fines and their assessment according to some reasonable criteria, such as levels of national wealth, or even more refined measures based on the diminishing utility of wealth, equality of sacrifice, or other considerations.

While all these developments are occurring, we can count on the continuation of the process that has been going on since the consolidation of the Russian Revolution and especially since the death of Stalin—and not only in the Soviet Union. The Russians have not given up their ultimate objective of establishing communism over the whole earth. But there can be just as little doubt that Russia has become more like America, or that America has in many respects become more like Russia. Fortunately the things that have been copied in both countries have mostly been good things. Over time, the Russians have gained considerably in individual security as well as in higher levels of consumption and in education. Americans have gained more social security, greater racial equality (not copying Russia's anti-semitism), a deeper recognition of government's social responsibilities, and recently also, some improvement in education and in attitudes toward scientists, science, and scholars.

Both we and the Russians have learned that the issue is not one of being hard or soft, but of being firm and yet flexible, and being able to do whatever needs to be done to achieve our aims of stabilizing coexistence without war until world order can be established. Many are afraid that our firm stand on Cuba will play into the hands of the die-hards who want a "tough" policy, but in fact the Cuba incident seems to have led to a keener awareness both of problems and of dangers, so that it will result not in blindly uncompromising attitudes but rather in more rational policies based on better understanding, and in greater firmness combined with flexibility.

It appears, too, that a comparable development in the understanding of the situation has gone on in the Soviet Union. It is even possible that the Soviet Union, believing as it does in the guarantee given to it by History that communism will triumph without war, may become even more flexible than the United States. (China, to be sure, is another story, since the Chinese seem to think that their guarantee by History stipulates a war.) Our long run hope must lie in the further development of the United States and the Soviet Union until they become much more like each other, and each has decided that it has won the world to its side. All that will then remain is the invention of a name that sounds like freedom in English and like socialism in Russian.

[4]

PROJECTING THE NEW ECONOMIC WORLD ORDER†

ABBA P. LERNER
Florida State University
Tallahassee, Florida, USA

Values

This sixth ICUS is the first for me; I feel I should begin my paper with a brief confession about the values underlying it. Some doubts I had had about ICUS were reawakened by the summary report of the fifth ICUS. Gratified by a complete identification with the hopes expressed in the introduction by the Reverend Moon that it would contribute to the realization of a "world of happiness, peace and love," I was surprised and slightly disturbed by my complete disagreement with Sir John Eccles' propositions about absolute values and absolute truth as well as with Max Jammer's belief (and apparent regret) that advances in physics have robbed us, allegedly for the first time, of an alleged "coherent and intellectually satisfying world picture." I am in full agreement with W.H. Thorpe's conclusion to the report—that belief in a "meaning" of the world, as distinct from scientific understanding, rests on religious faith or on an accepted system of myths. My confession is that I feel no need for a belief in a meaning of the universe or in the existence of absolute or universal values or in the possibility of absolute truth.

Yet I do not feel out of place in this conference because *shared* values are all that we need for cooperation for the advancement of the human welfare goals raised in the introduction. A search beyond these for *absolutes* not only takes time and energy away from the goals but carries with it a danger. A conviction that absolute values have been discovered or absolute truth achieved can easily lead, again, to a losing of the human welfare goals in a concentration on the condemnation of "wicked" values and the eradication of heresy.

†This article was made possible by the remarkable hospitality of the School of Social Sciences of the University of California, Irvine, during the summer of 1977.

The mobilization of shared values in the task of furthering human welfare is best served by Occam's Razor: demand only the *minimum* necessary, require only those *essential* for cooperation and only those that are needed for the cooperation that is *feasible,* and be prepared to work only with those who share these values.

Economics

Having settled the matter of basic values—at least to my own (current) satisfaction, I turn to the basic economics. I do not like the expression "closing the gap" between the rich and the poor since this suggests equal concern for pulling down the rich as for raising up the poor. I am concerned only with eliminating poverty. Taking from the rich (which usually turns out to be mainly taking from the not-quite-so-poor) can contribute to this end, but any real solution must be found elsewhere. Two basic well-established economic propositions are:

1. Raising the level of living of the poor of the world to any satisfactory standard must come primarily from increased production.
2. No feasible increase in production will be able to provide this for all if the world's population keeps on growing.

A third basic proposition, not so well established is:

3. Productive efficiency is not enough. *Distributive efficiency* is just as necessary. Raising productive efficiency alone, leaving unchanged the relative distribution of income and wealth, would be almost completely swallowed up by higher intensities of "keeping up with the Joneses."

Productive Efficiency

Productive efficiency is achieved automatically in a free market economic system to the degree that it is perfectly competitive. Government action is required only to correct for imperfections of competition and of the market and to adjust for externalities. Since this "correction" covers all socially beneficial government activity, including the institutions necessary for the market to work, the economic system can also be considered as government planning which only uses the market to correct for bureaucratic imperfections. But whether the capitalist or the socialist language is preferred, it is the market mechanism that achieves productive efficiency. It causes *preferred output* to be produced wherever possible by shifting productive factors from where the value of their marginal product is less to where it is greater until *the value of the marginal product (VMP) of every factor of production is the same in all its possible uses.* Such further improvements are then no longer available. Productive efficiency is achieved.

There is a value postulate underlying the desirability of *productive efficiency:*

1. It is better to use resources to produce what the consumer prefers *as between different products.* But no consideration is given to different degrees of need (for products in general) by *different consumers.*

Distributive Efficiency

The consideration of the degrees of need by different consumers is the province of *distributive efficiency.* It is concerned with the use of income to satisfy more important, or more strongly felt, human needs rather than less important, or less strongly felt, needs, and it calls for two additional value postulates:

2. All people feel satisfactions or enjoy utilities that are comparable to those felt or enjoyed by oneself and by others.

3. All people rationally choose to satisfy more important needs rather than less important ones at least part of the time.

From these additional utility postulates we can derive *the principle of diminishing marginal utility of income.* Successive increases in income permit the addition of only less important items since only these still remain to be purchased. From this follows further the basic principle of distributive efficiency:

The efficient distribution of a given income is one that equalizes the marginal utility of income of all the individuals. As long as any two marginal utilities of income are unequal, the transfer of a dollar from where its marginal utility is less to where it is greater will yield a gain in utility greater than the loss. This is an improvement in distributive efficiency. By virtue of the principle of diminishing marginal utility of income it will also lower the greater of the two marginal utilities and raise the lesser one. The continuation of such transfers will continue to improve the distribution but the difference between the marginal utilities will keep diminishing. When this difference has disappeared altogether, the marginal utilities will have been equalized and complete distributional efficiency will have been reached. Of course, this analysis can be compelling only for those who accept the underlying utility postulates—but very few would admit to the arrogance implied in rejecting them.

Distributive efficiency is parallel to productive efficiency. It calls for equalizing marginal utilities of income instead of VMP's. While the market mechanism works automatically towards equalizing VMP's, it does not work at all towards equalizing marginal utilities. Distributive efficiency can be achieved only by governmental equalization of the marginal utilities by redistributing income from where its marginal utility is less to where it is greater.

Equality

The lack of any objective measure of marginal utility had seemed to block completely any practical conclusions from this approach. But I have shown*, and other economists have shown in somewhat different ways, that a policy guideline can be developed from the utility postulates on which distributive efficiency is based. Every shift of a dollar from a larger to a smaller income entails a *probable* increase in the utility of the poorer individual greater than the *probable* decrease in the utility of the richer one. Utilitarian Marginalism thus enables us to derive the policy guidelines:

> *The best that anyone can do who is aiming at distributive efficiency is to spread a given income equally.*

But here we meet another obstacle. The distributive efficiency principle seems to be in direct conflict with the productive efficiency principle. The market equalizes the VMP's of productive factors by making these equal to its uniform *price*. Where the factor is labor, the price of the factor is also the wage, and this serves not only to guide the labor to where its VMP is greatest, but also as an incentive to the worker to provide the service. If equal incomes are provided, there will be no material incentive for the worker to work or for managers to manage, and there would certainly be much less available for distribution. The distributive principle would destroy the productive principle!

*Lerner, *The Economics of Control,* New York: Macmillan, 1944; "Nozick, Rawls, and Utilitarian Marginalisms," to appear in a symposium on ethics and income distributors in the forthcoming January 1977 number of *The Eastern Economic Journal,* edited by Professor Raymond E. Canterbury of Florida State University and the late Professor Harry Johnson of the University of Chicago.

This is a misinterpretation. The distributive principle applies strictly only to the distribution of a *given* income. The argument is valid only as long as a dollar taken from one person permits a whole dollar to be given to the other, i.e., only if the total income is unchanged or "given." But does not this alone suffice to destroy the usefulness of the notion of distributive efficiency?

"Given" Income

It does not do so because a great deal of the income *is* "given" in the relevant sense. The prices *paid* for productive resources have to be as high as the market sets them to discourage their use where the VMP is less than in alternative uses. But there is no need for the *owners* of the resources to enjoy all such payments as their *income*. They need get only the payment for that part of the *human* resources—the *work* (including the efforts in economical management) *which, if not paid for, would have been devoted to the enjoyment of leisure* or to more pleasant but less useful work. All the rest is "given." It is available for efficient distribution. Economists of all schools have long recognized this as "rent" or "surplus."

The equalization of the VMP's (for productive efficiency) is indeed achieved by making them equal to the pay. But there is no need for this VMP to be received for *all* the units of a factor. It is necessary *only at the margin*. It may seem natural to pay for all the units, but this is only because it is our habit to start counting from zero, and that is arbitrary. We could start counting the daily hours of *paid* work only after, say, four hours of work had been done. The worker's income would then consist of his equal share of the "social surplus" *plus* the VMP of the hours he works in excess of the four hour norm (or minus the VMP of any reduction of hours worked below the norm). The worker would thus be free to work up to the point or margin where his wage (equal to his VMP) just compensates him for the disutility of his work, every employer would maximize the profits of his firm by employing each type of worker, and every other factor, up to the point where the wage or the payment for the factor is equal to its VMP, and productive efficiency would be unimpaired.

Degrees of Distributive Efficiency

Distributive efficiency would not be complete, the degree of distributive efficiency depending upon the number of "unpaid hours." The extension of distributive efficiency by raising the norm of unpaid working time (and thus increasing the surplus available for efficient distribution) is limited not by the requirements of productive efficiency but by the willingness of workers to supply the norm of unpaid work for the sake of the pay for work beyond the norm. There is a minimum necessary *income* without which the worker will not be available for the job. This is determined by the alternative occupations open to him. In a perfectly competitive economy there would be little if any scope for an employer to demand "unpaid hours" (not even from apprentices or medical interns). But where the alternative occupations are similarly subjected to the unpaid norm competition from alternative occupations is easily prevented.

Limits to Distributive Efficiency

The effective limit to the equalization of income in accordance with distributive efficiency is not in the necessity of maintaining productive efficiency. It is in the resistance of workers to equalizations of pay that they regard as "unfair" or as "too socialistic," as below the traditional minimum standard of living for each particular skill or profession required to induce conscientious work.

There is no *objective* basis for such "required" levels of reward. It is a matter of custom or culture and not of technology. The possible degree of distributional efficiency thus rests entirely on tradition and can be increased as people get used to greater income equality with the moderation or elimination of poverty.

Traditional pay differentials can be protected by political pressures, threats of strikes and most of all by the productive inefficiencies that grow out of feelings of resentment at whatever is felt to be "unjust," and are hard to distinguish from conscious or unconscious sabotage. Only as greater equality of income becomes socially acceptable can greater distributional efficiency be attained. But there is a wide range over which greater distributive efficiency need not damage productive efficiency.

Disappointing Slogans

I am now more than half way through my lecture without having even referred to the topic—Projecting the New Economic World Order. But I think that I have laid down some basic economic and moral guidelines, the absence of which has left much of the recent discussions without a proper foundation. The basic intent of the new economic world order is a raising of the economic condition of the poor people of the poorer countries. The Less Developed Countries, LDCs, is the paternalistic euphemism of the rich countries.* The sad observation that successful aid has been the exception rather than the rule led to a turn to the slogan of "trade not aid."

This was understandable as a protest against protectionist restriction of imports from the poor countries with their low wages (inevitable with their low VMPs)—although often weakened by accompanying defense of protectionist restrictions of imports from the rich countries with their low prices (due their high VMPs) which are just as essential for the benefits from trade. But the idea that "fair" trade could cure the poverty of the poor countries is based on the myth that the wealth of the rich countries is stolen from the poor by "unfair" or "unequal" exchanges, rather than produced by ability to make use of technology and of the resources of the earth (including some found in the poorer countries).

Recognition that trade was not enough led to the call for *foreign investment* which would raise VMPs and wages. But investment is undertaken only if the investor gets some gain from it too, and when a successful investment was completed and the foreign capital returned together with some earnings from the years of the investment, the investors naturally took out of the country more than they had brought in. The poor country's gains had, in some cases, merely increased the number rather than the living standard of the poor. This gave support to the myth that the wealth of the rich was obtained by robbing the poor. Foreign investment, denounced as imperialism or colonialism and discouraged by confiscations petered out before it could lead to successful development as in the United States and Canada.

Another turn was from depending on trade and on foreign investment towards *self help,* the rich countries only showing the poor countries *how* to be more productive. This was technical training—Point Four and the Peace Corps—and it too, turned out to be a great disappointment. Many cases of individual devotion and even heroism were sunk in cross-cultural misunderstandings, growing bureaucracy, disruption of cultural systems, and the absence of the infrastructure necessary for economic prosperity.

"Fair" Prices

The latest turn is a hope for a New Economic World Order through a reincarnation of "fair prices" as demonstrated by the quadrupling of oil prices by the cartel formed by OPEC, the Oil Producing and Exporting Countries. Although it is the poor countries which are beginning to develop that are hurt most grievously by the increase in the price of oil, and of the fertilizers made with it, resentment at the harm they suffer seems to be more than offset by gratitude to OPEC for having shown them a way of getting higher prices for what they sell to the rich countries while feeling that what they would be getting only is their right by virtue of market power and not from anybody's condescending gifts.

But this is an illusion on both counts. It is doubtful whether the market can be as helpful to any of the poor countries as it has been to OPEC, and it is clear that to many it will be of no help at all.

Conscience Money

In the United Nations General Assembly the poor nations are in the majority, and the rich countries seem willing to make sizeable contributions toward raising the income of the poor countries. But this seems mostly to be taking the form of accepting monopolistic restrictions (which are nothing but the combination of a gift to the restricting poor countries with a damage to world net product) or of gifts otherwise disguised as loans, or investments, or insurance policies, or public relations expenses and by many other aliases. It seems to me that this willingness betrays a vague awareness of the principle of distributive efficiency and a recognition that a large part of the world net product is "surplus," and that its appropriation by the rich is not required for productive efficiency and not justified by the productive efficiency principle. On the other hand, it was never the property of the poor and so it cannot be said to have been stolen from them. Only the distributive efficiency principle gives any indication where it should go—i.e., as surplus which an unbiased distributor would divide equally among all. Much of the income and wealth would therefore have to be transferred from the rich to the poor, but it would not really be *given* by the rich to the poor any more than it would be *given back* to the poor by the rich.

International Distributive Efficiency

I happen to be in a better position than most to point out that any new economic order, if it is to succeed in reducing world poverty, most include the sharing of the surplus. In 1945 I proposed that the United States devote

50 billion dollars of its wealth to the reconstruction of the post war world on a more egalitarian basis. This was considered so naively unrealistic that I could not even get the lecture published for several years until the proposal had been much surpassed by the Marshall Plan and other US economic aid. Even then I could get it published only in the "starry-eyed" *Bulletin of the Atomic Scientists*.

By 1945 the principle of sharing the surplus more in accordance with distributive efficiency had been accepted on a large scale, but only *domestically*—for fellow nationals. In the richer countries there were attempts to make taxation of the well-to-do progressive. More successful were some measures for raising the economic welfare of the poor. But the day had not yet dawned for the *international* application of the principle of distributive efficiency. The earlier suggested bases for the New World Economic Order: the return of riches robbed from poor countries, the dependence on foreign investment, the spreading of technical knowledge, and even the subsidizing of infrastructures, had largely bogged down in bureaucracy, corruption, and disillusionment because a crucial element was missing or underemphasized.

This missing element is provided by the utilitarian marginalism behind the concepts of productive and distributive efficiency. It is the concentration on *individuals*. It is not nations—the entities mainly dealt with in the earlier approaches—but only *individual human beings* that have utility and the marginal utility whose equalization, called for by distributive efficiency, is best served by the policy guideline of equal sharing of the surplus.

So thoroughly was this missing element suppressed that attempts by the countries granting economic aid to make sure that the poor people in the poor countries benefitted from it, and not those through whose hands it passed, were denounced as unacceptable "strings," rejected as undermining national sovereignty and attributed to imperialist or colonialist machinations. Even more bitter was the response to suggestions that the aid should be limited to raising the level of living of the poor and not spent where it would only increase their number.

Essential "Strings"

The transfer of surplus, to be acceptable and really to increase distributive efficiency, should certainly avoid entanglement with other objectives that might be attractive to the governments of the countries making the transfers. But the "strings" just mentioned are essential conditions for the successful achievement of the New Economic World Order.

Some recent research has shown these strings to be even more essential than appears from the general analysis. Careful econometric studies have shown that even where economic aid has overcome the bureaucratic hurdles, escaped corruption, and resulted in successful development, even where the development disease of poor countries aping the techniques appropriate to rich countries has been avoided, in most cases, more poor people lose than gain from economic development for a considerable time before the benefits trickle down to them. If this is to be prevented, special measures have to be taken to raise the economic level of the very poor *before* the development. This further evidence only shows more emphatically that the only consistent moral and philosophical basis for the objective of the New Economic World Order is the principle of distributive efficiency.

Finally a Projection

I have still not "projected" the New Economic World Order. I can only hope that the substitute will be considered more useful by serving future developments rather than present prophesies. What I would project if pressed to move up to the level of my incompetence is that there will be a continuing increase in helping the poor, with the benevolence continuing to be disguised as insurance and as conscience money for damage by monopolistic restrictions as in Arabian oil or American soy beans (and now in American wheat and shipping). It will be combined with political bidding for allies and for bases by the rival world powers, and this will force attention to the preference of the governments of the poor countries rather than to the needs of their impoverished citizens.

However, as the understanding spreads of the basic efficiency principles, the existing trend of raising minimum levels of living relatively as well as absolutely, will continue in the rich countries, and will spread to a similar raising of relative as well as absolute economic levels, both of the poorer countries and of their poorer inhabitants.

In the longer run I see in the capitalist countries a continuing decrease in the volume of rents and surpluses—the "un-necessary incomes"—being appropriated and justified as necessary for efficiency; and in the socialist countries a continuing increase in the volume of payments to workers and management recognized as *necessary* material incentives for industry and efficiency. As the spread of technological knowledge diminishes, the differences between the "capitalist" and the "socialist" economies, the economic basis for the ideological conflict will weaken. Communication between countries will improve technically as well as politically, and the chances of world peace may increase. But now I am indeed projecting far beyond my level of incompetence and perhaps beyond everybody else's.

BIBLIOGRAPHY

Journal Articles

"The Diagrammatical Representation of Cost Conditions in International Trade," *Economica*, August 1932.

"The Diagrammatical Representation of Elasticity of Demand," *The Review of Economic Studies*, October 1933.

"The Diagrammatical Representation of Elasticity of Substitution," *The Review of Economic Studies*, October 1933.

"A Note on the Elasticity of Substitution," *The Review of Economic Studies*, February 1934.

"The Concept of Monopoly and the Measurement of Monopoly Power," *The Review of Economic Studies*, June 1934.

"The Concept of Arc Elasticity of Demand," *The Review of Economic Studies*, June 1934.

"The Diagrammatical Representation of Demand Conditions in International Trade," *Economica*, August 1934.

"Economic Theory and Socialist Economy," *The Review of Economic Studies*, October 1934.

"Economic Theory and Socialist Economy: Rejoinder to Dobb," *The Review of Economic Studies*, February 1935.

"A Note on the Theory of Price Index Numbers," *The Review of Economic Studies*, October 1935.

"Further Notes on Index Numbers IV: A Reply," *The Review of Economic Studies*, February 1936.

"The Symmetry of the Elasticity of Substitution," *The Review of Economic Studies*, February 1936.

"The Symmetry between Import and Export Taxes," *Economica*, August 1936.

"Mr. Keynes' 'General Theory of Employment, Interest and Money'," *International Labour Review*, October 1936.

"A Note on Socialist Economics," *The Review of Economic Studies*, October 1936.

"Capital, Investment and Interest," *Proceedings of the Manchester Statistical Society*, 1936–37.

"Some Notes on Duopoly and Spatial Competition," *The Journal of Political Economy*, April 1937, (with H. W. Singer).

"Statics and Dynamics in Socialist Economies," *The Economic Journal*, June 1937.

"International Trade and Transfer," *Econometrica*, October 1937.

"A Rejoinder to Professor Cassel," *International Labour Review*, November 1937.

"Savings Equals Investment," *Quarterly Journal of Economics*, February 1938.

"A Undialectical Account of Dialectics," *Science and Society*, Spring 1938.

"Alternative Formulations of the Theory of Interest," *The Economic Journal*, June 1938.

"Theory and Practice in Socialist Economics," *The Review of Economic Studies*, October 1938.

"The Relation of Wage Policies and Price Policies," *The American Economic Review*, Supplement, March 1939.

"Equilibrium and Dynamic Concepts in the Theory of Employment," *Econometrica*, April 1939.

"Saving and Investment, Definitions, Assumptions, Objectives," *Quarterly Journal of Economics*, August 1939.

"From Vulgar Political Economy to Vulgar Marxism," *The Journal of Political Economy*, August 1939.

"Ex Ante Analysis and Wage Theory," *Economica*, November 1939.

"Professor Hicks' Dynamics," *Quarterly Journal of Economics*, February 1940.

"Vulgar Marxism: A Further Note," *The Journal of Political Economy*, April 1940.

"Some Swedish Stepping Stones in Economic Theory," *The Canadian Journal of Economics and Political Science*, November 1940.

"Peace and Finance," *The University Review* (Kansas City), Spring 1941.

"Full Employment and Total Democracy," *Social Change*, May 1941.

"The Economic Steering Wheel," *The University Review* (Kansas City), June 1941.

"Democratic Perspective," *The University Review* (Kansas City), September 1942.

"Functional Finance and the Federal Debt," *Social Research*, February 1943.

"Economic Liberalism in the Postwar World," *Postwar Economic Problems*, March 1943.

"User Cost and Prime User Cost," *The American Economic Review*, March 1943.

"Interest Theory—Supply and Demand for Loans or Supply and Demand for Cash," *Review of Economic Statistics*, May 1944.

"Government Spending, Public Debt, and Postwar Taxation," *International Postwar Problems*, January 1945.

"Planning and Freedom," *International Postwar Problems*, July 1945.

"Full Employment and the Atomic Bomb," *Commonsense*, October 1945.

"An Integrated Full Employment Policy," *International Postwar Problems*, January 1946.

"Monetary Policy and Fiscal Policy," *Review of Economic Statistics*, May 1946.

"The Problem of Full Employment—Discussion," *The American Economic Review*. Supplement, May 1946.

"How to Keep the Peace," *Bulletin of the Atomic Scientists*, September 1946.

"Geometrical Comparison of Elasticities," *The American Economic Review*, March 1947.

"The President Addresses the World," *Bulletin of the Atomic Scientists*, April–May 1947.

"Money as a Creature of the State," *American Economic Review Proceedings*, May 1947.

"Rising Prices" (in symposium, "Ten Economists on the Inflation), *The Review of Economics and Statistics*, February 1948.

"An Economist Comments on Daniel and Squires, 'Freedom Demands Responsibility'," *Bulletin of the Atomic Scientists*, October 1948.

"Does Control of Atomic Energy Involve a Controlled Economy?," *Bulletin of the Atomic Scientists*, January 1949.

"The Myth of the Parasitic Middleman," (originally in Yiddish, *Yivo Bleter*, January 1947, Journal of the Yiddish Scientific Institute), *Commentary*, July 1949.

"The Inflationary Process: Some Theoretical Aspects," *The Review of Economics and Statistics*, August 1949.

"Wage Policy in Full Employment," in "Report of the Varese Meeting of the Econometric Society," September 6–8, 1950, *Econometrica*, 1951.

"Fighting Inflation," *The Review of Economics and Statistics*, August 1951.

"Factor Prices and International Trade," *Economica*, February 1952.

"The Essential Properties of Interest and Money," *The Quarterly Journal of Economics*, May 1952.

"Discussion—Professor Hart's Criticisms of Mr. Brill's Paper," *Econometrica,* July 1952.

"Reply to review by W. S. Woytinsky, 'Economics of Employment'," *Industrial and Labor Relations Review,* October 1952.

"On the Marginal Product of Capital and the Marginal Efficiency of Investment," *The Journal of Political Economy,* February 1953.

"Should We Break our Biggest Monopoly," *Bulletin of the Atomic Scientists,* May 1953.

"Discussion on Social Choice Functions," *Econometrica,* September 1953.

"Stabilization and Economic Independence," *Riv'on le-Khalkalah,* August 1954.

"The Histadrut and the Israel Economy," *Midstream,* October 1957.

"Halting the Current Recession—A Proposal for Dealing with 'Sellers' Inflation," *Commentary,* February 1958.

"Planning for Israel's Solvency," *Midstream,* Summer 1958.

"Consumption-Loan Interest and Money," *The Journal of Political Economy,* October 1959.

"A Rejoinder," *The Journal of Political Economy,* October 1959.

"On Generalizing the General Theory," *The American Economic Review,* March 1960.

"Problems of Achieving and Maintaining a Stable Price Level," *The American Economic Review,* May 1960.

"Economics and the Control of Man—The Case of the Economist," *The American Scholar,* Summer 1960.

"The Burden of Debt," *The Review of Economics and Statistics,* May 1961.

"Discussion of Harry Johnson on 'Keynes after 25 years'," *The American Economic Review,* May 1961.

"A Note on the Rate of Interest and the Value of Assets," *The Economic Journal,* September 1961.

"Depression Administrada," *Revista de Economica Lationoamericana,* December 1961.

"Own Rates and the Liquidity Trap," *The Economic Journal,* June 1962.

"The Analysis of Demand," *The American Economic Review,* September 1962.

"Consumer's Surplus and Micro-Macro," *The Journal of Political Economy,* February 1963.

"Financial Institutions and Monetary Policy," *The American Economic Review,* May 1963.

"Let's Get Rid of Our Cross of Gold," *Challenge,* April 1964.

"The Cross of Gold," *Washington Post,* April 1964.

"Nuclear Symmetry as a Framework for Coexistence," *Social Research,* Summer 1964.

"Our Declining National Debt—Is it too Small?," *Banking,* November 1964.

"On Some Recent Developments in Capital Theory," *The American Economic Review,* May 1965.

"Professor Samuelson on Theory and Realism: Comment," *The American Economic Review,* December 1965.

"Conflicting Principles of Public Utility Price Regulations," *Journal of Law and Economics,* June 1966.

"Employment Theory and Employment Policy," *The American Economic Review,* May 1967.

"The Economist's Can Opener," *Western Economic Journal,* March 1968.

"The Death of the Gold Standard," *New Leader,* June 1968.

"Black Studies: The Universities in Moral Crisis," *The Humanist,* May–June 1969.

"The Enemy Within," *Measure,* September 1969.

''Consumer's Surplus and Micro-Macro: A Discussion. A Reply,'' *The Journal of Political Economy,* January–February 1970.

''Distributional Equality and Aggregate Utility—Reply,'' *The American Economic Review,* June 1970.

''Depression and Inflation in the 70's,'' *Hebrew Economic Quarterly,* 1971.

''The Ivory Tower,'' *The Humanist,* March 1971.

''Social Scientist Has No Special Right,'' *Freedom at Issue,* July–August 1971.

''The 1971 Report of the President's Council of Economic Advisors: Priorities and Efficiency,'' *The American Economic Review,* September 1971.

''A Note on 'Understanding the Marxian Notion of Exploitation','' *Journal of Economic Literature,* March 1972.

''The Economics and Politics of Consumer Sovereignty,'' *The American Economic Review,* May 1972.

''Group Think,'' *Freedom at Issue,* July–August 1972.

''Pollution Abatement Subsidies,'' *The American Economic Review,* December 1972.

''The Deformation of Affirmative Action,'' *Midstream,* April 1973.

''From the Treatise on Money to the General Theory,'' *Journal of Economic Literature,* March 1974.

''Priorities and Pollution,'' *The American Economic Review,* September 1974.

''Marxian Value, Surplus Value, and Surplus'' (in Hebrew), *Riv'on le-Khalkalah* (Economics Quarterly), December 1974.

''Stagflation,'' *Intermountain Economic Review,* Fall 1975.

''A Reluctant Keynesian,'' *Intermountain Economic Review,* Fall 1976.

''Marginal Cost Pricing in the 1930's,'' *The American Economic Review,* February 1977.

''Environment—Externalizing the Internalities?,'' *The American Economic Review,* March 1977.

''Utilitarian Marginalism (Nozick, Rawls, Justice, and Welfare),'' *Eastern Economic Journal,* January 1978.

''Stagflation: Its Cause and Cure,'' *Challenge,* September–October 1977.

''From Pre-Keynes to Post-Keynes,'' *Social Research,* Autumn 1977.

''The Scramble for Keynes' Mantle,'' *Journal of Post Keynesian Economics,* Fall 1978.

''A Wage Increase Permit Plan to Stop Inflation,'' *Brookings Papers on Economic Activity,* 1978.

''MAP—The Market Mechanism Cure for Stagflation,'' *Atlantic Economic Journal,* March 1979.

''On Keynes, Policy and Theory—A Grumble,'' *Social Research,* Winter 1979.

''OPEC—A Plan—If You Can't Beat Them, Join Them,'' *Atlantic Economic Journal,* September 1980.

''A Keynesian on Hayek,'' *Challenge,* September–October 1980.

''Incentive Anti-Inflation Plans'' (with David C. Colander), *Kyklos,* 1982. Fasc. 1

Contributed Papers in Chronological Order

''Budgetary Principles,'' *Cowles Commission Conference* (Report), July 1939.

''The American Way of Business'' with Oscar Lange, *The American Way of Business,* National Education Association, 1944.

''Bimetallism,'' ''Coinage,'' ''Economics,'' ''Money,'' *American Peoples Encyclopedia*, 1945.

''Money,'' *Encylopaedia Britannica*, 1946.

''Investment, Economic Aspects,'' *Encyclopaedia Britannica*, 1946.

''Foreign Economic Relations of the United States,'' *Saving American Capitalism*, edited by S. E. Harris, Knopf, 1948.

''The Burden of the National Debt,'' *Income, Employment and Public Policy Essays in Honor of Alvin H. Hansen*, edited by Lloyd A. Melzler, Norton, 1948.

''When Should Wages be Increased?,'' *Studies in Business Economics*, The Conference Board, January 1950.

''Immigration, Capital Formation and Inflationary Pressure,'' *The Economics of International Migration*, International Economics Association, Macmillan, 1958.

''Inflationary Depression and the Regulation of Administered Prices,'' *Joint Economic Committee Print*, Conference on Economic Stability and Growth, March 31, 1958.

''Meta Economics,'' *Study of the Soviet Economy: Its Place in American Education*, Indiana University Press, 1961.

''Macro-economics and Micro-economics,'' *Logic, Methodology and Philosophy of Science: Proceedings of the 1960 International Congress, 1962*, Stanford University Press, 1962.

''Consumer's Surplus,'' *Encyclopaedia Britannica*, 1962.

''The Death of the Class Struggle,'' *The Strategy of Deception*, edited by J. J. Kirkpatrick, Farrar, Straus, 1963.

''Sellers' Inflation and Administered Depression,'' *Administered Prices: A Compendium on Public Policy*, Subcommittee on Antitrust and Monoply of U.S. Senate, 1963.

''Keynesian Economics in the Sixties,'' *Keynes' General Theory—Reports of Three Decades*, edited by R. Lekachman, St. Martin's Press, 1964.

''Testimony before House Banking and Currency Committee,'' *The Federal Reserve After 50 Years* (Hearings), March 11, 1964.

''The Big Powers and Economic Development in the Middle East,'' *The Big Powers and Present Crisis in the Middle East*, Fairleigh Dickinson University Press, 1968.

''Micro-economic Theory,'' *Perspectives in Economics*, edited by J.W. Snow, Interstate, 1968.

''Capital,'' *International Encyclopaedia of the Social Sciences*, May 1968.

''On Instrumental Analysis,'' *Economic Means and Social Ends*, edited by R. L. Heilbroner, Prentice-Hall, 1969.

''Some Thoughts on Landauer's *Theory of National Economic Planning*,'' *Essays in Socialism and Planning in Honor of Carl Landauer*, edited by G. Grossman, Prentice-Hall, 1970.

''Money, Debt, and Wealth,'' *Econometrics and Economic Theory, Essays in Honor of Jan Timbergen*, edited by Willy Sellekaerts, International Arts and Sciences, 1973.

''Price Flexibility and the International Money Market,'' *Understanding Economics, Essays in Public Policy*, edited by Yung-Bing Chen, Little, Brown, 1974.

''Reflection on the Agonies of the University,'' *The Idea of a Modern University*, edited by Sidney Hook and others, Prometheus Books, 1974.

''Three Kinds of Inflation,'' *Policy Formation in an Open Economy*, edited by Mundell and van Snellenberg, University of Waterloo Press, 1974.

''Wages, Profits and Marginal Analysis,'' *Inflation, Trade and Taxes*, edited by Belsley, et al., Ohio University Press, 1975.

''The Transmissions of Inflations from Country to Country,'' *Geographical Aspects of Inflation-*

ary Process, Part One, edited by Peter B. Corbin, for American Geographical Society, Redgrave, 1976.

"Projecting the New Economic World Order," *The Search for Absolute Values in a Changing World,* International Cultural Foundation, 1978.

"Keynesianism: Alive, If Not So Well," *Fiscal Responsibilities in Constitutional Democracy,* edited by J. Buchanan and R. Wagner, Martinus Nijhoff, 1978.

"Introductory Remarks," *Limits to Redistribution,* Duncker & Humb, 1978.

"Some Questions and Answers About TIP," *Solutions to Inflation,* edited by David C. Colander, Harcourt Brace Jovanovitch, 1979.

"MAP: A Cure for Inflation" (with David C. Colander), *Solutions to Inflation,* edited by D. Colander, Harcourt Brace Jovanovich, 1979.

"There is a Cure for Inflation" (with David C. Colander), *Incomes Policies for the United States: New Approaches,* Martinus Nijhoff, 1980.

"A Mutation in the Macro-Mechanism of the Market Economy," *Proceedings of the Tel Aviv University Conference on Development in an Inflationary World,* June 16–19, 1979.

"The Market Anti-Inflation Plan: A Cure for Stagflation," *Essays in Post-Keynesian Inflation,* edited by J. Gapinski and C. Rockwood, Ballinger, 1979.

"A Note on the Diminishing Marginal Utility of Income," *Selected Economic Writings of Abba P. Lerner,* edited by D. Colander, New York University Press, 1983.

"Welfare Economics and the Scitovsky Paradox," *Selected Economic Writings of Abba P. Lerner,* edited by D. Colander, New York University Press, 1983.

"Paleo-Austrian Capital Theory," *Selected Economic Writings of Abba P. Lerner,* edited by D. Colander, New York University Press, 1983.

Book Reviews in Chronological Order

"*Marxism and Economics* by P. Sweezy and J. Robinson," *The Journal of Political Economy,* March 1945.

"*The Accumulation of Capital* by Joan Robinson," *The American Economic Review,* September 1957.

"*The Theory of International Economic Policy, Vol. II* by J. Meade," in Trade and Welfare and Mathematical Supplement, *The Journal of Political Economy,* October 1957.

"*The Failure of the 'New Economics'* by Henry Hazlitt," *The Review of Economics and Statistics,* May 1960.

"*A Program for Monetary Stability* by Milton Friedman," *Journal of the American Statistical Association,* March 1962.

"*The Problem of Rising Prices* by William Fellner, et al.," *The Journal of Political Economy,* August 1962.

"*Money in a Theory of Finance* by J. Gurley and Shaw," *Journal of the American Statistical Association,* September 1962.

"*Capitalism and Freedom* by Milton Friedman," *The American Economic Review,* June 1973.

"*John Maynard Keynes* by Hyman Minsky," *Challenge,* May–June 1976.

AUTHOR INDEX

SUBJECT INDEX